READINGS

IN CRIMINOLOGY

AND PENOLOGY

READINGS IN CRIMINOLOGY AND PENOLOGY

SECOND EDITION

Edited by DAVID DRESSLER

Columbia University Press

NEW YORK and LONDON 1972

Affectionately dedicated to M. Singh, M.D.

One of those rare physicians who heals with his heart as well as with the Materia Medica.

PREFACE

CULTURE IS constantly changing, a fact that in itself renders obsolete some of the contents of the first edition of this book, which appeared in 1964. Add to this that the rate of change has accelerated tremendously in the past decade or so, and there is the more reason for updating the compilation. The civil rights movement, the Vietnam war, the emergence of a youth drug culture, and other phenomena which have resulted in radical shifts in ways of looking at once-familiar things have necessarily also brought about new orientations in criminology and penology. The present, second, edition of this volume takes some of these changes into account.

It is addressed primarily to students taking courses in criminology, penology, juvenile delinquency, and police science. Hopefully, it will also be of service in certain courses offered in undergraduate and graduate social work curricula. It should also prove useful to correctional workers in the field and to administrators of in-service programs in correctional agencies.

Criminology as a study has traditionally been housed in departments of sociology, and indeed that discipline has contributed mightily to its development. However, invaluable contributions also come from biology, psychology, social work, public administration, law, and police science. For this reason, the present volume, while basically sociological in orientation, includes representative selections from other areas of investigation and practice.

Happily, theoreticians in criminology do not always agree. If they did, there would be no challenge, no incentive for change when change is indicated. Just as it would be a disservice to expose the student to but one discipline, so it seems ill-advised to offer him only what the compiler considers "best" or "soundest" or "most scientific" or "most advanced." For this reason, some of the divergences among theoreticians are presented.

And if there are differences among theoreticians, there is down-right hostility at times between them and field practitioners. It would give the reader an unrealistic picture if he were to put down his book believing that what the theoreticians point to as effective ways of thinking and doing are necessarily and always what the practitioner—the policeman, the judge, the prison warden, the probation or parole officer—thinks and does. Theory derives at least partly from practice, and practice is enriched by the application of theory, but in the nature of things, theory sometimes outstrips practice and vice versa. A book of readings is obligated to give the practitioner a chance to be heard. Someone said that a society that has contempt for either its philosophers or its plumbers is likely to find that neither its theories nor its pipes hold water.

Nor can an anthology of this sort afford to overlook the layman. Some lay opinion may be based exclusively on guesswork or prejudice; some may be grounded in firmer soil; but all of it constitutes the opinion of the people, and in a democracy, the voice of the people must be listened to and respected *as* the *vox populi*. Furthermore, as Samuel Johnson told us many years ago, "About things on which the public thinks long, it commonly attains to think right." It does not always work out that way, but it does often enough for us to have learned that the "experts" are not invariably expert, and the folk frequently cut through to the truth ahead of the scientists.

Lay opinion on certain subjects is given space in this compendium. A layman, as viewed here, may be a psychiatrist, an attorney, or a chemist. He is a layman, along with "the man in the street," where criminology and penology are concerned. Thus Eldridge Cleaver and Rev. Martin Luther King, Jr., both of whom are included in the book, are laymen in the sense indicated above. They are undoubtedly, however, highly qualified to discuss the rights and problems of blacks, as they do in the selections.

No compendium will please every reader. Space limitations make it impossible to be as exhaustive as one might be. Editorial judgments had to be exercised. No reader will find all he wants. Each will regret the omission of a particular item. Some will question the inclusion of specific readings. The compiler accepts responsibility for the final product.

Since journal articles and government documents are sometimes hard to get at, preference is given to them here. With some exceptions, books one would expect to find in a reasonably adequate library were not excerpted, on the theory the student does better to consult the original, in its entirety. Occasionally, however, material from an extant volume has been included, because excluding it would deprive the reader of a "classic" in the field or because the particular item states the matter at hand better than anything the editor was able to find in a journal.

Since the collection supports a text rather than being one in itself, subject matter covered extensively in practically every textbook in criminology, penology, and juvenile delinquency is treated sparingly or not at all.

Most of the items were selected because, in the editor's judgment, they were sound. Some exemplify research method as they present the product of research. Some are original contributions to theory. Some are primarily or purely descriptive. In some instances, a selection was included not because it represented sound scholarship but precisely because it did not, yet the ideas expressed are or had been influential in the field.

Titles are sometimes those of the original authors, sometimes of the compiler. Full attribution will be found in the editor's note. The title and affiliation of authors are shown in the editor's note if they appeared in the original publication. They are not necessarily current.

On occasion, articles were compressed; tables and diagrams were almost entirely deleted. In such instances, care was exercised not to rip words from context, and editorial devices show where deletions occurred. To economize on space, an author's footnotes were frequently omitted in whole or in part. Where only some were omitted the numbering of the footnotes in that selection may not follow those of the original. In general, footnotes used are reprinted as they appeared in the original, which explains differences in styling.

I received much help from numerous teaching colleagues, police and correctional officials, social workers, and in two instances, seasoned veterans of the underworld. I cannot list all of those who were so kind, but they know how grateful I am.

My wife, Belle Dressler, served as an informed layman, who often set me straight on a given subject, since she did not allow the "scientific method" to overawe her, and insisted on using common sense and heart. My son, Joshua, was of inestimable value as a representative and clear-eyed analyst of his generation. His knowledge of civil rights alignments, civil disobedience issues, the drug culture, and the New Left far surpasses mine. To Belle and Joshua, my heartfelt thanks.

David Dressler

California State College, Long Beach

CONTENTS

Part I

DEFINING AND MEASURING CRIME

INTRODUCTION

WHAT IS crime? Who is the criminal? Some definitions stem from religious concepts; others are philosophical, legal, anthropological, or psychological. From the sociological viewpoint, crime has been variously defined as deviant behavior, normative behavior, adjustive behavior, and so on. In Part I we offer several definitions of crime and, by extension, criminals.

Emile Durkheim theorizes that crime is a normal phenomenon of society, the natural and inevitable product of collective life and social evolution. The collective conscience of a people defines what is crime, he holds.

Thorsten Sellin, while acknowledging the utility and propriety of defining crime in legal terms, considers such a definition too restrictive. Crime, he argues, is a violation of culture norms, which is something beyond mere violation of law per se.

Paul Tappan has no quarrel with the proposal that we study conduct norms toward a fuller understanding of the phenomenon of crime. However, he finds the juristic orientation provides the only precise and administratively applicable definition. Only those are criminals who have been adjudicated as such by the courts. Beginning with this, he proceeds to present a strictly legal definition of crime.

As legally defined, how much crime do we have? J. Edgar Hoover perceives an alarming increase in crime, and Richard D. Knudton casts some doubt on any and all statistical measures of crime, pointing to their many inadequacies. He is one of many who have deplored the absence of comprehensive, accurate, and altogether believable criminal statistics.

The reader who wishes to pursue the subject further will find a thoroughgoing discussion in Marvin E. Wolfgang's "Uniform Crime Reports," *University of Pennsylvania Law Review*, 111 (April 1963), 708–738.

CRIME AS NORMAL BEHAVIOR

EMILE DURKHEIM

Emile Durkheim, *Rules of Sociological Method* (Glencoe, Ill.: The Free Press, 1950), pp. 65–73.

THERE IS no society that is not confronted with the problem of criminality. Its form changes; the acts thus characterized are not always the same everywhere; but everywhere and always, there have been men who have behaved in such a way as to draw upon themselves penal repression. If, in proportion as societies pass from the lower to the higher types, the rate of criminality, i.e., the relation between the yearly number of crimes and the population, tended to decline, it might be believed that crime, while still normal, is tending to lose this character of normality. But we have no reason to believe that such a regression is substantiated. Many facts would seem rather to indicate a movement in the opposite direction. . . . There is, then, no phenomenon that presents more indisputably all the symptoms of normality, since it appears closely connected with the conditions of all collective life. . . . No doubt it is possible that crime itself will have abnormal forms, as, for example, when its rate is unusually high. This excess is, indeed, undoubtedly morbid in nature. What is normal, simply, is the existence of criminality, provided that it attains and does not exceed, for each social type, a certain level, which it is perhaps not impossible to fix in conformity with the preceding rules. . . . To classify crime among the phenomena of normal sociology is not to say merely that it is an inevitable, although regrettable phenomenon, due to the incorrigible wickedness of men; it is to affirm that it is a factor in public health, an integral part of all healthy societies. This result is, at first glance, surprising enough to have puzzled even ourselves for a long time. Once this first surprise has been overcome, however, it is not difficult to find reasons explaining this normality and at the same time confirming it.

In the first place crime is normal because a society exempt from it is utterly impossible. Crime . . . consists of an act that offends certain very strong collective sentiments. In a society in which criminal acts are no longer committed, the sentiments they offend would have to be found without exception in all individual consciousnesses, and they must be found to exist with the same degree as sentiments contrary to them. Assuming that this condition could actually be realized, crime would not thereby disappear; it would only change its form, for the very cause which would thus dry up the sources of criminality would immediately open up new ones.

Indeed, for the collective sentiments which are protected by the penal law of a people at a specified moment of its history to take possession of the public conscience or for them to acquire a stronger hold where they have an insufficient grip, they must acquire an intensity greater than that which they had hitherto had. The community as a whole must experience them more vividly, for it can acquire from no other source the greater force necessary to control these individuals who formerly were the most refractory. For murderers to disappear, the horror of bloodshed must become greater in those social strata from which murderers are recruited; but, first it must become greater throughout the entire society. Moreover, the very absence of crime would directly contribute to produce this horror, because any sentiment seems much more respectable when it is always and uniformly respected.

One easily overlooks the consideration that these strong states of the common consciousness cannot be thus reinforced without reinforcing at the same time the more feeble states, whose violation previously gave birth to mere infraction of convention—since the weaker ones are only the prolongation, the attentuated form, of the stronger. Thus robbery and simple bad taste injure the same single altruistic sentiment, the respect for that which is another's. However, this same sentiment is less grievously offended by bad taste than by robbery; and since, in addition, the average consciousness has not sufficient intensity to react keenly to the bad taste, it is treated with greater tolerance. That is why the person guilty of bad taste is merely blamed, whereas the thief is punished. But, if this sentiment grows stronger, to the point of silencing in all consciousness the inclination which disposes man to steal, he will become more sensitive to the offenses which, until then, touched him but lightly. He will react against them, then, with more energy; they will be the object of greater opprobrium, which will transform certain of them from the simple moral faults that they were and give them the quality of crimes. For example, improper contracts, or contracts improperly executed, which only incur public blame or civil damages, will become offenses in law.

Imagine a society of saints, a perfect cloister of exemplary individuals. Crimes, properly so called, will there be unknown; but faults which appear venial to the layman will create there the same scandal that the ordinary offense does in ordinary consciousnesses. If, then, this society has the power to judge and punish, it will define these acts as criminal and will treat them as such. For the same reason, the perfect and upright man judges his smallest failings with a severity that the majority reserve for acts more truly in the nature of an offense. Formerly, acts of violence against persons were more frequent than they are today, because respect for individual dignity was less strong. As this has increased, these crimes have become more rare; and also, many acts violating this sentiment have been introduced into the penal law which were not included there in primitive times.

In order to exhaust all the hypotheses logically possible, it will perhaps be asked why this unanimity does not extend to all collective sentiments without exception. Why should not even the most feeble sentiment gather enough energy to prevent all dissent? The moral consciousness of the society would be present in its entirety in all the individuals, with a vitality sufficient to prevent all acts offending it—the purely conventional faults as well as the crimes. But a uniformity so universal and absolute is utterly impossible; for the immediate physical milieu in which each one of us is placed, the hereditary antecedents, and the social influences vary from one individual to the next, and consequently diversify consciousness. It is impossible for all to be alike, if only because each one has his own organism and that these organisms occupy different areas in space. That is why, even among the lower peoples, where individual originality is very little developed, it nevertheless does exist.

Thus, since there cannot be a society in which the individuals do not differ more or less from the collective type, it is also inevitable that, among these divergences, there are some with a criminal character. What confers this character upon them is not the intrinsic quality of a given act, but that definition which the collective conscience lends them. If the collective conscience is stronger, if it has enough authority practically to suppress these divergencies, it will also be more sensitive, more exacting; and, reacting against the slightest deviations with the energy it otherwise displays only against more considerable infractions, it will attribute to them the same gravity as formerly to crimes. In other words, it will designate them as criminal.

Crime is, then, necessary; it is bound up with the fundamental conditions of all social life, and by that very fact it is useful, because these conditions of which it is a part are themselves indispensable to the normal evolution of morality and law.

Indeed, it is no longer possible today to dispute the fact that law and morality vary from one social type to the next, nor that they change within the same type if the conditions of life are modified. But, in order that these transformations may be possible, the collective sentiments at the basis of morality must not be hostile to change, and consequently must have but moderate energy. If they were too strong, they would no longer be plastic. Every pattern is an obstacle to new patterns, to the extent that the first pattern is inflexible. The better a structure is articulated, the more it offers a healthy resistance to all modification; and this is equally true of functional, as of anatomical, organization. If there were no crimes, this condition could not have been fulfilled; for such a hypothesis presupposes that collective sentiments have arrived at a degree of intensity unexampled in history. Nothing is good indefinitely and to an unlimited extent. The authority which the moral conscience enjoys must not be excessive; otherwise no one would dare criticize it, and it would too easily congeal into an immutable form. To make progress, individual originality must be able to express itself.

In order that the originality of the idealist whose dreams transcend his century may find expression, it is necessary that the originality of the criminal, who is below the level of his time, shall also be possible. One does not occur without the other.

Nor is this all. Aside from this indirect utility, it happens that crime itself plays a useful role in this evolution. Crime implies not only that the way remains open to necessary changes but that in certain cases it directly prepares these changes. Where crime exists, collective sentiments are sufficiently flexible to take on a new form, and crime sometimes helps to determine the form they will take. How many times, indeed, it is only an anticipation of future morality—a step toward what will be! According to Athenian law, Socrates was a criminal, and his condemnation was no more than just. However, his crime, namely, the independence of his thought, rendered a service not only to humanity but to his country. It served to prepare a new morality and faith which the Athenians needed, since the traditions by which they had lived until then were no longer in harmony with the current conditions of life. . . . It would never have been possible to establish the freedom of thought we now enjoy if the regulations prohibiting it had not been violated before being solemnly abrogated. . . .

From this point of view the fundamental facts of criminality present themselves to us in an entirely new light. Contrary to current ideas, the criminal no longer seems a totally unsociable being, a sort of parasitic element, a strange and unassimilable body, introduced into the midst of society. On the contrary, he plays a definite role in social life. Crime, for its part, must no longer be conceived as an evil that cannot be too much suppressed. There is no occasion for self-congratulation when the crime rate drops noticeably below the average level, for we may be certain that this apparent progress is associated with some social disorder. Thus, the number of assault cases never falls so low as in times of want. With the drop in the crime rate, and as a reaction to it, comes a revision, or the need of a revision in the theory of punishment. If, indeed, crime is a disease, its punishment is its remedy and cannot be otherwise conceived; thus, all the discussions it arouses bear on the point of determining what the punishment must be in order to fulfill this role of remedy. If crime is not pathological at all, the object of punishment cannot be to cure it, and its true function must be sought elsewhere.

CRIME AS VIOLATION OF
CONDUCT NORMS

THORSTEN SELLIN

Excerpted from Thorsten Sellin, *Culture Conflict and Crime* (New York: Social Science Research Council, Bulletin 41, 1938), pp. 19–32. At the time of publication, Thorsten Sellin was Professor of Sociology at the University of Pennsylvania.

THE VERY foundation of studies in crime causation rests upon the definition of "crime" and "criminal." They are the subject matter of traditional criminology. Both are defined by law, but while the limitations which such definition imposes upon research has been lamented by the criminologist, it has not been seriously questioned. Even such astute critics of criminological research as Michael and Adler stated, "We cannot make empirical investigations of crime and criminals unless we have some basis for differentiating criminal from other behavior and criminals from other persons, which is so precise and definite that we will not confuse them in our observations. . . . The most precise and least ambiguous definition of crime is that which defines it as behavior which is prohibited by the criminal code. . . . Not only is the legal definition of a crime precise and unambiguous, but it is the *only possible* definition of crime." [1] These authors go even further in their interpretation of the concepts under discussion. While they recognize that a person who violates the criminal law thereby becomes a criminal, they add that "the most certain way . . . to distinguish criminals from non-criminals is in terms of those who have been convicted of crime and those who have not. . . . Both for practical and for theoretical purposes we must proceed as if that were true. . . . The

[1] Michael, Jerome, and Adler, Mortimer J., *Crime, Law, and Social Science.* New York: Harcourt, Brace & Co. 1933. Pp. 1–2 and note on p. 2.

criminologist is therefore quite justified in making the convict population the subject of his studies as he does." [2]

In a footnote in another section of their work, however, they
raised a question which should be noted here and which they
made no attempt to answer: "One of the crucial problems which
confronts the criminologist is whether this manner of distinguishing criminals from non-criminals is significant for his purposes." [3]
In designating this problem as a "crucial" one, the authors were
undoubtedly right. It is *the* crucial problem. It is, furthermore, one
to which little attention has been paid by criminologists. Criminology has become the study of crimes and criminals. The social demand for crime prevention and repression, the apparent precision
of the legal definitions, and the availability of concrete data, collected during the law enforcement process have all aided in fixing
the artificial boundaries of criminology. Such boundaries cannot be
recognized by science. Yet, specialization, a division of labor, is
obviously necessary in research. "The scientific study of any field of
phenomena," to quote George Catlin, "requires the general delimitation of that field," but that delimitation must "arise intrinsically
from the nature of the subject matter and [must] not be of a
purely fortuitous nature, based on some merely external similarities
in what is observed." [4] The legal definitions which circumscribe
criminological research fall into the class of "external similarities"
mentioned. Criminologists have defined the phenomena, which
they study "in terms of the most available . . . [data] thereby stul-
tifying . . . [their] entire theoretical concepts," to paraphrase a
statement by Frank Ross. [5] We shall attempt to show that the categories set up by the criminal law do not meet the demands of scientists because they are of "a fortuitous nature" and do not "arise
intrinsically from the nature of the subject matter."

[2] *Ibid.*, P. 3.
[3] *Ibid.*, P. 92.
[4] Catlin, George. "The Delimitation and Mensurability of Political Phenomena." *American Political Science Review.* 21:255–69. May 1937. The term
"delimitation" is not to be interpreted as fixing the boundaries of any field or
area of research, but as a manner of conceiving the intrinsic or natural properties of the objects studied.
[5] Ross, Frank. *Fields and Methods of Sociology.* Bernard, L. L. (ed.) 2nd
Ed., New York: Farrar & Rinehart. 1934. P. 463.

Crime Norms

Among the various instrumentalities which social groups have evolved to secure conformity in the conduct of their members, the criminal law occupies an important place, for its norms are binding upon all who live within the political boundaries of a state and are enforced through the coercive power of that state. The criminal law may be regarded as in part a body of rules, which prohibit specific forms of conduct and indicate punishments for violations. The character of these rules, the kind or type of conduct they prohibit, the nature of the sanction attached to their violation, etc. depend upon the character and interests of those groups in the population which influence legislation. In some states these groups may comprise the majority, in others a minority, but the social values which receive the protection of the criminal law are ultimately those which are treasured by dominant interest groups. In democratic states this essential character of the criminal law is not so easy to discern as in states with other forms of government, but even in democracies the importance of strong minority interest groups can be seen shaping some part of the criminal law. "Our legislators," says Manuel Gamio, in discussing the penal law of Mexico, ". . . make laws for the dominant minority, similar in race, tradition and civilization of the people of Europe . . . with the result that the laws are to a large degree copied from foreign patterns. . . . The social majorities, especially the indigenous peoples, remain outside the boundaries of these laws, which ignore their biological needs and the nature of their mental processes, their peculiar indo-hispanic culture, their economic status, aspirations and tendencies." [6] Among the examples he cites the law which makes the religious and the "natural" or common-law marriages illegal. In the Valley of Teotihuacan, 73 percent of the marriages are illegal, due to no conscious violation but "for the social minority, for whom the laws were made the 'natural' union is abnormal, although for the social majority . . . these unions are perfectly

[6] Gamio, Manuel. *Hacia un Mexico Nuevo*. Mexico City: Manuel Gamio. 1935. Pp. 186–87.

normal." [7] Similar lack of congruence between the laws of a state and the moral ideas of different social groups within its population may be observed wherever the standards of the dominant groups are at variance with those of subjected or submissive ones. The criminal norms, i.e. the conduct norms embodied in the criminal law, change as the values of the dominant groups are modified or as the vicissitudes of social growth cause a reconstitution of these groups themselves and shifts in the focus of power. Thus crimes of yesteryear may be legal conduct today, while crimes in one contemporary state may be legal conduct in another. This lesson of history makes it a safe prediction—an empirical generalization as well founded as any generalization in the natural sciences—that everything the criminal law of any state prohibits today, it will not prohibit at a given future time, unless complete social stagnation sets in, an experience unknown to the social historian.

As a matter of fact, the variability in the definition of crime—and consequently in the meaning attached to the noun "criminal"—is too familiar to the social scientist to require any demonstration. It should, however, raise in his mind the question of how such variability can permit the formulation of the universal categories required in all scientific research.

The unqualified acceptance of the legal definitions of the basic units or elements of criminological inquiry violates a fundamental criterion of science. The scientist must have freedom to define his own terms, based on the intrinsic character of his material and designating properties in that material which are assumed to be universal. There are indeed numerous instances where public policy, expressed in law, has temporarily restrained, frustrated, or fixed the social ends of scientific research in this or that field. There is also evidence to show the hampering effect which the weight of authority, ascribed to one or more scientists, has had upon the progress of research. In neither case, however, have scientists permitted non-scientists to define the basic *terms* of inquiry.

It should be emphasized at this point that the above comments do not imply that the criminal law or the data about crimes and criminals assembled in the process of its enforcement are not useful

[7] *Loc. cit.*

in scientific research. They are indeed a rich source for the scientist, but the application of scientific criteria to the selection and classification of these data independently of their *legal* form is essential to render them valuable to science. Nor is it claimed that the study of criminology as traditionally conceived has no value. On the contrary, the *social* value of such research may be at times very great even when the scientific validity of its conclusions is questionable. The results of such study may afford a basis for social action or public policy which is in harmony with dominant attitudes. They may furthermore give social prestige to the investigator and therefore have distinct value to him. What *is* claimed is that if a science of human conduct is to develop, the investigator in this field of research must rid himself of shackles which have been forged by the criminal law. If psychiatry had confined itself to the study of persons declared legally incompetent by criminal courts, it would no doubt have learned something about mental disease, but if courts had defined and thus classified various forms of mental diseases for reasons to be sought in public policy, the psychiatrist would have learned little indeed. It is because he has insisted on defining his own terms that he is now so frequently in conflict with the law, which serves socially defined ends and is not concerned solely with what scientists do. The legislator and the administrator on the one hand, the scientist on the other, speak different languages, fundamentally irreconcilable. This is as it should be, for they are pursuing essentially different ends. The scientist has to have a language of his own in which everyday words, if they are employed, carry a specific meaning significant to him although to others they may have no such import. Confinement to the study of crime and criminals and the acceptance of the categories of specific forms of "crime" and "criminal" as laid down in law renders criminological research theoretically invalid from the point of view of science. The data of the criminal law and the data about crimes and criminals now subservient to legal categories must be "processed" by the scientist before he can use them.

Conduct Norms

Man is born into a culture. He arrives biologically equipped to receive and to adapt knowledge about himself and his relationships to others. His first social contacts begin a life-long process of coordination during which he absorbs and adapts ideas which are transmitted to him formally or informally by instruction or precept. These ideas embody *meanings* attached to customs, beliefs, artifacts, and his own relationships to his fellow men and to social institutions. Looked upon as discrete units, these ideas may be regarded as *cultural elements,* which fit into patterns or configurations of ideas, which tend to become fixed into integrated systems of meanings. Embodied in the mind they become *personality elements,* and the sum total of all such elements may be conveniently called *personality,* as distinguished from the person's biological individuality or his inherited and acquired morphological and physiological traits. Personality then rests upon a biological foundation, which is of the greatest importance in the formation of personality. The biological make-up of an individual fixes limits to personality development, determines the character of the receptive and adaptive processes which transform cultural elements into personality elements, and influences the latter's expressions in social activity. . . .

If all individuals were biologically alike and subjected to identical cultural influences, all personalities would be identical. If all individuals were biologically alike, but each subjected to different cultural influences, each would present unique personality configurations. Since with the possible exceptions of identical twins, no two individuals can be found that possess the same biological equipment and since no two persons can ever be assumed to have been exposed to the same cultural influences, at least after the period of early infancy, each total personality is unique. Scientific research in the behavior field is therefore confronted with the problem of offering scientific descriptions of the growth and manifestations of unique personalities in unique biological individuals. The scientific method, however, is not applicable to the study of unique phenomena. It can only deal with classes, kinds, types. If a generalization were made on the basis of the findings in a study of a case assumed to be unique, the validity of that generalization could never be tested. Etiological research would be impossible if it could not assume that the data it employs may be grouped into classes, the units of which are identical or may at least be assumed to possess sufficient similarity to be classed together for research purposes.

Every person's existence may be regarded from one point of view at least as being made up of one choice after another. He is constantly faced with the need of deciding whether he should do this or do that. The vast majority of these choices are of an undramatic nature, involving the prosaic routine of daily life and so affected by habit that the deliberative element associated with the idea of "choice" has been submerged and the person's reaction has gradually become automatic. Such being the case, it is the new or the infrequently recurring situation in which he finds himself which most obviously calls into action the exercise of the will and compels him to balance against one another the various possible reactions which the life situation in question arouses, selecting the one he deems most suitable to him at the moment. Whether the manner in which a person responds in a life situation is the result of habit or of deliberation, his reaction may be regarded as an expression of his personality. The character of that reaction depends upon what the life situation involved *means* to him. Some of these life situations at least are sufficiently repetitious and socially so defined that they call for definite responses from the type of person who encounters them. There are attached to them, so to speak, norms which define the reaction or response which in a given person is approved or disapproved by the normative group. The social attitude of this group toward the various ways in which a person might act under certain circumstances has thus been crystallized into a rule, the violation of which arouses a group reaction. These rules or norms may be called *conduct norms*. All personal reaction or activity which they govern may be called *conduct*. The term behavior might well be reserved for all types of reactions—conduct then being a subtype—or for all types *not* defined as conduct.

Conduct, as defined above, can occur only in situations which are defined by some social group and governed by a rule of some sort. Furthermore, all conduct has been socially conditioned, since personality is a social product. Therefore it is unwise from a scientific point of view to speak of antisocial as opposed to social conduct. These terms belong to the language of social reform. It would seem best, in order to avoid misunderstanding, to speak instead of *normal* and *abnormal conduct,* i.e. conduct in accord with or deviating from a conduct norm.

Conduct norms are the products of social life. Social groups place on the activity of their members certain restrictions which aim to insure the protection of social values which have been injured by unrestricted conduct. A conduct norm is originally an *ex post facto* rule. Generally speaking "breach is the mother of law" [8] and equally a mother of conduct norms.

Every person is identified with a number of social groups, each meeting some biologically conditioned or socially created need. Each of these groups is normative in the sense that within it there grow up norms of conduct applicable to situations created by that group's specific activities. As a member of a given group, a person is not only supposed to conform to the rules which it shares with other groups, but also to those which are peculiarly its own. A person who as a member of a family group—in turn the transmitting agency for the norms which governed the groups from which the parents came—possesses all its norms pertaining to conduct in routine life situations, may also as a member of a play group, a work group, a political group, a religious group, etc., acquire norms which regulate specialized life situations and which sustain, weaken or even contradict the norms earlier incorporated in his personality. The more complex a culture becomes, the more likely it is that the number of normative groups which affect a person will be large, and the greater is the chance that the norms of these groups will fail to agree, no matter how much they may overlap as a result of a common acceptance of certain norms. A conflict of norms is said to exist when more or less divergent rules of conduct

[8] A phrase borrowed from Seagle, William. "Primitive Law and Professor Malinowski." *American Anthropologist.* 39:275–90. April–June 1937. P. 284.

govern the specific life situation in which a person may find himself. The conduct norm of one group of which he is a part may permit one response to this situation, the norm of another group may permit perhaps the very opposite response.

For every person, then, there is from the point of view of a given group of which he is a member, a normal (right) and an abnormal (wrong) way of reacting, the norm depending upon the social values of the group which formulated it. *Conduct norms are, therefore, found wherever social groups are found, i.e. universally. They are not the creation of any ONE normative group; they are not confined within political boundaries; they are not necessarily embodied in law.*

These facts lead to the inescapable conclusion that the study of conduct norms would afford a sounder basis for the development of scientific categories than a study of crimes as defined in the criminal law. Such study would involve the isolation and classification of norms into *universal categories,* transcending political and other boundaries, a necessity imposed by the logic of science. The study of how conduct norms develop, how they are related to each other and to other cultural elements, the study of changes and differentials in norm violations and the relationship of such violations to other cultural phenomena, are certainly questions which the sociologist by training and interest might regard as falling within his field. . . .

The need for finding some basis for criminological research which would extend beyond that of the law has been expressed before. Innumerable definitions of crime have been offered which if not read in their context would appear to go beyond the legal definition. Upon examination, however, almost all of them prove to be the legal norms clothed in a sociological language. Such is not the case, however, with the definition offered by Makarewicz, who can be said to use the term crime in the sense of a conduct norm. "A crime is an act by a member of a given social group, which by the rest of the members of that group is regarded as so injurious or as showing such a degree of antisocial attitude in the actor that the group publicly, overtly and collectively reacts by trying to abrogate some one of his rights (Güter)."[9] Znaniecki[10] also attempts to avoid the legal definition and in his latest work we find the following statement which presents his point of view.

Because a collective system has social validity in the eyes of each and all of those who share in it, because it is endowed with a special dignity which merely individual systems lack altogether, individual behavior which endangers a collective system and threatens to harm any of its elements appears quite different from an aggression against an individual (unless, of course, such an aggression hurts collective values as well as individual values). It is not only a harmful act, but an objectively evil act, a violation of social validity, an offense against the superior dignity of this collective system. . . . The best term to express the specific significance of such behavior is *crime*. We are aware that in using the word in this sense, we are giving it a much wider significance than it has in criminology. *But we believe, that it is desirable for criminology to put its investigations on a broader basis; for strictly speaking, it still lacks a proper theoretic basis.* . . . Legal qualifications are not founded on the results of previous research and not made for the purpose of future research; therefore they have no claim to be valid as scientific generalizations—nor even as heuristic hypotheses.[11]

This extension of the meaning of the term *crime* is not desirable. It is wiser to retain that term for the offenses made punishable by the criminal law and to use the term abnormal conduct for the violations of norms whether legal or not.

[9] Makarewicz, J. *Einführung in die Philosophie des Strafrechts.* Stuttgart: Enke, 1906. Pp. 79–80.

[10] Znaniecki, Florian. "Social Research in Criminology." *Sociology and Social Research.* 12:207–22. March–April 1928.

[11] Znaniecki, Florian. *Social Actions.* New York: Farrar & Rinehart. 1936. Pp. 350–52. (The italics are mine.)

CRIME AS A LEGAL CONCEPT

PAUL W. TAPPAN

Excerpted from Paul W. Tappan, "Who Is the Criminal?," *American Sociological Review*, XII (February 1947), 96–102. In 1947, Paul Tappan was affiliated with New York University.

WHAT IS crime? As a lawyer-sociologist, the writer finds perturbing the current confusion on this important issue. Important because it delimits the subject matter of criminological investigation. A criminologist who strives to aid in formulating the beginnings of a science finds himself in an increasingly equivocal position. He studies the criminals convicted by the courts and is then confounded by the growing clamor that he is not studying the real criminal at all, but an insignificant proportion of non-representative and stupid unfortunates who happened to have become enmeshed in technical legal difficulties. It has become a fashion to maintain that the convicted population is no proper category for the empirical research of the criminologist. Ergo, the many studies of convicts which have been conducted by the orthodox, now presumably outmoded criminologists, have no real meaning for either descriptive or scientific purposes. Off with the old criminologies, on with the new orientations, the new horizons!

This position reflects in part at least the familiar suspicion and misunderstanding held by the layman sociologist toward the law. To a large extent it reveals the feeling among social scientists that not all anti-social conduct is proscribed by law (which is probably true), that not all conduct violative of the criminal code is truly anti-social, or is not so to any significant extent (which is also undoubtedly true). Among some students the opposition to the traditional definition of crime as law violation arises from their desire to discover and study wrongs which are absolute and eternal rather than mere violations of a statutory and case law system which vary in time and place; this is essentially the old metaphysical search for the law of nature. They consider the dynamic and relativistic nature of law to be a barrier to the growth of a scientific system of hypotheses possessing universal validity.

Recent protestants against the orthodox conceptions of crime and criminal are diverse in their views: they unite only in their denial of the allegedly legalistic and arbitrary doctrine that those convicted under the criminal law are the criminals of our society and in promoting the confusion as to the proper province of criminology. It is enough here to examine briefly a few of the current schisms with a view to the difficulties at which they arrive.

I

A number of criminologists today maintain that mere violation of the criminal law is an artificial criterion of criminality, that categories set up by the law do not meet the demands of scientists because they are of a "fortuitous nature" and do not "arise intrinsically from the nature of the subject matter." [1] The validity of this contention must depend, of course, upon what the nature of the subject matter is. These scholars suggest that, as a part of the general study of human behavior, criminology should concern itself broadly with all anti-social conduct, behavior injurious to society. We take it that anti-social conduct is essentially any sort of behavior which violates some social interest. What are these social interests? Which are weighty enough to merit the concern of the sociologist, to bear the odium of crime? What shall constitute a violation of them?—particularly where, as is so commonly true in our complicated and unintegrated society, these interests are themselves in conflict? Roscoe Pound's suggestive classification of the social interests served by law is valuable in a juristic framework, but it solves no problems for the sociologist who seeks to depart from legal standards in search of all manner of anti-social behavior.

[1] See, for example, Thorsten Sellin, *Culture Conflict and Crime*, pp. 20–21 (1938).

However desirable may be the concept of socially injurious conduct for purposes of general normation or abstract description, it does not define what is injurious. It sets no standard. It does not discriminate cases, but merely invites the subjective value-judgments of the investigator. Until it is structurally embodied with distinct criteria or norms—as is now the case in the legal system —the notion of anti-social conduct is useless for purposes of research, even for the rawest empiricism. The emancipated criminologist reasons himself into a cul de sac: having decided that it is footless to study convicted offenders on the ground that this is an artificial category—though its membership is quite precisely ascertainable, he must now conclude that, in his lack of standards to determine anti-sociality, though this may be what he considers a real scientific category, its membership and its characteristics are unascertainable. Failing to define anti-social behavior in any fashion suitable to research, the criminologist may be deluded further into assuming that there is an absoluteness and permanence in this undefined category, lacking in the law. It is unwise for the social scientist ever to forget that all standards of social normation are relative, impermanent, variable. And that they do not, certainly the law does not, arise out of mere fortuity or artifice.

II

In a differing approach certain other criminologists suggest that "conduct norms" rather than either crime or anti-social conduct should be studied. There is an unquestionable need to pursue the investigation of general conduct norms and their violation. It is desirable to segregate the various classes of such norms to determine relationships between them, to understand similarities and differences between them as to the norms themselves, their sources, methods of imposition of control, and their consequences. The subject matter of this field of social control is in a regrettably primitive state. It will be important to discover the individuals who belong within the several categories of norm violators established and to determine then what motivations operate to promote conformity or breach. So far as it may be determinable, we shall wish to know in what way these motivations may serve to insure conformity to different sets of conduct norms, how they may overlap and reinforce the norms or conflict and weaken the effectiveness of the norms.

We concur in the importance of the study of conduct norms and their violation and, more particularly, if we are to develop a science of human behavior, in the need for careful researches to determine the psychological and environmental variables which are associated etiologically with non-conformity to these norms. However, the importance of the more general subject matter of social control or "ethology" does not mean that the more specific study of the law-violator is non-significant. Indeed, the direction of progress in the field of social control seems to lie largely in the observation and analysis of more specific types of non-conformity to particular, specialized standards. We shall learn more by attempting to determine why some individuals take human life deliberately and with premeditation, why some take property by force and others by trick, than we shall in seeking at the start a universal formula to account for any and all behavior in breach of social interests. This broader knowledge of conduct norms may conceivably develop through induction, in its inevitably very generic terms, from the empirical data derived in the study of particular sorts of violations. Too, our more specific information about the factors which lie behind violations of precisely defined norms will be more useful in the technology of social control. Where legal standards require change to keep step with the changing requirements of a dynamic society, the sociologist may advocate—even as the legal profession does—the necessary statutory modifications, rather than assume that for sociological purposes the conduct he disapproves is already criminal, without legislative, political, or judicial intervention. . . .

IV

Having considered the conceptions of an innovating sociology in ascribing the terms "crime" and "criminal," let us state here the juristic view: Only those are criminals who have been adjudicated as such by the courts. Crime is an intentional act in violation of the criminal law (statutory and case law), committed without defense or excuse, and penalized by the state as a felony or misdemeanor. In studying the offender there can be no presumption that arrested, arraigned, indicted, or prosecuted persons are criminals unless they also be held guilty beyond a reasonable doubt of a particular offense. Even less than the unconvicted suspect can those individuals be considered criminal who have violated no law. Only those are criminals who have been selected by a clear substantive and a careful adjective law, such as obtains in our courts. The unconvicted offenders of whom the criminologist may wish to take cognizance are an important but unselected group; it has no specific membership presently ascertainable. Sociologists may strive, as does the legal profession, to perfect measures for more complete and accurate ascertainment of offenders, but it is futile simply to rail against a machinery of justice which is, and to a large extent must inevitably remain, something less than entirely accurate or efficient.

Criminal behavior as here defined fits very nicely into the sociologists' formulations of social control. Here we find *norms* of conduct, comparable to the mores, but considerably more distinct, precise, and detailed, as they are fashioned through statutory and case law. The *agencies* of this control, like the norms themselves, are more formal than is true in other types of control: the law depends for its instrumentation chiefly upon police, prosecutors, judges, juries, and the support of a favorable public opinion. The law has for its *sanctions* the specifically enumerated punitive measures set up by the state for breach, penalties which are additional to any of the sanctions which society exerts informally against the violator of norms which may overlap with laws. *Crime* is itself simply the breach of the legal norm, a violation within this particular category of social control; the criminal is, of course, the individual who has committed such acts of breach.

Much ink has been spilled on the extent of deterrent efficacy of the criminal law in social control. This is a matter which is not subject to demonstration in any exact and measurable fashion, any more than one can conclusively demonstrate the efficiency of a moral norm. Certainly the degree of success in asserting a control, legal or moral, will vary with the particular norm itself, its instrumentation, the subject individuals, the time, the place, and the sanctions. The efficiency of legal control is sometimes confused by the fact that, in the common overlapping of crimes (particularly those *mala in se*) with moral standards, the norms and sanctions of each may operate in mutual support to produce conformity. Moreover, mere breach of norm is no evidence of the general failure of a social control system, but indication rather of the need for control. Thus the occurrence of theft and homicide does not mean that the law is ineffective, for one cannot tell how frequently such acts might occur in the absence of law and penal sanction. Where such acts are avoided, one may not appraise the relative efficacy of law and mores in prevention. When they occur, one cannot apportion blame, either in the individual case or in general, to failures of the legal and moral systems. The individual in society does undoubtedly conduct himself in reference to legal requirements. Living "beyond the law" has a quality independent of being non-conventional, immoral, sinful. Mr. Justice Holmes has shown that the "bad man of the law"—those who become our criminals—are motivated in part by disrespect for the law or, at the least, are inadequately restrained by its taboos.

From introspection and from objective analysis of criminal histories one can not but accept as axiomatic the thesis that the norms of criminal law and its sanctions do exert some measure of effective control over human behavior; that this control is increased by moral, conventional, and traditional norms; and that the effectiveness of control norms is variable. It seems a fair inference from urban investigations that in our contemporary mass society, the legal system is becoming increasingly important in constraining behavior as primary group norms and sanctions deteriorate. Criminal law, crime, and the criminal become more significant subjects of sociological inquiry, therefore, as we strive to describe, understand, and control the uniformities and variability in culture.

We consider that the "white collar criminal," the violator of conduct norms, and the anti-social personality are not criminal in any sense meaningful to the social scientist unless he has violated a criminal statute. We cannot know him as such unless he has been properly convicted. He may be a boor, a sinner, a moral leper, or the devil incarnate, but he does not become a criminal through sociological name-calling unless politically constituted authority says he is. It is footless for the sociologist to confuse issues of definition, normation, etiology, sanction, agency and social effects by saying one thing and meaning another.

V

To conclude, we reiterate and defend the contention that crime, as legally defined, is a sociologically significant province of study. The view that it is not appears to be based upon either of two premises: 1. that offenders convicted under the criminal law are not representative of all criminals and 2. that criminal law violation (and, therefore, the criminal himself) is not significant to the sociologist because it is composed of a set of legal, non-sociological categories irrelevant to the understanding of group behavior and/or social control. Through these contentions to invalidate the traditional and legal frame of reference adopted by the criminologist, several considerations, briefly enumerated below, must be met.

1. Convicted criminals as a sample of law violators:

a. Adjudicated offenders represent the closest possible approximation to those who have in fact violated the law, carefully selected by the sieving of the due process of law; no other province of social control attempts to ascertain the breach of norms with such rigor and precision.

b. It is as futile to contend that this group should not be studied on the grounds that it is incomplete or non-representative as it would be to maintain that psychology should terminate its description, analysis, diagnosis, and treatment of deviants who cannot be completely representative as selected. Convicted persons are nearly all criminals. They offer large and varied samples of all types; their origins, traits, dynamics of development, and treatment influences can be studied profitably for purposes of description, understanding, and control. To be sure, they are not necessarily representative of all offenders; if characteristics observed among them are imputed to law violators generally, it must be with the qualification implied by the selective processes of discovery and adjudication.

c. Convicted criminals are important as a sociological category, furthermore, in that they have been exposed and respond to the influences of court contact, official punitive treatment, and public stigma as convicts.

2. The relevance of violation of the criminal law:

a. The criminal law establishes substantive norms of behavior, standards more clear cut, specific, and detailed than the norms in any other category of social controls.

b. The behavior prohibited has been considered significantly in derogation of group welfare by deliberative and representative assembly, formally constituted for the purpose of establishing such norms; nowhere else in the field of social control is there directed a comparable rational effort to elaborate standards conforming to the predominant needs, desires, and interests of the community.

c. There are legislative and juridical lags which reduce the social value of the legal norms; as an important characteristic of law, such lag does not reduce the relevancy of law as a province of sociological inquiry. From a detached sociological view, the significant thing is not the absolute goodness or badness of the norms but the fact that these norms do control behavior. The sociologist is interested in the results of such control, the correlates of violation, and in the lags themselves.

d. Upon breach of these legal (and social) norms, the refractory are treated officially in punitive and/or rehabilitative ways, not for being generally anti-social, immoral, unconventional, or bad, but for violation of the specific legal norms of control.

e. Law becomes the peculiarly important and ultimate pressure toward conformity to minimum standards of conduct deemed essential to group welfare as other systems of norms and mechanics of control deteriorate.

f. Criminals, therefore, are a sociologically distinct group of violators of specific legal norms, subjected to official state treatment.

They and the non-criminals respond, though differentially of course, to the standards, threats, and correctional devices established in this system of social control.

g. The norms, their violation, the mechanics of dealing with breach constitute major provinces of legal sociology. They are basic to the theoretical framework of sociological criminology.

THE ALARMING INCREASE
IN CRIME

J. EDGAR HOOVER

Excerpted from J. Edgar Hoover, "The Faith of Free Men," *Vital Speeches of the Day*, XXXII, No. 3 (November 15, 1965), 71–74. At the time of publication J. Edgar Hoover was Director of the Federal Bureau of Investigation.

Is AMERICA as a nation being swept by an epidemic of spiritual malnutrition? I fervently hope not; but the danger signs are all too clear. I fear that the public may be coming to accept widespread lawlessness as an unavoidable adjunct to our way of life.

What has happened to the civic pride, the righteous indignation, of otherwise respectable citizens who turn their backs on helpless victims of beatings, robberies, and sex crimes? The incredibly indifferent attitude of these people is exacting a heavy toll. It has helped to turn the streets and parks of many cities into virtual jungles of fear—where, according to a recent survey, nearly one half of the residents are afraid to walk alone at night.

Despite the continuing efforts of some self-professed experts to minimize the crime problem, the undeniable fact remains that crime is increasing—in both numbers and intensity—at an alarming rate. It is growing six times as fast as our expanding population.

Last year, more than 2,600,000 serious offenses were reported to law enforcement agencies throughout the United States. This is the largest total on record. It means that more Americans felt the ravages of crime last year than ever before.

Today, the onslaught continues—with five serious offenses being recorded every minute. There is a vicious crime of violence—a murder, forcible rape or assault to kill—every 2½ minutes; a robbery, each 5 minutes, a burglary, every 28 seconds; and 52 automobiles are stolen every hour.

These figures are based on facts—unlike the illogical and inane criticism which has been voiced by the peculiar clique of sociologists and criminologists who are apparently suffering armchair fatigue. These impractical theorists who attempt to define away our crime problem should step from their paper castles into the world of reality. . . .

There is an urgent need today for realistic thought and realistic action in meeting the challenge of crime and immorality. This is especially true in the critical area of youthful criminality—where society has too long been asked to endure gross abuses of public and private trust by shallow-minded juvenile authorities.

The true meaning and intent of our great national holidays have been defiled by bands of defiant youths such as the arrogant young hoodlums who turned the Fourth of July this year into a nightmare of terror and destruction at resort communities in Ohio, Missouri, Iowa, and New York. Reports that participants in these orgies of lawlessness were being released after payment of small fine [sic] caused one great newspaper to observe, "About all that such slaps on the wrist will do is bring them out in force again next year. What they need, and what they ought to get, is 6 months at hard labor."

Whenever dangerous young hoodlums are encouraged to develop an attitude of "I can get away with anything—I'm a juvenile," society suffers and justice becomes a meaningless expression. Parental neglect, excessive weakness, categorical leniency, destroy respect for law and for those charged with its enforcement.

In complaining last year of what it termed "turnstile justice," a major newspaper in New York demanded, "it's time that the public was told just why so many young criminals and terrorists are passed through this turnstile and sent back to the streets to kill, rape, rob, and assault the innocent."

Exaggerated charges? Not in the least. From 1960 through 1964, no less than 225 police officers were killed in line of duty. Nearly one-third of the hoodlums arrested in connection with these murders were on parole or probation when the killings occurred.

The lives of six of these officers were claimed by criminals who had been paroled for a prior murder. Eleven lives were taken by offenders who had been paroled after confinement for felonious assault; and 32 of these officers were killed by paroled robbers.

We recently completed an examination of the records of nearly 93,000 criminals who were arrested in 1963 and 1964. This disclosed that 76 percent—more than three-quarters—had been arrested on at least one previous occasion. Over one-half of them had received lenient treatment, including parole, probation, and suspended sentences, at some point in their criminal careers—and these criminals recorded an average of more than three additional arrests after their first encounter with the school of soft justice and official leniency.

Forty-one years ago, an experienced attorney and jurist in New York issued a strong warning: "It is not the criminals, actual or potential, that need a neuropathic hospital. It is the people who slobber over them in an effort to find excuses for their crimes. The demand of the hour in America, above all other countries, is for jurors with conscience, judges with courage, and prisons which are neither country clubs nor health resorts."

The same "demands of the hour" continue to exist today. Tragically, the atmosphere of many courtrooms is still polluted by some jurors who deliberately close their minds to the evidence before them. Too many of our judges seek out technicalities rather than guilt or innocence. A trial should truly represent an enlightened search for truth so that deception, surprise, technicalities, and delay will be obliterated. The jousting in legal mumbo-jumbo resorted to by too many of our judges makes a farce of our judicial system.

But even if he should be convicted, the criminal knows that regardless of his past record there is steadily increasing hope for a suspended or a probationary sentence or an early release on parole.

The decent people in all sections of the country—East, West, North, and South—have suffered too long at the hands of terrorists set free with little more than a pretext of impartial consideration of their guilt.

They have tired of the street brawl tactics displayed by those lawyers—criminal [sic] who employ any means the courts will tolerate to defeat the interests of justice.

They are losing patience with systems of parole and probation that are little more than conveyor belts from our prisons and courts chambers back to the underworld.

And they have become nauseated by the irresponsible actions of other "sometime" Americans such as those fair-weather patriots who eagerly grasp every right and privilege which our country guarantees its inhabitants—while ignoring the duties and obligations that citizenship necessarily entails.

Those who seek equal rights under the law should be taught to assume equal responsibility before the law. Certainly, civil rights and individual dignity have their vital place in life, but what about the common good and the law and order that preserve us all from lapsing back into the jungle?

We must have a world ruled by law. I am not one of those who believe in adding a great many more laws. The crux of the problem is that we do not observe the laws we already have; nor is the spirit of these laws interpreted by our courts to give equal justice to the criminal and to law-abiding citizens who are the victims of the savagery perpetrated on our streets and highways.

During my early years, a strong and lasting impression was made on my life by a schoolteacher who told our class one day that, in order to receive passing grades and qualify for graduation, each of us would have to master the "three R's" of reading, writing and arithmetic. "But," she continued, "I hope you learn far more than that in my classroom because, in order to achieve true happiness and success in life, you will have to master an additional set of 'R's,' the 'three R's' of Americanism—reason, respect, and responsibility."

Then she added, "You will also find that there is a fourth 'R' which is sacred to America. It is religion."

Today, there is a most urgent need for Americans to rededicate themselves to the strong moral principles upon which our Nation was founded.

As Ralph Waldo Emerson said, "The true test of civilization is not the census, not the size of cities, nor the crops—no, but the kind of man the country turns out."

Faith dominated the atmosphere at Independence Hall in Philadelphia where the Declaration of Independence and the Constitution were framed.

Faith is our mainstay in the ideological struggle now raging between the camps of God-less communism and human freedom.

And faith remains our strongest bulwark against the criminal and subversive enemies who would destroy our priceless heritage of liberty and justice for all. But faith without work will be of no avail—there must be unity of purpose.

America will continue to progress in dignity and freedom so long as our people cherish liberty and justice and truth and honor God.

Faith in God. That is the fortress of free men.

OUR INADEQUATE CRIMINAL STATISTICS

RICHARD D. KNUDTON

Richard D. Knudton (ed.), *Criminological Controversies* (New York: Appleton-Century-Crofts, 1968), pp. 21–24. At the time of publication Richard D. Knudton was a member of the Sociology Department of Valparaiso University.

THE AMERICAN populace, regardless of the testimony of the experts, generally believes that society is becoming more criminal and more violent. However, this assumption is reached without complete or accurate data. Although the volume of criminal acts has risen, simple population growth accounts for much of this increase. Then, too, legislators have continued to define more events and acts as crimes. Barnes and Teeters once pointed out that more than 75 percent of all persons serving sentences in the United States in the 1950's could not have been incarcerated fifty years earlier because their violations were not then defined by law as crimes. As population has continued to grow and society to become more complex, the tendency to depend upon law rather than noninstitutionalized control mechanisms has led to the increased formalization of legal codes, which in turn has led to increased "crime."

In addition, a major difficulty in understanding the nature and extent of crime arises from the complexity of modern life because so many agencies are involved in the criminal process. Politicians legislate, policemen enforce, lawyers defend, prosecuting attorneys prosecute, judges adjudicate, prison officials maintain custody of the offender, and criminologists evaluate processes, procedures, and results. Each seeks to develop situations or environments which are most advantageous to his purpose. In no other area do theorists and practitioners come together with such frequency and so little understanding. Police commissioners, for example, have long been aware that the easiest way to gain funds for salary increases and equipment modernization is to make the public aware of increased criminal activity. But police enforcement itself reflects the cultural conditions and pressures of the local political and social system. The discrepancy between a life sentence for a physically disabled youth using narcotics and a fifteen-year sentence for the man who makes narcotics available for commercial profit vividly illustrates the gross inequalities possible within the legal and judicial process.

The problem of evaluating the extent of crime in the United States is, of course, the problem of gathering accurate statistics. But we face a clear paradox: Crime by its nature is secret. No one has ever been able to ascertain the exact volume of crime. Even the best index of criminal activity, the *FBI Uniform Crime Reports*, can only report the crimes *known* to police. Even then, the *Reports* do not reveal the occupation, employment status, social class, and ecological characteristics of the criminal. Organized crime, most costly of all crime in America, with its illegal gambling, narcotics, prostitution, labor racketeering, and gang activity remains largely unmeasured. Although the FBI data does not include information relating to the financial costs of crime, it does indicate the specific number of known violations by category.

Until 1958 the *Uniform Crime Reports* classified criminal homicide (including murder and nonnegligent and negligent manslaughter), rape (including statutory rape of persons underage), robbery, aggravated assault, burglary (or breaking and entering), larceny (or theft), and auto theft as serious (*index*) crimes. However, the removal in 1958 of manslaughter by negligence from the category of criminal homicides, the redefinition of rape to include only forcible rape, and the clarification of larceny to include only thefts involving $50 or more has made the accurate comparison of pre-1958 and post-1958 data in these areas largely impossible. But the assumption of the increased criminal orientation of the country is based upon such comparisons.

The usefulness of data in the *Uniform Crime Reports* is also limited because there is little or no data dealing with prison admissions and discharges, recidivism rates, or local and state actions and incarcerations. At best, present available data simply describes the general incidence of crime. As long as the data which constitutes the body of the *Reports* comes from enforcement agencies charged with maintaining the security of the community, the accuracy of the data remains a moot question. When the collection of crime statistics was shifted in 1950 from the individual precincts to a centralized bureau in New York City, the incidence of burglary rose from 2,726 to 42,491 and larceny from 7,713 to 70,949 within a matter of four years. The wide discretionary powers of the police, the prosecutors' office, and the courts all serve to confuse the statistical accuracy of data concerning crime.

Marvin E. Wolfgang, sociologist at the University of Pennsylvania, critically appraised the value of the *Uniform Crime Reports* in the *Pennsylvania Law Review*. The index of offenses gives a false impression of the meaning of "seriousness." Although the *Reports* categorize crimes as *index* (serious or major) crimes and *other* (less serious or minor) crimes, greater physical harm may come to a person in the commission of a less serious act. Offenses such as arson, kidnapping, and assault and battery, none of which are index crimes, may in fact involve more harm than forcible rape, aggravated assault, or larceny. In a study of over 13,000 delinquencies recorded in Philadelphia during one year, Thorsten Sellin and Marvin E. Wolfgang found that about 20 percent of the cases involving bodily injury were in crimes classified in the *Reports* as less serious offenses and normally defined to exclude the possibility of physical harm.

The data of the *Reports* is misleading in matters of damaged or stolen property. Embezzlement, a theft involving large amounts, remains unreported, while larcenies of smaller amounts are reported with seeming precision. Malicious mischief and disorderly conduct, absent from the index, potentially may involve more damage and loss than property offenses identified in the crime index. The *Reports* also fail to make a distinction between *reported* and *completed* criminal acts. Attempted burglaries, robberies, and rapes are included in the index even though no personal injury or property damage may have occurred. No distinction between auto theft and juvenile joy-riding is made, although the greatest number of auto thefts are simply the latter. The seriousness of the offense is also undifferentiated. A larceny over $50 is equated with premeditated murder in the index, although murder represents the infliction of ultimate harm to another person. Failure to distinguish between the seriousness of the offense and the completion or noncompletion of the act makes the data concerning the number of offenses in the seven categories of serious, index crime rather dubious. Because the distinction of index and other crimes is rather arbitrary, crime trends in the United States may be totally inaccurate.

Offenses against the person constitute about 13 percent of all index crimes; offenses against property account for the other 87 percent. The public generally believes the reverse of these statistics. Rather surprisingly, burglary accounts for more than 44 percent of the crimes measured by the crime index. It is possible that a decline in criminal homicide and rape may be offset by proportionally minor increases in burglary, larceny, and auto theft. For data purposes multiple crimes are only classified in the most serious category. Because the definition of "serious" crimes reflects the values of professional enforcement officers, the data of the *FBI Uniform Crime Reports* is hardly objective.

The classification system of the *Reports* illustrates the weakness of categorizing data without an adequate theoretical frame of reference. The data is represented quantitatively, but it lacks a qualitative dimension. The kinds of crime most likely to be reported and classified are those most likely to be completed by lower-class persons, a fact not revealed by the *Reports* data. "White collar" crime remains unreported, although it is of far greater cost to society. Because crimes are defined by laws, those who legislate, generally middle-class property owners, proliferate and expand laws dealing with crimes against property. Since the focus of the data-gathering process has been on the quantity of acts rather than the social costs and definition of criminal behavior, qualitative evaluation of the criminal process has been impossible.

A fundamental inadequacy of the *Reports* centers on the fact that the crime rate in each category must be related to a population base, usually 100,000 persons, if crime rates are to be compared. However, the accurate measurement of the population is undertaken only at ten-year intervals. Therefore, the attempt to compare 1960 and 1966 rates of criminal homicide using the base population of 1960 results in inaccurate comparisons. And yet such perversions of data are quite common in the *Reports* and in normal newspaper reporting. Crime will naturally increase as the population increases. However, crime rates are now determined by relating the *current* volume of criminal acts to the *past* size of the population. Therefore, crime statistics continue to rise for the first nine years of the census period only to undergo a major readjustment when new population figures become available. We can already expect a readjustment in the crime rates in 1970 and 1971 when the new population figures are available. Only then will we really be able to know whether the rapid crime increase is a fact or a myth. The present statistical rise in crime may be little more than the failure to gather statistics during intercensus years, or it may be the result of better detection and enforcement procedures within the community. Although ex-presidential nominee Barry Goldwater continues to consider "crime in the streets" a greater political issue than the war in Vietnam, the data does not support his underlying assumption that crime has risen. The public attitude is a paradox. When enforcement is most effective, i.e., when apprehensions are high, the public identifies a "rise" in crime. A crime wave can be manufactured at any time simply by enforcing laws with greater vigor. In like manner, it is also possible to "decrease" the amount of crime by limiting law enforcement. The proficiency of the local police, using new devices and trained in new techniques, must be recognized as a basic factor in the "increasing" crime rate. On the other hand, crime may *really* increase in a community because the community has refused to pay the costs of adequate police coverage.

Not only are the *FBI Uniform Crime Reports* generally biased in their conclusions, they are also statistically inaccurate in their categories. Although Thorsten Sellin criticized the FBI crime data

before its revision in 1958, his criticism that the United States has
the worst criminal statistics of any nation in the western world remains pertinent today. If data is to be valid, it must be free of the
biases which the current *Reports* perpetuate. As long as the gathering agency has a vested interest in the quantity and interpretation
of the data, such data must be suspect. We can freely admit that
crime is rising in incidence, but so is the population. Crime is an
activity of youth. As long as the birthrate continues at its present
level and the median age of the population continues to decline,
we will not know whether the American people are becoming more
criminal.

Part II

BEHAVIOR PATTERNS
OF OFFENDERS

INTRODUCTION

In PART I, Paul Tappan ("Crime as a Legal Concept") holds that in the strict legal sense a criminal is a person who, by court adjudication, is found to have committed an act that the law defines as a crime. But he agrees that the legal definition of a specific crime or act of delinquency does not tell us what motivated the individual to perpetrate it, what characteristics may be found in those who collectively fall within the offense category, or what social conditions or specific situations facilitate enactment of such offenses. In an effort to understand the etiology, control, and treatment of crime and delinquency, criminologists go beyond legal definitions to study conduct norms involved in illegal behavior, as elucidated by Sellin ("Crime as Violation of Conduct Norms") in Part I. Out of such thinking developed the idea of criminal typologies, i.e., attempts at classifying offenders and/or offenses in some sort of meaningful arrangement.

As far back as 1840, H. A. Frégier classified offenders according to the degree of violence employed. He also distinguished between professional thieves, occasional thieves, and thieves who stole from necessity. Cesare Lombroso, Enrico Ferri, and Raffaele Garofalo each established criminal typologies. In recent times, Sutherland suggested that *particular* criminal behaviors be studied; he hoped this might lead to revisions of extant generalizations regarding criminal behavior as a whole. They did contribute some understanding of the phenomenon of crime, but did not tell us enough. Thus Sutherland and Cressey proposed that illegal behavior be broken down into homogeneous units, that specific crimes and "sociological units" within the broader area be investigated.

Another stimulating discussion of this subject will be found in Marshall B. Clinard and Richard Quinney, *Criminal Behavior Systems: A Typology* (New York: Holt, Rinehart, and Winston, 1967).

Research into criminal behavior systems is still in its infancy. Many theoretical and methodological questions are as yet unanswered. Probably there is no one systematization that would meet with unanimous approval.

Here, in Part II, the objective is modest: to portray a limited variety of offenders classifiable in respective homogeneous units, and to explore the behavior systems involved to some extent. We describe the backgrounds, techniques, and behavior patterns of selected, legally definable categories of offenders. The purpose is simply to show the offender in action.

In "The Professional Thief," the protagonist speaks in the first part of the text, and Sutherland's commentary follows in the second. This is a classic in sociological literature, by Edwin Sutherland, who made immense contributions in more than one area of sociology and criminology. However, the book, *The Professional Thief,* from which the selection was taken, was published in 1937. Understandably, there have been changes since then. This is touched upon in the selection from the President's Commission on Law Enforcement, here titled "A More Recent Conception of Professional Crime."

"Maxie the Goniff" belongs in one subcategory of professional criminals, the pickpocket. In others are confidence men, heels and boosters (shoplifters), safecrackers (who are dying out), and counterfeiters.

Note that by Sutherland's definition, as well as other (but by no means all) criminologists, persons in organized crime would not be classed as professional criminals, even though they may devote every working day to it. This is because (1) the professional eschews violence if at all possible, where the gangster, for instance, does not, and (2) members of the hierarchy of professional crime identify themselves as such; they do not generally consider the racketeer or mobster a part of it. Nevertheless, a case can, and has been, made by eminent criminologists for the proposition that an individual committed to a fulltime and (he hopes) a lifetime of predatory crime of any nature is properly designated a professional.

However the reader may classify the individual in organized crime, we present the President's Commission statement on such operations, under the title "Organized Crime." This is followed by

"Boss of the Outfit," a dramatic description of one individual committed to this form of criminal endeavor.

Murderers certainly do not represent a homogeneous unit, for murder comes in various forms, by the hands of a variety of different individuals, activated by a number of radically disparate motivations. There is murder for hire. There is murder committed in a fit of ungovernable passion. Others kill in the perpetration of robberies; still others out of compulsion—they cannot restrain their urges.

We present only two kinds of killers, "The Normal Murderer," discussed by Guttmacher, and the compulsive sex slayer, exemplified in the psychiatric study of William Heirens, by Kennedy and associates.

It was Sutherland, again, who pioneered the concept of white-collar crime. "White-Collar Criminality" is one of his earliest statements on the subject. He made several revisions later, but the white-collar criminal, as a genre of offender, has come in for criticism, as for instance by Quinney, in "A Re-examination of White-Collar Criminality." The news story on the conviction of electrical company officials, "Crimes of Corporations and Executives," illustrates the genre.

In getting into the subject of drunkenness it must be emphasized that nowhere in the United States is either partaking of alcoholic beverages or drunkenness per se a criminal offense. The legal sanction is applied only against persons who are drunk and boisterous in *public*. But we have a shocking amount of public intoxication which makes it an appropriate subject of discussion in criminology. The heavy drinker and the alcoholic are more medical-psychiatric problems than criminal, but the fact remains that, under given circumstances, we are willing to treat sick people as malefactors.

The extreme of abuse of alcohol intake is alcoholism. Who is the alcoholic? How does he achieve that unhappy state? In "Becoming an Alcoholic," Jellinek describes the process. "An Alcoholic's Story" is the case history of a confirmed alcoholic. (He later became drug-addicted.)

Until comparatively recently, narcotic drugs were ingested in the shadows, in secret. After marijuana became known in the

United States in the late 1920s it was smoked in privacy; few users mentioned the fact. The "hard stuff," heroin, was the big problem. Marijuana was the pleasure, largely, of the lower socio-economic class.

Today, a new drug culture has developed. It is out in the open. Users are younger than formerly, and from all socio-economic levels of society. The youthful generation eschews heroin for the most part, but indulges in LSD and other forms of "acid" (hallucinogens). Marijuana appeals to middle-class youth now, as never in the past. Misconceptions about the effects of "grass" have been widely disseminated. There *are* serious dangers in the use of certain drugs, but the general public is not sure what they are; confusion is commonplace.

Here again, the addict may properly be considered a medical-psychiatric problem, and to a degree, government is beginning to recognize him as such. However, certain aspects of the drug traffic, use and abuse, run afoul of criminal statutes.

"Drugs of Abuse and Their Effects" will give the reader an idea of the results of using drugs of abuse.

The documentary "Drug User" is the statement of but one user. This is how he honestly analyzes his experience. But the nature of the drugs being what they are, one may deceive himself. To illustrate: I taped a dozen such documents. Some individuals insisted they had faultless perception of space while under marijuana—they did not wobble, they could drive cars. Others conclude that smoking marijuana did affect such function. Either some users are deceived, or the effects of smoking differ by individual and/or the conditions at the time of ingestion. Very possibly, both are true. On the other hand, all of the tapings report common experiences. All agree that when a person is "high" on marijuana, he has a strong desire to eat; that he does irrational things, such as putting mustard on cherry pie. All who used LSD saw the earth ripple and undulate. Thus, despite individual differences on some scores, the documents, including the one in this section, have a typicality that suggests authenticity.

The young man who speaks as a "Drug User" finds that nothing really deleterious resulted from his experimentations. An "outsider," Roszak, gives a more ominous picture in "The Use and Abuse of Psychedelic Experience." He is not simply guessing. As a college instructor he has been in position to observe youth in action.

The selection by Bordua, "The Gang as a Cultural Phenomenon," is one of the very best statements in this field of inquiry. "Gang Boy" depicts one youth in the setting of his particular kind of street gang.

THE PROFESSIONAL THIEF

A PROFESSIONAL THIEF

Excerpted from *The Professional Thief, By a Professional Thief, Annotated and Interpreted by Edwin H. Sutherland* (Chicago, University of Chicago Press, 1937), pp. 3–4, 10–11, 14, 24–25, 197, 200, 202, 206–7, 209–10, 211.

I

THE PROFESSIONAL THIEF is one who steals professionally. This means, first, that he makes a regular business of stealing. He devotes his entire working time and energy to larceny. . . . Second, every act is carefully planned. The selection of spots, securing of the property, making a getaway, disposing of the stolen property, and fixing cases in which he may be pinched (arrested) are all carefully planned. Third, the professional thief has technical skills and methods which are different from those of other professional criminals. Manual skill is important in some of the rackets, but the most important thing in all the rackets is the ability to manipulate people. The thief depends on his approach, front, wits, and in many instances his talking ability. The professional burglar or stickup man (robber with a gun), on the other hand, uses violence or threat of violence. . . . Fourth, the professional thief is generally migratory and may work in all the cities of the United States. He generally uses a particular city as headquarters, and when two professional thieves first meet, the question is always asked: "Where are you out of?". . . .

The professional thief has nothing in common with the amateur thief. . . . The professional thief will be in sympathy with the amateur's attempt to steal something but will not be interested in him, for they have no acquaintances or ideas of stealing in common. . . .

The professional thief has nothing in common with those who commit sex crimes or other emotional crimes and would not even be courteous to them if he should chance to meet them in the can. . . .

Sympathy and congeniality with professional burglars and stick-ups is nearly as close as between thieves in one racket. They are all thieves, and the fact that one has a different racket does not alter this feeling. To professional burglars whom he knows on the street he will tender ideas and spots. . . . He will render assistance to a professional burglar in fixing cases, securing bonds, or escaping from a jailhouse. . . .

There are few fixed rules of ethics, but there are some common understandings among thieves. . . .

It is understood that no thief must squawk (inform) on another. . . . If a thief should squawk, the other thieves would not descend to the same plane and squawk on him. They use better methods. The worst penalty is to keep him broke. This is done by spreading the news that he has squawked, which makes it impossible for him to get into any mob. That is the greatest disgrace and the greatest hardship that can befall a thief. . . .

A thief is not a professional until he is proficient. When a thief is taken on for unimportant tasks by some mob, he is not regarded as a professional. He may develop into a professional in the course of time if he does these unimportant jobs well enough to lead the mob to give him more important jobs. . . .

Members of the profession make their exit from the profession in various ways. Some die, some get too old to work and wind up in a home for old people, some develop a habit (drug) and become too inefficient to be professional thieves, some violate the ethics of the profession and are kicked out, some get in bad with the fix and can no longer get protection and are therefore useless as members of a mob, some become fixers in resort cities, some become big shots in gambling, vice, junk, or booze rackets, some get "the big one" (extraordinarily large theft), and some settle down to legitimate occupations without getting "the big one.". . . .

II

The essential characteristics of the profession of theft . . . are technical skill, status, consensus, differential association, and organization. Two significant conclusions may be derived from analysis of these characteristics. The first is that the characteristics of the profession of theft are similar to the characteristics of any other permanent group. The second is that certain elements run through these characteristics which differentiate the professional thieves sharply from other groups. . . .

The professional thief has a complex of abilities and skills, just as do physicians, lawyers or bricklayers. . . .

The professional thief, like any other professional man, has status. The status is based upon his technical skill, financial standing, connections, power, dress, manners, and wide knowledge acquired in his migratory life. . . .

The profession of theft is a complex of common and shared feelings, sentiments, and overt acts. Pickpockets have similar reactions to prospective victims and to the particular situations in which victims are found. This similarity of reactions is due to the common background of experiences and the similarity of points of attention. These reactions are like the "clinical intuitions" which different physicians form of a patient or different lawyers form of a juryman on quick inspection. Thieves can work together without serious disagreements because they have these common and similar attitudes. . . .

Differential association is characteristic of the professional thieves, as of all other groups. The thief is a part of the underworld and in certain respects is segregated from the rest of society. . . .

The final definition of the professional thief is found within this differential association. The group defines its own membership. A person who is received in the group and recognized as a professional thief is a professional thief. One who is not so received and recognized is not a professional thief, regardless of his methods of making a living. . . .

Professional theft is organized crime. It is not organized in the journalistic sense, for no dictator or central office directs the work of the members of the profession. Rather it is organized in the sense that it is a system in which informal unity and reciprocity may be found. . . .

The complex of techniques, status, consensus, and differential association . . . may be regarded as organization. More specifically, the organization of professional thieves consists in part of the knowledge which becomes the common property of the profession. Every thief becomes an information bureau. For instance, each professional thief is known personally to a large proportion of the other thieves. . . .

Similarly, the knowledge regarding methods and situations becomes common property of the profession. "Toledo is a good town," "The lunch hour is the best time to work that spot," . . . and similar mandates and injunctions are transmitted from thief to thief until everyone in the profession knows them. . . .

Informal social services are similarly organized. Any thief will assist any other thief in a dangerous situation. . . . In these services reciprocity is assumed, but there is no insistence on immediate or specific return to the one who performs the service.

A MORE RECENT CONCEPTION

OF PROFESSIONAL CRIME

Excerpted from the President's Commission on Law Enforcement and Administration of Justice, *Task Force Report: Crime and Its Impact— An Assessment* (Washington, D.C.: U.S. Government Printing Office, 1967), pp. 96–101.

EXISTING INFORMATION about professional crime is fragmentary, and much of it may be outdated. A primary source is Edwin H. Sutherland's classic description of theft as a way of life, "The Professional Thief," but that work, though helpful, was published in 1937 and describes the life of a thief in the period between 1905 and 1925. Other books published since have focused on particular types of criminal activity normally engaged in by professionals including confidence game operations, pickpocketing, professional robbery and burglary, and receiving stolen goods. These few studies provide the basic information on professional crime available in the literature. Although differences in emphasis and coverage exist among them, they present a reasonably coherent, though necessarily incomplete, description of certain types of professional criminal activity.

In order to supplement this material, the Commission sponsored a pilot field research study in four cities—Atlanta, Chicago, New York, and San Francisco—during the summer of 1966. The study differed from previous research in that it used police and prosecutors as well as professional criminals as primary informants. . . .

. . . The number of criminals interviewed varied from a low of eight in one city (Chicago) to 19 in another (San Francisco), with a total of 50 being interviewed. About two-thirds of the total number were in jail or prison at the time of their interviews. Although compared with prior studies the combined samples amounted to a relatively large number of informants, it is obvious that such a survey, conducted under . . . tight time limitations, could not result in a detailed comprehensive picture of professional crime in the United States. But the data collected are useful for obtaining some insights about professional criminals and the life they lead. Combined with relevant data from previous studies, they provide the basis for the material in this chapter.

For purposes of the Commission-sponsored study, professional crime was defined as: "Crime committed for personal economic gain by individuals whose major source of income is from criminal pursuits and who spend the majority of their working time in illegal enterprises." Organized crime and white-collar crime were specifically excluded. And while the definition was comprehensive enough to cover a variety of crimes such as killing or strong-arming for hire, professional arson and even prostitution, the principal emphasis of the Commission's study, following the pattern of earlier studies, was on essentially predatory crimes where the victim does not consent and where the actors usually function not as employees but as entrepreneurs. This approach tends to focus on theft and theft-related offenses, including such crimes as receiving stolen goods, shoplifting, pickpocketing, auto theft, burglary, forgery, confidence games, and various kinds of fraud.

This definition differs from traditional definitions in that it does not include any requirement that professionals have specially developed skills or that they have any particularly close association with other professionals. In Sutherland's classic study, the professional thief was described as having "a complex of abilities and skills °°° developed °°° by education" which "can be secured only in association with professional thieves." Obviously this difference in definition affected the characteristics found to be associated with professional criminals. Thus prior studies found that professional criminals were often highly specialized, and that they tended to be quite loyal to members of their professional groups. The Commission-sponsored study, on the other hand, found that professional criminals tended to be generalists, to operate in a variety of loose associations with other professionals, and to exhibit no particular loyalty to their fellows. There is no way of knowing whether these different findings reflect only the difference in definition, or whether they reflect in addition changes in the character of professional crime.

The purpose of this chapter is to summarize the concededly inadequate data regarding professional crime, contained in the available literature and in the report of the Commission's study, and to speculate about possible lines of fruitful inquiry. The chapter adopts the broad definition used by the Commission-sponsored study. The significance of professional criminals so defined lies in part simply in the amount of crime that they are apparently responsible for. It is obvious that any group which is engaged in criminal activity on a relatively full-time basis will be responsible for crime out of all proportion to its numbers. Moreover, unlike many occasional criminals, professionals typically make no significant contribution to society through legitimate activity. Their significance lies also in the fact that, compared to many of the criminal types dealt with in the Commission's report, professional criminals are a relatively rational and competent group of persons who are involved in crime because it is a profitable business. It would appear therefore that the traditional sanctions of the criminal law could be highly effective in dealing with many types of professional crime. . . .

The Extent of Professional Crime

There are no accurate statistics on the amount of professional crime. Published studies contain only estimates of career earnings of individual professional criminals, illustrative "touches," estimated average weekly earnings of various types of professional mobs, and other data of this order. . . .

. . . there is reason to believe that professional criminals are responsible for a large proportion of all property crimes committed and probably an even larger proportion of total property loss through such crimes. Available information indicates, for example, that there are a large number of professional criminals, all of whom, by definition, work at crime on a relatively full-time basis, and some of whom are reported to have very high incomes, sometimes exceeding $100,000. And it is apparent that thefts involving the loss of large amounts of valuable merchandise require the sorts of contacts with fences and commercial establishments that professionals develop.

There is evidence that the more successful professionals tend to spend substantial portions of their working time in developing lucrative opportunities and planning their criminal activity. A week, month, or even longer period may be spent in preparing for a particularly promising venture. As a result, "scores" tend to be good and the risk of apprehension low. The run-of-the-mill professional criminal, on the other hand, finds it necessary to spend more time in actual stealing to meet expenses and maintain himself at a comfortable and free-spending standard of living. Members of rackets, such as picking pockets and other forms of low-paying larceny, spend virtually all of their time this way.

The Commission's study produced some vivid descriptions of the day-to-day life of the typical professional, the flavor of which is captured by the term "hustling." For the small-time professional criminal, hustling means moving around the bars and being seen; it means asking "what's up." It means "connecting" in the morning with two others who have a burglary set up for the evening, calling a man you know to see if he wants to buy 10 stolen alpaca sweaters at $5 each, and scouting the streets for an easy victim. It means being versatile: passing checks, rolling a drunk, driving for a stickup, boosting a car, burglarizing a store. It is a planless kind of existence, but with a purpose—to make as much money as can be made each day, no holds barred. While the more successful professional criminals hustle to some extent, they can afford to be much more purposeful and choosy in their criminal activities.

The Commission's study revealed that run-of-the-mill professionals regularly gather at certain bars and restaurants which in effect function as criminal job placement centers. These centers do for the professional criminal what want ads, employment offices, and businessmen's luncheons do for legitimate business. Through contact with other criminals, professionals learn of jobs to be pulled and of openings in groups planning to pull them. Contacts of this type also enable the professional to keep abreast of the latest techniques, and to gather information regarding criminal opportunities.

These centers tend to attract the low-status professional criminal; apparently the successful practitioner in crime does not go to the employment office.

Characteristics of Professional Crime

SKILLS

Sutherland drew a sharp distinction between the professional and the amateur thief based upon their relative skills. Under his classification, a person might steal as a full-time occupation, but he would not be a professional if he lacked the comprehensive complex of technical skills, personal contacts, and knowledge necessary in order to make a good living at crime in comparative safety. Sutherland's professional thief was contemptuous of the amateur's crude techniques, low income, and inability to avoid arrest. He therefore avoided association with amateurs and excluded them from the complex of reciprocal expectations and services which characterized his own way of life. But even under this definition, the professional criminal's skills vary significantly in kind and degree. The big-time jewel thief and the "ropers" and "insidemen" who contrive to extract thousands of dollars from wealthy victims in the big con game are at one end of the spectrum. At the other are petty thieves, short con operators, and pickpockets who, though technically competent, lack the techniques needed to make big scores consistently.

Clearly there is an even greater range in skills when all persons who work at crime on a relatively full-time basis are classified as professionals. Nevertheless even this group is, as a whole, a relatively competent one. Many of its members possess, in addition to particular skills, the ability to plan and carry out detailed operations, to manipulate people, to analyze problems and implement solutions. It is clear that professional crime represents the loss to society of the potential contributions of a capable group of people, as well as the channeling of their energies into destructive activities.

SPECIALIZATION

There is evidence that some individual professional criminals tend to specialize in a limited number of related rackets. Many exclude certain kinds of activities: thus some of the professional criminals who were interviewed in the course of the Commission's study said that they would not use violence. But in general the Commission's study indicated that professionals in the middle and lower status levels tend to be versatile. Even the better professional criminal is not always free to follow his preferred line of work, since it may not be either profitable or safe at all times. Under these circumstances he may undertake activities at which he is not especially skilled.

GROUP ACTIVITY

Earlier studies described the relationship between professional criminals as relatively structured. Sutherland, in describing the professional thief of 40 years ago, and Maurer, in his treatment of professional confidence men and pickpockets, stressed the idea that professional criminals enjoy a sense of identity and solidarity and work within a set of well-defined norms and codes of loyalty, helpfulness, and honesty in dealing with one another.

The Commission-sponsored study, directed at a broader group of criminals, found that only the more successful members of this group could be so characterized. It found that the associations or gangs which run-of-the-mill professionals form to commit their crimes tend to be unstable, and that this instability results in part from the diversity of their activities. Different crimes require different kinds of personnel, amounts of financial backing, and types of fencing operations. Consequently, groupings and relations with loan sharks and fences may change from operation to operation. Even the few relatively stable groups which the consultants heard about brought in other professional criminals for certain jobs, and some members of the group might hire out from time to time on other jobs.

The shifting, transitory pattern of most professional criminals' working relationships was found to be accompanied by the absence of any strong ethical codes. Few . . . seemed to feel bound by any "no ratting" rule. Typically they appeared to take it for granted that others would do whatever necessary to protect themselves—to avoid imprisonment or reduce a sentence—and that they, therefore, should do likewise. As one professional criminal commented: "The one who gets his story told first gets the lightest sentence." There was little resentment expressed about this. It was treated like the weather—a fact of life. Further, criminals expected to be cheated by their colleagues, or by most colleagues. Many of those interviewed reported having been cheated by fences and even by their partners in a particular venture. Victimization of one professional group by another is apparently also fairly common, limited only by fear of reprisal.

There were exceptions to this general pattern, however. Some professional criminals stated that they had worked with certain individuals whom they trusted completely. And relative stability was found among the really successful professional criminals in New York and Chicago. In Chicago, for example, there is a group of between 50 and 200 "heavy" professional thieves who concentrate on such criminal activities as burglary, robbery, and cartage theft. It is said that this group, or at least the core members of the group, are quite stable and quite highly organized, and apparently they exert a considerable amount of control over their own regular members, as well as over persons who work with them only on occasional jobs.

Changing Criminal Opportunities

As conditions in society change, certain criminal occupations become relatively unprofitable, and other opportunities develop. The nature of crime will tend to change accordingly. Criminal activity like legitimate business activity may respond to the market, to supply and demand curves, and to technological developments. Professional crime, guided by the profit motive, can be expected to be particularly responsive to such factors. One example is the reported decline in safecracking. This is apparently due in part to such factors as increased law enforcement surveillance and mobility, and improvements in the design of safes. Undoubtedly the fact that safes no longer play as important a role has also contributed to the decline—modern economic transactions involve the transfer of credits much more than the transfer of cash. Thus it may have become both more difficult and riskier to rob safes, and also less profitable. At the same time, more promising opportunities for crime have arisen. One of these is check-passing. The Commission's study learned that nearly every burglar nowadays is also in the check business. One professional burglar said that in one period of several weeks between burglaries he passed over $20,000 of stolen checks. A generation ago burglars did not even look for checks to steal.

A good illustration of the effect of the development of a new market is auto theft and crimes relating to the automobile, such as auto stripping and auto "boosting" (stealing goods from parked cars), activities which are reported to be thriving in the cities surveyed. The Commission's study found also that there has been a rapid rise in recent years in home improvement and related frauds, a rise which corresponds roughly to the increase in privately owned homes. Some law enforcement officials think that in many cities these frauds currently constitute the most profitable source of income for professional criminals.

Professional criminals are also reported to be turning from robbing banks, picking pockets, and operating confidence games to other opportunities, but documentation for such new trends is scanty. . . .

Key Aspects of Professional Crime

The services of the fence and the loan shark appear to be essential to the operations of many professional criminals. Since a great many professionals may depend on a very few such figures, they may constitute a particularly vulnerable aspect of professional crime. The "fix" appears to be of similar importance to the success of professional criminality.

THE FENCE

Nearly all professional theft is undertaken with the aim of selling the goods thereafter. Although the thief himself may retail his stolen merchandise, he probably will prefer to sell to a fence. He thereby increases his safety by reducing the risk that he will be arrested with the goods in his possession, or that they will be stolen in turn from him. He also avoids the dangers associated with the disposal process itself. In addition, large quantities of goods which may be perishable or otherwise quickly lose their value, or for which there is a specialized demand, will require a division of labor and level of organization beyond the capacity of an individual thief operating as his own retailer. The professional thief thus needs a "middleman" in the same way and for some of the same reasons as the farmer, manufacturer, or other producer.

The types of thefts recorded by the Commission study staff in New York and Chicago suggest the presence of big-time fences who can handle large quantities of specialized goods. For example, in Chicago there recently occurred a cartage theft of $250,000 worth of merchandise and Green Stamps from a Sperry and Hutchinson warehouse and another cartage theft of copper metal valued at over $400,000. To dispose of such quantities of specialized goods requires connections with commercial firms. Most likely a highly accomplished fence served as a middleman between the thieves and the eventual buyers.

As an illustration of the level of efficiency which may be attained by professionals working in cooperation with fences, the Commission's study learned from the New York City police that within the space of approximately 1 month following the recent increase in that city's cigarette sales tax, an entire system for distributing bootlegged cigarettes had been set up and was operating smoothly. The out-of-state suppliers, the truckers, and both the wholesale and retail distributors had been organized, and the system was operating on a scale capable of handling full truckloads of untaxed cigarettes shipped in from the South.

Some fences engage in fencing as a supplement to their legitimate businesses, often on a more or less regular basis. The consultants learned of clothing and appliance dealers who regularly serve as outlets for stolen goods. The major outlets for stolen jewels in one of the cities studied were reported to be legitimate jewelry merchants. Other fences deal primarily or wholly in stolen goods, and are therefore professional criminals themselves.

Some narcotics pushers act as fences, taking stolen goods instead of cash for narcotics. While dealing with addicts is generally regarded as more dangerous than dealing with nonaddicts, it is also more profitable. The addict in need of a "fix" does not bargain well. . . .

THE LOAN SHARK

The loan shark also performs a key function by providing professional criminals with capital and emergency funds. The literature of professional crime contains few references to loan shark activity. Both Sutherland and Maurer describe a practice whereby members of a professional criminal gang establish their own emergency fund. Each member of the gang contributes an equal share to the fund which he may receive back if he leaves the gang. If he is arrested while working with the gang, he has access to as much of the fund as he needs for a bail bond, legal fees, or related expenses. This sort of arrangement appears to be an extension of the natural interdependence of a closely knit group and tends to reinforce the solidarity of the group.

The loan shark functions quite differently. He may meet professional criminals' needs for cash in emergencies, but his activity often has secondary effects which tend to be detrimental to his clients.

Professional criminals may turn to the loan shark to finance crimes which require extra amounts of capital—to buy the tools, or whatever may be needed for the operation, or to bribe public officials. The professional criminal may be willing to pay usurious interest rates (sometimes reported to be as high as 100 percent per week for highly risky loans) if he expects his activities to be particularly lucrative. He may also need emergency financing when apprehended, to pay bail and legal costs. To repay the money borrowed plus interest upon his release, the criminal will often engage in further criminal activities, often more risky than those he ordinarily undertakes. If rearrested, he must post bond again and incur additional legal fees. This pattern may be repeated a number of times before he is finally brought to trial. The high interest charged by the loan shark may thus itself precipitate criminal activity.

The interaction between loan sharking and professional crime doubtless is far more complicated than was discovered during the course of the Commission's brief study. The study staff was told that some "legitimate" businessmen provide loans to criminals occasionally. And there was some evidence that professional criminals regard loan sharking as a relatively safe and profitable racket, and that those who make a big score or otherwise accumulate enough capital frequently set themselves up as loan sharks. But further study is needed on these as well as other facets of the relationship between professional crime and the loan shark.

THE FIX

There is evidence that the professional criminal frequently bribes public officials to increase his security against law enforcement activity. The fix may be applied in advance to forestall intervention by the police and thereby reduce a major occupational hazard of his profession. Or it may be used after the fact to alleviate the usual consequences of apprehension—to obtain reduced charges or a lighter sentence, or to arrange for preferential treatment. In some communities the professional must himself deal directly with the appropriate officials. In others there may be a local "fixer" who has connections with the party in power and who may be tied in with organized crime. Here the professional criminal need only deal with the fixer as a middleman. . . .

Attorneys, bondsmen, politicians, and other ostensibly legitimate persons may be fixers. A fixer may also be a fence, the insideman in a big con game, or a member of organized crime. Cash is the usual commodity used to purchase immunity, but sometimes a case may be fixed for credit or as a favor.

The extent of fixing today is difficult to document. The Commission's study . . . encountered little evidence of the sort of fixing described here. The fact that police, judges, and prosecutors probably are better paid and trained today may mean that individually they are less susceptible to bribery. The increased bureaucratization of police operations and personnel practices may also make policemen less subject to corruption from above. And the decline of the big city political machine may have contributed to a decline in organized fixing. On the other hand, professional criminals still operate with considerable success, and it seems likely that they need some protection to do so.

Relations with Organized Crime

Professional crime may or may not be carried on in structured groups. In some ways it can be loosely analogized to legitimate business activity. But its essence is not business; it is outright theft or theft-related conduct. Organized crime, on the other hand, tends to bear a closer resemblance to the operations of business. It involves thousands of criminals working in well-organized, highly structured operations engaged in activities involving the supplying of illegal goods and services—such as gambling, narcotics, and prostitution—to cooperative customers; it often involves infiltration into legitimate businesses and labor unions.

Regrettably, little is known of the nature and extent of the relationship between professional and organized crime. . . . But it is apparent that a variety of working arrangements exist between professional criminals and organized crime, which are of substantial significance for both categories of crime. There is some evidence, for example, that the fences and loan sharks with whom professional criminals deal are frequently part of the organized crime operation. And there is some indication that organized crime exerts significant power and control over professional crime. The Commission's study staff was informed, for example, that in Chicago the syndicate occasionally provides the services of an arbitrator to settle disputes among the members of a large theft gang. And the syndicate apparently hires professional criminals, on occasion, to do particular jobs such as homicide. . . .

The professional criminal's energy and talents are devoted not merely to committing profitable crimes, but to avoiding the legal consequences of such activity. His methods range from simply taking full advantage of all rights accorded him by the system of criminal justice to actual corruption of the system. It is obvious that sophisticated methods of law enforcement are necessary to deal with the phenomenon of professional crime. A more sophisticated understanding of professional crime is a clear prerequisite.

MAXIE THE GONIFF

DAVID DRESSLER

Reprinted from *Parole Chief* (New York, Viking, 1951), pp. 243–47.

MAXIE THE GONIFF is a professional. Practically all cannons are. He is not very bright. His body is slight and springy; his fingers are long, tapering, and nervous. His face resembles a parrot's, the beak long and hooked downward. His eyes are furtive. He decided over fifty years ago that picking "pokes" was a fine way of making a living. He apprenticed himself to a master, studied hard, graduated with honors, and went on his own. He wouldn't tell me how old he was at the time we spoke, but my guess is that he was at least sixty-five. . . .

Like most of his kind, Maxie has a long criminal record. He has been arrested seventy-one times in twenty-two states.

"Doesn't speak so well for you, Maxie," I goaded him. . . .

He flushed angrily. "Every one of them pinches came after a whole season's work. In fifty years I done six years time. I'm living good—well, pretty good—for forty-four years and it cost me six years! You should have it so good!"

He claims that both his parents were alcoholics, that they put him out of the house when he was twelve, and that he has been on his own ever since. For a time he was a petty thief, then a shoplifter, and finally, while still a kid, he met a man who took him on as an apprentice dip and taught him the business.

Picking pockets *is* a business, Maxie insists. "You've got to figure a certain amount of risk in any business. Suppose I open a saloon. I'm taking a chance, no? I might go broke, I might have to pay too much protection—it's all business."

Like all commercial enterprises, Maxie's has its seasons. "Summers we work the resorts, like Coney Island and the buses and subways going to and from. Beaches are good too. Certain holidays is season for us. Before Easter and Christmas. There's lots of shopping. That's when I hit department stores. In the elevators or even on the floor."

When he has had a run of bad luck he will depart from his more accustomed beat and cover a church wedding. "You don't often find much dough on the guys, but brother! are they easy to take! They don't expect a thief in a church."

Occasional gravy is a convention or parade. Maxie plays the crowds. He loves American Legion groups because "half the time they don't even know *the next morning* whether they've been hooked or just spent the dough!" . . . .

Maxie takes pride in his technique. He has little use for the lone operator, although he admits there are some good ones. He considers they take too many risks. . . .

He likes to work in a mob of two or four people. Say you're on a subway or elevator. "You pick your mark and try to figure where he keeps his wallet. It ain't hard to find out. You just jostle the sucker and move off. Right away he puts his hand where he's got the wallet to see if it's there. He tips you off.

"Of course, if he don't fall for that, you've got to *fan* him. You feel around, very easy, until you locate the poke.

"Then comes pratting. You prat the guy around. That means you push him around, edge him around, not hard, gentle, just enough to distract his attention. Also to get him into position—the position you want him in for the score."

The man who does the pushing is the "stall." When the victim is in position, the "duke" (hand) of one thief extracts the poke. This man is called, variously, a "hook," "tool," "wire," or "instrument." He is the most skillful member of the team. The victim's attention is directed to the stall as the hook takes the wallet. Maxie is a hook.

"Funny thing," he said, chuckling. "Some guys look for a poke in a hip pocket. They like to take it from there. I'd rather score out of the breast pocket. Why? Because the sucker thinks he's cute, see?

. . . He thinks if he carries it in the breast pocket it's tough to take. It is, but a good thief likes that kind of meat. I always do." (I doubt it. Professional cannons are awful liars. Chances are, Maxie, good businessman that he is, will always go for the easier score when possible.)

While taking from the inside pocket, the wire "shades" the duke —covers his hand so the victim won't see it, perhaps with a newspaper. "What I do," says Maxie, "is 'put a throw' in his face. I shade my duke with a paper and annoy the guy by flappin' it under his nose. That makes 'im mad. He's concentratin' on the throw while I'm 'takin' off the score.'

"In a good crowd, on a hip job, the 'push grift' works. No shadin' the duke, nothin'. Everybody's pushing, so you push all you want, and the guy don't even see or feel your hand."

In digging for the wallet the "straight hoist" is commonly employed. The cannon puts the first two fingers, held stiffly, into the pocket. He stiffens his body, lifts up on his toes, and out comes the wallet.

The next step is "cleaning." "The stall distracts attention, say. Now the wire's got the poke. He has to get clean right away. . . . If the sucker 'blows' (discovers his loss) he's gonna figure right away it's the wire, because the wire was closest to him. So I pass the wallet on right away to one of my stalls—the one who will be first off the car or elevator. If the guy grabs me I'm clean. I beef like hell. If he goes for the stall, he drops the poke and he's clean. Or better yet, he plants it on some bystander and we take it back later."

Maxie is proudest of the fact that he is a specialist among specialists, "a left-breech hook." That's a man who can draw a score out of a left pants pocket. "There ain't many can do that. It's hard. Try it!"

I asked him how much he earned a year by grifting. He became very evasive, even apologetic. "Oh, I had my ups and downs. Why talk about it? You do all right, year in, year out, if you're good. Some years I run five, ten thousand. Other times not so good. . . ."

"Where did your money go? . . ."

"Well, the horses got a lot of it. Craps. Cards. Women. And I had to eat too." He forgot to mention that he has a wife and two children who are dependent upon him for their support.

I have never known an affluent pickpocket. I don't believe they make as much as Maxie claims, and their money seems to go fast. They live riotously. Some are drug addicts at times in their lives. Many have wives and children. I've never known one who wasn't a confirmed gambler or who wasn't fresh out of money every time I inquired.

Maxie is hurt because cannons are generally regarded with contempt, even in the professional underworld. He doesn't like to admit that contempt is earned. But the average dip is penny ante. Moreover, he is weak-willed, often turns in a pal to save his own skin. Perhaps because he is a weakling, the pickpocket is often a stool pigeon.

Maxie insists there is honor among thieves in his game. "Sure, a guy rats now and then. That don't prove nothin'. You'll always find a few rats. But most of us stick together. We help each other. We put up fall dough for a guy in trouble."

"Did you ever rat, Maxie?"

"Like I say, we stick together. We put up fall dough." . . . .

"Maxie," I asked, "if you had it to do over again, what would you be instead of a pickpocket?"

"What's wrong," he snapped, "with this racket?"

ORGANIZED CRIME

The President's Commission on Law Enforcement and Administration of Justice, *Task Force Report: Organized Crime, Annotations and Consultants' Papers* (Washington, D.C.; U.S. Government Printing Office, 1967), pp. 1–10.

ORGANIZED CRIME is a society that seeks to operate outside the control of the American people and their governments. It involves thousands of criminals, working within structures as complex as those of any large corporation, subject to laws more rigidly enforced than those of legitimate governments. Its actions are not impulsive but rather the result of intricate conspiracies, carried on over many years and aimed at gaining control over whole fields of activity in order to amass huge profits.

The core of organized crime activity is the supplying of illegal goods and services—gambling, loan sharking, narcotics, and other forms of vice—to countless numbers of citizen customers. But organized crime is also extensively and deeply involved in legitimate business and in labor unions. Here it employs illegitimate methods —monopolization, terrorism, extortion, tax evasion—to drive out or control lawful ownership and leadership and to exact illegal profits from the public. And to carry on its many activities secure from governmental interference, organized crime corrupts public officials.

Former Attorney General Robert F. Kennedy illustrated its power simply and vividly. He testified before a Senate subcommittee in 1963 that the physical protection of witnesses who had cooperated with the Federal Government in organized crime cases often required that those witnesses change their appearances, change their names, or even leave the country. When the government of a powerful country is unable to protect its friends from its enemies by means less extreme than obliterating their identities, surely it is being seriously challenged, if not threatened.

What organized crime wants is money and power. What makes it different from law-abiding organizations and individuals with those same objectives is that the ethical and moral standards the criminals adhere to, the laws and regulations they obey, the procedures they use are private and secret ones that they devise themselves, change when they see fit, and administer summarily and invisibly. Organized crime affects the lives of millions of Americans, but because it desperately preserves its invisibility many, perhaps most, Americans are not aware how they are affected, or even that they are affected at all. The price of a loaf of bread may go up one cent as the result of an organized crime conspiracy, but a housewife has no way of knowing why she is paying more. If organized criminals paid income tax on every cent of their vast earnings everybody's tax bill would go down, but no one knows how much.

But to discuss the impact of organized crime in terms of whatever direct, personal, everyday effect it has on individuals is to miss most of the point. Most individuals are not affected, in this sense, very much. Much of the money organized crime accumulates comes from innumerable petty transactions: 50-cent bets, $3-a-month private garbage collection services, quarters dropped into racketeer-owned jukeboxes, or small price rises resulting from protection rackets. A one-cent-a-loaf rise in bread may annoy housewives, but it certainly does not impoverish them.

Sometimes organized crime's activities do not directly affect individuals at all. Smuggled cigarettes in a vending machine cost consumers no more than tax-paid cigarettes, but they enrich the leaders of organized crime. Sometimes these activities actually reduce prices for a short period of time, as can happen when organized crime, in an attempt to take over an industry, starts a price war against legitimate businessmen. Even when organized crime engages in a large transaction, individuals may not be directly affected. A large sum of money may be diverted from a union pension fund to finance a business venture without immediate and direct effect upon the individual members of the union.

It is organized crime's accumulation of money, not the individual transactions by which the money is accumulated, that has a great and threatening impact on America. A quarter in a jukebox means nothing and results in nothing. But millions of quarters in thousands of jukeboxes can provide both a strong motive for murder and the means to commit murder with impunity. Organized crime exists by virtue of the power it purchases with its money. The millions of dollars it can invest in narcotics or use for layoff money give it power over the lives of thousands of people and over the quality of life in whole neighborhoods. The millions of dollars it can throw into the legitimate economic system give it power to manipulate the price of shares on the stock market, to raise or lower the price of retail merchandise, to determine whether entire industries are union or nonunion, to make it easier or harder for businessmen to continue in business.

The millions of dollars it can spend on corrupting public officials may give it power to maim or murder people inside or outside the organization with impunity; to extort money from businessmen; to conduct businesses in such fields as liquor, meat, or drugs without regard to administrative regulations; to avoid payment of income taxes or to secure public works contracts without competitive bidding.

The purpose of organized crime is not competition with visible, legal government but nullification of it. When organized crime places an official in public office, it nullifies the political process. When it bribes a police official, it nullifies law enforcement.

There is another, more subtle way in which organized crime has an impact on American life. Consider the former way of life of Frank Costello, a man who has repeatedly been called a leader of organized crime. He lived in an expensive apartment on the corner of 72d Street and Central Park West in New York. He was often seen dining in well-known restaurants in the company of judges, public officials, and prominent businessmen. Every morning he was shaved in the barbershop of the Waldorf Astoria Hotel. On many weekends he played golf at a country club on the fashionable North Shore of Long Island. In short, though his reputation was common knowledge, he moved around New York conspicuously and unashamedly, perhaps ostracized by some people but more often accepted, greeted by journalists, recognized by children, accorded all the freedoms of a prosperous and successful man. On a

society that treats such a man in such a manner, organized crime
has had an impact.

And yet the public remains indifferent. Few Americans seem to
comprehend how the phenomenon of organized crime affects their
lives. They do not see how gambling with bookmakers, or borrow-
ing money from loan sharks, forwards the interests of great criminal cartels. Businessmen looking for labor harmony or nonunion
status through irregular channels rationalize away any suspicions
that organized crime is thereby spreading its influence. When an
ambitious political candidate accepts substantial cash contributions from unknown sources, he suspects but dismisses the fact that
organized crime will dictate some of his actions when he assumes
office. . . .

The Types of Organized Criminal Activities

CATERING TO PUBLIC DEMANDS

Organized criminal groups participate in any illegal activity that
offers maximum profit at minimum risk of law enforcement interference. They offer goods and services that millions of Americans
desire even though declared illegal by their legislatures.

Gambling. Law enforcement officials agree almost unanimously
that gambling is the greatest source of revenue for organized
crime. It ranges from lotteries, such as "numbers" or "bolita," to
off-track horse betting, bets on sporting events, large dice games
and illegal casinos. In large cities where organized criminal groups
exist, very few of the gambling operators are independent of a
large organization. Anyone whose independent operation becomes
successful is likely to receive a visit from an organization representative who convinces the independent, through fear or promise of
greater profit, to share his revenue with the organization.

Most large-city gambling is established or controlled by organized crime members through elaborate hierarchies. Money is filtered from the small operator who takes the customer's bet,
through persons who pick up money and slips, to second-echelon
figures in charge of particular districts, and then into one of several

main offices. The profits that eventually accrue to organization leaders move through channels so complex that even persons who work in the betting operation do not know or cannot prove the identity of the leader. Increasing use of the telephone for lottery and sports betting has facilitated systems in which the bookmaker may not know the identity of the second-echelon person to whom he calls in the day's bets. Organization not only creates greater efficiency and enlarges markets, it also provides a systematized method of corrupting the law enforcement process by centralizing procedures for the payment of graft.

Organization is also necessary to prevent severe losses. More money may be bet on one horse or one number with a small operator than he could pay off if that horse or that number should win. The operator will have to hedge by betting some money himself on that horse or that number. This so-called "layoff" betting is accomplished through a network of local, regional, and national layoff men, who take bets from gambling operations.

There is no accurate way of ascertaining organized crime's gross revenue from gambling in the United States. Estimates of the annual intake have varied from $7 to $50 billion. Legal betting at racetracks reaches a gross annual figure of almost $5 billion, and most enforcement officials believe that illegal wagering on horse races, lotteries, and sporting events totals at least $20 billion each year. Analysis of organized criminal betting operations indicates that the profit is as high as one-third of gross revenue—or $6 to $7 billion each year. While the Commission cannot judge the accuracy of these figures, even the most conservative estimates place substantial capital in the hands of organized crime leaders.

Loan Sharking. In the view of most law enforcement officials loan sharking, the lending of money at higher rates than the legally prescribed limit, is the second largest source of revenue for organized crime. Gambling profits provide the initial capital for loan-shark operations.

No comprehensive analysis has ever been made of what kinds of customers loan sharks have, or of how much or how often each kind borrows. Enforcement officials and other investigators do have some information. Gamblers borrow to pay gambling losses;

narcotics users borrow to purchase heroin. Some small businessmen borrow from loan sharks when legitimate credit channels are
closed. The same men who take bets from employees in mass employment industries also serve at times as loan sharks, whose
money enables the employees to pay off their gambling debts or
meet household needs.

Interest rates vary from 1 to 150 percent a week, according to
the relationship between the lender and borrower, the intended
use of the money, the size of the loan, and the repayment potential.
The classic "6-for-5" loan, 20 percent a week, is common with small
borrowers. Payments may be due by a certain hour on a certain
day, and even a few minutes' default may result in a rise in interest
rates. The lender is more interested in perpetuating interest payments than collecting principal; and force, or threats of force of the
most brutal kind, are used to effect interest collection, eliminate
protest when interest rates are raised, and prevent the beleaguered
borrower from reporting the activity to enforcement officials. No
reliable estimates exist of the gross revenue from organized loan
sharking, but profit margins are higher than for gambling operations, and many officials classify the business in the multi-billion-
dollar range.

Narcotics. The sale of narcotics is organized like a legitimate im-
porting-wholesaling-retailing business. The distribution of heroin,
for example, requires movement of the drug through four or five
levels between the importer and the street peddler. Many enforcement officials believe that the severity of mandatory Federal narcotics penalties has caused organized criminals to restrict their activities to importing and wholesale distribution. They stay away
from smaller-scale wholesale transactions or dealing at the retail
level. Transactions with addicts are handled by independent narcotics pushers using drugs imported by organized crime.

The large amounts of cash and the international connections
necessary for large, long-term heroin supplies can be provided only
by organized crime. Conservative estimates of the number of addicts in the Nation and the average daily expenditure for heroin
indicate that the gross heroin trade is $350 million annually, of
which $21 million are probably profits to the importer and distrib-

utor. Most of this profit goes to organized crime groups in those few cities in which almost all heroin consumption occurs.

Other Goods and Services. Prostitution and bootlegging play a small and declining role in organized crime's operations. Production of illegal alcohol is a risky business. The destruction of stills and supplies by law enforcement officers during the initial stages means the loss of heavy initial investment capital. Prostitution is difficult to organize and discipline is hard to maintain. Several important convictions of organized crime figures in prostitution cases in the 1930's and 1940's made the criminal executives wary of further participation.

BUSINESS AND LABOR INTERESTS

Infiltration of Legitimate Business. A legitimate business enables the racket executive to acquire respectability in the community and to establish a source of funds that appears legal and upon which just enough taxes may be paid to avoid income tax prosecution. Organized crime invests the profit it has made from illegal service activities in a variety of businesses throughout the country. To succeed in such ventures, it uses accountants, attorneys, and business consultants, who in some instances work exclusively on its affairs. Too often, because of the reciprocal benefits involved in organized crime's dealings with the business world, or because of fear, the legitimate sector of society helps the illegitimate sector. The Illinois Crime Commission, after investigating one service industry in Chicago, stated:

There is a disturbing lack of interest on the part of some legitimate business concerns regarding the identity of the persons with whom they deal. This lackadaisical attitude is conducive to the perpetration of frauds and the infiltration and subversion of legitimate businesses by the organized criminal element.

Because business ownership is so easily concealed, it is difficult to determine all the types of businesses that organized crime has penetrated. Of the 75 or so racket leaders who met at Apalachin, N.Y., in 1957, at least 9 were in the coin-operated machine industry, 16 were in the garment industry, 10 owned grocery stores, 17 owned bars or restaurants, 11 were in the olive oil and cheese business, and 9 were in the construction business. Others were involved in automobile agencies, coal companies, entertainment, funeral homes, ownership of horses and race tracks, linen and laundry enterprises, trucking, waterfront activities, and bakeries.

Today, the kinds of production and service industries and businesses that organized crime controls or has invested in range from accounting firms to yeast manufacturing. One criminal syndicate alone has real estate interests with an estimated value of $300 million. In a few instances, racketeers control nationwide manufacturing and service industries with known and respected brand names.

Control of business concerns has usually been acquired through one of four methods: (1) investing concealed profits acquired from gambling and other illegal activities; (2) accepting business interests in payment of the owner's gambling debts; (3) foreclosing on usurious loans; and (4) using various forms of extortion.

Acquisition of legitimate businesses is also accomplished in more sophisticated ways. One organized crime group offered to lend money to a business on condition that a racketeer be appointed to the company's board of directors and that a nominee for the lenders be given first option to purchase if there were any outside sale of the company's stock. Control of certain brokerage houses was secured through foreclosure of usurious loans, and the businesses then used to promote the sale of fraudulent stock, involving losses of more than $2 million to the public.

Criminal groups also satisfy defaulted loans by taking over businesses, hiring professional arsonists to burn buildings and contents, and collecting on the fire insurance. Another tactic was illustrated in the recent bankruptcy of a meatpacking firm in which control was secured as payment for gambling debts. With the original owners remaining in nominal management positions, extensive product orders were placed through established lines of credit, and the goods were immediately sold at low prices before the suppliers were paid. The organized criminal group made a quick profit of three-quarters of a million dollars by pocketing the receipts from sale of the products ordered and placing the firm in bankruptcy without paying the suppliers.

Too little is known about the effects on the economy of organized crime's entry into the business world, but the examples above indicate the harm done to the public and at least suggest how criminal cartels can undermine free competition. The ordinary businessman is hard pressed to compete with a syndicate enterprise. From its gambling and other illegal revenue—on most of which no taxes are paid—the criminal group always has a ready source of cash with which to enter any business. Through union connections, the business run by organized crime either prevents unionization or secures "sweetheart" contracts from existing unions. These tactics are used effectively in combination. In one city, organized crime gained a monopoly in garbage collection by preserving the business's nonunion status and by using cash reserves to offset temporary losses incurred when the criminal group lowered prices to drive competitors out of business.

Strong-arm tactics are used to enforce unfair business policy and to obtain customers. A restaurant chain controlled by organized crime used the guise of "quality control" to insure that individual restaurant franchise holders bought products only from other syndicate-owned businesses. In one city, every business with a particular kind of waste product useful in another line of industry sold that product to a syndicate-controlled business at one-third the price offered by legitimate business.

The cumulative effect of the infiltration of legitimate business in America cannot be measured. Law enforcement officials agree that entry into legitimate business is continually increasing and that it has not decreased organized crime's control over gambling, usury and other profitable, low-risk criminal enterprises.

Labor Racketeering. Control of labor supply and infiltration of labor unions by organized crime prevent unionization of some industries, provide opportunities for stealing from union funds and extorting money by threats of possible labor strife, and provide funds from the enormous union pension and welfare systems for business ventures controlled by organized criminals. Union control also may enhance other illegal activities. Trucking, construction, and waterfront shipping entrepreneurs, in return for assurance that business operations will not be interrupted by labor discord, countenance gambling, loan sharking, and pilferage on company property. Organized criminals either direct these activities or grant "concessions" to others in return for a percentage of the profits.

Some of organized crime's effects on labor union affairs, particularly in the abuse of pension and welfare funds, were disclosed in investigations by Senator John McClellan's committee. In one case, almost immediately after receiving a license as an insurance broker, the son of a major organized crime figure in New York City was chosen as the broker for a number of such funds, with significant commissions to be earned and made available for distribution to "silent partners." The youthful broker's only explanation for his success was that he had advertised in the classified telephone directory.

In New York City, early in 1966, the head of one organized crime group was revealed to be a partner in a labor relations consulting firm. One client of the firm, a nationally prominent builder, said he did not oppose unions but that better and cheaper houses could be built without them. The question of why a legitimate businessman would seek the services of an untrained consultant with a criminal record to handle his labor relations was not answered.

Location of Organized Crime Activities

Organized criminal groups are known to operate in all sections of the Nation. In response to a Commission survey of 71 cities, the police departments in 80 percent of the cities with over 1 million residents, in 20 percent of the cities with a population between one-half million and a million, in 20 percent of the cities with between 250,000 and 500,000 population, and in over 50 percent of the cities between 100,000 and 250,000, indicated that organized criminal groups exist in their cities. In some instances Federal agency intelligence indicated the presence of organized crime where local reports denied it. Of the nine cities not responding to the commission survey, six are known to Federal agencies to have extensive organized crime problems. . . .

Organized crime in small cities is more difficult to assess. Law enforcement personnel are aware of many instances in which local racket figures controlled crime in a smaller city and received aid from and paid tribute to organized criminal groups located in a nearby large city. In one Eastern town, for example, the local racket figure combined with outside organized criminal groups to establish horse and numbers gambling grossing $1.3 million annually, an organized dice game drawing customers from four states and having an employee payroll of $350,000 annually, and a still capable of producing $4 million worth of alcohol each year. The town's population was less than 100,000. Organized crime cannot be seen as merely a big-city problem.

Corruption of the Enforcement and Political Systems

Today's corruption is less visible, more subtle, and therefore more difficult to detect and assess than the corruption of the prohibition era. All available data indicate that organized crime flourishes only where it has corrupted local officials. As the scope and variety of organized crime's activities have expanded, its need to involve public officials at every level of local government has grown. And as government regulation expands into more and more areas of private and business activity, the power to corrupt likewise affords the corrupter more control over matters affecting the everyday life of each citizen.

Contrast, for example, the way governmental action in contract procurement or zoning functions today with the way it functioned only a few years ago. The potential harm of corruption is greater today if only because the scope of governmental activity is greater. In different places at different times, organized crime has corrupted police officials, prosecutors, legislators, judges, regulatory agency officials, mayors, councilmen, and other public officials, whose legitimate exercise of duties would block organized crime and whose illegal exercise of duties helps it.

Neutralizing local law enforcement is central to organized crime's operations. What can the public do if no one investigates the investigators, and the political figures are neutralized by their alliance with organized crime? Anyone reporting corrupt activities may merely be telling his story to the corrupted; in a recent "investigation" of widespread corruption, the prosecutor announced that any citizen coming forward with evidence of payments to public officials to secure government action would be prosecuted for participating in such unlawful conduct.

In recent years some local governments have been dominated by criminal groups. Today, no large city is completely controlled by organized crime, but in many there is a considerable degree of corruption.

Organized crime currently is directing its efforts to corrupt law enforcement at the chief or at least middle-level supervisory officials. The corrupt political executive who ties the hands of police officials who want to act against organized crime is even more effective for organized crime's purposes. To secure political power organized crime tries by bribes or political contributions to corrupt the nonoffice-holding political leaders to whom judges, mayors, prosecuting attorneys, and correctional officials may be responsive. . . .

Membership and Organization of Criminal Cartels

Some law enforcement officials define organized crime as those groups engaged in gambling, or narcotics pushing, or loan sharking, or with illegal business or labor interests. This is useful to the extent that it eliminates certain other criminal groups from consideration, such as youth gangs, pickpocket rings, and professional criminal groups who may also commit many types of crimes, but whose groups are ad hoc. But when law enforcement officials focus exclusively on the crime instead of the organization, their target is likely to be the lowest-level criminals who commit the visible crimes. This has little effect on the organization.

The Commission believes that before a strategy to combat organized crime's threat to America can be developed, that threat must be assessed by a close examination of organized crime's distinctive characteristics and methods of operation.

National Scope of Organized Crime

In 1951 the Kefauver Committee declared that a nationwide crime syndicate known as the Mafia operated in many large cities and that the leaders of the Mafia usually controlled the most lucrative rackets in their cities.

In 1957, 20 of organized crime's top leaders were convicted (later reversed on appeal) of a criminal charge arising from a meeting at Apalachin, N.Y. At the sentencing the judge stated that they had sought to corrupt and infiltrate the political mainstreams of the country, that they had led double lives of crime and respectability, and that their probation reports read "like a tale of horrors."

Today the core of organized crime in the United States consists of 24 groups operating as criminal cartels in large cities across the Nation. Their membership is exclusively men of Italian descent, they are in frequent communication with each other, and their smooth functioning is insured by a national body of overseers. To date, only the Federal Bureau of Investigation has been able to document fully the national scope of these groups, and FBI intelligence indicates that the organization as a whole has changed its name from the Mafia to La Cosa Nostra.

In 1966 J. Edgar Hoover told a House of Representatives Appropriations Subcommittee:

La Cosa Nostra is the largest organization of the criminal underworld in this country, very closely organized and strictly disciplined. They have committed almost every crime under the sun. . . .

La Cosa Nostra is a criminal fraternity whose membership is Italian either by birth or national origin, and it has been found to control major racket activities in many of our larger metropolitan areas, often working in concert with criminals representing other ethnic backgrounds.

It operates on a nationwide basis, with international implications, and until recent years it carried on its activities with almost complete secrecy. It functions as a criminal cartel, adhering to its own body of "law" and "justice" and, in so doing, thwarts and usurps the authority of legally constituted judicial bodies. . . .

In individual cities, the local core group may also be known as the "outfit," the "syndicate," or the "mob." These 24 groups work with and control other racket groups, whose leaders are of various ethnic derivations. In addition, the thousands of employees who perform the street-level functions of organized crime's gambling, usury, and other illegal activities represent a cross section of the Nation's population groups.

The present confederation of organized crime groups arose after Prohibition, during which Italian, German, Irish, and Jewish groups had competed with one another in racket operations. The Italian groups were successful in switching their enterprises from prostitution and bootlegging to gambling, extortion, and other illegal activities. They consolidated their power through murder and violence. . . .

Recognition of the common ethnic tie of the 5,000 or more members of organized crime's core groups is essential to understanding the structure of these groups today. Some have been concerned that past identification of Cosa Nostra's ethnic character has reflected on Italian-Americans generally. This false implication was eloquently refuted by one of the Nation's outstanding experts on organized crime, Sgt. Ralph Salerno of the New York City Police Department. When an Italian-American racketeer complained to him, "Why does it have to be one of your own kind that hurts you?," Sgt. Salerno answered:

I'm not your kind and you're not my kind. My manners, morals, and mores are not yours. The only thing we have in common is that we both spring from an Italian heritage and culture—and you are the traitor to that heritage and culture which I am proud to be part of.

Organized crime in its totality thus consists of these 24 groups allied with other racket enterprises to form a loose confederation operating in large and small cities. In the core groups, because of their permanency of form, strength of organization and ability to control other racketeer operations, resides the power that organized crime has in America today.

INTERNAL STRUCTURE

Each of the 24 groups is known as a "family," with membership varying from as many as 700 men to as few as 20. Most cities with organized crime have only one family; New York City has five. Each family can participate in the full range of activities in which organized crime generally is known to engage. Family organization is rationally designed with an integrated set of positions geared to maximize profits. Like any large corporation, the organization functions regardless of personnel changes, and no individual —not even the leader—is indispensable. If he dies or goes to jail, business goes on.

The hierarchical structure of the families resembles that of the Mafia groups that have operated for almost a century on the island of Sicily. Each family is headed by one man, the "boss," whose primary functions are maintaining order and maximizing profits. Subject only to the possibility of being overruled by the national advisory group, which will be discussed below, his authority in all matters relating to his family is absolute.

Beneath each boss is an "underboss," the vice president or deputy director of the family. He collects information for the boss; he relays messages to him and passes his instructions down to his own underlings. In the absence of the boss, the underboss acts for him.

On the same level as the underboss, but operating in a staff capacity, is the *consigliere*, who is a counselor, or adviser. Often an elder member of the family who has partially retired from a career in crime, he gives advice to family members, including the boss and underboss, and thereby enjoys considerable influence and power.

Below the level of the underboss are the *caporegime*, some of whom serve as buffers between the top members of the family and the lower-echelon personnel. To maintain their insulation from the police, the leaders of the hierarchy (particularly the boss) avoid direct communication with the workers. All commands, information, complaints, and money flow back and forth through a trusted go-between. A *caporegima* fulfilling this buffer capacity, however, unlike the underboss, does not make decisions or assume any of the authority of his boss.

Other *caporegime* serve as chiefs of operating units. The number of men supervised in each unit varies with the size and activities of particular families. Often the *caporegima* has one or two associates who work closely with him, carrying orders, information, and money to the men who belong to his unit. From a business standpoint, the *caporegima* is analogous to plant supervisor or sales manager.

The lowest level "members" of a family are the *soldati,* the soldiers or "button" men who report to the *caporegime.* A soldier may operate a particular illicit enterprise, e.g., a loan-sharking operation, a dice game, a lottery, a bookmaking operation, a smuggling operation, on a commission basis, or he may "own" the enterprise and pay a portion of its profit to the organization, in return for the right to operate. Partnerships are common between two or more soldiers and between soldiers and men higher up in the hierarchy. Some soldiers and most upper-echelon family members have interests in more than one business.

Beneath the soldiers in the hierarchy are large numbers of employees and commission agents who are not members of the family and are not necessarily of Italian descent. These are the people who do most of the actual work in the various enterprises. They have no buffers or other insulation from law enforcement. They take bets, drive trucks, answer telephones, sell narcotics, tend the stills, work in the legitimate businesses. For example, in a major lottery business that operated in Negro neighborhoods in Chicago, the workers were Negroes; the bankers for the lottery were Japanese-Americans; but the game, including the banking operation, was licensed, for a fee, by a family member. . . .

There are at least two aspects of organized crime that characterize it as a unique form of criminal activity. The first is the element of corruption. The second is the element of enforcement, which is necessary for the maintenance of both internal discipline and the regularity of business transactions. In the hierarchy of organized crime there are positions for people fulfilling both of these functions. But neither is essential to the long-term operation of other types of criminal groups. The members of a pickpocket troupe or check-passing ring, for example, are likely to take punitive action against any member who holds out more than his share of the spoils, or betrays the group to the police; but they do not recruit or train for a well-established position of "enforcer."

Organized crime groups, on the other hand, are believed to contain one or more fixed positions for "enforcers," whose duty it is to maintain organizational integrity by arranging for the maiming and killing of recalcitrant members. And there is a position for a "corrupter," whose function is to establish relationships with those public officials and other influential persons whose assistance is necessary to achieve the organization's goals. By including these positions within its organization, each criminal cartel, or "family," becomes a government as well as a business.

The highest ruling body of the 24 families is the "commission." This body serves as a combination legislature, supreme court, board of directors, and arbitration board; its principal functions are judicial. Family members look to the commission as the ultimate authority on organizational and jurisdictional disputes. It is composed of the bosses of the Nation's most powerful families but has authority over all 24. The composition of the commission varies from 9 to 12 men. . . .

The commission is not a representative legislative assembly or an elected judicial body. Members of this council do not regard each other as equals. Those with long tenure on the commission and those who head large families, or possess unusual wealth, exercise greater authority and receive utmost respect. The balance of power on this nationwide council rests with the leaders of New York's 5 families. They have always served on the commission and consider New York as at least the unofficial headquarters of the entire organization.

In recent years organized crime has become increasingly diversified and sophisticated. One consequence appears to be significant organizational restructuring. As in any organization, authority in organized crime may derive either from rank based on incumbency in a high position or from expertise based on possession of technical knowledge and skill. Traditionally, organized crime groups, like totalitarian governments, have maintained discipline through the unthinking acceptance of orders by underlings who have respected the rank of their superiors. However, since 1931, organized crime has gained power and respectability by moving out of bootlegging and prostitution and into gambling, usury, and control of legitimate business. Its need for expertise, based on technical knowledge and skill, has increased. Currently both the structure and operation of illicit enterprises reveal some indecision brought about by attempting to follow both patterns at the same time. Organized crime's "experts" are not fungible, or interchangeable, like the "soldiers" and street workers, and since experts are included within an organization, discipline and structure inevitably assume new forms. It may be awareness of these facts that is leading many family members to send their sons to universities to learn business administration skills.

As the bosses realize that they cannot handle the complicated problems of business and finance alone, their authority will be delegated. Decisionmaking will be decentralized, and individual freedom of action will tend to increase. New problems of discipline and authority may occur if greater emphasis on expertise within the ranks denies unskilled members of the families an opportunity to rise to positions of leadership. The unthinking acceptance of rank authority may be difficult to maintain when experts are placed above long-term, loyal soldiers. Primarily because of fear of infiltration by law enforcement, many of the families have not admitted new members for several years. That fact plus the increasing employment of personnel with specialized and expert functions may blur the lines between membership and nonmembership. In organized crime, internal rebellion would not take the form of strikes and picketing. It would bring a new wave of internal violence.

CODE OF CONDUCT

The leaders of the various organized crime families acquire their positions of power and maintain them with the assistance of a code of conduct that, like the hierarchical structure of the families, is very similar to the Sicilian Mafia's code—and just as effective. The code stipulates that underlings should not interfere with the leader's interests and should not seek protection from the police. They should be "standup guys" who go to prison in order that the bosses may amass fortunes. The code gives the leaders exploitative authoritarian power over everyone in the organization. Loyalty, honor, respect, absolute obedience—these are inculcated in family members through ritualistic initiation and customs within the organization, through material rewards, and through violence. Though underlings are forbidden to "inform" to the outside world, the family boss learns of deviance within the organization through an elaborate system of internal informants. Despite prescribed mechanisms for peaceful settlement of disputes between family members, the boss himself may order the execution of any family member for any reason.

The code not only preserves leadership authority but also makes it extremely difficult for law enforcement to cultivate informants and maintain them within the organization. . . .

BOSS OF THE OUTFIT

Excerpted from *Life*, 63, No. 9 (September 1, 1967), 13, 42B–43; *Life*, 66, No. 21 (May 30, 1969), 45, 47.

CALL IT the Mob. The name fits, although any of a half-dozen others—the Outfit, the Syndicate, La Cosa Nostra, the Mafia—serves about as well. Whatever it's called, it exists, and the fact of its existence is a national disgrace. . . .

The Mob is a fraternity of thugs, but it holds such power, wealth and influence that in one way or another it poisons us all. It rigs elections and in so doing destroys the democratic process. More and more it is muscling into legitimate business—local, national and international—to the extent that nearly every American is paying into its treasury in countless unsuspected ways.

The 5,000 members of Costa Nostra are all of Italian background, and most of them are Sicilians. Abetting them is a larger army of nonmembers—of many creeds and origins—who wittingly or unwittingly do the Mob's bidding. The scale and sophistication of its operations challenge the imagination: the President's Crime Commission estimates the Mob's annual profit from illegal gambling alone at $6 to $7 billion. "Loan sharking," narcotics, labor racketeering, "skimming" and all the varieties of extortion in which it deals bring in enormous additional sums wrenched out of the poor and those least able to resist the exploiters. Through the mechanism of "the fix," it can, and too often does, control congressmen, state officials and law enforcement men. The Mob is in fact a government of its own, with its own laws, enforced with torture and murder. It is organized with ruthless efficiency to achieve its ends and protect its members from prosecution. At the top is a ruling body which settles internal disputes and preserves discipline. Beneath this supreme council are the officers and troops, the men who do the corrupting, bribing, extorting, terrorizing, robbing and killing.

The crime syndicate of today came into being with Prohibition and has continued to thrive and grow despite sporadic bursts of public concern. One of the principal reasons for this is that existing legal machinery is simply unable to cope with it. Criminal laws deal with individual crimes, not an international association. The Mob's multitiered hierarchy insulates its leaders from direct participation in the crimes they order. To the continuing despair of police agencies, it has also benefited vastly from recent court decisions limiting the admissibility of evidence. Most of all, the Mob has fattened itself on the public's appetite for its services—dope, sex and gambling—and apathy toward its evil. . . .

[Sam] Giancana took over the 300-member Chicago Cosa Nostra Family—the Outfit, as it is called locally—in 1957, after it became apparent to him that the incumbent Boss, Tony Accardo, was getting too slow and too rich. Giancana's decision was brought home to Accardo by a bullet fired over his head as Tony was entering his spacious $500,000 estate in suburban River Forest. He understood.

Sam Giancana is a frail, gnome-like man whose constant cigar smoking has deformed his upper lip into a permanent sneer. Back in World War II, when asked by the draft board what he did for a living, he replied, "I steal." He was adjudged a psychopath, and Sam figures it was bad rap. "I was telling them the truth," he said. Before he was old enough to vote, he'd been arrested three times for murder. He likes the girls—for one he purchased a remounted 30-carat stolen diamond from a fence in New York—and has made international headlines as the recurrent escort of singer Phyllis McGuire. He likes to play golf, and when FBI agents began bothering his game when they had him under surveillance in 1963, he went to federal court and got an order stipulating that the agents must stay two foursomes back.

Ultimately, the agents won that round. Giancana was called before a grand jury, granted immunity from prosecution stemming from anything he might say and, when he refused to answer questions, served a year in jail for contempt. Fearing another such sentence, he has stayed pretty much out of the country ever since. For a time, control of the Outfit fell to Giancana's lieutenants, but as federal prosecutions sent several of them to jail, Family matters demanded a more experienced hand at the helm. One current theory is that Accardo has come out of retirement to resume active control.

The truth is that Giancana is still running things by remote control from a hideout in Mexico, a posh castle near Cuernavaca where he poses as Riccardo Scalzetti. The real Scalzetti, Giancana's erstwhile chauffeur and courier, is more familiar to Chicagoans as Richard Cain, a well-known former Chicago policeman and more recently a private investigator.

In Chicago, where racketeering was perfected, the connection between the Mob and the politicians remains extensive and arrogant. From an office across from City Hall, there are men ready to carry out Giancana's wishes and attend to the clockwork of the Fix.

It is a matter of particular pride to Giancana and his boys that they are firmly in control of both the Democratic and the Republican political organizations in Chicago's famous First War, which includes the Loop with its glittering commerce and the West Side campus of the University of Illinois as well as a warren of flophouses, honky-tonks, pool halls, pawnshops and slums. It also enfolds City Hall, the Cook County courthouse, police headquarters, the federal courthouse, the Chicago Stock Exchange, the Board of Trade, most of the major office buildings, the largest hotels and the terminals of major railroads. The Democratic organizations of two other West Side wards—the 28th and the 29th—are also nominally chattels of the Mob. But the real gangster operative power, for obvious reasons, is in the First.

The First Ward Republican apparatus is a joke. Giancana's men permit it to exist only so they can have a foot in both parties. The hoods have been known to round up a few thousand G.O.P. votes in certain elections just to avoid embarrassing Democratic winners with heavy pluralities from a gangster-dominated political organization. But aside from being something to scratch matches on, Republicans in the First Ward are handy in other ways. In Mexico City this year, for example, Giancana and Miss McGuire tooled around in a white Oldsmobile licensed to Peter Granata, the present Republican committeeman in the First Ward.

Although Cosa Nostra control over the three wards is as well-known to many Chicagoans as the Water Tower, Mayor Richard J. Daley, the longtime guru of Cook County's Democrats, stays aloof. As Chicago mayors have always done, Mayor Daley tends to bristle at allegations of organized corruption in his city as being something less than patriotic. Leadership of ward organizations, he contends, is the exclusive concern of the people in the wards.

First Ward Democratic headquarters, just across LaSalle Street from City Hall, is a handily located, permanently established center of political corruption. Here politicians, policemen, newsmen and other useful people troop into the office for favors given and received. (As in few other cities, certain journalists are part and parcel of the First Ward Fix. The First Ward Democratic organization, if it serves the gangsters' needs, can—and on occasion does —swing enough influence in city rooms to get a story killed or softened to the point where it is almost an apology.) The principal disbursing officer, and Giancana's main liaison with the First Ward-heelers, is Pat Marcy, who served a prison term for robbery back before he became secretary of the First Ward Democratic organization.

Details of the First Ward's bribe trafficking were spelled out in a 1963 report on police corruption in Chicago by the U.S. Department of Justice. The report, naming names, disclosed specific payoffs that kept police from cracking down on centers of vice operated by the Giancana Mob. But Police Superintendent Orlando W. Wilson, a man with a reputation for incorruptibility, reacted in much the same manner as Mayor Daley, scoffing at the report as "gossip" and refusing to take any action against accused bribe-takers on the police force—including his administrative assistant, Sgt. Paul Quinn. (Wilson retired August 1. Quinn remains on the force as administrative assistant to Wilson's successor, James B. Conlisk Jr.)

Giancana rules the First Ward like a Tartar warlord. He can brush an alderman off the city council with a gesture of his hand —as he did in 1962, when he ordered the resignation of Alderman John D'Arco. (It was all brought to a head by a D'Arco *faux pas*. He and Giancana were seated at a restaurant table when an FBI agent, well-known to both men, approached. D'Arco, reacting as a politician, leaped to his feet and shook hands with the agent. Giancana disapproved. Exit Alderman D'Arco.) State Senator Anthony DeTolve, a relative of Giancana's late wife, was nominated to succeed D'Arco. Four days before the aldermanic election, the gang Boss capriciously decided that DeTolve would not do, either. In the ensuing confusion, the First Ward wound up without an alderman for a year. Not many constituents could discern any difference.

For seven years, U.S. Representative Roland Libonati was one of the tame congressmen from the First Ward. "Libby" got on the powerful House Judiciary Committee and became something of a Capitol Hill landmark. Tony Tisci, Giancana's son-in-law, was on the government payroll at $11,829.84 a year as Libonati's assistant. In 1962, for reasons still undisclosed, Giancana decided that Libonati was a liability. The hapless congressman submitted without a protest and for stated reasons of his wife's ill health, obediently did not run for re-election in 1964. Tisci stayed on as assistant to Libonati's successor, Frank Annunzio.

The grand jury investigation that jailed Giancana eventually dislodged Tisci from Annunzio's payroll. The disclosure that Tisci had refused to talk to the jury, pleading fear of self-incrimination, was followed by his resignation as Annunzio's aide. Marcy and D'Arco were also Fifth Amendment witnesses. But there, as might be expected, the matter rested. U.S. Attorney Edward V. Hanrahan, a Democratic appointee, did not extend immunity to Tisci, Marcy and D'Arco even though they, like Giancana, had balked at testifying. Immunity for them might have been embarrassing for Mayor Daley's Democratic machine. It would have given the three the choice of exposing the workings of Giancana's captive organization or, like him, going to jail.

For some years, Giancana's political courier was the master fixer of the Chicago Mob, the late, notorious Murray Humphreys. Using the name "Mr. Pope," he frequently delivered messages and packages to Libonati and other members of the Illinois congressional delegation. Humphreys died in 1965, and some of his political duties now fall to Gus Alex, who runs the rackets for Giancana in the First Ward.

Giancana, perhaps spellbound by his acquaintances among celebrities and his control over paid-for political hacks, has been known to overstep his own influence. Once, during a time of tight surveillance by the FBI, he dispatched his aide-de-camp, a hoodlum named Charles English, with a message for the G-men who were waiting outside for him to leave a saloon. The message was an invitation to Robert F. Kennedy, then the Attorney General, to sit down and talk over calling the agents off. English made quite a sales pitch. "Elected officials all over the country, hundreds of 'em, owe their jobs to 'Moe,'" he explained proudly. His parting words were equally blithe: "Moe says that if Kennedy wants to talk, he should get in touch with Frank Sinatra to set it up."

Kennedy passed up the bid—and along about that time Sinatra fell out of New Frontier favor. The FBI continued its investigations, resulting in a 1965 jail sentence for Giancana. . . .

Among political favors rendered by paid-for officials to Cosa Nostra are the passing along of information that comes over their desks, and the sending up of storm signals whenever official action against the Mob is threatened. In 1962, for example, Attorney General Kennedy sent his federal prosecutors a list of gangsters to be investigated, stipulating that the list be held in strict secrecy within the Department of Justice. In a matter of weeks a copy of the list turned up in a Michigan Avenue office used by Giancana and Alex.

Fans of Sinatra and Miss McGuire might reconsider their acceptance of Giancana as a social figure if they had heard a conversation which took place in Miami a few years ago among three Giancana employes. So, for that matter, might Sinatra and Miss McGuire. The subject was William Jackson, a grotesque slugger for the Outfit who weighed well over 350 pounds. Jackson somehow had gotten out of line and had to be dealt with. As faithfully related by an informant, James Torello and Fiore Buccieri were telling John (Jackie) Cerone with some glee how they'd gone about it.

"Jackson was hung up on that meat hook," said Torello. "He was so _____heavy he bent it. He was on that thing three days before he croaked."

Buccieri began to giggle. "Jackie, you shoulda seen the guy. Like an *elephant,* he was, and when Jimmy hit him in the_____with that electric prod . . ."

Torello interrupted excitedly. "He was floppin' around on that hook, Jackie. We tossed water on him to give the prod a better charge, and he's screamin'. . . ."

The conversation turned animatedly to other methods of dispensing Giancana's brand of justice—except for the revolting subject matter, they might have been men sitting around a bait shop discussing favorite fishing lures. "The stretcher is best," insisted Torello. "Put a guy on it with chains and you can stretch him until his joints pop. . . . Remember the guy that sweat so much he dried out? He was *always* wantin' water, water. . . . I think he died of thirst."

For sheer candor, a hidden microphone can't be beat. Law breakers and law enforcers know this better than anyone else. At one time or another during a six-year period beginning in 1959, federal agents had a microphone planted somewhere amid the tomato paste and olive oil cans in a back room of the Armory Lounge restaurant in Forest Park, Ill., headquarters of Momo (also known as Moe, Sam, Mooney) Giancana, Boss of the Chicago Mob. They had another bug at a Michigan Avenue tailor shop which served as a meeting place for major Chicago hoodlums. There were two more bugs in a mortgage firm at a mercantile company, where a Giancana lieutenant named Felix (Philly) Alderisio had a piece of the action. . . .

. . . The contents of the government logs . . . present as direct and startling a picture of Mob life as has yet been seen—gamey, gossipy, authentic, and in some cases terrifying. [Excerpts:]

NOTE: *In the following conversations,* **** *indicates that an obscenity has been omitted.*

TIME: Oct. 11, 1961

PLACE: Armory Lounge

CAST: Giancano; Lou Brady, a Florida hustler.

SUBJECT: The cancellation of a murder contract the gang issued for Brady. To avoid the killers, Brady had fled to Texas. Now he has emerged from hiding and is trying to convince Giancana that he had *not* made off with that $90,000 from the sale of the Florida home of another Chicago gangster, Paul DeLucia. Brady hopes to return to Florida without being killed if Giancana can be induced to put in a good word for him with the Florida branch of Cosa Nostra.

BRADY—I took and went to Texas . . . like a °°°° hermit, like the middle of Siberia, where you got to send away to get a °°°° pound of macaroni. Sam, all you got to do is make a phone call. Just make one call and say: "You know that fella [Brady], he's with me."

GIANCANA—I don't make telephone calls.

BRADY—All right, write a note, put it in an envelope, seal it and give it to me. I'll deliver it.

GIANCANA—That's all right. I'm going down there [to Miami] in a month anyway.

BRADY—What's the matter, Sam? You wouldn't write a note for me to carry?

GIANCANA—What the hell. All I have to do is go there.

No word has been heard from Brady in recent years. He was last reported seen headed out to sea on a boat with Florida Cosa Nostra Boss Santo Trafficante.

TIME: Feb. 11, 1962

PLACE: A Miami cottage rented by John (Jackie) Cerone, a sidekick of Accardo and an Alderisio associate.

CAST: Jackie Cerone; Davie Yaras, Miami charge d'affaires for the Chicago gang; Fiore (Fifi) Buccieri, leader of Giancana's assassination squads; and Jimmy Torello, one of Buccieri's killers.

SUBJECT: The proposed kidnaping and killing of Chicago Union boss Frank Esposito. He is being stalked but has been inconveniently spending most of his time basking with John D'Arco. The killers have no love for D'Arco but he presents logistic problems.

CERONE—They . . . lay there and watch, but that °°°° [Esposito] never left his °°°° porch. All he would do all day long is walk to the °°°° front and then walk to the back. He walked three or four miles every day, but that °°°° never left his porch.

YARAS—I wish °°°° we were hitting him [Esposito] now, right now. We could have hit him the other night. We went to prowl the house . . . there was just Philly and he.

CERONE—Yeah, that would have been a perfect spot to rub him out.

. . . Well, if we don't score by the end of the week . . . then we got to take a broad and invite him here.

YARAS—Leave it to us. As soon as he walks in the °°°° door, boom! We'll hit him with an °°°° ax or something. He won't get away from us.

BUCCIERI—. . . Now if he [Esposito] comes with D'Arco . . . we do everybody a favor. We would do everybody a favor if this °°°° D'Arco went [was killed] with him [Esposito].

CERONE—The only thing, he [D'Arco] weighs 300 °°°° pounds. (*Later, same conversation*)

CERONE—Get the boat tomorrow.

YARAS—I'll get the boat and everything else.

CERONE—We'll get him on the boat if he takes a walk—then it's nothing for me to call him.

YARAS—Yeah, then you can say: "Hey, Frank, what are you doing here?" You know what I figured we could do? Early in the morning we could go there in bathing suits. When we got him in the car, we don't have to do nothing to him in the car.

CERONE—All right. Here's what we do. Monday, we work. We start. Skippie [Frank Cerone, a kinsman of Jackie's] and Davie [Yaras] will work on it. Next morning we go out there and we do it all over again. Even I can go out there one morning. We can take turns. The guy must take a ride. Maybe he won't do it in a week, maybe the 10th or 11th day, he might take a ride alone. We can pull our car right alongside . . . we can all step in . . . even if it's daytime. One guy grabs the wheel, throws him in, let him holler.

BUCCIERI—Well, we got that knife and he's got to move, with us jabbing him with that knife.

CERONE—We'll put him on the floor and away we go. We can ride around with him. Before we do it.

BUCCIERI—Well, we got him **** after we get him in. We'll drive slow.

CERONE—Yeah, we can drive around and then we can find a prairie. We can have everything with us, the ax and everything.

BUCCIERI—We can't let any blood show. We got to keep the guy alive until we're in a good, safe spot.

CERONE—Oh, no, you can't touch the guy until we get to the car.

BUCCIERI—Yeah, we keep him alive until we're ready.

CERONE—Yeah, you can't afford to have a man dead on your hands. I got the contract [the murder assignment]. Did you know that?

BUCCIERE—Yeah.

Esposito's life was spared when the FBI notified Florida authorities of the murder plan. As they sat around Cerone's living room, planning to chop up Esposito, the gangsters talked of other jobs in other times, chatty and giggly as schoolgirls. Cerone recalled his attempt to murder Jim (Big Jim) Martin, a policy betting king, a job botched because Cerone was using out-dated ammunition.

CERONE—So when I banged the guy, I called him with a full load . . . but it had to go through a Cadillac. I blasted him twice. Joe [Accardo] says: "Is the guy dead?" And I said: "Sure, because when I nailed him, his head went like that, you know?" The next morning, the headlines are in the paper. The guy is still living . . . this double o [double-o buckshot, a shotgun load] was 10 years old . . . it wasn't fresh, so the guy lived.

YARAS—That's one thing, when I use that double o, I got to use fresh ones [shells].

CERONE—The guy [Martin] was a big nigger. He left the country and went to Mexico. That's what we wanted anyway. We wound up with all his policy [lottery] games. The next day, I'm on the corner [where Martin was shot]. I went to the place all dressed up. The squads [police] and the cars are all around. I'm right there. And everybody is talking and I say: "Oh, that's terrible. But them **** niggers, they're always fighting one another, you know."

Cerone always boasted that few people outside The Mob knew he was a triggerman.

CERONE—I wasn't known for a long time. I kept away. I wasn't seen with nobody, never mixed. I was always hidden, for many years.

Cerone chuckled about that. Then another killing crossed his mind.

CERONE—I remember one time we was on this guy for a week. You know, you get close and you blow it and then you try again. So this one night, we pull up on the guy and he's with his wife. So he [Cerone's partner in the crime] said: "What the °°°°, I'll get him." So I grabbed the wheel and he jumped out and chased the °°°° a half a block, but he nailed him. Remember that time you popped that guy and you rolled him over a couple of times and he lived?

YARAS—I didn't do that. . . . Oh, yeah, now I remember. I did that with Johnny. I'm gonna tell you a funny story. You know, I think that °°°° tried to hit me the same time I hit him. I swear. Because he put a shot right through the windshield.

It was Buccieri's turn, then, to reminisce about a victim he called Polecat.

BUCCIERI—I remember we had to hit him in the belly, then we had to burn him. We couldn't even get the handcuffs on him.

THE NORMAL MURDERER

MANFRED S. GUTTMACHER

Excerpted from Manfred S. Guttmacher, *The Mind of the Murderer* (New York: Farrar, Strauss and Cudahy, 1960), pp. 12–20.

SOCIETY'S GREATEST concern must be with the non-psychotic murderer; with the individual who exhibits no marked psychopathology, since by far the greatest numbers of homicides are committed by them. . . .

The late Paul Schilder, a man with a brilliant and a restlessly inquiring mind, published a series of studies on persons' attitudes toward death. In regard to the rather typical young slayer, the holdup man, the killer after an insignificant quarrel, Schilder made this observation: "It is rather that life and death do not seem to play an important part in the manifest content of psychic life. Persons of this kind seemingly kill as easily as children in their play, and they are not more concerned about their own death than children are. It almost seems that these 'normal murderers,' who are not otherwise so badly adapted to their reality, show particular infantile trends in their reaction to life and death. One may say they kill because they do not appreciate the deprivation they inflict upon others." [1] . . .

Criminological studies reveal that the great majority of the offenders of this type come from the economically and socially underprivileged strata of our society. Almost without exception one finds in their early backgrounds not only economic want, but cruelties and miseries of every kind. Such early conditioning predisposes to a marked under-valuation of life. To these individuals people are objects to be manipulated for predatory purposes. The

[1] Schilder, Paul, "The Attitude of Murderers Toward Death," Abnormal and Social Psychology, 31, 1936, 348.

Gluecks, in their important studies on juvenile delinquency, have found that the seriously delinquent child was involved in accidents far more frequently than the non-delinquent child. Disregard for their own safety came early and paralleled their disregard for the welfare of others. One can safely hypothesize that the amount of satisfying nurture that the child receives in its earliest years must be a fundamental element in the formation of its attitudes on the value of human life.

The denial of satisfying early nurture must in many instances have a positive aspect, that of frustration. Frustration is known to play an extremely important role in the creation of aggressive and destructive drives, elements in the personality structure of the greatest importance in homicide.

There are many murderers we have examined who could serve as prototypes for the young criminal with a reckless disregard for human life. Take for example Robert T., a twenty-one year old Negro, who shot and killed, in a fight, a male Negro twice his age. His father had died when he was five. His mother was an ineffectual woman who died at thirty-seven of heart disease. There were two illegitimate half-brothers who were given out for adoption. In his early life there was a great deal of poverty. He had lived much of the time with a woman he called his aunt, but he does not know whether she was actually related to him. He got to the fourth grade and was then transferred to a special class. He was a very active truant. Robert was twice knocked unconscious, once while a boy, by a toy pistol, and at twenty, by a "boyfriend who hit me in the head with a blackjack when we had a fight." He had had gonorrheal infections which he treated himself with pills from a drugstore.

He had a spotty work record, losing jobs because of absenteeism. The Navy kept him only eight weeks before discharging him. He gambled heavily and used both alcohol and marijuana. His temper was easily aroused, all arguments automatically ended in fights.

When he was eighteen he was fined twenty-five dollars for fighting. A youth had cleaned him out in a crap game. When he refused to return any of the money, a fight started. At nineteen he was sentenced to thirty days in jail because of a street fight in which many youths armed with knives participated. Two months later he robbed a white boy on the street of a small sum of money and was given a penal sentence of two years.

Two weeks before the murder he and the victim had jointly purchased a bottle of liquor. The other man asserted that he was drinking more than his share and jerked the bottle from his mouth; a fight ensued. According to the defendant, this man, at the conclusion of the fight, threatened to kill him.

Robert learned of a youth in his neighborhood who had paid a group of little children fifty cents for a pistol which they had found. He went to this youth and lied, insisting that the pistol was his, but magnanimously gave him fifty cents to reimburse him for what he had paid the children.

For two weeks he carried the loaded pistol in his belt. Then one night he saw the other man on the street, walking with a man and a woman. He shifted the pistol from his belt to his pocket as they approached. He claims that the victim made a menacing gesture. He instantly fired one fatal shot and fled to his girl friend's house, where he had been living.

Robert was given a life sentence in the penitentiary. A recent inquiry reveals that in the nine years that he has been there he has had eighteen disciplinary infractions, including an attempt to choke another inmate, striking an inmate on the head with a brick, and seven fist fights.

Let us consider another example of the "normal slayer." Alvin B. is a huge seventeen year old Negro boy nearly six feet tall and weighing two hundred and fifteen pounds, who murdered a policeman. In appearance, he resembles a fine future linesman for a professional football team. By psychological tests he is shown to have bright average intelligence. Some ten months before the homicide he quit in the second year of high school. He had never failed to pass a grade.

His medical history was marked by frequent trips to the accident rooms of the Baltimore hospitals. When he was fourteen, a gang of school boys robbed him of thirty cents and knocked him out, breaking his nose. At sixteen he contracted gonorrhea.

At fourteen he worked one entire summer at a grocery store. For some years he had helped his brother-in-law, who was engaged in gardening and grass cutting. A short time before his offense he worked for a few weeks as a porter in a drug store at $39 a week.

Alvin came from a broken home. He was told that his father left his mother before he was born. He met his father two or three times a month in bar rooms. "He'll give me money if I ask him, but he won't give me nothing unless I do ask." He knows very little about his father, except that he is a construction laborer. His mother does occasional day work. She is an active Baptist. He says of her, "She's a nice mother. She sacrificed herself for us all the time." Occasionally his mother beat him with a strap when he was a small boy. The stepfather, who had married the mother four years before, was a baker. The patient feels quite hostile toward him. "He just nags at you, that's all. He likes to make people feel stupid because he's got an education. He seems to think he's a perfect man, nothing ever suits him." The patient is the youngest of five. The eldest sister, a heavy drinker, had left her husband for another man. The eldest brother had served a five year sentence for selling narcotics. Alvin lived much of the time with a sister, seven years older than himself, and her husband. He seemed fond of them. He said they treated him well, even permitting him to take girls up to his room. The brother, Lee, who was two years older was involved with the patient in the offense that led to the homicide. Although only nineteen this brother was married and already had two children.

One gains the impression from this patient, as with others of his type, that there is a complete lack of family cohesiveness. His ignorance in regard to his mother's schooling, the occupations of his grandfathers, the name of the bakery in which his stepfather worked, his father's police record, the grade levels in school to which his sisters and brothers went, their church affiliation, etc., are characteristic.

When questioned about the things that give him most pleasure in life, he immediately responded, "girls." Attempts at heterosexual relations began at seven. He had lived with a twenty-six year old girl for nine months and then tired of her. He is a skillful pool player, often running all fifteen balls. He claims to have lost only one fight in his life and was known for his fighting prowess. His mother forced him to go to church regularly when he lived in her house.

The morning of the day on which the offense occurred the patient spent in the poolroom with his nineteen year old brother, Lee. That afternoon he went to see one of his girls. He was taking her to the movies when a friend, Ray, who does not work and has an extensive criminal record, sent word to him to come to his house. He got his brother to go along. When they arrived there they found Ray having sex relations with his wife. Not wishing to interrupt them, they called to him to meet them at the pool room. An hour later Ray arrived and asked them if they wanted to get some money. Alvin replied, "I guess so." They then went to get Slim. They found him in his car. The four of them rode around, stopping while Ray bought a pint of whiskey, which they drank. On their tour of the city they surveyed various liquor stores and finally picked out one to hold up. Alvin was carrying a loaded pistol, which he had secured sometime before through a burglary. Ray was also armed. Slim stayed in his car, the others went in. Three men and a porter were in the store. Ray ordered some whiskey and when the clerk turned around he was facing Ray's gun. Alvin covered the other men. Lee went behind the partition to see if there was a safe. Because of the recent robberies of liquor stores, a police officer had secreted himself in the rear. He grabbed Lee by the neck. Lee shouted "look out." Then the officer started blasting away at Ray, letting go of Lee, and they all fled. Alvin turned and fired at the officer until his gun was empty. Ray jumped into the car that took off. Alvin ran up an alley and met two policemen coming down toward him. He dropped his gun and threw up his hands. One officer shot him in the leg. He said,

I didn't feel much pain. There were lots of officers around me. They tore off my coat to see if they could find my name. They kept wanting to know who the other boys were. I told them I didn't know. Two cops picked me up and put me in an ambulance. They started to hit on my leg where the bullet was at and kept hitting on my head to tell them my name and the names of the others. Then I cussed them and they cussed me. One pulled out his gun and said, "I ought to kill you." I was scared so I hit him. I guess I dazed him and then I jumped the other one and grabbed the gun from his hand. He started toward me. That's when the gun went off. The next thing I knew I was out of the ambulance and running. I jumped into a taxi and told the driver to take off. He rammed into the ambulance. That shook me up and knocked the gun out of my hand. I got behind the wheel and tried to put it into reverse. The pain got real bad in my leg. Officers were coming up all around me. I started to run and got shot in the hip and the leg. Then I got shot in the neck as I stooped over. I jumped over a fence and crashed through the back window of a house. I saw a kitchen knife and grabbed it. I ran out the front of the house. There was a taxi with a woman in it. I got in, the woman eased out. The driver said, "Boy, you are bleeding. What's the matter, have the police been firing at you?" I said, "No, I was at a bar and got into a fight." He didn't want to take me. I told him if he didn't I'd run the knife through him. He must have had his blinker light on. A police car came up. I ducked down. Another one came up. They shot into the cab and I got hit in the arm, in the chest, and in the leg. I guess the one in the chest made me kind of dizzy.

The hospital report stated that he had seven separate bullet wounds.

When Alvin was asked how he began his involvement in serious crime, he said,

There was an older fellow, twenty-nine, named Slicklow, and me and him made quite a bit of money through burglary. I was around fifteen then. Everytime when I was coming from school, he was waiting for me. He got me cards for bar rooms and started me drinking. He didn't work. He was pimping off a woman. He always had women for me. I guess he just liked me. He said I didn't carry myself like a boy but like a man. I bought a lot of clothes and stuff. He crossed me up one time. He held out a couple of hundred dollars on me, so I told him I'd be his friend but I wasn't going to work with him like this any more. Then I did some hustling with Ray. We murphied a guy, you know, we told him we could get him a woman but it would take a lot of money. When he took out his roll we took it and ran. I done quite a series of robberies with Ray. I kept telling him we ought not to be doing it but he said he'd been doing it for a long time and got away with it pretty good.

The Clinic psychologist, on the basis of his projective tests, reported,

This patient has a somewhat paranoid view of the world, but possibly it has enough reality basis that one cannot say that it is more than a product of aggression. He sees the world as depriving and divides it clearly into the "haves" and the "have-nots." His own value system is based on this distinction. He has no compunction about taking from the "haves" since he is a "have-not." He does not feel that he is wrong because society has made him so. He has been deprived so now it is up to society to look after him and if they do not give it, he will take it. Stealing is therefore natural to him. Murder is incidental.

Despite the fact that he has murdered a policeman, Alvin's death sentence has been commuted to a life sentence because of his age.

Certainly one must admit that such individuals are maladjusted to society. But, in all probability, the genesis of such defective personality structure has resulted from the defective ethical standards which flourish in the social milieu in which they were spawned, rather than from hidden neurotic complexes.

WILLIAM HEIRENS:

SEX OFFENDER—KILLER

FOSTER KENNEDY,
HARRY R. HOFFMAN,
AND WILLIAM H. HAINES

Excerpted from Foster Kennedy, Harry R. Hoffman, and William H. Haines, "Psychiatric Study of William Heirens," *Journal of Criminal Law and Criminology*, XXXVIII (July, 1947), 311–41. Reprinted by special permission of the *Journal of Criminal Law, Criminology and Police Science*, Vol. XXXVIII, No. 4 (Copyright © 1947, by Northwestern University School of Law). At the time of publication, Dr. Kennedy was Professor of Clinical Medicine (Neurology), Cornell University and Director of Neurological Service—Bellevue Hospital, New York City. Dr. Hoffman was State Alienist, Department of Public Welfare, State of Illinois, and Associate Clinical Professor of Psychiatry (Rush), University of Illinois. Dr. Haines was Director of the Behavior Clinic, Criminal Court of Cook County and Assistant Clinical Professor of Psychiatry (Rush), University of Illinois.

WILLIAM HEIRENS was a 17-year-old University of Chicago student. On June 26, 1946, he was intercepted while making his getaway after an attempt at burglary in Chicago's north side. Prior to his arrest there had been many unsolved burglaries and atrocious murders. Among these was the murder of 6-year-old Suzanne Degnan, whose body was found dismembered in the city's sewers.

After his arrest he feigned insanity for a few days, then made a confession which he denied the following day, and admitted subsequently.

Prior to his trial a psychiatric examination was requested by his attorneys . . . and by William J. Touhy, State's Attorney of Cook County. Dr. Harry R. Hoffman and Dr. William H. Haines were selected. Later a third member, Dr. Foster Kennedy of New York City, was invited to collaborate in the examination and he agreed. It was felt that since Dr. Haines and Dr. Hoffman represented government agencies, the services of a neutral out-of-state psychiatrist should be obtained.

The doctors were given permission to make any report that they saw fit . . . regarding Heirens' mental status. They were all agreed that he was legally sane and they wrote a detailed joint report which was submitted to His Honor Judge Harold G. Ward, Chief Justice of the Criminal Court, September 3, 1946. . . .

Social History

The patient is 17.5 years old, white, born in Evanston, Ill., of native-born parents of Luxemburg descent. The family history, as given, is negative as to insanity, epilepsy, alcoholism, or mental defectiveness. The father grew up in floral business with his father, and opened a store and conservatory of his own soon after marriage. . . . The family occupied a flat in connection with the store. With the depression, the business failed and although several attempts were made to re-establish themselves in different locations, none was successful. After a period of irregular employment, the father secured work on the police force of Carnegie Steel Company, about eight years ago, and has now worked up to a position of special investigator. In addition, he works several evenings on the Lincolnwood Village Police Force. The mother has worked much of the time since marriage, both to supplement the income and because she enjoyed it, working in their own and other florist shops, in a bakery as a fancy pastry maker, and more recently designing and executing custom made clothes. The mother handles the family finances. The patient expressed some concern over his mother's work, feeling it was done to pay his school tuition, but she preferred to do it and to employ someone to do the housecleaning, etc.

The patient is the older of two brothers. Family religion is Roman Catholic. Early in the pregnancy of patient, the mother feared she would miscarry. Labor was long (62 hours) and delivery

difficult with high forceps employed. The patient weighed eight
pounds and five ounces and was 24 inches long at birth. Breast
feedings were inadequate and extremely painful to the mother so
that bottle feedings were supplemented almost from the beginning.
Weaning from the breast was completed by age of one month. He
presented a feeding problem from the beginning—he "vomited in a
gush"—after every feeding and was sickly and severely under-
weight for the first three months. Thereafter under different care
and diet he began to gain weight. Teething presented no problem.
The ages of walking and talking are unknown; the mother reports
"the usual age." The mother reported that toilet training was completed early; after eight months there was no nocturnal wetting
and by one year, daytime bladder and bowel control had been established. No relapses were reported.

At seven months, while unattended, he fell from his buggy to a
cement basement areaway 12 feet below and injured his head. He
was not unconscious when his mother found him. At age eight or
nine he fell from a trapeze and sustained a compound fracture of
the bones of the right arm necessitating an open reduction. When
about 12, he fell down some cement stairs at school, cutting his
head over the eye. Patient fainted then. At the age of eight, he had
a tonsillectomy with severe hemorrhage and some complications.
He also had chicken pox and measles as a child. In the summer of
1942 and again in the spring of 1946, he complained of severe
headaches. Otherwise, health history is negative.

He was a solitary child and youth, sensitive and difficult to
know. Apparently no one ever had a close or confidential relationship with him; certainly his parents did not. As a child he was
with his brother a good deal and had to fight his battles for him.
He never had any real friends and preferred to be alone. In the 7th
and 8th grades excessive day dreaming was reported. He had some
mechanical interests and considerable skill, according to the parents, repairing electric motors, repairing or making radios from old
parts. He was interested in collecting and recently had a considerable coin collection. Very early he was eager to earn his own
money—worked delivering orders for a food store the summer he
was 12, delivered for a liquor store the summer he was 14, and

worked in the steel mills with his father the summer of 1944 and 1945. He was very frugal with his money, spent little on himself— just saved it. His only "splurge" was in gifts for the family. He bought expensive presents out of proportion to his earnings. Very early he learned not to whimper or cry when hurt and could endure considerable physical pain.

He attended public school kindergarten for a few months at age five and entered parochial school at six. He attended three parochial elementary schools, as the family moved, and graduated from 8th grade (receiving his diploma in absentia since he was then in the Juvenile Detention Home) at age of 13.

In June, 1942, he was first apprehended by the police trying to break into a basement storeroom. Subsequently he admitted nine burglaries within the preceding six months. Following the Juvenile Court hearing, he was committed to Gibault School for Boys and remained there from July 5, 1942, to June 4, 1943. Except for an attempt to run home three weeks after commitment, he presented no discipline problem and exteriorly was a conformist according to report received. He was obedient and co-operative, with a good attitude toward authority. He completed his first year of high school here with scholastic averages all in the 80s. He was quiet and serious, "definitely an introvert," and would often be found away from campus completely alone. He had few friends and preferred to be by himself. He was not interested in athletics; team games especially did not appeal to him. He expressed a good attitude toward religious obligations, frequently took Holy Communion, went to confession less regularly at school than lately. He did not want to know anyone intimately.

Two months after his return from Gibault, he was again arrested, charged with burglary. In Juvenile Court the case was heard before a visiting Judge who acceded to the family's wishes. The patient was placed on probation to go to St. Bede's Academy at Peru, Illinois, where he remained from September, 1943, to May 27, 1945, but was at home for summer vacation in 1944 and 1945. He completed 2nd and 3rd years of high school there. This school report showed grades of "A" and "B" in all subjects for his sophomore year, from "A" to "F" (English) in junior year. His adjustment was good, no discipline problem. He had no confidential relationship with anyone and preferred to be alone. Probation was terminated January 19, 1945.

In September, 1945, he entered the University of Chicago, after taking placement tests, and remained there until his apprehension in the summer quarter of 1946. His scholastic record there was average and below. He had many absences from academic and physical education classes. According to the mother, he was active in the Calvert Club (a Catholic organization, social and religious). He seemed to have at least a superficial relationship with a few students and finally began to have a few "dates" with girls, though with no close friends.

According to the parents, the patient never displayed any of the usual sexual curiosity as a child nor displayed any jealousy of his brother three years younger. No sex instructions were given by the parents. At the age of about 13, there was an incident of sex play which patient witnessed in the boys' toilet at school and reported to his mother, at which time he was warned about venereal disease. This was a few months before the first known burglary. The parents were unaware of his delinquencies until after he was apprehended, but since his earlier court appearance have been constantly fearful of a repetition, though trying to trust him.

Physical Examination

. . . He is a well built young man weighing 159 pounds. . . . No evidence was found of any structural abnormality in the central, autonomic, or peripheral nervous systems. The hands were moist and over-cold and without tremor. There was a remarkable reduction to the perception of pin pricks, however strong, as "pain." This was present all over the body with the exception of the glans penis. Sharp pin pricks inside the nose on the mucous membrane and the soles of the feet was [*sic*] denied as being painful and no motion of withdrawal was made there or elsewhere. This was also true as regards the mucous membrane of the lip and the scrotum and body of the penis. A sharp needle could be pressed more than four millimeters under the nails without inducing pain or defense withdrawal movements. . . . The corneal reflexes at first were greatly reduced, and at the close of this examination had disappeared so that it became possible to tap the eyeballs with a closed safety pin without his winking or giving any motor sign of sensation. . . . The perception of vibration and the other forms of sensation were normal. The visual fields were found to narrow progressively as the test continued, so that they became finally almost pin-point. This phenomenon . . . is a positive objective indication of profound hysteria.

This striking reduction of power to appreciate painful stimulation as such, together with its remarkable deepening as the result of suggestion, is to us a clear proof of the patient's hysterical personality.

The blood pressure, heart, lungs, and abdomen were normal. He is powerfully built with fine muscular development; he excelled in wrestling.

Psychiatric Examination

. . . We propose now to give . . . an account of the significant actions and emotional reactions of this patient in so far as they could be discovered. When quotation marks are used, the quotations will be the patient's own words, or question and answer.

When aged nine, the patient began to be interested in "the feeling and color" and then "the stealing" of women's underclothing. He began to take these at first from clothes lines, then from basements, and later from strange houses, the doors of which he found open or ajar. Dresses or other articles of women's apparel made no appeal to him nor was he interested in the undergarments of his immediate family. Having secured a pair of women's panties or drawers, he would take it to a basement or home, put it on, experience excitement and sexual completion. Most garments he then threw away, some he replaced, and some he hoarded in his grandmother's attic.

We believed it important, if possible, by objective evidence to prove the truth of his statement of fetishism. An investigation brought to light, in the spot he had described, "a cardboard box" containing some forty pairs of women's old, used panties and drawers, mostly made of rayon and brightly colored.

When 12 or 13 years of age, he secured the desired garments by going into houses through windows. This furnished more excitement. After three such expeditions, he took objects ("guns or money") other than underclothes; a change which was again an added stimulation. "It seemed sort of foolish to break in and not take anything." When he had thus changed his objective, the interest in underclothes largely evaporated and was replaced by the excitement experienced on "making an entrance" through the window. Often he would struggle against his desire to leave his room at night, but the following dialogue shows this part of the picture better than we can describe it:

Q. Do you know when you get up from your room to go out, when you have surrendered to the urge to go out, what you are going out for?

A. Yes, they always were burglaries.

Q. Would you prowl around the streets in a state of suppressed sexual excitement looking for an entrance?

A. It wasn't that way. Maybe it's not excitement. It feels like it's further away in the distance. You don't seem to have any feeling of anything.

Q. When you saw the window you made a decision? You went into a state of sexual excitement?

A. Yes, there was sexual excitement. I always had an erection. . . .

Q. It was the act of going through the window?

A. Yes. . . .

Q. Did you get any sexual excitement out of taking loot in the suitcase?

A. No.

Q. It was just going through the window?

A. Yes.

Q. What you had taken out of the houses would not give you any pleasure afterwards?

A. No, it gave me a sense of depression.

Q. It wasn't exactly depression when you went further, and killed?

A. I had no feeling of having done it. Things were so vague.

Q. I object to your general statement that "things were so vague." You are not using the right term. Maybe they were "different" but not "vague." For instance, in the Degnan case, you were able to see there was somebody sleeping on the right hand side by your flash light. You saw that somebody sitting up and that she had long hair, and you were able to see that somebody begin to talk and you answered. You also saw that the door on the other side of the room was shut.

A. I didn't answer—(the child)

Q. You took the child and went out the window. Your word "vague" is wrong. You were in an unusual condition but not "vague." . . .

Q. On three occasions you were surprised by people seeing you and you immediately killed. Why did you do that?

A. It was the noise that set me off, I believe. I must have been in a high tension and the least bit of noise would disturb me in that manner.

Q. Are you sensitive to noise?

A. No, I wouldn't say that I was.

Q. When people are surprised doing something they should not be doing, their usual action is to retreat. When you saw the child . . . talking, why didn't you turn tail and go out?

A. I don't know.

Q. Did you have any conscious thoughts when the child spoke to you?

A. No.

Q. Of what you would do?

A. There was no deliberation at all.

Q. You just went over and strangled her?

A. Yes.

Q. Tell me, you didn't make any effort to take the bodies of the other two murders away?

A. No.

Q. Why did you take the child away?

A. I don't know that. I'm cooperating . . . to find out.

Q. You remember going out the window with the child?

A. Yes.

Q. And you carried the child with that extra strength you feel yourself possessed of at these times down the ladder and quite a long distance. You set the child down somewhere before you got to the basement?

A. I don't know. It is just like a floor with holes in it. I've tried to look through the holes to see what is down below. (Patient is referring to his memory here, its blocks and spaces.) There is just not enough holes to find out. . . .

Q. When did the headaches come into the picture?

A. When I tried to resist the urge to get outside and burglarize. It seemed as though I was in a dream. I did not have any feeling. It was like walking through darkness and pushing a mist aside. . . .

After assaulting Miss Peterson, he had an orgasm and without striking her again he left and returned to his room at the University. He later returned to the Peterson apartment, administered first aid, and tried by telephone to get help for her.

Q. When you had an emission you always felt you had done wrong?
A. Yes. In fact, that was the only time.

We believe, from other statements, by this remark he meant that only immediately after orgasm did he suffer from the pang of conscience. . . . [H]e at first denied ever having attempted any sex play with girls. Two days later with one of his rare shows of emotion he said, looking much ashamed, that twice, later correcting himself to eight times, he had touched girls "on the breasts" and then pressed "on the leg." Always having done this, he would immediately burst into tears and "be upset and unable to sleep." It should be noticed that no uncomfortable emotions followed either burglaries or murders. He forcibly [sic] denied ever having made any more intimate advances, except that he "kissed them" sometimes. "They wanted to kiss; I didn't."

It was clear that normal sex stimulation and experience were unpleasant, indeed "repulsive," to him, and these efforts after them created in him a negative emotional state. He found them improper in the conduct of others; he never spoke of them except in condemnation, as for example of the young men in the University who had brought a girl into their rooms at night.

He was interested in books on sex and crime. . . .

Q. What did you read about?
A. Nothing special about my case.
Q. What did you read?
A. Around the subject of masochism, fetichism, sadism, flagellation.
Q. Where did you read about this?
A. In books. I think Kraft-Ebbing mostly.
Q. And what else?
A. In Dreams—Freud—read some parts of that, and that's practically all.
Q. You once said you couldn't read Freud; it was so dirty.
A. I didn't read it because it was against the principles of the Catholic Church.
Q. What did you mean by dirty?
A. Did I say that?
Q. I think you did; it was transcribed. What did you mean by dirty?
A. It has to do with sex.

Q. Sex between the sexes?

A. No, not particularly.

Q. Sex between man and woman?

A. No, his whole theory is based on sex.

Q. Bill, before we leave, may I ask you one parting question, and I assume you are honest: If you had to choose between sex, burglaries, and murder, which would be the most obnoxious to you?

A. "Sex" and murder.

Q. And suppose you had to choose between "sex" and murder, which would be the more obnoxious to you?

A. Murder.

Q. Yet, after murder you did not burst into tears and become emotionally upset, and after a very small amount of sex play you *were* emotionally upset. Don't you think you are not giving the right answer?

A. They're the right answers.

Q. The right answers are that you hate sex more than burglary?

A. Yes.

Q. You hate sex more than burglary and you hate murder more than sex? But, Bill, this is factual. Now you tell us, quite honestly, after touching the breasts of some girl and the thighs of some girls, you cried, went home and had a great deal of chagrin and remorse, didn't you? After the murder of the Brown girl, the Degnan girl, and the Ross girl, did you cry? After the Degnan girl, you went home and had two breakfasts, attended all classes without any pangs of remorse?

A. No, no pangs of remorse.

Q. After the Brown affair?

A. No.

Q. So the sex concept to you is more important than the destroying of individuals?

A. No.

Q. Was it worse than burglary?

A. Yes, it was worse than burglary.

Q. Was it worse than carrying a loaded weapon?

A. Yes. . . .

Q. Bill, when doctor asked you the question, which was worse sex or murder, you answered no. In watching you, you nodded your head in the affirmative, and then said no.

A. Just said no.

Q. There was a nod of the head, yes.

A. I always do that, if you watch me. I nod my head when I talk, whether it is yes or no.

In observing the patient, he was noted not to nod his head in speaking. We believe that William Heirens nodded his head to indicate that subjectively he felt sex was worse than murder, but in verbalizing stated murder. . . .

Psychologist's Report

William Heirens was submitted to a series of carefully selected and conducted psychological tests, calculated to reveal trends, both conscious and underlying consciousness.

The quality of intellect was carefully tested and he was found to have an intelligence quotient of 110—an average figure. . . .

On none of the psychological tests was there any indication of a psychosis or of malingering.

On personality questionnaires he was found to be outgoing and dominant with a lack of self-consciousness or feelings of inferiority. It must be remembered, however, that these questionnaires represent the subject's own evaluation of himself and may not necessarily conform with his actual behavior.

An evaluation of all the psychological techniques used indicated a definite emotional insensitivity and instability severe enough to be considered abnormal, as well as a blunting of moral concepts.

The majority of tests tend to suggest hysteria. . . .

We believe that . . . William Heirens is not suffering from any psychosis nor mental retardation; that he has a deep sexual perversion and is as emotionally insensitive within, as he is incapable of feeling pain without. He is unstable, and hysterically unpredictable, and most of his actions can be swayed from time to time by the suggestions coming from his environment.

WHITE-COLLAR CRIMINALITY

EDWIN H. SUTHERLAND

Edwin H. Sutherland, "White-Collar Criminality," *American Sociological Review*, V (February, 1940), 1–12. In 1940, E. H. Sutherland was affiliated with Indiana University.

THIS PAPER is concerned with crime in relation to business. The economists are well acquainted with business methods but not accustomed to consider them from the point of view of crime; many sociologists are well acquainted with crime but not accustomed to consider it as expressed in business. This paper is an attempt to integrate these two bodies of knowledge. More accurately stated, it is a comparison of crime in the upper or white-collar class, composed of respectable or at least respected business and professional men, and crime in the lower class, composed of persons of low socioeconomic status. This comparison is made for the purpose of developing the theories of criminal behavior, not for the purpose of muckraking or of reforming anything except criminology.

The criminal statistics show unequivocally that crime, as *popularly conceived and officially measured,* has a high incidence in the lower class and a low incidence in the upper class; less than two percent of the persons committed to prisons in a year belong to the upper class. These statistics refer to criminals handled by the police, the criminal and juvenile courts, and the prisons, and to such crimes as murder, assault, burglary, robbery, larceny, sex offenses, and drunkenness, but exclude traffic violations.

The criminologists have used the case histories and criminal statistics derived from these agencies of criminal justice as their principal data. From them, they have derived general theories of criminal behavior. These theories are that, since crime is concentrated in the lower class, it is caused by poverty or by personal and social characteristics believed to be associated statistically with poverty, including feeblemindedness, psychopathic deviations, slum neighborhoods, and "deteriorated" families. This statement, of course, does not do justice to the qualifications and variations in the conventional theories of criminal behavior, but it presents correctly their central tendency.

The thesis of this paper is that the conception and explanations of crime which have just been described are misleading and incorrect, that crime is in fact not closely correlated with poverty or with the psychopathic and sociopathic conditions associated with poverty, and that an adequate explanation of criminal behavior must proceed along quite different lines. The conventional explanations are invalid principally because they are derived from biased samples. The samples are biased in that they have not included vast areas of criminal behavior of persons not in the lower class. One of these neglected areas is the criminal behavior of business and professional men, which will be analyzed in this paper.

The "robber barons" of the last half of the nineteenth century were white-collar criminals, as practically everyone now agrees. Their attitudes are illustrated by these statements: Colonel Vanderbilt asked, "You don't suppose you can run a railroad in accordance with the statutes, do you?" A. B. Stickney, a railroad president, said to sixteen other railroad presidents in the home of J. P. Morgan in 1890, "I have the utmost respect for you gentlemen, individually, but as railroad presidents I wouldn't trust you with my watch out of my sight." Charles Francis Adams said, "The difficulty in railroad management . . . lies in the covetousness, want of good faith, and low moral tone of railway managers, in the complete absence of any high standard of commercial honesty."

The present-day white-collar criminals, who are more suave and deceptive than the "robber barons," are represented by Krueger, Stavisky, Whitney, Mitchell, Foshay, Insull, the Van Sweringens, Musica-Coster, Fall, Sinclair, and many other merchant princes and captains of finance and industry, and by a host of lesser followers. Their criminality has been demonstrated again and again in the investigations of land offices, railways, insurance, munitions, banking, public utilities, stock exchanges, the oil industry, real estate, reorganization committees, receiverships, bankruptcies, and politics. Individual cases of such criminality are reported frequently, and in many periods more important crime news may be found on the financial pages of newspapers than on the front pages. White-collar criminality is found in every occupation, as can be discovered readily in casual conversation with a representative of an occupation by asking him, "What crooked practices are found in your occupation?"

White-collar criminality in business is expressed most frequently in the form of misrepresentation in financial statements of corporations, manipulation in the stock exchange, commercial bribery, bribery of public officials directly or indirectly in order to secure favorable contracts and legislation, misrepresentation in advertising and salesmanship, embezzlement and misapplication of funds, short weights and measures and misgrading of commodities, tax frauds, misapplication of funds in receiverships and bankruptcies. These are what Al Capone called "the legitimate rackets." These and many others are found in abundance in the business world.

In the medical profession, which is here used as an example because it is probably less criminalistic than some other professions, are found illegal sale of alcohol and narcotics, abortion, illegal services to underworld criminals, fraudulent reports and testimony in accident cases, extreme cases of unnecessary treatment, fake specialists, restriction of competition, and fee-splitting. Fee-splitting is a violation of a specific law in many states and a violation of the conditions of admission to the practice of medicine in all. The physician who participates in fee-splitting tends to send his patients to the surgeon who will give him the largest fee rather than to the surgeon who will do the best work. It has been reported that two thirds of the surgeons in New York City split fees, and that more than one half of the physicians in a central western city who answered a questionnaire on this point favored fee-splitting.

These varied types of white-collar crimes in business and the professions consist principally of violation of delegated or implied trust, and many of them can be reduced to two categories: misrepresentation of asset values and duplicity in the manipulation of power. The first is approximately the same as fraud or swindling; the second is similar to the double-cross. The latter is illustrated by the corporation director who, acting on inside information, purchases land which the corporation will need and sells it at a fantastic profit to his corporation. The principle of this duplicity is that the offender holds two antagonistic positions, one of which is a position of trust, which is violated, generally by misapplication of funds, in the interest of the other position. A football coach, permitted to referee a game in which his own team was playing, would illustrate this antagonism of positions. Such situations cannot be completely avoided in a complicated business structure, but many concerns make a practice of assuming such antagonistic functions and regularly violating the trust thus delegated to them. When compelled by law to make a separation of their functions, they make a nominal separation and continue by subterfuge to maintain the two positions.

An accurate statistical comparison of the crimes of the two classes is not available. The most extensive evidence regarding the nature and prevalence of white-collar criminality is found in the reports of the larger investigations to which reference was made. Because of its scattered character, that evidence is assumed rather than summarized here. A few statements will be presented, as illustrations rather than as proof of the prevalence of this criminality.

The Federal Trade Commission in 1920 reported that commercial bribery was a prevalent and common practice in many industries. In certain chain stores, the net shortage in weights was sufficient to pay 3.4 percent on the investment in those commodities. Of the cans of ether sold to the Army in 1923–1925, 70 percent were rejected because of impurities. In Indiana, during the summer of 1934, 40 percent of the ice cream samples tested in a routine manner by the Division of Public Health were in violation of law. The Comptroller of the Currency in 1908 reported that violations of law were found in 75 percent of the banks examined in a three months' period. Lie detector tests of all employees in several Chicago banks, supported in almost all cases by confessions, showed that 20 percent of them had stolen bank property. A public accountant estimated, in the period prior to the Securities and Exchange Commission, that 80 percent of the financial statements of corporations were misleading. James M. Beck said, "Diogenes would have been hard put to it to find an honest man in the Wall Street which I knew as a corporation lawyer" (1916).

White-collar criminality in politics, which is generally recognized as fairly prevalent, has been used by some as a rough gauge by which to measure white-collar criminality in business. James A. Farley said, "The standards of conduct are as high among office-holders and politicians as they are in commercial life," and Cermak, while mayor of Chicago, said, "There is less graft in politics than in business." John Flynn wrote, "The average politician is the merest amateur in the gentle art of graft, compared with his brother in the field of business." And Walter Lippmann wrote, "Poor as they are, the standards of public life are so much more social than those of business that financiers who enter politics regard themselves as philanthropists."

These statements obviously do not give a precise measurement of the relative criminality of the white-collar class, but they are adequate evidence that crime is not so highly concentrated in the lower class as the usual statistics indicate. Also, these statements obviously do not mean that every business and professional man is a criminal, just as the usual theories do not mean that every man in the lower class is a criminal. On the other hand, the preceding statements refer in many cases to the leading corporations in America and are not restricted to the disreputable business and professional men who are called quacks, ambulance chasers, bucket-shop operators, dead-beats, and fly-by-night swindlers.

The financial cost of white-collar crime is probably several times as great as the financial cost of all the crimes which are customarily regarded as the "crime problem." An officer of a chain grocery store in one year embezzled $600,000, which was six times as much as the annual losses from five hundred burglaries and robberies of the stores in that chain. Public enemies numbered one to six secured $130,000 by burglary and robbery in 1938, while the sum stolen by Krueger is estimated at $250,000,000, or nearly two thousand times as much. The New York *Times* in 1931 reported four cases of embezzlement in the United States with a loss of more than a million dollars each and a combined loss of nine million dollars. Although a million-dollar burglar or robber is practically unheard of, these million-dollar embezzlers are small-fry among white-collar criminals. The estimated loss to investors in one investment trust from 1929 to 1935 was $580,000,000, due primarily to the fact that 75 percent of the values in the portfolio were in securities of affiliated companies, although it advertised the importance of diversification in investments and its expert services in selecting safe securities. In Chicago, the claim was made six years ago that householders had lost $54,000,000 in two years during the administration of a city sealer who granted immunity from inspection to stores which provided Christmas baskets for his constituents.

The financial loss from white-collar crime, great as it is, is less important than the damage to social relations. White-collar crimes violate trust and therefore create distrust, which lowers social morale and produces social disorganization on a large scale. Other crimes produce relatively little effect on social institutions or social organization.

White-collar crime is real crime. It is not ordinarily called crime, and calling it by this name does not make it worse, just as refraining from calling it crime does not make it better than it otherwise would be. It is called crime here in order to bring it within the scope of criminology, which is justified because it is in violation of the criminal law. The crucial question in this analysis is the criterion of violation of the criminal law. Conviction in the criminal court, which is sometimes suggested as the criterion, is not adequate because a large proportion of those who commit crimes are not convicted in criminal courts. This criterion, therefore, needs to be supplemented. When it is supplemented, the criterion of the crimes of one class must be kept consistent in general terms with the criterion of the crimes of the other class. The definition should not be the spirit of the law for white-collar crimes and the letter of the law for other crimes, or in other respects be more liberal for one class than for the other. Since this discussion is concerned with the conventional theories of the criminologists, the criterion of white-collar crime must be justified in terms of the procedures of those criminologists in dealing with other crimes. The criterion of white-collar crimes, as here proposed, supplements convictions in the criminal courts in four respects, in each of which the extension is justified because the criminologists who present the conventional theories of criminal behavior make the same extension in principle.

First, other agencies than the criminal court must be included, for the criminal court is not the only agency which makes official decisions regarding violations of the criminal law. The juvenile court, dealing largely with offenses of the children of the poor, in many states is not under the criminal jurisdiction. The criminologists have made much use of case histories and statistics of juvenile delinquents in constructing their theories of criminal behavior. This justifies the inclusion of agencies other than the criminal court which deal with white-collar offenses. The most important of these agencies are the administrative boards, bureaus, or commissions, and much of their work, although certainly not all, consists of cases which are in violation of the criminal law. The Federal Trade Commission recently ordered several automobile companies to stop advertising their interest rate on installment purchases as 6 percent, since it was actually 11½ percent. Also it filed complaint against *Good Housekeeping,* one of the Hearst publications, charging that its seals led the public to believe that all products bearing those seals had been tested in their laboratories, which was contrary to fact. Each of these involves a charge of dishonesty, which might have been tried in a criminal court as fraud. A large proportion of the cases before these boards should be included in the data of the criminologists. Failure to do so is a principal reason for the bias in their samples and the errors in their generalizations.

Second, for both classes, behavior which would have a reasonable expectancy of conviction if tried in a criminal court or substitute agency should be defined as criminal. In this respect, convictability rather than actual conviction should be the criterion of criminality. The criminologists would not hesitate to accept as data a verified case history of a person who was a criminal but had never been convicted. Similarly, it is justifiable to include white-collar criminals who have not been convicted, provided reliable evidence is available. Evidence regarding such cases appears in

many civil suits, such as stockholders' suits and patent-infringe-
ment suits. These cases might have been referred to the criminal
court but they were referred to the civil court because the injured
party was more interested in securing damages than in seeing punishment inflicted. This also happens in embezzlement cases, regarding which surety companies have much evidence. In a short
consecutive series of embezzlements known to a surety company,
90 percent were not prosecuted because prosecution would interfere with restitution or salvage. The evidence in cases of embezzlement is generally conclusive, and would probably have been sufficient to justify conviction in all of the cases in this series.

Third, behavior should be defined as criminal if conviction is
avoided merely because of pressure which is brought to bear on
the court or substitute agency. Gangsters and racketeers have been
relatively immune in many cities because of their pressure on prospective witnesses and public officials, and professional thieves,
such as pick-pockets and confidence men who do not use strong-
arm methods, are even more frequently immune. The conventional
criminologists do not hesitate to include the life histories of such
criminals as data, because they understand the generic relation of
the pressures to the failure to convict. Similarly, white-collar criminals are relatively immune because of the class bias of the courts
and the power of their class to influence the implementation and
administration of the law. This class bias affects not merely present-
day courts but to a much greater degree affected the earlier
courts which established the precedents and rules of procedure of
the present-day courts. Consequently, it is justifiable to interpret
the actual or potential failures of conviction in the light of known
facts regarding the pressures brought to bear on the agencies
which deal with offenders.

Fourth, persons who are accessory to a crime should be included
among white-collar criminals as they are among other criminals.
When the Federal Bureau of Investigation deals with a case of kidnapping, it is not content with catching the offenders who carried
away the victim; they may catch and the court may convict twenty-five other persons who assisted by secreting the victim, negotiating the ransom, or putting the ransom money into circulation. On

the other hand, the prosecution of white-collar criminals frequently stops with one offender. Political graft almost always involves collusion between politicians and business men but prosecutions are generally limited to the politicians. Judge Manton was found guilty of accepting $664,000 in bribes, but the six or eight important commercial concerns that paid the bribes have not been prosecuted. Pendergast, the late boss of Kansas City, was convicted for failure to report as a part of his income $315,000 received in bribes from insurance companies but the insurance companies which paid the bribes have not been prosecuted. In an investigation of an embezzlement by the president of a bank, at least a dozen other violations of law which were related to this embezzlement and involved most of the other officers of the bank and the officers of the clearing house were discovered but none of the others was prosecuted.

This analysis of the criterion of white-collar criminality results in the conclusion that a description of white-collar criminality in general terms will be also a description of the criminality of the lower class. The respects in which the crimes of the two classes differ are the incidentals rather than the essentials of criminality. They differ principally in the implementation of the criminal laws which apply to them. The crimes of the lower class are handled by policemen, prosecutors, and judges, with penal sanctions in the form of fines, imprisonment, and death. The crimes of the upper class either result in no official action at all, or result in suits for damages in civil courts, or are handled by inspectors, and by administrative boards or commissions, with penal sanctions in the form of warnings, orders to cease and desist, occasionally the loss of a license, and only in extreme cases by fines or prison sentences. Thus, the white-collar criminals are segregated administratively from other criminals, and largely as a consequence of this are not regarded as real criminals by themselves, the general public, or the criminologists.

This difference in the implementation of the criminal law is due principally to the difference in the social position of the two types of offenders. Judge Woodward, when imposing sentence upon the officials of the H. O. Stone and Company, bankrupt real estate firm in Chicago, who had been convicted in 1933 of the use of the mails to defraud, said to them, "You are men of affairs, of experience, of refinement and culture, of excellent reputation and standing in the business and social world." That statement might be used as a general characterization of white-collar criminals for they are oriented basically to legitimate and respectable careers. Because of their social status they have a loud voice in determining what goes into the statutes and how the criminal law as it affects themselves is implemented and administered. This may be illustrated from the Pure Food and Drug Law. Between 1879 and 1906, 104 pure food and drug bills were presented in Congress and all failed because of the importance of the persons who would be affected. It took a highly dramatic performance by Dr. Wiley in 1906 to induce Congress to enact the law. That law, however, did not create a new crime, just as the federal Lindbergh kidnapping law did not create a new crime; it merely provided a more efficient implementation of a principle which had been formulated previously in state laws. When an amendment to this law, which would bring within the scope of its agents fraudulent statements made over the radio or in the press, was presented to Congress, the publishers and advertisers organized support and sent a lobby to Washington which successfully fought the amendment principally under the slogans of "freedom of the press" and "dangers of bureaucracy." This proposed amendment, also, would not have created a new crime, for the state laws already prohibited fraudulent statements over the radio or in the press; it would have implemented the law so it could have been enforced. Finally, the Administration has not been able to enforce the law as it has desired because of the pressures by the offenders against the law, sometimes brought to bear through the head of the Department of Agriculture, sometimes through congressmen who threaten cuts in the appropriation, and sometimes by others. The statement of Daniel Drew, a pious old fraud, describes the criminal law with some accuracy, "Law is like a cobweb; it's made for flies and the smaller kinds of insects, so to speak, but lets the big bumblebees break through. When technicalities of the law stood in my way, I have always been able to brush them aside easy as anything."

The preceding analysis should be regarded neither as an assertion that all efforts to influence legislation and its administration are reprehensible nor as a particularistic interpretation of the criminal law. It means only that the upper class has greater influence in moulding the criminal law and its administration to its own interests than does the lower class. The privileged position of white-collar criminals before the law results to a slight extent from bribery and political pressures, principally from the respect in which they are held and without special effort on their part. The most powerful group in medieval society secured relative immunity by "benefit of clergy," and now our most powerful groups secure relative immunity by "benefit of business or profession."

In contrast with the power of the white-collar criminals is the weakness of their victims. Consumers, investors, and stockholders are unorganized, lack technical knowledge, and cannot protect themselves. Daniel Drew, after taking a large sum of money by sharp practice from Vanderbilt in the Erie deal, concluded that it was a mistake to take money from a powerful man on the same level as himself and declared that in the future he would confine his efforts to outsiders, scattered all over the country, who wouldn't be able to organize and fight back. White-collar criminality flourishes at points where powerful business and professional men come in contact with persons who are weak. In this respect, it is similar to stealing candy from a baby. Many of the crimes of the lower class, on the other hand, are committed against persons of wealth and power in the form of burglary and robbery. Because of this difference in the comparative power of the victims, the white-collar criminals enjoy relative immunity.

Embezzlement is an interesting exception to white-collar criminality in this respect. Embezzlement is usually theft from an employer by an employee, and the employee is less capable of manipulating social and legal forces in his own interest than is the employer. As might have been expected, the laws regarding embezzlement were formulated long before laws for the protection of investors and consumers.

The theory that criminal behavior in general is due either to poverty or to the psychopathic and sociopathic conditions associated with poverty can now be shown to be invalid for three reasons. First, the generalization is based on a biased sample which omits almost entirely the behavior of white-collar criminals. The criminologists have restricted their data, for reasons of convenience and ignorance rather than of principle, largely to cases dealt with in criminal courts and juvenile courts, and these agencies are used principally for criminals from the lower economic strata. Consequently, their data are grossly biased from the point of view of the economic status of criminals and their generalization that criminality is closely associated with poverty is not justified.

Second, the generalization that criminality is closely associated with poverty obviously does not apply to white-collar criminals. With a small number of exceptions, they are not in poverty, were not reared in slums or badly deteriorated families, and are not feebleminded or psychopathic. They were seldom problem children in their earlier years and did not appear in juvenile courts or child guidance clinics. The proposition, derived from the data used by the conventional criminologists, that "the criminal of today was the problem child of yesterday" is seldom true of white-collar criminals. The idea that the causes of criminality are to be found almost exclusively in childhood similarly is fallacious. Even if poverty is extended to include the economic stresses which afflict business in a period of depression, it is not closely correlated with white-collar criminality. Probably at no time within fifty years have white-collar crimes in the field of investments and of corporate management been so extensive as during the boom period of the twenties.

Third, the conventional theories do not even explain lower class criminality. The sociopathic and psychopathic factors which have been emphasized doubtless have something to do with crime causation, but these factors have not been related to a general process which is found both in white-collar criminality and lower class criminality and therefore they do not explain the criminality of either class. They may explain the manner or method of crime— why lower class criminals commit burglary or robbery rather than false pretenses.

In view of these defects in the conventional theories, an hypothesis that will explain both white-collar criminality and lower class criminality is needed. For reasons of economy, simplicity, and logic, the hypothesis should apply to both classes, for this will make possible the analysis of causal factors freed from the encumbrances of the administrative devices which have led criminologists astray. Shaw and McKay and others, working exclusively in the field of lower class crime, have found the conventional theories inadequate to account for variations within the data of lower class crime and from that point of view have been working toward an explanation of crime in terms of a more general social process. Such efforts will be greatly aided by the procedure which has been described.

The hypothesis which is here suggested as a substitute for the conventional theories is that white-collar criminality, just as other systematic criminality, is learned; that it is learned in direct or indirect association with those who already practice the behavior; and that those who learn this criminal behavior are segregated from frequent and intimate contacts with law-abiding behavior. Whether a person becomes a criminal or not is determined largely by the comparative frequency and intimacy of his contacts with the two types of behavior. This may be called the process of differential association. It is a genetic explanation both of white-collar criminality and lower class criminality. Those who become white-collar criminals generally start their careers in good neighborhoods and good homes, graduate from colleges with some idealism, and with little selection on their part, get into particular business situations in which criminality is practically a folkway and are inducted into that system of behavior just as into any other folkway. The lower class criminals generally start their careers in deteriorated neighborhoods and families, find delinquents at hand from whom they acquire the attitudes toward, and techniques of, crime through association with delinquents and in partial segregation from law-abiding people. The essentials of the process are the same for the two classes of criminals. This is not entirely a process of assimilation, for inventions are frequently made, perhaps more frequently in white-collar crime than in lower class crime. The inventive geniuses for the lower class criminals are generally professional criminals, while the inventive geniuses for many kinds of white-collar crime are generally lawyers.

A second general process is social disorganization in the community. Differential association culminates in crime because the community is not organized solidly against that behavior. The law is pressing in one direction, and other forces are pressing in the opposite direction. In business, the "rules of the game" conflict with the legal rules. A business man who wants to obey the law is driven by his competitors to adopt their methods. This is well illustrated by the persistence of commercial bribery in spite of the strenuous efforts of business organizations to eliminate it. Groups and individuals are individuated; they are more concerned with their specialized group or individual interests than with the larger welfare. Consequently, it is not possible for the community to present a solid front in opposition to crime. The Better Business Bureaus and Crime Commissions, composed of business and professional men, attack burglary, robbery, and cheap swindles, but overlook the crimes of their own members. The forces which impinge on the lower class are similarly in conflict. Social disorganization affects the two classes in similar ways.

I have presented a brief and general description of white-collar criminality on a framework of argument regarding theories of criminal behavior. That argument, stripped of the description, may be stated in the following propositions:

1. White-collar criminality is real criminality, being in all cases in violation of the criminal law.

2. White-collar criminality differs from lower class criminality principally in an implementation of the criminal law which segregates white-collar criminals administratively from other criminals.

3. The theories of the criminologists that crime is due to poverty or to psychopathic and sociopathic conditions statistically associated with poverty are invalid because, first, they are derived from samples which are grossly biased with respect to socioeconomic status; second, they do not apply to the white-collar criminals; and third, they do not even explain the criminality of the lower class, since the factors are not related to a general process characteristic of all criminality.

4. A theory of criminal behavior which will explain both white-collar criminality and lower class criminality is needed.

5. An hypothesis of this nature is suggested in terms of differential association and social disorganization.

A RE-EXAMINATION OF WHITE-COLLAR CRIMINALITY

EARL R. QUINNEY

Excerpted from Earl R. Quinney, "The Study of White Collar Crime: Toward a Reorientation in Theory and Research," *Journal of Criminal Law, Criminology and Police Science,* 55, No. 2 (June 1964), 208–214. At the time of publication Earl R. Quinney was Assistant Professor of Sociology in the University of Kentucky.

WHITE COLLAR crime as a unique form of illegal behavior has received a great deal of attention since Sutherland introduced the concept in his 1939 presidential address to the American Sociological Society. White collar crime—the violation of criminal law by a person of high socio-economic status in the course of occupational activity—has been focused upon in several ways. For instance, a number of research studies of white collar crime have been initiated, the legal character of the violations has been questioned, the sociological relevance of the concept has been doubted, the theoretical and research significance of the concept has been indicated, critiques and summaries have been written, and in most criminology textbooks considerable space has been devoted to a discussion of white collar crime. Most important to the field of criminology, use of the concept of white collar crime has led to the reexamination of the grounds on which generalizations about crime and criminals are made. Although controversy still occurs, the majority of criminologists regard white collar crime as a legitimate subject for criminological research.

Because the validity of white collar crime as a form of crime has been a subject of severe controversy, the question of conceptual clarity has largely been ignored. Today, as a result, the meaning of the concept is not always clear. In addition to the lack of conceptual clarity, a satisfactory explanation of the diverse behaviors sub-sumed under the concept does not exist. . . .

Unit of Analysis

The first problem stems from the fact that the legal category of crime includes many different kinds of behavior, and it follows that it is unlikely that the different behaviors are subject to a common explanation. Several writers have attempted to correct this diffi-culty by delineating various behaviors within the legal definition of criminal behavior. Law violators have been placed into behavior units that are more homogeneous than those provided in the legal definitions.

Arguments for the delineation of types of white collar crime have been made on several occasions. Aubert noted a few years ago that, similar to the concept of crime, white collar crime proba-bly covers a range of behaviors and each type of behavior may need a different causal explanation. . . . As a starting point in de-lineating types of white collar crime, Bloch and Geis suggested that it might be desirable to separate white collar crimes commit-ted (1) by individuals as individuals (e.g., lawyers, doctors), (2) by employees against the corporation (e.g., embezzlers), and (3) by policy-making officials for the corporation (as in the recent anti-trust cases).

In a somewhat different manner, Geis in a recent article, after recommending that white collar crimes be grouped into forms of behaviors that analytically resemble one another both in their manifestation and in terms of the ingredients which appear to enter into their origin, suggested that the concept of white collar crime be restricted to "corporate violations." He concluded that "unless the concept of white collar crime is restricted, in line with the above or similar ideas, it will continue to remain prey to the legitimate criticisms of numerous scholars . . . , and it will con-tinue to be so broad and indefinite as to fall into inevitable desuetude." [1]

---

[1] Geis, *Toward a Delineation of White Collar Offenses,* 32 *Sociological In-quiry* 171 (1962).

It is apparent, then, that such efforts to distinguish categories of white collar crime, or to restrict the definition of white collar crime itself, must be undertaken in order to give the concept any scientific utility. Various principles of classification should be considered. Possible classifications could include such factors as a more elaborate indication of the kind of occupation and the source of employment, the position of the occupation in the occupational structure, the occupational role or roles of the offender, and the institutional nature of the occupation or organization (political, business, industrial, medical, etc.). Also, classifications could be based on the nature and recency of the law itself and the relation of the offense to societal values. . . .

However, before white collar typologies can be developed, a more pressing problem must be faced and that is that the concept of white collar crime today rather indiscriminately covers a diverse, wide, and oftentimes uncertain and inconsistent range of behaviors. The result is that we are not entirely certain what behaviors constitute white collar crime. This is due in part to Sutherland's definition and to his own subsequent use of the concept. The research and writing of others on the subject have done little to clarify the concept. We remain uncertain as to (1) the importance of the social status of the offender, (2) the exact meaning of occupational activity, and (3) the possibility of including deviant behaviors which are not strictly legal violations.

SOCIAL STATUS OF THE OFFENDER

Sutherland conceptually limited white collar crime to violation of the criminal laws regulating occupations by persons who are "respectable" or of the "upper socioeconomic class." His reason for emphasizing social status was primarily for the purpose of illustrating that persons of high status commit crimes and may be included in the study of criminal behavior—thus altering the picture of crime as well as the usual conception of the pathological criminal. While the limitation of white collar crime to a particular status group may be of historical significance in the reformulation of criminological theory, it appears to have little theoretical merit today, except to point to procedural differences in the administration of justice. Newman, in his critique of white collar crime, suggested that "farmers, repairmen, and others in essentially non-white collar occupations, could through such illegalities as watering milk for public consumption, making unnecessary 'repairs' on television sets, and so forth, be classified as white collar violators." Such an expansion of the concept to include all violations that occur in the course of occupational activity—regardless of the offender's social status—would increase the utility of the concept. It would then be advisable to change the term to *occupational crime.*

OCCUPATIONAL ACTIVITY

The exact meaning of occupational activity is drawn into question when one reviews the writings on white collar crime. One cannot quarrel with the fact that the study of such offenses as embezzlement, price fixing, over-pricing in time of war, misrepresentation in advertising, unfair labor practices, and medical fee-splitting involve behaviors that occur directly in the course of one's occupational activities. It is another thing, however, to include certain forms of such acts as income tax evasion, rent control violation, and violation of welfare compensation laws in the category of occupational crime. These latter behaviors usually do not strictly occur in the course of occupational activity, except, for example, in the case of income tax evasion which is carried out for a corporation or in the case of rent control violation when it can be established that one pursues renting as an occupation. The important point here is that the behavior must be directly related to the violator's occupational activities if it is to be included in white collar crime or occupational crime. Such precision will reduce conceptual problems in future theory and research.

CRIME AND DEVIANT BEHAVIOR

Those who have argued against the inclusion of white collar crime in criminology have stressed that the violations are not crimes because they are not in violation of the traditional criminal code and, what is more, that the violations are not crimes because the offenders are not usually convicted in a court of criminal law. The advocates of the concept of white collar crime have argued

that the behaviors are nevertheless in violation of laws and regulations which contain provisions for punishment. They also argue that
the fact that cases are usually processed differently is of no scientific interest, at least for the purpose of explanation.

Although the controversy no longer seems to be of primary concern, ambiguities arise because some writers on white collar crime,
Sutherland included, have been interested in behaviors which are
not punishable by law, for example, "sharp" business practices and
contract violation. It is important that only behaviors which are
punishable by law be included in the concept of white collar crime
(or occupational crime). On the other hand, the student of occupational crime could gain much by focusing on any deviations in occupational activity, be they criminal or not. It would be valuable,
then, to employ the concept of *occupational deviation.* In keeping
with recent conceptualization of deviant behavior in general, occupational deviation represents departures from expectations that are
shared and recognized as legitimate within an occupation. Occupational deviation includes all occupational behavior that violates
the institutionalized expectations of an occupation, that is, deviant
behavior that occurs in the course of occupational activity. It
should be made explicit at all times, however, whether or not the
behavior in question is criminal as well as a deviation from occupational norms.

By thus expanding the concept beyond the limits set by legal
definitions, but still noting if the behaviors are illegal or not, it
would be possible to handle the heretofore unmanageable fact that
violations of the legal norms are not necessarily violations of other
(non-legal) norms. . . .

Therefore, a shift to the concept of occupational deviation would
allow researchers to investigate actual departures from occupational norms without having to rely upon the otherwise necessary
inference that violations of legal norms are also deviations from occupational norms. It would also be possible to study occupational
deviations that have not been formalized into law. . . .

Another interesting observation arises when the criminologist
views the relationship between legal norms and occupational
norms. There is the special case in which most of the occupational

behaviors are defined as criminal by persons outside of the occupation. To the incumbents, however, the behaviors may be legitimate according to their own standards, yet there are entirely different behaviors which they regard as occupational deviations. These are the illegitimate (and usually illegal) occupations which are organized around criminal activity. Crime is pursued by the members as a career and as a regular day-by-day means of livelihood, as in the case of professional theft and the various forms of organized crime. These criminal occupations are known to have their own norms and deviations. The criminal code, for example, presents the professional criminal with the rules that one criminal should not inform on another and that there should be an honest division of the loot with partners in crime. The study of occupational crime and occupational deviation among these illegitimate occupations would certainly present the researcher with two separate and distinct behaviors. Of course, it is not unlikely that the criminal behaviors of illegitimate occupations are also supported by some legitimate occupations.

CRIMES OF CORPORATIONS
AND EXECUTIVES

ANTHONY LEWIS

Anthony Lewis, "7 Electrical Officials Get Jail Terms in Trust Case,"
The New York *Times*, February 7, 1961, pp. 1, 26. Reprinted with permission from The New York *Times*.

PHILADELPHIA, Feb. 6—Seven executives of the country's
leading electrical manufacturing companies received jail sentences
today for violating the antitrust laws. Federal District Judge J.
Cullen Ganey sent each to prison for thirty days.

In addition, Judge Ganey imposed fines totaling $931,500 on in-
dividuals and corporations in what the Government has called the
largest of all criminal antitrust cases. . . .

Among those drawing prison terms were vice presidents of the
General Electric Company and the Westinghouse Electric
Corporation—the two largest companies in the industry. Aside
from those going to jail, twenty men drew suspended prison sentences.

All the defendants had pleaded guilty or no defense to charges
of fixing prices and rigging bids on heavy electrical equipment,
such as power transformers. Sales of the products involved totaled
$1,750,000,000 a year.

But the real drama in the courtroom today arose not from the
money or the corporations involved. It lay with the men who stood
before Judge Ganey to hear their fate.

They were middle-class men in Ivy League suits—typical business men in appearance, men who would never be taken for law-
breakers. Over and over their lawyers described them as pillars of
their communities.

Several were deacons or vestrymen of their churches. One was president of his local Chamber of Commerce, another a hospital board member, another chief fund raiser for the Community Chest, another a bank director, another director of the taxpayer's association, another an organizer of the local Little League.

Lawyer after lawyer said his client was "an honorable man"—a victim of corporate morality, not its creator. To a degree Judge Ganey agreed.

"The real blame," the judge said in an opening statement, "is to be laid at the doorstep of the corporate defendants and those who guide and direct their policy."

Judge Ganey said the typical individual defendant was "the organization or the company man, the conformist, who goes along with his superiors and finds balm for his conscience in additional comforts and the security of his place in the corporate set-up."

Judge Ganey imposed jail sentences only on men he thought were high enough in their companies to make policy. Jail sentences of any kind are unusual, though not unprecedented, in antitrust cases.

These sentences were below the statutory maximums—a $50,000 fine on each count and a year in jail for the individual defendants. Most were also below Justice Department recommendations, which were for the most part short of the maximums.

The recommendations were sent to Judge Ganey Jan. 19, the day before the new Administration took office. But the acting chief of the department's antitrust division, W. Wallace Kirkpatrick, read the court a statement by the new Attorney General, Robert F. Kennedy.

Mr. Kennedy said he had reviewed the cases and considered the crimes "so willful and flagrant that even more severe sentences would have been appropriate." He suggested, "under the circumstances," that "sentences at least as severe as those recommended be imposed."

Forty-five individuals and twenty-nine corporations were named as defendants in the package of twenty indictments.

Today sentence was imposed on the thirty-six men and twenty-one companies. Some of the same defendants figure in the cases to be handled tomorrow.

The corporate defendants today drew a total of $822,500 in fines. The largest figures were $185,000 for General Electric, in five cases, and $180,000 for Westinghouse, in six.

All of the individual defendants also drew fines, ranging from $1,000 to $12,500. The total for them was $109,000. . . .

Judge Ganey said he had suspended the sentences of some other defendants "reluctantly," and only because of their age or bad health.

He repeatedly rejected pleas by counsel to the effect that their clients were not deeply involved. He would cut in crisply to remark that the defendant had been an "aggressive competitor" in a shocking case.

The formal charge in all the cases was violation of the Sherman Antitrust Act, which prohibits conspiracies in restraint of trade. That is a common charge, but the Government said these conspiracies were unusually elaborate and damaging.

The defendants were said to have held frequent secret meetings, and used codes. They allegedly parceled out Government contracts among each other, submitting low bids in rotation under a scheme called "the phase of the moon." . . .

Gerhard A. Gesell of Washington, counsel for G.E., took vigorous exception to Judge Ganey's comment about corporate responsibility for the violations.

He noted that G.E. had a company rule, known as Regulation 20.5, directing strict obedience to the antitrust laws. And he observed that the company had demoted all officials involved before any indictments were brought.

"It is simply not a fact that there was a way of life at General Electric that permitted, tolerated, or winked at these violations," Mr. Gesell said. "The company abhors, sought to prevent, and punished this conduct."

But Judge Ganey disagreed with Mr. Gesell. He said he thought General Electric's Rule 20.5 "was honored in its breach rather than its observance."

Mr._____was the first individual defendant called. A small man with gold-rimmed glasses, he stood with head slightly bowed as his attorney, Philip H. Strubing of Philadelphia, sought leniency.

"No further punishment is needed to keep these men from doing what they have done, again," Mr. Strubing said.

"These men are not grasping, greedy, cut-throat competitors. They devote much of their time and substance to their communities."

Mr. Strubing listed Mr._____'s activities—senior warden of his church, benefactor of charities for crippled children and cancer victims, fellow of an engineering society. . . .

Next was Mr._____, tall and distinguished in appearance. His attorney, Henry T. Reath of Philadelphia, also made a general attack on the Government's demand for jail terms.

He said Government lawyers were "cold-blooded" and did not understand what it would do to a man like Mr._____to "put him behind bars" with "common criminals who have been convicted of embezzlement and other series [sic] crimes."

In contrast to Mr. Gesell, Mr. Reath insisted that Mr._____had only followed long-established company policy by getting together with supposed competitors to arrange their business.

Mr. Reath said Mr._____was chairman of the building fund for a new Jesuit novitiate in Lenox, Mass.; a director of the Schenectady, N.Y. boy's club, and a member of Governor Rockefeller's Temporary State Committee on Economic Expansion.

"It would be a great personal tragedy for this fine man" to go to jail, Mr. Reath concluded. Judge Ganey took only a few seconds to mark Mr._____down for thirty days in prison.

And so it went. Lawyers spoke of their clients' long years with one company, of their daughters in prominent colleges, of the shame that publicity had already caused.

Judge Ganey ordered the seven who were given jail sentences to begin their terms Monday at 10 A.M.

BECOMING AN ALCOHOLIC

E. M. JELLINEK

Excerpted from E. M. Jellinek, "Phases of Alcohol Addiction," *Quarterly Journal of Studies on Alcohol*, 13, No. 4 (December 1952), 673–84. The author, a specialist on alcohol and alcoholism, has done research on the subject at Yale University under the Research Council on Problems of Alcohol. The present article, published in the *Quarterly Journal*, is a summary of lectures, as published under the auspices of the Alcoholism Subcommittee of the World Health Organization. (Expert Committee on Mental Health, Alcoholism Subcommittee, Second Report, Annex 2, *The Phases of Alcohol Addiction*. World Health Organization techn. Rep. Ser., No. 48, August 1952.)

Introduction

ONLY CERTAIN forms of excessive drinking—those which in the present report are designated as alcoholism—are accessible to medical-psychiatric treatment. The other forms of excessive drinking, too, present more or less serious problems, but they can be managed only on the level of applied sociology, including law enforcement. . . .

The conditions which have been briefly defined by the Subcommittee as alcoholism are described in the following pages in greater detail, in order to delimit more definitely those excessive drinkers whose rehabilitation primarily requires medical-psychiatric treatment. . . .

THE DISEASE CONCEPTION OF ALCOHOL ADDICTION

The Subcommittee has distinguished two categories of alcoholics, namely, "alcohol addicts" and "habitual symptomatic excessive drinkers." For brevity's sake the latter will be referred to as non-addictive alcoholics. Strictly speaking, the disease conception attaches to the alcohol addicts only, but not to the habitual symptomatic excessive drinkers.

In both groups the excessive drinking is symptomatic of underlying psychological or social pathology, but in one group after several years of excessive drinking "loss of control" over the alcohol intake occurs, while in the other group this phenomenon never develops. The group with the "loss of control" is designated as "alcohol addicts." . . .

The disease conception of alcohol addiction does not apply to the excessive drinking, but solely to the "loss of control" which occurs in only one group of alcoholics and then only after many years of excessive drinking. There is no intention to deny that the nonaddictive alcoholic is a sick person; but his ailment is not the excessive drinking, but rather the psychological or social difficulties from which alcohol intoxication gives temporary surcease.

The "loss of control" is a disease condition per se which results from a process that superimposes itself upon those abnormal psychological conditions of which excessive drinking is a symptom. The fact that many excessive drinkers drink as much as or more than the addict for 30 or 40 years without developing loss of control indicates that in the group of "alcohol addicts" a superimposed process must occur.

Whether this superimposed process is of a psychopathological nature or whether some physical pathology is involved cannot be stated as yet with any degree of assurance, the claims of various investigators notwithstanding. Nor is it possible to go beyond conjecture concerning the question whether the "loss of control" originates in a predisposing factor (psychological or physical), or whether it is a factor acquired in the course of prolonged excessive drinking.

The fact that this "loss of control" does not occur in a large group of excessive drinkers would point towards a predisposing X factor in the addictive alcoholics. On the other hand this explanation is not indispensable as the difference between addictive and nonaddictive alcoholics could be a matter of acquired modes of living—for instance, a difference in acquired nutritional habits.

THE MEANING OF SYMPTOMATIC DRINKING

The use of alcoholic beverages by society has primarily a symbolic meaning, and secondarily it achieves "function." Cultures which accept this custom differ in the nature and degree of the "functions" which they regard as legitimate. The differences in these "functions" are determined by the general pattern of the culture, e.g., the need for the release and for the special control of aggression, the need and the ways and means of achieving identification, the nature and intensity of anxieties and the modus for their relief, and so forth. The more the original symbolic character of the custom is preserved, the less room will be granted by the culture to the "functions" of drinking.

Any drinking within the accepted ways is symptomatic of the culture of which the drinker is a member. Within that frame of cultural symptomatology there may be in addition individual symptoms expressed in the act of drinking. The fact that a given individual drinks a glass of beer with his meal may be the symptom of the culture which accepts such a use as a refreshment, or as a "nutritional supplement." That this individual drinks at this given moment may be a symptom of his fatigue, or his elation or some other mood, and thus an individual symptom, but if his culture accepts the use for these purposes it is at the same time a cultural symptom.

In this sense even the small or moderate use of alcoholic beverages is symptomatic, and it may be said that all drinkers are culturally symptomatic drinkers or, at least, started as such.

The vast majority of the users of alcoholic beverages stay within the limits of the culturally accepted drinking behaviors and drink predominantly as an expression of their culture, and while an individual expression may be present in these behaviors its role remains insignificant.

For the purpose of the present discussion the expression "symptomatic drinking" will be limited to the predominant use of alcoholic beverages for the relief of major individual stresses.

A certain unknown proportion of these users of alcoholic beverages, perhaps 20 per cent, are occasionally inclined to take advantage of the "functions" of alcohol which they have experienced in the course of its "cultural use." At least at times, the individual motivation becomes predominant and on those occasions alcohol loses its character as an ingredient of a beverage and is used as a drug.

The "occasional symptomatic excessive drinker" tends to take care of the stresses and strains of living in socially accepted—i.e., "normal"—ways, and his drinking is most of the time within the cultural pattern. After a long accumulation of stresses, however, or because of some particularly heavy stress, his tolerance for tension is lowered and he takes recourse to heroic relief of his symptoms through alcoholic intoxication. Under these circumstances the "relief" may take on an explosive character, and thus the occasional symptomatic excessive drinker may create serious problems. No psychological abnormality can be claimed for this type of drinker, although he does not represent a well-integrated personality.

Nevertheless, within the group of apparent "occasional symptomatic excessive drinkers" there is a certain proportion of definitely deviating personalities who after a shorter or longer period of occasional symptomatic relief take recourse to a constant alcoholic relief, and drinking becomes with them a "mode of living." These are the "alcoholics" of whom again a certain proportion suffer "loss of control," i.e., become "addictive alcoholics."

The proportion of alcoholics (addictive and nonaddictive) varies from country to country, but does not seem to exceed in any country 5 per cent or 6 per cent of all users of alcoholic beverages. The ratio of addictive to nonaddictive alcoholics is unknown.

The course of alcohol addiction [to be discussed] is based on an analysis of more than two thousand drinking histories of male alcohol addicts. Not all symptoms occur necessarily in all alcohol addicts, nor do they occur in every addict in the same sequence. The "phases" and the sequences of symptoms within the phases are characteristic, however, of the great majority of alcohol addicts and represent what may be called the average trend.

For alcoholic women the "phases" are not as clear-cut as in men and the development is frequently more rapid.

The "phases" vary in their duration according to individual characteristics and environmental factors. . . .

THE PREALCOHOLIC SYMPTOMATIC PHASE

The very beginning of the use of alcoholic beverages is always socially motivated in the prospective addictive and nonaddictive alcoholic. In contrast to the average social drinker, however, the prospective alcoholic (together with the occasional symptomatic excessive drinker) soon experiences a rewarding relief in the drinking situation. The relief is strongly marked in his case because either his tensions are much greater than in other members of his social circle, or he has not learned to handle those tensions as others do.

Initially this drinker ascribes his relief to the situation rather than to the drinking and he seeks therefore those situations in which incidental drinking will occur. Sooner or later, of course, he becomes aware of the contingency between relief and drinking.

In the beginning he seeks this relief occasionally only, but in the course of 6 months to 2 years his tolerance for tension decreases to such a degree that he takes recourse to alcoholic relief practically daily.

Nevertheless his drinking does not result in overt intoxication, but he reaches toward the evening a stage of surcease from emotional stress. Even in the absence of intoxication this involves fairly heavy drinking, particularly in comparison to the use of alcoholic beverages by other members of his circle. The drinking is, nevertheless, not conspicuous either to his associates or to himself.

After a certain time an increase in alcohol tolerance may be noticed, i.e., the drinker requires a somewhat larger amount of alcohol than formerly in order to reach the desired stage of sedation.

This type of drinking behavior may last from several months to 2 years according to circumstances and may be designated as the prealcoholic phase, which is divided into stages of occasional relief-drinking and constant relief-drinking.

THE PRODROMAL PHASE

The sudden onset of a behavior resembling the "blackouts" in anoxemia marks the beginning of the prodromal phase of alcohol addiction. The drinker who may have had not more than 50 to 60 g. of absolute alcohol and who is not showing any signs of intoxication may carry on a reasonable conversation or may go through quite elaborate activities without a trace of memory the next day, although sometimes one or two minor details may be hazily remembered. This amnesia, which is not connected with loss of consciousness, has been called by Bonhoeffer the "alcoholic palimpsests," with reference to old Roman manuscripts superimposed over an incompletely erased manuscript.

"*Alcoholic palimpsests*" may occur on rare occasions in an average drinker when he drinks intoxicating amounts in a state of physical or emotional exhaustion. Nonaddictive alcoholics, of course, also may experience "palimpsests," but infrequently and only following rather marked intoxication. Thus, the frequency of "palimpsests" and their occurrence after medium alcohol intake are characteristic of the prospective alcohol addict.

This would suggest heightened susceptibility to alcohol in the prospective addict. Such a susceptibility may be psychologically or physiologically determined. The analogy with the "blackouts" of anoxemia is tempting. Of course, an insufficient oxygen supply cannot be assumed, but a malutilization of oxygen may be involved. The present status of the knowledge of alcoholism does not permit of more than vague conjectures which, nevertheless, may constitute bases for experimental hypotheses.

The onset of "alcoholic palimpsests" is followed (in some instances preceded) by the onset of drinking behaviors which indicate that, for this drinker, beer, wine and spirits have practically ceased to be beverages and have become sources of a drug which he "needs." Some of these behaviors imply that this drinker has some vague realization that he drinks differently from others.

Surreptitious drinking is one of these behaviors. At social gatherings the drinker seeks occasions for having a few drinks unknown to others, as he fears that if it were known that he drinks more than the others he would be misjudged: those to whom drinking is only a custom or a small pleasure would not understand that because he is different from them alcohol is for him a necessity, although he is not a drunkard.

Preoccupation with alcohol is further evidence of this "need." When he prepares to go to a social gathering his first thought is whether there will be sufficient alcohol for his requirements, and he has several drinks in anticipation of a possible shortage.

Because of this increasing dependence upon alcohol, the onset of *avid drinking* (gulping of the first or first two drinks) occurs at this time.

As the drinker realizes, at least vaguely, that his drinking is outside of the ordinary, he develops *guilt feelings about his drinking behavior* and because of this he begins to *avoid reference to alcohol* in conversation.

These behaviors, together with an *increasing frequency of "alcoholic palimpsests"* foreshadow the development of alcohol addiction; they are premonitory signs, and this period may be called the prodromal phase of alcohol addiction.

The consumption of alcoholic beverages in the prodromal phase is "heavy," but not conspicuous, as it does not lead to marked, overt intoxications. The effect is that the prospective addict reaches toward evening a state which may be designated as emotional anesthesia. Nevertheless, this condition requires drinking well beyond the ordinary usage. The drinking is on a level which may begin to interfere with metabolic and nervous processes as evidenced by the frequent "alcoholic palimpsests."

The "covering-up" which is shown by the drinker in this stage is the first sign that his drinking might separate him from society, although initially the drinking may have served as a technique to overcome some lack of social integration.

As in the prodromal phase rationalizations of the drinking behavior are not strong and there is some insight as well as fear of possible consequences, it is feasible to intercept incipient alcohol addiction at this stage. In the United States of America, the publicity given to the prodromal symptoms begins to bring prospective alcoholics to clinics as well as to groups of Alcoholics Anonymous.

It goes without saying that even at this stage the only possible modus for this type of drinker is total abstinence.

The prodromal period may last anywhere from 6 months to 4 or 5 years according to the physical and psychological makeup of the drinker, his family ties, vocational relations, general interests, and so forth. The prodromal phase ends and the crucial or acute phase begins with the onset of loss of control, which is the critical symptom of alcohol addiction.

THE CRUCIAL PHASE

Loss of control means that any drinking of alcohol starts a chain reaction which is felt by the drinker as a physical demand for alcohol. This state, possibly a conversion phenomenon, may take hours or weeks for its full development; it lasts until the drinker is too intoxicated or too sick to ingest more alcohol. The physical discomfort following this drinking behavior is contrary to the object of the drinker, which is merely to feel "different." As a matter of fact, the bout may not even be started by any individual need of the moment, but by a "social drink."

After recovery from the intoxication, it is not the "loss of control" —i.e., the physical demand, apparent or real—which leads to a new bout after several days or several weeks; the renewal of drinking is set off by the original psychological conflicts or by a simple social situation which involves drinking.

The "loss of control" is effective after the individual has started drinking, but it does not give rise to the beginning of a new drinking bout. The drinker has lost the ability to control the quantity once he has started, but he still can control whether he will drink on any given occasion or not. This is evidenced in the fact that after the onset of "loss of control" the drinker can go through a period of voluntary abstinence ("going on the water wagon").

The question of why the drinker returns to drinking after repeated disastrous experiences is often raised. Although he will not admit it, the alcohol addict believes that he has lost his will power and that he can and must regain it. He is not aware that he has undergone a process which makes it impossible for him to control his alcohol intake. To "master his will" becomes a matter of the greatest importance to him. When tensions rise, "a drink" is the natural remedy for him and he is convinced that this time it will be one or two drinks only.

Practically simultaneously with the onset of "loss of control" the alcohol addict begins to *rationalize his drinking behavior:* he produces the well-known alcoholic "alibis." He finds explanations which convince him that he did not lose control, but that he had a good reason to get intoxicated and that in the absence of such reasons he is able to handle alcohol as well as anybody else. These rationalizations are needed primarily for himself and only secondarily for his family and associates. The rationalizations make it possible for him to continue with his drinking, and this is of the greatest importance to him as he knows no alternative for handling his problems.

This is the beginning of an entire "system of rationalizations" which progressively spreads to every aspect of his life. While this system largely originates in inner needs, it also serves to counter *social pressures* which arise at the time of the "loss of control." At this time, of course, the drinking behavior becomes conspicuous, and the parents, wife, friends and employer may begin to reprove and warn the drinker.

In spite of all the rationalizations there is a marked loss of self-esteem, and this of course demands compensations which in a certain sense are also rationalizations. One way of compensation is the *grandiose behavior* which the addict begins to display at this time. Extravagant expenditures and grandiloquence convince him that he is not as bad as he had thought at times.

The rationalization system gives rise to another system, namely the "system of isolation." The rationalizations quite naturally lead to the idea that the fault lies not within himself but in others, and this results in a progressive withdrawal from the social environment. The first sign of this attitude is a *marked aggressive behavior*.

Inevitably, this latter behaving generates guilt. While even in the prodromal period remorse about the drinking arose from time to time, now *persistent remorse* arises, and this added tension is a further source of drinking.

In compliance with social pressures the addict now goes on *periods of total abstinence*. There is, however, another modus of control of drinking which arises out of the rationalizations of the addict. He believes that his trouble arises from his not drinking the right kind of beverages or not in the right way. He now attempts to control his troubles by *changing the pattern of his drinking*, by setting up rules about not drinking before a certain hour of the day, in certain places only, and so forth.

The strain of the struggle increases his hostility toward his environment and he begins to *drop friends* and *quit jobs*. It goes without saying that some associates drop him and that he loses some jobs, but more frequently he takes the initiative as an anticipatory defence.

The isolation becomes more pronounced as his entire *behavior becomes alcohol-centered,* i.e., he begins to be concerned about how activities might interfere with his drinking instead of how his drinking may affect his activities. This, of course, involves a more marked egocentric outlook which leads to more rationalizations and more isolation. There ensues a *loss of outside interests* and a *reinterpretation of interpersonal relations* coupled with *marked self-pity.* The isolation and rationalizations have increased by this time in intensity and find their expression either in contemplated or actual *geographic escape.*

Under the impact of these events, a *change in family habits* occurs. The wife and children, who may have had good social activities, may withdraw for fear of embarrassment or, quite contrarily, they may suddenly begin intensive outside activities in order to escape from the home environment. This and other events lead to the onset of *unreasonable resentments* in the alcohol addict.

The predominance of concern with alcohol induces the addict to *protect his supply,* i.e., to lay in a large stock of alcoholic beverages, hidden in the most unthought-of places. A fear of being deprived of the most necessary substance for his living is expressed in this behavior.

Neglect of proper nutrition aggravates the beginnings of the effects of heavy drinking on the organism, and frequently the *first hospitalization* for some alcoholic complaint occurs at this time.

One of the frequent organic effects is a *decrease of the sexual drive* which increases hostility toward the wife and is rationalized into her extramarital sex activities, which gives rise to the well-known *alcoholic jealousy.*

By this time remorse, resentment, struggle between alcoholic needs and duties, loss of self-esteem, and doubts and false reassurance have so disorganized the addict that he cannot start the day without steadying himself with alcohol immediately after arising or even before getting out of bed. This is the beginning of *regular matutinal drinking*, which previously had occurred on rare occasions only.

This behavior terminates the crucial phase and foreshadows the beginnings of the chronic phase.

During the crucial phase intoxication is the rule, but it is limited to the evening hours. For the most part of this phase drinking begins sometime in the afternoon and by the evening intoxication is reached. It should be noted that the "physical demand" involved in the "loss of control" results in continual rather than continuous drinking. Particularly the "matutinal drink" which occurs toward the end of the crucial phase shows the continual pattern. The first drink at rising, let us say at 7 A.M., is followed by another drink at 10 or 11 A.M., and another drink around 1 P.M., while the more intensive drinking hardly starts before 5 P.M.

Throughout, the crucial phase presents a great struggle of the addict against the complete loss of social footing. Occasionally the aftereffects of the evening's intoxication cause some loss of time, but generally the addict succeeds in looking after his job, although he neglects his family. He makes a particularly strong effort to avoid intoxication during the day. Progressively, however, his social motivations weaken more and more, and the "morning drink" jeopardizes his effort to comply with his vocational duties as this effort involves a conscious resistance against the apparent or real "physical demand" for alcohol.

The onset of the "loss of control" is the beginning of the "disease process" of alcohol addiction which is superimposed over the excessive symptomatic drinking. Progressively, this disease process undermines the morale and the physical resistance of the addict.

THE CHRONIC PHASE

The increasingly dominating role of alcohol, and the struggle against the "demand" set up by matutinal drinking, at last break down the resistance of the addict and he finds himself for the first time intoxicated in the daytime and on a weekday and continues in that state for several days until he is entirely incapacitated. This is the onset of *prolonged intoxications,* referred to in the vernacular as "benders."

This latter drinking behavior meets with such unanimous social rejection that it involves a grave social risk. Only an originally psychopathic personality or a person who has later in life undergone a psychopathological process would expose himself to that risk.

These long-drawn-out bouts commonly bring about *marked ethical deterioration* and *impairment of thinking* which, however, are not irreversible. True *alcoholic psychoses* may occur at this time, but in not more than 10 per cent of all alcoholics.

The loss of morale is so heightened that the addict *drinks with persons far below his social level* in preference to his usual associates—perhaps as an opportunity to appear superior—and, if nothing else is available, he will *take recourse to "technical products"* such as bay rum or rubbing alcohol.

A *loss of alcohol tolerance* is commonly noted at this time. Half of the previously required amount of alcohol may be sufficient to bring about a stuporous state.

Indefinable fears and *tremors* become persistent. Sporadically these symptoms occur also during the crucial phase, but in the chronic phase they are present as soon as alcohol disappears from the organism. In consequence the addict "controls" the symptoms through alcohol. The same is true of *psychomotor inhibition,* the inability to initiate a simple mechanical act—such as winding a watch—in the absence of alcohol.

The need to control these symptoms of drinking exceeds the need of relieving the original underlying symptoms of the personality conflict, and the *drinking takes on an obsessive character.*

In many addicts, approximately 60 per cent, some *vague religious desires develop* as the rationalizations become weaker. Finally, in the course of the frequently prolonged intoxications, the rationalizations become so frequently and so mercilessly tested against reality that the entire *rationalization system fails* and the addict admits defeat. He now becomes spontaneously accessible to treatment. Nevertheless, his obsessive drinking continues as he does not see a way out.

Formerly it was thought that the addict must reach this stage of utter defeat in order to be treated successfully. Clinical experience has shown, however, that this "defeat" can be induced long before it would occur of itself and that even incipient alcoholism can be intercepted. As the latter can be easily recognized it is possible to tackle the problem from the preventive angle.

The "Alcoholic Personality"

The aggressions, feelings of guilt, remorse, resentments, withdrawal, etc., which develop in the phases of alcoholic addiction, are largely consequences of the excessive drinking, but at the same time they constitute sources of more excessive drinking.

In addition to relieving, through alcohol, symptoms of an underlying personality conflict, the addict now tends to relieve, through further drinking, the stresses created by his drinking behavior.

By and large, these reactions to excessive drinking—which have quite a neurotic appearance—give the impression of an "alcoholic personality," although they are secondary behaviors superimposed over a large variety of personality types which have a few traits in common, in particular a low capacity for coping with tensions. There does not emerge, however, any specific personality trait or physical characteristic which inevitably would lead to excessive symptomatic drinking. Apart from psychological and possibly physical liabilities, there must be a constellation of social and economic factors which facilitate the development of addictive and nonaddictive alcoholism in a susceptible terrain.

The Nonaddictive Alcoholic

Some differences between the nonaddictive alcoholic and the alcohol addict have been stated passim. These differences may be recapitulated and elaborated, and additional differential features may be considered.

The main difference [might be shown] in a diagram which suggests a progressive exacerbation of the use of alcohol for symptom relief and of the social and health consequences incumbent upon such use, but without any clear-cut phases.

The prealcoholic phase is the same for the nonaddictive alcoholic as for the alcohol addict, i.e., he progresses from occasional to constant relief of individual symptoms through alcohol.

The behaviors which denote that alcohol has become a drug rather than an ingredient of a beverage occur also in the nonaddictive drinker, but, as mentioned before, the "alcoholic palimpsests" occur rarely and only after overt intoxication.

"Loss of control" is not experienced by the nonaddictive alcoholic, and this is the main differentiating criterion between the two categories of alcoholics. Initially, of course, it could not be said whether the drinker had yet reached the crucial phase, but after 10 or 12 years of heavy drinking without "loss of control," . . . the differential diagnosis is rather safe.

The absence of "loss of control" has many involvements. First of all, as there is no inability to stop drinking within a given situation there is no need to rationalize the inability. Nevertheless, rationalizations are developed for justifying the excessive use of alcohol and some neglect of the family attendant upon such use. Likewise, there is no need to change the pattern of drinking, which in the addict is an attempt to overcome the "loss of control." Periods of total abstinence, however, occur as a response to social pressure.

On the other hand, there is the same tendency toward isolation as in the addict, but the social repercussions are much less marked as the nonaddictive alcoholic can avoid drunken behavior whenever the social situation requires it.

The effects of prolonged heavy drinking on the organism may occur in the nonaddictive alcoholic too; even delirium tremens may develop. The libido may be diminished and "alcoholic jealousy" may result.

Generally, there is a tendency toward a progressive dominance of alcohol resulting in greater psychological and bodily effects. In the absence of any grave initial psychopathy, however, the symptoms of the chronic phase as seen in addicts do not develop in the nonaddictive alcoholic. In the presence of grave underlying psychopathies a deteriorative process is speeded up by habitual alcoholic excess, and such a nonaddictive drinker may slide to the bottom of society.

AN ALCOHOLIC'S STORY

ANONYMOUS

Tape recording of a series of interviews between the anonymous subject and David Dressler. Identifying features have been altered.

I'M A drug addict, but actually I began as an alcoholic. I have the double problem. I don't know why. I had fine folks, every opportunity. They did too much for me. My father was a very in-fluential politician in New York. Any time I got in a scrape he got me out. I started drinking in grade school. I got in plenty of scrapes. My parents always shielded me. I was one of five boys. No girls. My parents thought the world of all of us. They gave us the best of everything. There was no dissension at home. We loved each other. A close Catholic family. I can't tell you why I was a drunk by the time I was 13.

I was in prep school, coming home from parties three in the morning, banging up cars, getting arrested and put in jail. Always my father got me out. This gave me a crutch.

I was a five-letter man at school and I was given the opportunity to go into professional football. I quit school and signed up. My parents had to sign because I was a minor.

The first week in training, living in a beautiful hotel, it cost $50 a day, I had the conveniences of all millionaires, I was invited out to a party and never returned to the hotel until about four in the morning, breaking one of the strictest rules they had in football. I crept up the back stairway, reached the fourth floor, and I slipped and fell, fell the four floors down the stairs. The noise was some-thing, and next day I was brought before the manager and the owner of the club and really given a going over. I said it wouldn't happen again.

Somehow, it hurt my ego to have been talked to like that. Naturally, that called for action. I woke up six in the morning lying on the grass in back of the playing field. I had got drunk and blacked out. I was fired.

This started me on a nine year cross-country binge. I was hired and fired from teams. It seemed that every time I was fired there was a telegram waiting for me, inviting me to join another club. They thought they could dry me out, give me some guidance, and that would eventually net them a lot of money. I was always told I had ability, and I proved this on different occasions. I have been a national star, setting records that were reported in every paper in the United States. Once I won a game practically by myself. The funny thing was I was completely ignorant of the fact. I was loaded. Drunk.

I stayed with one club almost the whole season. Then I was fired. Again I'd broken training rules. I jumped on the train and went to Florida. I had a lot of money. I was paid off. Naturally, with big-shotitis, I went to the $50 a day hotel where I started, forgetting that back then the club was paying the freight. Carousing. Night clubs. Money ran short and I went to a middle class hotel. Then to a small hotel. Then to a room.

I finally started selling my wardrobe. Hocking my clothes. I finally wound up with one suit and a pair of bathing trunks.

I was really in the throes of alcoholism at that time. I had seen men living on the beach, so I sold my last suit and put on my trunks and went to live on the beach.

Now I was living on the beach. We were making it the best we could. One of the boys I hung around with came up with the idea that I'd been to a lot of fine houses where the ball team had been invited, that I'd know the layout of the houses, and would know how to break in and grab some liquor off. Or whatever we could use. Well, I didn't want to steal anything, but I would do anything to get that drink, so we broke into this home, and I knew exactly where they kept their liquor. We got away with this kind of thing for quite some time, but finally we were caught.

Again the long arm of politics, and again my crutch came to my rescue. I was given a lecture and told to go back to playing football. To quit drinking and behave myself.

I did go back to playing football, and I stayed sober for a while. Then I started nightclubbing and got myself fired for good.

About then I met Harriet. She was a showgirl, very beautiful, a good drinker, and we hit it off right away. We got married. And I made up my mind I was going to make the grade. I got a job as a salesman. I traveled. Short trips. I tried to stay sober. I fought it like mad. I'd be like a caged lion in the rooms at night, in hotels. I'd try to sleep. Then it would start all over again, that mental obsession from hearing the music coming from the main dining room and bar. It would drive me crazy until from sheer exhaustion I would fall alseep.

One time in San Francisco I met a friend, we went out and had a sandwich and a bottle of beer, and this one bottle set me off again, and I went on drinking whiskey and at four in the morning I came back to the hotel and created such a disturbance the manger telephoned the company and I was fired.

I got back to LA without a dime. My wife and I were together. We had been going along for five years beautifully, never had an argument. She was an everyday drinker and an everynight drinker. We'd sit around to two, three o'clock in the morning. Finally we got to the stage where we had to sit around holding hands, because if we let go, we'd kill each other. I'd go down to the store, maybe to buy a newspaper or sandwiches, and I wouldn't come home for three or four days. And every time I picked up the phone to call my wife she'd never ask me where I'd been or what happened to me. She'd always say, "Bring me something." Booze. If I could keep her well supplied with alcohol I could stay away for weeks at a time. Finally it became very aggravating to me, that she didn't care what happened to me, when I'd finally call, all she'd say was, "Bring me something."

By this time the war had started. Pearl Harbor was bombed. I was put in 3A. I came home this time and again found my wife completely on the floor and the whole rug full of blood. I rushed my wife to the hospital. I, in a drunken stupor, was standing out in the corridor of the hospital. The doctor come up and put the papers in my hand. He said, "Sign these. I've got to operate on your wife to save her life." And I signed them and didn't know what I was signing. I found out next day. The doctor said she would live but we would never be able to have a child.

This was a thing that contributed to my alcoholism, and later my drug addiction, that all my life I dreamed about having a boy, and wanting him to become a great athlete. Now here was my chance of ever having a child gone.

Then I found that I had gone downtown with three other boys to enlist in the army. We all had been drinking. They were all single and in 1A. After the examinations we all met outside, waiting for the returns. All three of them had got turned down and I had been accepted.

I was shipped to the ETO and eight months later I was hurt. They brought me back to the states in a semi-paralyzed condition and operated on my chest and took out two ribs that were paralyzing my nerves and stopping my head from going from side to side. This is where I was introduced to morphine and HMCs and I found this to be a great comfort. I became an addict at this time.

I was in the hospital for quite some time and all this time they gave me drugs to relieve the terrific pain that I had in the back of my head. That was what I wanted. Narcotics. After I got out of the hospital they gave me a letter to another one, where I reported to, and there I was given all the sedation and medication I needed. Between this and alcohol I soon became a raving maniac. I acquired five 502s [citations for drunk driving]. I was thrown into jails. I was handcuffed to the bars.

Drugs absolutely crazed me. I'd go days and not remember a thing. I don't remember trying to push my wife out of the automobile going at 90 miles an hour, and police chasing me. These were complete, total blackouts. I don't even remember the time my wife had to hide in the cement mixer for over five hours, where I had been stalking her like a lion with a big butcher knife. She said I tried to kill her.

Incidentally, my father passed away about this time. I knew I had lost my crutch. At this particular time something seemed to come into my mind. I knew this was going to wind up, this marriage, this way of life we were leading, me full of drugs, she drunk all the time. I had been given every opportunity in life, and here, right now, I knew I had lost my crutch, my father. From now on anything I would do, I was on my own. It seemed that the whole world had been taken away from me. I was full of nothing but utter despair, because now I knew this was the end.

It came into my mind that if I could get my wife straightened out, if I tried to do one last act of decency, something that was human, to help her, not to leave her stranded . . . I wanted to run away, and end it all, end of the line for me, but I wanted to find some way to take care of my wife.

Now understand. All this while I'm up to the ears in dope. I came upon the idea that I would take my last possession, my automobile, and I would sell it, and I would go to the race track at Delmar and make a lot of money. Then I would have money for my wife to live on, and I would take my discharge papers with me, and I would go on and end it some place in the world, which I didn't know and I didn't care, and the government would bury me. It seemed logical. I was hopped up, you understand.

I did this. I sold my car. I went to Delmar. And the first thing I did was register at the Delmar Hotel and get a $17 a day room. I got a cab and went out to the race track. I remember, when I got there, looking around for somebody to score off of.

Anyway, I awoke next morning at three in the morning, on the beach. I had paid $17 for a room, and here I wound up sleeping on the beach. The first thing, I reached into my pocket, and there, that horror, that feeling, that lost moment came upon me that I was penniless. I didn't have any money at all.

I picked myself up and went back into the room. I waited and found some friends of mine, borrowed a few dollars, got a fix, ran into another dear friend of mine, who gave me another fix and put me up for a week or so.

We went to Tijuana and brought back stuff. I was holed in somewhere. I never saw the sun. Just fixing and sleeping and fixing.

I have no idea who got me out of there and put me on a bus for LA, but I arrived there and went home and found my wife on a terrible drunk. She didn't ask where I had been, just asked, "Did you bring something?" Then she started crying and said she couldn't possibly go on living this way and I had to do something about it. So I took her downtown to a friend of mine, who let her sleep on a couch until I could find a way to send her back East, where her folks were.

As I was going along Hollywood Boulevard I ran into a friend by the name of Sandy, who had talked to me for a number of years about this wonderful way of life that he had found in Alcoholics Anonymous. I said, "This is it. I tell you what you can do. My wife is very, very sick right now, and she's blind drunk out there. Maybe you can call her up, maybe she'll go to a meeting, maybe you could help her out."

He said, "Let's do that."

I said, "Well, you do it."

He said, "We usually don't do this. You call her."

I says, "No. It would be better if you call her."

So he called and asked her. At this particular time he had caught her at her lowest ebb. She had just but one drink left. When the phone rang she was sitting there deciding whether to drink this or save it, because she had no other money, she had hocked everything in the house, and we had overdrawn all of our credit. So she consented that she would go, she would do anything. She said, "What about Hal?"

He said, "Don't worry about him. I got him with me." He said, "We'll take care of him later, but first we'll get you straightened out, because that's what he wants to do."

She says, "Well, I'll go if he goes."

He told me he could get her to go to the meeting tonight if I consented to go along. I said, "I don't have to go along. I don't want any part of it. It's just for her."

He said, "No, it'll be much better if you go along for company sake."

I had this thing started now, so I didn't want anything to hinder it, so I decided I would go along. I thought, what the hell, what have I got to lose? My wife's an alcoholic. She needs this. Me, alcohol was second to narcotics, and anyhow I could quit anytime, only I didn't want to quit right now.

Well, I met him and Harriet at the AA meeting that night, and by this time I'm up to the ears. I've had so much I'm itching, my nose is running and I'm half ready to fall asleep, like always with junkies. I went into the AA meeting. I was in a complete daze. I didn't hear anything. Not a word they said. But it seemed that my wife enjoyed this, and it was quite different from what she had expected.

After, she and Sandy sat up to three in the morning, he was explaining about this disease of alcoholism, and I'm bored to death.

I went to the meeting with her for the next seven nights—to make sure *she* got there. I never heard anything. I was loaded each time I went.

Finally, this one night, they sat me in the middle of the room. The leader started it off. Then it seemed about eight or nine men got up and talked. The first five that got up were describing themselves as former athletes. They had done all these things, had stolen, been fired from the different clubs. And I turned to my wife and I said, "What did you do, have this thing all planned? Just for me?"

She said no, would I just please listen.

It seemed that every guy that got up hit me between the eyes and told my story. Every one was an athlete, most were pro football players until they went under. This was from drink, not drugs, but I was sore that they were telling my story and pretending it happened to them.

Then the leader said something that in my dazed condition made some sort of impression on me. He said AA could show a new way of life. It was a sort of challenge. After all, I was an alcoholic, too, not just a junkie. It was a challenge and I was sort of used to a challenge in athletics.

They asked was there any newcomers in the meeting. My right hand went up. The rest of the people applauded and said they were glad to have the newcomers there.

My wife grabbed my arm and said, "What a wonderful thing! You really going to become a member?"

I says, "What do you think I raised my arm for?"

Actually, I had no intention of raising my arm or letting anyone know that I was defeated by alcohol *or* narcotics. So I was still

phoney. But I wouldn't let her know I raised my arm without realizing it.

She was tickled skinny. We talked to the leader after the meeting. He asked if I could stop drinking a day at a time. I thought
so. I didn't tell him I was on drugs, too.

I started attending Alcoholics Anonymous meetings regularly
and they made sense to me, when I was sober. It wasn't long and I
was off alcohol. I was in AA and believed in it. Then I admitted I
had this other habit. I knew by then there were others in AA who
had the double problem, and they had stopped drinking and using.
I asked how they did it. They said what worked for the one thing
worked for the other. You quit using an hour at a time, a day at a
time, and you followed the AA Twelve Steps. I tried it and it
worked, and I quit using for almost seven months.

Then my old injury came back. I was rushed to the hospital and
shot full of morphine, and there I was all over again.

I was deep in despair. I'd come into Alcoholics Anonymous with
32 cents. I'd just got on my feet, I was ready to start work on a fine
job, I had started to repay my debts—then this.

I was put in traction for a long time. Then they said I could go
home. I got into my car and was driving home, feeling real sorry
for myself, full of self pity. I started to cry. Well, I'm not ashamed
of that. Here I had lost a wonderful chance to make a lot of
money. To clear up all my old debts.

I reach into the glove compartment to get a handkerchief, and
right in there is a half bottle of brandy, some chlorohydrate, and
some "pills." I withdrew my hand, because at AA I had learned alcohol was cunning, baffling, and powerful, it was very patient, it
would wait for you, until you were low, in a state of self pity. It
was always there, waiting. Here was the challenge now, and it was
another decision. I could take this drink. I could take this "medicine." I could take these "pills."

I quickly shut the door and drove as fast as I could to the AA
clubhouse and talked to the members there and they told me I had
done the right thing.

I went home and told my wife. A very funny thing. All this time
my wife knew about this job I was working toward, that would

take me all over the country, and she had been praying for me not to go, because she was afraid I would return to the old way of life. It took me quite a long time to figure this out, later, that God had answered her prayers and had not answered mine.

She accepted this and went out and got a job. Then I found out I could get disability insurance. From then on we had no trouble about the material way of life. Everything seemed to happen for the good. Now we didn't have to have so much money to live upon. We didn't have to have big-shotitis, didn't entertain, because all our time was taken up with going to meetings, doing Twelfth Step work helping others.

I went back to the hospital. They put me in a brace for a year. One morning I woke up and I couldn't move. The doctors said if they didn't operate I would become paraplegic. I was operated on, and when I came out of the anesthetic and saw through the haze, I saw my wife at my bedside. That was a wonderful thing. Here was this woman, that I had tried to destroy, tried to kill for no reason at all, here she was, right beside my bed, holding my hand. I went back to sleep again.

Another wonderful thing happened. Every day there was bundles and bundles of mail. Close to 850 postal cards. Flowers. Different members of AA would come in. Once a blank check was left on my bed, with a note to fill in whatever amount I needed.

And of all the people I had drank with over the years, spent money with, bought drugs from, not one,—no—only but one, came out, spent five minutes and left.

I decided then I would devote the rest of my life to helping other people. The rest of my life I would not think of myself first. This is what I've tried.

At AA meetings, some of us realized there were people like me, suffering from a two-headed disease, or three-headed disease. They had gone from alcoholism into sedation and from sedation into narcotics. These people, although they had given up the alcoholism, were restorting to sedation and narcotics.

And in AA the "narcotics" were being ostracized, to some extent. Because in AA they say we deal in alcohol. But in my humble opinion this philosophy and way of life can help anyone suffering from any disease, by omitting the word "alcohol" where it says, "I admitted that I was powerless over . . ." and substituting "drugs."

You see, the alcoholic looks down on the narcotic. He thinks taking drugs is just disgusting. The narcotic looks down on the alcoholic, he considers him a juicehead, a sissy. He considers himself smarter, cleaner than the drunk. So the narcotic and the alcoholic didn't really get together much.

So we got this idea. Why shouldn't a few of us that had this two-headed problem meet by ourselves and follow the AA program for alcohol and also narcotics? So that's how Narcotics Anonymous got started out here. I found out later that somebody in the East had thought of the same thing and they had the same idea out there, before we started our group. But we hadn't heard about it at the time.

For nine years now I haven't had a drink or touched a pill or taken a narcotic of any kind. My wife has stayed sober all this time. For the first time in my life I own a little home, my car is paid for, I don't have any debts. I work regularly. God sees to that.

People ask how people like us got started on drugs. We don't worry about that too much. We worry about staying clean a day at a time, not how we got addicted. After a time, though, you get to analyzing things. And I still don't know.

There was the fact my father was a crutch, always got me out of things. But over and above everything, all us alcoholics and narcotics are running away from something. That's why we drink, why we take drugs. What was I running from? I'm not sure. Maybe a hidden fear, of not being able to get to the top. My father was at the top, in politics. Always being put up for this office and that office. Me, I'd start to the top, time and again, and not quite make it.

A narcotic, a junkie, he builds up an expensive habit and he has to have the stuff. I never met a junkie that couldn't get what he needed. I've known some that had a $250 a day habit—I'm not kidding. Somehow, they got the money. You have to. You chisel, borrow, steal. Any addict will give another one just a little fix if he has anything extra, because someday he'll be hard up, he'll feel those grappling hooks in his stomach, and he wants to be able to get something from another addict.

An addict will arrive in a town he's never been in. He walks down the main stem, and in the hour he has scored. He has found a pusher. Don't ask me how they do it. They do.

These laws they're talking about, to give the death penalty to peddlers. That's nonsense. It won't get the big guys, the wholesalers, the importers, the smugglers. Know who'll get the gas chamber? The user. The junkie. Because more than likely he pushes on the side, to support his habit. He buys the stuff, cuts it down, sells part so he'll be able to have a fix tomorrow off the profits.

An addict will find somebody who doesn't use. He'll get him to chippy around until he's hooked. Now he has to have the stuff, he'll do anything for it. He buys from the junkie that started him off.

You would think all anyone would ever have to do to stay off drugs is just watch somebody kick it. The agony. The fits. The vomiting. The cramps. They go crazy. Every person I ever knew who got hooked wanted more than anything else in the world to quit. There's no enjoyment in using. The addict doesn't have beautiful dreams, so far as I ever could recall. All he has is sores all over his body, a running nose, and a pain in the belly. And still he'll use. That's what he means when he says, "I've got a monkey on my back." There's very few of us can shake that monkey off, believe me.

DRUGS OF ABUSE AND
THEIR EFFECTS

PREPARED BY SMITH KLINE
AND FRENCH LABORATORIES
AND THE NATIONAL
EDUCATION ASSOCIATION

Excerpted from *Drug Abuse: Escape to Nowhere* (Washington, D.C.: National Education Association, 1967), Chapter 2.

SUBSTANCES WITH abuse potential range from simple kitchen spices through common flowers and weeds to highly sophisticated drugs. All these substances may be divided into five categories: 1) narcotics, 2) sedatives, 3) tranquilizers, 4) stimulants, and 5) hallucinogens.

Medically defined, narcotics are drugs which produce insensibility or stupor due to their depressant effect on the central nervous system. Included in this definition are opium, opium derivatives (morphine, codeine, heroin) and synthetic opiates (meperidine, methadone). As regulated by Federal narcotic laws, however, the term "narcotics" also embraces the coca leaf and its derivative, cocaine. Pharmacologically, this drug is a stimulant, not a depressant, but for law enforcement purposes it is considered a narcotic. All other drugs susceptible to abuse are non-narcotics.*

Whatever their classification, most of these drugs have important legitimate applications. Narcotic, sedative, tranquilizing and stimu-

---

* This includes marijuana. Popularly regarded as a narcotic drug, it is not so considered either medically or under law. The confusion, in part, stems from the fact that the drug is controlled by the Federal Bureau of Narcotics.

lant drugs are essential to the practice of modern medicine. Hallucinogens are used in medical research. To the abuser, though, these same medically useful drugs have a compelling attribute: they affect the nervous system, producing a change in his emotional responses or reactions. The abuser may feel intoxicated, relaxed, happy or detached from a world that is painful and unacceptable to him.

With repeated use, many drugs cause *physical dependence*. This is an adaptation whereby the body learns to live with the drug, tolerates ever-increasing doses, and reacts with certain withdrawal symptoms when deprived of it. The total reaction to deprivation is known clinically as an abstinence syndrome. The symptoms that appear depend on the amount and kind of drug used. Withdrawal symptoms disappear as the body once again adjusts to being without the drug—or if the drug is reintroduced.

With many drugs, the chronic user finds he must constantly increase the dose in order to obtain an effect equal to that from the initial dose. This phenomenon, called *tolerance*, represents the body's ability to adapt to the presence of a foreign substance. Tolerance does not develop for all drugs or in all individuals; but with drugs such as morphine, addicts have been known to build up great tolerance very quickly. It is interesting to note, however, that tolerance does not develop for all the possible effects of a given drug. For example, tolerance develops to the euphoric-like effects of heroin, but only slightly to the constricting effects on the pupil of the eye. *Complete* tolerance may not develop to a drug's toxic effects; accordingly, no matter how high his tolerance, an addict may still administer a lethal dose to himself. Tolerance can occur without physical dependence.

A more important factor in keeping the abuser enslaved by his habit is the *psychic* or *psychological dependence* present in most cases of drug abuse. Psychic dependence is an emotional or mental adaptation to the effects of the drug. The abuser not only likes the feeling from the drug and wants to reexperience it—he feels he cannot function normally without the drug. It enables him to escape from reality—from his problems and frustrations. The drug and its effects seem to provide the answer to everything, including disenchantment and boredom. With the drug, all seems well. It is the *psychological* factor which causes an addict who has been withdrawn from his physical dependence to return to drug abuse.

All substances with abuse potential can produce changes in behavior, particularly when large amounts are improperly used. The abuser may be withdrawn and solitary, or sociable and talkative. He may be easily moved to tears or laughter. He may be quick to argue or believe that "someone is out to get him." These changes in behavior may be harmless or may constitute a danger to both the abuser and society. Much of the public concern about drug abuse stems from widely publicized changes in behavior accompanying the use of drugs.

Three frequently confused terms encountered in drug abuse discussions are "addiction," "habituation" and "drug dependence." *Addiction* has been defined as a state of periodic or chronic intoxication produced by the repeated consumption of a drug and involves tolerance, psychological dependence, usually physical dependence, an overwhelming compulsion to continue using the drug, and detrimental effects on both the individual and society. *Habituation* has been defined as a condition, resulting from the repeated consumption of a drug, which involves little or no evidence of tolerance, some psychological dependence, no physical dependence, and a desire (but not a compulsion) to continue taking the drug for the feeling of well-being that it engenders. Detrimental effects, if any, are primarily on the individual.

Through the years, the terms addiction and habituation have frequently been used interchangeably—and erroneously so, with the result that discussions of drug abuse have been fraught with semantic difficulties. Accordingly, the World Health Organization (WHO) recently recommended that these terms be replaced by a single and more general term—"drug dependence." *Drug dependence* is described as "a state arising from repeated administration of a drug on a periodic or continuous basis." Since many different kinds of drugs can be involved in drug dependence, the term is further qualified in accordance with the particular drug being used: Examples: "drug dependence of the morphine type," "drug dependence of the barbiturate type."

Although it was hoped that the newer terminology involving "drug dependence" and its various qualifiers would eventually replace the older terms of "addiction" and "habituation," from a practical standpoint this is not possible. The language of laws (international, national and local) which governs drugs subject to abuse encompasses the terms "addiction" and "habituation." As it would be difficult to set these laws aside, it appears that all three terms will become a part of drug abuse terminology, with "drug dependence" being favored by medically oriented groups and "addiction" and "habituation" being favored in legislative and law enforcement circles.

Morphine-like Narcotics (Opiates)

Medical Use. Natural and synthetic morphine-like drugs are the most effective pain relievers in existence and are among the most valuable drugs available to the physician. They are widely used for short-term acute pain resulting from surgery, fractures, burns, etc., and in the latter stages of terminal illnesses such as cancer. Morphine is the standard of pain relief by which other narcotic analgesics are evaluated.

The depressant effect of opiates produces drowsiness, sleep and a reduction in physical activity. Side effects can include nausea and vomiting, constipation, itching, flushing, constriction of pupils and respiratory depression.

Manufacture and distribution of medicinal opiates are stringently controlled by the Federal government through laws designed to keep these products available only for legitimate medical use. One aspect of the controls is that those who distribute these products are registered with Federal authorities and must comply with specific record-keeping and drug security requirements.

Abuse. The appeal of morphine-like drugs lies in their ability to reduce sensitivity to both psychological and physical stimuli and to produce a sense of euphoria. These drugs dull fear, tension or anxiety. Under the influence of morphine-like narcotics, the addict is usually lethargic and indifferent to his environment and personal situation. For example, a pregnant addict will usually continue drug abuse despite the fact that her baby will likewise be addicted —and probably die shortly after birth unless medical treatment is undertaken at once.

The price tag on the abuse of these drugs is high. Chronic use may lead to both physical and psychological dependence. Psychological dependence is the more serious of the two, since it is still operative after drug use has been discontinued. With chronic use, tolerance develops and ever-increasing doses are required in order to achieve a desired effect. As the need for the drug increases, the addict's activities become increasingly drug-centered. When drug supplies are cut off, characteristic withdrawal symptoms may develop.

Symptoms of withdrawal from narcotic analgesics include:

Nervousness, anxiety, sleeplessness.
Yawning, running eyes and nose, sweating.
Enlargement of the pupils, "gooseflesh," muscle twitching.
Severe aches of back and legs, hot and cold flashes.
Vomiting and diarrhea.
Increase in breathing rate, blood pressure and temperature.
A feeling of desperation and an obsessional desire to secure a "fix."

The intensity of withdrawal symptoms varies with the degree of physicul dependence. This, in turn, is related to the amount of drug customarily used. Typically, the onset of symptoms occurs about 8–12 hours after the last dose. Thereafter, symptoms increase in intensity, reach a peak between 36–72 hours, and then gradually diminish over the next 5–10 days. However, weakness, insomnia, nervousness, and muscle aches and pains may persist for several weeks. In extreme cases, death may result.

Because increasing pressure by law enforcement authorities has made traffic in heroin more difficult, "street" supplies have tended to contain increasingly low percentages of active ingredient. (The heroin content of a "bag" now ranges between 3 and 10%. Pure heroin is "cut"—diluted—with milk sugar.) As a consequence, many present-day narcotic addicts experience relatively mild withdrawal symptoms unless they are consuming many bags per day. On the other hand, narcotic addicts can die from overdosage when the supplies they buy in the "street" contain more than the customary low percentage of heroin. (Addict deaths from overdosage at a rate of one a day have been reported in New York City.) . . .

Depressants (Sedatives)

This group includes a variety of old and new drugs which have a depressant effect on the nervous system. Within this group, the most commonly abused products are the barbiturates. The "street" term for this type of product is "goofball."

Medical Use. The barbiturates are among the most versatile depressant drugs available. They are used for epilepsy, high blood pressure, insomnia and in the treatment and diagnoses of mental disorders. They are used before and during surgery. Alone or in combination with other drugs, they are prescribed for almost every kind of illness or special situation requiring sedation. Used under medical supervision, barbiturates are impressively safe and effective.

Abuse. The abuser takes barbiturates orally, intravenously or rectally. Although barbiturate intoxication closely resembles alcoholic intoxication, barbiturate abuse is far more dangerous than alcohol abuse or even narcotic abuse. Unintentional overdosage can easily occur. Convulsions, which may follow withdrawal, can be fatal. Overindulgence in alcohol before barbiturate ingestion may result in fatal depression of respiratory and cardiovascular systems.

The barbiturate abuser exhibits slurred speech and staggering gait. His reactions are sluggish. He is emotionally erratic and may be easily moved to tears or laughter. Frequently, he is irritable and antagonistic. Sometimes, he has impressions of euphoria. Because he is prone to stumble or drop objects, he often is bruised and has cigarette burns.

Chronic misuse of barbiturates is accompanied by the development of tolerance and both psychological and physical dependence. Physical dependence appears to develop only with continued use of doses much greater than those customarily used in the practice of medicine. In a physically dependent barbiturate abuser, abrupt withdrawal is extremely dangerous. Withdrawal from the drug should *always* be supervised by a physician.

In withdrawal, during the first 8–12 hours after the last dose, the barbiturate abuser who has become physically dependent appears to improve. After this, there are signs of increasing nervousness, headache, anxiety, muscle twitching, tremor, weakness, insomnia, nausea and a sudden drop in blood pressure when the person stands abruptly (he often faints). These symptoms are quite severe at about 24 hours. There are changes in the electroencephalographic readings and, within 36–72 hours, convulsions resembling epileptic seizures may develop. Such convulsions occasionally occur as early as the sixteenth hour of withdrawal or as late as the eighth day.

Convulsions, which can be fatal, are an ever-present danger with barbiturate withdrawal and distinguish barbiturate from narcotic withdrawal. (Narcotic addiction is not characterized by a failure of muscular coordination or by convulsions upon drug withdrawal.) Whether or not convulsions occur, there may be a period of mental confusion. Delirium and hallucinations similar to the delirium tremens (DT's) may develop. Delirium may be accompanied by an extreme agitation that contributes to exhaustion. The delirium may persist for several days followed by a long period of sleep. (Delirium may also develop early in the course of withdrawal.) . . .

Tranquilizers

The term "tranquilizer" refers to a rather large group of drugs introduced since the early 1950's. Unlike barbiturate-type sedatives, tranquilizers can be used to counteract tension and anxiety without producing sleep or significantly impairing mental and physical function.

All tranquilizers are not alike. In general, they may be divided into two groups—"major" or "minor"—based on their usefulness in severe mental disorders (psychoses). "Major" tranquilizers are those with antipsychotic activity. These include primarily the phenothiazine and reserpine-type drugs. Reserpine also is used to treat high blood pressure. The antipsychotic tranquilizers are not known to produce physical dependence. Abuse of this type of tranquilizer is practically nonexistent.

The "minor" group of tranquilizers includes a number of chemically quite different drugs. For the most part, they are not effective in psychotic conditions. They are widely used, however, in the treatment of emotional disorders characterized by anxiety and tension. Many are useful as muscle relaxants.

Through the years, it has been found that some members of this second group of tranquilizers occasionally have been abused. The two drugs most often reported have been meprobamate and chlordiazepoxide. Chronic abuse of these drugs, involving increasingly larger daily doses, may result in the development of physical and/or psychological dependence. Symptoms during misuse and following abrupt withdrawal closely resemble those seen with barbiturates. Chronic use of high doses can result in convulsions if the drugs are suddenly withdrawn. In order to combat abuse of this category of tranquilizers, the FDA has requested more stringent controls on meprobamate, chloridiazepoxide and diazepam. To date, abuse of tranquilizers has been infrequent and has not become a "street" problem. Abuse supplies usually are obtained by having prescriptions refilled in excess of normal needs.

Stimulants

This group includes drugs which directly stimulate the central nervous system. The most widely known stimulant in this country is caffeine, an ingredient of coffee, tea, cola and other beverages. Since the effects of caffeine are relatively mild, its usage is socially acceptable and not an abuse problem. The synthetic stimulants such as amphetamine and other closely related drugs are more potent and can be abused. Another dangerous stimulant is cocaine.

COCAINE

Cocaine is obtained from the leaves of the coca bush found in certain South American countries. It is an odorless, white crystalline powder with a bitter taste, producing numbness of the tongue.

(The word "coca" is often confused with "cacao." The two are not related. Cacao is the name of a tree from which cocoa and chocolate are derived.)

Medical Use. Cocaine was once widely used as a local anesthetic. Its place in medicine, however, has been largely taken by newer, less toxic drugs.

The stimulant effect of cocaine results in excitability, talkativeness and a reduction in the feeling of fatigue. Cocaine may produce a sense of euphoria, a sense of increased muscular strength, anxiety, fear and hallucinations. Cocaine dilates the pupils and increases the heartbeat and blood pressure. Stimulation is followed by a period of depression. In overdosage, cocaine may so depress respiratory and heart function that death results.

Abuse. International control measures have greatly reduced the abuse of cocaine, although the chewing of coca leaves in some South American countries is still common. Cocaine is either sniffed or injected directly into a vein. The abuse of cocaine tends to be more sporadic than the abuse of heroin. The intense stimulatory effects usually result in the abuser voluntarily seeking sedation. This need for sedation has given rise to a practice of combining a depressant drug such as heroin with a drug such as cocaine ("speedball") or alternating a drug such as cocaine with a depressant. In some persons, cocaine produces violent behavior. Cocaine does not produce physical dependence. Tolerance does not develop and abusers seldom increase their customary dose. When drug supplies are cut off, the cocaine user does not experience withdrawal symptoms, but he does feel deeply depressed and hallucinations may persist for some time. Strong psychological dependence on the drug and a desire to reexperience the intense stimulation and hallucinations cocaine produces lead to its chronic misuse.

AMPHETAMINE

Medical Use. Amphetamine has been available since the early 1930's. First used medically as a nasal vasoconstrictor in treatment of colds and hay fever, amphetamine was later found to stimulate the nervous system. This stimulating activity is the primary basis for its uses in medicine today. Amphetamine is used for narcolepsy (a disease characterized by involuntary attacks of sleep) and to counteract excessive drowsiness caused by sedative drugs. But in the main, amphetamine is used in obesity, where the drug exerts an anti-appetite effect, and to relieve mild depression such as that accompanying menopause, convalescence, grief and senility. Paradoxically, this drug tends to calm hyperactive, noisy, aggressive children, thus producing a more normal behavior.

Amphetamine may produce a temporary rise in blood pressure, palpitations, dry mouth, sweating, headache, diarrhea, pallor and dilation of the pupils. Such effects are generally seen only with high doses or as occasional side effects with therapeutic doses. Amphetamine drugs seldom cause death, even in acute overdosage.

Abuse. Amphetamine is a stimulant. It increases alertness, dispels depression and superimposes excitability over feelings of fatigue. It also produces an elevation of mood and a feeling of well-being. All these are factors underlying amphetamine abuse— and explain its popular name, "pep pill."

Amphetamine usually is taken orally in the form of tablets or capsules. However, there have been reports of intravenous use in which amphetamine is dissolved in water and then injected. With this route of administration, the effects of the drug are felt almost immediately.

Most medical authorities agree that amphetamine does not produce physical dependence, and there is no characteristic abstinence syndrome upon abrupt discontinuation of drug use. Mental depression and fatigue, however, are frequently experienced after the drug has been withdrawn. Psychological dependence is common and is an important factor in continuance of and relapse to amphetamine abuse. The development of tolerance permits the use of many times the usual therapeutic dose.

An acute psychotic episode may occur with intravenous use, or a drug psychosis may develop with the chronic use of large doses. Symptoms include extreme hyperactivity, hallucinations and feelings of persecution. These bizarre mental effects usually disappear after withdrawal of the drug.

Generally, misuse is associated with milder symptoms. The abuser is talkative, excitable and restless, and experiences a "high."

He suffers from insomnia, perspires profusely, has urinary frequency and exhibits a tremor of the hands. . . .

Hallucinogens

Distortions of perception, dream images and hallucinations are characteristic effects of a group of drugs variously called hallucinogens, psychotomimetics, dysleptics or psychedelics. These drugs include mescaline, d-lysergic acid diethylamide (LSD), psilocybin and dimethyltryptamine (DMT). At present, they have no general clinical medical use—except for research applications. However, they are being encountered with increasing frequency as drugs of abuse.

Marijuana, while chemically distinct from the foregoing, is also considered a hallucinogen. Pharmacologically, it is *not* a narcotic although its control under the Marijuana Tax Act of 1937—and later laws—is somewhat similar to the control imposed on narcotics. Also, like narcotic law enforcement, marijuana law enforcement is handled by the Federal Bureau of Narcotics as well as certain state and local law enforcement agencies.

MARIJUANA (CANNABIS)

According to the Commission on Narcotic Drugs of the Economic and Social Council of the United Nations, marijuana abuse is more widespread, from a geographical standpoint, than abuse of any other dangerous drug. Widely encountered in North and South America, Africa, Southeast Asia and the Middle East, it is known as bhang or ganja in India, hashish in the Middle East, dagga in South Africa and maconha or djamba in South America.

The intoxicating substance which gives marijuana its activity is found primarily in a resin from the flowering tops and leaves of the female plant. The potency of marijuana varies with the geographical location in which the plant grows, time of harvest, and the plant parts used. For example, hashish is stronger than American marijuana because the former contains more resin.

Medical Use. At one time, marijuana had a minor place in the practice of medicine. But because the safety and effectiveness of newer drugs so outweigh the limited utility of marijuana, it is no longer considered medically respectable in the United States. . . .

Abuse. Marijuana may be smoked, sniffed or ingested, but effects are experienced most quickly with smoking. The mental effects include a feeling of euphoria, exaltation and a dreamy sensation accompanied by a free flow of ideas. Senses of time, distance, vision and hearing are distorted. Sometimes panic and fear are experienced. Hallucinations may develop with large doses. In the company of others, the marijuana user is talkative and laughs easily. When alone, he is more often drowsy and quiet. The initial period of stimulation is frequently followed by a moody reverie and drowsiness. The user's ability to perform many tasks normally or safely —particularly automobile driving—is seriously impaired.

Other effects of marijuana include dizziness, dry mouth, dilated pupils and burning eyes, urinary frequency, diarrhea, nausea and vomiting, and hunger, particularly for sweets.

Marijuana does not produce physical dependence or an abstinence syndrome. Once the user has established the amount of marijuana needed to achieve his particular "high," there is little tendency to increase the dose, indicating that tolerance doesn't develop. Moderate to strong psychic dependence can develop in accordance with the user's appreciation of the drug's effects.

In terms of some effects on behavior, use of marijuana is roughly comparable to moderate abuse of alcohol (also a drug). Like alcohol, it tends to loosen inhibitions and increase suggestibility, which explains why an individual under the influence of marijuana may engage in activities he would not ordinarily consider. Although the marijuana smoker sometimes feels himself capable of extraordinary physical and mental feats, he seldom acts to accomplish them for fear of disrupting his "euphoric" state. But what he does not realize is that the drug can have unpredictable effects—even on persons accustomed to its use.

To date, available information indicates that marijuana has few detrimental effects on an individual's *physical* health. Psychic dependence and the drug's effects, however, may lead to extreme lethargy, self-neglect and preoccupation with use of marijuana to a degree that precludes constructive activity. Additionally, the use of marijuana may precipitate psychotic episodes or cause impulsive behavior in reaction to fear or panic. . . .

MESCALINE, PSILOCYBIN, DMT

For centuries, various Indian tribes have used mescaline (derived from the Mexican cactus, peyote) in religious ceremonies. Mescaline is available on the illicit market as a crystalline powder in capsules or as a liquid in ampuls or vials. It may also be obtained as whole cactus "buttons," chopped "buttons" in capsules, or as a brownish-gray cloudy liquid. The drug is generally taken orally, but may be injected. Because of its bitter taste, the drug is often ingested with tea, coffee, milk, orange juice or some other common beverage.

Psilocybin is derived from certain mushrooms found in Mexico. It has been used in Indian religious rites as far back as pre-Columbian times. It is not nearly as potent as LSD, but with adequate doses, similar hallucinogenic effects are produced. Psilocybin is available in crystalline, powdered or liquid form.

DMT (dimethyltryptamine) is a more recent addition to the list of presently abused hallucinogenic agents. Although prepared synthetically, it is a natural constituent of the seeds of certain plants found in the West Indies and South America. Powder made from these seeds is known to have been used as a snuff as far back as the arrival of Columbus in the New World—and is still used by some Indian tribes of South America. DMT produces effects similar to those of LSD, but much larger doses are required.

Some varieties of morning glory seeds are also abused for their hallucinogenic effects. The bizarre behavioral effects produced upon ingestion are probably attributable to LSD-like components.

LSD

LSD (lysergic acid diethylamide) was synthesized in 1938 from lysergic acid present in ergot, a fungus that grows on rye. LSD is the most potent of the hallucinogens. On the illicit market, the drug may be obtained as a small white pill, as a crystalline powder in capsules, or as a tasteless, colorless or odorless liquid in ampuls. Frequently, it is offered in the form of impregnated sugar cubes, cookies or crackers. LSD is usually taken orally, but may be injected.

LSD primarily affects the central nervous system, producing changes in mood and behavior. The user may also exhibit dilated pupils, tremor, elevated temperature and blood pressure, and hyperactive reflexes. Tolerance to the behavioral effects of LSD may develop with several days of continued use, but physical dependence does not occur. Although psychic dependence may develop, it is seldom intense. Accordingly, most LSD devotees will use the drug when available, but do not seem to experience a serious craving when LSD cannot be obtained.

In general, the LSD experience consists of changes in perception, thought, mood and activity. Perceptual changes involve senses of sight, hearing, touch, body image and time. Colors seem to itensify or change, shape and spatial relation appear distorted, objects seem to pulsate, two-dimensional objects appear to become three dimensional and inanimate objects seem to assume emotional import. Sensitivity to sound increases but the source of the sound is elusive. Conversations can be heard but may not be comprehended. There may be auditory hallucinations of music and voices. There may be changes in taste and food may feel gritty. Cloth seems to change texture, becoming coarse and dry or fine and velvety. The subject may feel cold or sweaty. There are sensations of light-headedness, emptiness, shaking, vibrations, fogginess. Subjects lose awareness of their bodies with a resultant floating feeling. Arms or legs may be held in one position for extended periods of time. Time seems to race, stop, slow down or even go backwards. Changes in thought include a free flow of bizarre ideas including notions of persecution. Trivial events assume unusual significance and importance. An inspiration or insight phenomenon is claimed by some LSD adherents.

The mood effects of LSD run the gamut. There may be bursts of tears, of laughter, or the subject may feel no emotion at all. A state of complete relaxation and happiness, not apparent to an observer, may be experienced. A feeling of being alone and cut off from the world may lead to anxiety, fear and panic. Accordingly, the LSD session is frequently monitored by an abstaining LSD-experienced friend to prevent flight, suicidal attempts, dangerous reaction to panic states, and impulsive behavior, such as disrobing. There may be a feeling of enhanced creativity, but this subjective feeling rarely seems to produce objective results.

After a number of hours, the effects of LSD begin to wear off. Waves of the LSD experience, diminishing in intensity, alternate with periods of no effects at all, until all symptoms disappear. Some fatigue, tension, and recurrent hallucinations may persist long after ingestion of the drug. Psychological changes induced by the drug can persist for indefinite periods.

There is, at present, no approved general medical use for LSD. Some interesting results have been obtained with the drug in certain medically supervised research programs—particularly in the treatment of chronic alcoholism and terminal illness. However, the Food and Drug Administration now takes the position that LSD has insufficient clinical utility to warrant either prescription or non-prescription use. Consequently, LSD is now subject to controls similar to those for any unproven investigational drug.

Medical warnings notwithstanding, large quantities of the drug have become available on an illicit basis for use in "mind expansion"—an application not even contemplated in medical research programs undertaken to date. Those using LSD for this purpose advocate unrestricted use of the product. They state that the drug is not inherently dangerous, claiming either personal use without complication or citing safe use by various notables from many fields. Although it may be true that some individuals have had LSD experiences without apparent ill effect, growing medical evidence shows the drug can cause very serious, and often damaging reactions in many. Hospital admissions of persons with acute LSD-induced psychoses are on the increase. Bizarre behavior in public, panic, fear, and homicidal and suicidal urges have been reported. Psychotic states have been induced through use of the drug —both with emotionally unstable individuals and with persons in whom no sign of emotional instability had been evident. Although most LSD-induced psychotic episodes have occurred in persons initially experimenting with the drug, untoward results have also occurred with "experienced" abusers. What's more, "casualties" have happened even when the drug has been taken under supervision, both medical and nonmedical. LSD also can produce delayed psychotic reactions in some individuals. In some instances, hallucinations have recurred for weeks after the drug was taken. . . .

DRUG USER

ANONYMOUS

Transcript of a recorded interview conducted by the editor. Identifying features have been changed.

TED'S STORY differs in some respects from statements of other drug users who were interviewed by the editor. The differences among the interviewees have to do mostly with how a particular drug affected a particular function, such as ability to drive or sexual feeling. Possibly, given drugs produce different effects in different people. It is also possible that self-deception plays a part, the user believing he maintained his equilibrium, for instance, when in fact he did not. Finally, research suggests that the same person will react differently in different environments—pleasant, unpleasant, peaceful, hostile.

Despite individual differences reported by interviewees, they all mentioned certain phenomena as characteristic of the drug experience. All marijuana smokers, for instance, became very hungry and got exceptional enjoyment from eating. All of them felt "relaxed" in the early stages of a smoking session. All marijuana and LSD users heard pitches in music not caught by the human ear otherwise. All LSD users reported seeing the ground "ripple," "surge," or undulate and "breathe."

Thus, the typical user of the drugs under examination here, has both common and individual experiences. Ted is quite typical in this sense.

Q: Tell me something about yourself, Ted. How old are you?
A: Twenty-one.

Q: And you're a college student, at Lennox College. What's your major?

A: Psychology, but I'm not certain.

Q: How many children in your family?

A: Four.

A: I haven't had a real good childhood. My mom died when I was eleven, and my father always told me that I was fucked.

Q: That you were what?

A: That I was fucked. No good, you know. Those were his words. He's a drunk, you know. And he's an inadequate personality. But as I was growing up I didn't understand too much about that. I just never got along with him at all. Because he'd be drinking. He'd have his friends there drinking with him, and I just never got along with him at all. After we'd be around each other, there'd be bad vibrations. Bad feelings toward each other. And he'd keep telling me I was fucked, and I'd tell him his liver's fucked, you know, to get back at him. So we just never got along too well, and I just never communicated too well.

Q: What year are you in at school?

A: This is my third semester. Because I started late. When I got out of high school I went to Calvert Junior College. My dad kicked me out when I was 17, and so I was really on the line, not knowing whether I was going to exist. I just didn't have time to think about school, you know. So I finally just quit going to my classes. I picked up a couple of Fs, and I dropped out.

Then I got a job as a gardener and I worked for a few years, and I got enough money together so that I really don't have to worry about eating. So now I can study better. And so far, in two semesters, I have a 3.5 grade point average.

Q: You live by yourself?

A: Yeah.

A: There's some real bad stuff I have to tell you. I have reformed. This stuff I did was when I was 18, right after I moved out, I turned on. I was afraid of everything, then, including the draft. At that time I was idealistic, you know, and I felt war was immoral. Now I realize there's nothing I can do about it, but then

I felt, well, I'm going to go to Canada, like a lot of kids did. So I needed to make some money. So I sold a little, too.

Q: Almost everybody who uses seems to push a little.

A: Yeah. If you use it regularly, you start. But generally, it's maybe lids and stuff.

Q: What did you start on?

A: The first time I ever used any kind of a drug or narcotic was marijuana. It was at Pearl River. I had to smoke six of them before I was what they call stoned.

Q: How did you happen to start? Where did you get it? Were there others with you?

A: My older brother had a friend named Tex, a real nice person. He's married now. He works with computers and he makes pretty good money. He has a boat. And he has some land by the river. We went to the river with him. Let's see, it was Tex and me, and . . . it must have been Ben, and someone else. Oh, yeah—Hal.

They had already been smoking grass. They were used to it. We were sitting on the shore and they split about three joints between the four of us. I was really disappointed, or frustrated. They were all going wild—"This is a mind blower! Wow! This is really groovy!" And me—nothing. So I went and rolled another one, and then I rolled about three more, and smoked them all myself. And then I really felt it. So I just lay down.

I remember it all real clear. Ramsey Lewis was on Tex's tape deck; they were playing music, because they generally do when they smoke grass. I just lay down, and there was music, and I felt just like I was floating in the air, and I could see an ocean, breaking in waves, and it was just a great experience.

And then I remember we went to get something to eat, and we went across the river in this boat, and then we walked across this golf course. The first time you experience grass, they say the time goes slow. Yes. It seemed like forever, just walking across that golf course, like I was never going to get through, you know.

Q: Was it a pleasant experience?

A: Yeah.

Q: Could you walk all right?

A: I could do everything that I normally could do. I felt more alive than ever. Normally, you just walk across a golf course, like, you know, but this time you're walking across, and everything is just going wild, man, and it seems like it never ends. And as for functioning, I could function better than ever. Perhaps my mind was aware, perceiving more things better. Perhaps my motor abilities wouldn't have been as good if I was driving a car, but as for stumbling or anything, I wasn't stumbling.

Q: Could you understand what your companions were saying to you?

A: I could understand.

Q: And could you answer? Did your voice get slurred? Do you know?

A: My voice was perhaps slower. I would answer, but I would think longer. Normally, I'd answer real quick. Now, they'd say something, and I'd be thinking, and then I'd integrate what they had been saying with what I was thinking, and slowly come up with something. But it wasn't slurred. My voice wasn't slurred. On beer, you slur. But this, it wasn't slurring. You just take a little more time to answer, because you're thinking. I was thinking about life, or thinking about existence and what not, where before I never really had. I didn't believe in God before, and now it starts you thinking about it, and I've become more of an agnostic rather than an atheist.

Q: This happened the first time you smoked marijuana?

A: Not the God thing. That came later.

I remember that as we were eating, when they would talk, I was like in my own world, and I remember that they were mostly talking among themselves. They'd ask me something, and I was like separated from them. When they did ask me something, I would hear what they said, and take a while to tear apart what they said, and put it together again, and tell them what my answer was. Before, I'd come back with an answer, spontaneously. I was stoned, you know. That's how I reflect upon it now. But I remember my talk wasn't slurred or anything.

Q: Then what?

A: We went back and went to bed. Next morning I got up and

it was a great experience, in recollection. I wanted to do it again.

Before, I never got drunk much. I never was a drinker. I was always fairly studious. I always got Bs in high school. I'd get drunk then, because everyone else did. We'd go to a party and you'd have to break down the reality thing, to be able to meet the girls and things. And so, whenever I'd go to a party, and everybody was getting drunk, I'd get drunk, too. But I never liked drinking. Because my old man was a drunk. I had a thing against it. And then, with grass, it got to where I could go out, and I'd get high, and now I could escape a little from reality, and not have to be drunk.

I read in a magazine about that kid who got 20 years back east. When he first turned on he was twenty. He thought it was the greatest thing in the world. Because you're freed a little from all your conditioning. All your life, going through high school and everything, you're going through all this conditioning, all this propagandizing. You don't have a real identity, if you haven't had the chance. You can develop it, but if you didn't have the chance, like most kids I knew, who grew up in lower class, not even hardly middle class, they didn't have any real identity. I could really relate when I read that article about that kid, because he said he was just thrilled, and that it was like a whole new world opened to him. And that's how it is, at first. But it wears off. The novelty wears off.

Q: A friend of mine, about 22 years old, smoked about four times, I think. He told me that when he smokes, aside from the fact that he feels terribly exhilarated, very good, very happy, things take on an intensity that they don't have otherwise. He says that eating is a new experience entirely, that it isn't the same as eating when you haven't been smoking grass. He couldn't find the precise words to describe it, but he said it's there, something very intense. What about that? Do you agree?

A: As I see it now, it's more electrical activity, or something like that. When you eat, everything is more intense, everything tastes better. Like when we went to eat the first time. It's like everything, the first time is the greatest. Well, when we went across that golf course to eat, and we ate tacos, well, man, it was like it was the first time I ever ate tacos. And the only thing I can relate it to now is, your taste things must be operated with your mind, and it's some kind of release of energy, either electrical or something.

Q: What about hearing? Some smokers say you hear sounds that you normally would not hear. They say they hear music at a pitch that people ordinarily don't catch. Did you experience anything like that?

A: I don't know musical language. The only thing I can say is that I enjoyed music more. I don't know about strange pitches, but before I smoked grass I'd hear the Beatles, and there was just a few words and some music. While I'm stoned it seems like I can hear every separate part. Like, with the Beatles, I can hear John or George, or who's playing the guitar, how the drum's going, all at the same time. It seems to probably release some kind of activity in your brain. Or perhaps—the way I think about it now—perhaps it releases something in your endocrine system. In this society, as you grow up, you never use your endocrine system. But before, in the course of evolution, when we were cave men, every day you'd experience your endocrine glands, to keep you alive, and to defend against all the animals. As you grew up, it was probably a daily experience. Now, as you grow up, you just go to school, sit, do nothing, you never experience anything. Therefore, it could be you never really use your potential in this society. At least in my generation. Well, marijuana, and for sure LSD, stimulate these glands. Or stimulate your brain, which then stimulates your glands, because your pituitary system is controlled by your brain, and your brain is controlled by it, to a degree. LSD and like that—no one's sure how LSD works—but I think it has some effect upon your brain or your pituitary gland. Probably both. And it starts all your evolutionary life processes going, for the kids of this generation, that have never used them.

Q: What about sexuality? Does smoking marijuana increase sexuality and sexual feeling?

A: In my opinion it does. It really isn't so much that it increases it, although it does, a little. It's just that everything you experience is a little more intense. The thing is that you want sex more. It gets to be a basic thing, you know. I've heard kids say, "Wow! Yeah! It really makes it something." But actually, it's just that you want it more when you're under the influence. It isn't that, when you experience sex, it's so very much different from what it is when you haven't been smoking.

Q: I've been told that it's like the case with alcohol. That after you've had some drinks, the inhibitions are down, the desire is there, but the actual ability to perform the sex act is not as good, not as successful, as when you haven't been drinking alcohol. The same, I'm told, can be said about marijuana.

A: Well, that's a very nebulous thing, there. For me, I would have to agree with that, to the degree that if you just kept smoking number after number after number, and if it was any kind of strong grass, well then you'd eventually get so you were just like a blob, you know. Which would be similar to drinking. But if you just smoked one or two, you could still perform.

Q: Now, this first time you smoked, just how did it come about? Here you were, with your friends. Did they come right out and ask how you would like to try smoking a joint?

A: Yeah. They were going to the river, and they said, "Do you want to go?"

I said, "Yeah."

And they said, "Well, Tex has got some grass and we're going to smoke some when we get there."

And I said, "OK. I'll try it." I was 18, I think. Either 17 or right after I turned 18. And I thought, well, that will be great. It'll be fun. I'd heard Tex tell stories, and it was all good, and it wasn't anything bad. It wasn't near as bad as booze. And I'd drunk beer and things, and I didn't like that at all. And they said, "Well, this is better than booze. You don't get sick, that sort of thing."

So it was fine with me, and I wanted to experience it. I'd read a lot about it, in magazines.

That really promotes it, all those articles. Because you're a kid, and you read, like, here's all these kids, this article is about these kids who have done it. They may say they're against it now, but you read how these kids experienced it, and how they liked it, and, you know, your curiosity is aroused. And the thing is that it really doesn't hurt you. Physically, I believe it doesn't hurt one any more than tobacco. But any accidents or similar things that might occur due to the lessening of one's motor abilities will hurt oneself and society.

The bad part is that you get busted. But I read those magazines and I could hardly wait.

Q: When was the next time you had experience with any drug?

A: After the first time it was every once in a while. I was living with my older brother, and we'd have a few numbers around. We'd buy numbers then. Three numbers for a dollar. After you do it once, one number does it, if it's good grass. So we would get three or six numbers, and on the weekends we'd do it. It got to be a weekend thing.

I just never got along with my brother, so I moved out.

And then I bought some lids and started selling numbers. Like I'd buy a lid and roll 30, 40 numbers, and sell enough numbers to get my money back, and then have the other numbers to smoke, and to give some to my friends when they'd come over to my little apartment.

And then I got to where I bought six lids for $40. I sold four of them and got two lids free, because of the profit. You know, that's how it starts, if you're not a Mafia type guy. I just happened to meet these guys, at the Hamburger Shack. They used to stand around and talk about things, about going to the beach. And then there'd be some guy selling numbers, selling acid and stuff. I figured I'd do the same, buy and sell grass by the lid.

My first experience with other drugs, was a friend of mine named Clem used to take benzedrine—they call them "uppers." He took it to be able to work. He's a real studious guy. He goes to Gregory University and he's real stable. He used to take them every once in a while, to work, and because they made him feel good. So he turned me on to two of them, me and a friend of mine. We ate them with some coffee, and then I was up all night. I was really stimulated and I thought it was great.

That was the first experience.

Then I met some guy who was dealing bricks, and quantities of acid.

Q: What are bricks?

A: They're 2.2 pounds of marijuana. They are bricks, kilograms. We usually just call them bricks.

So I started buying. Then, with LSD, a friend of mine that moved in next door to the apartment where I was at, Frankie, he had a friend that was about 30. He was turned on to LSD and said it was good. So Frankie wanted to try it. He wanted me to do it with him because we were friends, you know. So I said OK. The other guy was going to be our guide—stay with us and see that nothing went wrong. So we each took half a cap, and it was a real happy experience. Listening to sounds. We came alive, from just being dead. Basically, from just being dead you come alive. That's the only way I can describe it. I don't regret it at all, because it tears down your ego, or tears down all your conditioning, and you build up from that. Perhaps I would have done that through the growth process and maturing, without LSD, but I don't regret ever having taken it.

That was half a cap. And then we took a whole cap. And since then I've taken it about 20 times.

Q: Did you hallucinate during the experience?

A: Some people have experienced seeing monsters and things. I never experienced that, but things are so intense. It's a blood thing, when you're peaking on it. Your blood is flowing, and taking it to your brain and to your sense organs. Things go like this: bong! bong! Just like with your heart beat. If the lights are low or something, if they're red or something, the red will take over and as your heart beats, it will go boom! boom! That's how I remember.

But I also remember, one day I took it about five minutes before the sun came out. I got up on top of the house—I was living in, like, a nature place, in the woods. And I took LSD and got up on top of my house, and was just coming on to it as the sun came up. That was the longest experience I ever had. The whole time the sun was up, about twelve hours, I was under the effect of the drug. Due to the normal time of six to eight hours, the psychological effect of "coming on" to the LSD as the sun was just rising seems to have extended the euphoric feeling for a longer period.

And I was hallucinating. For instance I'd look at the ground, and the ground would seem to breathe. It surged up and down, as if it were breathing. And the little house next door, it was surging up and down, like it was breathing. And the air conditioning metal on top of the house. It just looked like it was flowing. It was galvanized metal, so you could see reds and blues and greens. And it was flowing. And little greens and reds would just shoot out, go tshhh!, you know. Like sparklers. Tshoo! Tshoo! And it was flowing. It would keep flowing around and around and around, and flowing. And you know, for having to grow up in this society, and being poor, and not really being able to experience anything, it was one of the greatest experiences ever.

Q: Ever feel any fear under LSD?

A: I never did. There are certain persons, with a certain psychological state of mind, who can't handle narcotics, especially LSD. A friend of mine took it, I forget if it was his second or third time, and he lost all contact with reality, or whatever is existence. I had to stay up all night with him.

He didn't see how he could go on living in the state of mind he was in at that time. You see, he was peaking on the acid. We call it peaking when it has the strongest effect upon you. Then it wears off as your system uses it up. But he was peaking, and he couldn't see how he would ever come back down, be what we call normal; how he would get up the next day and think normally, think as a human being, instead of as a person on LSD. He couldn't see ever coming down, because he was peaking. He couldn't see going on living, either, because to him, it wasn't living, it wasn't existing, being in the state of mind he was in. He just kept walking around, and it was almost like he just wanted to lay down and die, because he didn't want to exist in that state.

So I sat up all night with him. A friend of mine next door had some tranquilizers, so I got some, but that didn't help too much. Finally, the effects started wearing off. As far as I know, he's never taken LSD again. It's been about a year now.

Q: In the 20 times that you took LSD, you never had a bad trip?

A: I'm trying to remember. I've never, like, flipped out, or experienced what my friend went through. But now I do remember one bad experience. While I was on it I was thinking, "Wow! I don't want to do this any more." Because it was getting to be so physical. I felt, "Wow! It's not good for my body and my system." When I first took it I didn't think of death or anything, because I was so young. You don't see how finite you are. But finally, the last few times, it got to where, "Wow! If I take any more . . ."

I've known people who've taken it hundreds of times and they still didn't feel this way. But me, finally I figured, "Gee! If you just keep taking this kind of thing, physically you're going to be torn apart. You're going to be worn away or something." And so, when I'd finally come back down, I'd say, "Wow! I'm glad that's over, and I won't take it again." And I haven't. But never a regret, you know, of having done it.

Q: What was unhappy, or bad, about the sort of trip that caused you to quit?

A: It got to my ego. When I'd come down, it was bad. You're euphoric on it, when you first come on to it. You just get extremely euphoric. Reality goes out of you—what I call reality. The everyday work and materialistic striving to be somebody, make a name for yourself. It all goes away. I'm not materialistic, but I want to make a name, write books, like you do. But when I would first come on to LSD, all the reality, and the thing of making a name, all of it would go out of me. I'd just enjoy existence, being alive, and perceiving everything that you perceive under it. Then, as I started to get over the peak, it got to the ego thing of, "Gee! What am I going to do when I come down? What am I really doing to make a name for myself?" I'd worry about having thrown out reality, just been enjoying myself. That would be when I was starting to come back a little to reality, when I was coming down.

That's the bad part, the reality is thrown away. Basically, the drug thing is an escape, and that's what I was doing. But it was still a great experience.

Q: In other words, if I understand you correctly, when you are peaking on LSD, you feel great, euphoric. You escape from reality, from the harsh realities of life?

A: Yes.

Q: And then, when you start "coming down," you come back to

reality enough to dread returning to the demands of life? And you realize you have only escaped temporarily, and soon will have to get back to the business of living in this world, so to speak?

A: Yes. When you first take it, the escape from reality is very much in effect. But then, as you come down, reality starts hitting you, really hard. Your ego, or what you want in life, or what you want to be, is bolstered as you first take off. It's like, "Wow! I can do anything!" I'm God, or whatever. You get a feeling of being able to be anything, be a doctor, or whatever you apply yourself to, whatever you want. Then, as you start coming down, as you get over, then reality starts coming back. And that's why, the last few times, I decided it's no good.

Besides being physical, there's the thing of, "Now wait a minute! You've just taken this. You're just as good as everyone else. You won't listen when the system tries to put you down, when it says, 'Look, be a carpenter. Or just be a part of the whole thing. The mass product thing.'"

And then, as you get over it, you say, "Wait a minute. This taking LSD isn't building your personality, building your ability. It's just an escape. It's an ego builder. But then when you get back to reality, it lets you down."

Q: So that the bad part of the trip, for you, is when you're down? Not during it?

A: For me, it was after I started coming down, and started thinking, "Hey, now! Tomorrow I've got to get up and go to work." Which is fine, but what am I accomplishing by taking acid? Nothing, really, you know?

Some people, they just keep taking it, I don't know why. But for me, I experienced it about 20 times, and then I had to go on from there, quit it and face reality. I had a lot of inadequate feelings, because of how my mom had died, really an experience of having no home base. A mother is a home base, you know. Like, you go home to mother. And you're able to go out the next day, see the world, and then come home to mother. I had no home base.

But for me, LSD did it. It was one aspect of my maturing process, biologically and mentally, that has helped me get to the point that I now am at. I feel very adequate and able to become a functioning part of society rather than a dropout. I go to school now. I'm going to join the Scholastic Society. I can go there, and if they don't like me, that's just their tough luck, you know. But always, before, I've gotten bad vibrations from people. Because I didn't have any family.

So for me, LSD was great, because it gave me a home base.

Q: You just decided to quit, and did? There was no struggle?

A: No struggle. It was a thing of I got sick. I got the flu. My resistance to illness was low. Taking the drugs uses up all your defenses, you know. Up until that time I'd never been sick. I'd always been very healthy. But drugs use up your physical defenses. Against flu. Any kind of bug. Your defenses are really beat down. Especially a heroin addict. If they're around any kind of disease they're going to get it. I never fix. But if you keep taking any drug, like LSD, your defenses are used up.

Q: When one goes off LSD or a similar hallucinogenic drug, he doesn't feel the sort of body craving that the heroin user does?

A: No, not at all.

Q: Is there a psychological drive to get back to it? Do some people become habituated to it? They'd like to quit but can't?

A: Not that I know of. I've never known anyone who wanted to quit and couldn't.

Q: If they keep taking LSD for a long, long time, will they hurt themselves physically?

A: Of course, I'm not an expert, but I would have to say, "Definitely." It will hurt you physically, after a while. It's so heavy on you. Not just psychologically but physically. Maybe if you're 30, 40, you can take it 100, 200 times, but not at my age, the way I was when I got sick. But I still feel right now that my mind has benefited from the experience.

Q: Will you tell me a little more about that? Why, as you've said, you don't regret having had the experience?

A: It's because of this "base" thing, having a base. Now I can go to school, and my ego will go against the teacher's ego and I'll come out of it with an A or a B. Whereas before, when I was 17, 18, when I started at junior college, I was like a little frightened animal. Now, LSD has built up my ego. And my base. To where I can say, "Gee! I can go to school. I can be a professor. I can be whatever I want to be, if I apply myself." So LSD benefited me. But if I took it 20 more times, it might hurt me.

Q: How long since you used any LSD?

A: A little over a year.

Q: Did you quit grass when you went to LSD? Or did you keep on with grass, too?

A: I kept on with it.

Q: Did you ever stop using grass?

A: I still smoked grass after I put down on acid. But when I got into school, I said, "Wow, man! This grass is just a waste of time and I can't study. So I put down almost completely. I do smoke now and then. Like when I go and see my little brother, or if I go and see some of my old friends. I do it socially. Just like you take a drink. Because that way I can be in with them and be their friends.

I'm trying to help them. A lot of them need help. Like my little brother. Someone's been turning him on to reds, "downers." So I've been going over there. When I try to tell him things if he's getting high and I'm not, there's that rebellious thing. A thing of "I'll get high *because* everybody says not to." So I'll smoke it socially, you know. Otherwise it would be like the man trying to tell kids, "Don't do it." Well, that just never is going to work.

Q: Do you think that continuous, longtime smoking of marijuana does as much harm to the organism as LSD can?

A: No. Smoking marijuana all your life would never do what taking LSD all your life would do. But if you started as a kid, smoking marijuana, well, you're never going to apply yourself and become a professor, a doctor, a lawyer. Not a very efficient one, I don't think. Because it's just like alcohol, like my old man. He drinks. As soon as he's off work he's got his scotch and he's drinking it until he goes to bed. He's always under the influence, because it never gets out of his system. The same thing with marijuana. When you smoke it every day, or two or three times a week, you're in a kind of apathy. You can't be apathetic and be a doctor. But it wouldn't hurt you any more than smoking cigarettes, physically, I don't think.

Q: Let's consider LSD again. You've suggested that there are certain types of personality that have bad trips on LSD. But I gather there's no one personality type, no individual, whatever his personality may be, who is almost certain to become a confirmed LSD user. The alcoholic has a compulsion for drink. He's got to have it. The man hooked on heroin has got to have it, no matter what. I gather this is not true of LSD users, no matter how often they have used? They don't develop a compulsive need for it, or perhaps a body hunger for it?

A: No, but now, marijuana, there's a little of what you're saying there.

Q: How so?

A: People who just smoke it all the time. Like the guy who needs it the minute he gets up. With LSD, you couldn't be that way. Because it's too physical, its effect on you. But like, take, the guy who the minute he gets up needs a drink, some guys want to hit a number. They're practically hitting a number all day long.

Q: But suppose their supply were cut off. Would they be in misery? In pain? Running around, desperately trying to get it?

A: No, but I imagine there would be a lot of anxiety. They'd bite their fingernails—"What am I going to do?" They'd probably go and get some wine, or else beer.

Q: To the best of your knowledge, is it largely young people who smoke grass or use LSD? Or is there an older group?

A: Generally it's the young, but there's a few older people. But young people, if they had turned on as kids, they won't keep doing it as adults. You find the kids doing it until they grow up a little.

Q: In your experience, have many young people moved from marijuana or LSD to hard stuff, like heroin?

A: No. Not any of my friends or contemporaries. The only people I knew that used heroin were a few of the pushers. And, well, a few of the friends of friends of mine. Like, when I was dealing, I'd go to their homes, and there would be some smack freaks there. They might be fixing.

A: I was lucky. I was always pretty stable as I grew up, even if I didn't have much of a family. I was always in school. I believed in the right things. But I didn't believe in going to Viet Nam and killing.

Q: Why do you figure you turned out this way?

A: That's a big question. The only thing I can figure out is that I loved my mother before she died, and that must have gotten me through it.

I always missed my mom. That's one of the biggest things in life. Everyone else has mothers and I don't. I've always remembered my mother as just loving her so much. When she died, I remember they told us, and I just started laughing, because it just blew my mind. Like, everyone else was crying, but I started laughing, because I wouldn't accept it. I always flash back on it. Like I always remember seeing her in the casket, and stuff like that. Real clear. And all of that was taken away from me, all that love, and what I really needed.

I'd go and try to play football at school, and everyone else's parents were there, and there I was, just nothing, man. They'd say, "Well, don't you have any parents?" I'd tell them there was my dad, but he was doing something, he was busy. I'd give an excuse, a lie.

So, for a year, every day I got home, all I heard from my old man was that I was fucked. My only escape, I think, was thinking about my mom. I didn't feel sorry for myself, but I always wanted to go to other people's houses to see their moms. I'd think it was groovy to go to a guy's house, because I could see his mom, and talk to her, and see what effect I had upon her. I've always wanted them to like me. I think that's why I've gotten through without stealing, because I always wanted to go see people's moms, and I always wanted them to like me. I would think, "How could I go to see somebody's mom if I was robbing somebody's house the day before?"

A: I plan to do graduate work if I'm not drafted. I used to dread that, getting drafted. I felt then that it was my idealism that made me think Viet Nam was wrong. But probably I was just scared. Now I'm in the frame of mind where if I can stay out, I will. I don't think it's a right war. But if I have to, I'll go rather than go to jail. If I don't go, I'll probably go to graduate school.

THE USE AND ABUSE OF PSYCHEDELIC EXPERIENCE

THEODORE ROSZAK

Excerpted from Theodore Roszak, *The Making of a Counter Culture* (Garden City, New York: Doubleday and Company, 1969), pp. 155–164.

AT THE bohemian fringe of our disaffected youth culture, all roads lead to psychedelia. The fascination with hallucinogenic drugs emerges persistently as the common denominator of the many protean forms the counter culture has assumed in the post-World War II period. Correctly understood (which it all too seldom is), psychedelic experience participates significantly in the young's most radical rejection of the parental society. Yet it is their frantic search for the pharmacological panacea which tends to distract many of the young from all that is most valuable in their rebellion, and which threatens to destroy their most promising sensibilities.

If we accept the proposition that the counter culture is, essentially, an exploration of the politics of consciousness, then psychedelic experience falls into place as one, but only one, possible method of mounting that exploration. It becomes a limited chemical means to a greater psychic end, namely, the reformulation of the personality, upon which social ideology and culture generally are ultimately based.

This was the spirit in which, at the turn of the century, both William James and Havelock Ellis undertook their study of hallucinogenic agents. The prospectus of these early experimenters—James using nitrous oxide and Ellis, the newly discovered peyote (on which James was able to achieve only bad stomach cramps)—was highly exuberant with respect to the cultural possibilities that might flow from an investigation of hallucinatory experience. Ellis, reporting to the Smithsonian Institution in 1898 on his introduction to the "saturnalia for the specific senses," observed that:

If it should ever chance that the consumption of mescal becomes a habit, the favorite poet of the mescal drinker will certainly be Wordsworth. Not only the general attitude of Wordsworth, but many of his most memorable poems and phrases cannot—one is almost tempted to say—be appreciated in their full significance by one who has never been under the influence of mescal. On all these grounds it may be claimed that the artificial paradise of mescal, though less seductive, is safe and dignified beyond its peers.[1]

James was even more emphatic in hailing the philosophical importance of the non-intellective powers he had discovered not only directly through his experiments with narcotics, but more academically by way of his ground-breaking survey *The Varieties of Religious Experience*. The enthusiasm on James' part is especially noteworthy since, as a founder of both pragmatism and behavioral psychology, he was much beholden to the standard forms of cerebration that belong to the scientific world view. Still, James was convinced that:

. . . our normal waking consciousness, rational consciousness as we call it, is but one special type of consciousness, whilst all about it, parted from it by the filmiest of screens, there lie potential forms of consciousness entirely different. . . . No account of the universe in its totality can be final which leaves these other forms of consciousness quite disregarded. . . . they forbid a premature closing of our accounts with reality.[2]

When, some fifty years later, Aldous Huxley and Alan Watts undertook psychedelic experiments that were destined to have far greater social influence than those of Ellis and James, the investigations were still characterized by the same controlled samplings and urbane observations. Once again, the object was to gain a new, internal perspective on modes of consciousness and on religious traditions that the narrowly positivist science of the day had

[1] Quoted in Robert S. DeRopp, *Drugs and the Mind* (London: Gollancz, 1958), pp. 55–56.
[2] William James, *The Varieties of Religious Experience* (New York: Modern Library, 1936), pp. 378–79.

swept into an outsized pigeonhole labeled "mysticism"—meaning . . . "meaningless." The exercise Watts and Huxley had set themselves was therefore essentially one of synthesis and assimilation. In much the same spirit in which Freud had set out to reclaim the dream as a form of evidence that could bear the weight of scientific speculation, Watts and Huxley wanted to recapture the value of neglected cultural traditions for which no disciplined method of study existed. The method they proposed was the systematic cultivation of states of abnormal consciousness that approached these traditions by outflanking the discursive, logic-chopping intellect.

The hypothesis Ellis and James, Watts and Huxley were testing has always seemed to me wholly sensible, even from the most rigorously scientific viewpoint. If the province of science is the disciplined examination of human experience, then surely abnormal (or transnormal) states of consciousness must also constitute a field of scientific study. As James had contended, the mystics, by relating their insights to direct personal experience, would seem to qualify as rigorous empiricists. Why then should their experience and the knowledge that appears to flow from it be screened out by science as somehow illegitimate? Is it perhaps the case that the mystics, in accepting the fullness of human experience, have been more truly scientific than the conventional scientist, who insists that only what makes itself apparent to an arbitrarily limited range of consciousness deserves attention? Such a prejudice would seem all the more untenable once artificial chemical agents have been developed which provide discriminate access to these transnormal forms of consciousness. Why should they not be used as a kind of psychic depth charge with which to open up courses of perception that have become severely logjammed due to the entrenched cerebral habits of our Western intelligence?

As an intellectual proposition, such experimentation may have been sound. But the experiments were destined to become more than a form of exotic psychological research. Instead, they have been sucked into the undertow of a major social movement—and in this context, their influence has been far from wholesome.

With hindsight, it is clear enough what went wrong. Both Huxley and Watts drew the analogy between the drug experience and such exploratory devices as the microscope. Accordingly, the hallucinogens were to function as a lens through which the shadowy layers of consciousness could be studied. But a microscope in the hands of a child or the laboratory janitor becomes a toy that produces nothing but a kind of barbarous and superficial fascination. Perhaps the drug experience bears significant fruit when rooted in the soil of a mature and cultivated mind. But the experience has, all of a sudden, been laid hold of by a generation of youngsters who are pathetically a-cultural and who often bring nothing to the experience but a vacuous yearning. They have, in adolescent rebellion, thrown off the corrupted culture of their elders and, along with that soiled bath water, the very body of the Western heritage —at best, in favor of exotic traditions they only marginally understand; at worst, in favor of an introspective chaos in which the seventeen or eighteen years of their own unformed lives float like atoms in a void.

I think one must be prepared to take a very strong line on the matter and maintain that there are minds too small and too young for such psychic adventures—and that the failure to recognize this fact is the beginning of disaster. There is nothing whatever in common between a man of Huxley's experience and intellectual discipline sampling mescaline, and a fifteen-year-old tripper whiffing airplane glue until his brain turns to oatmeal. In the one case, we have a gifted mind moving sophisticatedly toward cultural synthesis; in the other, we have a giddy child out to "blow his mind" and bemused to see all the pretty balloons go up. But when all the balloons have gone up and gone pop, what is there left behind but the yearning to see more pretty balloons? And so one reaches again for the little magic tube . . . and again and again.

At the level of disaffiliated adolescence, the prospect held forth by psychedelic experience—that of consciousness expansion—is bound to prove abortive. The psychedelics, dropped into amorphous and alienated personalities, have precisely the reverse effect: they diminish consciousness by way of fixation. The whole of life comes to center despotically on one act, one mode of experience. Whether or not marijuana, LSD, and amphetamine are addictive remains a moot point—largely because of the ambiguity of the term "addiction." Are fingernails addictive? We all know people who bite them constantly and compulsively. Is chess addictive? There are players who will go without food or drink rather than abandon the board. Where does the dependency of compulsive fascination leave off and addiction begin?

What *is* obvious, however, is that the psychedelics are a heavyweight obsession which too many of the young cannot get over or around. For them, psychic chemistry is no longer a means for exploring the perennial wisdom; it has become an end in itself, a source of boundless lore, study, and esthetic elaboration. It is becoming the whole works. It is not that the young have all become hopheads; it is rather that, at the bohemian fringe, they are in the process of trying strenuously to inflate the psychedelics to the size of an entire culture. Ironically, the vice is typical of the worst sort of American commercialism. Start with a gimmick; end with a *Weltanschauung*. Madison Avenue's strategy of strategies: don't just sell them a new can opener; sell them a new way of life. . . .

If the psychedelic obsession were no more than a symptom of cultural impoverishment, things would be bad enough. But one must complete the grim picture by adding the sweaty, often vicious, and, in a few instances, even murderous relationships that inevitably grow up around any illegal trade. Money is still what it takes to survive in an urban environment, even if one is only eking out a subsistence. And narcotics, with their subsidiary merchandise, are what brings the money into communities like the East Village and the Haight-Ashbury. In a perceptive series on the Haight-Ashbury dope commerce written for the Washington *Post* (October 15–29, 1967), Nicholas Von Hoffman was forced to the unhappy conclusion that, whatever else they may take themselves to be, the hippies constitute, willy-nilly, "the biggest crime story since prohibition." The account he has to offer is far from pretty. Even if most of the flower children manage to steer clear of the more cynical and criminal aspects of the trade, their communities have nevertheless become a market more and more dominated by hard-nosed entrepreneurial interests that have about as much concern for expanding consciousness as Al Capone had for arranging Dionysian festivals.

To be sure, the authorities with their single-minded determination to treat the use of psychedelics as a police problem, and the mass media with their incorrigible penchant for simplifying and sensationalizing, are both to blame for turning the often innocent curiosity of the young into ugly and furtive channels. But the young bear a primary responsibility for letting themselves be trapped in the vicious ambience that the dominant society has created. One must insist that, on their own terms, they are old enough to know better than to let themselves be driven into the same bag with drug merchandisers, who are only the criminal caricature of the American business ethos, and who will scarcely be reformed by being given docile new populations to exploit.

THE GANG AS A CULTURAL
PHENOMENON

DAVID J. BORDUA

Excerpted from David J. Bordua, "Delinquent Subcultures: Sociological Interpretations of Gang Delinquency," *Annals of the American Academy of Political and Social Science*, CCCXXXVIII (November 1961), 120–36. At the time of publication, D. J. Bordua was a member of the Department of Sociology in the University of Michigan.

IN ITS more well-developed and extreme forms, gang or subcultural delinquency has been heavily concentrated in the low status areas of our large cities. The theoretical interpretations I will discuss all confine themselves to gang delinquency of this sort.

The Classical View

Still the best book on gangs, gang delinquency, and—though he did not use the term—delinquent subcultures is *The Gang* by Frederic M. Thrasher, and his formulations are the ones that I have labeled "the classical view." Not that he originated the basic interpretative framework, far from it, but his application of the theoretical materials available at the time plus his sensitivity to the effects of social environment and his willingness to consider processes at all behavioral levels from the basic needs of the child to the significance of the saloon, from the nature of city government to the crucial importance of the junk dealer, from the consequences of poverty to the nature of leadership in the gang still distinguish his book.

Briefly, Thrasher's analysis may be characterized as operating on the following levels. The ecological processes which determine the structure of the city create the interstitial area characterized by a variety of indices of conflict, disorganization, weak family and neighborhood controls, and so on. In these interstitial areas, in response to universal childhood needs, spontaneous play groups develop. Because of the relatively uncontrolled nature of these groups—or of many of them at least—and because of the presence of many attractive and exciting opportunities for fun and adventure, these groups engage in a variety of activities, legal and illegal, which are determined, defined, and directed by the play group itself rather than by conventional adult supervision.

The crowded, exciting slum streets teem with such groups. Inevitably, in a situation of high population density, limited resources, and weak social control, they come into conflict with each other for space, playground facilities, reputation. Since many of their activities, even at an early age, are illegal, although often not feloniously so—they swipe fruit from peddlers, turn over garbage cans, stay away from home all night, and steal milk and cakes for breakfast, play truant from school—they also come into conflict with adult authority. Parents, teachers, merchants, police, and others become natural enemies of this kind of group and attempt to control it or to convert it to more conventional activities. With some groups they succeed, with some they do not.

If the group continues, it becomes part of a network of similar groups, increasingly freed from adult restraint, increasingly involved in intergroup conflict and fighting, increasingly engaged in illegal activities to support itself and to continue to receive the satisfactions of the "free" life of the streets. Conflict, especially with other groups, transforms the play group into the gang. Its illegal activities become more serious, its values hardened, its structure more determined by the necessity to maintain eternal vigilance in a hostile environment.

By middle adolescence, the group is a gang, often with a name, usually identified with a particular ethnic or racial group, and usually with an elaborate technology of theft and other means of self-support. Gradually, the gang may move in the direction of adult crime, armed robbery, perhaps, or other serious crimes.

Prior to that time, however, it is likely to have engaged in much stealing from stores, railroad cars, empty houses, parents, drunks, almost anywhere money or goods are available. The ready access to outlets for stolen goods is of major importance here. The junk dealer, especially the junk wagon peddler, the convenient no-questions-asked attitudes of large numbers of local adults who buy "hot" merchandise, and the early knowledge that customers are available all help to make theft easy and profitable as well as morally acceptable.

It is appropriate at this point to deal with a matter that has become important in the discussion of more recent theories of group delinquency. This is Albert K. Cohen's famous characterization of the delinquent subculture as nonutilitarian, by which he seems to mean that activities, especially theft, are not oriented to calculated economic ends.[1]

Thrasher makes a great point of the play and adventure quality of many illegal acts, especially in the pregang stages of a group's development, but he also describes many cases where theft has a quite rational and instrumental nature, even at a fairly early age.

The theft activities and the disposition of the loot make instrumental sense in the context of Thrasher's description of the nature of the group or gang. Much theft is essentially for the purpose of maintaining the group in a state of freedom from adult authority. If a group of boys lives days or even weeks away from home, then the theft of food or of things which are sold to buy food is hardly nonutilitarian. . . .

Such youngsters may, of course, spend the two dollars gained from selling stolen goods entirely on doughnuts and gorge themselves and throw much of the food away. I think this largely indicates that they are children, not that they are nonutilitarian.[2]

[1] Albert K. Cohen, *Delinquent Boys: The Culture of the Gang* (Glencoe: The Free Press, 1955), pp. 25, 26.

[2] The examples cited above are all in Thrasher. . . . In general, views of the nature of gang activity have shifted quite fundamentally toward a more irrationalist position. Thus, the gang's behavior seems to make no sense. Underlying this shift is a tendency to deal almost entirely with the gang's subculture, its values, beliefs, and the like, to deal with the relationships between this subculture and presumed motivational states which exist in the potential gang members before the gang or protogang is formed, and to deal very little with the developmental processes involved in the formation of gangs. Things which make no sense without consideration of the motivational consequences

Let us look a little more systematically at the Thrasher formulations, however, since such an examination can be instructive in
dealing with the more recent theories. . . .

At the level of the local adult community, we may say that the
social structure is permissive, attractive, facilitative, morally supportive of the gang development process.

It is permissive because control over children is weak; attractive
because many enjoyable activities are available, some of which are
illegal . . . but all of which can be enjoyed only if the child manages to evade whatever conventional controls do exist.

In another sense, the local environment is attractive because of
the presence of adult crime of a variety of kinds ranging from organized vice to older adolescents and adults making a living by theft.
The attraction lies of course, in the fact that these adults may have
a lot of money and live the carefree life and have high status in the
neighborhood.

The local environment is facilitative in a number of ways. There
are things readily available to steal, people to buy them, and
places to hide without adult supervision.

The environment is morally supportive because of the presence
of adult crime, as previously mentioned, but also for several additional reasons. One is the readiness of conventional adults to buy
stolen goods. . . . The prevalence of political pull, which not only
objectively protected adult crime but tended to undercut the
norms against crime, must be mentioned then as now. The often
bitter poverty which turned many situations into matters of desperate competition also contributed.

Additionally, many gang activities, especially in the protogang
stage, are not seriously delinquent and receive adult approval.
These activities include such things as playing baseball for "side

---

of gang membership are not necessarily so mysterious given Thrasher's highly
sensitive analysis of the ways in which the nature of the gang as a group led
to the development—in relation to the local environment—of the gang culture.
Current theory focuses so heavily on motive and culture to the exclusion of
group process that some essential points are underemphasized. It would not
be too much of a distortion to say that Thrasher saw the delinquent subculture as the way of life that would be developed by a group becoming a gang
and that some recent theorists look at the gang as the kind of group that
would develop if boys set about creating a delinquent subculture.

money" and much minor gambling such as penny pitching. Within limits, fighting lies well within the local community's zone of tolerance, especially when it is directed against members of another ethnic group.

At the level of the adolescent and preadolescent groups themselves, the environment is essentially coercive of gang formation. The presence of large numbers of groups competing for limited resources leads to conflict, and the fullfledged adolescent gang is pre-eminently a conflict group with a high valuation of fighting skill, courage, and similar qualities. Thus, the transition from spontaneous group to gang is largely a matter of participating in the struggle for life of the adolescent world under the peculiar conditions of the slum.

At the level of the individual, Thrasher assumes a set of basic needs common to all children. He leans heavily on the famous four wishes of W. I. Thomas, security, response, recognition, and new experiences, especially the last two. Gang boys and boys in gang areas are, in this sense, no different from other boys. They come to choose different ways of satisfying these needs. What determines which boys form gangs is the differential success of the agencies of socialization and social control in channeling these needs into conventional paths. Thus, due to family inadequacy or breakdown or school difficulties, coupled with the ever present temptations of the exciting, adventurous street as compared to the drab, dull, and unsatisfying family and school, some boys are more available for street life than others.

Finally, it should be pointed out that the gang engages in many activities of a quite ordinary sort. Athletics are very common and highly regarded at all age levels. Much time is spent simply talking and being with the gang. The gang's repertory is diverse— baseball, football, dice, poker, holding dances, shooting the breeze, shoplifting, rolling drunks, stealing cars. . . .

I have purposely attempted to convey the distinctive flavor of essentially healthy boys satisfying universal needs in a weakly controlled and highly seductive environment. Compared to the deprived and driven boys of more recent formulations with their status problems, blocked opportunities (or psychopathologies if one takes a more psychiatric view), Thrasher describes an age of innocence indeed.

This is, perhaps, the most important single difference between Thrasher and some—not all—of the recent views. Delinquency and crime were attractive, being a "good boy" was dull. . . .

Working Class Boy and Middle Class Measuring Rod

If Thrasher saw the gang as being formed over time through the attractiveness of the free street life and the unattractiveness and moral weakness of the agencies of social control, Albert K. Cohen sees many working class boys as being driven to develop the delinquent subculture as a way of recouping the self-esteem destroyed by middle-class-dominated institutions.

Rather than focusing on the gang and its development over time, Cohen's theory focuses on the way of life of the gang—the delinquent subculture. A collective way of life, a subculture, develops when a number of people with a common problem of adjustment are in effective interaction, according to Cohen. The bulk of his basic viewpoint is the attempted demonstration that the common problem of adjustment of the lower class gang boys who are the carriers of the delinquent subculture derives from their socialization in lower class families and their consequent lack of preparation to function successfully in middle class institutions such as the school.

The institutions within which the working class boy must function reward and punish him for acceptable or unacceptable performance according to the child-assessing version of middle class values. The middle class value pattern places great emphasis on ambition as a cardinal virtue, individual responsibility (as opposed to extreme emphasis on shared kin obligations, for example), the cultivation and possession of skills, the ability to postpone gratification, rationality, the rational cultivation of manners, the control of physical aggressions and violence, the wholesome and constructive use of leisure, and respect for property (especially respect for the abstract rules defining rights of access to material things).

The application of these values adapted to the judgment of children constitutes the "middle class measuring rod" by which all children are judged in institutions run by middle class personnel —the school, the settlement house, and the like. The fact that working class children must compete according to these standards is a consequence of what Cohen, in a most felicitous phrase, refers to as the "democratic status universe" characteristic of American society. Everyone is expected to strive, and everyone is measured against the same standard. Not everyone is equally prepared, however, and the working class boy is, with greater statistical frequency than the middle class boy, ill prepared through previous socialization.

Social class for Cohen is not simply economic position but, much more importantly, a set of more or less vertically layered cultural settings which differ in the likelihood that boys will be taught the aspirations, ambitions, and psychological skills necessary to adjust to the demands of the larger institutions.

Cohen goes on to describe this predominantly lower working class cultural setting as more likely to show restricted aspirations, a live-for-today orientation toward consumption, a moral view which emphasizes reciprocity within the kin and other primary groups, and correlatively less concern with abstract rules which apply across or outside of such particularistic circumstances. In addition, the working class child is less likely to be surrounded with educational toys, less likely to be trained in a family regimen of order, neatness, and punctuality. Of particular importance is the fact that physical aggression is more prevalent and more valued in the working class milieu.

When a working class boy thus equipped for life's struggle begins to function in the school, the settlement, and other middle-class-controlled institutions and encounters the middle class measuring rod, he invariably receives a great deal of disapproval, rejection, and punishment. In short, in the eyes of the middle class evaluator, he does not measure up. This is what Cohen refers to as the problem of status deprivation which constitutes the fundamental problem of adjustment to which the delinquent subculture is a solution.

But this deprivation derives not only from the negative evaluations of others but also from self-derogation. The working class boy shares in this evaluation of himself to some degree for a variety of reasons. The first of these is the previously mentioned democratic status universe wherein the dominant culture requires everyone to compete against all comers. Second, the parents of working class boys, no matter how adjusted they seem to be to their low status position, are likely to project their frustrated aspirations onto their children. They may do little effective socialization to aid the child, but they are, nevertheless, likely at least to want their children to be better off than they are. Third, there is the effect of the mass media which spread the middle class life style. And, of course, there is the effect of the fact of upward mobility as visible evidence that at least some people can make the grade.

In short, the working class boy is subjected to many social influences which emphasize the fact that the way to respect, status, and success lies in conforming to the demands of the middle class society. Even more importantly, he very likely has partly accepted the middle class measuring rod as a legitimate, even superior, set of values. The profound ambivalence that this may lead to in the individual is simply a reflection of the fact that the larger culture penetrates the lower working class the world in many ways. . . .

This, then, is the common problem of adjustment. Given the availability of many boys similarly situated, a collective solution evolves, the delinquent subculture. This subculture is characterized by Cohen as nonutilitarian, malicious, and negativistic, characterized by versatility, short-run hedonism, and an emphasis on group autonomy, that is, freedom from adult restraint.

These are, of course, the direct antitheses of the components of the middle class measuring rod. The delinquent subculture functions simultaneously to combat the enemy without and the enemy within, both the hated agents of the middle class and the gnawing internal sense of inadequacy and low self-esteem. It does so by erecting a counterculture, an alterntive set of status criteria.

This subculture must do more than deal with the middle-class-dominated institutions . . . and the feelings of low self-esteem. . . . It must also deal with the feelings of guilt over aggression, theft, and the like that will inevitably arise. It must deal with the fact that the collective solution to the common problem of adjustment is an illicit one in the eyes of the larger society and, certainly, also in the eyes of the law-abiding elements of the local area.

It must deal, also, with the increasing opposition which the solution arouses in the police and other agencies of the conventional order. Over time, the subculture comes to contain a variety of definitions of these agents of conventionality which see them as the aggressors, thus legitimating the group's deviant activities.

Because of this requirement that the delinquent subculture constitute a solution to internal, psychological problems of self-esteem and guilt, Cohen sees the group behavior pattern as being overdetermined in the psychological sense and as linking up with the mechanism of reaction formation.

Thus, the reason for the seeming irrationality of the delinquent subculture lies in the deeply rooted fears and anxieties of the status deprived boy. I have already discussed the shift from Thrasher's view of delinquency as attractive in a situation of weak social control to the views of it as more reactive held by some modern theorists. Cohen, of course, is prominent among these latter, the irrationalists. It is extremely difficult to bring these viewpoints together at all well except to point out that Cohen's position accords well with much research on school failure and its consequences in damaged self-esteem. It does seem unlikely . . . that the failure of family, school, and neighborhood to control the behavior of Thrasher's boys would result in their simple withdrawal from such conventional contexts without hostility and loss of self-regard.

Cohen emphasizes that not all members of an ongoing delinquent group are motivated by this same problem of adjustment. Like any other protest movement, the motives which draw new members at different phases of its development will vary. It is sufficient that a core of members share the problem.

The analysis of the delinquent subculture of urban working class boys set forth in *Delinquent Boys* has been elaborated and supplemented in a later article by Cohen and James F. Short.[3]

Responding to the criticism that there seemed a variety of kinds of delinquent subcultures, even among lower class urban youth,

[3] Albert K. Cohen and James F. Short, Jr., "Research in Delinquent Sub-Cultures," *Journal of Social Issues*, Vol. 14 (1958), No. 3, pp. 20–36.

Cohen and Short distinguish the parent-male subculture, the conflict-oriented subculture, the drug addict subculture, and a subculture focused around semiprofessional theft.

The parent subculture is the now familiar subculture described
in *Delinquent Boys*. Cohen and Short describe it as the most common form.[4]

We refer to it as the parent sub-culture because it is probably the most
common variety in this country—indeed, it might be called the "garden
variety" of delinquent sub-culture—and because the characteristics listed
above seem to constitute a common core shared by other important var-
iants.

In discussing the conditions under which these different subcultures arise, Cohen and Short rely on a pivotal paper published in
1951 by Solomon Kobrin.[5] Dealing with the differential location of
the conflict-oriented versus the semiprofessional theft subculture,
Kobrin pointed out that delinquency areas vary in the degree to
which conventional and criminal value systems are mutually integrated. In the integrated area, adult criminal activity is stable and
organized, and adult criminals are integral parts of the local social
structure—active in politics, fraternal orders, providers of employment. Here delinquency can form a kind of apprenticeship for
adult criminal careers with such careers being relatively indistinct
from conventional careers. More importantly, the interests of organized criminal groups in order and a lack of police attention would
lead to attempts to prevent the wilder and more untrammeled
forms of juvenile violence. This would mean, of course, that crime
in these areas was largely of the stable, profitable sort ordinarily
associated with the rackets.

Lower Class Boy and Lower Class Culture

The interpretation of the delinquent subculture associated with
Albert Cohen . . . contrasts sharply in its main features with what

---

[4] *Ibid.*, p. 24. The characteristics are those of maliciousness and so on that I
have listed previously.
[5] Solomon Kobrin, "The Conflict of Values in Delinquency Areas," *American Sociological Review*, Vol. 16 (October, 1951), No. 5, pp. 653–61.

has come to be called the lower class culture view associated with Walter B. Miller. Miller disagrees with the Cohen position concerning the reactive nature of lower class gang culture.[6]

In the case of "gang" delinquency, the cultural system which exerts the most direct influences on behavior is that of the lower class community itself—a long-established, distinctively patterned tradition with an integrity of its own—rather than a so-called delinquent sub-culture which has arisen through conflict with middle class culture and is oriented to the deliberate violation of middle class norms.

What, then, is the lower class culture Miller speaks of and where is it located? Essentially, Miller describes a culture which he sees as emerging from the shaking-down processes of immigration, internal migration, and vertical mobility. Several population and cultural streams feed this process, but, primarily, lower class culture represents the emerging common adaptation of unsuccessful immigrants and Negroes.

It is the thesis of this paper that from these extremely diverse and heterogeneous origins (with, however, certain common features), there is emerging a relatively homogeneous and stabilized native-American lower class culture; however, in many communities the process of fusion is as yet in its earlier phases, and evidences of the original ethnic or locality culture are still strong.[7]

In his analysis, Miller is primarily concerned with what he calls the hard core group in the lower class—the same very bottom group referred to by Cohen as the lower-lower class. The properties of this emerging lower class culture as described by Miller may be divided into a series of social structural elements and a complex pattern of what Miller calls focal concerns.

The first of the structural elements is what Miller calls the female-based household, that is, a family form wherein the key relationships are those among mature females (especially those of different generations but, perhaps, also sisters or cousins) and between these females and their children. The children may be by

---

[6] Walter B. Miller, "Lower Class Culture as a Generating Milieu of Gang Delinquency," *Journal of Social Issues,* Vol. 14 (1958), No. 3, pp. 5–19.

[7] Walter B. Miller, "Implications of Urban Lower Class Culture for Social Work," *The Social Service Review,* Vol. 33 (September, 1959), No. 3, pp. 219–36.

different men, and the biological fathers may play a very inconsistent and unpredictable role in the family. Most essentially, the family is not organized around the expectation of stable economic support provided by an adult male.

The relationship between adult females and males is characterized as one of serial mating, with the female finding it necessary repeatedly to go through a cycle of roles of mate-seeker, mother, and employee.

Closely related to and supportive of this form of household is the elaboration of a system of one-sex peer groups which, according to Miller, become emotional havens and major sources of psychic investment and support for both sexes and for both adolescents and adults. The family, then, is not the central focus of primary, intimate ties that it is in middle class circles.

In what is surely a masterpiece of cogent description, Miller presents the focal concerns of lower class culture as trouble, toughness, smartness, excitement, fate, and autonomy. . . .

Trouble is what life gets you into—especially trouble with the agents of the larger society. The central aspect of this focal concern is the distinction between law-abiding and law-violating behavior, and where an individual stands along the implied dimension either by behavior, reputation, or commitment is crucial in the evaluation of him by others. Toughness refers to physical prowess, skill, masculinity, fearlessness, bravery, daring. It includes an almost compulsive opposition to things seen as soft and feminine, including much middle class behavior, and is related, on the one hand, to sex-role identification problems which flow from the young boy's growing up in the female-based household and, on the other hand, to the occupational demands of the lower class world. Toughness, along with the emphasis on excitement and autonomy, is one of the ways one gets into trouble.

Smartness refers to the ability to "con," outwit, dupe, that is, to manipulate things and people to one's own advantage with a minimum of conventional work. Excitement, both as an activity and as an ambivalently held goal, is best manifested in the patterned cycle of the week end night-on-the-town complete with much drink and sexual escapades, thereby creating the risk of fighting and trouble. Between week ends, life is dull and passive. Fate refers to the conception of many lower class individuals that their lives are determined by events and forces over which they have little or no control. It manifests itself in widespread gambling and fantasies of "when things break for me." Gambling serves multiple functions in the areas of fate, toughness, smartness, and excitement.

The last focal concern described by Miller is that of autonomy —concern over the amount, source, and severity of control by others. Miller describes the carrier of lower class culture as being highly ambivalent about such control by others. Overtly, he may protest bitterly about restraint and arbitrary interference while, covertly, he tends to equate coercion with care and unconsciously to seek situations where strong controls will satisfy nurturance needs.

What is it like to grow up in lower class culture? A boy spends the major part of the first twelve years in the company of and under the domination of women. He learns during that time that women are the people who count, that men are despicable, dangerous, and desirable. He also learns that a "real man" is hated for his irresponsibility and considered very attractive on Saturday night. He learns, too, that, if he really loves his mother, he will not grow up to be "just like all men" but that, despite her best efforts, his mother's pride and joy will very likely turn out to be as much a "rogue male" as the rest. In short, he has sex-role problems.

The adolescent street group is the social mechanism which enables the maturing boy to cope with a basic problem of feminine identification coupled with the necessity of somehow growing up to be an appropriately hated and admired male in a culture which maximizes the necessity to fit into all male society as an adult. The seeking of adult status during adolescence, then, has a particular intensity, so that manifestations of the adult culture's focal concerns tend to be overdone. In addition, the street group displays an exaggerated concern with status and belongingness which is common in all adolescent groups, but becomes unusually severe for the lower class boy.

The street group, then, is an essential transition mechanism and training ground for the lower class boy. Some of the behavior involved is delinquent, but the degree to which the group engages in specifically delinquent acts, that is, constructs its internal status criteria around the law-violating end of the trouble continuum, may vary greatly depending on local circumstances. These include such things as the presence and salience of police, professional criminals, clergy, functioning recreational and settlement programs, and the like.

Like Thrasher, Miller emphasizes the wide range of activities of a nondelinquent nature that the gang members engage in, although, unlike Thrasher's boys, they do not do so because of poor social control, but because of the desire to be "real men." . . .

Miller's approach, like the approaches of Thrasher and Cohen, has its strengths and weaknesses. Miller has not been very successful in refuting Cohen's insistence on the clash between middle class and lower class standards as it affects the sources of self-esteem. To be sure, Cohen's own presentation of just what the lower class boy has or has not internalized is considerably confused. . . . Cohen seems to be saying that a little internalization is a dangerous thing. Miller seems to be saying that the involvements in lower class culture are so deep and exclusive that contacts with agents of middle class dominated institutions, especially the schools, have no impact.

Actually, resolution of this problem does not seem so terribly difficult. In handling Cohen's formulations, I would suggest that previous internalization of middle class values is not particularly necessary, because the lower class boys will be told about them at the very time they are being status-deprived by their teachers and others. They will likely hate it and them (teachers and values), and the process is started. On the other hand, it seems unlikely that Miller's lower class boys can spend ten years in school without some serious outcomes. They should either come to accept middle class values or become even more antagonistic of both, and this should drive them further into the arms of lower class culture. . . .

Miller also seems to be weak when he insists upon seeing what he calls the hard core of lower class culture as a distinctive form and, at the same time, must posit varieties of lower class culture to account for variations in behavior and values. This is not necessarily a factually untrue position, but it would seem to underemphasize the fluidity and variability of American urban life. It is necessary for him to point out that objectively low status urban groups vary in the degree to which they display the core features of lower class culture, with Negroes and Irish groups among those he has studied displaying it more and Italians less.

Miller seems so concerned that the features of lower class culture, especially the female-based household, not be seen as the disorganization of the more conventional system or as signs of social pathology that he seems to overdo it rather drastically. He is very concerned to show that lower class culture is of ancient lineage and is or was functional in American society. Yet, at the same time, he says that lower class culture is only now emerging at the bottom of the urban heap. He also forgets that none of the low status groups in the society, with the possible exception of low status Negroes, has any history of his female-based household, at least not in the extreme form that he describes.

A closely related problem is posed by Miller's citation of cross-cultural evidence, for example, "The female-based household is a stabilized form in many societies—frequently associated with polygamy—and is found in 21 per cent of world societies." [8] . . . I question the implication that the female-based household as the household form, legitimated and normatively supported in societies practicing polygamy, can be very directly equated with a superficially similar system existing on the margins of a larger society and clearly seen as deviant by that larger society. Surely, in primitive societies, the household can count on the stable economic and judicial base provided by an adult male. The very fact that such a household in the United States is under continuous and heavy pressure from the law, the Aid to Dependent Children worker, and nearly all other agents of the conventional order must make for a very different situation than in societies where it is the accepted form. In such societies, would mothers generally regard men as "unreliable and untrustworthy" and would the statement "all men are no good" be common? Surely, such an attitude implies some awareness that things should be otherwise.

[8] *Ibid.*, p. 225 fn.

All this is not to argue that tendencies of the sort Miller describes are not present nor to underestimate the value of his insistence that we look at this way of life in its own terms—a valuable contribution indeed—but only to ask for somewhat greater awareness of the larger social dynamics that produce his lower class culture.

Finally, a last criticism of Miller's formulations aims at the use of the focal concerns material. There seems more than a little danger of tautology here if the focal concerns are derived from observing behavior and then used to explain the same behavior. One would be on much safer ground to deal in much greater detail with the structural roots and reality situations to which lower class culture may be a response. Thus, for example, Miller makes no real use of the vast literature on the consequences of prolonged instability of employment, which seems to me the root of the matter.

These criticisms should not blind us to very real contributions in Miller's position. Most importantly, he tells us what the lower class street boys are for, rather than just what they are against. In addition, he deals provocatively and originally with the nature of the adult culture which serves as the context for adolescent behavior. Finally, he alerts us to a possible historical development that has received relatively little attention—the emergence of something like a stable American lower class. This possibility seems to have been largely neglected in studies of our increasingly middle class society.

Success Goals and Opportunity Structures

The last of the major approaches to the problem of lower class group delinquency to be considered here is associated with Richard A. Cloward and Lloyd E. Ohlin.[9] Stated in its briefest form, the theory is as follows: American culture makes morally mandatory the seeking of success goals but differentially distributes the

[9] The full statement of the approach is in Richard A. Cloward and Lloyd E. Ohlin, *Delinquency and Opportunity* (Glencoe: The Free Press, 1960); see also Richard A. Cloward, "Illegitimate Means, Anomie and Deviant Behavior," *American Sociological Review*, Vol. 24 (April, 1959), No. 2, pp. 164–76.

morally acceptable means to these success goals, the legitimate opportunities that loom so large in the approach.

This gap between culturally universalized goals and structurally
limited means creates strain among lower class youths who aspire
to economic advancement. Such strain and alienation leads to the
formation of delinquent subcultures, that is, normative and belief
systems that specifically support and legitimate delinquency,
among those boys who blame the system rather than themselves for
their impending or actual failure. The particular form of delinquent subculture—conflict, criminal, or retreatist (drug-using)—
which results depends on the nature of the local neighborhood
and, especially, on the availability of illegitimate opportunities,
such as stable crime careers as models and training grounds.

The criminal subculture develops in stable neighborhoods with
much regularized crime present; the conflict form develops in
really disorganized neighborhoods where not even illegitimate opportunities are available; the retreatist, or drug-use, subculture develops among persons who are double failures due either to internalized prohibitions against violence or theft or to the objective
unavailability of these solutions.

Intervening between the stress due to blocked aspirations and
the creation of the full-fledged subculture of whatever type is a
process of collectively supported "withdrawal of attributions of legitimacy from established social norms."

This process, coupled with the collective development of the relevant delinquent norms, serves to allay whatever guilt might have
been felt over the illegal acts involved in following the delinquent
norms.

Since the argument in *Delinquency and Opportunity* is, in many
ways, even more complicated than those associated with Cohen,
Short, and Miller, I will discuss only a few highlights.

On the question of who aspires to what, which is so involved in
the disagreements between Cohen and Miller, Cloward and Ohlin
take the position that it is not the boys who aspire to middle class
status—and, therefore, have presumably partially internalized the
middle class measuring rod—who form the raw material for delin-

quent subculture, but those who wish only to improve their economic status without any change in class membership. Thus, it is appropriate in their argument to say that the genitors of the delinquent subcultures are not dealing so much with an internal problem of self-esteem as with an external problem of injustice. Cohen says, in effect, that the delinquent subculture prevents self-blame for failure from breaking through, the reaction formation function of the delinquent subculture. Cloward and Ohlin say that the delinquent norm systems are generated by boys who have already determined that their failures, actual or impending, are the fault of the larger social order.

This insistence that it is the "system blamers" who form the grist for the subcultural mill leads Cloward and Ohlin into something of an impasse, it seems to me. They must, of course, then deal with the determinants of the two types of blame and choose to say that two factors are primarily relevant. First, the larger culture engenders expectations, not just aspirations, of success which are not met, and, second, there exist highly visible barriers to the fulfillment of these expectations, such as racial prejudice, which are defined as unjust.

These do not seem unreasonable, and, in fact, in the case of Negro youth, perhaps, largely fit the case. Cloward and Ohlin, however, are forced for what seems overwhelmingly polemical reasons into a position that the feeling of injustice must be objectively correct. Therefore, they say (1) that it is among those actually fitted for success where the sense of injustice will flourish and (2) that delinquent subcultures are formed by boys who do not essentially differ in their capacity to cope with the larger institutions from other boys. This point deserves some attention since it is so diametrically opposed to the Cohen position which states that some working class boys, especially lower working class boys, are unable to meet the demands of middle-class dominated institutions.

It is our impression that a sense of being unjustly deprived of access to opportunities to which one is entitled is common among those who become participants in delinquent subcultures. Delinquents tend to be persons who have been led to expect opportunities because of their potential ability to meet the formal, institutionally-established criteria of evaluation. Their sense of injustice arises from the failure of the system to fulfill these expectations. Their criticism is not directed inward since they regard themselves in comparison with their fellows as capable of meeting the formal requirements of the system. It has frequently been noted that delinquents take special delight in discovering hypocrisy in the operation of the established social order. They like to point out that it's "who you know, not what you know" that enables one to advance or gain coveted social rewards. They become convinced that bribery, blackmail, fear-inspiring pressure, special influence, and similar factors are more important than the publicly avowed criteria of merit.[10]

On the same page in a footnote, the authors go on to say that the research evidence indicates "the basic endowments of delinquents, such as intelligence, physical strength, and agility, are the equal of or greater than those of their nondelinquent peers."

The material in these quotations is so riddled with ambiguities it is difficult to know where to begin criticism, but we can at least point out the following. First, Cloward and Ohlin seem to be confusing the justificatory function of delinquent subcultures with their causation. All of these beliefs on the part of gang delinquents have been repeatedly reported in the literature, but, by the very argument of *Delinquency and Opportunity*, it is impossible to tell whether they constitute compensatory ideology or descriptions of objective reality.

Second, Cloward and Ohlin seem to be victims of their very general tendency to ignore the life histories of their delinquents.[11] Thus, there is no way of knowing really what these subcultural beliefs may reflect in the experience of the boys. Third, and closely related to the ignoring of life history material, is the problem of assessing the degree to which these gang boys are in fact prepared to

[10] Richard A. Cloward and Lloyd E. Ohlin, *Delinquency and Opportunity, op. cit.*, p. 117.

[11] This is the most fundamental weakness in the book. The delinquents in Thrasher, Cohen, and Miller were, in varying degrees, once recognizably children. Cloward and Ohlin's delinquents seem suddenly to appear on the scene sometime in adolescence, to look at the world, and to discover, "Man, there's no opportunity in my structure." It is instructive in this connection to note that the index to *Delinquency and Opportunity* contains only two references to the family. One says that the family no longer conducts occupational training; the other criticizes Miller's ideas on the female-based household.

meet the formal criteria for success. To say that they are intelligent, strong, and agile is to parody the criteria for advancement. Perhaps Cohen would point out that intelligent, agile, strong boys who begin the first grade using foul language, fighting among themselves, and using the school property as arts and crafts materials do not meet the criteria for advancement.

It is quite true that members of highly sophisticated delinquent gangs often find themselves blocked from whatever occupational opportunities there are, but this seems, often, the end product of a long history of their progressively cutting off opportunity and destroying their own capacities which may begin in the lower class family, as described by either Cohen or Miller, and continue through school failure and similar events. By the age of eighteen, many gang boys are, for all practical purposes, unemployable or need the support, instruction, and sponsorship of trained street-gang workers. Participation in gang delinquency in itself diminishes the fitness of many boys for effective functioning in the conventional world.

If, indeed, Cloward and Ohlin mean to include the more attitudinal and characterological criteria for advancement, then it seems highly unlikely that any large number of boys trained and prepared to meet these demands of the occupational world could interpret failure exclusively in terms which blame the system. They would have been too well socialized, and, if they did form a delinquent subculture, it would have to perform the psychological function of mitigating the sense of internal blame. This, of course, would make them look much like Cohen's boys.

In short, Cloward and Ohlin run the risk of confusing justification and causation and of equating the end with the beginning.

All of this is not to deny that there are real obstacles to opportunity for lower class boys. There are. These blocks on both the performance and learning sides are a major structural feature in accounting for much of the adaption of lower class populations. But they do not operate solely or even primarily on the level of the adolescent. They create a social world in which he comes of age, and, by the time he reaches adolescence, he may find himself cut off from the larger society. Much of the Cloward and Ohlin approach seems better as a theory of the origins of Miller's lower class culture. Each generation does not meet and solve anew the problems of class structure barriers to opportunity but begins with the solution of its forebears. This is why reform efforts can be so slow to succeed.

The positive contributions of the Cloward-Ohlin approach seem to me to lie less on the side of the motivational sources of subcultural delinquency, where I feel their attempts to clarify the ambiguities in Cohen have merely led to new ambiguities, but more on the side of the factors in local social structure that determine the type of subcultural delinquency.

The major innovation here is the concept of illegitimate opportunities which serves to augment Kobrin's almost exclusive emphasis on the differentially controlling impact of different slum environments. I do think that Cloward and Ohlin may make too much of the necessity for systematic, organized criminal careers in order for the illegitimate opportunity structure to have an effect, but the general argument has great merit.

In addition to the concept of illegitimate opportunities and closely related to it is the description, or speculation, concerning historical changes in the social organization of slums. Changes in urban life in the United States may have truly produced the disorganized slum devoid of the social links between young and old, between children and older adolescents which characterized the slums described by Thrasher. Certainly, the new conditions of life seem to have created new problems of growing up, though our knowledge of their precise impact leaves much to be desired.

Conclusion

. . . As I have indicated, there have been some profound changes in the way social theorists view the processes of gang formation and persistence. These, I believe, derive only partially . . . from changes in the facts to be explained. Indeed, we must wait for a study of gangs which will approach Thrasher's in thoroughness before we can know if there are new facts to be explained. Nor do I believe that the changes in viewpoint have come about entirely because old theories were shown to be inadequate to old facts. Both Cohen and Cloward and Ohlin feel that older theorists did not deal with the problem of the origins of delinquent subcultures, but only with the transmission of the subculture once developed. A careful reading of Thrasher indicates that such is not the case.

All in all, though, it does not seem like much fun any more to be a gang delinquent. Thrasher's boys enjoyed themselves being chased by the police, shooting dice, skipping school, rolling drunks. It was fun. Miller's boys do have a little fun, with their excitement focal concern, but it seems so desperate somehow. Cohen's boys and Cloward and Ohlin's boys are driven by grim economic and psychic necessity into rebellion. It seems peculiar that modern analysts have stopped assuming that "evil" can be fun and see gang delinquency as arising only when boys are driven away from "good."

GANG BOY

Except for material in brackets, which is interpolation by the editor, this is part of a tape recording made by him. All names and certain other identifying features have been changed.

[WHEN THE following was recorded, Hank was 18 and no longer attending school. He lived with his parents in a small, rented, tract house "on the wrong side of the tracks" in a western city of some 100,000 population. Hank was unemployed. He had never worked for pay to any extent, perhaps a total of two weeks in his entire life.]

I was born in Cleveland. My folks come from there. My dad didn't have much education. He used to be a day laborer, then he commenced driving a cab. When the war broke out he come to Dixville here to work in a defense plant. Them days he did real well. The money come rolling in. We bought a house, a new car. Then, boom! The war's over, he loses his job, we sell the house and go live in this crummy place.

Still in all, the old man ain't doing bad. He drives truck. We don't worry about eating. One thing. We ain't never been on relief, that's for damn sure!

My dad's all right. When you talk to him, maybe he sounds kind of rough, but that's just the way he has. He don't mean nothing by it. He don't drink or fight. He never misses church. If I had his habits I'd be all right.

Ma's the nervous type, she worries a lot. But I guess I give her plenty of room to worry.

I got two brothers that are older than me. Ralph's married. I guess he was a little wild when he was young. He's been to Statesville twice, for armed robbery. I didn't learn no habits from him, though. He was too old for me to hang with. I didn't see too much of him.

Morris, he's single. I guess he's been in a little trouble, too. Been picked up by the Juvenile Detail a few times. I never knew what for. Right now he's in federal pen for drugs. There's a bum rap! The cops had it in for him. They kept tailing him and shaking him down, over and over and over. Just because once, when they give him a frisk, he got snotty and cracked wise to them. So they never forgot it. Every time they seen him on the street they stopped him and shook him down. They planted heroin in his car, they grabbed him and sent him up. That's why kids feel they've been robbed by the cops.

I've got an older sister, Caroline. She don't live in town. She got married a long time ago. She lives in Chicago. I guess she's doing all right.

I come after Caroline, then comes my brother George, then Mary. George is 15, I guess. Mary's 14.

I'll tell you this. We all get along. You don't hear no loud hollering and throwing things and like that. We get along good and we help each other.

I always got along good at home. Except, you know how it is, I've got a little sister. It was there a while, but no more. But you know how they are when they're little. Go past them, don't even touch them,—"Ma! He hit me!" Then your mother is after you, naturally. She don't want you hitting her little baby. But we get along good now.

My folks wasn't too strict when I was little. Later, they commenced clamping down. They got tighter and tighter. They didn't want me running around. But all my life I think I only got about three lickings. Three good ones.

I found out I dassen't tell Ma certain things. It made her nervous. But my dad, if I done something wrong, the best thing was to run right to him and tell him before somebody else did. If he found out from me he'd even help me out of trouble. But if he got it from somebody else, then I caught hell.

Rat Packs

[Q.] *Is the bunch you hang out with what the papers call a rat pack?*

[A.] Christ, no! I been running around since I was in grade school. I've been on probation, in county jail and reformatories. I been arrested, Christ! It must be 125, maybe 150 times. Still, that don't make me a rat pack hoodlum.

Take this fight we had out in Portertown. This kid Pete, he just had an operation on his eyes, he belongs in our outfit. He was going to get his eyesight back, you know, but it was pretty poor. He went out to see this girl out in Portertown. This other guy come up, and I guess he liked this girl pretty well, and he didn't want Pete hanging around. They got in a fight. The bastard blinded Pete in one eye, damn near blinded him in the other. Now he's worse off in both eyes than he was before.

So Pete told this Portertown jerk we'd be out there to meet them. The guy says any time, any place, if we wanted to fight it out, they'd be ready.

So we spread it around there was going to be a gang fight and we'd meet in a certain drive-in restaurant. Word spreads like wildfire any time there's going to be a good fight or a party. Gangs from other towns, they come over to help us. We had quite a little bundle of guys, about two hundred. Good God! You should have seen it! We must have had 40 cars. They was stacked up four blocks back. There wasn't a foot between each bumper. We went all the way out there that way, and if the first car cleared a corner, all the others piled right through. We didn't stop for a thing. It was like a funeral. It was going to be one, too, if we could lay hands on them guys!

We walked down this street, coming toward where the fight was supposed to take place, and here they were. They had hot pokers and clubs and hooks and knives and 'most everything you could think of. So we walked up to this white picket fence, a guy just got through painting it, everybody gathered around, and when we walked away, good God! All that was sitting there was the four corner posts. The rest, everybody held in their hands. Of course, we had tire irons, too, and some knives. One guy had a zip gun, one of them homemade things, but they shoot good.

We jumped them guys and kicked the shit out of them. We knocked them all over the lot. One of our guys kicked a Portertowner in the head and stomped up and down on him until there wasn't nothing left of his face but bloody meat. You couldn't see his eyes no more. There was busted heads, busted arms, teeth all over the street—it was a bloody mess.

Right away, the papers called us a rat pack. We wasn't no such a thing. What I call a rat pack is like the Death Heads. From Lawrence. There's 300 of them. To get in you've got to have done time. Most of them have been in Statesville, but you can get in if you've been to the Ref, too. Those guys, they've been away for robbery, burglary, there's even a couple done time for murder. Those guys, they'll see a harmless fellow on the street, they'll make it their business to kick his ass. Just for the hell of it. They'll steal anything that ain't nailed down. They'll bust up a party and tear up the house.

[Q.] *Well, haven't you done some of those things?*

[A.] Yeah, but with them it's night after night after night! They make a *business* of it! They *mean* to be ornery. They're *looking* for trouble. *That's* a rat pack. My gang's not like that. Guys don't go out and just naturally look for a fight. If they've been drinking, if they run into trouble, sure, they'll fight. But they don't beg for it. What we done in Portertown, that wasn't rat-packing. Pete wasn't out there looking for trouble. When this jerk jumped him there wasn't nothing left for us to do but fight. Either that or be called chicken shit. You let one guy run you off and the rest of them are going to try it. If you let one, you let them all. You damn sure ain't going to get along doing that!

What burns me is, for every rat pack there must be 500 decent gangs. Every neighborhod's got a dozen. Still, let any five, six boys be seen together and we're a rat pack.

A rat pack is more or less what the older folks laid on kids. Believe me, there's a lot of harm done by the papers and people calling us all rat-packers. You lay a name like that on a kid and he'll start living up to it.

They lay all this stuff on kids alone. Well, what about these old guys that's committing all these sex crimes and murders and stuffing bodies in trunks and all like that? What kids do ain't half that!

Beginnings of Street Life

[Q.] *How did you first start hanging out, do you remember?*
[A.] You wouldn't believe it, but when I was nine, ten, I used to be bashful. I just didn't want to go nowhere. We didn't even have no television then, but I'd just lay around by the radio, listen to that all night. 'Till time to go to bed. Or I'd read. Fiction. True stuff. All them old books, like *Smoke Blows West*, *Daniel Boone*, westerns, stuff like that. Mysteries. Football stories. Baseball stories. Comics once in a while. You couldn't get me out of the house. My ma would say, "For Pete's sake! Why don't you go outside and play?"

I was about eleven, twelve, when I commenced going out a little. There was these guys I went to school with. We'd ride home together on our bike. One of us would say, "Where you going tonight?" "Where *you* going?" "Well," he'd say, "let's go over and get Johnny. He'll go riding with us." So we'd go get him. There'd be three, four guys that way. There wasn't nothing else to do. You don't want to stay home all the time.

After a while it wasn't just bike riding. We'd maybe go to a show. Or we'd get together some money and go to Ferry's [a concession park], ride the roller coaster.

Hanging out happens gradual. You don't realize you're starting a gang. You feel jittery at home. You don't know what to do with yourself. You know the other guys will be on a certain corner. Or a malt shop. You say, "Hell! I haven't nothing better to do. I'll just walk over and kick it around a little with the fellows." You get so you head for that spot 'most every night.

Then, from hanging around, you commence cutting up now and then. When I was twelve, thirteen, we used to think it was smart to walk past a newsstand and when the guy turned his back we'd snatch a bunch of papers. If he seen us we'd throw them in his face and run. We just did it to be ornery. You did what the others did.

The first thing I ever took to amount to anything was when I was twelve. Me and Sloppy started out to make a night of it. Well, that night seemed awful long, boy, once you got in the middle of it! We didn't have nothing to do. We was kind of sleepy, we wanted to keep going, so naturally, we was going to find something to do.

We was sitting around, and we seen this bicycle parked up on a lawn, right in front. It was a real keen deal, one of them English makes. The guy left it out there where it had no business being, so we jumped on it and took off. Sloppy was driving it. I hung on the back. We hadn't had it no more than a couple of hours, when zooooom! The juvenile officers come around the corner in a car. We tried to get away but we hit some gravel and slid and fell, ass over tea kettle. We busted out a couple of spokes. They took us downtown and called our folks to come down. The guy that owned the bike come down, too. He was a grown guy. The cops told him they didn't think we realized how serious it was, what we done— and we didn't, at the time. So they let us go after our folks paid for the damage.

By this time we had quite a few fellows that was hanging around regular. There was never any meetings. Just: "You going to be in the malt shop tonight?" "Yeah!" There was nothing else you could do.

[Q.] *What about that Boys' Club about a mile away from your house? Ever go there when you had nothing else to do?*

[A.] You can't go to no Boys' Club. There was probably some kids that went there, to shoot pool or something, but we didn't go. A club, you want to be taken for what you are. You don't want to have to keep your hands clean and do this and don't do that. That's what gets some guys down. They just don't go for stuff like that. These sissy places, a couple guys go there, and they're shooting pool, say. And the cue slips, and one of them says, "Oh, shit!" That's all, boy! Out! They throw you out.

So we kept on hanging out. And the trouble commenced. Picked up for hitching rides. Picked up for curfew. A couple of us was feeling ornery one night, didn't have nothing to do, so we went over and let the air out of some guy's tires. Quite a few times we got picked up for drinking. We got throwed in jail a couple times for fighting at a party. We wasn't fighting, we was arguing. You know, you get a couple, three deals like that and you get so you haven't got a bit of use for cops.

There's another thing. They lock us up for having beer in the car. Why don't they do something about the grownups that sell us the stuff? They're more at fault than we are. If they wasn't to sell it to us we wouldn't be getting drunk, would we?

It's gone on and on like that. I been downtown maybe 125 or 150 times. They just suspended my license, for drunk driving. I run into the side of a house. I got 30 days, license suspended, and now I have to drive without a license.

[Q.] *Hank, were there any guys your age, when you started hanging out, who found other things to do? Who didn't hang out?*

[A.] Oh, yeah! I'll tell you why that is. Everybody *wants* to hang out when he's a certain age, because he's got to get away from the monotony. Some *don't* hang out because they're scared. They hear you get put in jail if you belong to a gang.

[Q.] *You mean there's nobody at all that age who just wouldn't care to belong to a street gang?*

[A.] Oh, them! They're scared the group wouldn't accept them. They're the studious type, book worms. What do they do for fun? They go to the show. Make popcorn at home. Cook fudge or something.

[Q.] *Well, why would this fellow want to do that while you fellows want to be on the street?*

[A.] I don't know what would make you want to hang out. Maybe just one night you went out and had some fun at a party or something and kept on going like that. Maybe you think that's more fun than making fudge. *I* for damn sure don't care to make fudge!

Gang Organization and Behavior as Hank Sees Them

The papers talk about a gang like it's a club, with officers and regular members and all. There are groups like that, but for every one of them there's hundreds of the other kind.

My gang don't have a name. It's just the gang. A fellow wants to hang out with us, he belongs. Anybody from our part of town can belong. I couldn't tell you how many is in our gang because it don't work that way. Today we might have ten, next week twenty guys. That don't mean we don't have a certain number of more or less regulars, that you see 'most every night. And if you was to ask me if a certain guy belongs with us I could pretty well tell you. But we didn't vote him in. He just got in. And he can leave any time.

We don't have officers and we don't have dues, and we don't have regular meetings. We don't have no rules.

You know which side of town a guy comes from, and if he's from your side he can belong. Now, there's no offense in a guy's being from a different side of town. Some of them fellows come over to our side and we get along fine with them. But they wouldn't really be part of our gang.

You meet a guy and ask, "Where are you from?" The other guy says, "I'm from the north side." Another guy says the south side. Them are more or less the gangs—the side of town you come from.

But even on our side, there's thousands of fellows we wouldn't consider part of our gang. Our fellows are the ones you more or less have dealings with. If there's a party or something, you'd rather mention it to them than somebody else. You got to know them in school or from the neighborhood. They're your buddies.

There's some guys don't get in with us. He's got to be our kind, a good sport. I wouldn't want to go with a guy, if he seen a girl, if you go to her house, he'd have to use the roughest language. I wouldn't want to go around with a guy like that because, you go to a girl's house, and he starts that crap, and then they say, "So-and-so come over last night with so-and-so, and boy, I mean to say, they were using the rottenest language!" *They* were. And *you* didn't use that language.

It don't make any difference how much money a fellow has or hasn't got. Lots of guys from rich neighborhoods, you couldn't find better guys. But then there's got to be a couple of wise guys in there that thinks just because their folks has provided for them a better car, better than you could provide for yourself, well, they think they're it. Well, you got to consider who paid for the car. If you paid for it, you're entitled to a higher standing, because you bought it, it wasn't provided for you. If I have a $500 car and you have a $500 car, but I paid for mine and you didn't, I deserve to rate higher. I got more to boast about.

Now, a guy don't have to be a good fighter to belong, at least not so far as I'm concerned. I don't even care if he's a sissy, so long as he minds his own business. If trouble starts, he don't have to be a Joe Louis, but he can't run off. I myself, I like to go out with a guy that isn't going to run from it. Now, a lot of times you run into guys that aren't going to have nothing to do with that fight. That's the kind of guy I don't like to go out with. I wouldn't want him part of my gang, because if it's your fight, you don't want to chicken out.

A fellow like that, if he hangs around, you don't drop him, because we don't have rules about dropping guys. What'll happen is this. He'll come up and say, "Where are you going tonight? Let's go get drunk." And I'll say, "Nah! I don't feel like it now. I think I'll go to a show." And if he says, "Good! I'll go, too," then you go and pick up a paper and look through and say, "Aw, shit! There ain't a thing here I want to see. Oh, well, I guess I'll go home and go to bed. Well, I'll see you later." So he'll take off and you'll go to a show or a girl's house. Only you didn't want him around. He'll catch on sooner or later.

A guy can belong, no matter who he is, if he's a right guy. If there's a colored fellow, or a Puerto Rican, or an Italian, that don't make a bit of difference. I don't go for that stuff about only certain fellows can belong. Everybody's as good as the next one, so long as he does what's expected.

Nobody is the leader, the boss, in our gang. When we decide to do something, each time it's somebody, spur of the moment, that sets it up. He's the leader. Next time another guy says, "Let's do this and that." He's the leader.

Very seldom do we plan something in advance. We don't say, "Let's do this and that tomorrow." Usually we decide it a minute in advance. Oh, once in a while a guy will say, "Let's meet tomorrow night and go out and snatch some hubcaps." But usually you don't plan that far ahead.

I seen an article by one of them *experts*. He says every gang is supposed to have a president and a secretary. He says there's a social president and a fighting president. Well, I never ran into a club like that. He says there's one guy they call a war counselor. I never heard of it. But I guess that could happen in a gang that wanted to be known as the roughest gang around.

In name gangs, more or less, you have to be voted in. Some, you get in on how tough you are. Name gangs, like the Dirty Dozen, the Coffin Chasers, they're likely to get pretty tough. They're more than likely the rat-packers. One gang fights another. That happens very often. When these clubs go by a name, then one gang has got to be the underdog. And that one don't want to take that name.

ABOUT FIGHTS

Every now and then it's fun to have a fight. It's like going to a party. You enjoy going to a party and you enjoy a fight every now and then.

There's two types of gang fights. One is where somebody from a gang gets hurt by a guy from another outfit. So the two gangs arrange to meet and have it out. The other kind is where two name gangs always consider each other enemies. They're going to fight every time they meet, any place, any time.

I don't consider it one bit smart to go around looking for a fight. But if you've got to mix it up, you want to be the ones that are able to walk away when it's over.

ABOUT GIRLS

All us guys have three hobbies: Girls, parties, cars. And fights, because any of them three can start a fight.

I used to be bashful with girls, all thumbs, but I damn sure got over it. I go with lots of girls and I've got a kind of steady girl. And I wouldn't marry a goddamn one from this whole town. They're all the same. They're none of them any good.

[Q.] *Oh, now! You don't really mean that?*

[A.] The hell I don't! We'll take three or four of them out on a party, and before the night's over, Christ! Each of us has laid the same girl. There ain't a girl in this town, if you took her out more than twice, that you couldn't get it. I'll bet you ten to one! Because there isn't a girl here you can't kiss. And you ask anybody—if you can kiss a girl, you can make her. Or if you can't, you didn't pull the right tactics.

I'm no angel, but I wouldn't marry a girl that I heard this guy and that guy had. I'd marry one that had dates, but she can't have gone all the way, with a different guy every night. No, sir!

With us, there's two kinds of girls. There is *your* girl and *just* a girl. You don't mess around with somebody else's *your* girl. You talk to her at parties but you don't date her. Then there are *just* girls—everybody's property. Any fellow in the gang can date them. Even ten guys could take the one girl out and all have her. Them kind are out-and-out lays.

I've got this steady girl. That don't mean I don't go with other girls. But they're *just* girls, pigs.

[Q.] *How about your steady girl? Don't you expect you might marry her some day?*

[A.] Nope! I go with her just for kicks. I'm not serious about her. I don't intend to marry her. But she don't know that. She'd like to marry me, but right now she's satisfied with what she's getting.

I'll tell you something. I'm afraid of women. I don't mean *afraid*. I'm afraid of their *ways*. The reason I don't want to get married too soon is you're liable to get hold of the wrong girl. You think you're doing everything that's all right; then, when you get married, get a home, why you find out she's been running around with another guy. Then you're going to break up, and there goes everything you ever worked for.

I'll tell you who I would marry, when I'm ready. A nice girl. A nice girl, she's more or less like a school girl. Lived out in the country. Don't like to run around. Doesn't lead a fast life. A good girl. I'd marry that kind. She was home with her mother, or going to night school, or working nights. I'd much rather go with something like that than with these things down here. If a girl was run-

ning around when you married her, she's going to be running
around after you married her.

PARTIES

You hear a lot of nonsense about party crashing. Well, there's
not a party that hasn't been crashed, and there isn't a girl that run
one that didn't expect it to be crashed. That don't make it right,
but they've done it to our parties, we can just as well do it to
theirs.

It doesn't necessarily mean trouble to crash a party. A lot of
them, the guys are good natured, everybody has a good time. But
then there's some places that just don't want other guys around. I
don't know whether it's because they can't handle their girls themselves, they can't keep them, or what. That's what causes a lot of
party fights, boy!

Last Friday we heard about this party the other side of town.
We goes over there. We kept driving around in front of the place
and finally we decided to go in. These fellows kept staring at us.
Popping off. They wouldn't pop off loud enough so we could hear
them. So we went over and asked them what the hell they was
staring at us for. Then this one guy told our guy to shut his mouth,
that it wasn't any of his business.

So he said, "Well, I'm gonna make it my business!"

The other guy said, "Well, let's see you and me go out in the
back and we'll find out who's gonna make it whose business!"

So they did. Pretty soon everybody wanted a go at it. It was true
blue, I mean! When the cops come, everybody scattered. Nobody
got caught. I wouldn't say there was too much damage. Maybe a
couple of black eyes and busted lips. That's about all.

Some of these smart guys, they think the tougher you are at a
party, the higher you rate. They try to show off in front of the
girls. If everybody would mind their own business and try to get
along, I think the party would be much more fun. But when these
guys are popping off about they're going to do this, do that, well,
they're not going to do nothing! Because nobody's going to stand
for it. Me, I don't think it's a bit smart to get tough at a party.

Another thing I can't see is when you go to a party and some girls leave their purses in the bedroom, there's got to be one wise guy that's going to go in and rifle them purses. That causes a lot of trouble. If you're at a party, Christ! That stuff isn't yours. You've been invited to the party, they've been nice enough to invite you, why the hell don't you keep hands off things that don't belong to you? Leave with what you come in with? But no! A lot of guys won't do that.

THE GANG AND CRIME

Most of the stuff me and the gang get into is just fun, raising hell, or orneriness. You wouldn't call it crime. But I guess we've done things you could. There ain't a kid that hasn't stolen something—cigarettes or a can of beer or a comic. Hub caps.

I remember there was three Chevvies sitting out there on Marlin Boulevard once, where the aircraft plant is. Well, three of our gang had Chevvies. We all went down there one night and when we was through, good God! We had all them cars stripped down to bare metal. We took the engines, wheels, dashboard equipment, steering wheels, every goddamn thing but the shell. You should have seen them silly things sitting there after we left!

I might roll a drunk, maybe get in a robbery. Snatch me some hubcaps. But certain things I wouldn't do, gang or no gang. Shaking down fags—that's dirty business. I wouldn't peddle dope. And I wouldn't commit one of them sex offenses, messing with little girls. I've got absolutely no use for that and I wouldn't give the time of day to any bastard that would do a thing like that. There's a limit.

ABOUT COPS

I don't hate all cops. The cops that kids hate earn it. Figure it out. I'll bet there isn't but three out of every ten people in the country that hasn't been pinched at least once. Now, that's a lot of people. If there's one bad cop, there's a lot of people hating him. Cops should think of that.

There's some decent cops. Let you get away with stuff. Dixville isn't too bad that way, as long as you're not living in the bad part of town, where we live. That's where you get the lousy cops.

What I mean by a good cop is he don't look to be hauling you in right away. Say you're under age, you're drinking. A cop is supposed to run you in. A decent cop won't run you in just for drinking. A cop you could get along with would be one, he'd say, "Well, as long as you fellows are only drinking beer, go ahead." I'd rather see kids sitting around with a can of beer than I would with a marijuana cigarette!

I've got nothing against cops or judges or probation officers, so long as they're decent. I just don't like to be robbed.

GOOD DEEDS

Why do people only tell about the bad things? Why don't they mention that gangs do good? If a guy has a blowout, you help him fix it. If you're working in a gas station and one of your buddies is broke, you let him drive his car in and give him a couple gallons of gas when the boss isn't around. Many a kid that wasn't living home, got kicked out, I've taken out, bought hamburgers for, fed him in the morning. You never hear them college professors tell about the good things gangs do.

Leaving the Gang

[Q.] *Sooner or later, you're going to move out of the gang, aren't you? You don't expect to be around the same bunch the rest of your life?*

[A.] Oh, yeah! You give it up after a while. I'm about ready to quit this kind of life. Get me a job. Settle down.

[Q.] *Is that what happens to most of the fellows you know about? They get a little older and settle down?*

[A.] Oh, yeah! They wisen up and begin to see their mistakes. I guess you wouldn't call it mistakes. It's just you look back and see what you had done before. When you was a kid.

[Q.] *Hank, you talk about kids a lot. When does a fellow stop being a kid and become a man, settle down, take responsibilities, work, make a living, support a family, things like that?*

[A.] I'd say when you get married.

[Q.] *You're a kid until you get married?*

[A.] Yeah. Because until you get married you're going to keep on doing the same things.

Summing Up

[Q.] *Hank, if someone were going to do a character sketch of you, describe what you're like, say "Hank's a good fellow, Hank's a bad fellow," this, that. If you were describing yourself, what would you say?*

[A.] Oh, I don't know. Just a kid that lives on the worst side of town in terms of where to live. Likes to go out with girls. Interested in cars all the time. That's about the main interests. Cars and women.

[Q.] *Is this fellow a good sport?*

[A.] Oh, yeah!

[Q.] *Is he honest?*

[A.] Yeah. With his friends.

[Q.] *Is he a good citizen?*

[A.] What do you mean by that?

[Q.] *Works, supports his family, helps keep his community decent. And so on. Being a good citizen might mean you carry your own freight.*

[A.] Oh, yeah! I say yes to that. He's a good citizen, this guy.

[Q.] *Suppose a young fellow—a kid—came to you and asked if it would be a good thing, a smart thing, for him to get in with a gang something like yours. Imagine he asks your advice. What would you tell him?*

[A.] Knowing what I know, I'd tell young guys to kind of hold it down a little bit. Go with the gang, but don't be so damn wild as I was, because when you're as wild as I was, it's hard on your folks, they worry a lot. I'd just hold it down to a mild roar if I had it to do all over again. But I sure as hell wouldn't advise him to make fudge. But books, there's no harm in reading books. I read books myself. But I don't go overboard with it. I'd advise him to finish high school. If he has a chance, go to college.

[Q.] *Do you ever worry about the way you've been going, up to now?*

[A.] Yeah. I was always worried one of these days I'm going to end up in the can for a long, long time.

[Q.] *But still, that hasn't stopped your hanging out.*

[A.] No, but it's made me stop and think for quite a bit. I'm going to show my will power very shortly.

Part III

THE SEARCH FOR EXPLANATIONS

INTRODUCTION

A MAJOR undertaking of criminology is the accretion of data on the etiology of delinquency and crime. What turns men to murder and robbery? Why does one man commit crime while his brother remains law-abiding? Questions like these have intrigued man since time immemorial. He has answered by guess, wishful thinking, superstitious belief, philosophy, and occasionally by reasonably scientific investigation.

The student of criminology wants to know, "What causes delinquency and crime?" The realistic answer is, we don't know. Not all of our investigations, taken together, have yielded up a single *cause* of delinquency and crime, if we define cause as an *invariant relationship*, as Dressler does in this section.

But if we know of no *cause*, we have been able to demonstrate the existence of *correlations* between certain factors on the one hand and delinquency and crime on the other.

Turning to a search for correlations, for clues as to the etiology of law-violating behavior, we turn first to biological factors. Delinquency and criminality are not inherited; there is no gene in the chromosomes for either. On the other hand, a consideration of biological inheritance is not altogether irrelevant in studying the genesis of illegal or antisocial behavior. Ashley Montagu reviews and criticizes latter-day Lombrosians and others who, in his estimation, overemphasize the role of biological and constitutional factors in determining conduct. He does not denigrate those factors, but he does insist that culture is the controlling influence and that crime is essentially of social origin.

What is roughly termed *race* is a biological condition. Much attention has been directed to the differential crime rate among the several racial groups, sometimes on the assumption that because an individual is of a given race he is therefore more (or less) likely to become criminal than is a person of another race. The article by

Green investigates comparative law-violation rates of whites and blacks.

We next consider evidence and conjecture on the etiology of deviant behavior from the psychological-psychiatric point of departure. Intelligence, which is determined only partly by inheritance, has received intensive study. Shulman's "Intelligence and Delinquency" reviews the results.

What part do other mental states play? Dr. Manfred S. Guttmacher's interpretation will be found in "The Psychiatric Approach to Crime and Correction."

For centuries man has been fascinated by the seeming fact that climate, seasonal variations in temperature, and other features of the physical environment influence human behavior. Lombroso discussed this in relation to the incidence of criminal behavior, and in our century, *Uniform Crime Reports,* published by the F.B.I., have frequently reported that the commission of certain categories of crime increases and decreases quite consistently with changing seasons. More sophisticated observers have attempted to interrelate physical environment and sociocultural phenomena. In "Geography and Crime," Joseph Cohen presents provocative data along this general line.

Another approach to the investigation of the interrelations of physical environment has been the study of human ecology. The contribution by Clifford R. Shaw and H. D. McKay is a trail-blazing report of early research oriented to the ecological concept of "delinquency areas." The excerpt covers findings for Chicago only, but the work itself included other urban communities. The conclusions, given in Part III, apply to all cities studied by Shaw and McKay.

Bernard Lander reexamines the ecological interpretations of Shaw, McKay, and others. His study, conducted in Baltimore, finds support for the thesis that delinquent behavior is related dynamically to the community, but no support for the hypothesis that the processes of city growth, as such, provide the basic explanation of differential delinquency rates in a metropolitan community. Lander concludes that the delinquency rate is fundamentally related to the *anomie* that develops under conditions of urban life.

Given an area of high delinquency rate, why do some youthful residents become delinquent while others do not? One answer is provided by Walter C. Reckless and Simon Dinitz in "Self-Concept as an Insulator Against Delinquency."

Broken homes, long assumed to have a bearing on delinquency and perhaps criminality, are the subject of Thomas Monahan's contribution. He reviews earlier studies, reports on his own, and revises some notions on the subject generally.

Glaser and Rice offer one of the best research explanations of the relations among crime and certain economic factors in their article, "Crime and Economic Condition."

The balance of Part III, devoted to theoretical formulations, begins with Sellin's "Culture Conflict and Crime."

Sutherland's "The Theory of Differential Association" has been very influential in criminological thinking. It is a general theory attempting to explain all of criminal behavior. Probably those who followed Sutherland have claimed more for it than did Sutherland himself. And he has had his critics, the selection by Sheldon Glueck being an example.

Robert K. Merton's "Social Structure and Anomie" is included here under the title "The Doctrine of 'Socially Derived Sin.'" It is useful as an approach to a general theory not only of crime causation but of other aspects of contemporary life.

THE CONCEPT OF CAUSE

DAVID DRESSLER

David Dressler, *Sociology: The Study of Human Interaction* (New York: Alfred A. Knopf, Inc., 1969), pp. 569–570.

IF YOU accept the statements of those who claim to know, crime and delinquency are "caused" by:

1. Too much parental affection during the individual's childhood.
2. Not enough parental affection during the individual's childhood.
3. Too much corporal punishment in the home.
4. Not enough corporal punishment in the home.
5. Inconsistent corporal punishment in the home.
6. Underprivileged childhood.
7. Overprivileged childhood.
8. Too much education.
9. Insufficient education.
10. Absence of religious training.
11. Overstringent religious training.
12. Broken homes.
13. Unbroken homes when they would have been more wholesome if broken by divorce.
14. Poverty.
15. Affluence.
16. Tough police.
17. Overpermissive police.
18. Feeblemindedness.
19. Intellectual brilliance.
20. Comic books.
21. Depiction of violence in movies and on TV.

Every one of these "causes" has been advanced at one time or another, by a supposed "expert" before an official body investigating crime and delinquency. Obviously, the persons testifying cannot all have been correct, since so much of the testimony is contradictory. What can we believe?

In the first place, we *know* we have found no cause of crime or delinquency if by cause is meant an *invariant relationship*. A factor, let us say broken homes, would have to be present, without any exception, in every instance where an individual is found to have committed an illegal act. And not a single instance of a broken home must be found among those who have not committed illegal acts. Only then could we properly claim to have a cause of crime or delinquency. We have none.

According to reasonably scientific data we do have some *causal* or *etiological* factors that seem to be *correlated* with crime and delinquency. That is, they appear more frequently, per capita, among the non-law-abiding than in the general population. The inference is that they play some part in producing illegal behavior. Among these are personality disturbances and certain family conditions, neighborhood influences, peer group associations, and economic circumstances.

THE BIOLOGIST LOOKS AT CRIME

M. F. ASHLEY MONTAGU

M. F. Ashley Montagu, "The Biologist Looks at Crime," *Annals of the American Academy of Political and Social Science*, CCXVII (September 1941), 46–57. At the time of publication, Ashley Montagu was Associate Professor of Anatomy in Hahnemann Medical College and Hospital, in Philadelphia.

As A biologist, interested in the origin, the development, and the functioning of man, I have always laid it down as a fundamental principle, from which no deviation could be allowed, that man must be studied as a *whole*. Man is an organism whose physical and mental functioning is *very* considerably influenced by cultural factors. This cultural influence is so great, and begins its unremitting action so early, that its effects, to a very large extent, become incorporated in the tissues of those who have been exposed to such influence. It is not merely a matter of the cultural effect being added to, or superimposed upon, the physical organism but an actual incorporation of the effects of these cultural influences into the physical organism so that they become an inseparable part of it.

Whatever lip service may be paid to this view in theory, I am not aware that it is given much attention in practice. Yet a full understanding of this view seems to me of the first importance for all social scientists, and more particularly for criminologists.

It is, in my view, due principally to a lack of the understanding of the relationship which exists between the physical organism and the influence of culture upon it that so many of the investigations and interpretations which have been made of the causes of crime have fallen into serious error. For this reason it seems to me of importance to discuss the essentials of this relationship here, before proceeding further.

The Biologist's View of Criminal Behavior

Criminal behavior is, from the viewpoint of a purely mechanistic biologist (which, for methodological reasons, I sometimes am), behavior like any other behavior, and is mechanistically to be explained in precisely the same terms. From the standpoint of the mechanistic biologist, criminal behavior is a form of behavior which, like most others, serves the purposes of the organism, but which has been arbitrarily delimited by a social group and termed "criminal." The biologist may fully recognize that the behavior which a particular society terms "criminal" may have important social consequences for the group, but since these consequences are not likely to produce either a temporary or a permanent change in the biological character of the group, such social consequences are no concern of his. The "criminal" behavior which is socially recognized still remains behavior which, from his standpoint, cannot be differentiated from any other *normal* behavior of the organism.

I emphasize ·*normal* here, because I wish to draw attention to the fact that criminal behavior is, from the biological standpoint, as normal as any other form of behavior. Thus, for example, many acts "committed" by lower animals, and by our anthropoid relations, within the social groups of which they are members, would in most human societies be regarded as "criminal." The taking of food which others have secured for themselves, the combat for females often resulting in the death of the weaker animal, to name but two common acts, are normal forms of behavior among many mammalian groups. In practically all human societies the "stealing" of food from another is regarded as a crime. In some human societies combat for females is allowable, and even the death of one of the combatants does not render the act a crime. But in most human societies such an act *is* regarded as a crime.

Without multiplying examples, it should be clear, then, that any segment of normal behavior can by a social group be made unallowable, and its overt expression be defined as a "crime."

Behavior defined as criminal does not render such behavior abnormal from either the biological or the social viewpoint. It merely renders it socially undesirable, and its undesirability is emphasized by the punishments which are prescribed for its expression, and which are supposed to serve as deterrents to its performance. From the standpoint of the biologist it is, nonetheless, perfectly normal behavior.

This is a fact which, when judgments of "criminal" behavior are made, is often neglected. Many students of crime tend rather to approach the study of criminal behavior as if such behavior were in itself abnormal, as if there were something intrinsically "wrong" with the organism exhibiting this "wrong" behavior. The persistent and practically serious error committed here is, quite unjustifiably, to translate a judgment of social value into one of biological value. Much of the thinking and writing about crime, in America as in Europe, is vitiated by this serious error. It is this error which has to a very large extent been responsible for the belief that there exists some relation between criminal behavior and the biological structure of the organism. Some recent examples of this will be dealt with a little later in this article. Meanwhile, it remains necessary to deal with the relationship existing between the organism and the effect of culture upon it.

Relationship of Body, Mind, and Behavior

The physical basis of those structures which are subsequently organized to function as mind are to a large extent inherited, precisely as are all other structures of the body. This is an assumption, but it seems a perfectly legitimate one to make. The qualification "to a large extent" is a very necessary one, since, in man, the nervous system continues to develop long after birth, and is therefore appreciably influenced by the experience of the individual.

There is every reason to believe, as Edinger has pointed out, "that in certain parts of the nervous mechanism new connections can always be established through education." [1] And as Ranson has added, "The neurons which make up the nervous system of an adult man are therefore arranged in a system the larger outlines of

[1] Quoted in S. W. Ranson, *The Anatomy of the Nervous System* (Philadelphia: W. B. Saunders Co., 1939), p. 56.

which follow an hereditary pattern, but many of the details of which have been shaped by the experiences of the individual." [2] It is evident that experience must play a considerable role in the development of the *structure* of the nervous system, and it should also be clear that the form of the nervous system which we know as *mind*—behavior—is dependent upon the interaction of several factors. These are primarily the inherited, *incompletely developed,* structure of the nervous system, and the *character of the external developing influences.*

Mind is a social product. It represents the social organization of previously unorganized nervous tissue, and the expression of that nervous tissue according to the cultural pattern of its organization, that is, in behavior. The hereditary determinants of the morphological character of the nervous system do not make a mind, but merely provide the cellular elements from which a mind may be organized. It is the cultural organization of such nervous cellular elements that *creates* mind. Genes do not create mind, but they do provide every individual with a somewhat different basic morphological pattern of cellular tissues. So that if it were possible to keep all other factors constant, differences in behavior, that is in mind, would still serve to distinguish every individual from every other individual. Such differences would express the action of the genetic differential and nothing else.

There is every reason to believe that the genetically determined nervous morphological differential is, in any human population, as variable as any of its physical characters. But once this has been granted, it must be said that there is equally good reason to believe—and this is the important point—that the observable differences in the behavior between different individuals is to a far larger extent determined by cultural factors than by the total number of biological factors which operate from within the individual. Chief among these biological factors is the microscopic structure of the nervous system itself, and it cannot here be too often emphasized that that very structure is itself, to the most important extent, structurally and physiologically, organized by the action, from birth to maturity, of cultural influences. It is principally to this

[2] S. W. Ranson, *loc. cit.*

unique capacity that the species Homo sapiens owes most of those qualities which are implied in the term "human being."

Therefore, the character of a human being's mind will to the most considerable extent depend upon the nature of the cultural influences to which it has been exposed. And as the cultural influences have varied, so will the mind, for the most part, vary. It should be obvious, too, that those cultural influences which exert their action earliest will have the most permanent effect upon the behavior of the individual. It has, of course, long been known that, with respect to the formation of habits, the earliest years of development are the most important.

If these statements have not yet been proved up to the hilt, it seems to me, as a human biologist and ecologist, that as a working hypothesis they represent the best approach which the student of crime can make to the understanding of "criminal" behavior in human societies. At the very least, if he is to lay any claim to being scientific in his work, it is a hypothesis which he must never cease to bear in mind and to apply. By so doing he will avoid the pitfalls of the extreme biologistic interpretation of criminal behavior on the one hand and of the extreme environmentalist interpretation on the other.

As a biologist it seems to me that the principal fact which all students of human behavior must continually hold before their minds is that man, alone among the members of the animal kingdom, is more dominantly and prominently a creature influenced by his cultural history than by his ancestral or individual biological history. And in this fact lies the uniqueness of man.

It is upon the failure to recognize this fact that all attempts to prove the dominance of the biological factor in the causation of crime have foundered. And we may now turn to an examination of some of the most recent of these attempts.

The Lombrosian Theory

Almost all scientific movements are as much the children of their time as the scientists through whom they have their being. One of the earliest schools of criminology, the Italian school, beginning with, and most prominently represented by, Lombroso, is a case in point. Lombroso, a physician, grew up in the age of Darwinism and Natural Selection. In Italy the fortification of Darwinism took the form of the collection of examples of vestigial structures which could be explained only on the basis that they had been derived from some earlier ancestral form. The Italians also particularly busied themselves with the collection of "atavistic" characters, that is, abnormal characters which were taken to be a reversion to an ancestral condition. When Darwin published the second edition of *The Descent of Man* in 1884, his references to such characters were for the most part supplied him by two Italian workers, Canestrini and Ottolenghi. Interestingly enough, under the influence of Lombroso, these two workers became leading criminologists. It need hardly be said that all three brought a strong biological bias to the study of the criminal. All three were physicians and all were strong supporters of Darwinism, Canestrini and Ottolenghi being actively interested in proving the origin of present from past forms by means of vestigial and "atavistic" structures. Is it any wonder, then, that in such a period and with such interests the school of Lombroso should have devoted itself to the attempt to prove that criminals, as a class, are characterized by a significantly higher proportion of vestigial and atavistic characters than is the normal population? Such characters were termed "stigmata of degeneration."

Among the "stigmata of degeneration" listed by Lombroso and his school were such characters as asymmetry of the head and skull, projecting eyebrows and jaws, high-pointed head, low retreating forehead, an unusually large or an unusually small head . . . and so on.

The interesting thing about such so-called "stigmata of degeneration" is that they are all perfectly normal characters distributed throughout the populations with which the Lombrosians dealt. When Lombroso's student Ferri found that 63 per cent of soldiers showed the stigmata of degeneration, Lombroso attempted to explain this startling discovery away by the suggestion that when the stigmata "are found in honest men and women, we may be dealing with criminal natures who have not yet committed the overt act because the circumstances in which they have lived protected them against temptation."

Thus, what in the end Lombroso stated was that individuals exhibiting stigmata will be prone to commit crimes under certain environmental conditions. Since almost all individuals exhibit one or another of these so-called "stigmata," we may unreservedly agree. But what Lombroso meant, and always reiterated, was that, in almost all cases, it was not the unfavorable environment which led to the commission of the crime, but the biological predisposition to commit it, externally advertised by the presence of stigmata. The stigmata were, by Lombroso, taken to be marks of biological inferiority, proof of the reversion to more primitive forms of biological organization which, in behavior, was reflected in primitive levels of response. This criminal behavior was inseparably associated with biological inferiority. The biological inferiority was held to be the cause of criminal behavior.

Professor Hooton's Conclusions

Interestingly enough, the most recent investigator of the relation between physical structure, as exhibited by external characters, and crime, Professor E. A. Hooton,[3] has come to conclusions very similar to those arrived at by Lombroso. Hooton is a physical anthropologist who has for many years been interested in the origin and evolution of man, and in the description, measurement, and analysis of the physical characters of skeletal and living groups. The interest and bias of his studies, like Lombroso's, have always been exclusively biologistic. Hence, when Hooton's report on 4,212 native white Old American prisoners and 313 native white civilians was published, the carry-over of his extreme biological bias to the planning of his investigation and the interpretation of his results was not altogether unexpected. . . . The errors of method and interpretation committed by Lombroso are all repeated by Hooton, except that Hooton does not specifically define the marks, or "stigmata," of biological inferiority but takes them to be *any of the*

[3] E. A. Hooton, *The American Criminal: An Anthropological Study,* Harvard University Press, 1939; *Crime and the Man,* Harvard University Press, 1939.

characters which are distinctive of the criminal aggregate when
compared with the civilian sample. . . .

Unlike Lombroso, Hooton did not commence with any precon-
ceived ideas of the nature of physical marks of inferiority, but was
content to allow the greater frequency with which certain physical
characters occurred in his criminal series as against his civilian series to indicate this.

In connection with Hooton's study it requires to be said that in
order to make any biological test of differential behavior, it is necessary that both the criminal series and the check noncriminal series investigated be in every respect similar except in the one condition of behavior. The two series must be drawn from the same
population or populations, from the same areas, and must come
from the same social, economic, occupational, and domestic levels.
When these requirements have been satisfied and a significantly
higher frequency of certain physical characters are found among
the criminals than among the noncriminals, it may legitimately be
inferred that there is some significant *association* between criminal
behavior and the presence of a high frequency of such characters
in an individual or in a group. But to infer from this that such
characters reflect the *cause* of criminal behavior is to misunder-
stand the nature of causation.

In his investigation Hooton did not satisfy the requirement of
equating the conditions of his two groups in all but those in which
they were being compared, and he did fall into the error of taking
one of the elements of a statistical association to be a cause of the
other. From Hooton's results it might, with more justice than is apparent in his choice of a cause, be said not only that is biological
inferiority not the cause of crime, but that crime is the cause of bi-.
ological inferiority. But even though a case could be made out for
it, such reasoning would be quite invalid.

For his criteria of "stigmata," Lombroso took characters which
were for the most part apelike. An examination of the characters
studied by Hooton by the biological standards of what are generally accepted to be advanced, primitive, and indifferent human
characters, yields results which are by no means surprising. By
such standards we find that Hooton's criminal series show, for the

combined anthropometric, indicial, and morphological characters, only 4 per cent of primitive, 15.8 per cent of indifferent, and the astonishing amount of 49.5 per cent of *advanced* characters, more frequently than the noncriminal population.

By biological standards, therefore, we see that Hooton's findings actually make his criminal series a considerably more advanced group biologically than his noncriminal series! Whatever this may mean, it will be obvious that from the standpoint of the biologist analyzing and judging Hooton's protocols, the criminal group reported upon by him is, on the whole, a physically more "superior" group than his noncriminals!

A Recent Investigation

In connection with this conclusion it may be of interest to note here that the most recent long-term study of juvenile delinquents of white, Negro, and mulatto stock has yielded very similar results. . . .

To investigate the possible relationships between biologic and constitutional factors and delinquent behavior in boys, a carefully controlled study was made at the Institute for Juvenile Research in Chicago by Drs. B. Boshes, S. Kobrin, E. Reynolds, and S. Rosenbaum, respectively a physician, a sociologist, a physical anthropologist, and a statistician. Four thousand boys were examined and measured in the grade schools of two socially and economically homogeneous delinquency areas in Chicago. The data obtained consisted of findings of a thorough medical examination and neurologic review, a series of sixty-three anthropometric measurements, indices, and modules, and extensive social and morphologic data.

The examiners had no prior knowledge of the behavior status of the subjects. For the purpose of this study, the legal definition of delinquency was considered inadequate. The delinquent groups here include, in addition to the apprehended or "official" delinquents, those boys who were known to have been engaged in delinquent practices in the community. The identifications of these latter delinquents were made by co-operating persons and agencies operating in the areas, but after the examination had been made. The total sample was separated into (1) three principal racial groupings—Caucasoid, Negroid, and Mexican; (2) two behavior categories—delinquent and nondelinquent; (3) age groups ranging from six to seventeen years. Social, economic, racial, and age variables were thus carefully controlled.

The findings of this as yet unpublished study indicate, briefly, the following: Although no significant physical differentiation between the behavior groups of white boys compared in metric and indicial items is apparent, such differentiation is found to exist between the Negro groups, especially in those items which are most indicative of racial membership. The analysis of extensive morphological data reveals that gross appearance is the selective factor which consistently accounts for these differences. In general, delinquents from a delinquency area are less heavily endowed with the so-called "stigmata of degeneracy" than are nondelinquents. The former are found to be superior from a medical and neurological standpoint both as to current health status and as to the reported illnesses previously incurred. Intelligence, as measured by intelligence tests previously given, does not appear as a differentiating factor between the behavior groupings.

The study offers new hypotheses concerning the biologic determination of antisocial conduct which may be briefly stated as follows: The factors producing differentiation in comparable behavior groups are socially determined and operate through a mechanism involving the gross appearance of the individuals. The most rational and consistent explanations of physical differentiation on a behavior basis do not require or include innate biological tendencies as causal factors in the determination of social misconduct.

Analysis of Chicago Data

These are extremely interesting results and conclusions. And if, on the basis of the Chicago data, we were to admit that the whites as a rule possess a higher frequency of biologically superior characters than the Negroes—an admission which we cannot, however, for a moment allow—the conclusions would be clear that the more "biologically superior" a Negro becomes, the more likely is he to become a delinquent! The Chicago delinquents of Negroid stock were, for example, in many physical respects superior, and in no way inferior, to the nondelinquents. The fact, however, is that from the general biological standpoint, white and Negro stand about on a par as regards the distribution of advanced and primitive characters. But if in the present instance we take the view of the human ecologist, and hold that in a white cultural area the possession of white physical characters confers definite advantages upon their possessors, and since in the Negroid population these advantages are fewest for those possessing the most Negro-like features, and gradually increase with the increase of resemblance to whites, then white characters must be regarded as biological characters conferring a social advantage upon the possessor. They are socially, not biologically, superior characters. In the Chicago culture-area, therefore, even the more socially valued physical characters are associated with a higher frequency of delinquency than are the less socially esteemed physical characters!

The fact is that all the available evidence indicates that there is no significant relation whatsoever between visible morphological and mental characters. This, of course, is not the same thing as saying that there exists no relation between heredity and mental characters. But it is a statement of the fact that such characters as the Lombrosians, for the most part erroneously, described as anomalies and vestiges, and their appeal to purely metaphysical and utterly unfounded conceptions such as "atavism," have no biological connection with crime.

The Individual and Society

That such characters may have a social connection with crime is in many cases possible. It has frequently been pointed out, for example, that in our culture, individuals who exhibit any unprepossessing physical characters are at something of a social disadvantage. The more marked such socially labeled physical defects may be, either individually or in combination, the more frequently will such an individual be made to feel that society has no very marked

interest in him, and the more likely is he to exhibit some active resentment against society. Add to such physical "defects" the conditions of a poor upbringing—both in the social and in the economic
senses—a bad physical and cultural environment, a disorganized
domestic environment, and a disorganized society, and antisocial
behavior of some sort is well-nigh inevitable.

A society which is anti-individual will always produce antisocial
individuals. Those who have felt the anti-individuality of their social group either migrate to other social areas in which their individuality is better appreciated, or they become social reformers of
one sort of another in their own group, or they take refuge in neu-
rosis, or—to omit naming the thousand and one other forms of
response—they find themselves forced into forms of conduct which
their particular society regards as criminal. Is the latter class distinguishable from the former classes by the possession of any physical or heritable characters whatsoever?

Some investigators have in recent years thought that they had
found a definite answer to this question, as well as a rebuttal of the
suggestion, at least as far as criminal behavior is concerned, that
there is no significant relation between morphological and mental
characters. This they believe they have discovered in the evidence
provided by the findings on twins. We may now briefly examine
this evidence and the claims which have been made for it, before
concluding this discussion.

Criminality in Twins

Twins are of two kinds, those deriving from one egg and those
deriving from two separate eggs. In the former case they are genetically alike, in the latter they are genetically unalike. If heredity
has anything whatsoever to do with behavior, one-egg twins
should be very much alike in behavior, at least significantly more
so than two-egg twins. Several investigators have . . . investigated
the concordance of criminal behavior of one-egg twins as compared with two-egg twins. When both members of a twin pair were
found to be similar with respect to the commission of one or more
crimes, they were termed "concordant"; when dissimilar, that is,

when one was found to have committed a crime and the other not, they were termed "discordant. . . ." I have summarized the findings of one American and four European investigators [4] on such adult twins. . . .

[Of] 104 pairs of one-egg twins examined, 70 were concordant and 34 were discordant. The concordant were almost exactly twice as numerous as the discordant pairs. On the other hand, the two-egg twins showed a discordance almost exactly twice as great as the concordance shown in this group of 112 pairs. These are impressive figures, but what do they mean? . . . . Newman, the latest writer on this subject, and our leading authority on twinning, believes that these figures prove "beyond question that hereditary factors bulk large among the causes of criminal behavior." [5] This is the opinion of all the investigators mentioned, but in reality such studies do not prove any connection whatsoever between hereditary factors and criminal behavior. Of this, Newman, who has perhaps observed more twins than anyone else living, is quite aware, for he writes:

The only serious criticism I have known to be aimed at the twin method of studying the factors of crime is that one-egg twins far more than two-egg twins are close companions in their social activities and are therefore more likely to encounter together such social influences as might lead to criminal behavior. This is one more instance of lack of control features in nature's scientific experiments, for it can hardly be maintained that the social environment of two-egg pairs is as closely similar as that of one-egg pairs. Therefore, environmental similarities may to some extent account for the close concordance in crime of one-egg twins, while lack of any such similarity in environment may to an equal extent account for lack of concordance in crime of two-egg twins. Undoubtedly the study of crime by means of the twin method is less simple than it seemed at the outset.[6]

[4] J. Lange, *Verbrechen und Schicksal: Studien an Kriminellen Zwillingen,* Leipzig, 1929. (English translation, by Charlotte Haldane, *Crime and Destiny,* New York, 1930.)

A. M. Legras, *Psychose en Criminaliteit bij Tweelingen,* Utrecht, 1932. ("Psychose und Kriminalität bei Zwillengen," *Zeitschrift für gesamte Neurologie und Psychiatrie,* Bd. 144, 1933.)

H. Kranz, *Lebenschicksal Krimineller Zwillinge,* Berlin, 1936.

F. Stumpfl, *Die Ursprunge des Verbrechens,* Leipzig, 1936.

A. J. Rosanoff, *et al.,* "Criminality and Delinquency in Twins," *Journal of Criminal Law and Criminology,* Vol. 24 (1934), pp. 923 ff.

[5] H. H. Newman, *Multiple Human Births* (New York, 1940), p. 160.

[6] *Ibid.*

This is, of course, the crucial point. The factor of environment has been virtually completely omitted from these studies of criminal behavior in twins. Hence, the attribution of the behavior of such twins to hereditary factors may be written off as yet another illustration of the fallacy of *false cause*.

If the hereditary theory is to be consistent, the proportion of two-egg twins who are both affected should be higher than the proportion of one-egg twins where only one is affected. The actual proportions, however, are almost identical, being 33.0 per cent for two-egg concordance, and 32.7 per cent for one-egg discordance. Furthermore, as Reckless has pointed out, "If biological determination of destiny is correct, a discordant monozygotic [one-egg] twin set should be impossible, whereas discordant dizygotic [two-egg] sets should be frequent." [7] The actual findings, however, reveal that one-third of the one-egg pairs of twins investigated were discordant. Why did not the hereditary factor for crime declare itself in one of the members of this one-third of single-egg twins? If the answer is that an environmental factor was probably operative in these cases, a factor which was absent in the case of the criminal sibling, then the theory of the hereditary cause of crime collapses beyond repair; for it then becomes obvious that it was the absence of such environmental factors, or the presence of others, that was the one indispensable condition in the causation of the criminal behavior!

It appears, then, that just as it takes environmental conditions to organize and to produce a mind, so, too, does it take environmental conditions to organize hereditarily determined elements of the nervous system to develop and function, or not, in ways which society terms "criminal." There is not the slightest evidence to believe that anyone ever inherits a tendency to commit criminal acts. Crime is a social condition, not a biological condition.

The Endocrine Glands and Criminality

It need hardly be said that the endocrine glands have provided innumerable writers with a wonderful quarry in which to dig for explanations of criminal behavior. In a book devoted to this sub-

[7] W. C. Reckless, *Criminal Behavior* (New York, 1940), p. 186.

ject, appropriately entitled *The New Criminology,* the authors claim "that the glandular theory of crime accounts for all the discrepancies, errors, oversights, and inadequacies of the earlier explanations." [8] The literature on the relation between the endocrine glands and criminality is now enormous, and it would obviously be impossible to deal with it here.

There exists abundant evidence to show that the glands of the endocrine system are intimately connected with the make-up of the personality. "But," as Hoskins authoritatively writes, "before psychology, sociology, and criminology can be convincingly rewritten as merely special aspects of endocrinology, many more facts than are now available will have to be collected and integrated." [9]

Writing now as a student of scientific method, I should venture the opinion that not one of the reports on the alleged relationship between glandular dysfunctions and criminality has been carried out in a scientific manner, and that all such reports are glaring examples of the fallacy of *false cause.* To illustrate with but a single example: Morris reports that the examination of the bodies of 192 inmates of state institutions in West Virginia revealed "persistence" of the thymus gland in 22 cases. Of these 22 cases, 19 were first- and second-degree murderers, and I was a rapist. Morris concluded that there was therefore some relationship between persistence of this gland and criminal behavior. [10]

It has only to be pointed out that "persistence" of the thymus gland, in more or less of a juvenile condition, will be found in at least 10 per cent of every cadaver population of the dissecting room, but that no anatomist has yet propounded the theory that that was the reason why these subjects eventually landed in the dissecting room! As every anatomist knows, the mass and size of the thymus is extremely variable, and finally, it is extremely doubtful whether the thymus is to be regarded as an endocrine gland at all!

The fact is that as far as the endocrine system and its relation to

[8] M. G. Schlapp and E. H. Smith, *The New Criminology* (New York, 1928), p. 72.
[9] R. G. Hoskins, *Endocrinology* (New York, 1941), p. 348.
[10] S. J. Morris, "The Relation of the Persistent Thymus Gland and Criminology," *Medical Record,* Vol. 99, p. 438.

personality and behavior are concerned, we are still almost completely in a world of the unknown, and that to resort to that system for an explanation of criminality is merely to attempt to explain the known by the unknown.

Social Origin of Crime

Habitual crime seems to me to be a trade or profession, licitly or illicitly pursued, like any other; a trade or profession which is entered and pursued because, in many cases, it was the only one which was offered or open to those who adopted it—socially open, *not* biologically open. Everyone agrees that there is a high correlation between poverty and crime, although, of course, criminals are by no means exclusively drawn from the poorer classes. Poverty itself is rarely a cause of crime, but in the group of necessary conditions which constitute the cause of crime in any one instance, it is of very frequent occurrence. This in itself would suggest that the larger proportion of crimes are committed by individuals who are making an effort to survive. Taken together with all the evidence —cultural, physical, and biological—it would suggest that crime is an adaptive form of behavior which is, in most cases, resorted to by the individual in order to stave off the possibility, real or imagined, of a vital insecurity. From the biological standpoint, therefore, criminal behavior, with relatively few exceptions, represents a successful adaptation to a difficult situation. From the social viewpoint, such behavior cannot be regarded as unsuccessful; it can only be regarded as undesirable and socially unallowable. I suggest that ultimately most crimes can be reduced to the uncomplicated status of a response to some form of personal insecurity.

It is not the individual who creates a crime, but society. Nor is it the individual who generally creates the conditions which lead him to commit a crime, but it is society which creates those conditions. From the viewpoint of the student of the biological bases of human society, our society is a disorganized and disharmonious one. We talk in terms of the greatest good of the greatest *number*, but neglect to act in terms of the greatest good of the greatest number of *individuals*. Opportunities for the social development of their biological potentialities are withheld from large numbers of individuals. These are virtually left to shift for themselves. Maleducation and malnutrition have frequently been their lot. To the lack of cultural and nutritional organization from which so many of them have suffered, society adds very little opportunity and guidance to stand, by licit means, on their own two feet.

I speak of "society," but that is not exactly what I mean. It is not societies, but certain kinds of social systems which, to me as a biologist, appear clearly to produce "criminal" behavior in many individuals. And until these systems have been modified where they most require modification, many human beings will continue to default. But it is not human beings or their biology that is at fault, but the social disorganization which renders such behavior possible.

RACE, SOCIAL STATUS,
AND CRIMINAL ARREST

EDWARD R. GREEN

Excerpted from "Race, Social Status, and Criminal Arrest," *American Sociological Review*, 35, No. 3 (June 1970), 476–490. At the time of publication, Edward R. Green was associated with Eastern Michigan University.

Introduction

THE RECURRENTLY higher official arrest rate of Negroes over
whites poses a persistent issue in the study of deviance relative to
ethnicity. Although it is well established that criminogenic conditions such as poverty, family instability, slum residence, and migration are much more concentrated among Negroes than whites, the
extent to which the differential accounts for the racial variance in
crime rates remains problematical. One point of view holds out the
prospect that under comparable circumstances the white and
Negro crime rates would not differ substantially, a presumption
which finds some support in the historical experience of lower class
white migrant groups who as recent arrivals on the American urban
scene also incurred high arrest rates which later declined in relation to their upward social movement and cultural assimilation. A
less sanguine view holds that the circumstances of whites and Negroes are not fully comparable, that the experience of the Negro in
America differs not only in degree but in kind from that of lower
class white ethnic minorities. Thus even under equivalent socioeconomic conditions, racial crime rates would materially differ: the
disabilities produced by discrimination add to the incidence of
Negro crime by engendering frustrations which find expression in

explosive assaults or repeated acts of predatory crime; racial discrimination in law enforcement exaggerates the official record of Negro crime by artificially inflating Negro rates of arrest and conviction.

The latter point of view is supported by the results of Moses' controlled investigation. He approached the problem by means of a comparison of arrest rates in two pairs of contiguous white and Negro neighborhoods in Baltimore partially equated with respect to selected socioeconomic characteristics of the inhabitants. The white and Negro neighborhoods were alike in regard to the racial homogeneity of their populations, the dominance of lower occupational and educational levels, and the average size of households. They differed greatly, however, in the percentage of home owners —whites exceeding Negroes 7 to 1 in one pair of neighborhoods, and 10 to 1 in the other. The results show that Negroes exceeded whites in arrest rates for felonies by a ratio of 6 to 1, a disparity which Moses attributes to racial proscriptions accentuating the burden of low socioeconomic status. It does not appear, however, that the social and economic differences between the two racial groups are sufficiently controlled to justify this conclusion. Although there was a dominance of blue collar workers among both races, whites predominated as foreman, craftsmen, and kindred workers, whereas Negroes predominated as laborers. Further, the employment data do not take account of the distribution of the unemployed which in all likelihood was greater among Negroes than whites. Perhaps more significantly, the whites were largely of eastern European extraction and the Negroes, of southern native American origin. Hence, it is hardly likely that the populations in the white and Negro neighborhoods were nearly alike in all analytically significant respects save race. Rather the comparison involves two culturally disparate groups whose relatively low economic status confers upon them only a superficial resemblance.

This study will reexamine the connection between race and crime in the light of racial differences in status characteristics related to variations in crime rates. Instead of comparing the crime rates of two racially distinct subcommunities like in the frequency distribution of the social traits of their inhabitants, as Moses attempted to do, we directly compare the arrest rates of whites and Negroes equated with respect to the variables of sex, age, and especially, occupation, employment status, and nativity as indices of social status.

Research Setting

The locus of the study, Ypsilanti, is a small industrial city lying close to the boundaries of the Detroit and Ann Arbor metropolitan areas in southeastern Michigan. With an estimated population of 25,000 in 1968, residing in an incorporated area of only four square miles, Ypsilanti reproduces in microcosm many of the features of urban transition—the trends of demographic and ecological changes and, particularly, the rapidly rising official rates of crime —characteristic of large northern industrial cities during the past quarter of a century.

War-time and post-war economic development, attracting migrants to the area, and rising birth rates swelled the city's population from 12,121 in 1940 to 18,312 by 1950 and 20,957 by 1960, a net increase of 73% over 1940, and to an estimated 23,000 in 1965. Ypsilanti Township bounding the city on the east, west, and south provides the city with a suburban fringe whose population increased more than six-fold between 1940 and 1960, from 4,153 to 26,000, surpassing in size the population within the city of Ypsilanti. In 1960, the first census year for which data on the state of birth of residents were published for individual communities, 42% of Ypsilanti's inhabitants were born outside of the state. Slightly more than 20%, or 4,671, of the city's population in 1960 consisted of Negroes of whom 2,471 or 52.9% were not native to the state. Nearly half of the white majority migrated from other states, a very large percentage originating in the Appalachian region. The high percentage of southern migrants in both races and the virtual absence of foreign-born among the whites heighten the cultural equivalency of the two racial groups, thus facilitating a rigorously controlled analysis of racial crime rates.

Official records of the Ypsilanti police show a pronounced increase in crime rates between the period just prior to the United

States' entry into World War II and 1966. Official reports for 1941 list a total of 227 arrests for assorted crimes, a rate of 1,870 per hundred thousand of population. The number of arrests skyrocketed during the war years, 1942–1945, to an average of 1,653 per year, a fantastic rate of 10,804 per hundred thousand, as the community received an influx of migrants seeking jobs in local war industries. The average annual arrest rate declined during the postwar period of 1946–1955 to 4,764, owing in part to the departure of many temporary war-time residents. But many of the migrants remained, and by 1956 the crime index had resumed an upward trend, rising to such an extent that by 1966 Ypsilanti's arrest rate of 6,428.5 for all offenses exceeded by 32% the average rate of 4,884.7 for the 51 largest American cities over 250,000 in population with the highest average arrest rate of all classes of cities. The arrest rate of 163.4 for crimes against the person—felonious homicide, forcible rape, aggravated assault, and robbery—fell between the average of 228.7 for cities over 250,000 in population, and the average of 134.0 for cities 100,000 to 250,000 in population, and was two and one-half times higher than the average rate of 61.0 for cities in its own size class.

Ypsilanti's rate (4,902 per hundred thousand in 1966) of serious crimes known to the police (criminal homicide, including manslaughter by negligence, forcible rape, robbery, aggravated assault, burglary and breaking or entering, all cases of larceny, and auto theft) was twice as great as the average of other cities in its size class and even greater than the average (4,554.6) of the 55 largest cities in the nation with populations of over 250,000.[1]

The Sample

The data comprise two bodies of materials. The first consists of the personal and legal information given in the records of all arrests, exclusive of juvenile detentions, in 1942, the first year that systematic records of all arrests were kept, the census years of

[1] A very large portion of the remarkable increase in crime rates in Ypsilanti derives demonstrably from improved police procedures for recording and labelling crimes.

1950, and 1960, and 1965. The cases are classified by the seriousness of the offense under two categories: (1) *Index crimes,* arrests for serious offenses constituting the crime index of the Federal Bureau of Investigation—murder and nonnegligent manslaughter, forcible rape, robbery, burglary, larceny over $50, and auto theft; and (2) *other crimes,* preponderantly arrests for minor offenses. Since arrests for Index crimes make up only one-tenth of the cases, in order to have a broader basis for inference concerning racial arrest rates for the more serious offenses, an additional body of data on all arrests for high misdemeanors and felonies in 1950–1959 and 1961–1964 has been combined with the cases of felonies and high misdemeanors for 1960 and 1965. These cases are classified by the character of the offense into (1) crimes against the person, (2) crimes against property, and (3) "others," predominantly crimes against the public welfare. The distinction between felonies and high misdemeanors on the one hand and ordinary misdemeanors on the other is legally crucial. The latter are tried in the municipal court, a lower trial court of limited criminal jurisdiction, and are punishable by prison sentences of no more than 90 days. The former are heard in the circuit court, a tribunal of countywide criminal jurisdiction, and are subject to prison terms as high as life imprisonment.

Rates of arrest are computed per hundred thousand of population, even though Ypsilanti's population did not exceed 25,000 by 1966, in order to render them comparable to the rates given in official statistics of crime published by the Justice Department.

Results

Criminal statistics published annually in the *Uniform Crime Reports* perennially demonstrate the powerful effect of *age, sex,* and *race* on crime rates. Males constituting half of the population make up about 90% of the persons arrested for serious crimes; young people age 11–25, comprising less than 25% of the population, account for almost 75% of the persons arrested for serious crimes; and Negroes, only 11% of the population, contribute 30% of the arrestees for serious crimes. Very similar results emerge locally.

Table 1 [deleted] records a disproportionately high number of arrests for Negroes compared with whites, men compared with women, and youths 17 to 24 years of age compared with persons age 25 and over. It also shows a much greater likelihood of arrest for persons in low status occupations and the unemployed, compared with those in high status occupations, and for persons born out-of-state, compared with those born in Michigan.

The trend of Negro arrest rates during the 25-year period covered by this study strongly suggests the acculturation, quantitatively and qualitatively, of the Negro to the white man's criminal behavior pattern. The percentage of Negroes among those arrested for Index crimes fluctuated downward from 53.2 in 1942 to 48.4 in 1950, 39.7 in 1960, and 44.7 in 1965. The percentage of Negroes among those arrested for lesser crimes fluctuated upward from 22.4 in 1942 to 34.1 in 1950, 28.7 in 1960, and 33.7 in 1965. For all offenses combined, the percentage of Negroes arrested increased from 24.2% in 1942 to 34.5% in 1965, a 42% increase over the 25-year period. But the Negro arrest figures did not keep pace proportionately with the growth in Negro population, which increased by 60% between 1940 and 1960—from 13.9% in 1940 to 19.7% in 1950, to 22.6% in 1960, and undoubtedly, to an even higher level in 1965.

Males in each sample year of the study constitute slightly less than half of the population but regularly produce over nine-tenths of the arrests for Index and non-Index crimes.

The percentage of persons age 17 to 24 and over 24, respectively, arrested for non-Index crimes in each sample year closely approximates the percentage distribution of these two age categories in the population of an age of criminal responsibility which begins at 17 in Michigan. With respect to Index crimes, youths age 17 to 24 comprising from one-fifth to one-third of the population over 16 years of age consistently account for two-thirds of the arrests. In view, however, of the steady increase in the percentage of youths by more than half, from 19.7 in 1940 to 31.2 in 1960, and an estimated 34.0 in 1965, the findings signify an actual decline in the youth arrest rate for serious crimes.

We cannot compare Ypsilanti to similar urban settings with respect to the effect of socioeconomic variables on arrest rates since the *Uniform Crime Reports* do not contain pertinent data. In each sample year the labor force constitutes just over one-half of the population 14 years of age or more, but contributes 95% of all arrests of persons over 16 years of age. The lower occupational strata comprising semiskilled and unskilled workers—operatives, service workers, and laborers—and the unemployed make up almost half of the labor force, but are arrested for non-Index offenses in the various sample years from 7–13 times as frequently as the white collar workers—professionals, managers, entrepreneurs, sales and clerical personnel—and craftsmen who, combined, make up slightly more than one-half of the labor force. The disparity between the upper and lower occupational groupings is even greater in the proportion of arrests for Index crimes, the latter exceeding the former by about 40 times in 1942; 22 in 1950; 12 in 1960; and 26 in 1965.

During the period surveyed, the percentage of arrests contributed by the employed, particularly the white-collar and skilled category, declined in relation to the proportion of the employed in the labor force; conversely, the percentage of all arrests contributed by the unemployed more than doubled from 7.5% in 1942 to 10% in 1950, 18.3% in 1960, and 16.7% in 1965.

The criminogenic effect of migration has been challenged by a Philadelphia study, which found that Negro youths native to Philadelphia became delinquent more frequently than those born elsewhere. The results in Ypsilanti show, to the contrary, that migrants, defined as persons born outside of Michigan, and particularly those who originate in the rural South, are much more likely to be arrested than natives. Between 1940 and 1960 the migrant population increased to two-fifths of the total population. Concomitantly, . . . in each sample year migrants accounted for the bulk of arrests for Index and non-Index crimes, the percentage climbing, for all cases, from 54.3 in 1942 to 70.5 in 1950, and leveling at 66.7 in 1960 and 67.3 in 1965. There is no indication, and no reason to assume, that between 1940 and 1965 the proportion of migrant arrests increased more than the proportion of migrants in the population.

The 1960 census data permit a direct assessment of the effect of migration on arrests. . . . [M]igrants accounted for 41.7% of the population of Ypsilanti, 67.3% of persons arrested for non-Index crimes, and 60.3% of those arrested for Index crimes. Southerners predominate among migrant arrestees, comprising four-fifths of those arrested for non-Index crimes and two-thirds of those arrested for Index crimes.

Thus, of all of the above criteria of demographic classification—age, sex, race, occupation, and nativity—only one grouping, namely, the occupational category of the unemployed, increased its arrest rate more rapidly than its rate of growth during the period studied. Certain elements of the population with a high suscepti-bility to criminal arrest—Negroes, youths, and migrants—increased in size proportionately more than groups with a rela-tively low likelihood of arrest—whites, older persons, and natives. Such trends in population composition, locally and in other highly urbanized areas, have contributed to a rise in general arrest rates but not necessarily to a rise in arrest rates for specific elements of the population.

Turning to the effect of sex, age, occupation, and nativity on ra-cial arrest rates, we find that we may not attribute the racial dis-parity in arrests to a dissimilarity between white and Negro in sex ratio inasmuch as the census reports for 1940, 1950, and 1960 show that the races are virtually equal in this regard. Neither may we impute the disparity to differences between the races in age distri-bution since in each of the three census years, the white popula-tion, with a lower arrest rate than the Negro population, consists of a smaller proportion of persons under 17, a larger proportion of persons in the high arrest rate age category of 17 to 24, and about an equal proportion of persons over 24.

A strong presumption arises, however, that sociocultural differ-ences, measured by the indices of occupation and nativity, account for much of the racial variance in arrest rates. United States Cen-sus data for Ypsilanti confirm that a much higher proportion of Ne-groes than whites is found in the high crime rate categories at the lower end of the occupational scale, among the unemployed and the migrants. In the 1940 Census whites are represented propor-

tionately twice as frequently as Negroes in the white collar and
skilled occpations, 51.3% to 24.1%; and in the 1950 and 1960 census, respectively, about three times as frequently, 62.5% to 22.4%
and 57.5% to 17%. The percentage of whites in the semiskilled
and unskilled occupations declined between 1940 and 1960 from
42.6 to 32.9, while the percentage of Negroes at that level increased from 44.7 to 61.9. The proportion of Negro unemployed
greatly exceeded the proportion of white unemployed in each census year: 28.3% to 5.1% in 1940, 12.2% to 3.1% in 1950, and
16.5% to 6.3% in 1960.

The data on nativity provided in the 1960 census indicate that a
much larger proportion of Negroes compared with whites were
born outside of Michigan, 53.5% to 38.3%.

Holding constant the effect of *occupation* or *nativity* as shown in
Table 2 [deleted] sharply reduces the racial variance in arrest
rates. At the level of the white-collar and skilled workers, both the
number and rate of arrests per hundred thousand of population for
Index crimes are small for both races; in the four sample years
combined, there were only eight cases, six white and two Negro.
For non-Index offenses the difference between whites and Negroes
in the white-collar and skilled occupations was practically nil in
1942, 3,780 to 3,600; and in 1950, 920 to 960; in 1960 and 1965, respectively, Negroes pulled ahead of whites, 4,200 to 1,190 and
3,750 to 850.

At the semiskilled and unskilled occupational level in 1942, Negroes exceeded whites by six times in rates of Index crimes, 5,440
to 890, and by two times in rates of non-Index crimes, 44,880 to
22,580. In the ensuing sample years the differential markedly declined. The Negro rate of arrests for Index crimes approximately
doubled the white rate in each sample year: 770 to 380 in 1950, 980
to 400 in 1960, and 1,140 to 560 in 1965. The racial arrest rates for
non-Index crimes more nearly approached parity: Negroes exceeded whites in 1950—13,300 to 9,860, but yielded to whites in
1960—8,620 to 11,960 and very closely approximated them in
1965—15,000 to 14,700. In view of the depth of the occupational
stratum denoted by the category semiskilled and unskilled—which
includes at the top "affluent" blue-collar factory operatives with se-

niority, steady work, and high wages, and at the bottom, the marginally employed—it is likely that the results tend to overstate the amount of Negro criminality relative to the criminality of whites in the same occupational class inasmuch as whites tend to predominate at the higher levels of blue-collar work, and Negroes, at the lower levels.

However, in the white-Negro comparison on the level of unemployment, all other things are nearly equal, since in a period of economic expansion and prosperity the unemployed of both races are likely to be equated at the bottom of the socioeconomic scale. In 1942 unemployed Negroes scored substantially higher than unemployed whites in arrest rates for Index crimes, 3,060 to 330, although the actual number of cases involved was insignificant, six Negroes and one white,[2] but arrests for non-Index offenses, totaling 52, were proportionately much higher for whites than Negroes yielding rates of 12,210 to 7,650. In 1950 whites exceeded Negroes in arrest rates for Index crimes, 2,120 to 1,740, and non-Index crimes, 15,370 to 8,700. In 1960, the white rate barely exceeded the Negro rate for Index crimes, 2,940 to 2,900 but decidedly surpassed the Negro rate for non-Index crimes, 16,590 to 11,600. In 1965 the Negro rate for Index crimes slightly surpassed the white rate, 2,250 to 2,090, but for non-Index crimes trailed considerably behind, 17,860 to 10,000. It is doubtful, however, that at the lowest socioeconomic level Negroes are less prone to commit minor (non-Index) crimes than whites. As most crime is intraracial in the offender-victim relationship and in the neighborhood setting, it is likely that Negro victims of Negro offenders or Negroes adversely affected by the crimes of Negroes are less apt to complain to the police than whites victimized by whites, due possibly to a greater tolerance of neighborhood disturbances, a distrust of police, or a lesser likelihood that the property loss of Negroes is covered by insurance.

The frequency of arrests of persons not in the labor force is relatively small in each sample year, although the Negro rate generally

[2] The inconsequential number of Index crimes reflects imprecision in official police recording procedures in 1942 rather than civil tranquillity, a matter to be treated in a subsequent report.

exceeds the white rate. Since this category does not, however, represent a social class level but rather a cross-section of the class structure of each group—the retired, homemakers, students, and the like—the higher Negro rate likely reflects the comparatively lower socioeconomic level of the Negro population.

The racial difference in nativity inflates the general arrest rate of the Negro much more than that of the white. In 1960, the first census year for which data on the nativity of residents of Ypsilanti were published, 44.1% of the Negro population compared with a somewhat larger 60.1% of the white population of Ypsilanti were born in Michigan. Since migrants contribute more heavily to crime rates than nonmigrants, and Negroes include a higher proportion of migrants than whites, holding constant the factor of migrant status effects a reduction in the racial difference in arrest rates. In 1960 the Negro superiority over whites in arrest rates for Index crimes declines from a ratio of 2.25 to 1, uncontrolled, (570 to 250) to 1.50 to 1 for the Michigan born (290 to 190), and remains slightly more than twice as high as the white rate (740 to 340) for those born out-of-state. The racial difference in rates of non-Index crimes declines from a ratio of 4 to 3 in favor of the Negro (4,660 to 3,280) to near parity, a slightly higher white rate among the native born—1,850 to 1,710, and a moderately higher Negro rate among those born elsewhere—6,840 to 6,040.

The data on arrests for felonies and high misdemeanors in 1950–1965 add another dimension to the analysis showing, in Table 3 [deleted], the effect of the type of offense—personal, property, or *other* (mainly crimes against the "public")—singly and interactively with each of the demographic variables of sex, age, occupation, and nativity on racial differences in the average annual arrest rate. The racial variance in arrest rates differs widely among the different types of offenses. Crimes against the person display a ratio of Negro to white arrest rates of about 6 to 1 (117.5 to 18.8); "other" crimes, a ratio of nearly 3 to 1 (236.3 to 86.9); and crimes against property, about 1.5 to 1.0 (134.4 to 85.0). Differences in racial arrest rates, expectedly, persist at a high level within each sex and age category. The control of the variables of occupation and nativity as shown in Table 3, however, markedly reduces the racial arrest rate differential. During the 16-year period the average annual rate per hundred thousand of population for crimes against the person is much higher in all occupational categories for Negroes than for whites. The racial differential for property crimes is negligible at all levels of occupational status among the employed; among the unemployed the white rate is higher, 997.5 to 743.1. For "other" offenses, Negroes show a much higher rate at the white collar and skilled level, 122.5 to 37.5; and semiskilled and unskilled level, 591.3 to 337.5. Among the unemployed, whites slightly exceed Negroes, 498.8 to 471.3.

The control of the effect of nativity somewhat reduces the excess of Negro over white arrest rates in all offense categories, except cases of property crimes committed by natives, wherein the Negro superiority increases slightly.

Since *race*, *occupation*, and *nativity*, each displays a close association with arrest rates and since a much higher proportion of Negroes than whites is found at low status occupational levels including the unemployed and among migrants, we proceed to an investigation of the joint effects of *occupation* and *nativity* on racial differences in arrest rates. As already noted, the census did not issue figures on State of birth by individual communities until 1960. Hence the analysis is restricted to the cases of arrest in 1960 and 1965. In calculating the 1965 rates, proportional increases were made in the 1960 figures to reflect the general growth of the population, although no adjustments were made to express estimated changes during the five-year period in the racial-occupational-nativity distribution. In computing the average annual rates for the high misdemeanor and felony arrests in 1950–1965, the census figures for 1960 were used, inasmuch as the 1960 population data very closely approximate the average of the 1950 census data and the estimates for 1965.

The 1960 census report does not supply data on the number of persons native to the State of residence and elsewhere, respectively, in each occupational category. Hence we have devised estimates by applying the percentage distribution of occupations for each race uniformly to those born in the State of arrest and those born elsewhere. The resulting figures are used as bases for the computation of arrest rates for each racial-occupational-nativity group. Since the natives of each race are more likely to be found in greater proportion at the upper occupational level than the non-natives, this procedure may have the effect of slightly over-estimating the arrest rate of the natives at the upper occupational level (white collar and craftsmen) and the migrants at the lower occupational level (semiskilled, unskilled, and unemployed), and slightly underestimating the arrest rate of the natives at the lower occupational level and the migrants at the upper occupational level because it reduces the size of the base used in calculating rates for the former categories and enlarges it for the latter categories.

The results, as shown in Table 4 [deleted], indicate that among groupings of persons more or less homogeneous with respect to *occupation* and *nativity* there is no consistent trend of racial difference in arrest rates. Considering first the arrests of the native-born persons for Index crimes in 1960, we observe that at each occupational level whites incur higher arrest rates than Negroes, although the total number of cases (N=20) is too small to justify any firm inference. For non-Index crimes, the white arrest rate substantially exceeds the Negro rate at the level of semiskilled and unskilled occupations, 6,060 to 3,000, and at the level of the unemployed, 8,670 to 6,000, but falls somewhat short of the Negro rate, 810 to 1,250, among white collar and skilled workers. Among persons born out-of-state, white rates for Index crimes exceed Negro rates slightly at the level of the white collar and skilled, and rather markedly at the level of the unemployed, 5,500 to 3,890. In turn, Negro rates greatly exceed white rates among the semiskilled and unskilled, 1,710 to 440. With respect to rates of arrest for non-Index crimes, whites yield to Negroes, 1,710 to 6,840, in the category of the white collar and skilled workers, but greatly surpass Negroes in the categories of the semiskilled and unskilled workers, 22,890 to 12,710, and the unemployed, 28,890 to 15,560.

The summary of the statistical analysis of the 1960 data (with Index and non-Index crimes consolidated) shows a high degree of interaction among the three independent variables of race, occupation, and migration, and a marked reduction in the racial imbalance in arrest rates when this interaction is taken into account.

The racial difference for persons born in the state is not statistically significant in three out of the four occupational categories—white collar and skilled, the unemployed, and those not in the labor force—but is significantly higher for whites than for Negroes among the semiskilled and unskilled. For persons born out-of-state, the white rate significantly surpasses the Negro rate among the semiskilled and unskilled workers and the unemployed, but falls significantly short of the Negro rate at the level of white collar and skilled workers and persons not in the labor force.

The results of the analysis of the 1965 data . . . closely follow the results for the 1960 data. Among the native-born people the racial difference in arrest rates at each occupational level fails to achieve significance. The racial difference is more pronounced in the migrant population: Negroes significantly exceed whites at the level of white collar workers and craftsmen, and among persons not in the labor force, but fall significantly short of the whites at the level of the unemployed. Among the semiskilled and unskilled, the white rate surpasses the Negro rate, though not significantly.

The data on the high misdemeanor and felony cases given in Table 5 [deleted] yield similar findings concerning the interrelationships among the variables of occupation, migration, and racial arrest rates. Arrest rates are highest for the miscellaneous category of other offenses, predominantly victimless crimes, followed in descending order by property crimes and crimes against the person. Within each offense category, taking each demographic variable singly, arrest rates are decidedly higher for the migrant than for the native, the lower occupational levels than for the higher occupational levels, the unemployed than for the employed, and the Negro than for the white. Controlling simultaneously for *occupation* and *nativity*, however, markedly reduces the racial differential, although not equally in all offense categories.

In crimes against the person, the number of arrests at the white collar and skilled level for those native to the state of residence and those born elsewhere is negligible, two whites and two Negroes. In the category of semiskilled and unskilled workers, Negroes have much higher arrest rates than whites both among the natives, 93.8 to 29.4, and the migrants, 392.5 to 125.0. The rate of arrest for personal crimes differs little by race for the native born unemployed, 86.3 for whites and 83.1 for Negroes, and is low in comparison with the rate for the unemployed with out-of-state origins who exhibit a statistically nonsignificant excess of Negro over white arrest rates, 571.9 to 341.3.

The effect of the racial factor on arrest rates for property crimes is astonishingly low. At the white collar and skilled level the racial difference in arrest rates is negligible for native and migrant. At the semiskilled and unskilled level the white rate is higher than the Negro rate both for natives and migrants, 166.9 to 145.6 and 367.5 to 294.4, respectively. Among the native unemployed, Negroes slightly exceed whites, 916.9 to 861.9; among the nonnative unemployed the Negro arrest rate is little more than half the white arrest rate, 629.4 to 1,228.8.

In cases of "other" crimes the racial factor is significant only for the employed born out-of-state, with Negroes exceeding whites 197.5 to 47.5 among the migrant white collar and skilled, and 955.6 to 541.9 among the migrant semiskilled and unskilled. Among the native-born persons at all occupational levels and the out-of-state unemployed, the differences are slight.

The statistical summary of the data in Table 5 condenses the occupational classification, excluding those not in the labor force, into two categories, *employed* and *unemployed*. The results support, generally, the statistical hypothesis of no significant difference in crime rates between the races, showing that in only three comparisons out of twelve do arrest rates differ significantly: the Negro arrest rate exceeds the white arrest rate among the native-born employed and the nonnative employed suspected of crimes against the person and the nonnative employed suspected of "other" crimes. In the other nine comparisons whites display the higher rate in five instances and Negroes, in four instances, but the differences are neither statistically nor anlytically significant.

Summary and Conclusions

This investigation confirms the hypothesis that the higher official rate of crime for Negroes compared with whites results predominantly from the wider distribution among Negroes of lower social class characteristics associated with crime. The findings, based on an analysis of official police records, spanning the period 1941–1965 in a small industrial community in the Great Lakes region, show, for both white and Negro, disproportionately high arrest rates for males, youths age 17 to 24, persons in low income occupations (semiskilled and unskilled workers), the unemployed, and persons not native to the State, predominantly Southerners. The racial variance in arrest rates does not reflect differences between the races in the distribution of the sexes or age groups since the races are about equal in sex ratio and whites have a somewhat higher proportion of persons in the age category most vulnerable to arrest, youths 17 to 24. The races differ greatly, however, in the distribution of occupational and natal characteristics; with these variables controlled, the arrest rates of the races tend toward parity and in several instances a higher rate for whites.

Even for serious crimes of violence including robbery, with a greater preponderance of Negro over white arrests than any other major category of crimes, migrant whites incur substantially higher arrest rates than native-born (Michigan) Negroes at each occupational level. This difference reflects the effect of the southern regional culture pattern which the southern migrant transplants to his new abode in the urban industrial center. Rates of felonious assault and homicide have been regularly higher in the South than elsewhere in the nation and express a heritage which southerners of both races share in common.

The findings lend no credence to the explanation of the Negro-white crime rate differential in terms of some distinctive aspect of Negro culture or in terms of racial conflict, whether viewed as the Negro's reaction to the frustrations resulting from racial discrimination or the expression of racial bias by the police. To be sure, we cannot ignore the interdependence between the depressed socioeconomic status and the racial discrimination endured by the Negro. The effect of socioeconomic status on arrest rates, however, appears to operate independently of race. Likewise we cannot surmise that police officers are innocent of racial prejudice or that the victims of racial prejudice endure their burden without rancor.

Nevertheless, there is no indication here, or systematic evidence elsewhere, of the transformation of racial prejudice into racial discrimination in the enforcement of the law or of the transformation of the frustrations produced by racial inequality into criminal behavior. Indeed, the data suggest the converse: during the period 1940 to 1965, certainly a period of rising expectations and militancy on the part of Negro Americans, the proportion of Negroes in the total population of the community increased to a greater extent than the proportion of Negroes among persons arrested for all offenses while the proportion of Negroes among persons arrested for Index crimes actually decreased.

INTELLIGENCE AND DELINQUENCY

HARRY M. SHULMAN

Excerpted from Harry M. Shulman, "Intelligence and Delinquency," *Journal of Criminal Law and Criminology*, XLI (March–April 1951), 763–81. Reprinted by special permission of the *Journal of Criminal Law, Criminology and Police Science*, Vol. XLI, No. 6 (Copyright © 1951, by Northwestern University School of Law).

. . . THE APPLICATION of . . . early crude intelligence tests to samplings of institutionalized offenders in prisons, reformatories and juvenile training schools and the finding that a very large proportion of those tested could be diagnosed as mental deficients, led to the single-factor theory of mental deficiency as the greatest cause of delinquent conduct. Thus Harry H. Goddard, one of America's most distinguished adherents of the psychological school of crime causation, was impelled to state, as late as 1919, that "It is no longer to be denied that the greatest single cause of delinquency and crime is low-grade mentality, much of it within the limits of feeble-mindedness." A similar declaration was made by Dr. William Healy, while Dr. Charles Goring, the English investigator into Lombroso's claims, declared more conservatively that defective intelligence was a vital constitutional factor in the aetiology of crime.

While there was substantial agreement as to the facts, there was considerable divergence as to the interpretation of the test findings, leading to such theories as: (1) the mental defective is a type of "born criminal," i.e., the "moral idiot"; (2) feeble-mindedness is a hereditary unit-character following Mendel's law, accounting for the preponderance of male defective offenders; (3) the feeble-minded characteristically commit dangerous crimes of assault and sex assault; (4) feeble-minded individuals commit crimes, in the absence of inhibiting social factors, because they lack the capacity to grasp the social values of their culture, including its social and legal definitions of right and wrong; (5) the feeble-minded cannot foresee the consequences of their actions, hence cannot be deterred by the threat of punishment laid down for crimes; (6) feeble-minded are suggestible, and so respond to the criminal leadership of brighter persons; (7) feeble-mindedness in individuals reared in families and neighborhoods where delinquent example is common, leads to delinquency.

Thus the elaborations of proponents of this single-factor theory ranged from the biological to the bio-social. The biological concept of the mental defective as a moral idiot or a Mendelian criminal type preceded in historical sequence the bio-social view of the mentally deficient offender as a product of social interaction. During the early decades of the 20th century there was still a predisposition to think fatalistically of mental deficiency, delinquency, and dependency as inevitably associated phenomena. . . .

Today, the concept that mental deficiency is necessarily a product of a tainted heredity is no longer accepted as wholly true. Evidence exists that perhaps one-half of all mental deficiency is the effect of non-germinal toxic and mechanical damage during the intra-uterine period and at birth. Mental deficients are found among all social classes and in every parental occupational and educational level. Nor is the concept any longer accepted that mental deficients must necessarily be behavior risks. . . .

Despite a changing outlook upon the relationship between mental defect and delinquency there remain a number of questions regarding which it is essential to have scientific evidence, such as: (1) The proportion of mental defectives among delinquents compared to the general population; (2) significant differences in general mental ability between delinquents and the general population; (3) criminal patterns and tendencies toward recidivism among defectives compared to non-defective offenders; (4) the relationship between level of intelligence and treatability. . . .

Problems in the Testing of Intelligence

Despite the proliferation of individually applied verbal tests for general intelligence, their standardization in nearly every tongue and their application to millions of school children, certain fundamental problems in intelligence testing remain unsolved. . . .

The evidence to date is that within a probable error of perhaps 2.5 points in either direction, *under conditions of constant cultural stimulation,* the IQ does not vary with age. But such factors as serious illness, or irregularity in exposure to learning situations, or other factors that affect opportunity for learning, do appear to affect the learning growth rate, and the IQ. Thus, there is evidence that children transferred from inferior to superior cultural environments appreciate in their learning rate, and gain in IQ, and that children returned from superior to inferior cultural environments tend to regress in learning rate and in IQ to the level previously established in the inferior social environment.

The product of learning growth known as "native" general intelligence is thus not alone dependent upon nature, but on nature and nurture. As a result, general intelligence must be viewed as a product of bio-social interaction. This introduces the problem of the significance of cultural differences in the determination of intelligence levels. This factor is of significance for the relation between intelligence and delinquency. Since the accurate measurement of general intelligence is dependent upon constancy of cultural stimulation, factors tending to differentiate the cultural background levels of delinquents and non-delinquents would lead to the under-estimation or over-estimation of the intelligence of one group or the other. Thus a finding as to the relative mental status of delinquents and non-delinquents requires holding constant the factor of cultural stimulation. Since this has not usually been done, a finding that delinquents are inferior in tested general intelligence to non-delinquents does not necessarily prove that intelligence and delinquency are causally related but only that the same antecedent factors that contributed an inferior nurture to the group from which the preponderance of delinquents were drawn, also led to the preponderance of that culture level in juvenile court arraignments. . . .

A final comment on the role of culture in the testing of general intelligence must stress the desirability of the homogeneity of culture backgrounds among delinquents compared with non-delinquents for mental status. Since delinquents are drawn disproportionately from urban areas, from among industrial groupings that include disproportionate numbers of children of ill-educated, bilingual and low-socio-economic status parentage, they should be compared in general intelligence, not to the whole child population, nor even to the total urban child population, but to samplings drawn from the same races, ethnic origins, socio-economic levels, and residence areas. . . .

The General Intelligence of Juvenile Delinquents

We have said that the earliest studies . . . of juvenile delinquents emphasized their retarded mentality as a class. Studies of more than 200 American samples of institutionalized delinquent children, on a literal translation of the original Binet-Simon scale, in connection with the knowledge that practically no institutionalized feeble-minded rated above twelve years in mental age, led to the conclusion that at least one-half of juvenile delinquents were mental defectives.[1]

Recent examinations, however, have tended to a reduction in the proportion of alleged mental defect among juvenile delinquents, in part as a result of newer tests having a higher mental age "ceiling," that permitted the testing of superior individuals, in part the greater skill of examiners and the use of more effective techniques for achieving motivation, and in part the extension of tests to broader samplings of juvenile delinquents to include non-committed as well as committed cases.

A study in 1928–29, of all the mental tests reported on criminals and delinquents, comprising some 350 reports on approximately 150,000 offenders, showed a decrease from an average of 50 per

[1] H. H. Goddard, *Human Efficiency and Levels of Intelligence*, Princeton, 1920, pp. 73–74.

cent of delinquents diagnosed as feeble-minded in the period 1910–1914 to an average percentage of 20 per cent in the period 1925–1928. The wide variation in test results was regarded as reflecting differences in test methods and scoring rather than differences in mental abilities of offenders.[2]

The Intelligence of Juvenile Delinquents and Total Juvenile Population

Attention has been directed during the two past decades to a comparison of the intelligence levels of juvenile delinquents as compared to the general juvenile population. Samples of juvenile delinquents, drawn for the most part from court-arraigned cases, have been found to be lower in tested general intelligence than the child population series upon which the major intelligence tests were standardized. Terman . . . found that approximately 50 per cent of his one thousand unselected American school children fell between an IQ of 93 and 108 and that the remainder fell above and below in equal proportion. Only .3 per cent had IQ's below 65 and only 2.6 per cent had IQ's below 75. In comparison, Healy and Bronner, in their 1926 court sample, reported 13.5 per cent of their cases as mentally deficient, Burt reported 8 per cent of a London, England, court sample as mentally deficient, and Merrill reported 23 per cent of 1,731 Los Angeles court delinquents as mentally deficient with IQ's below 70. Merrill, however, pointed out that her sample contained an unknown proportion of Mexican-born and Mexican ethnic stock children of presumed bi-lingual backgrounds. In a second California court sample of 500 cases from a territory having a more homogeneous ethnic stock, she reported 11.6 per cent as mentally deficient.[3]

Relatively similar findings have been reported for other delinquency samplings, some more selective and others less selective than total court intake. Kvaraceus reported 10.4 per cent of all

[2] Edwin H. Sutherland, *Mental Deficiency and Crime,* Ch. XV in Kimball Young (Editor), *Social Attitudes,* 1931, pp. 357–75.

[3] William Healy and Augusta Bronner, *Delinquents and Criminals,* 1926. Cyril Burt, *The Young Delinquent,* D. Appleton & Co., 1925. Maud Merrill, *Problems of Child Delinquency,* Boston, 1947.

public school problem children referred for guidance care as mentally deficient, with IQ's below 70. Sheldon and Eleanor Glueck reported 13.1 per cent of a sample referred by the Boston juvenile court to the Judge Baker foundation clinic for diagnostic study as mentally deficient. The New Jersey Juvenile Commission found 13 per cent of New Jersey children committed to juvenile training schools to have IQ's under 70.[4]

Zeleny, after equating the procedures of different examiners, concluded that the ratio of delinquents and general child population in respect to mental deficiency was about 1.2 to 1.[5]

Somewhat similar findings were reported for differences in *average intelligence* among delinquents and non-delinquents. Kvaraceus found an average intelligence quotient of 103 among unselected Passaic, New Jersey school children compared to an average IQ of 89 among 761 problem children referred by schools to a central guidance service. Eleanor Glueck, comparing 1,000 clinic-referred juvenile delinquents with 3,638 school children, found that only 41.6 per cent of the delinquents had average intelligence or better (IQ's over 90) compared to 79 per cent of the school children.[6]

Intelligence of Groups of Delinquents
Given Selective Treatment

Whereas contemporary interest in the relation of general intelligence and delinquency has continued unabated, instead of seeking a causal explanation of delinquency in intellectual inferiority, the tendency has been to explain the established test differences between delinquents and non-delinquents as a product of social selection. That is, inferior mentality is coming to be viewed as one of a series of attributes that characterize children whom society

[4] William C. Kvaraceus, *Juvenile Delinquency and the School,* Yonkers, 1945, pp. 122–23. New Jersey Juvenile Commission, *Justice and the Child in New Jersey,* 1939, p. 82. Sheldon and Eleanor Glueck, *One Thousand Juvenile Delinquents,* Cambridge, 1934, p. 102.
[5] L. D. Zeleny, "Feeble-mindedness and Criminal Conduct," *American Journal of Sociology,* 38:564–78, January, 1933.
[6] Kvaraceus, *ibid.* Glueck, *ibid.*

has selected out for formal adjudication as delinquents through the differential operation of the machinery of juvenile justice.

There is evidence that not only are juvenile delinquents nonrepresentative of the whole child population for social status, but that the selectivity of the delinquent group increases proportionately with the degree of authority applied to their handling. Thus they are found to be drawn in disproportionate numbers from (a) lower socio-economic groups, (b) Negroes, (c) foreign-born parentage, (d) groups disproportionately high in indices of mental disorder, dependency, and adult crime. Those dealt with unofficially, either through the courts or through the public and private child guidance facilities of schools and community appear to represent a group from higher socio-economic status than those officially arraigned or committed to juvenile training schools.

There is further evidence that the selective social characteristics of the officially arraigned delinquency group are accompanied by differential tested intelligence; and that as more selective screening takes place among the arraigned group, in terms of the severity of the subsequent controls applied, the greater the tested intelligence differential. . . .

As one progresses from court arraignment to training school commitments, the average IQ drops. . . .

There are two possible interpretations of these findings: (a) that greater maladjustment accompanies lower intelligence, resulting in the application of more extreme social controls; (b) that the greater maladjustment and the lower tested intelligence among official cases are both dependent upon inferior antecedent cultural backgrounds of delinquents as compared to general population samples.

The first interpretation leads to the conclusion that since a disproportionate number of severely maladjusted institutionalized delinquents tend to be dullards there is a correlation between mental backwardness and the social conditions within which delinquency is encouraged. From this conclusion it is an easy step to the view that mental dullness and social breakdown, as measured by such terminal indices as dependency, delinquency, and crime, are closely related phenomena.

The cultural interpretation rejects the adequacy of the initial findings, arguing that the very tests used for the measurement of general intelligence are discriminatory against the delinquent group. They are not culture-free tests, but tests depending largely upon skill in language expression, vocabulary, breadth of reading, exposure to conceptualized discussion, etc., involving a high level of training in the use of written and spoken English, and presuming an exposure to comparable linguistic cultural material in the family, among both delinquents and non-delinquents. But since we already know that a disproportionately large number of delinquents are of low socio-economic status . . . it may be inferred that their social backgrounds are not comparable to those of the general child population. Hence the general intelligence test results are not explicable by any fancied relation between intelligence and delinquency, but by a real relationship between court arraignment and low socio-economic and culture status.

Research evidence bearing upon both types of interpretation is at hand from studies of the differential intelligence levels of public school children in high and low delinquency areas. Shulman has shown, for New York City, that the tested intelligence of children in high delinquency areas tends to be lower than that of school children in low delinquency areas. In a recalculation of data from a series of group intelligence tests conducted among public school pupils by the Board of Education, he found that in five public schools in high delinquency areas, the median IQ's ranged from 88.5 to 98.5, with an average median of 91.5, while in seven public schools in low delinquency areas, the medians ranged from 95 to 115.5, with an average median of 103.5. Thus between the low delinquency areas and the high delinquency areas there was an IQ difference averaging 12 points favoring the low delinquency areas. . . .[7]

More pertinent to a cultural interpretation were the findings of Allison Davis, who devised a test for the measurement of untaught responses to problems in daily life outside of school. In an experimental study of school children from varying socio-economic back-

[7] Harry Manuel Shulman, *A Study of Problem Boys and Their Brothers,* New York State Crime Commission, Albany, 1929, pp. 18–22.

grounds, on standard intelligence tests, and on the test for daily life problems, he found that whereas on ten standard tests there was an average difference of nearly 8 points in IQ between the high and the low socio-economic groups, favoring the former, these differences vanished when the tests for daily life problems were applied.[8] He concluded that the standard tests did not truly measure the problem-solving potentialities of children from low socio-economic backgrounds.

Delinquents and Matched Control Samples

The controversy as to the role of native and cultural factors . . . has led some authorities to suggest that comparisons of delinquents and non-delinquents in samplings in which socio-economic status is held constant might be helpful in resolving this problem.

In this connection, Lichtenstein and Brown are reported to have found among 658 grade school children from a high delinquency area, 10 per cent with IQ's below 70. Use of this figure as a control percentage for the general population in a high delinquency area would not be unfavorable to the theory that delinquents are of the same tested mental potential as non-delinquents when equated for socio-economic background. Some of Merrill's findings lend additional weight to this theory. Among 300 delinquents of both sexes compared to 300 non-delinquent controls from the same communities and public schools, she found an average IQ for the controls only slightly and not significantly higher (89.3–86.7) but on the other hand she found among the delinquents almost twice as many IQ's below 70 as among the controls.[9]

However, the findings of other investigators controvert this point of view. Burt's delinquents and controls from the same districts and public schools in London showed differences favoring the controls, with 1.2 per cent in the defective group (IQ's 50–70) compared to 7.6 per cent in the delinquents, a ratio of better than six to one; and IQ's above 115 among only 2.5 per cent of the delin-

[8] From New York *Times*, March 23, 1950.

[9] For Lichtenstein and Brown, see Milton Metfessel and Constance Lovell, "Recent Literature on Individual Correlates of Crime," *Psychological Bulletin*, 1942, *34*, 153–60. Merrill, *ibid.*, pp. 169–70.

quents and 8.5 per cent of the controls, a reverse ratio of better than three to one. . . .[10]

A difficulty in equating culture backgrounds in terms of socio-economic status or area of residence is that within the same area of residence . . . or within the same income group, there are significant familial variations in culture level. A stricter measure of cultural homogeneity is afforded when delinquents and non-delinquents within the same families are compared for general intelligence. Healy and Bronner, in 105 court-arraigned delinquency cases, compared to a like number of non-delinquent siblings matched closely for age and usually for sex, found differences slightly favoring the non-delinquents. Their data sought to exclude mental defectives and were therefore valid only for IQ's above 70. Their findings (figures for delinquents given first) were: IQ above 110, 13–17 per cent; 90–110, 52–57 per cent; 72–90, 30.8–22.6 per cent.[11] These differences were not calculated for significance. Shulman, in a smaller matched sample of siblings, found that for 28 pairs, delinquents averaged IQ 75 and non-delinquents IQ 86.[12] Thus, both studies favored the theory that delinquents tend toward lower tested intelligence than non-delinquents, when equated for culture level. It is suggested that in the interest of a resolution of this question of the relation of intelligence and delinquency, further studies concern themselves with the intelligence of delinquent and non-delinquent siblings, with emphasis upon the analysis of those physical and emotional factors that might affect learning, mental growth, and motivation to maximum test output. . . .

[10] Cyril Burt, *ibid.*
[11] William Healy and Augusta Bronner, *New Light on Delinquency and Its Treatment*, New Haven, 1936, p. 75.
[12] Harry Manuel Shulman, *A Study of Problem Boys and Their Brothers*, New York State Crime Commission, Albany, 1929, p. 61.

THE PSYCHIATRIC APPROACH
TO CRIME AND CORRECTION

MANFRED S. GUTTMACHER

Excerpted from Manfred S. Guttmacher, "The Psychiatric Approach to Crime and Correction," *Law and Contemporary Problems*, XXIII (Autumn 1958), 633–49. At the time this article was published, Dr. Guttmacher was Chief Medical Officer, Supreme Bench of Baltimore.

BOTH THE treatment and the prevention of disease progresses haltingly until its pathology is established. In most instances, the great strides must wait upon the discovery of aetiology. As far as crime is concerned, whether it be normal criminality, which is essentially a social disease, or crime dependent on mental morbidity, its pathology is poorly understood and its aetiology is essentially unknown. We find ourselves in a position similar to that of the systematists of the eighteenth century; we must be satisfied largely with description and classification.

One of the greatest difficulties in psychiatry is its esoteric vocabulary. Its special terminology not only makes communications with other disciplines difficult, but its technical terms have varying connotations and, in some instances, even varying denotations for psychiatrists. In the writer's efforts to understand the criminals that he examines, he has grouped them under several categories. But no classification which he has come upon seems adequate. At present, he would suggest the following:

1. The normal criminal, the dysocial group made up of individuals who have identified with the asocial elements in our society, generally with morally and socially defective parental figures. They compose seventy-five to eighty per cent of criminals.

2. The accidental or occasional criminal, the individual with an

essentially healthy superego who has become overwhelmed by a special set of circumstances. This is a very small group. On the basis of claims made by offenders and their families, this group would appear to be much larger than it actually is. Nearly every mother whose youthful son becomes involved in criminal behavior asserts that he is a good boy, but the momentary victim of bad associates. On investigation, one generally learns that he had for years been a serious school behavior problem and a well-known client of the juvenile court. The bank officials whom the writer has met in prison all had pretty shady reputations before their convictions.

3. The organically or constitutionally predisposed criminal, forming a disparate group which constitutes a small portion of the total number of criminals and is comprised of numerous subgroups: the intellectually defective, the postencephalitic, the epileptic, the senile deteriorative, the posttraumatic, etc. Of course, the vast majority of persons with these maladies are noncriminal.

The role of head injury in the genesis of antisocial behavior is unclear. The high incidence of head injury in the criminal population is probably related to their general heedlessness resulting in their being accident-prone, rather than being an important causative factor in their delinquency. Why individuals, presumably exposed to identical injurious agents develop varying resultant behavioral patterns is uncertain. The effect is probably dependent on the basic structure of the premorbid personality to a greater degree than on the exact nature and location of the injury.

4. The psychopathic or sociopathic criminal,° the individual who is not psychotic (insane), but who indulges in irrational, antisocial behavior, probably resulting from hidden unconscious neurotic conflicts which constitute the driving dynamic force underlying his criminal conduct. This is a complex group, comprising ten to fifteen per cent of criminals. Among them are to be found some of the most malignant and recidivistic offenders. For purposes of

° Since this article appeared, psychiatric classification has undergone some change, following a major revision of the *Diagnostic and Statistical Manual of Mental Disorders*, published by the American Psychiatric Association in 1968. The term *antisocial personality* replaces *psychopathic personality* and *sociopathic personality*. Editor.

exposition, it is desirable to attempt to isolate discrete subgroups based primarily on behavioral manifestations. Until there is a deeper understanding of the psychopathology and some knowledge of aetiological factors, no really satisfactory subclassification of this important criminal group can be devised.

There is the sociopathic type, described so fully in Hervey Cleckley's *Mask of Sanity*.[1] They have shown evidences of life-long social maladjustment reaching back into early childhood. Dr. Robert Lindner used the very apt phrase "rebel without cause" to describe them.[2] They are in conflict with society in all areas. Benjamin Rush, the first psychiatrist in America and one of the signers of the Declaration of Independence, called the condition "anomia," a term derived from the Greek word for lawlessness.[3] He postulated the existence of a congenital defect of the moral sense in conjunction with normal, or even superior, intellectual powers. English writers have designated these individuals "moral imbeciles" or "moral defectives."

They are often very bright, attractive, and superficially ingratiating. But this amiability is a skillful masking of an overwhelming hostility. They are socially irresponsible. Other persons are merely objects to be manipulated for their own hedonistic purposes. Distant goals are sacrificed for immediate expediency. It has been suggested that they possess a peculiar incapacity to conceptualize, particularly in regard to time. They possess no loyalties and are suspicious of others. Indeed, this incapacity for establishing satisfying and meaningful relationships with other individuals is their nuclear defect. This makes psychiatric treatment so difficult, for psychotherapy—to be effective—requires that the patient establish a significant degree of identification with the therapist.

There is no agreement as to the causative factors involved in the development of such a crippling personality deformity. The most plausible hypothesis is that these individuals were deprived of deep and nurturing parental affection during their earliest years of life and that, as children, they instinctively developed, as a defense

[1] Hervey Cleckley, The Mask of Sanity (3d ed. 1955).

[2] See Robert M. Lindner, Rebel Without a Cause (1944).

[3] See J. C. Bucknill & D. H. Tuke, A Manual of Psychological Medicine (1858).

against this deprivation, an aggressive, insensitive relationship toward other individuals. This lack of early love objects with whom strong identification could be established became the crucial defect in their personality development. Bender maintains that a very critical break in total family identification during the second, third and fourth years may produce the same personality distortion.[4] The same hypothesis has been advanced to account for the development of certain schizophrenic disorders. Indeed, the two conditions have marked similarities.

Sociopaths seemingly do not learn by experience, since despite admonitions and punishments, they continue their same pattern of objectionable conduct. This is one of the characteristics that suggests that their disorder is essentially neurotic, since the repetitive element is constantly present in disturbances that are neurotic in origin. Many of the check forgers, swindlers, and confidence men are recruited from their ranks. Dr. Cleckley maintains that these individuals are no better able to conform to society's demands than are the frankly psychotic and that, therefore, it would be only just to treat them as irresponsible.

Karpman has published important studies on these character disorders.[5] He divides them into primary and symptomatic psychopaths. He finds the latter to be in great preponderance—these are the neurotic characters who act out their basic conflicts against society. Their unbearable tension and anxiety is temporarily abated by their antisocial acts. The smaller group, the primary psychopaths, he terms anethopaths. They are the completely amoral, conscienceless individuals who have a grossly deficient superego development. They seem incapable of developing anxiety, even in their dreams. Karpman cannot find significant psychogenetic factors in the backgrounds of many of the anethopaths. In his opinion, their malfunction, in all probability, is the result of an organic brain defect.

There are, of course, many other types of psychopathic offenders.

[4] Bender, *Psychopathic Behavior Disorders in Children,* in Robert M. Lindner & Robert V. Seliger (eds.), Handbook of Correctional Psychology 360, 362 (1947).

[5] Karpman, *The Myth of the Psychopathic Personality,* 104 Am. J. Psychiatry 523.

Among them are the violently aggressive and sadistic criminals. In most instances, they have been subjected to harsh cruelties during their formative years in the guise of parental discipline. Life is for them not a very precious commodity—neither their own nor that of other persons.

Most of the sexual offenders, too, are neurotic criminals. It is believed that their abnormalities generally stem from subtly distorting emotional relationships with parental figures in early life. Both the abnormally seductive mother and the mother who is forbiddingly punitive and suppressive may cripple her son in his sexual development. It is now well-recognized by criminologists that many crimes that appear to be nonsexual in nature originate in psychosexual pathology. The number of offenses of this type is probably far greater than we realize.

There is a subcategory of offenders whose crimes arise from what are known as personality trait disturbances who also belong in the large, heterogeneous group of neurotic offenders. Chief among them are the passive-aggressive personalities. In this group, one finds the unusually passive, long-suffering, and nonprotesting people who occasionally, under apparently slight provocation, explode with volcanic force.

Franz Alexander, again, has written widely and informatively on the group of offenders, originally described by Freud, who engage in antisocial behavior in order to achieve punishment at the hands of the law.[6] These are individuals who are in constant conflict with themselves because of intense guilt feelings over some deeply-buried early-life experience or emotional attitude which is below the level of consciousness. Punishment by the authorities for an offense, which is frequently symbolically related to the source of their guilt, gives them surcease from their relentless self-condemnation. Their crimes are often marked by a clumsy stupidity which makes their apprehension easy and certain. They enjoy peace of mind while under incarceration, which is lacking when living in the community. Doubtless offenders of this type exist, but in this author's experience, they are relatively rare.

[6] Franz Alexander, Fundamentals of Psychoanalysis 238 (1948); 4 Sigmund Freud, Collected Papers 342 (1949).

The writer has been impressed by another small group of neurotic offenders who appear to court capture by the authorities. These are immature individuals who feel helpless before their own antisocial impulses and compulsions and have a real fear of them. Like the small child who runs to his parents to fix things, they turn to the authorities, feeling that in some magical way, they can help them gain control. This type of reaction is most likely to occur in sex offenders.

Heedlessness, although fundamentally self-destructive in nature, does not necessarily originate from an inner need for punishment. Great segments of the population display an amazing degree of heedlessness in their daily living, which stems from an inability or unwillingness to face issues realistically. In every city, long queues form on the day that old automobile licenses expire, waiting for hours to buy new ones, despite the fact that at the cost of a few pennies, they could have received them well in advance by mail. And one need only consider the number of persons living precariously beyond their means, who lose the many possessions they are purchasing on the installment plan as soon as they are without a job. In professional gambling, the gambler is more likely to lose than to win. Some people are psychologically motivated in their incessant gambling by a need to punish and destroy themselves. But there is little reason to believe that most excessive gamblers are of this type. A more frequent dynamic pattern in the neurotic gambler is his need to triumph over others and to achieve disproportionate and immediate rewards from what he sees as his small investment.

5. The psychotic criminal, the individual whose antisocial behavior is a symptom of his insanity. He suffers from one of the major mental disorders. These insanities are marked by regressive behavior in which the ego is overwhelmed by primitive aggressive drives. These may be directed against himself or against others. As bizarre and as unintelligible as much of insane behavior appears to be, it has an economic utility for the individual. Were we wise enough, its meaning and significance could in every instance be deciphered.

Only one and a half to two per cent of criminals are definitely psychotic. There is, of course, no sharp dividing line between health and disease. At what point the psychological disorganization of the individual reaches sufficient proportions to be designated a psychosis is a matter of judgment. This problem presents its greatest difficulty in cases of short-lived psychosis. There are cases of temporary insanity. Alcoholic deliria and confusional states associated with epilepsy are widely recognized as such. Combat psychiatrists saw men who succumbed under great stress for brief periods successfully mobilize their psychological defenses and rapidly regain their stability.

THE GEOGRAPHY OF CRIME

JOSEPH COHEN

Excerpted from Joseph Cohen, "The Geography of Crime," *Annals of the American Academy of Political and Social Science*, CCXVII (September 1941), 29–37. At the time of publication, J. Cohen was Assistant Professor of Sociology in the University of Washington.

DURING THE past forty years students have become less and less disposed to posit new hypotheses concerning the influences of *physical* geography upon crime, and have become either skeptical of the old hypotheses or disinterested in them. The observations and brilliant speculations concerning the general effects of the geographical environment made by a continuous succession of social philosophers and social geographers following Montesquieu (1689–1755) and Buckle (1821–62) culminated during the 1890s in the extended empirical investigations of Albert Leffingwell and E. G. Dexter. The latter two studied the effects of separate phases of weather upon specific classes of behavior and upon crime in particular. The four succeeding decades in the twentieth century have not witnessed any comparable research efforts to check or amplify the theories of meteorological influence.

As a consequence of the rich development of psychology, anthropology, and sociology, especially since the first World War, significant explanations of criminal conduct have been sought in individual traits and attitudes, in factors of the material and nonmaterial culture, and in conditions of social organization. Geographical and temporal variations in crime rates are now generally interpreted as expressions of involved social situations in which physical elements are present as components, but not as direct and primary causal influences. A geographical approach to crime at the present time is usually employed to determine with what social factors, or combi-

nations of social and physical factors, variations in crime rates are
associated. The high homicide rates of the South, for example, are
recognized as effects of a complex set of historical and contempo-
raneous circumstances in the development of which the factors of
natural resources, topography, temperature, barometric pressure,
aqueous tension, precipitation, sunshine, rain, and wind velocity
are elemental but not decisive. The physical factors and influences
are believed by prevailing expert opinion within the field of criminology not to operate directly upon individual conduct, but to be
mediated by conditions of personality, culture, and social organization.

Nineteenth-Century Studies

Almost the whole range of hypotheses which impute direct
causal influence to the elements of the physical environment were
enunciated at one time or another during the nineteenth
century. . . .

M. de Guerry de Champneuf, Director of Criminal Affairs in the
French Ministry of Justice (1821–35), collected the records of the
different types of crimes committed in the eighty-six departments
of France during the years 1825 to 1830. It is interesting that he
used the number of persons accused of crime, rather than convictions, as an index of criminality, the wisdom of which is confirmed
by critical authority today. On the basis of de Champneuf's figures
on the geographical distribution of crime, Parmelee draws the following conclusion: "While there are for every 100 crimes against
the person 181.5 crimes against property in northern France, there
are in southern France for every 100 crimes against the person
only 48.8 crimes against property." [1] Concerning his data, de
Champneuf stated:

There is the influence of climate, and there is the influence of seasons,
for whereas the crimes against persons are always more numerous in the
summer, the crimes against property are more numerous in winter—so of
the crimes committed in the South, the crimes against the person are far
more numerous than those against property, while in the North the

[1] Maurice Parmelee, *Criminology* (New York: Macmillan, 1923), p. 45.

crimes against property are, in the same proportion, more numerous than those against the person.[2]

Lombroso, Ferri, and Aschaffenburg corroborated the South-North gradient trend for later periods in Italy, France, and Germany, and also cited statistical evidence for those countries, showing that crimes of violence against the person tend to increase in the summer months, and crimes against property in the winter.

None of these men believed that the physical influences are the exclusive or even the principal causes of delinquency. Lombroso was, of course, the author and outstanding advocate of the theory of the born criminal, whose tendencies, he asserted, are inhibited or facilitated by varying environmental influences. Ferri believed that there are criminal types in addition to the "born criminal," and, as a socialist, laid considerable stress upon economic influences.

Climate was believed by these writers to exert its influence in diverse ways. The warmer temperature of summer and the continuous warmth of the southern latitudes were regarded as affecting the physical mechanism directly, heightening emotion, stimulating activity, and, according to Lombroso, encouraging "quarrels, brawls, and stabbing affrays." The more abundant food supply and the minimum need for clothing were believed to account for the decrease in acts of criminal appropriation during the summer months and in the lush southern areas. Sex crimes, which were reported to be at a maximum during May and June, were regarded as related to an inherent biological periodicity of sexual interest.

This covergence of belief concerning the intimate causal relation between climate and crime, on the part of students who were otherwise of the most divergent opinion, was formulated by Adolphe Quetelet into the thermic law of delinquency, according to which crimes against the person predominate in warmer areas and during the warmer months, while crimes against property increase in cooler areas and in the winter time. Peter Kropotkin went much further. He attempted the formulation of a mathematical statement

[2] Quoted by M. C. Elmer, "Century Old Ecological Studies in France," *American Journal of Sociology*, Vol. XXXIX, No. 1, p. 65.

of the functional dependence of crime upon temperature and humidity. Bernaldo de Quiros quotes him as follows:

By the statistics of previous years one could foretell with astonishing exactness the number of crimes to be committed during the following year in every country of Europe. Through a very simple mathematical operation we can find a formula that enables us to foretell the number of crimes merely by consulting the thermometer and the hygrometer. Take the average temperature of the month and multiply it by seven, then add the average humidity, multiply again by two and you will obtain the number of homicides that are committed during the month.[3]

This notion represents the fantastic expectation of some that there could be found a simple formula for the explanation of behavior in terms of immediate and measurable geographic influences.

DEXTER'S CONCLUSIONS

The most challenging statement concerning the nature and the extent of physical influences upon crime—and the study which thirty-seven years after its publication is still the most frequently quoted—is contained in some of the chapters of Edwin Grant Dexter's *Weather Influences: an Empirical Study of the Mental and Physiological Effects of Definite Meteorological Conditions*.[4] Dexter's data included records of nearly 40,000 cases of assault and battery by men and women in New York City during the years 1891 to 1897; 184 murders in Denver between 1884 and 1896; and 3,891 cases of disciplinary action in New York prisons between 1891 and 1897. Dexter's principal conclusions are given in the following paragraphs in some detail because they constitute a full statement of the manner in which physical influences are still thought by some "geographic determinists" to cause variations in crime rates. No essential additions or modifications in the theory have been made since Dexter:

a) "Temperature, more than any other condition, affects the emotional states which are conducive to fighting" (p. 143). Under some circumstances the positive association between temperature

[3] Bernaldo de Quiros, *Modern Theories of Criminality* (Boston: Little, Brown and Co., 1911), p. 34.
[4] Edwin Grant Dexter, *Weather Influences*, New York: Macmillan, 1904.

and crime is not maintained, but the exceptions are easily explained. A warm day in April, with a mean temperature of, say, 75, following a cooler spell "might have a disastrous effect upon conduct" (p. 148), whereas the same temperature or even a higher one in August after a very hot spell would reduce the number of arrests for assault and battery. Changes in temperature during the summer bring about more marked variations in violence than corresponding variations in the winter time.

b) "Periods of low barometric pressure are proved to be the hardest season for the bluecoats" (pp. 149–50). As barometric pressure goes down, crimes of violence increase. Dexter believed that it is not the actual weight of the atmosphere that affects people, but the "feel" that many persons have that a storm is coming. . . .

c) The evidence of forty thousand cases is held to be conclusive that as humidity increases, acts of violence decrease.

The reason is undoubtedly this. Days of high humidity are not only emotionally but vitally depressing. . . . On such days we perhaps feel like fighting, but such a thing is altogether too much exertion, and the police records are none the wiser (p. 151).

d) Mild winds of between 150 and 200 miles per day are associated with the greatest release of energy in pugnacious assaults, as well as in other types of activity. This is easily accounted for by the fact that the usual excess of carbon monoxide in the air of cities is dispelled, and the increased oxygen brought in by winds heightens emotional and physical activity. . . .

e) Rainy weather has ambivalent influences upon the organism. It puts people "out of sorts," but also deprives them of the energy necessary to indulge their sulky moods. The number of crimes of violence is, therefore, minimized by rain.

Dexter believed that the weather operates directly upon the emotional and physiological activities of the individual, producing various anomalies of behavior. In his printed reports he only infrequently suggested the possible indirect effects of weather, and when he did, it was largely to dismiss or minimize the plausibility of such interpretations.

Since the publication of Dexter's study in 1904 no investigator has attempted systematically to relate crime to factors of climate and geography. The geographers are apparently not sufficiently interested in crime to study the relationship, and the criminologists are not disposed to regard investigations of the physical phases of geography and climate as promising much insight into criminal behavior. . . . This is especially surprising in view of the definitely seasonal and regional character of many crimes, as indicated by such sources as the *Uniform Crime Reports*.

Evidence of the Uniform Crime Reports

CRIMES OF VIOLENCE

The most comprehensive and reliable contemporary sources of data on seasonal aspects of crime are the *Uniform Crime Reports* of the Federal Bureau of Investigation and, for homicides, the state and Federal reports on vital statistics. . . .

The monthly trend of aggravated assault in 1935–40 shows a remarkably close resemblance to the 1891–97 arrest data of assault and battery gathered in New York City by Dexter. In each case the low point came in January; the annual average per day was approximated early in May; the peak was reached in midsummer; there was a gradual and continuous decline through November; and December showed a minor, "holiday" rise. The index numbers of aggravated assault for the separate years did not differ considerably from the six-year average.

The monthly rates for homicide also show a definite seasonal pattern, the general features of which are the same as in the case of aggravated assault. The highest rates occurred in July, August, September, and October. After tapering off during November, the figures rose during December, and then dipped decidedly to a low point in January. The rates rose gradually and consistently from January to July. The monthly rates for homicide are shown . . . to have varied less on the average than the rates for aggravated assault. In no case did the figures for a month deviate as much as 10 per cent from the mean annual rate.

In the case of the homicide rates there were marked fluctuations in the monthly trend from year to year. October was the high month three times, July twice, and August once. January, February, March, April, June, and November were in various years either lowest in their rates or tied for that position.

When the data from the *Uniform Crime Reports* on monthly variations of homicides are compared with data from other sources, particularly the vital statistics on homicides gathered by Federal and state vital statistics bureaus, the conclusion is reinforced that, *in general, murders are committed more frequently during the summer than during the winter, but there is marked variation in peak and low months from year to year and from area to area.*

Brearley made a study of the 1,601 homicides that occurred in South Carolina during the period 1920–26, and correlated them by months with the mean temperature. He found practically no association between them.[5] He also measured the relation between crime and changes in temperature, with similar results.[6] If this lack of correlation is confirmed in other studies, we shall have to conclude either that physical influences other than temperature are responsible for the seasonal variations, or that social factors associated with season are responsible.

CRIMES AGAINST PROPERTY

The observation, first made at the beginning of the nineteenth century, that crimes against property reach their peak during the winter and fall off during the summer is clearly established by the data of the *Uniform Crime Reports* for the offense of robbery, and somewhat less decisively for burglary and auto theft. . . .

The amounts of robbery receded and rose from the beginning of the year to the end with a symmetry that is rare in the statistics of social data. This catenary curve for the six-year average was closely approximated for each of the separate years.

The peak incidence of robbery occurred in December. The rate decreased each month until July, when it was almost 50 per cent lower than the maximum. After July the rate increased regularly through the remainder of the summer, the autumn, and until the

---

[5] H. C. Brearley, *Homicide in the United States* (Chapel Hill: Univ. of North Carolina Press, 1932), pp. 177–79. The Pearsonian coefficient of correlation (r) was +.128, with a probable error of .078.

[6] The coefficient was +.135, with a probable error of .072.

middle of the winter. The pattern of regular ebb and flow remained constant from year to year. Sometimes the curve rose or fell more markedly or less markedly, and sometimes the high point or the low point was reached a month earlier or later.

The rates for burglary, though definitely seasonal, were not so regular as those for robbery. From January through March there was a slight rise in rates. The rates were relatively constant during August, September, and October. There was not nearly so much difference between low and high months as in robbery. The pattern varied from year to year, but, in general, rates were consistently low in the middle of the year and consistently high in midwinter. In the remaining two offenses for which monthly data are available from the *Uniform Crime Reports* seasonality was present, but in a less marked manner than in the case of robbery.

Thus, we find that the data from many countries, gathered for well over a century, show incontrovertibly that crime is a seasonal phenomenon; that is, crimes against the person tend, on the whole, to increase in the summer time, while crimes against property predominate in the winter. . . .

That many influences are at work causing these fluctuations is abundantly clear when one scrutinizes the data in detail. Research has yet to reveal the factors with which these seasonal variations are associated. By what we must now regard as crude methods . . . Dexter attempted, as we have seen, to relate assault and battery and drunkenness to meterological influences, particularly temperature. With little more than a gesture he brushed aside the possibilities of "cultural" determination of the seasonal variations.

Reasons for Lack of Interest in Seasonal Variations

It appears very odd, on the surface, that such a promising line of research, in which many significant hypotheses could be tested, was not carefully investigated during a period that was marked otherwise by intensive research efforts. Some of the reasons for this lack of interest are the following:

a) Until the publication of the *Uniform Crime Reports* very little confidence was reposed in the available statistical data showing

the incidence of crime. . . . How could one account for variations
when the existence of variation was itself in doubt?

b) Associated with this skepticism of published statistical data
was the disrepute of all theories that rested on an alleged consonance between the fluctuation of crime and other social variables.
All sorts of implausible and contradictory theories were bolstered
by the demonstration of a close mutual fluctuation in time between
crime and a factor asserted to be its cause.

c) Especially since the war, interest has centered upon the individual, his antecedents, traits, and motivations. The method of co-
relation of crime as a mass phenomenon with other mass phenom-
elation of crime as a mass phenomenon with other mass phenomena did not seem, in the light of prevailing interests, to be directed
at significant causes. The typical objection from this point of view
was that this method does not explain why one individual commits
robbery and another does not, or why one individual commits robbery and another assault and battery. This is, of course, a superficial objection, since a scientific principle may be adequate if it explains mass variations, without accounting for the vagaries of
individual instances.

d) A great deal of seasonal variation is undoubtedly explained
by obvious, common-sense considerations which do not call for investigation at all. For example, as the days become longer the possibility of burglary decreases. Over 90 per cent of nonresidential
burglaries are committed at night. In a certain sense, winter and
night are more in the nature of occasions for increased burglary
than significant causes, just as summer is an occasion for baseball
and autumn for football. The pickpocket functions most favorably
in a standing, moving, out-of-door crowd, which is commonly a
summer rather than a winter phenomenon. Again, both summer
and the particular type of crowd are very favorable occasions for
this offense. Variations in crime that are related to such factors as
these are of immense practical importance to the police and other
law enforcement agencies, for obvious reasons, but they do not afford serious problems to science.

Sectional Differences

The diversities in the amount and type of crime found at different seasons of the year are exceeded by the diversities that are found between the different states and sections of the country. If the thermic law of crime were valid on a territorial basis, we should expect that states and cities which have high crime rates for assault and murder would have low rates for robbery, burglary, larceny, and auto theft. This negative association was reported as characteristic of some European countries, as we have noted earlier. The territorial phase of Quetelet's law does not prove sound when tested by American experience. States and cities which have rates above the average for assault and murder more frequently than not have rates for crimes against property which are also above the average. In general, however, the areas having extremely high rates for crimes of violence have moderate, and in some cases even low, rates for robbery, burglary, and similar offenses against property. These variations are not in consonance with the early European findings. The geographic distribution of offenses is not so simple and clear as to fall within the framework of any single law.

Crimes of violence have a definitely regional distribution. The highest rates for murder and assault are found in the South. The fourteen states with the highest per capita rates, according to the *Uniform Crime Reports,* are grouped contiguously in the southeast quarter of the country. The next group is the tier to the north which includes Pennsylvania, Ohio, Indiana, Illinois, Missouri, and Kansas. New York, New Jersey, and the far western states have relatively low rates. Human life is safest from homicide in New England and the northern prairie states. To a surprising extent, these groups of states form contiguous blocs, states of nearly equal rates lying adjacently. Data from the United States Division of Vital Statistics show essentially the same distribution.

The studies that have been made of the regional distribution of homicide in this and other countries do not give us much confidence in any explicit theory. Brearley found low correlation be-

tween homicide rates and such social phenomena as illiteracy, in-
dustrialization, farm tenancy, density of rural population, church
membership, and business conditions. We can take refuge behind a
generalization like "regional tradition," remembering that this explains nothing, but is itself in need of explanation.

The distribution by states of property offenses is characterized
with respect to each class by low rates in the New England states.
Most of the high rates for larceny are found west of the Mississippi. Robbery rates have their peak in Illinois, Kentucky, and
Tennessee, with an axis running westward to the coast states. In
either direction from this axis, the rates tend to diminish. Otherwise, no definite spatial pattern is distinguishable.

The evidence from the best available evidence shows that crime
rates vary according to definite seasonal and spatial patterns. The
explanation of these patterns has undergone a development from
an emphasis upon meterology and factors of physical environment
to an emphasis upon community structure, social organization, and
tradition. Criminological research cannot be said to have discovered as yet with which specific factors in the environment the temporal and spatial variations in crime are associated. This is one of
its important tasks for the future. . . . These differences, undoubtedly, are measures of significant social forces, and present a challenge to research men and scholars, as they do to those men of
practical affairs who presume to exercise leadership in advancing
the local and national welfare.

AN ECOLOGICAL APPROACH TO
JUVENILE DELINQUENCY

CLIFFORD R. SHAW
AND HENRY D. McKAY

Excerpted from Clifford R. Shaw and Henry D. McKay, *Juvenile Delinquency and Urban Areas, A Study of Rates of Delinquents in Relation to Differential Characteristics of Local Communities in American Cities* (Chicago: University of Chicago Press, 1942), pp. 50–54, 435–41.

A. *The Distribution of Alleged Delinquents Brought before the Juvenile Court of Cook County*

I. THE 1927–33 JUVENILE COURT SERIES

Series Studied. These 8,411 different alleged male delinquents were brought before the Juvenile Court of Cook County from Chicago. . . . They are all separate individuals, as duplications from year to year, as well as within the separate years, have been eliminated from the series.

Distribution of Delinquents. Map 7 . . . [deleted] shows the distribution by place of residence of the . . . delinquents. Each dot represents the home address of one delinquent boy. . . .

It will be observed . . . that there are areas of marked concentration of delinquents, as compared with other areas where the dots are widely dispersed. These concentrations are most obvious immediately north and northwest of the Loop along the North Branch of the Chicago River, in the areas some distance south of the Loop along State Street, and in the areas immediately outside and extending westward from the northern part of the Loop. . . .

This distribution . . . is closely related to the location of industrial and commercial areas and to the composition of the population. In the first place . . . the areas of heaviest concentration are, in general, not far from the central business district, within or near the areas zoned for light industry or commerce. As one moves outward, away from these areas into the residential communities, the cases are more and more scattered until, near the periphery of the city, they are, in general, widely dispersed.

The concentrations of delinquents not adjacent to the central business district are, for the most part, near outlying heavy industrial areas. . . . Comparison [of maps] reveals further that the alleged delinquents are concentrated mainly in areas characterized by decreasing population and low rentals, with high percentages of families on relief. Here, too, industrial workers predominate. The population in these neighborhoods was . . . largely foreign born, with high proportions of recent arrivals, aliens, and migrants from the rural South.

As to national heritage, the area of concentration of delinquents on the Near North Side was, during the period covered, predominantly Italian; the lower Northwest Side, mainly Polish; the Near West Side, Italian and American Negro; and the Lower West Side chiefly Czechoslovakian. Among the more outlying areas, the Humboldt Park population included Poles, Swedes, Italians, and Russian Jews; the Back of the Yards district was Polish and Lithuanian; while the predominant nationalities in South Chicago were Polish, Italian, Hungarian, Mexican, and Yugoslavian. . . .

In order to compare the number of delinquents by areas and to relate this number in each instance to the population of the same age and sex, the city was divided into 140 areas. . . .

When the distribution of the 8,411 delinquents is analyzed in terms of these 140 square-mile areas, wide differences are evident. In each of 3 areas there are more than 300 delinquents, while 8 have more than 150 each. At the other extreme, there is 1 area from which only 3 delinquents were taken to court, 15 with fewer than 10, and 25 with fewer than 15 delinquents. . . . The theoretical significance of these facts is at least twofold. First, they reveal the wide variation in distribution; second, they indicate, quite apart from density of population, the differential probability of a boy's having contact with other delinquent boys in the same area or of observing their activities.

Rates of Delinquents. . . . These rates represent the number of alleged delinquents taken to the Juvenile Court from each area during 1927–33, per hundred of the aged 10–16 male population in that area as of 1930. . . .

The range . . . is from 0.5 to 18.9. The median is 2.5 and the rate for the city as a whole, 4.2. Three of the 140 areas have rates above 17.0, and 14 below 1.0. . . . This comparison brings out two fundamental facts, namely, that there are wide differences among areas and that the number of areas with low rates far exceeds the number where they are high. . . .

It is clear from the data included in this volume that there is a direct relationship between conditions existing in local communities of American cities and differential rates of delinquents and criminals. Communities with high rates have social and economic characteristics which differentiate them from communities with low rates. Delinquency—particularly group delinquency, which constitutes a preponderance of all officially recorded offenses committed by boys and young men—has its roots in the dynamic life of the community.

It is recognized that the data . . . may be interpreted from many different points of view. However, the high degree of consistency in the association between delinquency and other characteristics of the community . . . appears to establish that all community characteristics, including delinquency, are products of the operation of general processes more or less common to American cities. Moreover, the fact that in Chicago the rates of delinquents for many years have remained relatively constant in the areas adjacent to centers of commerce and heavy industry, despite successive changes in the nativity and nationality composition of the population, supports emphatically the conclusion that the delinquency-producing factors are inherent in the community.

From the data available it appears that local variations in the conduct of children, as revealed in differential rates of delinquents, reflect the differences in social values, norms, and attitudes to which the children are exposed. In some parts of the city attitudes which support and sanction delinquency are, it seems, sufficiently extensive and dynamic to become the controlling forces in the development of delinquent careers among a relatively large number of boys and young men. . . .

This tradition is manifested in many different ways. It becomes meaningful to the child through the conduct, speech, gestures, and attitudes of persons with whom he has contact. Of particular importance is the child's intimate association with predatory gangs or other forms of delinquent and criminal organization. . . .

In these communities many children encounter competing systems of values. Their community, which provides most of the social forms in terms of which their life will be organized, presents conflicting possibilities. A career in delinquency and crime is one alternative, which often becomes real and enticing to the boy because it offers the promise of economic gain, prestige, and companionship and because he becomes acquainted with it through relationships with persons whose esteem and approbation are vital to his security and to the achievement of satisfactory status. . . .

In cases of group delinquency it may be said, therefore, that from the point of view of the delinquent's immediate social world, he is not necessarily disorganized, maladjusted, or antisocial. Within the limits of his social world and in terms of its norms and expectations, he may be a highly organized and well-adjusted person.

The residential communities of higher economic status, where the proportion of persons dealt with as delinquents and criminals is relatively low, stand in sharp contrast to the situation described above. Here the norms and values of the child's social world are more or less uniformly and consistently conventional. Generally speaking, the boy who grows up in this situation is not faced with the problem of making a choice between conflicting systems of moral values. . . .

It is important to ask what the forces are which give rise to these significant differences in the organized values in different communities. Under what conditions do the conventional forces . . . become so weakened as to tolerate the development of a conflicting system of criminal values? Under what conditions is the conventional community capable of maintaining its integrity and exercising such control over the lives of its members as to check the development of the competing system? Obviously, any discussion of this question . . . must be tentative. The data presented in this volume, however, afford a basis for consideration of certain points which may be significant.

It may be observed . . . that the variations in rates of officially recorded delinquents in communities of the city correspond very closely with variations in economic status. The communities with the highest rates . . . are occupied by those segments of the population whose position is most disadvantageous in relation to the distribution of economic, social, and cultural values. . . .

The communities with the lowest rates . . . occupy a relatively high position in relation to the economic and social hierarchy of the city. . . .

Despite these marked differences in the relative position of people in different communities, children and young people in all areas, both rich and poor, are exposed to the luxury values and success patterns of our culture. In school and elsewhere they are also exposed to ideas of equality, freedom, and individual enterprise. Among children and young people residing in low-income areas, interests in acquiring material goods and enhancing personal status are developed which are often difficult to realize by legitimate means. . . .

This disparity in the facilities available to people in different communities . . . is particularly important in relation to delinquency and crime in the urban world. In the city, relationships are largely impersonal. Because of the anonymity in urban life, the individual is freed from much of the scrutiny and control which characterize life in primary-group situations in small towns and rural communities. Personal status and the status of one's community are, to a very great extent, determined by economic achievement. Superior status depends not so much on character as on the possession of those goods and values which symbolize success. Hence, the kind of clothes one wears, the automobile one drives . . . become of great importance to the person. . . . The urban world . . . provides a general setting particularly conducive to the development of deviations in moral norms and behavior practices.

In the low-income areas, where there is the greatest deprivation and frustration . . . the development of crime as an organized way of life is most marked. Crime, in this situation, may be regarded as one of the means employed by people to acquire, or to attempt to acquire, the economic and social values generally idealized in our culture, which persons in other circumstances acquire by conventional means. . . . The power and affluence achieved . . . by many persons involved in crime and illegal rackets are well known to the children and youth of the community and are important in determining the character of their ideals. . . .

It should be observed that, while the tradition of delinquency and crime is thus a powerful force in certain communities, it is only a part of the community's system of values. As was pointed out previously, the dominant tradition in every community is conventional, even in those having the highest rates of delinquents. The traditionally conventional values are embodied in the family, the church, the school, and many other such institutions and organizations. Since the dominant tradition in the community is conventional, more persons pursue law-abiding careers than careers of delinquency and crime, as might be expected.

In communities occupied by Orientals, even those communities located in the most deteriorated sections of our large cities, the solidarity of Old World cultures and institutions has been preserved to such a marked extent that control of the child is still sufficiently effective to keep at a minimum delinquency and other forms of deviant behavior. . . .

It is the assumption of this volume that many factors are important in determining whether a particular child will become involved in delinquency, even in those communities in which a system of delinquent and criminal values exists. Individual and personality differences, as well as differences in family relationships and in contacts with other institutions and groups, no doubt influence greatly his acceptance or rejection of opportunities to engage in delinquent activities. It may be said, however, that if the delinquency tradition were not present and the boys were not thus exposed to it, a preponderance of those who become delinquent in low-income areas would find their satisfactions in activities other than delinquency.

In conclusion, it is not assumed that this theoretical proposition applies to all cases of officially proscribed behavior. It applies primarily to those delinquent activities which become embodied in groups and social organizations. For the most part, these are offenses against property, which comprise a very large proportion of all the cases of boys coming to the attention of the courts.

A DIVERGENT ECOLOGICAL VIEW ON DELINQUENCY

BERNARD LANDER

Excerpted from Bernard Lander, *Towards an Understanding of Juvenile Delinquency* (New York: Columbia University Press, 1954), pp. 77–90.

Conclusion

. . . The statistical findings in themselves do not supply the answer to the causal basis of the differential delinquency rate, but do provide a map which if analyzed with care and caution, may suggest some directions and answers. They enable us to test and suggest hypotheses. Statistical techniques and their results are effective aids in the quest for understanding. At best, however, they provide only clues, and if used without caution may in many instances even be misleading. . . .

In this monograph, we have dealt primarily with prediction, rather than with causation. With the exception of the factor analysis, our statistical techniques have primarily dealt with the discovery of the independent variables that are statistically significant in predicting the differential delinquency rate. Yet even successful prediction does not guarantee understanding. Prediction is based on the description of a statistically significant concomitant relationship between two or more variables. It does not tell us *why* this relationship exists or what it represents.

Prediction and causation, while closely related, are separate goals of sociological research. In a prediction study, we examine each factor in terms of *how much* it contributes to the variance of the dependent variable. In a causation study, our primary interest is not how much each factor contributes to the computation of a rate, but how the factors interact and are meaningfully related to differentials in the dependent variable.

The statistical analysis of the data available to us has a static character. It provides a snapshot of a relationship frozen in time. Causation, however, is dynamic. A study of causation entails an examination of the interaction of forces and resistances in the social situation—and in the individual—as they make for the acceptance or rejection of the norms of society with regard to juvenile conduct. . . .

Major Statistical Findings and Their Interpretation

HOUSING

The findings of this monograph confirm the many studies that have indicated a close correspondence between the delinquency rate and the housing characteristics of an area. In Baltimore, the zero order correlations between overcrowding, substandard housing conditions, and the juvenile delinquency rate are $r = +.73$ and $+.69$.

On the basis of similar zero order correlation coefficients, many investigators have argued that bad housing has a direct causal effect on the delinquency rate. The implication has been: "Remove the slums and you remove the social ills!"

More careful analysis however indicates the insufficiency of this interpretation. The fact that in ranking delinquency areas there is a frequency of overcrowding and bad housing does not in itself suggest a causal nexus to any greater extent than the frequency of tuberculosis or child mortality in these areas suggest these variables as causal bases of the delinquency rate. Furthermore, causation is not established unless we can indicate *how* the physical aspects of housing are related to the delinquency rate and *why* there is so much less delinquency in many rural areas or urban communities characterized in terms of our housing standards by primitive and very much substandard housing. It is germane to note that several tracts, namely, Tracts 1–4 and 2–3 in which 84% or more of the homes are substandard, are not even included in the group of tracts comprising the first quartile of the ranking delinquency areas. In Tract 25–6, 98% of the housing is substandard, the median estimated or contract monthly rental of $11.81 is the lowest in the city, more than 80% of the area is zoned for industry, and the residential district is almost completely surrounded by heavy industry yet there are 25 tracts in Baltimore with higher delinquency rates. As a matter of fact, in this study, the indices of partial correlation between overcrowding, substandard housing, and delinquency are reduced to zero when the other variables are held constant and their influence eliminated. Despite the high zero order correlation coefficients, the partial correlations suggest that there is no *real* or substantive relationship between the delinquency rate and the physical aspects of housing as such. The findings of the regression analysis in this respect are also amply confirmed by the factor analysis. On the other hand, our regression analysis indicates that home-ownership is significantly associated even on the .01 significance level with the presence of juvenile delinquency. We have hypothesized the frequency of home-ownership in Baltimore as a measure of community stability. The factor analysis also confirms the existence of a fundamental relationship between delinquency and social stability as measured by home-ownership and the lack of such a relationship with housing as measured by its physical or economic aspects. Thus, the primary significance of housing in the understanding of delinquency is not in its physical aspects or merely in the area's economic position in the city which its rentals reflect, but primarily and fundamentally in its social aspects as a measure of or contributor to social stability or *anomie*.

OTHER SOCIO-ECONOMIC VARIABLES

The zero order correlation between the median years schooling of a tract's population and its delinquency rate is $r = -.51$, and between median rentals and delinquency, $r = -.53$. The regression analysis and the factor analysis, however, clearly indicate that these variables are not fundamentally related to the prediction and/or understanding of juvenile delinquency.

Our analysis deals with the varying *area* rates. It is in this context that we find that economic variables are not significant in the prediction and understanding of the differential delinquency rate. As we have emphasized earlier these findings bear no necessary implication for a study of the prediction or understanding of the conduct patterns of a specific individual. The findings . . . do not gainsay the possible significance of any or all the variables studied as direct or indirect determinants of the behavior of individuals. Thus, one may well argue . . . that poverty may compel the individual to live in the kind of community in which other factors conducive to delinquency operate. Presumably, however, if such variables as poverty do enter into the determination of individual behavior with respect to delinquency, they do so in different ways, for different individuals—i.e., the fact of poverty presumably has different significance and differing consequences for different individuals. Else one would expect them to show up significantly in the area statistics. Individual differences in response to such variables as poverty would tend to cancel one another out and, hence, to disappear in the area statistics. For an understanding of the total causal analysis of juvenile delinquency there is need for a study of the determinants of individual conduct as they operate in and interact with the social situation.

POPULATION COMPOSITION

In Chicago and other American urban areas, Shaw found that high rates of delinquency characterized areas populated by large concentrations of foreign-born groups. This finding is not true for Baltimore. As a matter of fact there is if anything an *inverse* relationship between delinquency and the presence of foreign-born groups. . . . The 1903 Federal Slum Survey found delinquency concentrated primarily in sections populated by the foreign-born; in 1940, delinquency was a characteristic of areas inhabited by the native-born. In 1940, many of the foreign-born groups were well integrated culturally and economically into the Baltimore community and were characterized by a high degree of home-ownership and social stability. At least two of these ethnic groups, the Jews and the Chinese, were characterized by almost a complete absence of any recorded delinquency. During the study period, it was the Negro, a native-born group, that contributed a large proportion of Baltimore's recorded crime and delinquency.

During the 1939–1942 study period, Negro children comprised 49% of Baltimore's delinquents although they only constituted approximately 20% of the comparable age grouping in the general population. In the regression and factor analysis the percentage of Negroes in a tract is significantly related to the prediction and understanding of the differential delinquency rate. On the basis of these analyses one might erroneously impute a causal significance to race per se. However, the following evidence amply supports the hypothesis that race as such is not a significant factor in the understanding of delinquency.

The racial factor does not explain the wide variation in Negro delinquency rates. This rate varies as widely as does the white rate, indicating large differences in behavior patterns that cannot be ascribed as an effect of race per se. It is also of interest to note that the Negro delinquency rate increases from 8% in areas in which the Negro population concentration is less than 10% of the total population to 13 and 14% in tracts with 10–29.9 and 30–49.9 Negro population percentages. However, as the Negro population concentration increases beyond 50%, the Negro delinquency rate decreases to 7% in areas with 90% or more Negro population. Thus, in the areas with the greatest Negro population proportion, the Negro delinquency rate is lowest. A similar pattern of delinquency frequency also characterizes the white group in relation to the proportion of Negroes.

The net regression line which describes the relationship between the presence of Negroes and the delinquency rate when the influence of the other variables is eliminated also indicates a similar pattern. As the Negro proportion of the total tract population increases to 50%, the delinquency rate increases. As the percentage of Negroes increases beyond 50%, the delinquency rate correspondingly decreases. Thus, when other factors are held constant, delinquency rates in Baltimore are highest in areas of maximum racial heterogeneity. In areas of total Negro occupancy the delinquency rate is no higher than in similar areas of total white occupancy. This does not necessarily mean that high rates . . . are inevitable in racially heterogeneous areas. It means simply that under the conditions of racial heterogeneity found in Baltimore, such heterogeneity is associated with factors that effect an increased delinquency rate. The factor analysis suggests that, in Baltimore, the percentage of Negroes in an area is best viewed in the grouping of variables which define the *anomic* factor. The examination of the regression analysis, however, further suggests that the percentage of Negroes in an area is a curvilinear correlate of the *anomic* factor. Areas of maximum racial heterogeneity are characterized by the largest extent of social instability and *anomie*. In the areas of maximum Negro population concentration there is observable a corresponding increase of social stability and a decrease in delinquency.

Furthermore, there are many areas in which the Negro delinquency rate is substantially lower than the corresponding white rate. . . .

The evidence cited amply demonstrates that Negro delinquency is not a function or effect of race as such but is a reflection of social instability. In sections characterized by *anomie*, the Negro delinquency rate is high; in areas of social stability, the Negro . . . rate is of the same order as the corresponding white rate. . . .

THE CONCENTRIC ZONE AND GRADIENT HYPOTHESES

Many studies of the distribution and etiology of delinquency and other social pathologies have been stimulated by and prepared within the framework of the Park and Burgess ecological hypotheses. . . .

We summarize below the findings of the present study which relate to these hypotheses.

1. a) The location of industrial land use sections in Baltimore does not conform to the Burgess zonal hypothesis. There is no general tendency of heavy industry to surround or to be located near the central business district. . . .

b) The delinquency rates in or near several industrial areas are considerably higher than the city mean rate. This is in conformity with the Burgess-Shaw hypothesis. Strikingly at variance with this hypothesis, however, is the fact that some of the city's lowest delinquency rates occur in or near industrial areas. Also, in the seven tracts in which the major land use or zoning is industrial, the mean tract delinquency rate is lower than the city's delinquency mean. On the other hand, the mean delinquency rate for the twelve tracts which are predominantly or in part zoned for commercial use is almost twice the mean for the city at large.

c) According to the zonal hypothesis, the central business and industrial section is surrounded by the, [sic] zone in transition, or slum area which is characterized by the greatest frequency of delinquency, bad housing, and poverty. The following concentric district is the zone of workingmen's homes.

The findings of this monograph suggest that zones in transition from residence to business and industry are not limited to the innermost zones but are also found in the city's peripheral districts. Also, that areas characterized by poverty, bad housing and workingmen's homes while frequently near the center of the city are found in every zone. . . .

Furthermore, Baltimore's . . . "zone in transition," in the years 1939–42 contained districts with very high delinquency rates, but also areas in which the delinquency rate is close to zero. . . .

d) Shaw allocates the central and basic role in the understanding of the differential delinquency rate to the "invasion" of residential neighborhoods by business and industry in the process of city growth. In this study we have calculated and plotted the residual errors in order to analyze the significance of such factors of the delinquency rate, measures of which had not been included in the regressions equation. The examination of the distribution of the residual errors indicates that in many instances, especially in tracts adjoining retail commercial concentrations, the higher actual than predicted delinquency rates may suggest the influence of actual or impending changes in land-use as a causal factor of the delinquency rate. On the other hand, the majority of the tracts in the . . . "areas of transition" are characterized by predicted delinquency rates which are higher than the actual rates. In other words in the majority of tracts within the "zones of transition," there is no evidence to suggest that the delinquency rate is a function of the "invasion" of industry or commerce. We do not wish to deny the importance of changes in land-use in the understanding and/or prediction of the delinquency rate. The "invasion" . . . may, undoubtedly, in many instances weaken the social controls or consensus of the area and thus affect its delinquency rate. But our findings do not support a hypothesis which gives this factor the central role in the explanation of the differential delinquency rate. . . .

The findings of this study do support Shaw's thesis, "that delinquent behavior is related dynamically to the community and that because of the anonymity in urban life, the individual is freed from much of the scrutiny and control which characterize life in primary group situations in small towns and rural communities." But our findings do not support . . . Shaws [sic] hypothesis that the processes of city growth, as such, provides the basic explanation of a city's wide variations in delinquency rates.

2. a) An examination of the zonal distribution rates superficially and in a general fashion supports the Burgess gradient hypothesis. Zone 1 is characterized by the highest delinquency rate. There is decrease—although it is not a *regular* one—in the delinquency rate with progression from Zone 1 to Zone 7. . . .

An examination of the distribution of delinquency rates by census tracts shows that the zonal hypothesis oversimplifies the actual pattern of delinquency distribution. Each zone includes high and low delinquency rate areas. . . .

b) The Baltimore zonal areas cannot be designated as "natural areas." They are not characterized by a homogeneity of cultural and economic characteristics. Although low rental areas are found near the city center, they are by no means confined there but are found in every zone. . . . Similarly, with regards to the median years of schooling, in the inner zone are found tracts characterized by the city's highest and lowest educational medians. . . .

The data of this study also indicate that we cannot apply to Baltimore the attempt by Burgess to designate the successive zones as the zone of transition . . . of workingmen's homes . . . middle-class dwellers, and the commuters zone. Concentric zones in Baltimore are not characterized by any homogeneity in land-use. Workingmen's and middle-class homes are found in all zones. Industrial concentrations are not confined to the inner zones, but are also found in the so-called commuters zone.

3) We find no support for the assumption that seems to be more or less tacit in the work of some ecologists that physical space or locale per se is an independent or causal factor in the predictions or understanding of delinquency. . . .

4) The factor analysis based on the correlations among the variables indicates that there are *two* independent and underlying factors. This finding contrasts with Burgess' assumption of one general basic factor, namely, social disorganization of which delinquency, poverty, bad housing, and tuberculosis are equally manifestations. The basic factors in our study are closely associated with each other but are nonetheless different in character. Our evidence indicates that "social disorganization" (we prefer the concept "anomie") is perhaps a basic underlying factor of delinquency, but that this factor is not sufficient to account for a complex matrix of social interrelationships. A second, independently operating, factor is socio-economic in character.

Summary and Interpretation

. . . In our search for the understanding of the differential delinquency rate, we suggest that the nearer the explanation of this social phenomenon is to the direct motivation of behavior, the nearer it is to being an adequate explanation of the deviant behavior. We hypothesize an explanation of the differential delinquency rate in terms of the concept of *anomie*. When the *group norms* are no longer binding or valid in an area or for a population sub-group, in so far is individual behavior likely to lead to deviant behavior. Delinquency is a function of the stability and acceptance of the group norms with legal sanctions and the consequent effectiveness of the social controls in securing conforming juvenile behavior. . . .

The factor analysis indicates, and this finding is supported by our correlational analysis, that the delinquency rate is fundamentally related only to the *anomie* and not specifically to the socio-economic conditions of an area. The delinquency rate in a *stable* community will be low in spite of . . . bad housing, poverty, and propinquity to the city center. On the other hand, one would expect a high delinquency rate in an area characterized by normlessness and social instability. . . .

Emile Durkheim was one of the earliest sociologists to suggest that a differential crime rate is a reflection of differential degrees of social cohesion and the corresponding social control. Durkheim stresses that the breakdown of social cohesion frees the individual from the pressure of public opinion and the informal social controls which, in more solidary groups, operate to secure conformity to the norms of conventional behavior.

In a stable community a child is born and raised in a context of established norms which are supported by a social consensus. He tends to interiorize these norms, and they contribute to the establishment of his psychological field of needs, goals, and motivations. Generally, the child acts to satisfy his needs in a manner which has the approval of society. If he acts in a deviant fashion, formal and informal controls—including his own ego with its interiorized norms—act to deter the child from further deviant conduct.

Unstable community conditions and the consequent weakening of social controls that are congruent with the dominant culture provide fertile ground for the emergence of variant norms and group standards. It is erroneous to conceive of high delinquency areas as being devoid of norms and group controls or standards. . . . The controls and mores of a gang are highly regulatory of the behavior of its members. However, these norms may not be congruent with those of the larger society.

A deeper understanding of the differential juvenile delinquency rate will necessitate further research on *how* community stability or instability is meaningfully and dynamically related to the differential behavior of various types of individual children. Community or situational factors ultimately influence the delinquency rate only as they affect the needs, values, goals, and behavior of individual children.

SELF-CONCEPT AS AN INSULATOR
AGAINST DELINQUENCY

WALTER C. RECKLESS
AND SIMON DINITZ

Excerpted from Walter C. Reckless and Simon Dinitz, "Pioneering with Self-Concept as a Vulnerability Factor in Delinquency," *Journal of Criminal Law, Criminology and Police Science*, 58, No. 4 (December 1967), 515–23. At the time of publication Walter C. Reckless was Professor of Sociology at Ohio State University. Simon Dinitz was Professor of Sociology and Research Associate in Psychiatry at Ohio State University.

THIS PAPER presents a retrospective assessment of a pioneering line of research on the self-concept as an insulator against delinquency. The authors were in search of a clue—a possible self-factor—which might shed light on what it is that steers youths in high delinquency areas of a large city away from involvement in delinquency. Certainly, criminologists and sociologists are well aware of the simple fact that a large percentage of adolescents in high delinquency areas manage to keep out of official trouble with the law, walk around the street-corner gang and avoid its so-called "sub-culture," stay in school rather than drop out, identify with the norms and values of the dominant society, and turn their backs on the availability of illegitimate means to ends in their neighborhood environment. What, then, are the components which enable adolescents to develop and maintain nondelinquent patterns of conduct despite the adversities of family, class position, and neighborhood?

It was decided that the best subjects for an initial inquiry would be the sixth-grade boys in high delinquency areas. Attention was focused on white sixth-grade boys, so as not to complicate the research design with race and sex variables. One might well ask:

why sixth-grade boys? The answer is that they are approximately 12 years of age and are at the threshold of adolescence as well as the threshold of officially complained-upon delinquency. Complaints on boys for delinquency begin to increase at this age and keep on increasing through the succeeding years of adolescence. In addition, it begins to be feasible to interview a child, at the age of 12, about himself and his world as he sees it. . . .

As a start, the authors in 1955 gained permission to ask sixth-grade teachers in predominantly white elementary schools in high delinquency areas of Columbus, Ohio—teachers who interact with their pupils the entire school day for an entire school year—to indicate from among the white boys in their classes those who would never get into trouble with the law. Despite the fact that most of the teachers were middle-class females, the authors maintain—and we think very rightly so—that they have a sense of the direction in which their pupils are going. Kvaraceus' work in developing a delinquency proneness measure certainly bears out our contention that teachers' behavior ratings, evaluations, or prognostications are quite accurate.

A Close Look at Sampling and Procedure

Thirty sixth-grade teachers nominated 192 white boys in their classes who in their opinion would not experience police or juvenile court contact. The range was from 15 to 100 percent of the white boys in the 30 classes and the average per class was 6.4 boys.

The teachers at the time for making their nominations of the so-called "good boys" were asked to give their reasons for each nomination. They mentioned 1,033 reasons or 5.4 reasons per boy; 45 percent represented favorable personal characteristics, attitudes, and interests; 27 percent, one or more aspects of favorable home situations; 20 percent, participation in character-building youth organizations, religious activities, conforming in-school behavior, after-school employment; 7 percent, negative evaluations such as being excessively timid, naive, or overprotected so as to preclude involvement in delinquent behavior.

Sixteen of the 192 "good boys," constituting 8.3 percent of the teachers' nominees, turned out to have had, after clearance was made, previous contact with the police or the juvenile court. In 13 of the 16 cases, one or more members of the family had also had contact with the courts. Members of 42 additional families also had court contact, although the boys were not involved.

The authors eliminated these 16 boys, who already had contact with the law, from their "good boy" sample. In addition, when interviewers tried to locate the remaining 176 boys (out of the original 192), they could not find 51 boys, probably due in small part to wrong address, but in most part to removal of the family from the community in the interim of the several months between the teachers' nominations and the field follow-up. The project was left with a sample of 125 (192 minus 16 minus 51).

A schedule was developed to be administered on an individual basis to each of the 125 good boys in their own homes. Among other formal scales and inventories included in the schedule were 50 items which attempted to assess the boy's perception of himself in relation to his family, friends, school, and possible involvement with the law. We called these items self-concept items, because the responses represented the boy's perception of himself in reference to the significant others in his immediate world.

Two research interviewers contacted the mother at home and obtained permission to interview her and her son. The one interviewer administered the schedule to the boy in one room; the other interviewer administered a specially prepared schedule to the mother in an another room simultaneously.

The following school year, namely 1956, the authors returned to the same 30 sixth-grade classrooms and asked the teachers, most of whom were the same ones they interviewed in 1955, to nominate the white boys in their rooms, who would, in their opinion, almost certainly experience police or juvenile-court contact in the future.

The teachers named 108 white boys, constituting about 25 percent of the eligible boys. Twenty-four of the 108 nominated "bad boys" (23 percent) had already had contact with the police and juvenile court (as against 8.3 percent of the "good boy" nominees). In view of a much shorter time span between teacher nomination and home interview, we only lost 7 boys in the "bad boy" sample, reducing it to 101 cases. The interview schedules for the boy and the mother were the same in the 1956 101-bad-boy sample as in the 125-good-boy sample of the previous year.

The scores on the two directionally-oriented scales of the California Psychological Inventory (*De* scale and *Re* scale), which were included in the schedule administered to each boy, were different in the expected directions: significantly more favorable for the good-boys than for the bad-boys or more unfavorable for the bad-boys than the good-boys. Because the *De* scale of the CPI (now called the Socialization scale, measuring directionality toward and away from delinquency) and the *Re* scale of the CPI (measuring directionality toward social responsibility) are standardized scales, with national and even some international norms, the authors felt that the convincingly and significantly more favorable showing of the good, and the more unfavorable showing of the bad-boy sample, tended to validate the teacher's nominations. Likewise, these scale scores provided corroboration for the more favorable answers on the self-concept items received from the good than from the bad boys. In addition to these associations, the answers of the mothers to questions about their sons, paralleling virtually all of the questions used in the self-concept inventory for the boys, also added an additional dimension of validation. Thus, the teachers, the mothers, the *De* and *Re* Scales, and the boys' responses to the self-concept questions were highly consistent.

Follow-up Four Years Later

Four years after initial contact (1959 for the good and 1960 for the bad boys), the authors set about determining how many of the boys were known to the juvenile court. Out of the total of 125 in the 1955 sample of good boys, they were able to locate and assess 103; out of the 101 in the 1956 sample of bad boys, 70. . . .

Twenty-seven of the 70 bad boys (39 percent) had contact with the juvenile court for delinquency in the four year follow-up period—not including the court contacts in the instance of 24 out of the original 101 sample, prior to our study. Each of the twenty-seven out of the traceable 70 bad boys averaged over 3 contacts with the juvenile court throughout the four-year period or from the time the boys were approximately 12 to the time they were 16 years of age.

In contrast, just four out of the 101 good boys who were followed had a one-time record in the juvenile court in the ensuing four-year period of follow-up—and only for very minor offenses. Ninety-nine of the 103 good boys were still in school, although half of them had passed legal age for drop-out. Of the 99 still in school, all but four impressed their teachers as unlikely to get into future difficulty. Their responses to the readministered self-concept items were quite favorable, just as favorable as they were four years previously and the mothers' evaluations were just as favorable as four years earlier.

There was a remarkable four-year cohort stability on all of the directional indicators in both the good- and bad-boy samples: self-concept projections, teachers' prognostications, mothers' evaluations, scores on the *De* and *Re* scales of the CPI.

Furthermore, the authors were able to compare the traceable 103 good, and 70 bad boys, on the Nye-Short self-reporting delinquency check list (using 7 of the original Nye-Short items) and they found that the latter scored more unfavorably than the former. (This self-reporting check list was not available to us in 1955 and 1956.) Hence, "professed" involvement corroborated reported involvement in delinquency as well as the direction of the self-concept responses, and the teachers' expectations.

At this point it is important to duplicate the theoretical underpinning of our quest to discover what insulates a boy in the high delinquency areas against involvement in delinquency.

In our quest to discover what insulates a boy against delinquency in a high delinquency area, we believe we have some tangible evidence that a good self-concept, undoubtedly a product of favorable socialization, veers slum boys away from delinquency, while a poor self-concept, a product of unfavorable socialization, gives the slum boy no resistance to deviancy, delinquent companions, or delinquent sub-culture. We feel that components of the self-strength, such as a favorable concept of self, act as an inner buffer or inner containment against deviancy, distraction, lure, and pressures. Our operational assumptions are that a good self-concept is indicative of a residual favorable socialization and a strong inner self, which in turn steers the person away from bad companions and street corner society, toward middle class values, and to awareness of possibility of upward movement in the opportunity structure. Conversely, the poor concept of self is indicative of a residual unfavorable socialization (by 12 years of age probably not the result of participation in delinquency subculture) and indicative of weak inner direction (self or ego), which in turn does not deflect the boy from bad companions and street corner society, does not enable him to embrace middle class values, and gives him an awareness of being cut off from upward movement in the legitimate opportunity system. . . .

Cross-Sectional Studies

In 1957, the authors administered 717 schedules to sixth-grade children in 24 classes in eleven elementary schools of Columbus, Ohio, chosen according to census tract indexes of socio-economic status as well as high and low delinquency. Eight of the schools (with 17 sixth-grade classes) served disadvantaged areas with high delinquency rates, while 3 served middle-class areas where delinquency rates were low. All the sixth-grade pupils present in class on the appointed day were administered a schedule. The schedule consisted of 46 items from the *De* scale, 38 items from the *Re* scale (both from the California Psychological Inventory which is a factor-analyzed version of the Minnesota Multiphasic Inventory), 56 self-concept items, plus certain social background items. During the administration of the inventories, the sixth-grade room teacher was interviewed elsewhere by a research assistant. With her cumulative record cards before her, the teacher rated each child in her class as either headed for trouble with the law, not sure, or not headed for trouble with the law.

Since the schedule was administered in school, a standard introductory statement requesting cooperation and allaying fears was used. On the front page of the schedule the following statement appeared in bold type: *Remember this is not a test. We simply want to know how you feel about things. There are no right or wrong answers. The right answer for you is how you feel about things.* Dr. Dinitz read aloud each question, reminding the pupils of the response pattern: true or false; yes or no.

Dr. Ernest Donald analyzed 354 boys' schedules from among the total of 717. Because the teachers nominated too few girls as headed for trouble with the law to warrant comparison, the Donald analysis applied only to white and colored sixth-grade boys in both the high and low delinquency areas of Columbus, Ohio in 1957.[1] . . .

It was possible to relate the favorable and unfavorable responses on each of the 56 self-concept items with the dichotomous nominations of the sixth-grade teachers (headed for trouble with the law, including not sure, versus not headed for trouble with the law). Table I lists 16 of the 56 self-concept items, used in the 1957 schedule, which were found to be differentiated by teacher nomination at the .05 level of confidence and beyond (9 items at the .001; 3, at the .01; 1, at the .02; and 3, at the .05 level of confidence). Note that the items through number 39 were answered by yes or no; items 42 and 46 were answered by a response format of often, sometimes, never; item 50, as will be seen on inspection, was answered by checking one out of three possibilities.

When the favorable and unfavorable responses on these 16 self-concept items were related to high and low scores on the *De* scale of the California Psychological Inventory (which also measures direction toward or away from delinquency), all but one item (number 25) reached the minimum .05 level of statistical significance. Certainly, there is corroboration here; teacher nomination, response to self-concept items, and scores on the *De* scale are going in the same direction.

Five of the 16 significant self-concept items according to teachers' nominations . . . were discriminated by the race of the sixth-

[1] Donald & Dinitz, *Self-Concept and Delinquency Proneness, Interdisciplinary Problems of Criminology; Papers of the Am. Soc. of Criminol.,* 1964 (Reckless & Newman, Eds.), 49–59 (1965).

TABLE I   Significant Self-Concept Items According to Teacher
Nomination, Associated With High and Low Scores on the
De Scale of the California Psychological Inventory

Original Schedule No.	*Self-Concept Items*
1	Will you probably be taken to juvenile court sometime?
2	Will you probably have to go to jail sometime?
6	If you found that a friend was leading you into trouble, would you continue to run around with him or her?
11	Do you plan to finish high school?
12	Do you think you'll stay out of trouble in the future?
17	Are grown-ups usually against you?
21	If you could get permission to work at 14 would you quit school?
23	Are you a big shot with your pals?
24	Do you think your teacher thinks you will ever get into trouble with the law?
25	Do you think your mother thinks you will ever get into trouble with the law?
26	Do you think if you were to get into trouble with the law, it would be bad for you in the future?
27	Have you ever been told that you were headed for trouble with the law?
39	Have most of your friends been in trouble with the law?
42	Do you confide in your father?
46	Do your parents punish you?
50	Do you think you are quiet _____ average _____ active _____.[2]

grade (1957) Columbus boys (items 2, 12, 23, 39, 52); seven,
by high and low delinquency area (items 1, 2, 12, 25, 26, 27, and
39). . . .

After having spotted the 16 significant self-concept items, it was
possible to obtain a total self-concept score on the 16. High total
scores were in the unfavorable (delinquency) direction. When the
mean (total) scores on the 16 self-concept items were computed for
various subgroups of the sixth-grade boy sample (1957), the differ-

[2] *Ibid.* 51.

ence in the means for white and colored boys was (a) slight (although significant statistically); (b) somewhat larger for boys by type of area (again statistically significant); (c) not significant for white boys in high and in low delinquency areas; (d) significant for white boys in good areas and colored boys in bad areas; and (e) not significant for white boys and Negro boys (both) in areas of high delinquency.

By way of comparison, the mean self-concept score for boys with high *De* scores and that for boys with low *De* scores differed most of all and at a significance level of .00001. In commenting on these findings relative to self-concept scores by various subgroups of the sixth-grade Columbus boys, Donald had this to say:

One is almost ready to hazard the guess that race and type of neighborhood, whatever they may signify in the accumulated socialization of 12-year-old boys, are relatively unimportant in determining self-concepts. On the other hand, a large mean score difference on the self-concept items is found when the sixth-grade boys are divided by favorable and unfavorable direction of socialization as measured by the scores on the *De* scale. Evidently the big thing which determines the boy's self-concept orientation is something other than race and neighborhood. Might we say that it is the quality of family interaction and impact, apart from class and race, plus the impact of other supplementary relationships found within the child's world? [3]

Conclusion

It is no longer sufficient for sociologists who study criminal and delinquent behavior to call attention to the possible impact of disorganized and disadvantaged neighborhoods, family tensions and insufficiencies, bad companions and street-corner gangs, and the availability of illegitimate means to ends. Who responds to carriers of patterns of delinquency and crime? Who resists and goes the other way? We live in a society of alternates, where the self has more and more opportunities for acceptance or rejection of available confrontations. Consequently, sociologists as criminologists must join the search for the self-factors which determine direction of behavior or choice among alternates and in this endeavor they

[3] *Ibid.*, 54.

must work with their colleagues in psychology and psychiatry in an effort to discover what self-factors actually determine the direction of behavior and how they can be controlled.

The proposal herein has been to explore the self-concept as one important self-factor which controls the direction of the person. There is certainly some preliminary evidence in the authors' work to date, to indicate that the self-concept might be one of the important self-factors in determining the "drift" toward or away from delinquency and crime. The authors do not presume that such a self-factor would operate in instances of deep character and emotional disturbances. But for the large majority of unofficial and official offenders as well as effective conformers to the dominant norms of a democratic, industrial, urban, mobile society, it is certainly feasible to operate on the hypothesis that self-factors determine direction of behavior toward or away from delinquency and deviance in general.

The authors feel they uncovered some corroborating evidence, namely that the self-concept of early adolescent [sic] might be one of the self-factors which controls directionality. Certainly, teachers' prognostications of sixth-grade boys—even the mothers' evaluations—plus the De scale (now called Socialization scale) indicate that directionality, toward or away from delinquent behavior, can be sensed and assessed. If, in the future, effective assessment of self-reported delinquency can be made, sociologists as well as behavioral-science researchers will have another effective instrument to gauge directionality of the youth.

It seems to the authors that these indicators of directionality toward or away from deviance point to the strong possibility of a favorable-to-unfavorable self-concept in the young person, which is acting as the controlling agent. Our large cross-sectional study in 1957 certainly indicated that self-concept factors, the teachers' prognostication of direction of the youth, the De scale's assessment of direction were interrelated. And the authors, if they might be spared glibness, do not think it is the subtle "rub-off" of the teacher's sense of the individual youth's direction which causes an internalization of a favorable image of himself (although this might happen in rare instances). And in the 1955 and 1956 samples, when the mother's projections of direction in which the son was travel-ling were obtained, the authors did not feel that in the overwhelm-ing majority of instances the mother's faith or lack of faith in the directional outcome of her boy was the "looking glass" which gave the boy his image (although this might happen in more instances than in the impact of the sixth-grade teacher's sense of direction on the boy). The authors believe that a youth in American society ob-tains his self-concepts from many experiential sources, inside and outside the home and school. . . .

Undoubtedly, there is a need for the development of an effective self-concept measure which can assess the direction toward or away from delinquency or deviant behavior generally. There is need also to develop measures of other self-factors which control directionality. When such factors are uncovered and when they are effectively measured, then it should be possible to chart workable programs to prevent delinquency and to re-enforce the components of self which enable the youth to be an effective conformer. . . .

BROKEN HOMES AND DELINQUENCY

THOMAS P. MONAHAN

Excerpted from Thomas P. Monahan, "Family Status and the Delinquent Child: A Reappraisal and Some New Findings," *Social Forces*, XXXV (March 1957), 250–58.

WHEN A child loses a parent through death, desertion, divorce, or long separation, some form of deprivation is bound to result. Where . . . the male parent is missing, the child is placed under an obvious economic handicap. Absence of either parent may also cause a certain affectional loss for the child. In addition, the complementary control, example, and guidance given by both parents is wanting and complete socialization of the child is rendered more difficult.

At the death of a parent no cultural opposition is imposed upon the situation. Rather, social and economic assistance . . . is readily forthcoming. . . .

But, in cases of desertion and divorce (and illegitimacy) we have an entirely different set of circumstances. Here we frequently find the child exposed to a highly emotionalized atmosphere of discontent and discord. The child most often remains with the mother only, financial support may be withheld by the father, or the parents may fight over the child's custody. In case of desertion no new father may legally become part of the child's home. And the subtle challenge of public disapproval of the family situation and the psychological impact of a seeming rejection by one's parents may becloud the child's outlook.

Divorce in many cases is indeed simply a formal recognition . . . of an already socially broken home, and it is generally appreciated that the home in constant discord might cause the child more harm than if the parental relationship were severed. Such reasoning has merit, but, interestingly enough, this argument has been used to justify divorce rather than to plead for the rehabilitation or prevention of unhappy families. Such a viewpoint . . . contradicts another social philosophy which holds that even a bad home is better than no home at all for the child.

There are many varieties of broken homes and many correspondingly different kinds of family relationships involved. Even the social disparateness in family structure which results from long-term hospitalization, military service, or employment of the breadwinner away from home, may bring about some serious consequences for the members of a family. On the other hand, the conventional family structure may cloak a host of baneful influences or situations harmful to a child's wholesome development. To say it in another way, all broken homes are not bad ones, and all conventional types are not good ones.

This article . . . is restricted to a consideration of the more evident types of broken homes as they relate to children who are apprehended for committing delinquent acts.

Delinquency Studies of Broken Homes

With the establishment of juvenile courts in the United States . . . and the compilation of social statistics on youth who were brought before these courts, observers were struck by the high proportion—40 to 50 percent—of all delinquent children who came from broken homes. Since it was far beyond normal expectancy that such a proportion of all youth was similarly disadvantaged, early writers saw broken homes to be an important, if not the greatest single proximate (causal) factor in understanding juvenile delinquency.

There was no denial that the broken home was only one of a number of factors to take into account and that the age of the child and the quality of the home life, as well as the mere fact of a break, were important. A number of studies have shown, however, that abnormal or defective family relationships are much more prevalent among families of delinquent children than among families of comparable children who do not become delinquent. . . .

Some of the early studies attempted to estimate the proportion of broken homes in the population at large from existing census data, to use for a comparison with their special groups of delinquent or institutionalized children. A common conclusion was that delinquent children had about twice the proportion of broken homes as did children in the general population. . . .

The first major attempt at a controlled comparison was made by Slawson in 1923, using delinquent boys in four state institutions and boys in three New York City public schools, from which he concluded that there were over twice as many broken homes in his delinquent group.[1] Concurrently, in England, Cyril Burt analyzed a group of misbehaving ("delinquent") children and public school children of the same age and social class. Although his classification of "defective family relationships" included other factors besides the broken home, he, too, found the problem children to be doubly disfavored.[2] And, in 1929, Mabel Elliott compared the family structure of her group of Sleighton Farm girls—mostly sex offenders—with that of a group of Philadelphia working-class—continuation school—girls, revealing the respective proportions of broken homes to be 52 and 22 percent.[3]

Even greater refinement was introduced into the question by Shaw and McKay when they compared boys against whom official delinquency petitions were filed in the juvenile court of Chicago in 1929, with other boys drawn from the public school population of the same city area.[4] They found that a rather high proportion (29 percent) of the school boys 10 to 17 years of age came from broken homes. After the school population data were carefully adjusted statistically for age and ethnic composition to make them compara-

[1] John Slawson, "Marital Relations of Parents and Juvenile Delinquency," *Journal of Delinquency*, VIII (September–November, 1923), 280–83.

[2] Cyril Burt, *The Young Delinquent* (New York: D. Appleton and Co., 1925), pp. 51, 90 ff.

[3] Mabel Elliott, *Correctional Education and the Delinquent Girl* (Harrisburg, Pennsylvania State Department of Welfare, 1929), p. 28.

[4] C. R. Shaw and H. D. McKay, *Report on the Causes of Crime, Vol. II, Social Factors in Juvenile Delinquency* (Washington, D.C.: National Commission on Law Observance and Enforcement, Government Printing Office, 1931), pp. 261–84, and Shaw and McKay, "Are Broken Homes a Causative Factor in Delinquency?" *Social Forces*, 10 (May, 1932), pp. 514–24, and discussion pp. 525–33.

ble with the delinquent group, the proportion of broken homes rose to 36.1 percent for the school group, as compared to 42.5 percent for the delinquent boys. This result, as Shaw and McKay interpreted it, "suggests that the broken home, as such, is not an important factor in the case of delinquent boys in the Cook County juvenile court," while other writers further interpreted the findings as showing that broken homes generally are "relatively insignificant in relation to delinquency."[5] Even accepting the above figures for Chicago, mathematical exception has been taken to such interpretations.

Disagreement among Authorities

Thus there arose a sharp divergence of opinion among sociologists as to the importance of the broken home as a factor in delinquency. . . .

Hodgkiss' study of Chicago girls, done at about the same time and in the same manner as the Shaw-McKay inquiry, disclosed that 67 percent of the delinquent girls and 45 percent of the controls came from broken homes.[6] These figures were less readily dismissed. Again the high percentage of broken homes among the control group is remarkable. Probably because of difficulties surrounding the collection of such data from school children, the studies have not been repeated in Chicago.

Other Studies

Six other investigations published after the Shaw-McKay report deserve special mention. First, Cavan, in her study of school children in 1930, placed in opposition information on several classes of children in the same locality. The proportion of broken homes increased consistently from the control group of boys (21 percent) to the predelinquent boys (35 percent), to the institutionalized boys

[5] Shaw and McKay, *Report on the Causes of Crime, loc. cit.*, p. 392; and Sutherland, *Principles of Criminology* (Philadelphia: J. B. Lippincott Co., 1947), p. 159.

[6] M. Hodgkiss, "The Influence of Broken Homes and Working Mothers," *Smith College Studies in Social Work*, 3 (March, 1933), pp. 259–74.

(49 percent), to the institutionalized girls (71 percent).[7] Second, in a study of Spokane, Washington, public school boys, 14 to 17 years of age, and delinquent boys in 1937, Weeks and Smith made a careful comparison only to find that broken homes among the delinquents (41 percent) were far more numerous than among the control group of boys (27 percent), even when refined according to a number of social categories.[8] Third, in the mid-1930s, Merrill matched 300 run-of-the-mill cases referred to the court of a rural California county with other children selected according to age, sex, and neighborhood (school). In this case 51 percent of the delinquents were found to come from broken homes versus 27 percent for the control group.[9] Fourth, Wittman and Huffman's study of teen-aged youth in Elgin, Illinois, disclosed that a very high disproportion of the institutionalized delinquents came from broken homes as compared to high school students in the same area.[10] Fifth, the Gluecks carefully paired 500 boys from the general school population with 500 delinquent (correctional school) boys in the Boston area. They found that only 50 percent of the delinquent boys had been living with their own parents, whereas the control group of boys were living with both parents in 71 percent of the cases.[11] Sixth, a study of pre-war delinquents was made in England by Carr-Saunders and others, using an individual-matching technique (boys under 16 years), with the following results: delinquents had a much higher proportion of broken homes than the controls (28 percent versus 16 percent), and there was a greater amount of separation and divorce in the delinquent group of broken homes.[12]

[7] R. S. Cavan, *The Adolescent in the Family* (New York: D. Appleton-Century Co., 1934), pp. 220–21.

[8] H. A. Weeks and M. G. Smith, "Juvenile Delinquency and Broken Homes in Spokane, Washington," *Social Forces*, 18 (October, 1939), pp. 48–55.

[9] M. Merrill, *Problems of Child Delinquency* (New York: Houghton-Mifflin Co., 1947), pp. 66, 311.

[10] M. P. Wittman and A. V. Huffman, "A Comparative Study of Developmental, Adjustment, and Personality Characteristics of Psychotic, Psychoneurotic, Delinquent, and Normally Adjusted Teen Aged Youths," *Journal of Genetic Psychology*, LXVI (June, 1945), 167–82.

[11] S. Glueck and E. Glueck, *Unraveling Juvenile Delinquency* (Cambridge, Massachusetts: Harvard University Press, 1950), p. 88.

[12] A. M. Carr-Saunders, H. Mannheim, E. Rhodes, *Young Offenders* (New York: Macmillan Co., 1944), pp. 60, 149.

A Partial Summation

Thus, in comparisons of delinquents with control samples, and in statistical adjustments of delinquency data for age, ethnic, and neighborhood biases, the children with intact families have shown a clear and persistent advantage over those from broken homes. This is especially true for the females. In addition to this, the home of the delinquent child appears to be much more "defective," "immoral," or "inadequate" than are homes in general. In broken homes one seems to find a conjunction of deprivations and positive influences toward criminal behavior.

From an over-all viewpoint it is well to remember that a large proportion of children from broken homes do not become delinquent, but this hardly refutes the inescapable fact that more children from broken homes, as compared to unbroken homes, become delinquent. . . .

A convergence of information from the other disciplines as to the deleterious effects of divorce and desertion or family separations upon the child, as well as a psychological appreciation of the different nature of these types of family disruption, brought a more unanimous acknowledgement of the importance of the *socially* broken home. In some quarters the recent "wave" of delinquency has been interpreted to be a result of the growth of divorce and separation. However, information on the particular family relationships of children in the community and those who become delinquent are generally lacking. We know that over the past 50 years there has been a lessening of orphanhood through improvement in life expectancy, and an upward rise in family dissolutions through desertion and divorce, until now there seems to have been a reversal in the relative importance of the two factors of death and social discord in the breaking up of a child's family. Oddly enough, in spite of the change in the nature of broken homes the high over-all proportion of delinquent children from broken homes apparently has not changed significantly.

A Six-Year Study of Philadelphia Records

In order to throw some additional light upon the subject of broken homes, some special tabulations were made of all delinquency charges—44,448 cases, of which 24,811 were first offenders—disposed of in the Philadelphia Municipal Court in the period 1949–1954.

METHODOLOGICAL PROBLEMS

Accuracy of Data. In cases which are adjusted before going to court or which receive no investigation, children are quite often the only source of some of the information recorded. The precision of the data suffers thereby, especially if one is interested in the details of family relationships. . . .

Types of Data. The proportion and types of broken homes among juvenile offenders are known to vary greatly according to racial or ethnic group, sex and age, and certain offenses. As one proceeds from first offenders to the recidivists, from those dismissed to those adjudged delinquent, and from the probationary types to those which require institutionalization, it may be expected that one will find an increasing proportion of broken homes. Unfortunately, very little attention has been given to the correspondence between the degree of broken homes and the type of data being studied. A number of early studies, for instance, were concerned exclusively with special types of offenders, recidivists and institutionalized children. Since chronic offenders represent a special class, and other cases may be institutionalized *because* they come from broken homes, there is a basic weakness in using such selective kinds of information to demonstrate a relationship between broken homes and unlawful behavior of juveniles.

Lack of Population Statistics. Perhaps the greatest stumbling block . . . has been the lack of population data which would show the family situation of children as a whole. For nearly 50 years this deficiency in census compilations has been bemoaned by many students of the subject, and a wide variety of crude estimates have been made. If such information were tabulated from census cards and classified according to governmental units for age, color, and neighborhood area (census tracts), we could begin to assess this problem with more certainty. Among different elements of the population the proportion and types of broken homes vary so greatly that one must be cautious in using particular kinds of data for comparative purposes. It should be recognized that the percentages of broken homes in some control groups (Shaw-McKay, Hodgkiss, and Glueck) do not purport to represent the condition prevailing among the population as a whole. In general, no more than 20 percent of all children of juvenile court age have broken homes, with the proportion among the nonwhites being about twice that for the whites.

FAMILY STATUS OF DELINQUENTS BY SEX AND COLOR

As shown in Table I [deleted], the proportion of broken homes among Negroes is considerably greater that among the whites, and girls in each group are more often from broken homes than are boys in each class. The range of broken homes extends from about one-third of all cases of white boys to three-fourths of the cases of Negro girls, with white girls and Negro boys showing less than 50 percent with intact families.

The families of first offenders show a lesser degree of fragmentation, whereas those who offended in a prior year . . . are from families particularly marked by a greater degree of orphanhood, illegitimacy, and social disruption. Including children who are recidivists increases the population of broken homes in the whole.

The parents of Negro delinquents are less often legally separated and more often unmarried or living apart than are the parents of white children. Girls, of course, with a higher proportion of broken homes also show a higher degree of orphanhood; but, except for a moderate excess of orphanhood of Negro boys as compared to white boys, the impact of death is not an outstanding element of difference between the two classes. Initial disorganization and informal social disorganization of family status is most characteristic of Negro delinquent children.

RECIDIVISM BY FAMILY STATUS

It is a reasonable conjecture that if a broken home predisposes a child to commit a delinquent act, then it follows, to state it simply, that lacking the necessary parental guidance and control in the first place this tendency toward misconduct will continue throughout the period of childhood and there will be a greater recurrence of offenses among children in broken homes. Some studies have, in fact, revealed a greater degree of recidivism among children in broken homes. One cannot ignore this evidence by assuming that there is a selective apprehension of youth on the basis of their home conditions rather than a direct operation of the law.

The deleterious effect of broken homes upon children as regards the repetition of their delinquencies is portrayed in Table II [deleted]. In all sex and color groups children who are living with both parents are much less likely to appear again on charges of delinquency. . . .

As between the types of marital status, further meaningful differences appear. The exceedingly high proportion of recidivism among institutional children is no doubt related to their unusual background of deprivation and their likelihood of offending by running away. For white boys the percentage of all cases in the recidivist class increases from 32 where both parents are married and living together, to 38 where the father is dead and the boy is with his mother, to 42 where both parents are dead and the child is with a surrogate family, to 46 percent where the parents are living apart and the child is with the mother, to 49 where the parents are divorced, to 55 where the boy is living with his unmarried mother. In general the same pattern holds for both sex and color groups except that the recidivism contrast among the types of broken homes for Negroes is not as well defined nor as great. This could betoken a greater ambiguity or inaccuracy of Negro data, or a lesser significance to the Negro child as to the specific manner by which his home is broken. . . .

Where the child, especially the girl, remains with the mother there appears to be less likelihood of recidivism. The death of the mother, as compared to the death of the father, also leads to somewhat greater recidivism; while the loss of both parents is particularly severe on the Negro girls. For the most part, a child living in another family home and not with one of his parents is more likely to commit repeated offenses.

DIFFERENTIAL TREATMENT BY FAMILY STATUS

In Philadelphia, except for the handling of complaints which are rather trifling, law officers routinely deliver all children who are apprehended in the commission of delinquent acts into the hands of juvenile court authorities. They do not adjudicate or dispose of cases in the police station. Hence, in Philadelphia, as compared to other areas of the country, a much higher proportion of allegedly delinquent children receive treatment by the court, and the information on these cases approaches a completeness and representativeness as regards all children apprehended in the commission of delinquent acts. There does not seem to be any great tendency for policewomen, who arrest nearly 30 percent of the girls, to turn girls over to their parents rather than to charge them with delinquency. Indeed, girls show the same excessively high proportion of broken homes no matter what the type of offense may be.

The same proportion of broken homes appears in both the minor and major offense groups. . . . However, children who are living with both parents are much more likely to be dismissed by the intake interviewing staff, whereas the children from broken homes are more often held for court. The parentless child (one or both natural parents absent from home) is more often adjudged delinquent or in need of care, and a rather high proportion of them are committed to institutions for delinquents.

From these figures on first offenders it should be evident that the use of court arraignment and institutional statistics can give a rather distorted picture regarding the family status of delinquent children in general.

POPULATION COMPARISONS

. . . The 1950 Census for Philadelphia revealed that 7 percent of the white children and 33 percent of the nonwhite children *under 18 years* of age were *not* in census-classified husband-wife families.

In 1940 the corresponding figures were 13 percent for the whites and 33 percent for the nonwhites. Any adjustment for the age factor does not seem warranted because the proportion of broken homes among delinquent first offenders, 1949–1954, is practically the same for children of all ages.

With *incomplete* families among *first offenders* (1949–1954) under 18 years of age amounting to 22 percent for the white boys and 49 percent for the Negro boys, it should certainly be apparent that in their respective groups broken homes predispose these boys to acts of delinquency. Among the females the proportions from incomplete families are so high (42 percent for white girls and 68 percent for Negro girls) that there can hardly be any doubt as to the importance of parental deprivation to them.

Conclusion

One large minority in the population consistently shows twice the average rate of socially broken homes and twice the average rate of delinquency. Other groups with strong family cohesiveness show below average rates of delinquency. Such apparent associations cannot be dismissed as happenstance.

On the whole very little disagreement has been expressed over the probable harmful influence of the socially broken home on the child. This does not gainsay, however, the deprivation consequent to the loss of a parent through death. Indeed, the same high proportions of delinquents were found to come from broken homes more than a generation ago when orphanhood loomed larger as the reason for family disruption. Of even more importance to the child than the nature of the break is the fact of a break in his home.

All in all, the stability and continuity of family life stands out as the most important factor in the development of the child. It would seem, therefore, that the place of the home in the genesis of normal or delinquent patterns of behavior should receive greater practical recognition. The relationship is so strong that, if ways could be found to do it, a strengthening and preserving of family life, among the groups which need it most, could probably accomplish more in the amelioration and prevention of delinquency and other problems than any other single program yet devised.

CRIME AND ECONOMIC CONDITION

DANIEL GLASER
AND KENT RICE

Excerpted from Daniel Glaser and Kent Rice, "Crime, Age, and Employment," *American Sociological Review*, XXIV (October 1959), 680–86. The authors were affiliated with the University of Illinois when this article was published.

A REVIEW of past research makes it clear that no marked and consistent relationships have been established between overall or specific crime rates and economic conditions. . . .

Hypotheses

Despite . . . notorious deficiencies of American crime statistics, we had reason to believe that significant and stable relationships between crime and economic conditions might be demonstrated if the criminal population were appropriately differentiated by age and by offense. Our initial hypotheses, and their principal sources, were as follows:

Hypothesis 1. *The frequency of crimes committed by juveniles varies inversely with unemployment rates.* Several local studies of delinquency in the United States, covering the period around the depression of the 1930s, suggest that a decrease in delinquency occurred at that time. Plant observed such a decrease in Essex County, New Jersey, which he explained by the presumption that unemployment increased the time available to the father to be a companion to his children.[1] We were impressed by this interpretation, as well as by evidence that concern for integration increases

[1] James S. Plant, *Personality and the Cultural Pattern*, New York: The Commonwealth Fund, 1937, p. 141.

in small collaborative groups under threat,[2] despite Komarovsky's allegation that the authority of the father often declines with unemployment.[3] The apparent increases in delinquency during World War II and since 1948 provided further suggestion that parent-child contacts are the intervening variables in an inverse relationship between unemployment and juvenile delinquency; these rises in delinquency generally accompanied a simultaneous decline of male labor force unemployment and increase of married women in the labor force.

Emphasis on family relations as a primary factor in delinquency has been growing. This interpretation is often identified with the view that the juvenile's basic personality or emotional adjustment is the product of his family relationships and, therefore, personality or emotional stability is the intervening variable between family relations and delinquency. Reckless, Glaser, and others, however, have presented research findings which suggest that enculturation may be the primary intervening variable. Like Plant, they view the family as the agency which provides the principal competition to delinquent peer groups in the inculcation of cultural or subcultural values.[4]

Our expectation that an inverse relationship between delinquency and unemployment would apply to all types of crimes committed by juveniles stems from the impression that delinquent subcultures promote a high valuation of deviant acts which are versatile and relatively nonutilitarian, and that a youth's internalization of deviant values is a function of the extent to which he and his parents live in different social and cultural worlds.

Our initial hypotheses were expressed in terms of unemployment

[2] Cf. John T. Lanzetta, "Group Behavior Under Stress," *Human Relations,* 8 (1955), pp. 29–52.

[3] Mirra Komarovsky, *The Unemployed Man and His Family,* New York: Dryden, 1940.

[4] Walter C. Reckless, S. Dinitz, and E. Murray, "Self Concept as an Insulator Against Delinquency," *American Sociological Review,* 21 (December, 1956), pp. 744–46; Reckless, Dinitz, and B. Kay, "The Self Concept in Potential Delinquency and Potential Non-Delinquency," *American Sociological Review,* 22 (October, 1957), pp. 566–70; Daniel Glaser, "A Reconsideration of Some Parole Prediction Factors," *American Sociological Review,* 3 (June, 1954), pp. 336–37.

rates because this is an aspect of economic conditions which impinges most directly on the life of that portion of the population most liable to arrest, the lower socio-economic classes.

Hypothesis 2. *The frequency of property crimes committed by adults varies directly with unemployment rates.* Since adults differ from juveniles in the extent to which they are economically self-sufficient and are committed to legitimate occupations, it was anticipated that adult crime rates would vary directly with the inability to secure employment. Presumably, this would be particularly true for property offenses. . . .

If both of our hypotheses are valid, their opposing effects might account for previous failures to find marked relationships between crime and economic conditions.

Tests by United States Data

Since our hypotheses deal with the age of persons committing crimes, we needed data on criminals rather than the most complete index of the volume of crime: "crimes known to the police." Arrest data were preferred to conviction data for American criminals because the former are available for longer periods of time, and because offenses adjudicated in juvenile courts are not recorded as convictions. Arrestees, however, include some presumably innocent persons who are not convicted. We assume that the proportion of the latter group is sufficiently small or uniform through all our time, age, and offense categories that it does not radically distort the relationships which we are investigating. . . .

One assumption in comparing arrest totals for different age groups is that any errors in reporting are uniformly distributed for all age groups. This assumption is known to be somewhat invalid since only the pre-1952 figures were based on fingerprints submitted to the F.B.I., and the movement against fingerprinting juveniles is believed to have resulted after World War II in a decline in the proportion of arrests reported for juveniles, especially in 1951. When the F.B.I., in 1952, changed its system of age-specific data procurement from fingerprints to logs of arrests, compiled at local police agencies, the number of juvenile arrests reported increased markedly. Because of these trends in the age-specific arrest figures, the hypotheses were tested only on F.B.I. statistics, from their inception in 1932 through 1950.

The age-specific arrest data could not be compared with unemployment rates for exactly corresponding groups because long-term arrest and unemployment figures are not reported for the same age categories. Accordingly, we compared age-specific arrest rates with both the total and the age-specific male civilian unemployment rates. As far as possible, the latter were broken down into the age groups with which the arrestees were believed to be in most direct economic competition. . . . [When this is done] the patterns of relationships between arrests and both of these unemployment indices are similar. Since the index of total unemployment was less discriminating, the age-specific unemployment rates for the imperfectly matched age groups were then used for all other comparisons with arrest rates.

The results of our first test of the hypotheses are presented in Tables 1 and 2. . . . [Table 1 shows "Correlation Coefficients Relating Age-Specific U.S. Property Offense Arrests, as Per Cent of All-Ages Arrests, to Per Cent of U.S. Male Labor Force Unemployed, 1932–1950." Table 2 shows "Correlation Coefficients Relating Age-Specific U.S. Arrests for Crimes Against Persons and for Personal Disorganization Misdemeanors, as Per Cent of All Ages Arrests, to Per Cent of U.S. Male Labor Force Unemployed, 1932–1950." In Table 1, property offense arrests are for larceny, burglary, robbery, and auto theft. In Table 2, arrests for crimes against persons are for intended homicide, assault, and rape; arrests for personal disorganization misdemeanors are for drunkenness, disorderly conduct, and vagrancy.] In Table 1 the first hypothesis is clearly verified. The second hypothesis is verified with respect to adults aged 19 through 34, but an unexpected inverse relationship was found between crime and unemployment for adults 35 and over, resembling the relationship predicted only for juveniles.

The correlation coefficients in Table 2 suggest that the relationships originally hypothesized for employment and property offenses hold equally well for major types of non-economic crimes.

Arrests of juveniles for rape, intended homicide, and assault are inversely related to their unemployment, while a direct relationship is shown for arrestees between the ages 21 and 34. Again, a low negative relationship was found for offenders 35 years of age and over.

We considered two possible sociological explanations of the unexpected finding of an inverse relationship between felonious crimes and unemployment in the older age groups. The first, analogous to Durkheim's interpretation of increased suicide with prosperity, is that personal disorganization or anomie develops among older people because of their inability to adjust to increased economic means. This interpretation seemed somewhat validated by the finding that arrests for "personal disorganization" midemeanors were negatively related, and strongly so, to unemployment for the older age groups, but not for juveniles. We also speculated that disorganization of older persons might increase with prosperity because parents are needed by adult children during depressions, but lose parental functions during prosperity when their older offspring can be more self-sufficient.

An obvious alternative explanation for both the juvenile and old-age inverse relationships is that they are artifacts resulting from our indication of United States age-specific arrest trends by shifts in the proportion of total arrests contributed by specific age groups. Any marked change in arrests for one age group, expressed as a percentage of all arrests, would produce an inverse change in the percentage contributed by other age groups. Thus a marked positive relationship between unemployment and arrests for the middle-age ranges would produce, as artifacts, negative relationships for the other age ranges, or *vice versa*. To eliminate this possibility, we needed data in which crime rates for different age groups would be independent of each other, which we sought in municipal reports.

Tests by Municipal Data

A survey of municipal reports revealed that sex and age-specific arrest rates, differentiated by offense, had been published for several decades in fairly consistent form by police departments of three major cities: Chicago, Cincinnati, and Boston. The Chicago figures were somewhat suspect because of occasional odd fluctuations. The Cincinnati series, dating from 1935, inspired confidence because of the outstanding reputation of its public administration. We inferred that Boston data were punctiliously compiled by a highly compulsive bureaucracy because archaic language forms, and other details of annual presentation, were remarkably unchanged over a fifty-year period.

Unfortunately, we could obtain only age- and sex-specific population data for these cities for census years. A linear interpolation was employed to estimate the age-specific male population for intercensal years. The age-specific arrests could then be expressed as a per cent of the corresponding age population. This linear interpolation somewhat distorts actual trends, however, particularly in the 1940–50 decade, when the annual change in municipal age-group population certainly was not constant. Some further imperfection of the data as a test of our hypotheses lay in the need to use the national age-specific unemployment rates, for municipal rates were available only for recent years (and regretably, United States pre-1930 unemployment data are not available).

The relationships between these independent arrest rates for different age groups in the three municipalities, and United States unemployment rates, are presented in Table 3 . . . [showing "Correlation Coefficients Relating Arrests of Males in Boston, Cincinnati, and Chicago by Type of Offense, to Per Cent of U.S. Male Labor Force Unemployed, 1930–1956"]. They consistently confirm our prior conclusions with respect to our second hypothesis: that property theft and unemployment are positively related for the middle-age ranges. Only the Chicago figures fail to repeat our earlier finding, using national data, of a similar direct relationship between unemployment and both crimes against persons and the "personal disorganization" misdemeanors. The differences among these three cities in the overall relationship between arrests and unemployment (the "All Ages" findings) make any similarity in the age-specific findings particularly noteworthy.

The municipal evidence is less clear-cut in supporting the first hypothesis, which predicted an inverse relationship between all juvenile offenses and unemployment. This hypothesis is buttressed for the 10–17 age categories in the Boston data, but with negative correlations that are not significantly below zero, although significantly below the positive correlations for the older age groups. The 18–20 age group in Boston follows the adult pattern of increased property offenses with unemployment, but shows an inverse pattern on other offenses. The Chicago and Cincinnati arrest reports do not differentiate ages younger than 20 throughout the period covered. Significant negative relationships between crimes of this youngest age group in these two cities and unemployment were found for crimes against persons and for misdemeanors, but not for property offenses. However, property offense arrests of those 20 and under in Chicago and Cincinnati were markedly less related to unemployment than were arrests of adults, and there is a continuous increase in this relationship from the 20 and under to the somewhat older groups. This suggests that negative correlations, such as those yielded by the Boston data, might also have been procured for property offenses if as fine an age breakdown as that procured for Boston were available. Of course, a major portion of youth over 17 are in the job market, like adults. In general, the consistent pattern of difference between the relationship of crime and unemployment for the youngest age group and this relationship for the age groups between 20 and 44 is more impressive support for our first hypothesis than the statistical significance of correlation coefficients for these data.

The unexpected finding, discussed above of a negative relationship between older age offenses and unemployment, was not repeated with the municipal figures. Indeed, the three cities and the various offense categories investigated are inconsistent with respect to correlations between older age offenses and unemployment. A possible partial explanation of these inconsistencies is the marked differentiation between the cities in fluctuation of age-specific population composition. Between 1940 and 1950 the population 45 and over of Cincinnati increased 95 per cent and that of Chicago increased 53 per cent, while there was only a 9 per cent increase in this age-category for Boston. The distortion from our linear interpolation assumption of a 9.5 per cent increase from the 1940 figures each year in Cincinnati may be particularly defective; we are safest in linear interpolation with the relatively stable Boston population. Data on the racial and cultural background of the new older-age population in Cincinnati and Chicago might help to explain the irregularities in our findings for these two cities. The deficiencies in the source data, as well as the curvilinear relationships between age and the arrest-unemployment correlation coefficients, deterred us from partial regression analysis, using age as a third variable. We must accept an artifactual explanation for the inverse correlations in our national findings for the older age categories in the absence of data required for a more refined and precise analysis.

That conditions other than economic circumstances are particularly relevant to an understanding of trends in juvenile arrest rates is suggested by the fact that these rates are more independent of unemployment conditions than are the arrest rates of other age groups. . . .

Conclusions

Despite large deficiences of available data, we have presented evidence which suggests that more pronounced and consistent relationships between crime and economic conditions than were reported by previous studies can be obtained by using age-specific statistics. Consistent support was presented for the hypothesis that adult crime rates vary directly with unemployment, particularly rates of property offenses by persons of 20 to 45 years of age. Less conclusive—but appreciable—evidence was presented for the hypothesis that juvenile crime rates vary inversely with unemployment. . . .

Most criminology textbooks cite the low relationship of economic conditions to non-age-specific criminality as a basis for refuting Marxian explanations for crime. Our findings could be used by Marxists to ascribe criminality, at least in young adults, to the economic insecurity inherent in capitalism. A more parsimonious explanation, however, in the sense that it fits a variety of deviant behavior, is provided by Merton's paradigm which views crime as an innovating reaction to anomie, and stipulates the conditions for its priority over alternative reactions. This paradigm not only may be employed to account for the young adult's recourse to criminal means for economic ends when faced with unemployment, but also has been used to explain non-economic aspects of juvenile delinquency.[5]

As economic insecurity is reduced, we may still expect criminality to be associated with status insecurity or other sources of anomie. The generality of this phenomenon under quite different economic systems is suggested by Deaton's argument that post-World War II juvenile delinquency in the U.S.S.R. is distinctly associated with the anomie of the children of middle-class Russian families. The offspring of Soviet managers and professionals, reared in permissive family homes rather than factory nurseries, are more "on their own" than children of the Soviet proletariat. They are particularly anomic and prone to develop delinquent sub-cultures in late adolescence when they must suddenly shift to the regimented life which lower-class Russian children have experienced from infancy.[6]

If the Merton paradigm is to be applied to diverse types of criminality, what of the dominant American sociological explanation for crime which views it as a consequence of differential association or identification with criminals? It seems to us that the two are complementary. The Merton paradigm provides a needed explanation for conversion from a criminal to a non-criminal "way of life," and *vice versa*. Changes in the opportunity structure, as a result of job market fluctuations, alter the relative accessibility of legitimate and illegitimate means. . . .

Once a person has been involved in criminality, whether because of early enculturation in delinquency or later conversion,

[5] Robert K. Merton, *Social Theory and Social Structure*, Glencoe, Ill.: Free Press, 1957, pp. 121–30; Richard A. Cloward, "Illegitimate Means, Anomie, and Deviant Behavior," *American Sociological Review*, 24 (April, 1959), pp. 164–76; also, forthcoming articles by Cloward and L. E. Ohlin in which different types of delinquent subcultures are interpreted as alternative solutions to problems of anomie.

[6] Robert B. Deaton, "Postwar Juvenile Delinquency in the Union of Soviet Socialist Republics," unpublished M.A. thesis, University of Illinois, 1955.

and particularly when he has been arrested, committed to penal institutions, and released with the stigma of a criminal record, his criminal norms and his access to criminal means have been reinforced by his differential association and identification. Thus Merton's sociology may be needed to explain conversion to crime, while Sutherland's criminology may be applied within Merton's frame of reference to explain persistence in crime. . . .

CULTURE CONFLICT AND CRIME

THORSTEN SELLIN

Excerpted from Thorsten Sellin, *Culture Conflict and Crime* (New York, Social Science Research Council, Bulletin 41, 1938), pp. 63–70.

Conflicts of Cultural Codes

There are social groups on the surface of the earth which possess complexes of conduct norms which, due to differences in the mode of life and the social values evolved by these groups, appear to set them apart from other groups in many or most respects. We may expect conflicts of norms when the rural dweller moves to the city, but we assume that he has absorbed the basic norms of the culture which comprises both town and country. How much greater is not the conflict likely to be when Orient and Occident meet, or when the Corsican mountaineer is transplanted to the lower East Side of New York. Conflicts of cultures are inevitable when the norms of one cultural or subcultural area migrate to or come in contact with those of another, and it is interesting to note that most of the specific researches on culture conflict and delinquency have been concerned with this aspect of conflict. . . .

Conflicts between norms of divergent cultural codes may arise (1) when these codes clash on the border of contiguous culture areas; (2) when, as may be the case with legal norms, the law of one cultural group is extended to cover the territory of another; or (3) when members of one cultural group migrate to another.[1]

---

[1] This is unfortunately not the whole story, for with the rapid growth of impersonal communication, the written (press, literature) and the spoken word (radio, talkie), knowledge concerning divergent conduct norms no longer grows solely out of direct personal contact with their carriers. And out of such conflicts grow some violations of customs and of law which would not have occurred without them.

. . . .We need only to recall the effect on the American Indian of the culture conflicts induced by our policy of acculturation by guile and force. In this instance, it was not merely contact with the white man's culture, his religion, his business methods, and his liquor, which weakened the tribal mores. In addition, the Indian became subject to the white man's law and this brought conflicts as well, as has always been the case when legal norms have been imposed upon a group previously ignorant of them. . . .

We have noted that culture conflicts are the natural outgrowth of processes of social differentiation, which produce an infinity of social groupings, each with its own definitions of life situations, its own interpretations of social relationships, its own ignorance or misunderstanding of the social values of other groups. The transformation of a culture from a homogeneous and well-integrated type to a heterogeneous and disintegrated type is therefore accompanied by an increase of conflict situations. Conversely, the operation of integrating processes will reduce the number of conflict situations. Such conflicts within a changing culture may be distinguished from those created when different cultural systems come in contact with one another, regardless of the character or stage of development of these systems. In either case, the conduct of members of a group involved in the conflict of codes will in some respects be judged abnormal by the other group.

The Study of Culture Conflicts

In the study of culture conflicts, some scholars have been concerned with the effect of such conflicts on the conduct of specific persons, an approach which is naturally preferred by psychologists and psychiatrists and by sociologists who have used the life history technique. These scholars view the conflict as internal. Wirth [2] states categorically that a culture "conflict can be said to be a factor in delinquency only if the individual feels it or acts as if it were present." Culture conflict is mental conflict, but the character of this conflict is viewed differently by the various disciplines which

[2] Wirth, Louis. "Culture Conflict and Misconduct." *Social Forces*. 9:484–92. June, 1931. P. 490.

use this term. Freudian psychiatrists regard it as a struggle between deeply rooted biological urges which demand expression and the culturally created rules which give rise to inhibitive mechanisms which thwart this expression and drive them below the conscious level of the mind, whence they rise either by ruse in some socially acceptable disguise, as abnormal conduct when the inhibiting mechanism breaks down, or as neuroses when it works too well. The sociologist, on the other hand, thinks of mental conflict as being primarily the clash between antagonistic conduct norms incorporated in personality. "Mental conflict in the person," says Burgess in discussing the case presented by Shaw in *The Jack-Roller*, "may always be explained in terms of the conflict of divergent cultures." [3]

If this view is accepted, sociological research on culture conflict and its relationship to abnormal conduct would have to be strictly limited to a study of the personality of cultural hybrids. Significant studies could be conducted only by the life-history case technique applied to persons in whom the conflict is internalized. . . .

The absence of mental conflict, in the sociological sense, may, however, be well studied in terms of culture conflict. An example may make this clear. A few years ago a Sicilian father in New Jersey killed the sixteen-year-old seducer of his daughter, expressing surprise at his arrest since he had merely defended his family honor in a traditional way. In this case a mental conflict in the sociological sense did not exist. The conflict was external and occurred between cultural codes or norms. We may assume that where such conflicts occur violations of norms will arise merely because persons who have absorbed the norms of one cultural group or area migrate to another and that such conflict will continue so long as the acculturation process has not been completed. Only then may the violations be regarded in terms of mental conflict.

If culture conflict may be regarded as sometimes personalized, or mental, and sometimes as occurring entirely in an impersonal way solely as a conflict of group codes, it is obvious that research should not be confined to the investigation of mental conflicts and

[3] Burgess, Ernest W. in Clifford R. Shaw's *The Jack-Roller*. Chicago: University of Chicago Press. 1930. Pp. 184–97, p. 186.

that contrary to Wirth's categorical statement that it is impossible to demonstrate the existence of a culture conflict "objectively . . . by a comparison between two cultural codes," [4] this procedure has not only a definite function, but may be carried out by researches employing techniques which are familiar to the sociologist.

The emphasis on the life history technique has grown out of the assumption that "the experiences of one person at the same time reveals the life activities of his group" and that "habit in the individual is an expression of custom in society." [5] This is undoubtedly one valid approach. Through it we may hope to discover generalizations of a scientific nature by studying persons who (1) have drawn their norms of conduct from a variety of groups with conflicting norms, or who (2) possess norms drawn from a group whose code is in conflict with that of the group which judges the conduct. In the former case alone can we speak of mental or internal culture conflict; in the latter, the conflict is external.

If the conduct norms of a group are, with reference to a given life situation, inconsistent, or if two groups possess inconsistent norms, we may assume that the members of these various groups will individually reflect such group attitudes. Paraphrasing Burgess, the experiences of a group will reveal the life activities of its members. . . .

In conclusion, then, culture conflict may be studied either as mental conflict or as a conflict of cultural codes. The criminologist will naturally tend to concentrate on such conflicts between legal and nonlegal conduct norms. The concept of conflict fails to give him more than a general framework of reference for research. In practice, it has, however, become nearly synonymous with conflicts between the norms of cultural systems or areas. Most researches which have employed it have been done on immigrant or race groups in the United States, perhaps due to the ease with which such groups may be identified, the existence of more statistical data recognizing such groupings, and the conspicuous differences between some immigrant norms and our norms.

[4] Wirth, Louis. *Op. cit.* P. 490. It should be noted that Wirth also states that culture should be studied "on the objective side" and that "the sociologist is not primarily interested in personality but in culture."

[5] Burgess, Ernest W. *Op. cit.* P. 186.

THE THEORY OF DIFFERENTIAL
ASSOCIATION

EDWIN H. SUTHERLAND

Adapted from Edwin H. Sutherland, *Principles of Criminology*, 4th ed. (Philadelphia, Lippincott, 1947), pp. 3–9. J. B. Lippincott Company. Reprinted by permission of the publishers.

ANY SCIENTIFIC explanation consists of a description of the conditions which are always present when a phenomenon occurs and which are never present when the phenomenon does not occur. Although a multitude of conditions may be associated in greater or less degree with the phenomenon in question, this information is relatively useless for understanding or for control if the factors are left as a hodgepodge of unorganized factors. Scientists strive to organize their knowledge in interrelated general propositions, to which no exceptions can be found. The heterogeneous collection of factors associated with a phenomenon may be reduced to a series of interrelated general propositions by two general methods.

First, the multiple factors operating at a particular moment may be reduced to simplicity and generality by abstracting from them the elements which are common to all of them. Negroes, urban-dwellers, and young-adult males all have comparatively high crime rates. What do they have in common that results in these high crime rates? Research studies of criminal behavior have shown that criminal behavior is associated in greater or less degree with the social and personal pathologies, such as poverty, bad housing, slum-residence, lack of recreational facilities, inadequate and demoralized families, feeblemindedness, emotional instability, and other traits and conditions. At the same time, these research studies have demonstrated that many persons with those pathological traits and conditions do not commit crimes. Also, these studies have shown that persons in the upper socio-economic class frequently violate laws, although they are not in poverty, do not lack recreational facilities, are not feebleminded, or emotionally unstable. Such factors are obviously inadequate as an explanation of criminal behavior, and no amount of calculation of the risks of different categories of persons will bring us much closer to an understanding of criminal behavior. An adequate explanation of criminal behavior can be reached only by locating the abstract mechanisms and processes which are common to both the rich and the poor, the emotionally stable and the emotionally unstable who commit crimes. In arriving at these abstract mechanisms and processes, some of the concrete factors can be reinterpreted in general terms. A motion picture several years ago showed two boys engaged in theft; they ran when they were discovered; one boy had longer legs, escaped, and became a priest; the other had shorter legs, was caught, committed to a reformatory, and became a gangster. In this comparison, the boy who became a criminal was differentiated from the one who did not become a criminal by the length of his legs. In general, however, no significant relationship has been found between criminality and length of legs and certainly many persons with short legs are law-abiding and many persons with long legs are criminals. In this particular case, the length of the legs is probably of no significance in itself and is significant only as it determines the subsequent experiences and associations of the two boys.

Second, the causal analysis must be held at a particular level in order to arrive at valid generalizations. Two aspects of this may be mentioned. The first is limiting the problem to a particular part of the whole situation, largely in terms of chronology. In the heterogeneous collection of factors associated with criminal behavior one factor is often the cause of another factor or at least occurs prior to the other. Consideration of the time sequences among the factors often leads to simplicity of statement. When physicists stated the law of falling bodies they were not concerned with the reasons why a body began to fall except as this might affect the initial momentum. It made no difference to the physicist whether a body began to fall because it was dropped from the hand of an experimental physicist or rolled off the edge of a bridge because of vibration caused by a passing automobile. Such facts were on a different level of explanation and were irrelevant to the problem with which they were concerned. Much of the confusion regarding human behavior is due to failure to define and hold constant the level of explanation. A second aspect of this problem is the definition of criminal behavior. The problem in criminology is to explain the criminality of behavior, not the behavior, as such. Criminal behavior is a part of human behavior, has much in common with non-criminal behavior, and must be explained within the same general framework as any other human behavior. However, an explanation of criminal behavior should be a specific part of that general theory of behavior and its task should be to differentiate criminal from non-criminal behavior. Many things which are necessary factors in behavior are not necessary for the criminality of behavior. Respiration, for instance, is necessary for any behavior but it is not a factor in criminal behavior, as defined, since it does not differentiate criminal behavior from non-criminal behavior.

The scientific explanation of a phenomenon may be stated either in terms of the factors which are operating at the moment of the occurrence of a phenomenon or in terms of the processes operating in the earlier history of that phenomenon. In the first case the explanation is mechanistic, in the second historical or genetic; both are desirable. The physical and biological scientists favor the first of these methods and it would probably be superior as an explanation of criminal behavior. Efforts at explanations of the mechanistic type have been notably unsuccessful, perhaps largely because they have been concentrated on the attempt to isolate personal and social pathologies. Work from this point of view has, at least, resulted in the conclusion that the immediate factors in criminal behavior lie in the person-situation complex. Person and situation are not factors exclusive of each other, for the situation which is important is the situation as defined by the person who is involved. The tendencies and inhibitions at the moment of the criminal behavior are, to be sure, largely a product of the earlier history of the person, but the expression of these tendencies and inhibitions is a reaction to the immediate situation as defined by the person. The situation operates in many ways, of which perhaps the least important is the provision of an opportunity for a criminal act. A thief may steal from a fruit stand when the owner is not in sight but refrain when the owner is in sight; a bank burglar may attack a bank which is poorly protected but refrain from attacking a bank protected by watchmen and burglar alarms. A corporation which manufactures automobiles seldom or never violates the Pure Food and Drug Law but a meat-packing corporation violates this law with great frequency.

The second type of explanation of criminal behavior is made in terms of the life experience of a person. This is an historical or genetic explanation of criminal behavior. This, to be sure, assumes a situation to be defined by the person in terms of the inclinations and abilities which the person has acquired up to that date. The following paragraphs state such a genetic theory of criminal behavior on the assumption that a criminal act occurs when a situation appropriate for it, as defined by a person, is present.

Genetic Explanation of Criminal Behavior

The following statement refers to the process by which a particular person comes to engage in criminal behavior.

1. *Criminal behavior is learned.* Negatively, this means that criminal behavior is not inherited, as such; also, the person who is not already trained in crime does not invent criminal behavior, just as a person does not make mechanical inventions unless he has had training in mechanics.

2. *Criminal behavior is learned in interaction with other persons in a process of communication.* This communication is verbal in many respects but includes also "the communication of gestures."

3. *The principal part of the learning of criminal behavior occurs within intimate personal groups.* Negatively, this means that the impersonal agencies of communication, such as picture shows and newspapers, play a relatively unimportant part in the genesis of criminal behavior.

4. *When criminal behavior is learned, the learning includes* (a) *techniques of committing the crime, which are sometimes very complicated, sometimes very simple;* (b) *the specific direction of motives, drives, rationalizations, and attitudes.*

5. *The specific direction of motives and drives is learned from definitions of the legal codes as favorable or unfavorable.* In some societies an individual is surrounded by persons who invariably define the legal codes as rules to be observed, while in others he is surrounded by persons whose definitions are favorable to the violation of the legal codes. In our American society these definitions are almost always mixed and consequently we have culture conflict in relation to the legal codes.

6. *A person becomes delinquent because of an excess of definitions favorable to violation of law over definitions unfavorable to violation of law.* This is the principle of differential association. It refers to both criminal and anti-criminal associations and has to do with counteracting forces. When persons become criminal, they do so because of contacts with criminal patterns and also because of isolation from anti-criminal patterns. Any person inevitably assimilates the surrounding culture unless other patterns are in conflict; a Southerner does not pronounce "r" because other Southerners do not pronounce "r." Negatively, this proposition of differential association means that associations which are neutral so far as crime is concerned have little or no effect on the genesis of criminal behavior. Much of the experience of a person is neutral in this sense, e.g., learning to brush one's teeth. This behavior has no negative or positive effect on criminal behavior except as it may be related to associations which are concerned with the legal codes. This neutral behavior is important especially as an occupier of the time of a child so that he is not in contact with criminal behavior during the time he is so engaged in the neutral behavior.

7. *Differential associations may vary in frequency, duration, priority, and intensity.* This means that associations with criminal behavior and also associations with anti-criminal behavior vary in those respects. "Frequency" and "duration" as modalities of associations are obvious and need no explanation. "Priority" is assumed to be important in the sense that lawful behavior developed in

early childhood may persist throughout life, and also that delinquent behavior developed in early childhood may persist throughout life. This tendency, however, has not been adequately demonstrated, and priority seems to be important principally through its selective influence. "Intensity" is not precisely defined but it has to do with such things as the prestige of the source of a criminal or anti-criminal pattern and with emotional reactions related to the associations. In a precise description of the criminal behavior of a person these modalities would be stated in quantitative form and a mathematical ratio be reached. A formula in this sense has not been developed and the development of such a formula would be extremely difficult.

8. *The process of learning criminal behavior by association with criminal and anti-criminal patterns involves all of the mechanisms that are involved in any other learning.* Negatively, this means that the learning of criminal behavior is not restricted to the process of imitation. A person who is seduced, for instance, learns criminal behavior by association but this process would not ordinarily be described as imitation.

9. *While criminal behavior is an expression of general needs and values, it is not explained by those general needs and values since non-criminal behavior is an expression of the same needs and values.* Thieves generally steal in order to secure money, but likewise honest laborers work in order to secure money. The attempts by many scholars to explain criminal behavior by general drives and values, such as the happiness principle, striving for social status, the money motive, or frustration, have been and must continue to be futile since they explain lawful behavior as completely as they explain criminal behavior. They are similar to respiration, which is necessary for any behavior but which does not differentiate criminal from non-criminal behavior.

It is not necessary, at this level of explanation, to explain why a person has the associations which he has; this certainly involves a complex of many things. In an area where the delinquency rate is high a boy who is sociable, gregarious, active, and athletic is very likely to come in contact with the other boys in the neighborhood, learn delinquent behavior from them, and become a gangster; in the same neighborhood the psychopathic boy who is isolated, introvert, and inert may remain at home, not become acquainted with the other boys in the neighborhood, and not become delinquent. In another situation, the sociable, athletic, aggressive boy may become a member of a scout troop and not become involved in delinquent behavior. The person's associations are determined in a general context of social organization. A child is ordinarily reared in a family; the place of residence of the family is determined largely by family income; and the delinquency rate is in many respects related to the rental value of the houses. Many other factors enter into this social organization, including many of the small personal group relationships.

The preceding explanation of criminal behavior was stated from the point of view of the person who engages in criminal behavior. It is possible, also, to state theories of criminal behavior from the point of view of the community, nation, or other group. The problem, when thus stated, is generally concerned with crime rates and involves a comparison of the crime rates of various groups or the crime rates of a particular group at different times. One of the best explanations of crime rates from this point of view is that a high crime rate is due to social disorganization. The term "social disorganization" is not entirely satisfactory and it seems preferable to substitute for it the term "differential social organization." The postulate on which this theory is based, regardless of the name, is that crime is rooted in the social organization and is an expression of that social organization. A group may be organized for criminal behavior or organized against criminal behavior. Most communities are organized both for criminal and anti-criminal behavior and in that sense the crime rate is an expression of the differential group organization. Differential group organization as an explanation of a crime rate must be consistent with the explanation of the criminal behavior of the person, since the crime rate is a summary statement of the number of persons in the group who commit crimes and the frequency with which they commit crimes.

A CRITICAL LOOK AT DIFFERENTIAL ASSOCIATION THEORY

SHELDON GLUECK

Sheldon Glueck, "Theory and Fact in Criminology," *British Journal of Delinquency*, VII (October 1956), 92–98. At the time of publication, S. Glueck was affiliated with Harvard University.

BEFORE AND after Lombroso published his theory of the "born criminal" in 1897, there have been attempts to attribute crime to some unilateral cause. Intellectual defect as an exclusive or major explanation followed atavism, degeneracy, and epilepsy; mental disease followed intellectual defect; the psycho-analytic concept of criminalism "from a sense of guilt" followed traditional psychiatric explanations. The older unilateral sociological explanations in terms of poverty, movements of the business cycle, and the like, were succeeded by the over-emphasis of residence in economically underprivileged and culturally conflicting "interstitial" urban areas.

In more recent years, the theory of "differential association" has been put forward by the late Professor E. H. Sutherland, a distinguished criminologist, and elaborated in Professor D. R. Cressey's new edition of Sutherland's popular text-book on criminology. This theory plays a prominent part in American criminological circles. The proponents of this view disclaim that they, like their forerunners, are resorting to a unilateral explanation of crime; they do not call differential association a cause but rather a "theory." The theory is alleged to explain crime not in terms of a single aetological influence but rather in terms of many variables which it supposedly "organizes and relates."

It is the thesis of this paper that the theory of differential association, supported by its related concept of "definitions of the situation," fails to organize and integrate the findings of respectable research and is, at best, so general and puerile as to add little or nothing to the explanation, treatment, and prevention of delinquency.

Simply stated, the theory explains criminality as the result of an excess of "definitions favourable to violation of the law over definitions unfavourable to violation of the law,"[1] learned by the prospective offender in social interaction with existing criminals. However, as stated in the text-books the theory is not too clear. One form of explanation (in the quotation that follows) seems to emphasize the individual rather than the *milieu,* and to include, thereby, early childhood experiences and perhaps even original natural endowment of the offender in the bringing about of delinquent behaviour; but, if this be so, the theory adds nothing but the excess baggage of confusing terminology to what is already well known and explainable without the benefit of theory:

In another sense, a psychological or sociological sense, the situation is not exclusive of the person, for the situation which is important is the situation as defined by the person who is involved. That is, some persons define a situation in which a fruitstand owner is out of sight as a "crime-committing" situation, while others do not so define it. Furthermore, the events in the person-situation complex at the time a crime occurs cannot be separated from the prior life experiences of the criminal. This means that the situation is defined by the person in terms of the inclinations and abilities which the person has acquired up to date. For example, while a person could define a situation in such a manner that criminal behaviour would be the inevitable result, his past experiences would for the most part determine the way in which he defined the situation. . . . The following paragraphs state such a genetic theory of criminal behaviour on the assumption that a criminal act occurs when a situation appropriate for it, as defined by the person, is present.[2]

While it is true that a person's "inclinations and abilities," and his prior experiences influence his latest experience, it is difficult to see what is added to understanding by all this talk about "defini-

[1] Sutherland, E. H., "Principles of Criminology," 5th edition, revised by D. R. Cressey, J. B. Lippincott Company, 1955, Chapter IV.
[2] *Ibid.,* p. 77.

tions of the situation." It comes down to saying that if a person's makeup and experiences are such as to incline him to criminalism he will consciously become a criminal—something with which nobody can quarrel except for the unwarranted exclusion of the subconscious and unconscious influences in behaviour. Why place major emphasis on a "definition of the situation" which the prospective offender supposedly goes through? The important question is what makes him a delinquent, or, if we must pay tribute to the sociological formula, what makes him define a situation as conducive to criminalism?

But another form of exposition of the differential association theory emphasizes the influence of the *milieu*. We are informed, first, of the discovery that "criminal behaviour is *learned*" and that

Negatively, this means that criminal behaviour is not inherited, as such; also, the person who is not already trained in crime does not invent criminal behaviour, just as a person does not make mechanical inventions unless he has had training in mechanics.[3]

Consider the first part of this statement. Does anybody nowadays believe that criminal behaviour "as such" is inherited? Did even Lombroso believe so? Those criminologists who call attention to variations in the strength of different hereditary drives and controlling mechanisms do not claim that criminalism *per se* is inherited, but merely point to the too often sociologically under-emphasized if not ignored biological fact that, in the eyes of nature, all men are not created equal and that some, because of certain traits useful to the kind of activities involved in criminal behaviour, probably have a higher delinquency *potential* than others.

Consider, now, the second part of the quotation, to the effect that a person cannot invent criminal behaviour or commit crime without training. This is so contrary to obvious fact that it is surprising to see it seriously advanced. It attributes all criminal conduct to indoctrination by other criminals or contagion by criminal-

---

[3] Sutherland-Cressey, *op. cit.*, p. 77. "The differential association theory, which is considered by most sociologists as the best formulation to date of a general theory of criminality, holds, in essence, that criminality is learned in interaction with others in a process of communication." Cressey, D. R., "The Differential Association Theory and Compulsive Crimes," *J. of Crim. Law, Criminology and Police Science*, Vol. 45 (May–June, 1954), p. 29.

istic "patterns" and utterly ignores such primitive impulses of aggression, sexual desire, acquisitiveness, and the like, which lead children to various forms of anti-social conduct before they have learned it from others. What is there to be learned about simple lying, taking things that belong to another, fighting, and sex play? Do children have to be taught such natural acts? If one takes account of the psychiatric and criminological evidence that involves research into the early childhood manifestations of anti-social behaviour, one must conclude that it is not delinquent behaviour that is learned; that comes naturally. It is rather *non*-delinquent behaviour that is learned. Unsocialized, untamed, and uninstructed, the child resorts to lying, slyness, subterfuge, anger, hatred, theft, aggression, attack, and other forms of asocial behaviour in its early attempts of self-expression and ego formation. What he is normally forced to learn in his earliest struggles with the adult environment, in order to develop a personality and win the affection and sense of security and approval he craves, is not the non-conforming behaviour of egoism and delinquency but the conventional behaviour of altruism and non-delinquency; not the expression of natural asocial, dissocial, or anti-social impulses and desires, but how to tame these primitive tendencies sufficiently to win parental love and approval. Law-abiding character formation is a hard-won process.

If, as the proponents of the "differential association" theory insist, "the person who is not already trained in crime does not invent criminal behaviour just as a person does not make mechanical inventions unless he has had training in mechanics," how account for a basic finding in *Unraveling Juvenile Delinquency*,[4] that the onset of delinquent behaviour occurred at the tender age of seven years or less in 44.4 per cent of the delinquents and at ten years or less in 87.6 per cent? [5] These are not theoretical speculations but carefully verified facts. Just where and when did these very young children "differentially associate" with delinquents or criminals in order to learn how to commit their delinquencies? True, another finding of *Unraveling* was that 56 per cent of the delinquents, com-

---

[4] Glueck, S., and E. T., "Unraveling Juvenile Delinquency," New York, The Commonwealth Fund, 1950.
[5] *Ibid.*, p. 28.

pared to only three individuals among the non-delinquents, became members of boy gangs; [6] but since nine-tenths of the delinquents were . . . committing offences at under eleven years of age,
and since the gang is an adolescent phenomenon, it cannot be said
that the delinquents learned their anti-social behaviour from the
gang.

If what is meant by the proponents of the "crime is learned"
school is that most criminals consolidate their anti-social attitudes
in contact with others, or learn *techniques* of various crimes from
others, there is less objection (although this does not account for
the *origins* of misconduct); but even this is exaggerated. We found
little evidence in our numerous solidly grounded follow-up studies
. . . that the great majority of these criminals would have failed to
pass from juvenile delinquency to adult criminalism had it not
been for "differential association," or that they learned their techniques from each other.

By way of further elucidation of the differential association concept, the crux of this theory is presented in the following words:

The specific direction of motives and drives is learned from definitions
of the legal codes as favourable or unfavourable. In some societies an individual is surrounded by persons who invariably define the legal codes
as rules to be observed, while in others he is surrounded by persons
whose definitions are favourable to the violation of the legal codes. In
our American society these definitions are almost always mixed, with the
consequence that we have culture conflict in relation to the legal codes.
A person becomes delinquent because of an excess of definitions favourable to violation of law over definitions unfavourable to violation of law.
This is the principle of differential association. [7]

The ratio between such definitions and others unfavourable to law violation determines whether or not a person becomes criminal. [8]

Consider these statements. In the first place, has anybody actually counted the number of definitions favourable to violation of
law and definitions unfavourable to violation of law, and demonstrated that in the predelinquency experience of the vast majority

[6] *Ibid.*, p. 163.

[7] Sutherland-Cressey, *op. cit.*, p. 78.

[8] Cressey, D. R., "Application and Verification of the Differential Association Theory," *J. of Crim. Law, Criminology and Police Science*, Vol. 43
(1952–53), p. 43.

of delinquents and criminals, the former exceed the latter? Indeed, it is highly probable that, by the very extent, frequency, and intensity of conventional home and school and church influences, and the very early stage of the development of character at which these influences operate, there is an excess of "definitions *un*favourable to violation of law" even in the case of most of those who become delinquent and criminal.

In the second place, the theory in question, by emphasizing a quantitative excess of "definitions," ignores the patent fact that the individual influences of the human and physical environment to which persons are subjected vary in their impact. But more seriously, it fails to take account of obvious differences in the somatic, temperamental, and characterological make-up of individuals subjected to a superficially similar environment.

Those sociological criminologists who have taken up the ideas of W. I. Thomas are not as discerning as was the master. For right at the threshold of Thomas' significant *Primitive Behaviour*, he points out that conditioning is only half the process, the other half being the varied natures of those conditioned; and that these involve both experience and original endowment:

The reaction of different individuals in the same culture to identical cultural influences will depend partly on their different trains of experience and partly on their biochemical constitutions and unlearned psychological endowments. Local, regional, nationalistic and racial groups are in turn conditioned, in the formation of their behaviour patterns and habits, by their several trains of experience and conceivably by their particular biochemical and psychological constitutions.[9]

He includes, among the problems of individual and group adjustment, the "capacity and opportunity of the individual to be adjusted (*constitutional* factors, incentives, social position)." [10]

But by emphasizing the *number* or *ratio* of "definitions" as controlling, the differential association theory treats all persons as *equally* influenced by stimuli of one kind or another—something patently contrary to elementary biology and psychology. If the

[9] Thomas, W. I., "Primitive Behavior, An Introduction to the Social Sciences," New York, McGraw-Hill Book Co., 1937, p. 1.
[10] *Ibid.*, p. 2. Italics supplied.

quantitative emphasis of the theory is sound, then, to press it to its logical conclusion, the biggest criminals of all would be professors of criminology, prison guards, and prison chaplains! They certainly spend a great deal of time and effort in numerous instances of "differential association" with criminals. These persons are not criminal but essentially law-abiding, because of their original endowment and early home influences and training; and to say they "define the situation" differently from criminals is to add no insight whatsoever to the understanding of delinquency and non-delinquency, but to state, in pseudo-scientific language, the fact that they are not criminally inclined or do not wish to be criminals.

However, the proponents of this theory want to have it both ways. They also tell us that "differential associations vary in frequency, duration, priority, and intensity." If these influences vary in these different ways, how can one say that it is a mere numerical excess of definitions favourable to criminality that determines the issue? In discussing "intensity," Professor Cressey says that " 'intensity' is not precisely defined but it has to do with such things as the prestige of the source of a criminal or anti-criminal pattern and with *emotional reactions related to the associations*." [11] (Italics supplied.) But if this be so, it is not the *stimulus* of the "differential association" that is crucial but rather the *response* in terms of the emotional reaction of the individual to such stimulus; and this response obviously must vary with differences in the bio-psychologic structure of those who make it. What is added to this by the *deus ex machina* of "definitions of the situation"? How much more illuminating is Dr. Bernard Glueck's formulation: "A factor is not a cause unless and until it becomes a motive."

[11] Sutherland-Cressey, *op. cit.*, pp. 78–79.

THE DOCTRINE OF "SOCIALLY DERIVED SIN"

ROBERT K. MERTON

Robert K. Merton, "Social Structure and Anomie," *American Sociological Review*, III (October 1938), 672–82. When his article was published, R. K. Merton was affiliated with Harvard University.

THERE PERSISTS a notable tendency in sociological theory to attribute the malfunctioning of social structure primarily to those of man's imperious biological drives which are not adequately restrained by social control. In this view, the social order is solely a device for "impulse management" and the "social processing" of tensions. These impulses which break through social control, be it noted, are held to be biologically derived. Nonconformity is assumed to be rooted in original nature.[1] Conformity is by implication the result of an utilitarian calculus or unreasoned conditioning. This point of view, whatever its other deficiencies, clearly begs one question. It provides no basis for determining the nonbiological conditions which induce deviations from prescribed patterns of conduct. In this paper, it will be suggested that certain phases of social structure generate the circumstances in which infringement of social codes constitutes a "normal" response.[2]

---

[1] E.g., Ernest Jones, *Social Aspects of Psychoanalysis*, 28, London, 1924. If the Freudian notion is a variety of the "original sin" dogma, then the interpretation advanced in this paper may be called the doctrine of "socially derived sin."

[2] "Normal" in the sense of a culturally oriented, if not approved, response. This statement does not deny the relevance of biological and personality differences which may be significantly involved in the *incidence* of deviate conduct. Our focus of interest is the social and cultural matrix; hence we abstract from other factors. It is in this sense, I take it, that James S. Plant speaks of the "normal reaction of normal people to abnormal conditions." See his *Personality and the Cultural Pattern*, 248, New York, 1937.

The conceptual scheme to be outlined is designed to provide a coherent, systematic approach to the study of socio-cultural sources of deviate behavior. Our primary aim lies in discovering how some social structures *exert a definite pressure* upon certain persons in the society to engage in nonconformist rather than conformist conduct. The many ramifications of the scheme cannot all be discussed; the problems mentioned outnumber those explicitly treated.

Among the elements of social and cultural structure, two are important for our purposes. These are analytically separable although they merge imperceptibly in concrete situations. The first consists of culturally defined goals, purposes, and interests. It comprises a frame of aspirational reference. These goals are more or less integrated and involve varying degrees of prestige and sentiment. They constitute a basic, but not the exclusive, component of what Linton aptly has called "designs for group living." Some of these cultural aspirations are related to the original drives of man, but they are not determined by them. The second phase of the social structure defines, regulates, and controls the acceptable modes of achieving these goals. Every social group invariably couples its scale of desired ends with moral or institutional regulation of permissible and required procedures for attaining these ends. These regulatory norms and moral imperatives do not necessarily coincide with technical or efficiency norms. Many procedures which from the standpoint of *particular individuals* would be most efficient in securing desired values, e.g., illicit oil-stock schemes, theft, fraud, are ruled out of the institutional area of permitted conduct. The choice of expedients is limited by the institutional norms.

To say that these two elements, culture goals and institutional norms, operate jointly is not to say that the ranges of alternative behaviors and aims bear some constant relation to one another. The emphasis upon certain goals may vary independently of the degree of emphasis upon institutional means. There may develop a disproportionate, at times, a virtually exclusive, stress upon the value of specific goals, involving relatively slight concern with the institutionally appropriate modes of attaining these goals. The limiting case in this direction is reached when the range of alternative procedures is limited only by technical rather than institutional considerations. Any and all devices which promise attainment of the all important goal would be permitted in this hypothetical polar case.[3] This constitutes one type of cultural malintegration. A second polar type is found in groups where activities originally conceived as instrumental are transmuted into ends in themselves. The original purposes are forgotten and ritualistic adherence to institutionally prescribed conduct becomes virtually obsessive.[4] Stability is largely insured while change is flouted. The range of alternative behaviors is severely limited. There develops a tradition-bound, sacred society characterized by neophobia. The occupational psychosis of the bureaucrat may be cited as a case in point. Finally, there are the intermediate types of groups where a balance between culture goals and institutional means is maintained. These are the significantly integrated and relatively stable, though changing, groups.

An effective equilibrium between the two phases of the social structure is maintained as long as satisfactions accrue to individuals who conform to both constraints, viz., satisfactions from the achievement of the goals and satisfactions emerging directly from the institutionally canalized modes of striving to attain these ends. Success, in such equilibrated cases, is twofold. Success is reckoned

[3] Contemporary American culture has been said to tend in this direction. See André Siegfried, *America Comes of Age*, 26–37, New York, 1927. The alleged extreme (?) emphasis on the goals of monetary success and material prosperity leads to dominant concern with technological and social instruments designed to produce the desired result, inasmuch as institutional controls become of secondary importance. In such a situation, innovation flourishes as the *range of means* employed is broadened. In a sense, then, there occurs the paradoxical emergence of "materialists" from an "idealistic" orientation. Cf. Durkheim's analysis of the cultural conditions which predispose toward crime and innovation, both of which are aimed toward efficiency, not moral norms. Durkheim was one of the first to see that "contrairement aux idées courantes le criminel n'apparait plus comme un être radicalement insociable, comme une sorte d'elément parasitaire, de corps étranger et inassimilable, introduit au sein de la société; c'est un agent régulier de la vie sociale." See *Les Règles de la Méthode Sociologique*, 86–89, Paris, 1927.

[4] Such ritualism may be associated with a mythology which rationalizes these actions so that they appear to retain their status as means, but the dominant pressure is in the direction of strict ritualistic conformity, irrespective of such rationalizations. In this sense, ritual has proceeded farthest when such rationalizations are not even called forth.

in terms of the product and in terms of the process, in terms of the outcome and in terms of activities. Continuing satisfactions must derive from sheer *participation* in a competitive order as well as from eclipsing one's competitors if the order itself is to be sustained. The occasional sacrifices involved in institutionalized conduct must be compensated by socialized rewards. The distribution of statuses and roles through competition must be so organized that positive incentives for conformity to roles and adherence to status obligations are provided *for every position* within the distributive order. Aberrant conduct, therefore, may be viewed as a symptom of dissociation between culturally defined aspirations and socially structured means.

Of the types of groups which result from the independent variation of the two phases of the social structure, we shall be primarily concerned with the first, namely, that involving a disproportionate accent on goals. This statement must be recast in a proper perspective. In no group is there an absence of regulatory codes governing conduct, yet groups do vary in the degree to which these folkways, mores, and institutional controls are effectively integrated with the more diffuse goals which are part of the culture matrix. Emotional convictions may cluster about the complex of socially acclaimed ends, meanwhile shifting their support from the culturally defined implementation of these ends. As we shall see, certain aspects of the social structure may generate countermores and antisocial behavior precisely because of differential emphases on goals and regulations. In the extreme case, the latter may be so vitiated by the goal-emphasis that the range of behavior is limited only by considerations of technical expediency. The sole significant question then becomes, which available means is most efficient in netting the socially approved value?[5] The technically most feasible procedure, whether legitimate or not, is preferred to the institutionally pre-

---

[5] In this connection, one may see the relevance of Elton Mayo's paraphrase of the title of Tawney's well known book. "Actually the problem *is not that of the sickness of an acquisitive society; it is that of the acquisitiveness of a sick society.*" *Human Problems of an Industrial Civilization,* 153, New York, 1933. Mayo deals with the process through which wealth comes to be a symbol of social achievement. He sees this as arising from a state of anomie. We are considering the unintegrated monetary-success goal as an element in producing anomie. A complete analysis would involve both phases of this system of interdependent variables.

scribed conduct. As this process continues, the integration of the society becomes tenuous and anomie ensues.

Thus, in competitive athletics, when the aim of victory is shorn of its institutional trappings and success in contests becomes construed as "winning the game" rather than "winning through circumscribed modes of activity," a premium is implicitly set upon the use of illegitimate but technically efficient means. The star of the opposing football team is surreptitiously slugged; the wrestler furtively incapacitates his opponent through ingenious but illicit techniques; university alumni covertly subsidize "students" whose talents are largely confined to the athletic field. The emphasis on the goal has so attenuated the satisfactions deriving from sheer participation in the competitive activity that these satisfactions are virtually confined to a successful outcome. Through the same process, tension generated by the desire to win in a poker game is relieved by successfully dealing oneself four aces, or, when the cult of success has become completely dominant, by sagaciously shuffling the cards in a game of solitaire. The faint twinge of uneasiness in the last instance and the surreptitious nature of public delicts indicate clearly that the institutional rules of the game *are known* to those who evade them, but that the emotional supports of these rules are largely vitiated by cultural exaggeration of the success-goal.[6] They are microcosmic images of the social macrocosm.

Of course, this process is not restricted to the realm of sport. The process whereby exaltation of the end generates a *literal demoralization*, i.e., a deinstitutionalization, of the means is one which characterizes many [7] groups in which the two phases of the social structure are not highly integrated. The extreme emphasis upon

[6] It is unlikely that interiorized norms are completely eliminated. Whatever residuum persists will induce personality tensions and conflict. The process involves a certain degree of ambivalence. A manifest rejection of the institutional norms is coupled with some latent retention of their emotional correlates. "Guilt feelings," "sense of sin," "pangs of conscience" are obvious manifestations of this unrelieved tension; symbolic adherence to the nominally repudiated values or rationalizations constitute a more subtle variety of tensional release.

[7] "Many," and not all, unintegrated groups, for the reason already mentioned. In groups where the primary emphasis shifts to institutional means, i.e., when the range of alternatives is very limited, the outcome is a type of ritualism rather than anomie.

the accumulation of wealth as a symbol of success [8] in our own society militates against the completely effective control of institutionally regulated modes of acquiring a fortune.[9] Fraud, corruption, vice, crime, in short, the entire catalogue of proscribed behavior, becomes increasingly common when the emphasis on the *culturally induced* success-goal becomes divorced from a coordinated institutional emphasis. This observation is of crucial theoretical importance in examining the doctrine that antisocial behavior most frequently derives from biological drives breaking through the restraints imposed by society. The difference is one between a strictly utilitarian interpretation which conceives man's ends as random and an analysis which finds these ends deriving from the basic values of the culture.[10]

Our analysis can scarcely stop at this juncture. We must turn to other aspects of the social structure if we are to deal with the social genesis of the varying rates and types of deviate behavior characteristic of different societies. Thus far, we have sketched three ideal types of social orders constituted by distinctive patterns of relations between culture ends and means. Turning from these types of *culture patterning*, we find five logically possible, alternative modes of adjustment or adaptation *by individuals* within the culture-bearing society or group.[11] These are schematically pre-

[8] Money has several peculiarities which render it particularly apt to become a symbol of prestige divorced from institutional controls. As Simmel emphasized, money is highly abstract and impersonal. However acquired, through fraud or institutionally, it can be used to purchase the same goods and services. The anonymity of metropolitan culture, in conjunction with this peculiarity of money, permits wealth, the sources of which may be unknown to the community in which the plutocrat lives, to serve as a symbol of status.

[9] The emphasis upon wealth as a success-symbol is possibly reflected in the use of the term "fortune" to refer to a stock of accumulated wealth. This meaning becomes common in the late sixteenth century (Spenser and Shakespeare). A similar usage of the Latin *fortuna* comes into prominence during the first century B.C. Both these periods were marked by the rise to prestige and power of the "bourgeoisie."

[10] See Kingsley Davis, "Mental Hygiene and the Class Structure," *Psychiatry*, 1928, I, esp. 62–63; Talcott Parsons, *The Structure of Social Action*, 59–60, New York, 1937.

[11] This is a level intermediate between the two planes distinguished by Edward Sapir; namely, culture patterns and personal habit systems. See his "Contribution of Psychiatry to an Understanding of Behavior in Society," *Amer. J. Sociol.*, 1937, 42:862–70.

sented in the following table, where (+) signifies "acceptance," (−) signifies "elimination," and (±) signifies "rejection and substitution of new goals and standards."

	Culture goals	Institutionalized means
I. Conformity	+	+
II. Innovation	+	−
III. Ritualism	−	+
IV. Retreatism	−	−
V. Rebellion [12]	±	±

Our discussion of the relation between these alternative responses and other phases of the social structure must be prefaced by the observation that persons may shift from one alternative to another as they engage in different social activities. These categories refer to role adjustments in specific situations, not to personality *in toto*. To treat the development of this process in various spheres of conduct would introduce a complexity unmanageable within the confines of this paper. For this reason, we shall be concerned primarily with economic activity in the broad sense, "the production, exchange, distribution, and consumption of goods and services" in our competitive society, wherein wealth has taken on a highly symbolic cast. Our task is to search out some of the factors which exert pressure upon individuals to engage in certain of these logically possible alternative responses. This choice, as we shall see, is far from random.

In every society, Adaptation I (conformity to both culture goals and means) is the most common and widely diffused. Were this not so, the stability and continuity of the society could not be maintained. The mesh of expectancies which constitutes every social order is sustained by the modal behavior of its members falling within the first category. Conventional role behavior oriented

[12] This fifth alternative is on a plane clearly different from that of the others. It represents a *transitional* response which seeks to *institutionalize* new procedures oriented toward revamped cultural goals shared by the members of the society. It thus involves efforts to *change* the existing structure rather than to perform accommodative actions *within* this structure, and introduces additional problems with which we are not at the moment concerned.

toward the basic values of the group is the rule rather than the exception. It is this fact alone which permits us to speak of a human aggregate as comprising a group or society.

Conversely, Adaptation IV (rejection of goals and means) is the least common. Persons who "adjust" (or maladjust) in this fashion are, strictly speaking, *in* the society but not *of* it. Sociologically, these constitute the true "aliens." Not sharing the common frame of orientation, they can be included within the societal population merely in a fictional sense. In this category are *some* of the activities of psychotics, psychoneurotics, chronic autists, pariahs, outcasts, vagrants, vagabonds, tramps, chronic drunkards, and drug addicts.[13] These have relinquished, in certain spheres of activity, the culturally defined goals, involving complete aim-inhibition in the polar case, and their adjustments are not in accord with institutional norms. This is not to say that in some cases the source of their behavioral adjustments is not in part the very social structure which they have in effect repudiated nor that their very existence within a social area does not constitute a problem for the socialized population.

This mode of "adjustment" occurs, as far as structural sources are concerned, when both the culture goals and the institutionalized procedures have been assimilated thoroughly by the individual and imbued with affect and high positive value, but where those institutional procedures which promise a measure of successful attainment of the goals are not available to the individual. In such instances, there results a twofold mental conflict insofar as the moral obligation for adopting institutional means conflicts with the pressure to resort to illegitimate means (which may attain the goal) and inasmuch as the individual is shut off from means which are both legitimate *and* effective. The competitive order is maintained, but the frustrated and handicapped individual who cannot

[13] Obviously, this is an elliptical statement. These individuals may maintain some orientation to the values of their particular differential groupings within the larger society or, in part, of the conventional society itself. Insofar as they do so, their conduct cannot be classified in the "passive rejection" category (IV). Nels Anderson's description of the behavior and attitudes of the bum, for example, can readily be recast in terms of our analytical scheme. See *The Hobo*, 93–98, *et passim*, Chicago, 1923.

cope with this order drops out. Defeatism, quietism, and resignation are manifested in escape mechanisms which ultimately lead the individual to "escape" from the requirements of the society. It is an expedient which arises from continued failure to attain the goal by legitimate measures and from an inability to adopt the illegitimate route because of internalized prohibitions and institutionalized compulsives, *during which process the supreme value of the success-goal has as yet not been renounced.* The conflict is resolved by eliminating *both* precipitating elements, the goals and means. The escape is complete, the conflict is eliminated and the individual is asocialized.

Be it noted that where frustration derives from the inaccessibility of effective institutional means for attaining economic or any other type of highly valued "success," that Adaptations II, III, and V (innovation, ritualism, and rebellion) are also possible. The result will be determined by the particular personality, and thus, the *particular* cultural background, involved. Inadequate socialization will result in the innovation response whereby the conflict and frustration are eliminated by relinquishing the institutional means and retaining the success-aspiration; an extreme assimilation of institutional demands will lead to ritualism wherein the goal is dropped as beyond one's reach but conformity to the mores persists; and rebellion occurs when emancipation from the reigning standards, due to frustration or to marginalist perspectives, leads to the attempt to introduce a "new social order."

Our major concern is with illegitimacy adjustment. This involves the use of conventionally proscribed but frequently effective means of attaining at least the simulacrum of culturally defined success, —wealth, power, and the like. As we have seen, this adjustment occurs when the individual has assimilated the cultural emphasis on success without equally internalizing the morally prescribed norms governing means for its attainment. The question arises: Which phases of our social structure predispose toward this mode of adjustment? We may examine a concrete instance, effectively analyzed by Lohman,[14] which provides a clue to the answer. Loh-

[14] Joseph D. Lohman, "The Participant Observer in Community Studies," *Amer. Sociol. Rev.*, 1937, 2:890–98.

man has shown that specialized areas of vice in the near north side of Chicago constitute a "normal" response to a situation where the cultural emphasis upon pecuniary success has been absorbed, but where there is little access to conventional and legitimate means for attaining such success. The conventional occupational opportunities of persons in this area are almost completely limited to manual labor. Given our cultural stigmatization of manual labor, and its correlate, the prestige of white collar work, it is clear that the result is a strain toward innovational practices. The limitation of opportunity to unskilled labor and the resultant low income can not compete *in terms of conventional standards of achievement* with the high income from organized vice.

For our purposes, this situation involves two important features. First, such antisocial behavior is in a sense "called forth" by certain conventional values of the culture *and* by the class structure involving differential access to the approved opportunities for legitimate, prestige-bearing pursuit of the culture goals. The lack of high integration between the means-and-end elements of the cultural pattern and the particular class structure combine to favor a heightened frequency of antisocial conduct in such groups. The second consideration is of equal significance. Recourse to the first of the alternative responses, legitimate effort, is limited by the fact that actual advance toward desired success-symbols through conventional channels is, despite our persisting open-class ideology,[15] relatively rare and difficult for those handicapped by little formal education and few economic resources. The dominant pressure of group standards of success is, therefore, on the gradual attenuation of legitimate, but by and large ineffective, strivings and the increasing use of illegitimate, but more or less effective, expedients

[15] The shifting historical role of this ideology is a profitable subject for exploration. The "office-boy-to-president" stereotype was once in approximate accord with the facts. Such vertical mobility was probably more common then than now, when the class structure is more rigid. (See the following note.) The ideology largely persists, however, possibly because it still performs a useful function for maintaining the *status quo*. For insofar as it is accepted by the "masses," it constitutes a useful sop for those who might rebel against the entire structure, were this consoling hope removed. This ideology now serves to lessen the probability of Adaptation V. In short, the role of this notion has changed from that of an approximately valid empirical theorem to that of an ideology, in Mannheim's sense.

of vice and crime. The cultural demands made on persons in this situation are incompatible. On the one hand, they are asked to orient their conduct toward the prospect of accumulating wealth and on the other, they are largely denied effective opportunities to do so institutionally. The consequences of such structural inconsistency are psychopathological personality, and/or antisocial conduct, and/or revolutionary activities. The equilibrium between culturally designated means and ends becomes highly unstable with the progressive emphasis on attaining the prestige-laden ends by any means whatsoever. Within this context, Capone represents the triumph of amoral intelligence over morally prescribed "failure," when the channels of vertical mobility are closed or narrowed [16] *in a society which places a high premium on economic affluence and social ascent for* all *its members.*[17]

This last qualification is of primary importance. It suggests that other phases of the social structure besides the extreme emphasis on pecuniary success, must be considered if we are to understand the social sources of antisocial behavior. A high frequency of deviate behavior is not generated simply by "lack of opportunity" or

[16] There is a growing body of evidence, though none of it is clearly conclusive, to the effect that our class structure is becoming rigidified and that vertical mobility is declining. Taussig and Joslyn found that American business leaders are being *increasingly* recruited from the upper ranks of our society. The Lynds have also found a "diminished chance to get ahead" for the working classes in Middletown. Manifestly, these objective changes are not alone significant; the individual's subjective evaluation of the situation is a major determinant of the response. The extent to which this change in opportunity for social mobility has been recognized by the least advantaged classes is still conjectural, although the Lynds present some suggestive materials. The writer suggests that a case in point is the increasing frequency of cartoons which observe in a tragi-comic vein that "my old man says everybody can't be President. He says if ya can get three days a week steady on W.P.A. work, ya ain't doin' so bad either." See F. W. Taussig and C. S. Joslyn, *American Business Leaders,* New York, 1932; R. S. and H. M. Lynd, *Middletown in Transition,* 67 ff., chap. 12, New York, 1937.

[17] The role of the Negro in this respect is of considerable theoretical interest. Certain elements of the Negro population have assimilated the dominant caste's values of pecuniary success and social advancement, but they also recognize that social ascent is at present restricted to their own caste almost exclusively. The pressures upon the Negro which would otherwise derive from the structural inconsistencies we have noticed are hence not identical with those upon lower class whites. See Kingsley Davis, *op. cit.,* 63; John Dollard, *Caste and Class in a Southern Town,* 66 ff., New Haven, 1936; Donald Young, *American Minority Peoples,* 581, New York, 1932.

by this exaggerated pecuniary emphasis. A comparatively rigidified class structure, a feudalistic or caste order, may limit such opportunities far beyond the point which obtains in our society today. It is only when a system of cultural values extols, virtually above all else, certain *common* symbols of success *for the population at large* while its social structure rigorously restricts or completely eliminates access to approved modes of acquiring these symbols *for a considerable part of the same population,* that antisocial behavior ensues on a considerable scale. In other words, our egalitarian ideology denies by implication the existence of noncompeting groups and individuals in the pursuit of pecuniary success. The same body of success-symbols is held to be desirable for all. These goals are held to *transcend class lines,* not to be bounded by them, yet the actual social organization is such that there exist class differentials in the accessibility of these *common* success-symbols. Frustration and thwarted aspiration lead to the search for avenues of escape from a culturally induced intolerable situation; or unrelieved ambition may eventuate in illicit attempts to acquire the dominant values.[18] The American stress on pecuniary success and ambitiousness for all thus invites exaggerated anxieties, hostilities, neuroses, and antisocial behavior.

This theoretical analysis may go far toward explaining the varying correlations between crime and poverty.[19] Poverty is not an isolated variable. It is one in a complex of interdependent social and cultural variables. When viewed in such a context, it repre-

[18] The psychical coordinates of these processes have been partly established by the experimental evidence concerning *Anspruchsniveaus* and levels of performance. See Kurt Lewin, *Vorsatz, Wille und Bedurfnis,* Berlin, 1926; N. F. Hoppe, "Erfolg und Misserfolg," *Psychol. Forschung,* 1930, 14:1–63; Jerome D. Frank, "Individual Differences in Certain Aspects of the Level of Aspiration," *Amer. J. Psychol.,* 1935, 47:119–28.

[19] Standard criminology texts summarize the data in this field. Our scheme of analysis may serve to resolve some of the theoretical contradictions which P. A. Sorokin indicates. For example, "not everywhere nor always do the poor show a greater proportion of crime . . . many poorer countries have had less crime than the richer countries. . . . The [economic] improvement in the second half of the nineteenth century, and the beginning of the twentieth, has not been followed by a decrease of crime." See his *Contemporary Sociological Theories,* 560–61, New York, 1928. The crucial point is, however, that poverty has varying social significance in different social structures, as we shall see. Hence, one would not expect a linear correlation between crime and poverty.

sents quite different states of affairs. Poverty as such, and consequent limitation of opportunity, are not sufficient to induce a conspicuously high rate of criminal behavior. Even the often mentioned "poverty in the midst of plenty" will not necessarily lead to this result. Only insofar as poverty and associated disadvantages in competition for the culture values approved for *all* members of the society is linked with the assimilation of a cultural emphasis on monetary accumulation as a symbol of success is antisocial conduct a "normal" outcome. Thus, poverty is less highly correlated with crime in southeastern Europe than in the United States. The possibility of vertical mobility in these European areas would seem to be fewer than in this country, so that neither poverty *per se* nor its association with limited opportunity is sufficient to account for the varying correlations. It is only when the full configuration is considered, poverty, limited opportunity, and a commonly shared system of success symbols, that we can explain the higher association between poverty and crime in our society than in others where rigidified class structure is coupled with *differential class symbols of achievement.*

In societies such as our own, then, the pressure of prestige-bearing success tends to eliminate the effective social constraint over means employed to this end. "The-end-justifies-the-means" doctrine becomes a guiding tenet for action when the cultural structure unduly exalts the end and the social organization unduly limits possible recourse to approved means. Otherwise put, this notion and associated behavior relfect a lack of cultural coordination. In international relations, the effects of this lack of integration are notoriously apparent. An emphasis upon national power is not readily coordinated with an inept organization of legitimate, i.e., internationally defined and accepted, means for attaining this goal. The result is a tendency toward the abrogation of international law, treaties become scraps of paper, "undeclared warfare" serves as a technical evasion, the bombing of civilian populations is rationalized,[20] just as the same societal situation induces the same sway of illegitimacy among the individuals.

[20] See M. W. Royse, *Aerial Bombardment and the International Regulation of War*, New York, 1928.

The social order we have described necessarily produces this "strain toward dissolution." The pressure of such an order is upon outdoing one's competitors. The choice of means within the ambit of institutional control will persist as long as the sentiments supporting a competitive system, i.e., deriving from the possibility of outranking competitors and hence enjoying the favorable response of others, are distributed throughout the entire system of activities and are not confined merely to the final result. A stable social structure demands a balanced distribution of affect among its various segments. When there occurs a shift of emphasis from the satisfactions deriving from competition itself to almost exclusive concern with successful competition, the resultant stress leads to the breakdown of the regulatory structure.[21] With the resulting attenuation of the institutional imperatives, there occurs an approximation of the situation erroneously held by utilitarians to be typical of society generally wherein calculations of advantage and fear of punishment are the sole regulating agencies. In such situations, as Hobbes observed, force and fraud come to constitute the sole virtues in view of their relative efficiency in attaining goals—which were for him, of course, not culturally derived.

It should be apparent that the foregoing discussion is not pitched on a moralistic plane. Whatever the sentiments of the writer or reader concerning the ethical desirability of coordinating the means-and-goals phases of the social structure, one must agree that lack of such coordination leads to anomie. Insofar as one of the most general functions of social organization is to provide a basis for calculability and regularity of behavior, it is increasingly limited in effectiveness as these elements of the structure become dissociated. At the extreme, predictability virtually disappears and what may be properly termed cultural chaos or anomie intervenes.

This statement, being brief, is also incomplete. It has not included an exhaustive treatment of the various structural elements which predispose toward one rather than another of the alternative

[21] Since our primary concern is with the socio-cultural aspects of this problem, the psychological correlates have been only implicitly considered. See Karen Horney, *The Neurotic Personality of Our Time,* New York, 1937, for a psychological discussion of this process.

responses open to individuals; it has neglected, but not denied the relevance of, the factors determining the specific incidence of these responses; it has not enumerated the various concrete responses which are constituted by combinations of specific values of the analytical variables; it has omitted, or included only by implication, any consideration of the social functions performed by illicit responses; it has not tested the full explanatory power of the analytical scheme by examining a large number of group variations in the frequency of deviate and conformist behavior; it has not adequately dealt with rebellious conduct which seeks to refashion the social framework radically; it has not examined the relevance of cultural conflict for an analysis of culture-goal and institutional-means mal-integration. It is suggested that these and related problems may be profitably analyzed by this scheme.

Part IV

THE ADMINISTRATION OF JUSTICE

INTRODUCTION

WHEN A crime or behavior constituting juvenile delinquency comes to the attention of law enforcement authorities, the machinery for the administration of justice is set into motion. We examine this machinery in Part IV.

It is activated by law. Our basic law is the Constitution of the United States. Certain amendments to the Constitution known as the Bill of Rights are germane to the administration of justice and are given here, with commentary.

The Bill of Rights and other Constitutional provisions provide guarantees of due process in arrest, search and seizure, and use of evidence. These guarantees, as further spelled out in court decisions, serve as a guide to trial procedure and are referred to as "the exclusionary rule." This rule is vigorously debated, police and prosecutors often taking one side, defense counsel and appellate courts the other. An excellent statement of the argument for the rule may be found in an article by Monrad G. Paulsen.[1] A contrary view, specifically in reply to Paulsen, is presented by F. J. McGarr.[2] Both are well worth reading.

One of the most fiercely debated questions arising out of the exclusionary rule is whether wiretapping for use as evidence of criminal activity should be unrestricted, confined to narrow limits, or altogether proscribed. On this subject we have the very important minority opinion rendered by Justice Holmes in *Olmstead v. U.S.* Eventually, Holmes's view prevailed.

District Attorney Edward Silver does not quarrel with it but points to adverse results which, he believes, derive from current interpretations of *Olmstead*.

---

[1] Monrad G. Paulsen, "The Exclusionary Rule and Misconduct by the Police," *Journal of Criminal Law, Criminology and Police Science*, LII (September–October 1961), 255–65.

[2] Frank J. McGarr, "The Exclusionary Rule: An Ill Conceived and Ineffective Remedy," *Journal of Criminal Law, Criminology and Police Science*, LII (September–October 1961), 266–70.

Do our appellate courts, including the U.S. Supreme Court, provide even justice? Do they protect the public adequately while safeguarding the rights of defendants? Daniel Gutman answers with an emphatic "No." Ralph Slovenko is of another mind in "Does the Supreme Court Impede Justice?"

Our society is in a social revolution, the full meaning and ultimate limits of which we perceive only inchoately. A manifestation of this upheaval that concerns criminologists is the nonviolent and violent disobedience of law incident to the civil rights struggle, the Vietnam war controversy, and other issues. It is impossible to present *the* position on any one issue. Nor can we present *the* position of advocates of either peaceful disobedience or of those who favor violent means of attaining their ends. The situation is so fluid that positions taken yesterday are obsolete today. Moreover, at any one time there are a number of positions, not one "official" position. The American New Left is by no means the only movement involved in this cultural ferment, but we might expect that at least it would provide a unified theoretical underpinning for its activities. Not so. As Massimo Teodori points out, the New Left "is a collective phenomenon, . . . nourished by the contributions of many different ideals . . ." This explains why "there is no one document or Sacred Text to refer to when we want to examine the 'theory' behind the New Left." [3]

Because of the fluidity and diversity explained above, it was possible in this Part to include only a series of position statements no one of which is typical of all shades of opinion and conviction. In these we illustrate the problems and cite individual answers to the basic question: Which forms of disobedience of law are justified? To be tolerated? To be suppressed? Inferentially or directly we have the opinions of Martin Luther King, Jr. (whose concept of peaceful civil disobedience is repudiated by some who live after him); Eldridge Cleaver (whose position has changed in certain respects since this was published); and former Associate Justice Abe Fortas (whose legal opinions are not shared by all members of the Supreme Court).

[3] Massimo Teodori (ed.), *The New Left, A Documentary History* (Indianapolis: Bobbs-Merill, 1969), p. 80.

The police are usually the first confrontation point of civil disorders and law violation. Recently the constabulary has been under fire, charged with brutality, among other sins of omission and commission. Is police brutality a fact? Albert J. Reiss, Jr., examines the question, as does Senator Robert C. Byrd. Their respective conclusions are disparate on some points.

Esselstyn's "The Social Role of a County Sheriff" sheds light on the social and professional status and role of the county law officer. Harry M. Caudill gives us a vivid picture of a little-known law official in "The Rural Judge."

Most apprehended offenders find themselves in court, in contact with the administrative machinery of justice. According to some, our adversary trial procedure provides the most efficient method for separating the innocent from the guilty. In "Trial by Combat in American Courts" I take a contrary position.

The mentally incompetent defendant is victim of the lag between the medical and the legal definition of insanity. Our courts follow the Rule of M'Naghten for the most part. It is set forth in this Part. *Durham v. U.S.* departed from the Rule of M'Naghten, at least to a degree closing the gap between the latter and a more contemporary understanding of medical insanity.

The most drastic sentence a court can impose upon a defendant is capital punishment, a practice concerning which there has been much debate. Here, Chief of Police Edward J. Allen states his convictions on the subject. Walter C. Reckless reviews and analyzes what evidence exists as to the efficacy of capital punishment.

The most revolutionary overhauling of juvenile court philosophy and practice since the inception of that tribunal came by action of the U.S. Supreme Court in 1967. Its epochal pronouncement, *In Re Gault*, is included in Part IV, followed by somewhat disaparate views of the meaning and effect of *Gault* in articles by Alfred D. Noyes and Alan Neigher. It is still too soon after the *Gault* decision, however, to grasp the full implication of the Court's pronouncement.

THE CONSTITUTION ON CIVIL LIBERTIES

Osmond K. Fraenkel, *The Supreme Court and Civil Liberties: How the Court Has Protected the Bill of Rights,* published for the American Civil Liberties Union (New York, Oceana, 1960), pp. 9–13.

The Bill of Rights

Here are the principal guarantees of the Bill of Rights with brief comment showing what the Supreme Court has done in interpreting them or limiting their application. Only the essential holdings of the Court are mentioned here.

Article I. Congress shall make no law respecting an establishment of religion, or prohibiting the free exercise thereof;

This prohibits interference with religious beliefs, and direct support of religious institutions. Religious practices deemed harmful to society, such as polygamy among the Mormons, may be prohibited.

or abridging the freedom of speech,

Utterances may be punished only if there is a "clear and present danger" that they will result in harmful action or if they are libelous or obscene.

or of the press,

Neither Congress nor the states may censor publications or motion pictures in advance except, perhaps, motion pictures for obscenity. Congress may deny mailing privileges to certain kinds of printed matter deemed harmful. Leaflet distribution on the streets may not be banned or taxed.

or the right of the people peaceably to assemble,

No one may be punished for participating in a peaceful assembly even when called by an organization charged with violation of law.

and to petition the government for a redress of grievances.

No issue has arisen under this clause.

(While the First Amendment is a restraint on the federal government only, the Supreme Court has held that the rights there specified are also protected under the due process clause of Amendment XIV against invasion by the States.)

Article IV. The right of the people to be secure in their persons, houses, papers, and effects, against unreasonable searches and seizures, shall not be violated,

This restraint affects only federal officers, and covers only "unreasonable" searches. Evidence obtained by an illegal search cannot be used in a federal criminal trial. Tapping telephone wires to get evidence is not an illegal "search." But evidence obtained by wiretapping made illegal by statute cannot be used in a federal court.

and no warrants shall issue, but upon probable cause . . .

Warrants must show the commission of a crime and the nature of the property to be seized.

Article V. No person shall be held to answer to a capital, or otherwise infamous crime, unless on a presentment or indictment of a grand jury . . .

This is a restraint only on federal courts, covering crimes punishable by a penitentiary sentence or hard labor.

nor shall any person be subject for the same offence to be twice put in jeopardy of life or limb;

A person once tried and acquitted cannot again be tried in a federal court for the same crime, but may be tried for different crimes arising out of the same act.

nor shall be compelled in any criminal case to be a witness against himself,

This prohibits the federal government from forcing an individual, as defendant or even as witness, to incriminate himself or to produce his documents, except where the documents are required to be kept by law.

> *nor be deprived of life, liberty, or property, without due process of law . . .*

This provision insures a fair trial.

> *Article VI. In all criminal prosecutions, the accused shall enjoy the right to a speedy and public trial by an impartial jury . . .*

This restraint on federal courts does not prevent Congress from permitting the trial of minor offenses in the District of Columbia without juries.

> *and to be informed of the nature and cause of the accusation; to be confronted with the witnesses against him; to have compulsory process for obtaining witnesses in his favor;*

These provisions have resulted in little litigation.

> *and to have the assistance of counsel for his defense.*

The denial of the right to counsel in a federal court vitiates a conviction. In a state court counsel may be denied in a non-capital case if defendant be not prejudiced. But the right to counsel can be waived at the trial or by a voluntary plea of guilty.

> *Article VIII. Excessive bail shall not be required, nor excessive fines imposed, nor cruel and unusual punishment inflicted.*

There have been very few decisions dealing with the subject of excessive bail. The general rule is that the capacity of the prisoner to give bail is a determining element in fixing it, although the enormity of the offense can also be taken into consideration.

The provision with regard to cruel and unusual punishments was intended to prevent punishment such as burning at the stake, and other medieval forms of torture. Attempts to invoke this provision against the use of electrocution failed. There is no indication in the books of what would be considered an excessive fine.

> *Article XIII. Neither slavery nor involuntary servitude, except as a punishment for crime whereof the party shall have been*

duly convicted, shall exist within the United States, or any place subject to their jurisdiction.

This restraint operates on Congress, on the states and on individuals. It outlaws forced labor contracts, except as to seamen.

Article XIV. . . . No state shall make or enforce any law which shall abridge the privileges or immunities of citizens of the United States;

This protection of citizens against discriminatory action by state authority affects only rights of national, not state, citizenship—such as the right to travel. Attempts by Congress to protect Negroes from discrimination by private individuals were declared beyond the scope of this amendment. But Congress may prevent such discrimination in interstate commerce.

The right to discuss national issues in public places is protected by this provision.

nor shall any state deprive any person of life, liberty, or property, without due process of law;

This provision to insure fair trials (as in the Fifth Amendment), has been widened to void laws violating fundamental rights such as freedom of religion, speech, press or assembly.

nor deny to any person within its jurisdiction the equal protection of the laws.

For a long time the Supreme Court had ruled that racial segregation was permissible so long as equal accommodations were afforded. The Court has now repudiated that doctrine.

Article XV. The right of citizens of the United States to vote shall not be denied or abridged by the United States or by any state on account of race, color or previous condition of servitude.

This restraint on the states does not prevent property or educational qualifications for voting and its intent is thus commonly frustrated.

(The Nineteenth Amendment in effect added the word "sex" to the Fifteenth.)

The following provisions of the original Constitution affect civil rights.

Article I, Section 9. . . . The privilege of the writ of habeas corpus shall not be suspended, unless when in cases of rebellion or invasion the public safety may require it.

This is a prohibition only on Congress, not on the states.

No bill of attainder or ex post facto law shall be passed.

A bill of attainder is a law which punishes a person without a trial, such as prohibiting persons who had engaged in rebellion from carrying on their professions.

The prohibition against ex post facto laws (making criminal an act not criminal when committed) does not affect aliens in deportation proceedings, since deportation is a civil action.

(*Both these last prohibitions are, in Article I, Section 10, made binding on the states.*)

"I THINK IT A LESS EVIL THAT SOME CRIMINALS SHOULD ESCAPE THAN THAT THE GOVERNMENT SHOULD PLAY AN IGNOBLE PART"

Olmstead v. United States, 277 U.S. 438, 469 (1928).

[*Olmstead v. United States* is important in the history of civil rights rulings by the United States Supreme Court. Actually, however, it was the minority position that was eventually to prevail, not the majority ruling as handed down by the then Chief Justice William Howard Taft.

Olmstead, who headed a bootlegging organization headquartered in Seattle, was convicted on evidence secured when federal Prohibition agents tapped his telephone wires over a period of months. He appealed, arguing that the wiretaps were illegal and that evidence so secured should have been ruled inadmissible at trial. Tapping of telephone wires, Olmstead urged, violated the guarantees against searches and seizures in the Fourth Amendment, and those against self-incimination in the Fifth.

In a five-to-four decision, the Supreme Court ruled against this argument. In upholding the conviction, Taft, speaking for the majority, held that wiretapping could not be classed as search and seizure, since neither Olmstead's home nor office was entered; all the Prohibition agents did was listen from an outside post.

Justices Holmes, Brandeis, Butler, and Stone dissented. Holmes gave his reasoning in the dissenting opinion quoted below. It won out in time. Subsequent Court decisions, beginning with *Nardone v. United States*, 302 U.S. 379 (1937), gradually translated his minority view as expressed in *Olmstead* into what is essentially the Supreme Court's majority opinion as it seems to be today.]

Olmstead v. U.S.

Holmes, J., dissenting:

My Brother Brandeis has given this case so exhaustive an examination that I desire to add but a few words. While I do not deny it, I am not prepared to say that the penumbra of the Fourth and Fifth Amendments covers the defendant, although I fully agree that courts are apt to err by sticking too closely to the words of a law where those words import a policy that goes beyond them. . . . But I think, as Mr. Justice Brandeis says, that apart from the Constitution the government ought not to use evidence obtained, and only obtainable, by a criminal act. There is no body of precedents by which we are bound, and which confines us to logical deduction from established rules. Therefore, we must consider the two objects of desire both of which we cannot have and make up our minds which to choose. It is desirable that criminals should be detected, and to that end that all available evidence should be used. It also is desirable that the government should not itself foster and pay for other crimes, when they are the means by which the evidence is to be obtained. . . . I can attach no importance to protestations of disapproval if it knowingly accepts and pays and announces that in future it will pay for the fruits. We have to choose, and for my part I think it a less evil that some criminals should escape than that the government should play an ignoble part.

For those who agree with me, no distinction can be taken between the government as prosecutor and the government as judge. If the existing code does not permit district attorneys to have a hand in such dirty business, it does not permit the judge to allow such iniquities to succeed. . . . And if all that I have said so far be accepted, it makes no difference that in this case wire tapping is made a crime by the law of the state, not by the law of the United States. It is true that a state cannot make rules of evidence for courts of the United States, but the state has authority over the conduct in question, and I hardly think that the United States would appear to greater advantage when paying for an odious crime against state law than when inciting to the disregard of its own. I am aware of the often repeated statement that in a criminal proceeding the court will not take notice of the manner in which papers offered in evidence have been obtained. But that somewhat rudimentary mode of disposing of the question has been overthrown by *Weeks v. United States* . . . and the cases that have followed it. I have said that we are free to choose between two principles of policy. But if we are to confine ourselves to precedent and logic the reason for excluding evidence obtained by violating the Constitution seems to me logically to lead to excluding evidence obtained by a crime of the officers of the law.

LEGALIZED WIRE-TAPPING
IS NECESSARY

EDWARD S. SILVER

Excerpted from Edward S. Silver, "To Combat Efficiency of Organized Crime: Legalized Wire-Tapping Is Absolutely Necessary," *The Police Chief*, XXVI (February 1959), 30–33. At the time of publication E. S. Silver was District Attorney of Kings County, Brooklyn, New York.

THERE IS a great deal of fuzzy thinking about the "dirty business" of wire-tapping that sorely needs clarification. Laymen, as well as lawyers, feel a lift when they throw the cloak of Justices Holmes and Brandeis about them, and brand wire-tapping as "dirty business." When they do so it is obvious that they did not read the *Olmstead* case. . . .

The *Olmstead* case involved illegal wire-tapping . . . in the state of Washington, where wire-tapping was declared to be a crime by a specific statute. What both great judges said was that law enforcing agents should not be permitted to violate the laws even if it succeeds in convicting criminals. . . .

Understanding . . . the clear and only basis for Justice Holmes' dissent, we can put the words "dirty business" in the proper light. I quote the Justice . . .

For those who agree with me, no distinction can be taken between the government as prosecutor and the government as judge. *If the existing code does not permit* district attorneys to have a hand in such dirty business, it does not permit the judge to allow such iniquities to succeed.

There are those who like to consider themselves as "Liberals," whatever that word really means. There is a feeling among those "Liberals" that to come within the aura of that term, they must be against wire-tapping without thinking clearly on the question whether the wire-tapping is done according to law, or as in the *Olmstead* case, in violation of the law. Nor do they address themselves to whether wire-tapping is or is not necessary in the present day fight against crime. One can well cite Mr. Justice Brandeis in the *Olmstead* case . . . where he says . . . "But 'time works changes, brings into existence new conditions and purposes.' "

I speak for the great majority of prosecutors, who are not only ardent advocates of civil rights, but do something about it.

It is very important to point out that the wire-tapping controversy is not between those who cherish civil liberties and those who are indifferent to them. Indeed the record shows that the district attorneys are alert to protect civil rights, indeed the civil rights of those who are charged with crime. It is they who are generally in greatest need of that protection. . . .

It should be made clear, too, that district attorneys are not in favor of granting any law enforcing agency the right to tap wires without a court order. . . .

In 1954, in a letter to a Senate Committee looking into the wire-tapping problem, I wrote. . . .

I understand that the Attorney General does not favor a provision in the proposed bill requiring a court order, based on a showing of reasonable cause, authorizing the tap. . . . I resort quite frequently . . . to wire-tapping in our fight against crime. Under our state statute, I am required to get a court order and I welcome it as a reasonable restraint.

Power is a heady thing, as Mr. Justice Jackson said in *McDonald v. United States*. . . . Just preceding that wise observation he remarked, "so that an objective mind might weigh the need . . . the right of privacy was deemed too precious to entrust to the discretion of those whose job is the detection of crime and the arrest of criminals."

As a district attorney, I must not forget that at times in the zealousness to solve a crime I might be tempted to thrust aside protective procedures that have come down to us as a result of many hard fought battles. . . .

I want to say that I strongly favor the Attorney General having the power to tap wires in his fight against subversives. We must get the modern tools for their nefarious purposes. Yet, with this necessary power should go the objective view of the court in granting an order permitting a tap.

. . . Why do we need this right to tap wires with court order? Simply, to fight crime—modern crime—organized crime. Where is the sense or logic to say that those engaged in crime may use the telephone in furtherance of their iniquitous operations, and they do, without let or interference?

Federal Judge . . . Robert P. Patterson, speaking on the subject of organized crime before the American Bar Association . . . put it well when he said, in part:

The underworld of today would rate Jesse James as a small-fry amateur. Crime has become big business. . . . Advantage has been taken of the most modern methods in business organization, *swift communications,* swift transportation. Advantage has also been taken of lagging organization of government. Law enforcement systems operating along lines good enough for 1851 or 1901 are too slow for the swifter pace of the times we are living in.

. . . All the district attorneys . . . that I have come in contact with in the National Association, feel most strongly that wiretapping is absolutely necessary if they are to be able to cope with the modern criminal.

Does the public wish this right taken from its servants in this fight against crime? We believe it does not.

THE CRIMINAL GETS THE BREAKS

DANIEL GUTMAN

Excerpted from Daniel Gutman, "The Criminal Gets the Breaks,"
New York Times Magazine, November 29, 1964, pp. 36, 120–23. At the
time of publication, Daniel Gutman was dean of the New York Law
School, New York City.

"UNDER OUR criminal procedure the accused has every advantage. While the prosecution is held rigidly to the charge, he need
not disclose the barest outline of his defense. He is immune from
question or comment on his silence; he cannot be convicted when
there is the least fair doubt in the minds of any one of the
twelve. . . . Our procedure has been always haunted by the ghost
of the innocent man convicted. It is an unreal dream. What we
need to fear is the archaic formalism and the watery sentiment
that obstructs, delays and defeats the prosecution of crime."

So Judge Learned Hand wrote more than 40 years ago. Today,
no one disputes that a mounting wave of criminal bestiality has become one of the nation's most serious problems. The streets, our
parks, our homes and places of business—all are equally insecure
against invasion, plunder and violence.

Every day in the week, criminals walk out of the courts, cockier
and more brazen than ever, and looking for new prey. They "beat
the rap"—a status achievement in the underworld. In many of
such cases, the acquittal or dismissal has resulted not from lack of
evidence, but from the fact that the evidence of crime was obtained by unapproved methods. A technicality has precluded its
use.

Any discussion on how to handle the crime problem must consider the moral argument that it is better to permit the guilty to escape than for the innocent to be punished. Granted. Faced with a

choice, most of us would certainly agree with this proposition. It must be remembered, however, that no reasonable rules of procedure can offer complete security against an occasional miscarriage of justice. The possibility of error will always be present until a means is devised for ascertaining truth with certainty. There is not much likelihood of such a development in the foreseeable future. In the meantime, let us not underestimate the potential danger that an unpunished guilty felon—one who "beat the rap"— represents to society.

It is regrettable that those who advocate measures that would enable us to deal more adequately with the repression of crime are accused, almost invariably, of being "opposed to due process." One need only suggest a study, the need for change, and he is open to a charge of taking short cuts with due process of law. Unsavory epithets are applied to those who take any position on this vital public question—"radical" or "reactionary," "leftist" or "Fascist," as the case may be. As a result, many intelligent citizens say nothing; they avoid the controversy, although they are disturbed by the growing rate of crime and the apparent inability of government to cope with it.

The structure of democratic government rests largely on the constitutional guarantee that no person shall be deprived of "life, liberty or property without due process of law." The function of our highest court is to enforce the requirements of law. This task it has done well. Controversy arises over cases in which the Supreme Court may have gone beyond the requirements of the constitutional mandate. The feeling that it may have does not justify the violent attacks that have been made on the Court, but does demand critical discussion of some decisions.

More serious, in their effect, are those procedural rules and some of our laws which circumscribe the determinations of the courts— and which must be changed, if at all, by the legislatures that promulgated them. A glance at some of the cases in which evidence pointing to guilt was held to have been improperly admitted will best serve to illustrate the problem.

Not long ago, in a United States District Court, a case collapsed for lack of evidence. Three times, the defendant, James W. Killough, had confessed to the murder of his wife. On one occasion, he had led the police to a dump upon which he had thrown his wife's body after the murder. Twice, he had been convicted of the slaying; twice, the convictions were reversed. And now the judge directed the jury to acquit, writing "finis" to the case. The principal evidence consisted of the confessions. But the confessions were ruled out, on appeal.

The reason was that the accused had been detained for some 26 hours after his arrest, in violation of a procedural rule that required his arraignment to take place "without unnecessary delay." Therefore, the confessions (although freely given) and *all evidence related to or growing out of them* were inadmissible.

"We know the man is guilty," said Federal Judge Hart, who presided at the trial, "but we sit here blind, deaf and dumb." Later, he added: "Felons will sleep better tonight."

Judge Hart's ruling was dictated by the oft-cited Mallory case. The defendant, suspected of a brutal raping, consented, after being questioned for an hour and a half, to submit to a lie-detector test. There was a delay of several hours before the test could be given. When confronted with the results, Mallory signed a full confession. By that time, seven hours had elapsed since his apprehension. It was then too late to arraign him in court, and that procedure was postponed until the following morning.

Despite the fact that there had been no coercion upon the suspect to take the lie-detector test or to admit the crime, the confession was held, on appeal to the Supreme Court, to be inadmissible. The Court decided that a rule requiring arraignment without unreasonable delay had been violated. "Unreasonable" is considered for practical purposes to require immediate arraignment. Mallory, who had been convicted by a jury, went free. He was never retried because, without the confession, there was not enough evidence to establish guilt.

Another landmark decision that enables many guilty felons to escape conviction was handed down in the case of *Mapp v. Ohio.* A seizure of pornographic literature had been made, without a search warrant, and Dollree Mapp, who was convicted of possession of the material, appealed. The conviction was sustained until the case reached the Supreme Court. There it was held that evidence obtained by state officers in violation of Constitutional requirements controlling search and seizure is inadmissible in any criminal action in state as well as Federal courts. Previously, this "exclusionary" rule had been held to apply only to prosecutions in courts of Federal jurisdiction.

The search in the Mapp case was illegal. Without question, it violated the defendant's Constitutional rights, and the Supreme Court had no alternative but to rule out the evidence which brought about the conviction.

The impact of the Mapp decision lies in its retroactive effect. It will apply not only to future prosecutions, but will also nullify prior convictions in state courts, in cases where evidence that had been obtained improperly was admitted despite the fact that such evidence was previously admissible in all but Federal courts, in accordance with earlier rulings of the United States Supreme Court.

Then there is the Massiah case. Massiah, a seaman, was arrested and indicted on a charge of smuggling narcotics into this country. An accomplice, Colson, was indicted with him. By arrangement with Federal agents, Colson went for a ride with Massiah in an automobile that had been wired with radio equipment. The talk between Massiah and Colson was relayed to the agents, who were in another automobile. Massiah's statements were introduced in evidence. The conversation was incriminating. Massiah was convicted.

The United States Supreme Court set aside the conviction on the ground that Massiah did not have the benefit of counsel when the conversation in the automobile took place. The Sixth Amendment of the Constitution provides that: "In all criminal prosecutions, the accused shall enjoy the right . . . to have the assistance of counsel for his defense."

The full effect of the Massiah ruling may be to preclude any admission made by a person charged with crime in the absence of his lawyer. Justice Harlan, in a dissenting opinion in which he was joined by other justices of the Court, wrote: "The Massiahs can breathe much easier, secure in the knowledge that the Constitution furnishes an important measure of protection against faithless compatriots, guarantees sporting treatment for sporting peddlers of narcotics."

In the Escobedo case, the defendant, charged with the murder of his brother-in-law, was not permitted to consult his attorney, who tried to see him at the police station. Escobedo's admissions to the police officers who were interrogating him led to conviction.

The Supreme Court held that the refusal to permit the defendant to receive the advice of counsel was in violation of his constitutional rights. The following is an interesting excerpt from the dissenting opinion:

"The decision is thus another major step in the direction of the goal which the Court seemingly has in mind—to bar from evidence all admissions obtained from an individual suspected of crime, whether involuntarily made or not. It does of course put us one step 'ahead' of the English judges who have had the good sense to leave the matter a discretionary one with the trial court."

Whether or not constitutional privilege bars only compulsory incrimination, and does not preclude self-incrimination by voluntary statements, the far-reaching effect of the ruling in this case is readily discernible.

Discussing these rulings, a high-ranking Federal jurist commented not long ago: "It means that, from now on, a police officer about to arrest a suspect had better say to him: 'I have to arrest you. Would you mind waiting here for me while I go and get you a lawyer?'"

To be guilty of perpetrating a crime and to be proved guilty are two different things. A person accused of crime must be proven guilty, beyond a reasonable doubt. The technical requirements for evidence cannot always be satisfied, and persons who are by no means innocent are permitted to go free.

One of the great loopholes for escape from conviction is found in the provisions regarding search and seizure. The strict application of these requirements is demonstrated in the case of Fahy against the State of Connecticut. The defendant admitted, before and at his trial, to painting swastikas on the exterior of a synagogue. But the paint and brush shown to have been used by him had been seized without warrant. Clearly, the seizure was illegal.

Fahy's position in court was that he had not violated the law and was not guilty of vandalism. The legality of the search and seizure was not questioned, and he was convicted.

On appeal, the high court of Connecticut upheld the conviction, and ruled that "harmless error" had been committed in receiving into evidence the articles that had been seized improperly. The United States Supreme Court reversed the conviction. The wrongful search and seizure was the underlying reason. Justices of the Court wrote, in a dissenting opinion, that the evidence of guilt was overwhelming, with or without the brush and paint.

The layman, as well as the lawyer, may find it difficult to understand the rationale that circumscribes action to be taken pursuant to a search warrant. The rule was laid down by the Supreme Court in the Marron case: "The requirement that warrants shall particularly describe the things to be seized makes general searches under them impossible and prevents the seizure of one thing under a warrant describing another. As to what is to be taken, nothing is left to the discretion of the officer executing the warrant."

Simply stated, this means that if law-enforcement officers, while making a lawful search, pursuant to a search warrant, discover evidence of another crime the evidence of such other crime cannot be used against the possessor. As to such evidence, *or any information derived from it,* the search is of no effect.

A typical case, of frequent occurrence, is presented when police, searching pursuant to a warrant for evidence of violations of the gambling laws, find a quantity of narcotics. The latter evidence cannot be used even if its discovery is followed by a confession. The search for narcotics was not authorized, and confessions or other proof of commission of the crime that flow from or are developed by it are considered "fruits of the poisoned tree." The "poisoned tree" is evidence obtained in violation of statutory or Constitutional rights, and anything that derives from or is discovered as a result of such evidence is characterized as its "fruits" and cannot be used to prove the crime.

No discussion of law enforcement would be complete without some reference to wire-tapping. By enactment in 1934 of Section 605 of the Federal Communictions Act, the Congress banned "in-

terception and divulgence" of telephone conversations for all purposes. Nonetheless, wire-tapping pursuant to a court order, on a
showing that there are reasonable grounds to believe that evidence
of crime could be obtained, is authorized by the laws of New York
State.

In the Benanti case, the United State Supreme Court precluded
the admission in the Federal courts of such evidence even when
obtained by local or state officers acting under authority of a state
law. . . . Some Justices of the New York State Supreme Court
have announced that they will not sign orders permitting wire-
tapping for evidence of a crime—even though the statutory requirements have been met. They reason that the decisions of the
highest court render illegal such orders and all actions taken under
them, under any circumstances.

The Congress for several years has been "studying" the wire-tapping problem, but no action has been taken to amend the Federal
laws. In the meantime, the activities of narcotics rings and other
groups of organized criminals continue unabated.

The cases of the guilty who are permitted to go free are legion.
The reader must remember that we are not speaking of those cases
where, after a trial, the jurors conclude that a reasonable doubt exists as to guilt. In such cases they should acquit. We speak of the
criminals who are able to get away with their crimes, and to go
free to commit further crimes. Nor do we disagree with the rules
excluding a confession, or other evidence, that has been obtained
by coercion of any type.

There is a reasonable case to be made for changing some of our
technical requirements. We do not solve the problem of dealing
with those who make crime their business by providing procedural
methods of escape for the guilty, to the detriment of the law-abiding who are victimized by the lawless. Some changes can be made
within the framework of the Constitution and the Bill of Rights.

These changes cannot be accomplished, however, without divest-
ing ourselves of the currently fashionable practice of being overso-
licitous of the criminal and indifferent to the rights of the citizenry
at large. Treating with crime is a serious business. We, our children, our possessions are its targets. It is an enemy that recognizes

no law but that which is spawned in its own corruption. It knows no moral code—it violates everything that is human and decent. It is not a theory—it is real, it is ugly—a deadly, ever-present enemy.

These steps can be taken—now:

1. Enactment by Congress of legislation to permit wire-tapping, pursuant to court order, for evidence of major crimes.

2. Recodification of procedural requirements for search and seizure, which are distinctive for ancient strictures no longer valid.

3. Extension of the right to detain and interrogate, with proper safeguards against coercion or violation of constitutional rights.

4. Clarification of the extent and application of the "right-to-counsel" concept.

5. Relaxation of the rule excluding all evidence improperly obtained, so as to vest discretion as to admission in the trial judge.

6. Convening in extraordinary session of ranking members of the judicial, legislative and executive branches of the Federal Government for thorough consideration of the problems of law enforcement.

The challenge is to the bar, the public and the lawmakers. The executive and the judiciary must cooperate. This is everybody's responsibility.

DOES THE SUPREME COURT
IMPEDE JUSTICE?

RALPH SLOVENKO

Excerpted from Ralph Slovenko, "The Bill of Rights, the Supreme Court
and Crime," Ralph Slovenko (ed.), *Crime, Law and Corrections* (Spring-
field, Ill.: Charles C Thomas, 1966), pp. 521–30. At the time of publication Ralph Slovenko was Professor of Law at the University of Kansas.

THE HUE and cry tells us that the United States Supreme
Court is responsible for our crime problem. Its decisions on criminal procedure and evidence beginning in 1923 are said to make
detection of criminals difficult and their conviction well-nigh impossible. In 1923 when the Supreme Court for the first time nulli-
fied a criminal conviction handed down by a state court—police
procedures invariably included arbitrary arrests, searches without
warrants, rubber-hose and jaw-breaking interrogations, and holding of suspects for weeks without arraignment or counsel. But now
many consider that the Court has acted in a manner more appropriate for a commissioner of police, and there are public cries that
"the pendulum has swung too far in favor of criminals."

In attempting to transform the paper promises of the constitution
into concrete fact, has the Supreme Court created a haven for
criminals? There is an old saying that the road to hell is paved
with good intentions. New York Police Commissioner Michael J.
Murphy maintains that much of the blame for the crime wave lay
with court decisions. He questions whether "this overprotection of
the individual at the expense of the community will lead to Utopia
or to a hell on earth." FBI Director J. Edgar Hoover says, "We are
faced today with one of the most disturbing trends I have witnessed in my years of law enforcement: an overzealous pity for the

criminal and an equivalent disregard for his victim." "The time has come," the Combined Council of Law Enforcement Officials of the State of New York says in one of its pamphlets, "to restore to the police their proper authority to effectively carry out their sworn duties. In these times of mounting danger from the criminal element, it is the height of foolishness to handcuff law enforcement at the expense of the public safety."

But is this the real problem? What actually has the Supreme Court done? No doubt, fingerprinting of everyone (say, at starting school) and wiretapping or eavesdropping would assist in the detection of crime. The Supreme Court however has never ruled on universal fingerprinting, which has not been attempted, and its decisions delimiting wiretapping have wide acceptance. To put it broadly, the court's decisions that have caused controversy are those requiring the police to bring a person who is arrested before a committing magistrate without undue delay, the exclusion of evidence which is obtained by illegal search and seizure, and the appointment of counsel for the indigent.

It is claimed that these rulings constitute a powerful factor in the growing crime rate, which statistics show is rising five times as fast as the population. It may be true that decisions of the Court may hamper investigation of crime, but to say that the Court is the cause or a major cause of our lawlessness is to give unwarranted weight to its decisions. . . .

Law enforcement measures for dealing with armed robbers and ex-convicts carrying concealed weapons are puny. One European commentator sardonically observed that while churches, schools and restaurants may be segregated in the United States, gunshops are open to one and all—black or white, moron or psychotic. More persons are murdered annually in the City of Baltimore than in the entire United Kingdom, in part due to the proliferation of guns. . . .

One news commentator observes, "Crime in the U.S. is a matter of national concern, but its punishment—and reduction—is mainly up to state and local police and prosecutors." The public pays (or is forced to pay) for police services, and then feels that it is excused from lending assistance. But the payment of police services is not enough to make a good and responsible citizen. The ordinary citizen has the power of arrest, so he can act himself as a policeman, or he may volunteer as a member of the auxiliary police, but he usually does not bother to assist or even report crime to the police. It ought not to be surprising [that] Anglo-American law tends to discourage people from helping others in peril by making no provision to compensate them for injuries or damages they may suffer, and by leaving them vulnerable to lawsuits.

Largely because of the attitude of witnesses, about 85 per cent of crimes actually committed, are not made known to the police. Unless directly injured, the ordinary citizen is apathetic about crime control or does not want to spend time or take any risk which may be involved in enforcing the law. The Supreme Court's decisions are fundamentally based on the philosophy that law-enforcement depends upon public cooperation with the police—the policeman is kept subservient to the public. Apart from preserving a man's home as his castle, the Court's ruling[s] are no serious obstacle to the investigation of crime, nor are they a serious obstacle to the prosecution of those apprehended. Investigation and prosecution are both dependent upon the cooperation of the public.

What happens to offenders who are apprehended? As always, the vast majority of accused persons brought before the bar of justice plead guilty. Statistics show that from 70 to 90 per cent of persons charged with crime, depending on the jurisdiction, do not contest the charge. (It is an extremely rare occurrence when an innocent person confesses to a crime that he did not commit.) Of the 33,381 criminal defendants whose cases were terminated in the United States district courts during 1964, a total of 29,170 or 87.4 per cent were disposed of by conviction and 4,211 or 12.6 per cent were disposed of by dismissal or acquittal. Of the 29,170 defendants convicted in 1964, 90.1 per cent plead guilty (6.7 per cent were convicted by a jury trial, and 3.2 per cent were convicted by court trial). In New York County, less than 100 serious criminal cases go to actual verdict before the nine judges of the Court of General Sessions—90 to 95 per cent of the cases are disposed of by a guilty plea. The United States has a larger percentage of its population in prison than any other Western country (in 1964, 118.3

Americans were in prison per 100,000, as compared with approximately 65 per 100,000 in England and Wales).

The Supreme Court's decisions have not stifled the guilty plea option, except to require that an attorney be present at the time of the guilty plea (which means that the arraignment stage in criminal proceeding is often reduced to a perfunctory entry of a plea of not guilty by the court on behalf of the defendant, as the defendant even now frequently appears without an attorney at this state of proceeding).

So, 70 to 90 per cent of criminal defendants are convicted and sentenced without the need of the State presenting evidence at a (judge or jury) trial. What then of the remaining 10 to 30 per cent of accused persons who plead not guilty? How difficult is it, under the Court's rulings, to prosecute these persons?

As ever, criminal justice in the United States depends very much or perhaps primarily on the defense lawyer. A recent *New Yorker* cartoon shows a lawyer with a briefcase full of papers saying to a criminal, "Just for laughs, we'll plead innocent." Every lawyer knows that the system would be hard put to withstand exploitation if all lawyers were to seek every possible continuance and postponement, make every objection, and frame unresponsive pleadings. It is proper to avail oneself of every legal defense, but as the Canons of Ethics point out, it is improper to use dilatory tactics to frustrate the cause of justice. The defense lawyer who resorts to frivolous pleas or continuances may obtain an acquittal for the defendant, but that serves neither the best interests of the defendant nor of society.

By the best interests of the defendant, I mean that we ought to consider the merit of a plea of not guilty in a situation where, outside the courtroom, denial of the commission of an act would be considered an outright falsehood. It has the effect of reinforcing denial, and denying responsibility, which is unhealthy from a psychological point of view. One might compare Alcoholics Anonymous, where a person must admit he is an alcoholic; the procedure encourages the addict to confront his "character defects." When guilt is admitted and felt, where there is frankness, there improvement may occur. Moreover, most of the severely unsocialized, aggressive persons—the people who flagrantly get into trouble with the law—usually cannot be effectively treated outside of an institution, because adequate control, which is essential in treatment, is impossible in the open democratically organized society, hence they ought to be confined for their own welfare as well as for the welfare of society.

And what about the role of the defense lawyer where there is no trial—in cases settled by plea bragaining? The defense lawyer often negotiates the case with the district attorney on the basis of what type of person the defendant is, without really any knowledge of the defendant, his family, or his situation. He buffs and he bluffs, and that is the usual extent of his presentation. As we all know, under the adversary system, the district attorney is not provided the opportunity to interview the defendant.

But what about the cases that actually go to trial? A majority of these cases end in conviction, so the Supreme Court's decisions have not frustrated the trial process. Of the 1,501 criminal defendants who were disposed of by court trial in the United States district courts during 1964, 942 or 62.8 per cent were convicted, and of the 2,671 disposed of by jury trial, 1,955 or 73.2 per cent were convicted. The percentage of convictions in state courts is approximately the same. Indeed, as one judge observed, the function of the jury (and judge) is not to find who is guilty—that is too easy a task—but to determine which guilty persons should be acquitted. Evidence of guilt is not by any means the crucial problem in the trial of cases.

A defense lawyer, of course, cannot enter a plea of guilty for his client, no matter how guilty he may be, unless the client wishes to so plead. But, in many such cases, when the defendant enters a plea of not guilty, the court is given scant opportunity to pass on the substantive merits of the issue. The Constitution guarantees the defendant a speedy trial but the guilty defendant especially does not want a speedy trial. With the passage of time, the victim may forgive or forget, and witnesses too may forget, or, even more fortunately for the defendant, disappear.

Defense lawyers know that the principal way to win their case, whether or not the defendant is guilty, is to delay it. Delay the case often or long enough and there may be no trial. As time passes, it becomes more and more difficult for the prosecutor to prove the case beyond a reasonable doubt, which is his burden. Witnesses not only become unavailable, but also the statute of limitations has run, and the result is a dismissal or nolle prosequi of the case.

No rule of law, however noble, is immune from abuse. A motion for a continuance or postponement of the case may be fairly justified, but abuse often underlies an apparently legitimate claim—the defense lawyer claims he is not ready for trial or cannot go to trial because he is ill, or because witnesses are out of town, or because he is unprepared, or because he must handle other matters (which may bring a larger fee). It is only appropriate for the judge to continue the case, although he may perhaps be unduly optimistic over the nature of man—the judge usually rules, "On the basis of what defense counsel says, I will continue the case." Moreover, to force the defense to trial following such allegations by defense counsel may result in reversal of any conviction that is obtained, as being a deprivation of the right to counsel or fair trial. Whatever the Supreme Court's rulings, which are the subject of so much discussion, the motion for continuance is used as ever to break the back of the prosecutor. When witnesses appear for trial and are told that the case is postponed, it is highly unlikely that thereafter they will be cooperative or return to testify, even on subpoena. Taken from their work, losing time and money, witnesses soon become apathetic or disgruntled. Witnesses frequently complain that they are not willing to waste hours just waiting around the courthouse. . . .

Thus, of the cases that go to trial, the main obstacle to prosecution stems not from the Supreme Court's rulings but from delaying tactics employed by too many defense lawyers. . . .

Some police officials maintain that quick detection and punishment is the way to deal with growing crime. O. W. Wilson, Superintendent of Chicago's police department, says: "If it would be possible to have every criminal get a sharp punch in the nose within five minutes of the crime, we would have a tremendous decrease in the amount of crime. Punitive treatment is certainly a factor in preventing crime—and it is not the severity of the punishment as

much as the swiftness and certainty of it that will deter crime."
But, whatever the rulings of the Supreme Court, of this century or
the last, people about to commit a crime do not really believe that
they are going to be caught. . . .

To blame the Supreme Court for our crime problem is to take a
mysteriously myopic view of the situation. In comedies the clown
is blamed for everything and is beaten. In the middle ages, the
witch was blamed and burned. Nowadays, the Supreme Court, and
other public officials, are castigated for unpleasant conditions that
exist.

The Supreme Court's decisions on law enforcement may perhaps
be a factor in promoting lawlessness, but if so, it is miniscule compared to the religious, social and economic factors that are operative in this land of plenty, with its fast and hectic mode of living.
We are exposed and influenced by numerous factors, and among
these, the Court's decisions are rather like a straw in the wind.

ON NONVIOLENT CIVIL DISOBEDIENCE AGAINST RACISM: LETTER FROM BIRMINGHAM CITY JAIL

MARTIN LUTHER KING, JR.

Excerpted from Martin Luther King, Jr., "Letter from Birmingham City Jail," Philadelphia: American Friends Service Committee, May 1963. Printed by permission of the American Friends Service Committee. At the time of publication the Reverend Martin Luther King, Jr., was president of the Southern Christian Leadership Conference. He was reacting to a letter from eight Alabama clergymen of Roman Catholic, Protestant, and Jewish denominations, deploring the "series of demonstrations by some of our Negro citizens, directed and led in part by outsiders." The clergymen were "convinced that these demonstrations are unwise and untimely."

My dear Fellow Clergymen,

While confined here in the Birmingham City Jail, I came across your recent statement calling our present activities "unwise and untimely.". . . [S]ince I feel that you are men of genuine goodwill and your criticisms are sincerely set forth, I would like to answer your statement in what I hope will be patient and reasonable terms.

I think I should give the reason for my being in Birmingham, since you have been influenced by the argument of "outsiders coming in." I have the honor of serving as president of the Southern Christian Leadership Conference, an organization operating in every Southern state, with headquarters in Atlanta, Georgia. We have some eighty-five affiliate organizations all across the South—one being the Alabama Christian Movement for Human Rights.

Whenever necessary and possible we share staff, educational and financial resources with our affiliates. Several months ago our local affiliate here in Birmingham invited us to be on call to engage in a nonviolent direct action program if such were deemed necessary. We readily consented and when the hour came we lived up to our promises. So I am here, along with several members of my staff, because we were invited here. I am here because I have basic organizational ties here.

Beyond this, I am in Birmingham because injustice is here. Just as the eighth century prophets left their little villages and carried their "thus saith the Lord" far beyond the boundaries of their home towns; and just as the Apostle Paul left his little village of Tarsus and carried the gospel of Jesus Christ to practically every hamlet and city of the Graeco-Roman world, I too am compelled to carry the gospel of freedom beyond my particular home town. Like Paul, I must constantly respond to the Macedonian call for aid.

Moreover, I am cognizant of the interrelatedness of all communities and states. I cannot sit idly by in Atlanta and not be concerned about what happens in Birmingham. Injustice anywhere is a threat to justice everywhere. We are caught in an inescapable network of mutuality, tied in a single garment of destiny. Whatever affects one directly affects all indirectly. Never again can we afford to live with the narrow, provincial "outside agitator" idea. Anyone who lives inside the United States can never be considered an outsider anywhere in this country.

You deplore the demonstrations that are presently taking place in Birmingham. But I am sorry that your statement did not express a similar concern for the conditions that brought the demonstrations into being. I am sure that each of you would want to go beyond the superficial social analyst who looks merely at effects, and does not grapple with underlying causes. I would not hesitate to say that it is unfortunate that so-called demonstrations are taking place in Birmingham at this time, but I would say in more emphatic terms that it is even more unfortunate that the white power structure of this city left the Negro community with no other alternative.

In any nonviolent campaign there are four basic steps:

1) Collection of the facts to determine whether injustices are alive. 2) Negotiation. 3) Self-purification and 4) Direct Action. We have gone through all of these steps in Birmingham. There can be no gainsaying of the fact that racial injustice engulfs this community.

Birmingham is probably the most thoroughly segregated city in the United States. Its ugly record of police brutality is known in every section of this country. Its unjust treatment of Negroes in the courts is a notorious reality. There have been more unsolved bombings of Negro homes and churches in Birmingham than any city in this nation. These are the hard, brutal and unbelievable facts. On the basis of these conditions Negro leaders sought to negotiate with the city fathers. But the political leaders consistently refused to engage in good faith negotiation.

Then came the opportunity last September to talk with some of the leaders of the economic community. In these negotiating sessions certain promises were made by the merchants—such as the promise to remove the humiliating racial signs from the stores. On the basis of these promises Rev. Shuttlesworth and the leaders of the Alabama Christian Movement for Human Rights agreed to call a moratorium on any type of demonstrations. As the weeks and months unfolded we realized that we were the victims of a broken promise. The signs remained. Like so many experiences of the past we were confronted with blasted hopes, and the dark shadow of a deep disappointment settled upon us. So we had no alternative except that of preparing for direct action, whereby we would present our very bodies as a means of laying our case before the conscience of the local and national community. We were not unmindful of the difficulties involved. So we decided to go through a process of self-purification. We started having workshops on non-violence and repeatedly asked ourselves the questions, "Are you able to accept blows without retaliating?" "Are you able to endure the ordeals of jail?" We decided to set our direct action program around the Easter season, realizing that with the exception of Christmas, this was the largest shopping period of the year. Knowing that a strong economic withdrawal program would be the by-product of direct action, we felt that this was the best time to bring pressure on the merchants for the needed changes. Then it occurred to us that the March election was ahead and so we speedily decided to postpone action until after election day. When we discovered that Mr. Connor was in the run-off, we decided again to postpone action so that the demonstrations could not be used to cloud the issues. At this time we agreed to begin our nonviolent witness the day after the run-off.

This reveals that we did not move irresponsibly into direct action. We too wanted to see Mr. Connor defeated; so we went through postponement after postponement to aid in this community need. After this we felt that direct action could be delayed no longer.

You may well ask, "Why direct action? Why sit-ins, marches, etc.? Isn't negotiation a better path?" You are exactly right in your call for negotiation. Indeed, this is the purpose of direct action. Nonviolent direct action seeks to create such a crisis and establish such creative tension that a community that has constantly refused to negotiate is forced to confront the issue. It seeks so to dramatize the issue that it can no longer be ignored. I just referred to the creation of tension as a part of the work of the nonviolent resister. This may sound rather shocking. But I must confess that I am not afraid of the word tension. I have earnestly worked and preached against violent tension, but there is a type of constructive nonviolent tension that is necessary for growth. Just as Socrates felt that it was necessary to create a tension in the mind so that individuals could rise from the bondage of myths and half-truths to the unfettered realm of creative analysis and objective appraisal, we must see the need of having nonviolent gadflies to create the kind of tension in society that will help men to rise from the dark depths of prejudice and racism to the majestic heights of understanding and brotherhood. So the purpose of the direct action is to create a situation so crisis-packed that it will inevitably open the door to negotiation. We, therefore, concur with you in your call for negotiation. Too long has our beloved Southland been bogged down in the tragic attempt to live in monologue rather than dialogue.

One of the basic points in your statement is that our acts are untimely. Some have asked, "Why didn't you give the new administration time to act?" The only answer that I can give to this inquiry is that the new administration must be prodded about as much as the outgoing one before it acts. . . . My friends, I must say to you that we have not made a single gain in civil rights without determined legal and nonviolent pressure. History is the long and tragic story of the fact that privileged groups seldom give up their privileges voluntarily. . . .

We know through painful experience that freedom is never voluntarily given by the oppressor; it must be demanded by the oppressed. Frankly, I have never yet engaged in a direct action movement that was "well timed," according to the timetable of those who have not suffered unduly from the disease of segregation. For years now I have heard the words "Wait!" It rings in the ear of every Negro with a piercing familiarity. This "Wait" has almost always meant "never." It has been a tranquilizing thalidomide, relieving the emotional stress for a moment, only to give birth to an ill-formed infant of frustration. We must come to see with the distinguished jurist of yesterday that "justice too long delayed is justice denied." We have waited for more than three hundred and forty years for our constitutional and God-given rights. The nations of Asia and Africa are moving with jetlike speed toward the goal of political independence, and we still creep at horse and buggy pace toward the gaining of a cup of coffee at a lunch counter. I guess it is easy for those who have never felt the stinging darts of segregation to say, "Wait." But when you have seen vicious mobs lynch your mothers and fathers at will and drown your sisters and brothers at whim; when you have seen hate-filled policemen curse, kick, brutalize and even kill your black brothers and sisters with impunity; when you see the vast majority of your twenty million Negro brothers smothering in an air-tight cage of poverty in the midst of an affluent society; when you suddenly find your tongue twisted and your speech stammering as you seek to explain to your six-year-old daughter why she can't go to the public amusement park that has just been advertised on television, and see tears welling up in her little eyes when she is told that Funtown is closed to colored children, and see the depressing clouds of inferiority begin to form in her little mental sky, and see her begin to distort her little personality by unconsciously developing a bitterness toward white people; when you have to concoct an answer for a five-year-old son asking in agonizing pathos: "Daddy, why do white people treat colored people so mean?"; when you take a cross country drive and find it necessary to sleep night after night in the uncomfortable corners of your automobile because no motel will accept you; when you are humiliated day in and day out by nagging signs reading "white" and "colored"; when your first name becomes "nigger" and your middle name becomes "boy" (however old you are) and your last name becomes "John," and when your wife and mother are never given the respected title "Mrs."; when you are harried by day and haunted at night by the fact that you are a Negro, living constantly at tip-toe stance never quite knowing what to expect next, and plagued with inner fears and outer resentments; when you are forever fighting a degenerating sense of "nobodiness"; then you will understand why we find it difficult to wait. There comes a time when the cup of endurance runs over, and men are no longer willing to be plunged into an abyss of injustice where they experience the blackness of corroding despair. I hope, sirs, you can understand our legitimate and unavoidable impatience.

You express a great deal of anxiety over our willingness to break laws. This is certainly a legitimate concern. Since we so diligently urge people to obey the Supreme Court's decision of 1954 outlawing segregation in the public schools, it is rather strange and paradoxical to find us consciously breaking laws. One may well ask, "How can you advocate breaking some laws and obeying others?" The answer is found in the fact that there are two types of laws: There are *just* and there are *unjust* laws. I would agree with Saint Augustine that "An unjust law is no law at all."

Now what is the difference between the two? How does one determine when a law is just or unjust? A just law is a man-made code that squares with the moral law or the law of God. An unjust law is a code that is out of harmony with the moral law. To put it in the terms of Saint Thomas Aquinas, an unjust law is a human law that is not rooted in eternal and natural law. Any law that uplifts human personality is just. Any law that degrades human personality is unjust. All segregation statutes are unjust because segregation distorts the soul and damages the personality. It gives the segregator a false sense of superiority, and the segregated a false sense of inferiority. To use the words of Martin Buber, the great Jewish philosopher, segregation substitutes an "I-it" relationship for the "I-thou" relationship, and ends up relegating persons to the status of things. So segregation is not only politically, economically and sociologically unsound, but it is morally wrong and sinful. . . . So I can urge men to disobey segregation ordinances because they are morally wrong.

Let us turn to a more concrete example of just and unjust laws. An unjust law is a code that a majority inflicts on a minority that is not binding on itself. This is difference made legal. On the other hand a just law is a code that a majority compels a minority to follow that it is willing to follow itself. This is sameness made legal.

Let me give another explanation. An unjust law is a code inflicted upon a minority which that minority had no part in enacting or creating because they did not have the unhampered right to vote. Who can say that the legislature of Alabama which set up the segregation laws was democratically elected? Throughout the state of Alabama all types of conniving methods are used to prevent Negroes from becoming registered voters and there are some counties without a single Negro registered to vote despite the fact that the Negro constitues a majority of the population. Can any law set up in such a state be considered democratically structured?

These are just a few examples of unjust and just laws. There are some instances when a law is just on its face and unjust in its application. For instance, I was arrested Friday on a charge of parading without a permit. Now there is nothing wrong with an ordinance which requires a permit for a parade, but when the ordinance is used to preserve segregation and to deny citizens the First Amendment privilege of peaceful assembly and peaceful protest, then it becomes unjust.

I hope you can see the distinction I am trying to point out. In no sense do I advocate evading or defying the law as the rabid segregationist would do. This would lead to anarchy. One who breaks an unjust law must do it *openly*, *lovingly* (not hatefully as the white mothers did in New Orleans when they were seen on television screaming "nigger, nigger, nigger"), and with a willingness to accept the penalty. I submit that an individual who breaks a law that conscience tells him is unjust, and willingly accepts the penalty by staying in jail to arouse the conscience of the community over its injustice, is in reality expressing the very highest respect for law. . . .

We can never forget that everything Hitler did in Germany was "legal" and everything the Hungarian freedom fighters did in Hungary was "illegal." It was "illegal" to aid and comfort a Jew in Hitler's Germany. But I am sure that if I had lived in Germany during that time I would have aided and comforted my Jewish brothers even though it was illegal. If I lived in a Communist country today where certain principles dear to the Christian faith are suppressed, I believe I would openly advocate disobeying these anti-religious laws. I must make two honest confessions to you, my Christian and Jewish brothers. First, I must confess that over the last few years I have been gravely disappointed with the white moderate. I have almost reached the regrettable conclusion that the Negro's great stumbling block in the stride toward freedom is not the White Citizen's Council-er or the Ku Klux Klanner, but the white moderate who is more devoted to "order" than to justice; who prefers a negative peace which is the absence of tension to a positive peace which is the presence of justice; who constantly says, "I agree with you in the goal you seek, but I can't agree with your methods of direct action"; who paternalistically feels that he can set the timetable for another man's freedom; who lives by the myth of time and who constantly advises the Negro to wait until a "more convenient season." Shallow understanding from people of goodwill is more frustrating than absolute misunderstanding from people of ill will. Lukewarm acceptance is much more bewildering than outright rejection. . . .

In your statement you asserted that our actions, even though peaceful, must be condemned because they precipitate violence. But can this assertion be logically made? Isn't this like condemning the robbed man because his possession of money precipitated the evil act of robbery? Isn't this like condemning Socrates because his unswerving commitment to truth and his philosophical delvings precipitated the misguided popular mind to make him drink the hemlock? Isn't this like condemning Jesus because His unique God-Consciousness and never-ceasing devotion to His will precipitated the evil act of crucifixion? We must come to see, as federal courts have consistently affirmed, that it is immoral to urge an individual to withdraw his efforts to gain his basic constitutional rights because the quest precipitates violence. Society must protect the robbed and punish the robber.

I had also hoped that the white moderate would reject the myth of time. I received a letter this morning from a white brother in Texas which said: "All Christians know that the colored people will receive equal rights eventually, but it is possible that you are in too great of a religious hurry. It has taken Christianity almost 2000 years to accomplish what it has. The teachings of Christ take time to come to earth." All that is said here grows out of a tragic misconception of time. It is the strangely irrational notion that there is something in the very flow of time that will inevitably cure all ills. Actually time is neutral. It can be used either destructively or constructively. I am coming to feel that the people of ill will have used time much more effectively than the people of goodwill. We will have to repent in this generation not merely for the vitriolic words and actions of the bad people, but for the appalling silence of the good people. We must come to see that human progress never rolls in on wheels of inevitability. It comes through the tireless efforts and persistent work of men willing to be co-workers with God, and without this hard work time itself becomes an ally of the forces of social stagnation. We must use time creatively, and forever realize that the time is always ripe to do right. Now is the time to make real the promise of democracy, and transform our pending national elegy into a creative psalm of brotherhood. Now is the time to lift our national policy from the quicksand of racial injustice to the solid rock of human dignity.

You spoke of our activity in Birmingham as extreme. At first I was rather disappointed that fellow clergymen would see my non-violent efforts as those of the extremist. I started thinking about the fact that I stand in the middle of two opposing forces in the

Negro community. One is a force of complacency made up of Negroes who, as a result of long years of oppression, have been so completely drained of self-respect and a sense of "somebodiness" that they have adjusted to segregation, and, of a few Negroes in the middle class who, because of a degree of academic and economic security, and because at points they profit by segregation, have unconsciously become insensitive to the problems of the masses. The other force is one of bitterness and hatred, and comes perilously close to advocating violence. It is expressed in the various black nationalist groups that are springing up over the nation, the largest and best known being Elijah Muhammad's Muslim movement. This movement is nourished by the contemporary frustration over the continued existence of racial discrimination. It is made up of people who have lost faith in America, who have absolutely repudiated Christianity, and who have concluded that the white man is an incurable "devil." I have tried to stand between these two forces, saying that we need not follow the "do-nothing-ism" of the complacent or the hatred and despair of the black nationalist. There is the more excellent way of love and nonviolent protest. I'm grateful to God that, through the Negro church, the dimension of nonviolence entered our struggle. If this philosophy had not emerged, I am convinced that by now many streets of the South would be flowing with floods of blood. And I am further convinced that if our white brothers dismiss as "rabble rousers" and "outside agitators" those of us who are working through the channels of nonviolent direct action and refuse to support our nonviolent efforts, millions of Negroes, out of frustration and despair, will seek solace and security in black nationalist ideologies, a development that will lead inevitably to a frightening racial nightmare.

Oppressed people cannot remain oppressed forever. The urge for freedom will eventually come. This is what happened to the American Negro. Something within has reminded him of his birthright of freedom; something without has reminded him that he can gain it. Consciously and unconsciously, he has been swept in by what the Germans call the *Zeitgeist,* and with his black brothers of Africa, and his brown and yellow brothers of Asia, South America and the Caribbean, he is moving with a sense of cosmic urgency toward the promised land of racial justice. Recognizing this vital urge that has engulfed the Negro community, one should readily understand public demonstrations. The Negro has many pent-up resentments and latent frustrations. He has to get them out. So let him march sometime; let him have his prayer pilgrimages to the city hall; understand why he must have sit-ins and freedom rides. If his repressed emotions do not come out in these nonviolent ways, they will come out in ominous expressions of violence. This is not a threat; it is a fact of history. So I have not said to my people "get rid of your discontent." But I have tried to say that this normal and healthy discontent can be channelized through the creative outlet of nonviolent direct action. Now this approach is being dismissed as extremist. I must admit that I was initially disappointed in being so categorized.

But as I continued to think about the matter I gradually gained a bit of satisfaction from being considered an extremist. Was not Jesus an extremist in love—"Love your enemies, bless them that curse you, pray for them that despitefully use you." . . . Was not Abraham Lincoln an extremist—"This nation cannot survive half slave and half free." Was not Thomas Jefferson an extremist—"We hold these truths to be self-evident, that all men are created equal." So the question is not whether we will be extremist but what kind of extremist will we be. Will we be extremists for hate or will we be extremists for love? Will we be extremists for the preservation of injustice—or will we be extremists for the cause of justice? In that dramatic scene on Calvary's hill, three men were crucified. We must not forget that all three were crucified for the same crime—the crime of extremism. Two were extremists for immorality, and thusly fell below their environment. The other, Jesus Christ, was an extremist for love, truth and goodness, and thereby rose above his environment. So, after all, maybe the South, the nation and the world are in dire need of creative extremists.

I had hoped that the white moderate would see this. Maybe I was too optimistic. Maybe I expected too much. I guess I should have realized that few members of a race that has oppressed another race can understand or appreciate the deep groans and passionate yearnings of those that have been oppressed and still fewer have the vision to see that injustice must be rooted out by strong, persistent and determined action. I am thankful, however, that some of our white brothers have grasped the meaning of this social revolution and committed themselves to it. They are still all too small in quantity, but they are big in quality. Some like Ralph McGill, Lillian Smith, Harry Golden and James Dabbs have written about our struggle in eloquent, prophetic and understanding terms. Others have marched with us down nameless streets of the South. They have languished in filthy roach-infested jails, suffering the abuse and brutality of angry policemen who see them as "dirty nigger lovers." They, unlike so many of their moderate brothers and sisters, have recognized the urgency of the moment and sensed the need for powerful "action" antidotes to combat the disease of segregation.

Let me rush on to mention my other disappointment. I have been so greatly disappointed with the white church and its leadership. Of course, there are some notable exceptions. I am not unmindful of the fact that each of you has taken some significant stands on this issue. I commend you, Rev. Stallings, for your Christian stand on this past Sunday, in welcoming Negroes to your worship service on a non-segregated basis. I commend the Catholic leaders of this state for integrating Springhill College several years ago.

But despite these notable exceptions I must honestly reiterate that I have been disappointed with the church. I do not say that as one of the negative critics who can always find something wrong with the church. I say it as a minister of the gospel, who loves the church; who was nurtured in its bosom; who has been sustained by its spiritual blessings and who will remain true to it as long as the cord of life shall lengthen.

I had the strange feeling when I was suddenly catapulted into the leadership of the bus protest in Montgomery several years ago that we would have the support of the white church. I felt that the white ministers, priests and rabbis of the South would be some of our strongest allies. Instead, some have been outright opponents, refusing to understand the freedom movement and misrepresenting

its leaders; all too many others have been more cautious than cou-
rageous and have remained silent behind the anesthetizing security
of the stained-glass windows.

In spite of my shattered dreams of the past, I came to Birmingham with the hope that the white religious leadership of this community would see the justice of our cause, and with deep moral
concern, serve as the channel through which our just grievances
would get to the power structure. I had hoped that each of you
would understand. But again I have been disappointed. I have
heard numerous religious leaders of the South call upon their wor-
shippers to comply with a desegregation decision because it is the
law, but I have longed to hear white ministers say, "Follow this
decree because integration is morally *right* and the Negro is your
brother." In the midst of blatant injustices inflicted upon the
Negro, I have watched white churches stand on the sideline and
merely mouth pious irrelevancies and sanctimonious trivialities. In
the midst of a mighty struggle to rid our nation of racial and economic injustice, I have heard so many ministers say, "Those are social issues with which the gospel has no real concern," and I have
watched so many churches commit themselves to a completely
other-worldly religion which made a strange distinction between
body and soul, the sacred and the secular.

So here we are moving toward the exit of the twentieth century
with a religious community largely adjusted to the status quo,
standing as a tail-light behind other community agencies rather
than a headlight leading men to higher levels of justice. . . .

There was a time when the church was very powerful. It was
during that period when the early Christians rejoiced when they
were deemed worthy to suffer for what they believed. In those
days the church was not merely a thermometer that recorded the
ideas and principles of popular opinion; it was a thermostat that
transformed the mores of society. Wherever the early Christians
entered a town the power structure got disturbed and immediately
sought to convict them for being "disturbers of the peace" and
"outside agitators." But they went on with the conviction that they
were "a colony of heaven," and had to obey God rather than man.
They were small in number but big in commitment. They were too

God-intoxicated to be "astronomically intimidated." They brought an end to such ancient evils as infanticide and gladiatorial contest.

Things are different now. The contemporary church is often a weak, ineffectual voice with an uncertain sound. It is so often the arch supporter of the status quo. Far from being disturbed by the presence of the church, the power structure of the average community is consoled by the church's silent and often vocal sanction of things as they are.

But the judgment of God is upon the church as never before. If the church of today does not recapture the sacrificial spirit of the early church, it will lose its authentic ring, forfeit the loyalty of millions, and be dismissed as an irrelevant social club with no meaning for the twentieth century. I am meeting young people every day whose disappointment with the church has risen to outright disgust.

Maybe again, I have been too optimistic. Is organized religion too inextricably bound to the status quo to save our nation and the world? Maybe I must turn my faith to the inner spiritual church, the church within the church, as the true *ecclesia* and the hope of the world. But again I am thankful to God that some noble souls from the ranks of organized religion have broken loose from the paralyzing chains of conformity and joined us as active partners in the struggle for freedom. They have left their secure congregations and walked the streets of Albany, Georgia, with us. They have gone through the highways of the South on tortuous rides for freedom. Yes, they have gone to jail with us. Some have been kicked out of their churches, and lost support of their bishops and fellow ministers. But they have gone with the faith that right defeated is stronger than evil triumphant. These men have been the leaven in the lump of the race. Their witness has been the spiritual salt that has preserved the true meaning of the Gospel in these troubled times. They have carved a tunnel of hope through the dark mountain of disappointment.

I hope the church as a whole will meet the challenge of this decisive hour. But even if the church does not come to the aid of justice, I have no despair about the future. I have no fear about the outcome of our struggle in Birmingham, even if our motives are presently misunderstood. We will reach the goal of freedom in Birmingham and all over the nation, because the goal of America is freedom. Abused and scorned though we may be, our destiny is tied up with the destiny of America. Before the pilgrims landed at Plymouth we were here. Before the pen of Jefferson etched across the pages of history the majestic words of the Declaration of Independence, we were here. For more than two centuries our foreparents labored in this country without wages; they made cotton king; and they built the homes of their masters in the midst of brutal injustice and shameful humiliation—and yet out of a bottomless vitality they continued to thrive and develop. If the inexpressible cruelties of slavery could not stop us, the opposition we now face will surely fail. We will win our freedom because the sacred heritage of our nation and the eternal will of God are embodied in our echoing demands.

I must close now. But before closing I am impelled to mention one other point in your statement that troubled me profoundly. You warmly commended the Birmingham police force for keeping "order" and "preventing violence." I don't believe you would have so warmly commended the police force if you had seen its angry violent dogs literally biting six unarmed, nonviolent Negroes. I don't belive you would so quickly commend the policemen if you would observe their ugly and inhuman treatment of Negroes here in the city jail; if you would watch them push and curse old Negro women and young Negro girls; if you would see them slap and kick old Negro men and young boys; if you will observe them, as they did on two occasions, refuse to give us food because we wanted to sing our grace together. I'm sorry that I can't join you in your praise for the police department.

It is true that they have been rather disciplined in their public handling of the demonstrators. In this sense they have been rather publicly "nonviolent." But for what purpose? To preserve the evil system of segregation. Over the last few years I have consistently preached that nonviolence demands that the means we use must be as pure as the ends we seek. So I have tried to make it clear that it is wrong to use immoral means to attain moral ends. But now I must affirm that it is just as wrong, or even more so, to use moral means to preserve immoral ends. . . . T.S. Eliot has said that there is no greater treason than to do the right deed for the wrong reason.

I wish you had commended the Negro sit-inners and demonstrators of Birmingham for their sublime courage, their willingness to suffer and their amazing discipline in the midst of the most inhuman provocation. One day the South will recognize its real heroes. They will be the James Meredith's, courageously and with a majestic sense of purpose facing jeering and hostile mobs and the agonizing loneliness that characterizes the life of the pioneer. They will be old, oppressed, battered Negro women, symbolized in a seventy-two year old woman of Montgomery, Alabama, who rose up with a sense of dignity and with her people decided not to ride the segregated buses, and responded to one who inquired about her tiredness with ungrammatical profundity: "My feet is tired, but my soul is rested." They will be the young high school and college students, young ministers of the Gospel and a host of their elders courageously and nonviolently sitting-in at lunch counters and willingly going to jail for conscience's sake. One day the South will know that when these disinherited children of God sat down at lunch counters they were in reality standing up for the best in the American dream and the most sacred values in our Judeo-Christian heritage, and thusly, carrying our whole nation back to those great wells of democracy which were dug deep by the founding fathers in the formulation of the Constitution and the Declaration of Independence. . . .

If I have said anything in this letter that is an overstatement of the truth and is indicative of an unreasonable impatience, I beg you to forgive me. If I have said anything in this letter that is an understatement of the truth and is indicative of my having a patience that makes me patient with anything less than brotherhood, I beg God to forgive me.

I hope this letter finds you strong in the faith. I also hope that circumstances will soon make it possible for me to meet each of you, not as an integrationist or a civil-rights leader, but as a fellow clergyman and a Christian brother. Let us all hope that the dark clouds of racial prejudice will soon pass away and the deep fog of misunderstanding will be lifted from our fear-drenched communities and in some not too distant tomorrow the radiant stars of love and brotherhood will shine over our great nation with all of their scintillating beauty.

Yours for the cause of Peace and Brotherhood,

Martin Luther King, Jr.

ON CIVIL DISOBEDIENCE
WITH VIOLENCE
THE DEATH OF MARTIN LUTHER
KING: REQUIEM FOR NONVIOLENCE

ELDRIDGE CLEAVER

Eldridge Cleaver, "The Death of Martin Luther King: Requiem for Non-violence," Eldridge Cleaver, *Post-Prison Writings and Speeches* (New York: A Ramparts Book, Vintage Books, a division of Random House, 1969), pp. 73–79. At the time of publication, Eldridge Cleaver, who had been Minister of Information of the Black Panther Party, was a fugitive, wanted for violation of parole in California.

THE MURDER of Dr. Martin Luther King came as a surprise—and surprisingly it also came as a shock. Many people, particularly those in the black community who long ago abandoned nonviolence and opted to implement the slogan of Malcolm X—"black liberation by any means necessary"—have been expecting to hear of Dr. King's death for a long time. Many even became tired of waiting. But that Dr. King would have to die was a certainty. For here was a man who refused to abandon the philosophy and the principle of nonviolence in face of a hostile and racist nation which has made it indisputably clear that it has no intention and no desire to grant a redress of the grievances of the black colonial subjects who are held in bondage.

To black militants, Dr. King represented a stubborn and persistent stumbling block in the path of the methods that had to be implemented to bring about a revolution in the present situation. And so, therefore, much hatred, much venom and much criticism was focused upon Dr. King by the black militants. And the contradiction in which he was caught up cast him in the role of one who was hated and held in contempt, both by the whites in America who did not want to free black people, and by black people who recognized the attitude of white America and who wanted to be rid of the self-deceiving doctrine of nonviolence. Still, black militants were willing to sit back and watch, and allow Dr. King to play out his role. And his role has now been played out.

The assassin's bullet not only killed Dr. King, it killed a period of history. It killed a hope, and it killed a dream.

That white America could produce the assassin of Dr. Martin Luther King is looked upon by black people—and not just those identified as black militants—as a final repudiation by white America of any hope of reconciliation, of any hope of change by peaceful and nonviolent means. So that it becomes clear that the only way for black people in this country to get the things that they want—and the things that they have a right to and that they deserve—is to meet fire with fire.

In the last few months, while Dr. King was trying to build support for his projected poor people's march on Washington, he already resembled something of a dead man. Of a dead symbol, one might say more correctly. Hated on both sides, denounced on both sides—yet he persisted. And now his blood has been spilled. The death of Dr. King signals the end of an era and the beginning of a terrible and bloody chapter that may remain unwritten, because there may be no scribe left to capture on paper the holocaust to come.

That there is a holocaust coming I have no doubt at all. I have been talking to people around the country by telephone—people intimately involved in the black liberation struggle—and their reaction to Dr. King's murder has been unanimous: the war has begun. The violent phase of the black liberation struggle is here, and it will spread. From that shot, from that blood. America will be painted red. Dead bodies will litter the streets and the scenes will be reminiscent of the disgusting, terrifying, nightmarish news reports coming out of Algeria during the height of the general violence right before the final breakdown of the French colonial regime.

America has said "No" to the black man's demand for liberation, and this "No" is unacceptable to black people. They are going to strike back, they are going to reply to the escalation of this racist government, this racist society. They are going to escalate their retaliation. And the responsibility for all this blood, for all this death, for all this suffering . . . well, it's beyond the stage of assigning blame. Black people are no longer interested in adjudicating the situation, in negotiating the situation, in arbitrating the situation. Their only interest now is in being able to summon up whatever it will take to wreak the havoc upon Babylon that will force Babylon to let the black people go. For all other avenues have been closed.

The assassin's bullet which struck down Dr. King closed a door that to the majority of black people seemed closed long ago. To many of us it was clear that that door had never been open. But we were willing to allow the hopeful others to bang upon that door for entry, we were willing to sit back and let them do this. Indeed, we had no other choice. But now all black people in America have become Black Panthers in spirit. There will, of course, be those who stand up before the masses and echo the eloquent pleas of Dr. King for a continuation of the nonviolent tactic. They will be listened to by many, but from another perspective: people will look back upon Dr. King and upon his successors with something of the emotions one feels when one looks upon the corpse of a loved one. But it is all dead now. It's all dead now. Now there is the gun and the bomb, dynamite and the knife, and they will be used liberally in America. America will bleed. America will suffer.

And it is strange to see how, with each significant shot that is fired, time is speeded up. How the dreadful days that we all somehow knew were coming seem to cascade down upon us immediately, and the dreadful hours that we thought were years away are immediately upon us, immediately before us. And all eternity is gone, blown away, washed away in the blood of martyrs.

Is the death of Dr. King a sad day for America? No. It is a day consistent with what America demands by its actions. The death of Dr. King was not a tragedy for America. America should be happy that Dr. King is dead, because America worked so hard to bring it about. And now all the hypocritical, vicious madmen who pollute the government of this country and who befoul the police agencies of this country, all of the hypocritical public announcements following the death of Dr. King are being repudiated and held in contempt, not only by black people but by millions of white people who know that had these same treacherous, political gangsters made the moves that clearly lay within their power to make, Dr. King would not be dead, nonviolence would prevail and the terror would not be upon us. These people, the police departments, the legislatures, the government, the Democratic Party, the Republican Party, those commonly referred to as the Establishment or the power structure, they can be looked upon as immediate targets and symbols of blame.

But it has been said that a people or a country gets the leaders and the government that it deserves. And here we have at the death of Dr. King a President by the name of Lyndon Baines Johnson who has the audacity to stand before this nation and mourn Dr. King and to praise his leadership and the nonviolence he espoused, while he has the blood of hundreds of thousands of people and the slaughtered conscience of America upon his hands. If any one man could be singled out as bearing responsibility for bringing about the bloodshed and violence to come, it would be Lyndon Baines Johnson. But not just Lyndon Baines Johnson. All of the greedy, profit-seeking businessmen in America, all of the conniving, unscrupulous labor leaders of America, all of the unspeakable bootlickers, the big businessmen of the civil rights movement and the average man on the streets who feels hatred instilled in his heart by this vicious and disgusting system—the blame is everywhere and nowhere.

Washington, D.C., is burning. My only thought at that is: I hope Stokely Carmichael survives Washington. Chicago is burning, Detroit is burning and there is fire and the sound of guns from one end of Babylon to the other.

Last night I heard Lyndon Baines Johnson admonishing his people, admonishing black people to turn away from violence, and not to follow the path of the assassins. And of all the corn pone that he spouted forth one thing struck me and I felt insulted by it. He was ringing changes on a famous statement made by Malcolm X in his speech, "The Ballot or the Bullet." Malcolm X had prophesied that if the ballot did not prevail in gaining black people their liberation, then the bullet would be made to prevail. And Lyndon Johnson said last night that he was going to prove to the nation and to the American people that the ballot and not the bullet would prevail. Coming from him, it was a pure insult.

Those of us in the Black Panther Party who have been reading events and looking to the future have said that this will be the Year of the Panther, that this will be the Year of the Black Panther. And now everything that I can see leaves no doubt of that. And now there is Stokely Carmichael, Rap Brown, and above all there is Huey P. Newton. Malcolm X prophesied the coming of the gun, and Huey Newton picked up the gun, and now there is gun against gun. Malcolm X gunned down. Martin Luther King gunned down.

I am trying to put a few words on tape because I was asked to do so by the editor of this magazine, to try to give my thoughts on what the assassination of Dr. King means for the future, what is likely to follow and who is likely to emerge as a new or a prevailing leader of black people. It is hard to put words on this tape because words are no longer relevant. Action is all that counts now. And maybe America will understand that. I doubt it. I think that America is incapable of understanding *anything* relevant to human rights. I think that America has already committed suicide and we who now thrash within its dead body are also dead in part and parcel of the corpse. America is truly a disgusting burden upon this planet. A burden upon all humanity. And if we here in America . . .

April 6, 1968

CIVIL DISOBEDIENCE AND THE RULE OF LAW

ABE FORTAS

Excerpted from Abe Fortas, *Concerning Dissent and Civil Disobedience* (New York: World Publishing Co., 1968), pp. 30–33, 47–58, 104–109. At the time of publication Abe Fortas was Associate Justice of the Supreme Court of the United States.

. . . [CONSIDER] the difficulty and subtlety of the legal issues involved in determining whether a particular form of protest is or is not protected by the Bill of Rights. The reason for the difficulty is that, unavoidably, the Constitution seeks to accommodate two conflicting values, each of which is fundamental: the need for freedom to speak freely, to protest effectively, to organize, and to demonstrate; and the necessity of maintaining order so that other people's rights, and the peace and security of the state, will not be impaired.

The types of protests and the situations in which they occur are of infinite variety, and it is impossible to formulate a set of rules which will strike the proper balance between the competing principles. The precise facts in each situation will determine whether the particular protest or activity is within the shelter of the First Amendment or whether the protesters have overstepped the broad limits in which constitutional protection is guaranteed. It is, accordingly, hazardous to set out general principles. But here are a few principles that in my opinion indicate the contours of the law in this subtle and complex field where the basic right of freedom conflicts with the needs of an ordered society:

(1) Our constitution protects the right of protest and dissent within broad limits. It generously protects the right to organize

people for protest and dissent. It broadly protects the right to assemble, to picket, to stage "freedom walks" or mass demonstrations, if these activities are peaceable and if the protesters comply with reasonable regulations designed to protect the general public without substantially interfering with effective protest.

(2) If any of the rights to dissent is exercised with the intent to cause unlawful action (a riot, or assault upon others) or to cause injury to the property of others (such as a stampede for exits or breaking doors or windows), and if such unlawful action or injury occurs, the dissenter will not be protected. He may be arrested, and if properly charged and convicted of law violation, he will not be rescued by the First Amendment.

(3) If the right to protest, to dissent, or to assemble peaceably is exercised so as to violate valid laws reasonably designed and administered to avoid interference with others, the Constitution's guarantees will not shield the protester. For example, he may be convicted for engaging in marching or picketing which blocks traffic or for sitting-in in an official's office or in a public or private place and thereby preventing its ordinary and intended use by the occupant or others. It is difficult to generalize about cases of this sort, because they turn on subtleties of fact: for example, Did the public authorities confine themselves to requiring only that minimum restriction necessary to permit the public to go about its business? Were there facilities available for the protest which were reasonably adequate to serve the lawful purposes of the protesters, and which could have been used without depriving others of the use of the public areas? . . .

. . . If I had been a Negro in the South, I hope I would have disobeyed the state and local laws denying to Negroes equal access to schools, to voting rights, and to public facilities. If I had disobeyed those laws, I would have been arrested and tried and convicted. Until the Supreme Court ruled that these laws were unconstitutional, I would have been a law violator.

As it turned out, my refusal to obey those laws would have been justified by the courts. But suppose I had been wrong. Suppose the Supreme Court had decided that the laws were constitutional. Despite the deep moral conviction that motivated me—despite the fact that my violation of the discriminatory racial laws would have been in a great cause—I would have been consigned to jail, with no possible remedy except the remote prospect of a pardon.

This may seem harsh. It may seem especially harsh if we assume that I profoundly believe that the law I am violating is immoral and unconstitutional, or and if we assume that the question of its constitutionality is close. *But this is what we mean by the rule of law:* both the government and the individual must accept the result of procedures by which the courts, and ultimately the Supreme Court, decide that the law is such and such, and not so and so; that the law has or has not been violated in a particular situation, and that it is or is not constitutional; and that the individual defendant has or has not been properly convicted and sentenced. . . .

The term "civil disobedience" has been used to apply to a person's refusal to obey a law which the person believes to be immoral or unconstitutional. John Milton's famous defiance of England's law requiring licensing of books by official censors is in this category. He openly announced that he would not comply with it. He assailed the censorship law as an intolerable restriction of freedom, contrary to the basic rights of Englishmen. . . .

. . . The motive of civil disobedience, whatever its type, does not confer immunity for law violation. Especially if the civil disobedience involves violence or a breach of public order prohibited by statute or ordinance, it is the state's duty to arrest the dissident. If he is properly arrested, charged, and convicted, he should be punished by fine or imprisonment, or both, in accordance with the provisions of law, unless the law is invalid in general or as applied.

He may be motivated by the highest moral principles. He may be passionately inspired. He may, indeed, be right in the eyes of history or morality or philosophy. These are not controlling. It is the state's duty to arrest and punish those who violate the laws designed to protect private safety and public order.

The Negroes in Detroit and Newark and Washington and Chicago who rioted, pillaged, and burned may have generations of provocation. They may have incontestable justification. They may have been pushed beyond endurance. In the riots following the assassination of Martin Luther King, Jr., the Negroes may have been understandably inflamed by the murder of their leading advocate of nonviolence. But that provides no escape from the consequences of their conduct. Rioters should be arrested, tried, and convicted. If the state does not do so, it is either because of a tactical judgment that arrest and prosecution would cause more harm than good, or because the state is incompetent.

The same principles apply to the police and officers of the law. They, too, are liable for their acts. The fact that they represent the state does not give them immunity from the consequences of brutality or lawlessness. They, like the rioters, may be motivated by long and acute provocation. It may be that their lawlessness was the direct product of fear, or of righteous anger. They may have been moved to violence by more pressure than they could endure. But they, too, are subject to the rule of law, and if they exceed the authorized bounds of firmness and self-protection and needlessly assaulted the people whom they encountered, they should be disciplined, tried, and convicted. It is a deplorable truth that because they are officers of the state they frequently escape the penalty for their lawlessness.

We are a government and a people under law. It is not merely *government* that must live under law. Each of us must live under law. Just as our form of life depends upon the government's subordination to law under the Constitution, so it also depends upon the individual's subservience to the laws duly prescribed. Both of these are essential.

Just as we expect the government to be bound by all laws, so each individual is bound by all the laws under the Constitution. He cannot pick and choose. He cannot substitute his own judgment or passion, however noble, for the rules of law. . . . A citizen cannot demand of his government or of other people obedience to the law, and at the same time claim a right in himself to break it by lawless conduct, free of punishment or penalty. . . .

The use of force or violence in the course of social protest is a far cry from civil disobedience as practiced by Gandhi. Gandhi's concept insists upon peaceful, nonviolent refusal to comply with a law. It assumes that the protester will be punished, and it requires peaceful submission to punishment.

Let me elaborate this by reference to an article written by Dr. Martin Luther King, Jr., and published in September 1961. In this article, Dr. King set forth the guiding principles of his approach to effective protest by civil disobedience. He said that many Negroes would disobey "unjust laws." These he defined as laws which a minority is compelled to observe but which are not binding on the majority. He said that this must be done openly and peacefully, and that those who do it must accept the penalty imposed by law for their conduct.

This is civil disobedience in a great tradition. It is peaceful, nonviolent disobedience of laws which are themselves unjust and which the protester challenges as invalid and unconstitutional.

Dr. King was involved in a case which illustrated this conception. He led a mass demonstration to protest segregation and discrimination in Birmingham. An injunction had been issued by a state court against the demonstration. But Dr. King disregarded the injunction and proceeded with the march as planned. He was arrested. He was prosecuted in the state court, convicted of contempt, and sentenced to serve five days in jail. He appealed, claiming that the First Amendment protected his violation of the injunction.

I have no doubt that Dr. King violated the injunction in the belief that it was invalid and his conduct was legally as well as morally justified. But the Supreme Court held that he was bound to obey the injunction unless and until it was set aside on appeal; and that he could not disregard the injunction even if he was right that the injunction was invalid. Dr. King went to jail and served his time.

I have no moral criticism to make of Dr. King's action in this incident, even though it turned out to be legally unjustified. He led a peaceable demonstration. He acted in good faith. There was good, solid basis for his belief that he did not have to obey the injunction—until the Supreme Court ruled the other way. The Court disagreed with him by a vote of five to four. I was one of the dissenters. Then Dr. King, without complaint or histrionics, accepted the penalty of misjudgment. This, I submit, is action in the great tradition of social protest in a democratic society where all citizens, including protesters, are subject to the rule of law. . . .

I have emphasized that our scheme of law affords great latitude for dissent and opposition. It compels wide tolerance not only for their expression but also for the organization of people and forces to bring about the acceptance of the dissenter's claim. Both our institutions and the characteristics of our national behavior make it possible for opposition to be translated into policy, for dissent to prevail. We have alternatives to violence. . . .

It would be idle and foolish to expect that . . . dissident groups —the Negroes and the youth-generation—would confine themselves to the polite procedures that the other segments of our society would wish. We can hardly claim that their deserving demands would be satisfied if they did not vigorously assert them. We certainly cannot claim that those demands would be satisfied just as soon without their strenuous insistence. But we can, I think, require that the methods which they adopt be within the limits which an organized, democratic society can endure.

An organized society cannot and will not long endure personal and property damage, whatever the reason, context, or occasion.

An organized society will not endure invasion of private premises or public offices, or interference with the work or activities of others if adequate facilities for protest and demonstration are otherwise available.

A democratic society should and must tolerate criticism, protest, demand for change, and organizations and demonstrations within the generally defined limits of the law to marshal support for dissent and change. It should and must make certain that facilities and protection where necessary are provided for these activities.

Protesters and change-seekers must adopt methods within the limits of the law. Despite the inability of anyone always to be certain of the line between the permissible and forbidden, as a practical matter the lines are reasonably clear.

Violence must not be tolerated; damage to persons or property is intolerable. Any mass demonstration is dangerous, although it may

be the most effective consitutional tool of dissent. But it must be
kept within the limits of its permissible purpose. The functions of
mass demonstrations, in the city or on the campus, are to communicate a point of view; to arouse enthusiasm and group cohesiveness among participants; to attract others to join; and to impress
upon the public and the authorities the point advocated by the
protesters, the urgency of their demand, and the power behind it.
These functions do not include terror, riot, or pillage. . . .

In my judgment civil disobedience—the deliberate violation of
law—is never justified in our nation, where the law being violated
is not itself the focus or target of the protest. So long as our governments obey the mandate of the Constitution and assure facilities
and protection for the powerful expression of individual and mass
dissent, the disobedience of laws which are not themselves the target of the protest—the violation of law merely as a technique of
demonstration—constitutes an act of rebellion, not merely of dissent.

Civil disobedience is violation of law. Any violated [sic] of law
must be punished, whatever its purpose, as the theory of civil disobedience recognizes. But law violation directed not to the laws or
practices that are the subject of dissent, but to unrelated laws
which are disobeyed merely to dramatize dissent, may be morally
as well as politically unacceptable.

At the beginning of this discussion, I presented the dilemma of
obedience to law and the need that sometimes may arise to disobey profoundly immoral or unconstitutional laws. This is another
kind of civil disobedience, and the only kind that, in my view, is
ever truly defensible as a matter of social morality.

It is only in respect to such laws—laws that are basically offensive to fundamental values of life or the Constitution—that a moral
(although not a legal) defense of law violation can possibly be
urged. Anyone assuming to make the judgment that a law is in this
category assumes a terrible burden. He has undertaken a fearful
moral as well as legal responsibility. He should be prepared to
submit to prosecution by the state for the violation of law and the
imposition of punishment if he is wrong or unsuccessful. He should
even admit the correctness of the state's action in seeking to en-

force its laws, and he should acquiesce in the ultimate judgment of the courts.

For after all, each of us is a member of an organized society. Each of us benefits from its existence and its order. And each of us must be ready, like Socrates, to accept the verdict of its institutions if we violate their mandate and our challenge is not vindicated.

POLICE BRUTALITY?

ALBERT J. REISS, JR.

"Police Brutality—Answers to Key Questions," *Trans-action*, 5, No. 8 (July–August 1968), 10–19. At the time this article was published, Dr. Reiss was professor of sociology, chairman of the department, and director of the Center for Research on Social Organization at the University of Michigan, Ann Arbor.

"For three years, there has been through the courts and the streets a dreary procession of citizens with broken heads and bruised bodies against few of whom was violence needed to effect an arrest. Many of them had done nothing to deserve an arrest. In a majority of such cases, no complaint was made. If the victim complains, his charge is generally dismissed. The police are practically above the law."

This statement was published in 1903, and its author was the Hon. Frank Moss, a former police commissioner of New York City. Clearly, today's charges of police brutality and mistreatment of citizens have a precedent in American history—but never before has the issue of police brutality assumed the public urgency it has today. In Newark, in Detroit, in Watts, in Harlem, and, in fact, in practically every city that has had a civil disturbance, "deep hostility between police and ghetto" was, reports the Kerner Commission, "a primary cause of the riots."

Whether or not the police accept the words "police brutality," the public now wants some plain answers to some plain questions. How widespread is police mistreatment of citizens? Is it on the increase? Why do policemen mistreat citizens? Do the police mistreat Negroes more than whites?

To find some answers, 36 people working for the Center of Research on Social Organization observed police-citizen encounters in the cities of Boston, Chicago, and Washington, D.C. For seven days a week, for seven weeks during the summer of 1966, these observers, with police permission, sat in patrol cars and monitored booking and lockup procedures in high-crime precincts.

Obtaining information about police mistreatment of citizens is no simple matter. National and state civil-rights commissions receive hundreds of complaints charging mistreatment—but proving these allegations is difficult. The few local civilian-review boards, such as the one in Philadelphia, have not produced any significant volume of complaints leading to the dismissal or disciplining of policemen for alleged brutality. Generally, police chiefs are silent on the matter, or answer charges of brutality with vague statements that they will investigate any complaints brought to their attention. Rank-and-file policemen are usually more outspoken: They often insinuate that charges of brutality are part of a conspiracy against them, and against law and order.

The Meaning of Brutality

What citizens mean by police brutality covers the full range of police practices. These practices, contrary to the impression of many civil-rights activists, are not newly devised to deal with Negroes in our urban ghettos. They are ways in which the police have traditionally behaved in dealing with certain citizens, particularly those in the lower classes. The most common of these practices are:

—the use of profane and abusive language,
—commands to move on or get home,
—stopping and questioning people on the street or searching them and their cars,
—threats to use force if not obeyed,
—prodding with a nightstick or approaching with a pistol, and
—the actual use of physical force or violence itself.

Citizens and the police do not always agree on what constitutes proper police practice. What is "proper," or what is "brutal," it need hardly be pointed out, is more a matter of judgment about what someone did than a description of what police do. What is important is not the practice itself but what it means to the citizen. What citizens object to and call "police brutality" is really the judgment that they have not been treated with the full rights and dignity owing citizens in a democratic society. Any practice that degrades their status, that restricts their freedom, that annoys or harasses them, or that uses physical force is frequently seen as unnecessary and unwarranted. More often than not, they are probably right.

Many police practices serve only to degrade the citizen's sense of himself and his status. This is particularly true with regard to the way the police use language. Most citizens who have contact with the police object less to their use of four-letter words than to *how* the policeman talks to them. Particularly objectionable is the habit policemen have of "talking down" to citizens, of calling them names that deprecate them in their own eyes and those of others. More than one Negro citizen has complained: "They talk down to me as if I had no name—like 'boy' or 'man' or whatever, or they call me 'Jack' or by my first name. They don't show me no respect."

Members of minority groups and those seen as nonconformists, for whatever reason, are the most likely targets of status degradation. Someone who has been drinking may be told he is a "bum" or a "shitty wino." A woman walking alone may be called a "whore." And a man who doesn't happen to meet a policeman's standard of how one should look or dress may be met with the remark, "What's the matter, you a queer?" A white migrant from the south may be called a "hillbilly" or "shitkicker"; a Puerto Rican, a "pork chop"; a young boy, a "punk kid." When the policeman does not use words of status degradation, his manner may be degrading. Citizens want to be treated as people, not as "non-persons" who are talked about as if they were not present.

That many Negroes believe that the police have degraded their status is clear from surveys in Watts, Newark, and Detroit. One out of every five Negroes in our center's post-riot survey in Detroit reports that the police have "talked down to him." More than one in ten says a policeman has "called me a bad name."

To be treated as "suspicious" is not only degrading, but is also a form of harassment and a restriction on the right to move freely.

The harassing tactics of the police—dispersing social street-gatherings, the indiscriminate stopping of Negroes on foot or in cars, and commands to move on or go home—are particularly common in ghetto areas.

Young people are the most likely targets of harassing orders to disperse or move on. Particularly in summer, ghetto youths are likely to spend lots of time in public places. Given the inadequacy of their housing and the absence of community facilities, the street corner is often their social center. As the police cruise the busy streets of the ghetto, they frequently shout at groups of teenagers to "get going" or "get home." Our observations of police practices show that *white as well as Negro youths* are often harassed in this way.

Frequently the policeman may leave the car and threaten or force youths to move on. For example, one summer evening as the scout car cruised a busy street of a white slum, the patrolmen observed three white boys and a girl on a corner. When told to move on, they mumbled and grumbled in undertones, angering the police by their failure to comply. As they slowly moved off, the officers pushed them along the street. Suddenly one of the white patrolmen took a lighted cigarette from a 15-year-old boy and stuck it in his face, pushing him forward as he did so. When the youngsters did move on, one policeman remarked to the observer that the girl was "nothing but a whore." Such tactics can only intensify resentment toward the police.

Police harassment is not confined to youth. One in every four adult Negroes in Detroit claims he has been stopped and questioned by the police without good reason. The same proportion claim they have been stopped in their cars. One in five says he has been searched unnecessarily; and one in six says that his car was searched for no good reason. The members of an interracial couple, particularly a Negro man accompanying a white woman, are perhaps the most vulnerable to harassment.

What citizens regard as police brutality many policemen consider necessary for law enforcement. While degrading epithets and abusive language may no longer be considered proper by either police commanders or citizens, they often disagree about other practices related to law enforcement. For example, although many citizens see "stop and question" or "stop and frisk" procedures as harassment, police commanders usually regard them merely as "aggressive prevention" to curb crime.

PHYSICAL FORCE—OR SELF-DEFENSE?

The nub of the police-brutality issue seems to lie in police use of physical force. By law, the police have the right to use such force if necessary to make an arrest, to keep the peace, or to maintain public order. But just how much force is necessary or proper?

This was the crucial problem we attempted to answer by placing observers in the patrol cars and in the precincts. Our 36 observers, divided equally between Chicago, Boston, and Washington, were responsible for reporting the details of all stiuations where police used physical force against a citizen. To ensure the observation of a large number of encounters, two high-crime police precincts were monitored in Boston and Chicago; four in Washington. At least one precinct was composed of primarily Negro residents, another primarily of whites. Where possible, we also tried to select precincts with considerable variation in social-class composition. Given the criterion of a high-crime rate, however, people of low socio-economic status predominated in most of the areas surveyed.

The law fails to provide simple rules about what—and how much—force that policemen can properly use. The American Bar Foundation's study *Arrest,* by Wayne La Fave, put the matter rather well, stating that the courts of all states would undoubtedly agree that in making an arrest a policeman should use only that amount of force he reasonably believes necessary. But La Fave also pointed out that there is no agreement on the question of when it is better to let the suspect escape than to employ "deadly" force.

Even in those states where the use of deadly force is limited by law, the kinds of physical force a policeman may use are not clearly defined. No kind of force is categorically denied a policeman, since he is always permitted to use deadly force in self-defense.

This right to protect himself often leads the policeman to argue

self-defense whenever he uses force. We found that many policemen, whether or not the facts justify it, regularly follow their use of
force with the charge that the citizen was assaulting a policeman
or resisting arrest. Our observers also found that some policemen
even carry pistols and knives that they have confiscated while
searching citizens; they carry them so they may be placed at a
scene should it be necessary to establish a case of self-defense.

Of course, not all cases of force involve the use of *unnecessary*
force. Each instance of force reported by our observers was examined and judged to be either necessary or unnecessary. Cases involving simple restraint—holding a man by the arm—were deliberately excluded from consideration, even though a policeman's
right to do so can, in many instances, be challenged. In judging
when police force is "unwarranted," "unreasonable," or "undue,"
we rather deliberately selected only those cases in which a policeman struck the citizen with his hands, fist, feet, or body, or where
he used a weapon of some kind—such as a nightstick or a pistol.
In these cases, had the policeman been found to have used physical force improperly, he could have been arrested on complaint
and, like any other citizen, charged with a simple or aggravated
assault. A physical assault on a citizen was judged to be "improper" or "unnecessary" only if force was used in one or more of
the following ways:

If a policeman physically assaulted a citizen and then failed to
make an arrest; proper use involves an arrest.

If the citizen being arrested did not, by word or deed, resist the
policeman; force should be used only if it is necessary to make the
arrest.

If the policeman, even though there was resistance to the arrest,
could easily have restrained the citizen in other ways.

If a large number of policemen were present and could have assisted in subduing the citizen in the station, in lockup, and in the
interrogation rooms.

If an offender was handcuffed and made no attempt to flee or
offer violent resistance.

If the citizen resisted arrest, but the use of force continued even
after the citizen was subdued.

In the seven-week period, we found 37 cases in which force was used improperly. In all, 44 citizens had been assaulted. In 15 of these cases, no one was arrested. Of these, 8 had offered no verbal or physical resistance whatsoever, while 7 had.

An arrest was made in 22 of the cases. In 13, force was exercised in the station house when at least four other policemen were present. In two cases, there was no verbal or physical resistance to the arrest, but force was still applied. In two other cases, the police applied force to a handcuffed offender in a field setting. And in five situations, the offender did resist arrest, but the policeman continued to use force even after he had been subdued.

Just how serious was the improper use of force in these 44 cases? Naturally there were differences in degree of injury. In about one-half of the cases, the citizen appeared little more than physically bruised; in three cases, the amount of force was so great that the citizen had to be hospitalized. Despite the fact that cases can easily be selected for their dramatic rather than their representative quality, I want to present a few to give a sense of what the observers saw and reported as undue use of force.

Observing on Patrol

In the following two cases, the citizens offered no physical or verbal resistance, and the two white policemen made no arrest. It is the only instance in which the observers saw the same two policemen using force improperly more than once.

The police precinct in which these incidents occurred is typical of those found in some of our larger cities, where the patrolmen move routinely from gold coast to slum. There are little islands of the rich and poor, of old Americans and new, of recent migrants and old settlers. One moves from high-rise areas of middle- and upper-income whites through an area of the really old Americans—Indians—to an enclave of the recently arrived. The recently arrived are primarily those the policemen call "hillbillies" (migrants from Kentucky and Tennessee) and "porkchops" (Puerto Ricans). There are ethnic islands of Germans and Swedes. Although there is a small area where Negroes live, it is principally a precinct of whites. The police in the district are, with one exception, white.

On a Friday in the middle of July, the observer arrived for the 4 to 12 midnight watch. The beat car that had been randomly chosen carried two white patrolmen—one with 14 years of experience in the precinct, the other with three.

The watch began rather routinely as the policemen cruised the district. Their first radio dispatch came at about 5:30 p.m. They were told to investigate two drunks in a cemetery. On arriving they found two white men "sleeping one off." Without questioning the men, the older policeman began to search one of them, ripping his shirt and hitting him in the groin with a nightstick. The younger policeman, as he searched the second, ripped away the seat of his trousers, exposing his buttocks. The policemen then prodded the men toward the cemetery fence and forced them to climb it, laughing at the plight of the drunk with the exposed buttocks. As the drunks went over the fence, one policeman shouted, "I ought to run you fuckers in!" The other remarked to the observer, "Those assholes won't be back; a bunch of shitty winos."

Not long after they returned to their car, the policemen stopped a woman who had made a left turn improperly. She was treated very politely, and the younger policeman, who wrote the ticket, later commented to the observer, "Nice lady." At 7:30 they were dispatched to check a suspicious auto. After a quick check, the car was marked abandoned.

Shortly after a 30-minute break for a 7:30 "lunch," the two policemen received a dispatch to take a burglary report. Arriving at a slum walkup, the police entered a room where an obviously drunk white man in his late 40s insisted that someone had entered and stolen his food and liquor. He kept insisting that it had been taken and that he had been forced to borrow money to buy beer. The younger policeman, who took the report, kept harassing the man, alternating between mocking and badgering him rhetorical questions. [sic] "You say your name is Half-A-Wit [for Hathaway]? Do you sleep with niggers? How did you vote on the bond issue? Are you sure that's all that's missing? Are you a virgin yet?" The man responded to all of this with the seeming vagueness and joviality of the intoxicated, expressing gratitude for the policemen's help as they left. The older policeman remarked to the observer as they left, "Ain't drunks funny?"

For the next hour little happened, but as the two were moving across the precinct shortly after 10 p.m. a white man and a woman in their 50s flagged them down. Since they were obviously "substantial" middle-class citizens of the district, the policemen listened to their complaints that a Negro man was causing trouble inside the public-transport station from which they had just emerged. The woman said that he had sworn at her. The older policeman remarked, "What's a nigger doing up here? He should be down on Franklin Road!"

With that, they ran into the station and grabbed the Negro man who was inside. Without questioning him, they shoved him into a phone booth and began beating him with their fists and a flashlight. They also hit him in the groin. Then they dragged him out and kept him on his knees. He pleaded that he had just been released from a mental hospital that day and, begging not to be hit again, asked them to let him return to the hospital. One policeman said: "Don't you like us, nigger? I like to beat niggers and rip out their eyes." They took him outside to their patrol car. Then they decided to put him on a bus, telling him that he was returning to the hospital; they deliberately put him on a bus going in the opposite direction. Just before the Negro boarded the bus, he said, "You police just like to shoot and beat people." The first policeman replied, "Get moving, nigger, or I'll shoot you." The man was crying and bleeding as he was put on the bus. Leaving the scene, the younger policeman commented, "He won't be back."

For the rest of the evening, the two policemen kept looking for drunks and harassing any they found. They concluded the evening by being dispatched to an address where, they were told, a man was being held for the police. No one answered their knock. They left.

The station house has long been suspected of harboring questionable police practices. Interrogation-room procedures have been attacked, particularly because of the methods the police have used to get confessions. The drama of the confession in the interrogation room has been complete with bright lights and physical torture.

Whether or not such practices have ever existed on the scale suggested by popular accounts, confessions in recent years, even by accounts of offenders, have rarely been accompanied by such high drama. But recently the interrogation room has come under fire again for its failure to protect the constitutional rights of the suspect to remain silent and to have legal counsel.

Backstage at the Station

The police station, however, is more than just a series of cubicles called interrogation rooms. There are other rooms and usually a lockup as well. Many of these are also hidden from public view. It is not surprising, then, that one-third of all the observations of the undue use of force occurred within the station.

In any station there normally are several policemen present who should be able to deal with almost any situation requiring force that arises. In many of the situations that were observed, as many as seven and eight policemen were present, most of whom simply stood by and watched force being used. The custom among policemen, it appeared, is that you intervene only if a fellow policeman needs help, or if you have been personally offended or affronted by those involved.

Force is used unnecessarily at many different points and places in the station. The citizen who is not cooperative during the booking process may be pushed or shoved, have his handcuffs twisted with a nightstick, have his foot stomped, or be pulled by the hair. All of these practices were reported by policemen as ways of obtaining "cooperation." But it was clear that the booking could have been completed without any of this harassment.

The lockup was the scene of some of the most severe applications of force. Two of the three cases requiring hospitalization came about when an offender was "worked over" in the lockup. To be sure, the arrested are not always cooperative when they get in the lockup, and force may be necessary to place them in a cell. But the amount of force observed hardly seemed necessary.

One evening an observer was present in the lockup when two white policemen came in with a white man. The suspect had been handcuffed and brought to the station because he had proved obstreperous after being arrested for a traffic violation. Apparently he had been drinking. While waiting in the lockup, the man began to urinate on the floor. In response, the policeman began to beat the man. They jumped him, knocked him down, and beat his head against the concrete floor. He required emergency treatment at a nearby hospital.

At times a policeman may be involved in a kind of escalation of force. Using force appropriately for an arrest in the field seemingly sets the stage for its later use, improperly, in the station. The following case illustrates how such a situation may develop:

Within a large city's high-crime rate precinct, occupied mostly by Negroes, the police responded to an "officer in trouble" call. It is difficult to imagine a call that brings a more immediate response, so a large number of police cars immediately converged at an intersection of a busy public street where a bus had been stopped. Near the bus, a white policeman was holding two young Negroes at gun point. The policeman reported that he had responded to a summons from the white bus-driver complaining that the boys had refused to pay their fares and had used obscene language. The policeman also reported that the boys swore at him, and one swung at him while the other drew a screwdriver and started toward him. At that point, he said, he drew his pistol.

The policemen placed one of the offenders in handcuffs and began to transport both of them to the station. While driving to the station, the driver of one car noted that the other policeman, transporting the other boy, was struggling with him. The first policeman stopped and entered the other patrol car. The observer reported that he kept hitting the boy who was handcuffed until the boy appeared completely subdued. The boy kept saying, "You don't have any right to beat me. I don't care if you kill me."

After the policemen got the offenders to the station, although the boys no longer resisted them, the police began to beat them while they were handcuffed in an interrogation room. One of the boys hollered: "You can't beat me like this! I'm only a kid, and my hands are tied." Later one of the policemen commented to the observer: "On the street you can't beat them. But when you get to the station, you can instill some respect in them."

Cases where the offender resists an arrest provide perhaps the most difficulty in judging the legitimacy of the force applied. An encounter that began as a dispatch to a disturbance at a private residence was one case about which there could be honest difference in judgment. On arrival, the policemen—one white, the other Negro—met a white woman who claimed that her husband, who was in the back yard and drunk, had beaten her. She asked the policemen to "take him in." The observer reported that the police found the man in the house. When they attempted to take him, he resisted by placing his hands between the door jamb. Both policemen then grabbed him. The Negro policeman said, "We're going to have trouble, so let's finish it right here." He grabbed the offender and knocked him down. Both policemen then wrestled with the man, handcuffed him, and took him to the station. As they did so, one of the policemen remarked, "These sons of bitches want to fight, so you have to break them quick."

A Minimal Picture?

The reader, as well as most police administrators, may be skeptical about reports that policemen used force in the presence of observers. Indeed, one police administrator, indignant over reports of undue use of force in his department, seemed more concerned that the policemen had permitted themselves to be observed behaving improperly than he was about their improper behavior. When demanding to know the names of the policemen who had used force improperly so he could discharge them—a demand we could not meet, since we were bound to protect our sources of information —he remarked, "Any officer who is stupid enough to behave that way in the presence of outsiders deserves to be fired."

There were and are a number of reasons why our observers were able to see policemen behaving improperly. We entered each department with the full cooperation of the top administrators. So far as the men in the line were concerned, our chief interest was in how citizens behave toward the police, a main object of our study. Many policemen, given their strong feelings against citizens, fail to see that their own behavior is equally open to observation. Furthermore, our observers are trained to fit into a role of trust—one that is genuine, since most observers are actually sympathetic to the plight of the policeman, if not to his behavior.

Finally, and this is a fact all too easily forgotten, people cannot change their behavior in the presence of others as easily as many think. This is particularly true when people become deeply involved in certain situations. The policeman not only comes to "trust" the observer in the law-enforcement situation—regarding him as a source of additional help if necessary—but, when he becomes involved in a dispute with a citizen, he easily forgets that an observer is present. Partly because he does not know what else to do, in such situations the policeman behaves "normally." But should one cling to the notion that most policemen modify their behavior in the presence of outsiders, one is left with the uncomfortable conclusion that our cases represent a minimal picture of actual misbehavior.

Superficially it might seem that the use of an excessive amount of force against citizens is low. In only 37 of 3826 encounters observed did the police use undue force. Of the 4604 white citizens in these encounters, 27 experienced an excessive amount of force—a rate of 5.9 for every 1000 citizens involved. The comparable rate for 5960 Negroes, of whom 17 experienced an excessive amount of force, is 2.8. Thus, whether one considers these rates high or low, the fact is that the *rate of excessive force for all white citizens in encounters with the police is twice that for Negro citizens.*

A rate depends, however, upon selecting a population that is logically the target of force. What we have just given is a rate for *all* citizens involved in encounters with the police. But many of these citizens are not logical targets of force. Many, for example, simply call the police to complain about crimes against themselves or their property. And others are merely witnesses to crimes.

The more logical target population consists of citizens whom the police allege to be offenders—a population of suspects. In our study, there were 643 white suspects, 27 of whom experienced undue use of force. This yields an abuse rate of 41.9 per 1000 white suspects. The comparable rate for 751 Negro suspects, of whom 17 experienced undue use of force, is 22.6 per 1000. If one accepts these rates as reasonably reliable estimates of the undue force against suspects, then there should be little doubt that in major metropolitan areas the sort of behavior commonly called "police brutality" is far from rare.

Popular impression casts police brutality as a racial matter—white police mistreating Negro citizens. The fact is that white suspects are more liable to being treated improperly by the police than Negro suspects are. This, however, should not be confused with the chances a citizen takes of being mistreated. In two of the cities we studied, Negroes are a minority. The chances, then, that any Negro has of being treated improperly are, perhaps, more nearly comparable to that for whites. If the rates are comparable, then one might say that the application of force unnecessarily by the police operates without respect to the race of an offender.

Many people believe that the race of the policeman must affect his use of force, particularly since many white policemen express prejudice against Negroes. Our own work shows that in the police precincts made up largely of Negro citizens, over three-fourths of the policemen express prejudice against Negroes. Only 1 percent express sympathetic attitudes. But as sociologists and social psychologists have often shown, prejudice and attitudes do not necessarily carry over into discriminatory actions.

Our findings show that there is little difference between the rate of force used by white and by Negro policemen. Of the 54 policemen observed using too much force, 45 were white and 9 were Negro. For every 100 white policemen, 8.7 will use force; for every 100 Negro policemen, 9.8 will. What this really means, though, is that about one in every 10 policemen in high-crime rate areas of cities sometimes uses force unnecessarily.

Yet, one may ask, doesn't prejudice enter into the use of force? Didn't some of the policemen who were observed utter prejudiced statements toward Negroes and other minority-group members? Of course they did. But the question of whether it was their prejudice or some other factor that motivated them to mistreat Negroes is not so easily answered.

Still, even though our figures show that a white suspect is more liable to encounter violence, one may ask whether white policemen victimize Negroes more than whites. We found, for the most part, that they do not. Policemen, both Negro and white, are most likely to exercise force against members of their *own* race:

67 percent of the citizens victimized by white policemen were white.

71 percent of the citizens victimized by Negro policemen were Negro.

To interpret these statistics correctly, however, one should take into account the differences in opportunity policemen have to use force against members of their own and other races. Negro policemen, in the three cities we studied, were far *less* likely to police white citizens than white policemen were to police Negroes. Negro policemen usually policed other Negroes, while white policemen policed both whites and Negroes about equally. In total numbers, then, more white policemen than Negro policemen used force against Negroes. But this is explained by the fact that whites make up 85 percent of the police force, and more than 50 percent of all policemen policing Negroes.

Though no precise estimates are possible, the facts just given suggest that white policemen, even though they are prejudiced toward Negroes, do not discriminate against Negroes in the excessive use of force. The use of force by the police is more readily explained by police culture than it is by the policeman's race. Indeed, in the few cases where we observed a Negro policeman using unnecessary force against white citizens, there was no evidence that he did so because of his race.

The disparity between our findings and the public's sense that Negroes are the main victims of police brutality can easily be resolved if one asks how the public becomes aware of the police misusing force.

The Victims and the Turf

Fifty years ago, the immigrants to our cities—Eastern and Southern Europeans such as the Poles and the Italians—complained about police brutality. Today the new immigrants to our cities—mostly Negroes from the rural south—raise their voices through the civil rights movement, through black-nationalist and other race-conscious organizations. There is no comparable voice for white citizens since, except for the Puerto Ricans, they now lack the nationality organizations that were once formed to promote and protect the interests of their immigrant forbears.

Although policemen do not seem to select their victims according to race, two facts stand out. All victims were offenders, and all were from the lower class. Concentrating as we did on high-crime rate areas of cities, we do not have a representative sample of residents in any city. Nonetheless, we observed a sizable minority of middle- and upper-status citizens, some of whom were offenders. But since no middle- or upper-class offender, white or Negro, was the victim of an excessive amount of force, it appears that the lower class bears the brunt of victimization by the police.

The most likely victim of excessive force is a lower-class man of either race. No white woman and only two Negro women were victimized. The difference between the risk assumed by white and by Negro women can be accounted for by the fact that far more Negro women are processed as suspects or offenders.

Whether or not a policeman uses force unnecessarily depends upon the social setting in which the encounter takes place. Of the 37 instances of excessive force, 37 percent took place in police-controlled settings, such as the patrol car or the precinct station. Public places, usually streets, accounted for 41 percent, and 16 percent took place in a private residence. The remaining 6 percent occurred in commercial settings. This is not, of course, a random sample of settings where the police encounter suspects.

What is most obvious, and most disturbing, is that the police are very likely to use force in settings that they control. Although only 18 percent of all situations involving suspects ever ended up at the station house, 32 percent of all situations where an excessive amount of force was used took place in the police station.

No one who accepts the fact that the police sometimes use an excessive amount of force should be surprised by our finding that they often select their own turf. What should be apparent to the nation's police administrators, however, is that these settings are under their command and control. Controlling the police in the field, where the policeman is away from direct supervision, is understandably difficult. But the station house is the police administrator's domain. The fact that one in three instances of excessive force took place in settings that can be directly controlled should cause concern among police officials.

The presence of citizens who might serve as witnesses against a policeman should deter him from undue use of force. Indeed, procedures for the review of police conduct are based on the presumption that one can get this kind of testimony. Otherwise, one is left simply with a citizen complaint and contrary testimony by the policeman—a situation in which it is very difficult to prove the citizen's allegation.

In most situations involving the use of excessive force, there were witnesses. In our 37 cases, there were bystanders present three-fourths of the time. But in only one situation did the group present sympathize with the citizen and threaten to report the policeman. A complaint was filed on that incident—the only one of the 37 observed instances of undue force in which a formal complaint was filed.

All in all, the situations where excessive force was used were devoid of bystanders who did not have a stake in being "against" the offender. Generally, they were fellow policemen, or fellow offenders whose truthfulness could be easily challenged. When a policeman uses undue force, then, he usually does not risk a complaint against himself or testimony from witnesses who favor the complainant against the policeman. This, as much as anything, probably accounts for the low rate of formal complaints against policemen who use force unnecessarily.

A striking fact is that in more than one-half of all instances of undue coercion, at least one other policeman was present who did not participate in the use of force. This shows that, for the most part, the police do not restrain their fellow policemen. On the contrary, there were times when their very presence encouraged the use of force. One man brought into the lockup for threatening a policeman with a pistol was so severely beaten by this policeman that he required hospitalization. During the beating, some fellow policemen propped the man up, while others shouted encouragement. Though the official police code does not legitimate this practice, police culture does.

Victims—Defiant or Deviant

Now, are there characteristics of the offender or his behavior that precipitate the use of excessive force by the police? Superficially, yes. Almost one-half of the cases involved open defiance of police authority (39 percent) or resisting arrest (9 percent). Open defiance of police authority, however, is what the policeman defines as *his* authority, not necessarily "official" authority. Indeed in 40 percent of the cases that the police considered open defiance, the policeman never executed an arrest—a somewhat surprising fact for those who assume that policemen generally "cover" improper use of force with a "bona-fide" arrest and a charge of resisting arrest.

But it is still of interest to know what a policeman *sees* as defiance. Often he seems threatened by a simple refusal to acquiesce to his own authority. A policeman beat a handcuffed offender because, when told to sit, the offender did not sit down. One Negro woman was soundly slapped for her refusal to approach the police car and identify herself.

Important as a threat to his authority may appear to the policeman, there were many more of these instances in which the policeman did *not* respond with the use of force. The important issue seems to be whether the policeman manages to assert his authority despite the threat to it. I suspect that policemen are more likely to respond with excessive force when they define the situation as one in which there remains a question as to who is "in charge."

Similarly, some evidence indicates that harassment of deviants plays a role in the undue use of force. Incidents involving drunks made up 27 percent of all incidents of improper use of force; an additional 5 percent involved homosexuals or narcotics users. Since deviants generally remain silent victims to avoid public exposure of their deviance, they are particularly susceptible to the use of excessive force.

It is clear, though, that the police encounter many situations involving deviants where no force is used. Generally they respond to them routinely. What is surprising, then, is that the police do not mistreat deviants more than they do. The explanation may lie in the kind of relationships the police have with deviants. Many are valuable to the police because they serve as informers. To mistreat them severely would be to cut off a major source of police intelligence. At the same time, deviants are easily controlled by harassment.

Clearly, we have seen that police mistreatment of citizens exists. It is, however, on the increase? [sic]

Citizen complaints against the police are common, and allegations that the police use force improperly are frequent. There is evidence that physical brutality exists today. But there is also evidence, from the history of our cities, that the police have long engaged in the use of unneccessary physical force. No one can say with confidence whether there is more or less of it today than there was at the turn of the century.

What we lack is evidence that would permit us to calculate comparative rates of police misuse of force for different periods of American history. Only recently have we begun to count and report the volume of complaints against the police. And the research reported in this article represents the only attempt to estimate the amount of police mistreatment by actual observation of what the police do to citizens.

Lack of Information

Police chiefs are notoriously reluctant to disclose information that would allow us to assess the nature and volume of complaints against the police. Only a few departments have begun to report something about citizen complaints. And these give us very little information.

Consider, for example, the 1966 Annual Report released by the New Orleans Police Department. It tells us that there were 208 cases of "alleged police misconduct on which action was taken." It fails to tell us whether there were any allegations that are *not* included among these cases. Are these all the allegations that came to the attention of the department? Or are they only those the department chose to review as "police disciplinary matters"? Of the 208 cases the department considered "disciplinary matters," the report tells us that no disciplinary action was taken in 106 cases. There were 11 cases that resulted in 14 dismissals; 56 cases that resulted in 72 suspensions, fines, or loss of days; and 35 cases involving 52 written or verbal "reprimands" or "cautionings."

The failure of the report to tell us the charge against the policeman is a significant omission. We cannot tell how many of these allegations involved improper use of force, how many involved verbal abuse or harassment, how many involved police felonies or misdemeanors, and so on. In such reports, the defensive posture of the nation's police departments is all too apparent. Although the 1966 report of the New Orleans Police Department tells us much about what the police allege were the felonies and misdemeanors by citizens of New Orleans, it tells us nothing about what citizens allege was misconduct by the police!

Many responsible people believe that the use of physical brutality by the police is on the wane. They point to the fact that, at least outside the South, there are more reports of other forms of police mistreatment of citizens than reports of undue physical coercion. They also suggest that third-degree interrogations and curbstone justice with the nightstick are less common. It does not seem unreasonable, then, to assume that police practices that degrade a citizen's status or that harass him and restrict his freedom are more common than police misuse of force. But that may have always been so.

Whether or not the policeman's "sense of justice" and his use of unnecessary force have changed remains an open question. Forms may change while practices go on. To move misuse from the street to the station house, or from the interrogation room to the lockup, changes the place but not the practice itself.

Our ignorance of just what goes on between police and citizens poses one of the central issues in policing today: How can we make the police accountable to the citizenry in a democratic society and yet not hamstring them in their legitimate pursuit of law and order? There are no simple answers.

Police departments are organizations that process people. All people-processing organizations face certain common problems. But the police administrator faces a problem in controlling practice with clients that is not found in most other organizations. The problem is that police contact with citizens occurs in the community, where direct supervision is not possible. Assuming our unwillingness to spend resources for almost one-to-one supervision, the problem for the police commander is to make policemen behave properly when they are not under direct supervision. He also faces the problem of making them behave properly in the station house as well.

Historically, we have found but one way—apart from supervision—that deals with this problem. That solution is professionalization of workers. Perhaps only through the professionalization of the police can we hope to solve the problem of police malpractice.

But lest anyone optimistically assume that professionalization will eliminate police malpractice altogether, we should keep in mind that problems of malpractice also occur regularly in both law and medicine.

POLICE BRUTALITY OR
PUBLIC BRUTALITY?

HON. ROBERT C. BYRD

Excerpted from "Police Brutality or Public Brutality?" *The Police Chief,*
XXXIII, No. 2 (February 1966), 8–10. At the time of publication Robert
C. Byrd was a member of the United States Senate.

LAW ENFORCEMENT in America is in trouble.

To me, this situation reflects that our entire country is in trouble,
because when our law enforcers are weakened and made impotent,
then the laws which govern our Nation are in danger of collapsing.

For any number of reasons and alleged lofty causes the men and
women of the law enforcement establishment are being made ineffectual. Alarmingly, a long parade of individuals with odious tactics are straining the tolerance of our Constitution to the breaking
point.

At the same time, this small cadre of confused idealists and irresponsible extremists are seeking to tear down respect for law and
for the law enforcement officer.

The American public is more and more being subjected and exposed to every conceivable kind of outrage by hordes of rag-tag
beatniks, agitators and professional troublemakers who insist upon
lying down in the streets, blocking traffic, forming human walls in
front of business establishments, swarming over private property,
and staging noisy sit-ins and demonstrations. All of this is supposedly being done in order to "dramatize" grievances against our society and against the policies of the American Government at
home and abroad.

This small band of demonstrators have so successfully cloaked
themselves in the mantle of martyrdom that few people have dared

to voice an objection for fear of being labeled "bigot." They have succeeded in mesmerizing large segments of our population to the extent that representatives of law and order have become pictured as the villains while lawless marchers and sit-downers have become the figures for compassion.

One of the unfortunate by-products of this curious public attitude is the denigration of the law enforcement officer. There is a great deal of furor these days over discrimination against Negroes and other minorities. Few stop to think, however, that a group most discriminated against today is the law enforcement officer. He is constantly the subject of usually unsubstantiated charges of police brutality. His will and his morale are being shattered because the clamor of such charges is not counteracted by support from law-abiding, decent citizens. He is being psychologically assailed and physically assaulted, and few responsible individuals have come to his aid. . . .

It seems everyone is concerned with police brutality and yet no one is concerned over what I like to term "public brutality"; that is, the maltreatment of our officers of the law by citizens of every type. Until the American public realizes the brutality which is being inflicted upon our police officers, the law, which is the cornerstone of our Republic, will continue to be flaunted and diluted.

I am appalled at the lengths to which some charlatans are going as they take advantage of sometimes legitimate civil rights protests. Piteously, they cry of persecution by police who use what they term, of all things, "oral brutality." At the same time, however, they themselves delight in using the same type of brutality against police officers by characterizing them as gestapo, fuzz and in terms too opprobrious to be printed. It is truly amazing that as far as these insincere street marchers are concerned, there is only one side to the coin. They are the only ones persecuted; the policeman wears the uniform of authority—which, in itself, is anathema to the hoodlum element—and, as an officer, he becomes a ready target for oral abuse, vituperation, and, yes, physical assaults. To overly militant leaders, a Negro policeman should not wince when he is called an "Uncle Tom" or a "handkerchief head," because he is on the side of the law.

To the exploiters of the strife which America is enduring, the only victims are the rioters, the looters, the arsonists, the snipers, the thieves, and the murderers who commit vicious crimes while falsely wrapping themselves in the banner of the civil rights movement. I do not mean to imply that Negroes and other minorities in this country have not been discriminated against nor that they have escaped injustices at the hands of the majority. As Mr. Quinn Tamm, Executive Director of the International Association of Chiefs of Police, has said, however, "We are tired of the cry that because one segment of our population has been deprived for 100 years the balance of society must accept a hundred years of anarchy." The majority happens to have some rights also, and it, too, has suffered some injustices.

In the last several years, the law has been made to work quite effectively for the benefit of the downtrodden. It seems, however, that the more the workable processes of democratic justice have been applied to right grievous wrongs, the more greedy and impatient some factions in our society have become. Not satisfied with what the law has done for them, they seem bent upon destroying the only truly effective safeguard they have.

This incongruous philosophy is also apparent in the activities of those who protest the overseas policies and activities of the U.S. Government. Again, the police are the prime targets of weird individuals who have infiltrated groups sincerely concerned about our involvement in Vietnam and elsewhere. We have seen these ideologically confused individuals storm the White House, the very ramparts of our country's dignity; we have seen them, in effect, pledging allegiance to the Government of Hanoi by holding aloft Vietcong flags and promoting blood banks for the enemy; we have seen attempts in Oakland, California, at thwarting the movement of military goods to our fighting men in Vietnam; we have seen police officers assaulted, cursed, spat upon, and bitten by so-called non-violent demonstrators allegedly seeking academic and political freedom on the campus of the University of California in Berkeley.

In these situations, the police have stolidly suffered the unjustified charge of "brutality" and "gestapo." To my way of thinking, the police in all of these incidents have handled their responsibili-

ties with restraint, patience and a gentleness which would be unknown in most any other country in the world. Meanwhile, however, pseudoliberal organizations continue to harp upon the
necessity that it is the duty of the police to insure that both protes-
tors and counter-protesters each have the opportunity to express
their views. The galling aspect of this admonition is that the police
are already aware of this. They are men of the law and know more
about their responsibilities than many of their detractors.

I wish to reiterate that the police have done an outstanding job
of protecting all factions. Of course, there have been exceptions,
and there will always be. Police are supposed to be impartial; yes,
but at the same time, they are not automatons. They are men of
emotions who happen to be wearing uniforms. It takes a man of
steel to ignore a Vietcong flag on America's streets. It takes an im-
perturbable man to calmly witness bearded idiots trampling the
Constitution and Bill of Rights. It takes a strong man to hold his
temper as he is spat upon and reviled by unwashed, scraggly-
haired revolutionaries and uncouth, insolent, irresponsible hoodlums.

When it is borne in mind that the police are a militarylike organization, it is surprising that they are able to maintain any degree
of composure in the face of such senseless rebellion. Many of them
have sons and brothers in Vietnam, and a draft card burner to
them is anathema—but they are not allowed to show it. Police also
have a great deal of sympathy with the troops in Vietnam because
they fight a similar type of dirty war in which the enemy is forever
striking from the shadows. The police know guerrilla warfare because they fight it day in and day out with criminals in America's
streets. They also know that among the chief goals of communism
and other un-American ideologies is that public faith in the police
must be destroyed in order for the seeds of dissension to be
planted.

The police also know that the campaigns against them are not
reckless ones. They are well planned, and there are pamphlets
written to educate militant demonstrators in ways of skirmishing
with police in order to make the law enforcement officer appear to
be the brutal aggressor.

The police accept this. They also accept the fact that it is their sworn duty to uphold the law and that they cannot be dissuaded from their responsibilities by the fact that they are made to *look* bad in the eyes of the public.

Since the beginning days of the modern sit-ins, wade-ins and sleep-ins, the police have worked through their professional organization, the International Association of Chiefs of Police, to devise means of counteracting these despicable tactics. Of course, the simple answer would be retaliation, but the police officer of today is more professional, and, through conferences, research and study, he is getting closer to devising means of nullifying these tactics; that is, carrying out the letter of the law with as little violence as possible despite the efforts made to place him in an untenable position.

So-called civil disobedience cannot be countenanced by the law enforcement officer. Under our legal system, when there is an intent to break a law the act which follows the intent constitutes a crime and the individual should be punished. Unfortunately, those who seek martyrdom do not wish to understand this. They prefer to violate the law and then receive amnesty. Civil disobedience and lawlessness cannot be excused. We cannot allow one American to blithely burn his draft card while another bravely gives his life for the honor of his country in Vietnam.

The enigma surrounding the exhibitionists who seek martyrdom is compounded by the fact that some well-intentioned souls, understandably worried about the dangers present in an age of nuclear energy and a day when injustice to minorities still exists, will continue to demonstrate as they have in the past. To people who act in a mature and sincere manner, I say it is their Constitutional right to peaceably and lawfully assemble and to petition the government, but laws must be obeyed and police officers respected by all. With regard to those who counsel and perpetrate unlawful acts, the majority of Americans must react with vigilance, sterness, [sic], and speed in the dispensing of just and legal deserts for the offenders.

I am appalled when I hear or read statements to the effect that this gang of hirsute ragmuffins [sic] is so small and their impact so negligible that they should be ignored. That this is not so is the reason this type of lawlessness must be stopped. The morale of our troops in Vietnam is obviously affected. The North Vietnamese concept of the American will is without question of misconstruction since the Hanoi Government believed such attitudes to be so widespread that it issued commemorative stamps depicting Americans picketing against the war and even went so far as to picture the grisly self-immolation by that unfortunate man on the grounds of the Pentagon as an indication of American beliefs.

Persons responsible for aiding our enemies and destroying Americans' faith in other Americans must be punished. Not the least among the reasons for this is the fact that our police who bear the first brunt of these activities must be supported by their community officials, by the press, and by the public. What does it avail a police officer, moreover, to risk life and limb in arresting rioters and unlawful protesters if they are freed and even lauded, by the courts and when our Constitution and Bill of Rights are twisted well beyond any meaning that our forefathers attempted to convey?

Recent events have emphasized that there has been a violent breach of two cardinal principles of our American society—the respect for law and order and the recourse to orderly process of law to seek redress of wrongs. There is a great cry that the police of this Nation must hew to the letter of the law, whereas others who do not agree with it have the right to break the law with impunity. The vast majority of the 300,000 men and women of the police service in this country are remaining within the framework of the law in the face of great provocation daily. When we reach the stage that the other side can break the law without punishment while the police must continue to use Marquis of Queensbury rules, then it is obvious which will be the loser. The loser will be John Q. Citizen—you and me, our wives and children, old and young, black and white, in city and hamlet all over America.

Our country cannot stand firm upon laws that are manipulated like clay. America can endure only so long as it has as its foundation solid bedrock. And, that bedrock is the law and the men and women who enforce it.

If the police of this Nation are not supported now, the law will perish, and this Republic cannot endure long thereafter.

THE SOCIAL ROLE OF A
COUNTY SHERIFF

T. C. ESSELSTYN

T. C. Esselstyn, "The Social Role of a County Sheriff," *Journal of Criminal Law, Criminology, and Police Science*, XLIV (July–August 1953), 177–84. Reprinted by special permission of the *Journal of Criminal Law, Criminology and Police Science*, Vol. XLIV, No. 2 (Copyright © 1953, by Northwestern University School of Law). In 1953, the author was a member of the Department of Sociology and Anthropology in Illinois State University.

RURAL CRIME is a neglected field in criminology. Standard texts devote scant space to it. Few research projects have focused upon it. Rural sociologists are concerned with other matters. . . .

For these and for many other reasons, it would seem that some idea of space and function should be substituted for the term rural in criminology. The substitute offered in this present article is the *open country*. It would be defined as the region beyond the metropolis as measured by daily commuting and marketing. Agriculture and other extractive industries are prominent features of its economy and these enterprises play an important part in the attitudes and social organization of the people who live there. It includes the towns, villages, and small cities—the trade and service centers of varying size that stud it. This is the composite region on which the relevant tables in the *Uniform Crime Reports* are actually based. . . . This area is what we probably have in mind when we say "rural."

An open country crime would be any crime on which an open country law enforcement officer takes action. One way to study such crime would be to see how that officer acts. Several types of officers could be selected but the one recommended is the county sheriff because for many parts of the United States he is still important in open country crime control. A convenient method for this purpose would be to follow Znaniecki's concept of a social role, breaking it down into its four components: the social circle, the social person, the social status or office, and the social function.[1]

What follows is a summary of a larger study in which this method was used.[2] The region selected was "Star County," Illinois, a fictitious name for an actual county which lies in the open country as defined earlier. The sheriff whose role was analysed served there between 1946 and 1950. No pretense is made that what obtains in Star County obtains in all open country areas, for a sufficient body of inductive studies executed along similar lines is not at hand. . . .

Star County, Illinois

The principal city of Star County is Hopkins, the county seat with some 37,000 inhabitants. Hopkins is an independent police district. Apart from operating the county jail there, the sheriff carries on none of his peace-keeping functions within its limits. The remaining 50,000 persons in the population are dispersed among twenty-two minor civil divisions and eighteen towns including the rural areas. A little over twelve percent of the employed population is engaged in agriculture. This is the largest single field of employment. . . .

Star County . . . may be characterized briefly as a wealthy corn belt county with a cash-grain economy in which corn and livestock are the principal features. Money, volume output, quick turnover, and high profits from farm produce mark the worthy man. The pattern setter in the social order of Star County is the successful farmer. There is a continual drift from his ranks to the villages and small cities where he takes up residence in his declining years. He

---

[1] Znaniecki, Florian W., *The Social Role of the Man of Knowledge*, New York, Columbia University Press, 1940.

[2] Esselstyn, T. C., *Crime and Its Control in the Hinterland*, unpublished dissertation submitted in partial fulfillment of the requirements for the degree of Doctor of Philosophy, New York University, February, 1952.

brings with him the values and attitudes of responsibility, individualism, initiative, and the outward evidences of success and favor by which these are shown. His influence thus permeates all levels of Star County life and he is perhaps the chief referent in the "social circle" whom the sheriff serves.

The class structure discernible here appears to follow in general the four-way split discovered in other regions in Illinois.[3] This comes to bear on the sheriff because law breaking often involves class-linked behavior patterns. As to the adult, the social and recreational outlets available to Classes I and II are seldom policed. The counterparts for Classes III and IV are usually taverns and these the sheriff watches closely, not only on his own initiative but also on demand of the proprietors. Trouble is expected and trouble happens. The result is that adult crime in Star County, like crime elsewhere, is preponderantly associated with the less privileged.

As to the juvenile, the reaction pattern of the parent shows a generally stable connection with class position. Parents from Classes I and II characteristically rally to the side of the juvenile or express a readiness to take remedial action. Parents from Classes III and IV are usually overwhelmed or are resigned in the face of the child's delinquency to the point of relative inaction. The result is an over-loading of court cases and juveniles in the county jail from the latter two classes. Popularly, this result is attributed to favoritism. Functionally, the consequence flows from patterns acquired by the parent largely through class membership.

Social groups are perhaps of greater importance to law enforcement in Star County than social class. The number and kinds of groups are legion. Some, like the churches, certain occupational groups, service clubs, school boards, fraternal orders, and the like, are important agents for transmitting the value scheme. Open country life is channeled, controlled, and structured by their activities. Where the sheriff fails to take cognizance of their activities, he risks his strength.

Other groups are important because they exert a measure of strategic dominance over open country law enforcement. There are

[3] Warner, W. Lloyd, et al., Democracy in Jonesville, New York, Harper and Brothers, 1949.

several groups of this kind but the only one that will be mentioned here is the political party. This is a kind of closed corporation wherein assignments and duties are distributed with an eye to group victory on election day. Obligations incurred during the campaign are discharged by appointments as deputies or jailers, court house jobs, and other types of patronage. Yet curiously, the spoils system is self-limiting. There is a recognized point beyond which these preferential agreements violate the central values of personal worth and individualism, and thus constitute a threat to party survival. Short of that, the effect of the political party can be seen in the constituency of the sheriff's force.

The Sheriff as a Social Type

Before the spring primaries in 1950, an effort was made to learn something of the voting habits of Star County. Informants were asked what kind of a man they felt would best fill the office of sheriff. The replies stressed a reputation for "fairness and good judgment." He should know the county intimately and should be fairly mature. He should know "how to get along with people." A candidate would present evidence of this by prosperity and success in business or farming.

The incumbent sheriff replied independently and in quite the same way. Looking back upon his own victory in 1946, he felt that the candidate should symbolize success in life first of all, for this aroused the voter's confidence and was an index of reliability. He should be mature and, of course, free of scandal. Beyond these—

Experience in law enforcement would come last. The people assume your ability to be a good sheriff if they check you off on the other three things. If you can show you have got along with people all your life, that you are moral and are old enough to be a little wise about things, they will be able to judge whether you will be a sheriff who is stern and mean and hard on people, or whether you will be kind and decent and treat people right, yet all the time honest and doing the job the best way you can. You can say what you would do if you were sheriff, but usually in Star County the candidates never have had experience in law enforcement and the public doesn't expect it.

The social type that the voters have in mind as an ideal construct is thus almost identical to the construct which the sheriff had derived. He himself conformed to the desired social type. When he went before the people in 1946, he had thirty years' experience in the wholesale and retail meat trades, had prospered also as a handler of bulk petroleum products, and had held minor public offices by which he had established himself with the political party. He was well-known in the county, was equipped with many of the criteria on which Star County judges the worthy man, and could point to his business success as proof that he knew "how to get along with people." The "social person" in large measure reflected the values of the "social circle" by these means.

The Office of Sheriff

Sheriffs throughout the nation have been criticized so often in the popular press and in learned journals that a restatement would serve no purpose. Yet it should be clear by now that in many parts of the country, the office is almost impregnable.

In Illinois, the powers and duties of the sheriff are set forth in Chapter 125 of the revised statutes but these are extended and modified by other provisions liberally sprinkled elsewhere in the law. The resulting confusion places the sheriff in a position where he can interpret his job however he will. This means that he must exercise discretion, and in the process both the favored and the disaffected tend to regard him as both arbitrary and corrupt at one and the same time. The dilemma is especially marked over such issues as gambling and prostitution. Complaints are made to the sheriff ". . . but no one will swear out a warrant. We can't just go in there on suspicion. This is a free country. You can't search without a warrant and if no one will sign a complaint we can't do anything." Whatever the merits of this position, the point is that it prevails among sheriffs in Illinois and will persist until relevant statutes are codified. In the meantime, the sheriff is immune from attack on this score because this interpretation has the backing of both custom and court decisions.

From another point of view, the office is impregnable in Illinois because of the vital part it plays in the system of county government. The reference here is not to the way in which it controls crime, but to the jobs and moneys involved in its share of the local bureaucracy. In Star County, twenty-two persons were awarded jobs on the deputy force, in the jail, and in the court house in partial recognition of support to the sheriff during the 1946 campaign. As to finance, the annual reports of the county auditor, on at least one interpretation, suggest that the sheriff directed the income and outgo of about $100,000 a year during his term. Some of this went to salaries and allowed fees. About sixty percent of the income was applied to expenses incurred in court house and jail maintenance. The implication is not that these payments were improper or excessive. The only inference is that many middlemen participate in the sheriff's affairs. They have an understandable stake in the perpetuation of the office as a fixture and can be relied upon to support it regardless of how well or how poorly it controls crime.

A third support to the office can be found in open country attitudes. Here the sheriff is seen as symbolizing local control over local problems—another bulwark against the encroachments of centralized state power. A fourth support grows out of the associations, both local and statewide, which the sheriff sets up while in office. In the discharge of duty, he maintains local contacts which can be depended upon to further whatever other political hopes he may have. Formal contacts beyond the county line with other sheriffs and informal contacts through the Illinois Sheriff's Association help entrench the office. By these means it becomes the repository for specialized police crafts with exclusive dominance over open country crime control. Coupled with the legal chaos which surrounds it and the control it holds over jobs and finances, these factors make the sheriff's office one of the most powerful links in the system of county government. Against these defenses, the assaults of critics avail but little.

Conserving the Peace

The social function of conserving the peace is influenced by the three broad components just reviewed. It is influenced also by the actual experience of peace-keeping. Within the sheriff's ranks a body of knowledge significant for open country law enforcement is gradually built up by trial and error. Prominent in this lore are the following six elements: terrain features and climatic changes; shifting public demand; the amenability of deputies to superior orders; their individual initiative; their knowledge of typical habit patterns; and a general guide for conduct in all trouble-cases.

The first five are self-explanatory. The last is more complex. In order to guard against the needless dissipation of energies, every sheriff must devise some effective principle to show him when to act. The Star County sheriff developed the following solution:

Public safety is our rule. If you were driving sixty miles an hour through a zoned area late at night with no traffic in the road, it would be against the law, but it's not morally wrong and you wouldn't be hurting the public safety. So we don't arrest you. But if you did that in day time when a lot of cars are on the highway, you would be a menace to yourself and everyone else. We would have to pull you in not only for the public's safety but for yours too. That's how we decide all these things.

This is another word for discretion. As stated earlier, its exercise becomes extremely involved when the conflict of interest is more subtle.

The dynamics of crime control in Star County are traceable to these six factors. Their product is what the *Uniform Crime Reports* call "offenses known." What of offenses not known? Informants who had reported offenses were interviewed and in almost every case they disclosed other offenses which they had not reported. As a general practice, the rule of silence is invoked in four circumstances: where the theft or offense "didn't amount to much," or where it was felt that a report "won't do any good"; where the threat of a report is countered by an apology, an offer of marriage, or restitution; where there is fear of reprisal, real or imagined; and where a report might threaten community harmony. This last involves extreme cases such as unexplained deaths, suspected incest, fires or explosions of unknown origin, and the like. It is impossible to get specific facts in these instances. However, accounts of these events are transmitted to the young and to the objective investigator in a context designed to show the limits beyond which it is regarded as unwise to resort to formal legal sanctions—unwise because it is felt that ultimate justice has or will be done, or because of the fear that group life will be shattered if neighbor must testify against neighbor.

In these "offenses not known" there is the suggestion that the open country has a fairly high tolerance for lawlessness. A further issue remains. Offenses associated with the conduct of agriculture are often reported in the local press and in various local farm journals. These take many forms and many are embraced by the criminal code. None was ever reported to the sheriff and he made no arrests for these offenses between 1946 and 1950. When committed, such offenses are handled by administrative agencies. The effect is to so condition local attitudes as to regard offenses running with agriculture as something other than crimes. . . .

Conclusions—
Tentative Characteristics of Open Country Crime

An analysis of 5,700 offenders arrested by the sheriff in Star County between 1945 and 1949 shows many things, a few of which are these:

1. The annual arrest rate for persons from Hopkins (population 37,000) who committed offenses beyond the city limits was 1373.62 per 100,000. The comparable rate for all other Star County residents was 448.43.

It is doubtful whether these figures by themselves confirm older views on the excessive criminality of the urban dweller. The rate may be normal for an open country town like Hopkins. Then too, factors such as class status and the pattern of leisure time behavior need to be considered before the excess can be established generally.

2. Rates for reported offenses occuring *in* the open country vary according to the characteristics of each community. Communities in Star County outside of Hopkins varied in their average annual reported rates from 691.0 to 8,000.0.

3. The relatively high proportion of offenses against the person, long cited for rural areas, seems to hold for Star County viewed as an open country region. Thirteen percent of all arrests were for offenses against the person, the rest were for offenses against property. This would probably change if the reporting habits of the open country were considered. The inclusion of offenses against property not now reported would reduce the ratio.

4. Persons engaged in agriculture are represented among known offenders in about one half their chance share. However, a whole host of offenses associated with agriculture are eliminated from the sheriff's function by custom. If these were included, the crime rate of the agricultural class would go up.

5. Offenders arrested by the Star County sheriff appear to be from three to five years younger on the average than for the country as a whole. This seems to be due chiefly to the jail confinement of juveniles, whose inclusion in this study depressed the mean. Any sheriff in Illinois can probably refuse to receive juveniles in his jail on the grounds that the intent of the "Dependent, Neglected, and Delinquent Children's Act" makes it unlawful. However, such refusals are unknown.

6. The preponderant tendency is for all offenders to leave the jail at the end of the second day. Seventy-five percent leave within ten days. About three percent of all offenders are sentenced to jail as punishment. An additional five percent are sentenced to the state penal farm for periods of less than one year. Thus eight percent of all offenders receive a jail or like sentence.

In the main, offenders are disposed of in routine fashion. There is little concern over the causes of their crimes or the conditions surrounding their occurrence. As is true everywhere else, the administration of criminal justice in Star County is trapped by ritual. This is a commentary, not upon the sheriff nor upon the county judge nor the local state's attorney. It is a commentary upon the system of which they are parts.

These findings from Star County suggest that open country crime does not conform in all particulars to general ideas of crime beyond the metropolis thus far advanced. However, generalizations can hardly be made until further studies have been conducted along similar lines. Important by-products of such studies will probably be a fresh understanding of the law and of law enforcement. These may be even more important than the actual delineation of open country crime.

THE RURAL JUDGE

HARRY M. CAUDILL

Harry M. Caudill, *Night Comes to the Cumberlands* (Boston: Little, Brown, 1962), pp. 353–361. Harry M. Caudill, a lawyer, has served in the Kentucky House of Representatives.

THE OFFICE of the county judge [in rural Kentucky] is the nerve center of the courthouse. In addition to being a judicial official charged with the trial of misdemeanors and minor civil actions, His Honor is the chief executive officer of the county. He presides over the fiscal court, directs the spending of county funds and is generally the chief "contact man" with Frankfort in political matters pertaining to the county.

His office consists of two dingy rooms. The long unpainted walls are peeling and paint hangs in scales from the ceiling. The rays of the sun struggle with small success to pierce the dirty, rain-streaked windowpanes. In the corner of the outer room a tobacco-stained cardboard box serves as a waste can.

The outer room contains the desk of his secretary and a half-dozen chairs are lined up along the walls. No matter how harassed she may be by the constant procession of callers, his secretary never fails to smile ingratiatingly—because even the smallest frown may offend a voter. From 8:30 in the morning when the office opens until 4:30 when the doors are locked, there is seldom a moment when a group of people are not waiting to "see the judge."

A day spent with the county judge in such an office in a plateau county is a revealing experience. It tells a story of the breakdown of Democracy and of the growing dependence and futility of the population. If Democracy is to eventually prevail over totalitarian ideologies the individual citizen must be able to shoulder a multitude of responsibilities and to discharge them out of a sense of duty. To do this he must possess the ability to meet social and economic problems and the willingness to grasp them. Until a generation ago the mountaineer was accustomed to "turn out" for road workings and other undertakings for community betterment. He was not paid and he did not expect to be. His willingness to work on roads and other essential projects was a holdover from the frontier where no government or government largesse existed. However, as government expanded and its benefits multiplied the old sturdiness began to dissolve. Though many frontier modes and outlooks survive and are sharply impressive, the traumas of fifty years have left a lasting imprint on the character of the mountaineer. His forefathers lived by the frontier maxim "root hog or die." They would be astounded if they could return in the spirit to behold their descendants thronging the office of the county judge to implore his assistance in a multitude of situations which, in an earlier time, would have been met by the citizens without its once occurring to them that help from any quarter was either possible or desirable.

A moment after the judge unlocked the door to his office an elderly woman darted in behind him. The judge greeted her with an affable smile and after a moment of smalltalk about her family and community, he inquired her business. She drew a paper from her purse and displayed it to him. On it was scrawled in longhand: "*We the undersigned persons have contributed to help——who is sick and has to stay at home.*" Below this caption four or five courthouse officeholders and county-seat merchants had written their names. Each of them had noted his contribution of $1.00 to the sufferer. The old lady explained that her son had a family and had been sick for a long time. "The doctors," she said, "can't find out what's the matter with him, and as fer me, I'm almost certain it's cancer. You know, judge, how we've always voted fer you every time you ever run for anything and will again just as shore as you run. If you can help him out now when he's having such bad luck, we shore will appreciate it."

The judge sighed ruefully, because such pleas are routine, but he added his name to the list and handed the woman a dollar bill.

A moment later the secretary arrived and callers began to fill the chairs in the waiting room. Some said they had just dropped by to shake hands with the judge and had no business in particular, but three very determined gentlemen were ushered into his office. Dressed in mud-spattered overalls, they lived on a creek some eleven miles from the county seat. The state had built a rural highway into the community in 1949 and later hand-surfaced it. But long neglect had allowed the road to deteriorate badly. The spokesman for the group, a tall, raw-boned mountaineer, told their story:

Judge, you know what kind of a shape our road is in and that it's prac'ly impossible to travel it. The ditch lines are all stopped up and there are holes all over it big enough to set a washtub in. One feller broke an axle right in the middle of the road last week. Now you know our precinct has always been one of the best in the county and you never come up there electioneering in your life that you didn't git a big vote, but if you can't do something for us now we'll sure as hell remember it if you ever run for anything else again. We ain't got no governor or he wouldn't let the roads get in the shape they're in now. We've just got to have the ditch lines cleaned out and the holes filled up.

The judge attempted to mollify his angry visitors, for this was not their first visit to his office on the same business. He pointed out very courteously, however, that funds were short and that a new coat of surfacing was out of the question. He promised to send a scraper to clean out the drainage ditches, and pledged an application of gravel for the worst places in the road. He warned them, however: "The roads all over this county are going to pieces, and we simply don't have the money to keep them up. We are doing everything in our power to maintain the roads, but we just don't have the money to do a decent job."

Somewhat mollified, the men departed—but not before dropping another threat of retribution at the polls if some effective relief did not ensue.

As they left, the county attorney rapped on the door and then entered the judge's private office. The Grand Jury had adjourned the day before and, as their predecessors had done for a good many years, the jurors had blasted the county officials for allowing the courthouse and jail to fall into filthy ruin. In a report to the circuit judge they declared that they had inspected the jail and found that structure wholly "unfit for human occupancy." The walls were cracked and broken, the roof leaked and the cells were inadequately heated. The commodes were without seats and the coal-black mattresses were without sheets. The entire facility reeked of excrement, urine and sweat. They recommended that the jail be closed and not reopened until completely renovated. They found the courthouse in almost equally foul condition, and said so in scathing terms.

The judge and the county attorney went over the report together line by line and agreed with the sentiments expressed in it. The county attorney remarked that it was a good report. "They would have been a lot more helpful, though," he said, "if they had told us where to get the money to do something about it." The judge reminded him that in several mountain counties the question of a bond issue for the construction of a new jail and courthouse had been referred to the people and sternly rejected at the polls. The county attorney opined: "If the same issue was placed on the ballot in this county you wouldn't get three votes for it out of that grand jury panel."

While he and the judge talked, proof of the jury's criticism was manifested by a vile stench which crept into the office from the public toilet in the basement of the courthouse.

When the county attorney was gone one of the county's justices of the peace brought his son-in-law to meet the judge. The justice pointed out that the fiscal court would soon have to add another man to the county road crew, and that his son-in-law desperately needed the job. The judge and justice were political allies, and His Honor agreed that the jobless son-in-law was ideally suited for the position. When this happy accord had been reached his secretary informed the judge a deputy sheriff had arrested a speeder and that the culprit was awaiting trial. Whereupon the judge walked into the unswept little courtroom near his office and sat down behind the judicial desk.

A middle-aged man and his wife were sitting on the front bench in the section of the courtroom reserved for spectators. Nearby sat a man in overalls and an open-collared, blue workshirt. He wore a baseball player's cap and an enormous star-shaped badge was pinned to the bib of his overalls. Strapped to his side was a German Luger pistol, a memento of some distant battlefield. The judge cleared his throat and asked the officer the nature of the charge against the defendant. The deputy stood up and came forward.

"Judge," he said, "this man was driving in a very reckless way. I got behind 'im and follered 'im about four mile, and I seen his car cross the yaller line at least three times. I want a warrant chargin' 'im with reckless driving."

His Honor turned to the offender and asked what he had to say. He was from New Jersey and was on his way to visit his son in Virginia. He and his wife had decided to turn aside and see the Kentucky mountains, about whose beauty they had heard so much. They had driven neither recklessly nor rapidly, and if their automobile had crossed the center line at any time it had been done inadvertently and on a relatively straight stretch of road where no other vehicles were in view.

It was obvious that the judge was impressed by the "violator's" sincerity and that he believed what he had said. He paused for a long moment and reflected upon the situation and, to one versed in mountain politics, his silent cogitations left a plainly discernible track. He weighed the fact that on the one hand he was dealing with a deputy who voted in the county and whose kinsmen and friends were equipped with razor-sharp votes. He knew that if the motorist paid no fine the deputy would be offended. The officer made his living from the fees collected in cases such as this one. If the New Jersey motorist paid a fine he must also pay the costs, six dollars of which would go into the pocket of the deputy. The guardian of the public peace would take unkindly to a dismissal of the case after he had gone to the trouble to capture the man and bring him three miles to the county seat. Weighed on the other end of the scale was a stranger who would never be here again and who, even if he paid a small fine, perhaps unjustly, would not suffer irreparably. These considerations produced the inevitable conclusion. His Honor decreed the minimum fine allowed under the statute. The total came to eighteen dollars and fifty cents. When justice had thus been meted out the judge did not return to his office but took advantage of the opportunity to escape for lunch. When he returned at 1:00 P.M. the callers had increased in number and their problems had grown even more vexatious.

A fifty-year-old man, his wife and her father had come to tell the judge that the Welfare worker had denied his claim for public assistance. He wanted the judge to talk to her and, if necessary, to go to Frankfort and see if the claim couldn't be straightened out. He said:

Judge, I just can't work. I can't do nary thing. I'm sick and I've got a doctor's certificate to prove it. I worked in the mines for twenty-five years before they shut down but you know I got into bad air and ever since then when I git hot or a little bit tired I git so nervous I can't hardly stand it. I don't have a thing in the world to live on and they've turned down my claim, and I know that if you will get onto the people at Frankfort you can get it straightened out. There's a sight of people in this county that ain't as bad off as I am and they didn't have any trouble gettin' it and I'm sure not a-goin' to give up on it without seeing into it a little further.

At this juncture the man's father-in-law, a gentlemen of approximately seventy-five, chimed in. He had lived with his daughter and son-in-law for three years and never had known anybody who was a harder worker. He had seen the man work an hour or two in his vegetable garden and get so nervous that he would spill his coffee when he came into the house to rest. He assured the judge that he would be the first to say so if he thought his son-in-law was "putting on."

The judge heard this tale of woe with deep respect and assured his visitors that they had his sympathy and that he would make every effort to help them. He hedged by pointing out that public assistance is administered by a state agency over which he had no control. The Welfare Department had a lot of stubborn people on its staff, some of whom, unfortunately, were quite unreasonable. He remembered that the sick man had always been his friend and had stood by him in bygone years. He summed up his gratitude with the assertion, "You've scratched my back in the past and I'll try to scratch yours now. You know, turn about is fair play."

Highly gratified, the nervous man, his wife and his father-in-law left, after again reminding the judge that they sure would appreciate his help.

The next caller had been drawing State Aid but his check had been discontinued because his children had not been attending school regularly. He explained that his young-'uns had been sick. "Not sick enough to have a doctor, but feelin' bad and I just couldn't make 'em go to school a-feelin' bad. As soon as they got to feelin' better they went right back to school, and I don't know what we'll do if we don't git some help fer 'em again."

He promised that if the judge could prevail upon the Welfare worker to restore his check he would make an affidavit to send his children to school on each day when they were well enough to go.

About 3:30 in the afternoon the county truant officer (known officially by the horrendous title of Director of Pupil Personnel) made his appearance. A warrant had been sworn out charging a father with failing to send his children to school and the trial was set for that hour. The defendant was already present in the little courtroom. A few moments later the county attorney appeared to prosecute the case for the state. The truant officer explained that the defendant was the father of six children, all of whom were of elementary school age. They had not been to school in the preceding month despite his pleas that the father keep them in regular attendance. The county attorney asked the Court to impose a fine or jail sentence. The judge asked the defendant why he had not been sending his children to school. The man stalked forward and gazed around him with the uncertainty of a trapped animal. He was dressed in tattered overalls to which many patches had been affixed. He was approximately forty-five years old and it was obvious from his huge hands and stooped shoulders that he had spent many years under the low roof of a coal mine. He pleaded his defense with the eloquence of an able trial lawyer. With powerful conviction he said:

I agree with everything that's been said. My children have not been going to school and nobody wants them to go any more than I do. I've been out of work now for four years. I've been all over this coalfield and over into Virginia and West Virginia looking for work. I've made trip after trip to Indianny, Ohio and Michigan and I couldn't find a day's work anywhere. I drawed out my unemployment compensation over three years ago and the only income I've had since has been just a day's work now and then doing farm work for somebody. I sold my old car, my shotgun, my radio and even my watch to get money to feed my family. And now I don't have a thing in the world left that anybody would want. I'm dead-broke and about ready to give up. I live over a mile from the schoolhouse and I simply don't have any money to buy my children shoes or clothes to wear. I own a little old four-room shanty of a house and twenty acres of woreout hillside land. Last spring the coal company that owns the coal augered it and teetotally destroyed the land. I couldn't sell the whole place for five hundred dollars if my life depended on it. Me and my eldest boy have one pair of shoes between us, and that's all. When he wears 'em I don't have any and when I wear 'em he don't have any. If it wasn't for these rations the gover'ment gives us, I guess the whole family would of been starved to death long afore now. If you want to fine me I ain't got a penny to pay it with and I'll have to lay it out in jail. If you think puttin' me in jail will help my young-'uns any, then go ahead and do it and I'll be glad of it. If the county attorney or the truant officer will find me a job where I can work out something for my kids to wear I'll be much obliged to 'em as long as I live.

At the conclusion of this declaration the judge looked uneasily around, eying the county attorney and the truant officer in the hope that some help would come from that quarter. Both gentlemen remained silent. At length the judge plied the defendant with questions. The man had a third-grade education. He had worked in the mines for a total of twenty years and had spent three years as an infantry soldier in the war against Japan. He had been fortunate, however, and had received no wounds. Consequently, he drew no pension or compensation from the Veterans' Administration. The factories to which he had applied for employment had insisted on men with more education than he possessed. They also wanted younger men. Finally the county attorney demanded to know whether he had any skill except mining coal. The answer was an emphatic "No." Then he blurted out:

Judge, I'm not the only man in this fix on the creek where I live. They's at least a dozen other men who ain't sent their children to school for the same reason mine ain't a-goin'. They can't send 'em cause they can't get hold of any money to send 'em with. Now the county attorney and the truant officer are trying to make an example out of me. They think that if I go to jail for a week or two the rest of 'em will somehow find the money to get their kids into the schoolhouse.

He looked intently at the truant officer and demanded, "Ain't that so?" to which the truant officer hesitantly assented.

The judge mulled the problem over for a moment or two and then "filed away" the warrant. He explained that it was not being dismissed, but was being continued upon the docket indefinitely. "If the case is ever set for trial again I will write you a letter well in advance of the trial date and tell you when to be here," he said. "In the meantime go home and do the best you possibly can to make enough money to educate your children. If they don't go to school they'll never be able to make a living and when they get grown they'll be in just as bad a fix as you are in now."

The defendant thanked the judge, picked up his battered miner's cap and walked to the door. There he paused and looked back at judge, attorney and truant officer for a long moment, as though framing a question. Then he thought better of it and closed the door behind him. His Honor had had enough for one day, and decided to go home.

TRIAL BY COMBAT IN AMERICAN COURTS

DAVID DRESSLER

David Dressler, "Trial by Combat in American Courts," *Harper's Magazine*, CCXXII (April 1961), 31–36.

THE AVERAGE criminal trial, said the late Judge Jerome Frank, is a "sublimated brawl." A decade ago, few of Judge Frank's colleagues bothered to defend their profession when he made the charge in his crusading book, *Courts on Trial;* today many progressive lawyers and judges are battling for the very reforms he championed, and in some Federal and state courts the ancient rituals are changing. But even now in the United States, despite our prevailing respect for the scientific search for truth, trial techniques are as unscientific as an appendectomy performed with a tomahawk. . . .

Unfortunately for advocates of reform, most lawyers are proud of this instance of cultural lag. Our so-called adversary theory against which Judge Frank inveighed sets the rules of trial procedure. It stems from medieval trial by combat and is basic both to English common law and to American legal codes. In the old days accuser and accused met on the field of battle and had at each other. . . . If the accused fell, he was guilty. If the accuser died, that proved he didn't have a just cause to begin with. Thus was "truth" revealed.

Today, instead of fighting with lethal weapons, we use legal arguments. Where combatants formerly met face to face, they now have surrogates—attorneys—who fight for them. The judge acts as referee, theoretically protecting the contenders against foul blows.

The jury decides which "side" fought the better fight. But fight it is and the object is to win, not necessarily to reveal the truth.

The heart of the adversary system—and the source of many of the evils which the reforms now in progress aim to eliminate—is "surprise," a technique which some lawyers call "trial from ambush." The intent of surprise is to time a sudden blow so as to throw the opposition off balance and overwhelm it before it can recover.

A Chicago attorney, Luis Kutner, was in Federal Court defending William Henderson, who had been charged with piracy on the high seas. Henderson had boarded a sight-seeing motor launch operating on Lake Michigan and, when it left its moorings, pulled a pistol and robbed the passengers. At trial, thirty erstwhile passengers positively identified the defendant as their assailant. Kutner cross-examined diffidently, as if his cause were hopeless. He presented no evidence on his own, and listened respectfully as United States Attorney Al Bosworth summed up and rested his case, by which time Henderson's guilt was plain as a wart.

Then Kutner addressed Judge James H. Wilkerson: "Your Honor, the defense moves for a directed verdict of acquittal, on grounds this court lacks competent jurisdiction." Under Federal law, counsel, pointed out, the port of registry of a vessel determines jurisdiction. "The boat in question is registered out of Milwaukee. Chicago is therefore not the venue of the crime."

The judge ordered acquittal.

Now . . . Kutner knew all along that the case belonged in a Milwaukee court. He could have moved for change of venue before the trial opened in Chicago. Instead, he let it run its course. He allowed the prosecution to rest its case, confident it had won. Then he sprang his trap. . . . In the eyes of the law, Kutner's conduct was entirely ethical. Under the adversary theory he was an advocate, which is to say he was obliged to be strictly partisan. As a partisan, he was entitled to use surprise.

Tongue in cheek, attorneys insist that the adversary system guarantees revelation of all facts bearing on an issue, and so it furthers the scientific method in trial practice. A lawyer buried beneath a mountain of books in the Los Angeles County Law Library told me,

I am here seeking the matter that will win a certain action. My opponent is here, too, with the same purpose. I search with fervor and frenzy. Nothing favorable to my position will escape me. The same is true of my opponent, dammit! He and I will search and together we will bring in facts so plain that even a jury of potato peelers and peanut vendors will understand them.

Maybe. But I have been in and out of courts for years and most of the time I have felt those potato peelers and peanut vendors were licked. They would not get at the truth because it lay hidden behind a curtain of flimflam and obfuscation. Each attorney was out to help his side and his side only, at almost any cost. Each wanted the jury to believe that he and he alone was the bearer of the Holy Grail, while his opponent was a knave out to suppress the truth. Each witness swore he was telling nothing but the truth, even when his story was directly contrary to what a witness for the other side swore was true. No witness was permitted to tell all he knew, although under oath to tell "the whole truth." No witness could tell what he did tell in his own way. The attorney on his side suggested by his questions what the witness should say. In cross-examination the opposing lawyer tried to trap him into saying something else. Each counselor hoped to cajole the jury into disregarding everything the other lawyer or witnesses said. The net outcome, all too often, probably was that the talesmen agreed with the wag who said that cases are decided only "according to the preponderance of the perjury." They voted for the side that seemed to tell fewer lies.

Juries might get at the truth if counsel researched cases scientifically. When two research men investigate causes of cancer they make a hypothesis and check it with an open mind. They may pursue different courses but they clear their findings with each other.

Not so in criminal trial practice. According to the late eminent attorney, Charles P. Curtis, the counsel who sets out to build evidence "will waste a lot of time if he goes with an open mind." Unlike a scientist, he will not sit down with his opposite number and say, "Here is what I found. What did you find? We are both after the same thing—truth. What can we agree on, in the interest of justice?" Instead, he squirrels away his evidence, citations, and arguments—his putative "facts"—hoping his opponent will be overwhelmed by them in the courtroom.

An attorney told a Bar Association audience:

Of course surprise elements should be hoarded. Your opponent should not be educated as to matters concerning which you believe he is still in the dark. Obviously, the traps should not be uncovered. Indeed, you may cast a few more leaves over them so that your adversary will step more boldly on the low ground believing it is solid.

The leaves over the low ground are yellowed pages of musty law books containing ancient trial decisions, which serve as precedents. Precedents are hallowed. What was good enough for great-great-grandpappy is all the better today because it is aged-in-the-book. . . .

The precedents often fail to go to the heart of a matter. They award a decision, not on the essence of a case—that is, whether the defendant is guilty or not—but more frequently on mere technicality. If, as happened in one Florida case, the judge simply has to leave the bench to answer the call of nature while counsel is summing up for the jury, the opposing lawyer will make no demur. He has an early precedent up his sleeve that holds if a judge has to go, the trial should be recessed, even though all the evidence is in and only summation is in progress. Then, if the verdict is against his side, the lawyer will jostle the precedent loose and demand a new trial.

There are literally hundreds of thousands of technicalities that have won cases in the past. Many of them are contradictory. The lawyer who can't find the special one that fits his case had better turn in his diploma. . . .

In one case, the advocate found just what he needed to defend his client, a North Carolinian who had fired across the state line and killed a man in Tennessee. When North Carolina attempted to charge him, the attorney cried foul. The act, he pointed out, was completed in Tennessee, and the law requires a man be tried where the act was completed. North Carolina had to agree. Tennessee then tried to extradite the killer as a fugitive from justice.

Impossible, counsel fumed. Since his client had never been in Tennessee how could he be a fugitive from that state? Tennessee gave up. Thus, remarks Roscoe Pound, dean of legal philosophers, "The state which had him could not try him, while the state which could try him did not have him and could not get him."

If, by amazing mischance, a counselor finds no precedent, *circa* 1800, to prove his case, he might try another form of surprise, the hit-run tactic. He may fire an improper question at a witness, knowing it must be withdrawn. It will be expunged from the record but not from the recollection of the jurors.

When the Teamsters' president James R. Hoffa was tried for bribery in 1957, his attorney, Edward Bennett Williams, was content to have eight Negroes on the jury. . . . John Cye Cheasty, a prosecution witness, came up for cross-examination. Out of a clear sky, Williams asked him if he had not once been engaged by a bus line to investigate the National Association for the Advancement of Colored People during a Florida labor dispute.

The horrified prosecutor jumped to his feet, protesting that the question was altogether immaterial to the matter at issue. The judge sustained the objection and ordered the jury to disregard the question—one of many neat legal fictions is that jurors can forget what they have heard. Actually, the damage was done. It seems reasonable to assume that at least eight veniremen considered Cheasty's testimony as the biased mouthings of an enemy of labor and minorities.

Soon after, another dramatic surprise staggered the prosecution. Ex-champion Joe Louis sauntered into the courtroom, put an arm around Hoffa, and explained to newsmen, "I just came over to say hello to my friend Jimmy." Acquittal for the friend of the oppressed followed.

While in the Hoffa case surprise benefited the defense in court, the prosecution usually has a distinct advantage in preparing certain surprises before trial. For example, the findings of the police laboratory are available to it, rarely to the defense.

In one Los Angeles case, a defendant charged with murder convinced his attorney he was absolutely innocent. Although some attorneys consider it their duty to defend guilty clients, and the can-

ons of the bar hold that this is the one way to assure that
mitigating circumstances will be put before a jury, this particular
attorney prefers not to handle such cases. . . . At trial, the state
produced a police witness who testified he photographed the latent
print of the palm of a hand, found on the window sill over which
the slayer climbed to gain entrance. The print was the defendant's.
Had defense been apprised of this before trial, it might have prepared a better argument in favor even of a guilty client. Taken by
surprise, it surrendered the decision to the prosecution. Almost certainly a guilty man was convicted in this instance, but it is our
theory that even a guilty man is entitled to the best possible defense.

When I asked a Los Angeles police official whether police findings should not be shared with the defense, he replied, "Do the
Dodgers give the Giants their signals?" No, but human beings are
not baseballs, trials are not baseball games, and the stakes are not
pennants. The liberty and perhaps the life of a defendant is at
stake in every criminal trial. Police science should be employed in
the interest of truth and justice, not to win a battle for one side.

Because adversary methods sanction a battle of wits rather than
a search for truth, a few leaders in the law have become restive.
They know that we have at hand methods of finding evidence scientifically, that trials can be made more truthful and just than they
usually are at present. Largely as a result of their efforts, the
American Bar Association has at long last instituted reforms in the
adversary method, though much more remains to be done. The first
attack was on surprise. To minimize the unfairness and inefficiency
of this technique, the American Bar Association produced what it
calls "discovery."

Judge Frank likened surprise to a cat-and-mouse game. He
thought the mouse should at least have "a peek at the cat's claws."
That peek is now provided by discovery. This is, in essence, legal
machinery by which one side is required to inform the other, in advance of trial or sufficiently in advance during trial, that certain
evidence will be introduced. Forewarned, the other side has time
to prepare its case.

As far back as 1848, England provided a first step in discovery.

By changes in procedure, the prosecution was obliged to place before a magistrate all the evidence it planned to produce at trial. The defense was to be present and thus would have the information and could prepare adequately. The U.S. waited almost a century to follow suit. But in 1946, Federal Courts began operating under revised Rules of Criminal Procedure, developed under the sponsorship of the American Bar Association. For the first time, some discovery was officially sanctioned in criminal cases before Federal tribunals. Under the new Rules, defense may move, and the court order, that the Government shall show to the defendant's counsel specific documents and tangible objects material to preparation of the case for the accused.

Suppose John Smith is charged with kidnaping a child in violation of Federal statutes. The father is to be the principal Government witness. He has given the United States Attorney a sworn statement that the kidnaper sent him a ransom note. The note itself is in the prosecutor's possession. Defense counsel goes before a Federal judge, in the presence of the U.S. Attorney, and asks to see the statement. He also wants a photostat of the ransom note, so the handwriting may be compared with his client's.

The requested data would be essential to a reasonable defense in this instance, and would probably be furnished. This would not always be the case. It is not the purpose of discovery to facilitate "fishing expeditions" that will give away the Government's case in each and every respect. . . . Counsel must satisfy the judge that the requested information is material to building a defense and that denial would place the defendant in an untenable position at trial. Only then will discovery be ordered.

Because it is and undoubtedly should remain discretionary with the court, discovery was rarely granted in the first decade under the revised Rules. Beginning about the late 1950s Federal Courts became more liberal, but even now discovery is the exception rather than the rule.

But the trend has begun. The American Law Institute has stimulated the states to follow the Federal example. California, Delaware, Florida, Maryland, Michigan, New Jersey, and Ohio have enacted statutes authorizing some degree of discovery, and in the past several years the effects are being felt in state courts. In the majority of jurisdictions the prosecution must provide the defense with a list of its witnesses. In some states the substance of the expected testimony must also be revealed before trial.

Most discovery is in the interest of the defense, since it is the prosecution that brings the charge and believes it has evidence to sustain it. But some disclosure favors the prosecution. In several states the defense is required to notify the prosecutor when it plans to plead not guilty by virtue of insanity. Michigan, Arizona, Ohio, Kansas, Wisconsin, require that the prosecution be notified if the defense claims an alibi.

The disclosure of alibi was required by law even before 1946 in at least one state—Ohio. Its value is illustrated by the case of "Roaring Bill" Potter, a politician murdered in Cleveland. Racketeer Hymie Martin was arrested in Pittsburgh for the offense, and extradited. He would have escaped conviction but for the Ohio law which specified that the defendant must give three days' notice of a proposed alibi. County Prosecutor Ray T. Miller was so notified and, checking, learned that at the extradition hearing in Pittsburgh, Martin's attorney brought witnesses who swore the accused was in that city when Potter was murdered. The testimony apparently failed to convince.

At the trial in Cleveland, the same attorney presented different witnesses who testified Martin was in Akron the day of the murder. All the County Prosecutor had to do was place in evidence the testimony given at the extradition hearing. Since the defendant could not have been in Pittsburgh and Akron simultaneously, the conflict was obvious. The credibility of the alibi was destroyed and Martin was convicted.

Does discovery make it harder to convict the guilty? No so, says Maryland's Supreme Court. "We are not impressed by the fear. . . . It apparently has not had that effect."

The trend toward discovery is impressive but as yet limited. It continues to meet with resistance by a majority of attorneys. . . . [One of them] has explained why:

Some of the finest legal minds today are anxious for revolutionary changes in procedure, but they are as voices crying in the wilderness compared to the great unleavened mass of lawyers who are abundantly satisfied with things as they are. With even a slight modification of procedure in civil and criminal cases the United States could dispense with half her lawyers. The average citizen, therefore, need not expect the legal profession to commit hari-kari.

It will take an entirely new generation of lawyers, trained in a loftier philosophy, to bring a more effective justice into our courts. Most attorneys today come from law schools that imbue them with the theory of winning decisions at almost any cost. They have been taught to use not only surprise but every other questionable advantage which a complacent judge, himself a product of such schools, will allow.

Logic argues that a witness belongs to neither side. He should mount the stand to tell what he knows, whatever the outcome. But budding lawyers study textbooks that teach them to consider witnesses either "friendly" or "hostile." According to such texts, the hostile witness is an outsider and, as Charles P. Curtis says in *The Ethics of Advocacy,* "A lawyer is required to treat outsiders as if they were barbarians and enemies."

Is the hostile witness honest but egotistic? One text advises the cross-examiner he might "deftly tempt the witness to indulge in his propensity for exaggeration, so as to make him 'hang himself'." A truthful but irascible fellow? "Make him lose his temper and seem spiteful." One recent text by Lewis W. Lake has a section titled "How to Humiliate and Subdue a Recalcitrant Witness." Not a dishonest witness, mind you, but merely one who is recalcitrant, meaning he won't go along with the cross-examiner. The neophyte is instructed:

When you have forced the witness into giving you a direct answer to your question you really have him under control; he is off balance, and usually rather scared. This advantage should be followed up with a few simple questions such as, "You did not want to answer that question, did you?" If the witness says that he wanted to answer it, ask him in a resounding voice, "Well, why did you not answer it when I first asked you?" Whatever his answer is you then ask him, "Did you think that you were smart enough to evade answering the question?" Again, whatever the answer is you ask him, "Well, I would like for the jurors to know what you have behind all this dodging and ducking you have done!"

. . . This battering and legal-style "kicking the witness around" not only humiliates but subdues him.

We have barely emerged from the era of the self-made lawyer, who needed only a mail-order law book and a fireplace in front of which to study. That was good enough in Abe Lincoln's day, but we can do better today. This is an age of specialization, but one in which we believe the specifics of professional practice should be superimposed on a foundation of general education. Yet over half of today's attorneys are trained in the law without learning to understand the society for which law is created. They do not have college degrees. The majority attended schools of a type which a Columbia University dean called "vocational bargain basements." An investigator for the American Bar Association reported in 1954 that of nine law schools he inspected, six "showed no impact of the modern world whatsoever."

But a measure of improvement is on the way. The great universities now require a liberal-arts base for the law degree. They teach law as an institution of society, as a philosophy, a science, and a craft. When enough of their students have been graduated, law will be practiced with a sense of responsibility for the ethics of modern life. At any rate, there is a chance that lawyers will accept the obligation to make law serve society.

A Daumier print shows a lawyer arguing in court. Nearby sit a woman and child. The caption reads: "He defends the widow and orphan, unless he is attacking the orphan and the widow." That's trial by combat under adversary rules. We require much better in our time. Chief Justice Arthur T. Vanderbilt, of New Jersey, put it this way: "Justice in our courts shall be a search for truth, and not a mere battle of wits."

THE RULE OF M'NAGHTEN

Excerpted from Richard M. Bousfield and Richard Merrett, *Report of the Trial of Daniel M'Naghton at the Central Criminal Court, Old Bailey, (on Friday, the 3rd, and Saturday, the 4th of March, 1843) for Wilful Murder of Edward Drummond, Esq.* (London: Henry Renshaw, 1843), pp. V, VI, 1–6, 67–68, 73–74. Bousfield was "Student at Law" and Merrett listed himself as a "Shorthand Writer." The defendant's name has been variously spelled in the literature.

The Act

[DANIEL M'NAGHTEN, a North Ireland Protestant, developed the compulsive idea that a number of highly placed individuals, among them the Pope and the leader of the Tory Party in Great Britain, were plotting against him. Laboring under this delusion, in 1843 he purchased a pistol and proceeded to Downing Street in London, intent on shooting the Prime Minister, Sir Robert Peel. He did not know the Prime Minister by face, and when that official's private secretary, Edward Drummond, happened along, M'Naghten shot and killed him in the belief he was murdering Peel.]

[In the course of the trial, medical testimony was introduced to the effect that the defendant was insane when he committed the offense. The Solicitor-General concurring, Chief Justice Tindal halted further proceedings and addressed the jury.]

The Chief Justice Tindal.—Gentlemen of the Jury, in this important case . . . the point I shall have to submit to you is, whether on the whole of the evidence you have heard, you are satisfied that at the time the act was committed, for the commission of which the prisoner now stands charged, he had that competent use of his understanding as that he knew that he was doing, by the very act itself, a wicked and wrong thing? If he was not sensible at the time he committed that act, that it was a violation of the law of God or of man, undoubtedly he was not responsible for that act, or liable to any punishment whatever flowing from that act. Gentlemen, that is the precise point, which I feel it my duty to leave to you. . . . Now, gentlemen, I can go through the whole of the evidence . . . but I cannot help remarking, in common with my learned brethren, that the whole of the medical evidence is on one side, and that there is no part of it which leaves any doubt on the mind. It seems, almost unnecessary that I should go through the evidence. I am, however, in your hands; but if on balancing the evidence in your minds, you think the prisoner capable of distinguishing between right and wrong, then he was a responsible agent and liable to all the penalties the law imposes. If not so, and if in your judgment the subject should appear involved in very great difficulty, then you will probably not take upon yourselves to find the prisoner guilty. If that is your opinion, then you will acquit the prisoner. If you think you ought to hear the evidence more fully . . . I will state it to you, and leave the case in your hands. . . .

The Foreman of the Jury.—We require no more, my Lord.

The Chief Justice Tindal.—If you find the prisoner not guilty, say on the ground of insanity, in which case proper care will be taken of him.

The Foreman.—We find the prisoner *Not Guilty*, on the ground of insanity.

Aftermath of the Trial

THE M'NAGHTEN RULES *

[M'Naghten was hospitalized. The case was widely discussed and there was considerable feeling expressed that M'Naghten should have been hanged, that the trial court erred. The House of Lords drew up a list of questions concerning criminal responsibility of persons suffering from insane delusions. These were put to the fifteen High Court Judges, fourteen of whom replied on June 19, 1843. The reply constitutes what today are the M'Naghten Rules.]

* *M'Naghten's Case*, House of Lords (1843), 10 Cl & F. 200, 8 Eng. (Repr. 718).

Lord Chief Justice Tindal. My Lords, her Majesty's Judges, (with the exception of Mr. Justice Maule, who has stated his opinion to your Lordships), in answering the questions proposed to them by your Lordships' House, think it right, in the first place, to state that they have forborne entering into any particular discussion upon these questions, from the extreme and almost insuperable difficulty of applying those answers to cases in which the facts are not brought judicially before them. The facts of each particular case must of necessity present themselves with endless variety, and with every shade of difference in each case; and as it is their duty to declare the law upon each particular case, on facts proved before them, and after hearing argument of counsel thereon, they deem it at once impracticable, and at the same time dangerous to the administration of justice, if it were practicable, to attempt to make minute applications of the principles involved in the answers given by them to your Lordship's questions.

They have, therefore, confined their answers to the statement of that which they hold to be the law upon the abstract questions proposed by your Lordships; and as they deem it unnecessary, in this peculiar case, to deliver their opinions *seriatim*, and as all concur in the same opinion, they desire me to express such their unanimous opinion.

The first question proposed by your Lordships is this:

What is the law respecting alleged crimes committed by persons afflicted with insane delusion, in respect of one or more particular subjects or persons; as, for instance, where at the time of the commission of the alleged crime the accused knew he was acting contrary to law, but did the act complained of with a view, under the influence of insane delusion, of redressing or revenging some supposed grievance or injury, or of producing some supposed public benefit?

In answer to which question, assuming that your Lordships' inquiries are confined to those persons who labour under such partial delusions only, and are not in other respects insane, we are of the opinion that, notwithstanding the party accused did the act complained of with a view, under the influence of insane delusion, of redressing or revenging some supposed grievance or injury, or of producing some public benefit, he is nevertheless punishable according to the nature of the crime committed, if he knew at the time of committing such crime that he was acting contrary to law; by which expression we understand your Lordships to mean the law of the land.

Your Lordships are pleased to inquire of us, secondly,

What are the proper questions to be submitted to the jury, where a person alleged to be afflicted with insane delusion respecting one or more particular subjects or persons, is charged with the commission of a crime (murder, for example), and insanity is set up as a defence?

And thirdly, "In what terms ought the question to be left to the jury as to the prisoner's state of mind at the time when the act was committed?" And as these two questions appear to us to be more conveniently answered together, we have to submit our opinion to be, that the jurors ought to be told in all cases that every man is to be presumed to be sane, and to possess a sufficient degree of reason to be responsible for his crimes, until the contrary be proved to their satisfaction; and that to establish a defence on the ground of insanity, it must be clearly proved that, at the time of the committing of the act, the party accused was labouring under such a defect of reason, from disease of the mind, as not to know the nature and quality of the act he was doing; or, if he did know it, that he did not know he was doing what was wrong. The mode of putting the latter part of the question to the jury on these occasions has generally been, whether the accused at the time of doing the act knew the difference between right and wrong: which mode, though rarely, if ever, leading to any mistake with the jury, is not, as we conceive, so accurate when put generally, and in the abstract, as when put with reference to the party's knowledge of right and wrong in respect to the very act with which he is charged. If the question were to be put as to the knowledge of the accused solely and exclusively with reference to the law of the land, it might tend to confound the jury, by inducing them to believe that an actual knowledge of the law of the land was essential in order to lead to a conviction; whereas the law is administered upon the principle that every one must be taken conclusively to know it, without proof that he does not know it. If the accused was conscious that the act was one which he ought not to do, and if that act was at the same time contrary to the law of the land, he is punishable; and the usual course, therefore, has been to leave the question to the jury, whether the party accused had a sufficient degree of reason to know that he was doing an act that was wrong: and this course we think is correct, accompanied with such observations and explanations as the circumstances of each particular case may require.

The fourth question . . . is this: "If a person, under an insane delusion as to existing facts, commits an offence in consequence thereof, is he thereby excused?" To which question the answer must, of course, depend on the nature of the delusion: but, making the same assumption as we did before, namely, that he labours under such partial delusion only, and is not in other respects insane, we think he must be considered in the same situation as to responsibility as if the facts with respect to which the delusion exists were real. For example, if, under the influence of his delusion, he supposes another man to be in the act of attempting to take away his life, and he kills that man, as he supposes, in self-defence, he would be exempt from punishment. If his delusion was that the deceased had inflicted a serious injury to his character and fortune, and he killed him in revenge for such supposed injury, he would be liable to punishment.

The question lastly proposed . . . is:

Can a medical man conversant with the disease of insanity, who never saw the prisoner previously to the trial, but who was present during the whole trial and the examination of all the witnesses, be asked his opinion as to the state of the prisoner's mind at the time of the commission of the alleged crime, or his opinion whether the prisoner was conscious, at the time of doing the act, that he was acting contrary to law, or whether he was labouring under any and what delusion at the time?

In answer thereto, we state to your Lordships, that we think the medical man, under the circumstances supposed, cannot in strictness be asked his opinion in the terms above stated, because each of those questions involves the determination of the truth of the facts deposed to, which it is for the jury to decide, and the questions are not mere questions upon a matter of science, in which case such evidence is admissible. But where the facts are admitted or not disputed, and the question becomes substantially one of science only, it may be convenient to allow the question to be put in that general form, though the same cannot be insisted on as a matter of right.

THE DURHAM RULE: DEPARTURE
FROM M'NAGHTEN

Durham v. United States, 214 F. 2d 862 (1954).

BAZELON, Circuit Judge. Monte Durham was convicted of housebreaking by the District Court sitting without a jury. The only defense asserted at the trial was that Durham was of unsound mind at the time of the offense. We are now urged to reverse the conviction (1) because the trial court did not correctly apply existing rules governing the burden of proof on the defense of insanity, and (2) because existing tests of criminal responsibility are obsolete and should be superseded.

I

Durham has a long history of imprisonment and hospitalization. In 1945, at the age of 17, he was discharged from the Navy after a psychiatric examination had shown that he suffered "from a profound personality disorder which renders him unfit for Naval service." In 1947 he pleaded guilty to violating the National Motor Theft Act and was placed on probation for one to three years. He attempted suicide, was taken to Gallinger Hospital for observation, and was transferred to St. Elizabeths Hospital, from which he was discharged after two months. In January of 1948, as a result of a conviction in the District of Columbia Municipal Court for passing bad checks, the District Court revoked his probation and he commenced service of his Motor Theft sentence. His conduct within the first few days in jail led to a lunacy inquiry in the Municipal Court where a jury found him to be of unsound mind. Upon commitment to St. Elizabeths, he was diagnosed as suffering from "psychosis with psychopathic personality." After 15 months of treatment, he was discharged in July 1949 as "recovered" and was returned to jail to serve the balance of his sentence. In June 1950 he was conditionally released. He violated the conditions by leaving the District. When he learned of a warrant for his arrest as a parole violator, he fled to the "South and Midwest obtaining money by passing a number of bad checks." After he was found and returned to the District, the Parole Board referred him to the District Court for a lunacy inquisition, wherein a jury again found him to be of unsound mind. He was readmitted to St. Elizabeths in February 1951. This time the diagnosis was "without mental disorder, psychopathic personality." He was discharged for the third time in May 1951. The housebreaking which is the subject of the present appeal took place two months later, on July 13, 1951.

According to his mother and the psychiatrist who examined him in September 1951, he suffered from hallucinations immediately after his May 1951 discharge from St. Elizabeths. Following the present indictment, in October 1951, he was adjudged of unsound mind in proceedings . . . , upon the affidavits of two psychiatrists that he suffered from "psychosis with psychopathic personality." He was committed to St. Elizabeths for the fourth time and given subshock insulin therapy. This commitment lasted 16 months— until February 1953—when he was released to the custody of the District Jail on the certificate of Dr. Silk, Acting Superintendent of St. Elizabeths, that he was "mentally competent to stand trial and . . . able to consult with counsel to properly assist in his own defense."

He was thereupon brought before the court on the charge involved here. The prosecutor told the court:

So I take this attitude, in view of the fact that he has been over there [St. Elizabeths] a couple of times and these cases that were charged against him were dropped. I don't think I should take the responsibility of dropping these cases against him; then Saint Elizabeths would let him out on the street, and if that man committed a murder next week then it is my responsibility. So we decided to go to trial on one case, that is the case where we found him right in the house, and let him bring in the defense, if he wants to, of unsound mind at the time the crime was committed, and then Your Honor will find him on that, and in your decision send him back to Saint Elizabeths Hospital, and then if they let him out on the street it is their responsibility.

Shortly thereafter, when the question arose whether Durham could be considered competent to stand trial merely on the basis of Dr. Silk's ex parte statement, the court said to defense counsel:

I am going to ask you this, Mr. Ahern: I have taken the position that if once a person has been found of unsound mind after a lunacy hearing, an ex parte certificate of the superintendent of Saint Elizabeths is not sufficient to set aside that finding and I have held another lunacy hearing. That has been my custom. However, if you want to waive that you may do it, if you admit that he is now of sound mind.

The court accepted counsel's waiver on behalf of Durham, although it had been informed by the prosecutor that a letter from Durham claimed need of further hospitalization, and by defense counsel that ". . . the defendant does say that even today he thinks he does need hospitalization; he told me that this morning." [1] Upon being so informed, the court said, "Of course, if I hold he is not mentally competent to stand trial I send him back to Saint Elizabeths Hospital and they will send him back again in two or three months." In this atmosphere Durham's trial commenced.

His conviction followed the trial court's rejection of the defense of insanity in these words:

I don't think it has been established that the defendant was of unsound mind as of July 13, 1951, in the sense that he didn't know the difference between right and wrong or that even if he did, he was subject to an irresistible impulse by reason of the derangement of mind.

While, of course, the burden of proof on the issue of mental capacity to commit a crime is upon the Government, just as it is on every other issue, nevertheless, the Court finds that there is not sufficient to contradict the usual presumption of [sic] the usual inference of sanity.

There is no testimony concerning the mental state of the defendant as of July 13, 1951, and therefore the usual presumption of sanity governs.

While if there was some testimony as to his mental state as of that

---

[1] Durham showed confusion when he testified. These are but two examples:

"Q. Do you remember writing it? A. No. Don't you forget? People get all mixed up in machines.

"Q. What kind of a machine? A. I don't know, they just get mixed up.

"Q. Are you cured now? A. No, sir.

"Q. In your opinion? A. No, sir.

"Q. What is the matter with you? A. You hear people bother you.

"Q. What? You say you hear people bothering you? A. Yes.

"Q. What kind of people? What do they bother you about? A. (No response.)". . . .

*date to the effect that he was incompetent on that date, the burden of
proof would be on the Government to overcome it. There has been no
such testimony, and the usual presumption of sanity prevails.*

Mr. Ahern, I think you have done very well by your client and defended him very ably, but I think under the circumstances there is nothing that anybody could have done. [Emphasis supplied.]

We think this reflects error requiring reversal.

In Tatum v. United States we said, "When lack of mental capacity is raised as a defense to a charge of crime, the law accepts the
general experience of mankind and presumes that all people, including those accused of crime, are sane." [2] So long as this presumption prevails, the prosecution is not required to prove the defendant's sanity. But "as soon as 'some evidence of mental disorder
is introduced . . . sanity, like any other fact, must be proved as
part of the prosecution's case beyond a reasonable doubt.'" Here it
appears that the trial judge recognized this rule but failed to find
"some evidence." We hold that the court erred and that the requirement of "some evidence" was satisfied.

In Tatum we held that requirement satisfied by considerably less
than is present here. Tatum claimed lack of memory concerning
the critical events and three lay witnesses testified that he appeared to be in "more or less of a trance," or "abnormal," but two
psychiatrists testified that he was of "sound mind" both at the time
of examination and at the time of the crime. Here, the psychiatric
testimony was unequivocal that Durham was of unsound mind at
the time of the crime. Dr. Gilbert, the only expert witness heard, so
stated at least four times. . . . Intense questioning by the court
failed to produce any retraction of Dr. Gilbert's testimony that the
"period of insanity would have embraced the date July 13, 1951."
And though the prosecution sought unsuccessfully in its cross- and
recross-examination of Dr. Gilbert to establish that Durham was a
malingerer who feigned insanity whenever he was trapped for his
misdeeds, it failed to present any expert testimony to support this
theory. . . .

Apparently the trial judge regarded this psychiatric testimony as

[2] 1951, 88 U.S.App.D.C. 386, 389, 190 F.2d 612, 615.

"no testimony" on two grounds: (1) it did not adequately cover Durham's condition on July 13, 1951, the date of the offense; and (2) it was not directed to Durham's capacity to distinguish between right and wrong. We are unable to agree that for either of these reasons the psychiatric testimony could properly be considered "no testimony."

(1) Following Dr. Gilbert's testimony that the condition in which he found Durham on September 3, 1951, was progressive and did not "arrive overnight," Dr. Gilbert responded to a series of questions by the court:

Q. [Court.] Then it is reasonable to assume that it is not possible to determine *how far* this state of unsound mind had progressed by July 13th? Isn't that so? A. [Dr. Gilbert.] As to the seriousness of the symptoms as compared with them and the time I observed him, that's true, except that his travels were based, according to his statement to me, on certain of the symptoms and his leaving Washington, his giving up his job and work and leaving the work that he had tried to do.

Q. But you can't tell, can you, *how far* those symptoms had progressed and become worse by the 13th of July? A. No, not *how far* they were, that is correct. [Emphasis supplied.]

Thereafter, when the prosecutor on recross asked Dr. Gilbert whether he would change his opinion concerning Durham's mental condition on July 13, 1951, if he knew that Durham had been released from St. Elizabeths just two months before as being of sound mind, the court interrupted to say: "Just a minute. The Doctor testified in answer to my question that he doesn't know and he can't express a definite opinion as to his mental condition on the 13th of July." This, we think, overlooks the witness' unequivocal testimony on direct and cross-examination, and misconceives what he had said in response to questioning by the court, namely, that certain symptoms of mental disorder antedated the crime, although it was impossible to say how far they had progressed. . . .

(2) On re-direct examination, Dr. Gilbert was asked whether he would say that Durham "knew the difference between right and wrong on July 13, 1951; that is, his ability to distinguish between what was right and what was wrong." He replied: "As I have stated before, if the question of the right and wrong were pro-

pounded to him he could give you the right answer." Then the court interrupted to ask:

The Court. No, I don't think that is the question, Doctor—not whether he could give a right answer to a question, but whether he, himself, knew the difference between right and wrong in connection with governing his own actions. . . . If you are unable to answer, why, you can say so; I mean, if you are unable to form an opinion.

The Witness. I can only answer this way: That I can't tell how much the abnormal thinking and the abnormal experiences in the form of hallucinations and delusions—delusions of persecution—had to do with his anti-social behavior.

I don't know how anyone can answer that question categorically, except as one's experience leads him to know that most mental cases can give you a categorical answer of right and wrong, but what influence these symptoms have on abnormal behavior or anti-social behavior—

The Court. Well, your answer is that you are unable to form an opinion, is that it?

The Witness. I would say that that is essentially true, for the reasons that I have given.

Later, when defense counsel sought elaboration from Dr. Gilbert on his answers relating to the "right and wrong" test, the court cut off the questioning with the admonition that "you have answered the question, Doctor."

The inability of the expert to give categorical assurance that Durham was unable to distinguish between right and wrong did not destroy the effect of his previous testimony that the period of Durham's "insanity" embraced July 13, 1951. It is plain from our decision in Tatum that this previous testimony was adequate to prevent the presumption of sanity from becoming conclusive and to place the burden of proving sanity upon the Government. None of the testimony before the court in Tatum was couched in terms of "right and wrong."

Finally, even assuming *arguendo* that the court, contrary to the plain meaning of its words, recognized that the prosecution had the burden of proving Durham's sanity, there would still be a fatal error. For once the issue of insanity is raised by the introduction of "some evidence," so that the presumption of sanity is no longer absolute, it is incumbent upon the trier of fact to weigh and consider "the whole evidence, including that supplied by the presumption of sanity . . ." on the issue of "the capacity in law of the accused to commit" the crime.[3] Here, manifestly, the court as the trier of fact did not and could not weigh "the whole evidence," for it found there was "no testimony concerning the mental state" of Durham.

For the foregoing reasons, the judgment is reversed and the case is remanded for a new trial.

II

It has been ably argued by counsel for Durham that the existing tests in the District of Columbia for determining criminal responsibility, i.e., the so-called right-wrong test supplemented by the irresistible impulse test, are not satisfactory criteria for determining criminal responsibility. We are urged to adopt a different test to be applied on the retrial of this case. This contention has behind it nearly a century of agitation for reform.

A. The right-wrong test, approved in this jurisdiction in 1882, was the exclusive test of criminal responsibility in the District of Columbia until 1929 when we approved the irresistible impulse test as a supplementary test in Smith v. United States. The right-wrong test has its roots in England. There, by the first quarter of the eighteenth century, an accused escaped punishment if he could not distinguish "good and evil," i.e., if he "doth not know what he is doing, no more than . . . a wild beast." Later, in the same century, the "wild beast" test was abandoned and "right and wrong" was substituted for "good and evil." And toward the middle of the nineteenth century, the House of Lords in the famous M'Naghten case restated what had become the accepted "right-wrong" test in a form which has since been followed, not only in England but in most American jurisdictions as an exclusive test of criminal responsibility. . . .

As early as 1838, Isaac Ray, one of the founders of the American Psychiatric Association, in his now classic Medical Jurisprudence of Insanity, called knowledge of right and wrong a "fallacious" test

[3] Davis v. United States, 1895, 160 U.S. 469, 488, 16 S.Ct. 353, 358, 40 L.Ed. 499.

of criminal responsibility. This view has long since been substantiated by enormous developments in knowledge of mental life. . . .

Medico-legal writers in large number, The Report of the Royal Commission on Capital Punishment 1949–1953, and The Preliminary Report by the Committee on Forensic Psychiatry of the Group for the Advancement of Psychiatry present convincing evidence that the right-and-wrong test is "based on an entirely obsolete and misleading conception of the nature of insanity." [4] The science of psychiatry now recognizes that a man is an integrated personality and that reason, which is only one element in that personality, is not the sole determinant of his conduct. The right-wrong test, which considers knowledge or reason alone, is therefore an inadequate guide to mental responsibility for criminal behavior. . . . Nine years ago we said:

The modern science of psychology . . . does not conceive that there is a separate little man in the top of one's head called reason whose function it is to guide another unruly little man called instinct, emotion, or impulse in the way he should go.[5]

By its misleading emphasis on the cognitive, the right-wrong test requires court and jury to rely upon what is, scientifically speaking, inadequate, and most often, invalid and irrelevant testimony in determining criminal responsibility.

The fundamental objection to the right-wrong test, however, is not that criminal irresponsibility is made to rest upon an inadequate, invalid, or indeterminable symptom or manifestation, but that it is made to rest upon *any* particular symptom. In attempting to define insanity in terms of a symptom, the courts have assumed an impossible role, not merely one for which they have no special competence. As the Royal Commission emphasizes, it is dangerous

to abstract particular mental faculties, and to lay it down that unless these particular faculties are destroyed or gravely impaired, an accused person, whatever the nature of his mental disease, must be held to be criminally responsible. . . .[6]

[4] Royal Commission Report 80.

[5] Holloway v. United States, 1945, 80 U.S.App.D.C. 3, 5, 148 F.2d 665, 667, certiorari denied, 1948, 334 U.S. 852, 68 S.Ct. 1507, 92 L.Ed. 1774. . . .

[6] Royal Commission Report 114. And see State v. Jones, 1871, 50 N.H. 369, 392–93.

In this field of law as in others, the fact finder should be free to consider all information advanced by relevant scientific disciplines.

Despite demands in the name of scientific advances, this court refused to alter the right-wrong test at the turn of the century. But in 1929, we reconsidered in response to "the cry of scientific experts" and added the irresistible impulse test as a supplementary test for determining criminal responsibility. Without "hesitation" we declared, in Smith v. United States, it to be the law of this District that, in cases where insanity is interposed as a defense, and the facts are sufficient to call for the application of the rule of irresistible impulse, the jury should be so charged.[7] We said:

> The modern doctrine is that the degree of insanity which will relieve the accused of the consequences of a criminal act must be such as to create in his mind an uncontrollable impulse to commit the offense charged. This impulse must be such as to override the reason and judgment and obliterate the sense of right and wrong to the extent that the accused is deprived of the power to choose between right and wrong. The mere ability to distinguish right from wrong is no longer the correct test either in civil or criminal cases, where the defense of insanity is interposed. The accepted rule in this day and age, with the great advancement in medical science as an enlightening influence on this subject, is that the accused must be capable, not only of distinguishing between right and wrong, but that he was not impelled to do the act by an irresistible impulse, which means before it will justify a verdict of acquittal that his reasoning powers were so far dethroned by his diseased mental condition as to deprive him of the will power to resist the insane impulse to perpetrate the deed, though knowing it to be wrong.[8]

As we have already indicated, this has since been the test in the District.

Although the Smith case did not abandon the right-wrong test, it did liberate the fact finder from exclusive reliance upon that discredited criterion by allowing the jury to inquire also whether the accused suffered from an undefined "diseased mental condition [which] deprive[d] him of the will power to resist the insane impulse. . . ."[9] The term "irresistible impulse," however, carries the

---

[7] 1929, 59 App.D.C. 144, 146, 36 F.2d 548, 550, 70 A.L.R. 654.
[8] 59 App.D.C. at page 145, 36 F.2d at page 549.
[9] 59 App.D.C. at page 145, 36 F.2d at page 549.

misleading implication that "diseased mental condition[s]" produce only sudden, momentary or spontaneous inclinations to commit unlawful acts. As the Royal Commission found:

In many cases . . . this is not true at all. The sufferer from [melancholia, for example] experiences a change of mood which alters the whole of his existence. He may believe, for instance, that a future of such degradation and misery awaits both him and his family that death for all is a less dreadful alternative. Even the thought that the acts he contemplates are murder and suicide pales into insignificance in contrast with what he otherwise expects. The criminal act, in such circumstances, may be the reverse of impulsive. It may be coolly and carefully prepared; yet it is still the act of a madman. This is merely an illustration; similar states of mind are likely to lie behind the criminal act when murders are committed by persons suffering from schizophrenia or paranoid psychoses due to disease of the brain.[10]

We find that as an exclusive criterion the right-wrong test is inadequate in that (a) it does not take sufficient account of psychic realities and scientific knowledge, and (b) it is based upon one symptom and so cannot validly be applied in all circumstances. We find that the "irresistible impulse" test is also inadequate in that it gives no recognition to mental illness characterized by brooding and reflection and so relegates acts caused by such illness to the application of the inadequate right-wrong test. We conclude that a broader test should be adopted.

B. In the District of Columbia, the formulation of tests of criminal responsibility is entrusted to the courts and, in adopting a new test, we invoke our inherent power to make the change prospectively.

The rule we now hold must be applied on the retrial of this case and in future cases is not unlike that followed by the New Hampshire court since 1870. It is simply that an accused is not criminally responsible if his unlawful act was the product of mental disease or mental defect.

We use "disease" in the sense of a condition which is considered capable of either improving or deteriorating. We use "defect" in the sense of a condition which is not considered capable of either

[10] Royal Commission Report 110.

improving or deteriorating and which may be either congenital, or the result of injury, or the residual effect of a physical or mental disease.

Whenever there is "some evidence" that the accused suffered from a diseased or defective mental condition at the time the unlawful act was committed, the trial court must provide the jury with guides for determining whether the accused can be held criminally responsible. We do not, and indeed could not, formulate an instruction which would be either appropriate or binding in all cases. But under the rule now announced, any instruction should in some way convey to the jury the sense and substance of the following: If you the jury believe beyond a reasonable doubt that the accused was not suffering from a diseased or defective mental condition at the time he committed the criminal act charged, you may find him guilty. If you believe he was suffering from a diseased or defective mental condition when he committed the act, but believe beyond a reasonable doubt that the act was not the product of such mental abnormality, you may find him guilty. Unless you believe beyond a reasonable doubt either that he was not suffering from a diseased or defective mental condition, or that the act was not the product of such abnormality, you must find the accused not guilty by reason of insanity. Thus your task would not be completed upon finding, if you did find, that the accused suffered from a mental disease or defect. He would still be responsible for his unlawful act if there was no causal connection between such mental abnormality and the act. These questions must be determined by you from the facts which you find to be fairly deducible from the testimony and the evidence in this case.[11]

The questions of fact under the test we now lay down are as capable of determination by the jury as, for example, the questions juries must determine upon a claim of total disability under a policy of insurance where the state of medical knowledge concerning the disease involved, and its effects, is obscure or in conflict. In such cases, the jury is not required to depend on arbitrarily se-

[11] The court may always, of course, if it deems it advisable for the assistance of the jury, point out particular areas of agreement and conflict in the expert testimony in each case, just as it ordinarily does in summing up any other testimony.

lected "symptoms, phases, or manifestations" of the disease as criteria for determining the ultimate questions of fact upon which the claim depends. Similarly, upon a claim of criminal irresponsibility, the jury will not be required to rely on such symptoms as criteria for determining the ultimate question of fact upon which such claim depends. Testimony as to such "symptoms, phases, or manifestations," along with other relevant evidence, will go to the jury upon the ultimate questions of fact which it alone can finally determine. Whatever the state of psychiatry, the psychiatrist will be permitted to carry out his principal court function which, as we noted in Holloway v. U.S., "is to inform the jury of the character of [the accused's] mental disease [or defect]." [12] The jury's range of inquiry will not be limited to, but may include, for example, whether an accused, who suffered from a mental disease or defect did not know the difference between right and wrong, acted under the compulsion of an irresistible impulse, or had "been deprived of or lost the power of his will. . . ." [13]

Finally, in leaving the determination of the ultimate question of fact to the jury, we permit it to perform its traditional function which, as we said in Holloway, is to apply "our inherited ideas of moral responsibility to individuals prosecuted for crime. . . ." [14] Juries will continue to make moral judgments, still operating under the fundamental precept that "Our collective conscience does not allow punishment where it cannot impose blame." [15] But in making such judgments, they will be guided by wider horizons of knowledge concerning mental life. The question will be simply whether the accused acted because of a mental disorder, and not whether he displayed particular symptoms which medical science has long recognized do not necessarily, or even typically, accompany even the most serious mental disorder.

The legal and moral traditions of the western world require that those who, of their own free will and with evil intent (sometimes called *mens rea*), commit acts which violate the law, shall be criminally responsible for those acts. Our traditions also require that

[12] 1945, 80 U.S.App.D.C. 3, 5, 148 F.2d 665, 667.
[13] State v. White, N.M., 270 P.2d 727, 730.
[14] U.S.App.D.C. at page 5, 148 F.2d at page 667.
[15] 80 U.S. App. D.C. at pages 4–5, 148 F.2d at pages 666–67.

where such acts stem from and are the product of a mental disease or defect as those terms are used herein, moral blame shall not attach, and hence there will not be criminal responsibility. The rule we state in this opinion is designed to meet these requirements.

Reversed and remanded for a new trial.

A POLICE CHIEF'S VIEWS ON CAPITAL PUNISHMENT

EDWARD J. ALLEN

Excerpted from Edward J. Allen, "Capital Punishment: Your Protection and Mine," *The Police Chief,* XXVII (June 1960), 22, 24, 25–26, 28. At the time of publication, the author was Chief of Police in Santa Ana, California.

IN THE previous discussion on capital punishment (*The Police Chief,* March, 1960), it was pointed out that the wisdom of the ages, as revealed in Holy Scripture and spoken through the saints and sages, approved and advocated the death penalty for certain heinous crimes.

In our own times the people of California have repeatedly . . . turned back the constantly recurring repeal attempts of a militant minority and their malinformed minions. Yet, the present governor, with a seeming fixation, has vowed that he will foist the matter upon the California Legislature at succeeding sessions . . . and the same old tired arguments will be trotted out again:

1. Capital punishment does not deter crime.
2. It "brutalizes" human nature.
3. The rich and powerful often escape the death penalty.
4. Swift and certain punishment is more effective.
5. Society is to blame for the criminal's way of life, so we ought to be more considerate of him.

Let us, then, apart from the demands of pure justice, which should be the only determining factor, examine the above claims for validity and provability.

Capital Punishment Does Not Deter Crime?

If this be true, then why do criminals, even the braggadocian Chessman type, fear it most? Why does every criminal sentenced to death seek commutation to life imprisonment? Common sense alone, without the benefit of knowledge, wisdom, and experience, convinces that we are influenced to the greatest degree by that which we love, respect, or fear to the greatest degree—and that we cling most tenaciously to our most valued possessions. Life is indisputably our greatest possession. Additionally, there is no definitive proof anywhere that the death penalty is not a deterrent. There are merely the gratuitous statements of wishful thinkers, some of whom, because of the responsible duties of their positions, ought not be making unprovable or misleading statements.

Parole and probation people, an occasional governor, prison wardens (some prefer to be called penologists), criminal defense attorneys, and oftentime prison chaplains advance this "no deterrent" point of view. None doubts their sincerity, but they are hardly qualified to speak on the matter authoritatively or with pure objectivity. How can they *possibly* know how many people are NOT on death row because of the deterrent effect of the death penalty? Neither do they see the vicious, often sadistic despoiler or the cold-blooded professional killer plying their murderous trades. They encounter these predatory creatures after their fangs have been pulled. . . . Naturally, in their cages they behave more like sheep than ravenous wolves.

Prison wardens are housekeepers, custodians of criminals after they have been convicted. . . . It is neither the duty nor the prerogative of wardens or chaplains to decide matters of criminal justice. This has already been accomplished by the people. . . . True, it is altogether human to develop sympathy for even a depraved and chronic criminal. I suppose a zoo keeper develops a fondness for the wild animals which the taxpayers pay him to feed and guard. Yet, what kind of a zoo keeper would he be if he opened the cage doors and released the voracious beasts to prey upon the public? This very act would throw a community into terror and alarm. Even so, if a wild beast attacked a human being, there would be less guilt attached, since such an animal acts from instinct and not malice aforethought. Not so, a rational human being who deliberately murders or defiles his fellowman. It might serve a good purpose if these "bleeding hearts" could accompany those whose duty it is to examine first-hand . . . the gruesome handiwork of those for whom they intercede. . . .

It is also put forth, by those who would weaken our laws . . . that many murderers on death row claim they did not think of the death penalty when they committed their crimes. This is undoubtedly true. That is precisely the point. If they had thought of it, they would not have committed their crimes. . . . What of the countless others who *were* deterred from murder through fear of the penalty? . . . .

It Brutalizes Human Nature?

But the opposite is true. Wanton *murder* brutalizes human nature and cheapens human life, not the penalty for its perpetration. Capital punishment is the guarantee against murder and the brutalization of human nature. . . . To allow heinous criminals to commit their crimes without the commensurate reparation of the death penalty would surely brutalize and degrade human nature and reduce society to a state of barbarism. True Christian charity is based upon justice, the proper concern for the weak and innocent, not upon a soft-headed regard for despicable and conspiratorial killers. Let us resort to right reason and view retribution and reparation in proper perspective.

The Rich and Powerful Generally Escape?

There is truth in this statement and it is equally applicable to other penalties. . . . No one decries this discrimination more than law enforcement. . . . Since justice does not *always* prevail, ought we abandon our striving for its attainment? Who would advocate the abolition of the Ten Commandments because they are honored more in their breach than in their observance? . . . .

Specious Arguments

Two of the reasons advanced for the abolition of the death penalty have no validity whatsoever. One is an attempt to equate
human slavery with capital punishment. The argument is this:
Slavery was once rampant, but now an enlightened society favors
its abolition; therefore, we ought to do away with capital punishment, since we "moderns" are more "enlightened" than our forebears.

Firstly, slavery never was . . . morally right or justifiable or just.
The death penalty *is* morally right and justifiable and just. . . .
Here is another "beaut" from a university psychiatrist: The death
penalty could be society's way of "projecting its own crime into the
criminal." Now, I submit that the longer we permit this type of
nonsense to be spread abroad, the more ridiculous our nation is
going to appear in the eyes of the world. . . .

It is obvious to anyone who believes in the moral and natural
law . . . that first-degree murder requires personal premeditation
and the full consent of the will, hence, its punishment should be
meted out to the criminal or criminals personally responsible. To
argue otherwise is to argue the unnatural, but admittedly, this is
the day of the unnatural logician.

We argue that the unnatural in sex is natural and point to fables
for proof. Thus, we have the Oedipus and Electra complexes, situations culled from Greek drama and foisted upon us as Freudian
truisms. No use talking about free will, we just can't help ourselves. So today there is no crime, really, and no criminals—just
"complexes." And these "complexes" are so "complex" we must all
eventually succumb to their "complexity"—and employ a psy-
choanalyst. (Physician, heal thyself!) Truly, it is possible for people, even with exceptionally high IQ's, to be nuttier than fruit-
cakes, or vice versa, as the case may be. . . . [W]e will degenerate
further if we continue to give ear to certain types of
psychoanalytical professors and their automorphic automatons who
impute to all of us (including themselves?) the guilt for the personal crimes of individual criminals.

Swift and Certain Punishment

Swift and certain punishment is assuredly a crime deterrent, but only when coupled with commensurate severity. . . .

Individual States and Capital Punishment

. . . The proponents for abolition make much of the fact that there were seven states in 1958 . . . which have abolished capital punishment. These proponents make no mention of the fact that eight other states . . . once abolished capital punishment and have returned to it. . . . Of the states which have abolished capital punishment, two are now in New England: Maine and Rhode Island. Maine had one of the highest murder rates in New England in 1958, with an average of 2.5 per 100,000 population. . . . The six New England states have an average of 1.6, the lowest murder rate of any section of the country, yet only two of the six states have abolished the death penalty. . . .

The highest murder rate . . . was the southern group of 13 states. They had the exceptionally high rate of 9.0. Admittedly, the South has a problem, but the removal of the death penalty would only aggravate it. . . .

It would appear that the permeance of racial, ethnic, and religio-political cultures influence crime rates, including murder, in the various geographical sections of our country. Common sense dictates that more severe punitive sanctions are necessary in those states or sections where serious crime is more prevalent. . . . It would be the height of folly therefore to advocate the removal of the death penalty throughout the Southern States where the crime of murder is a serious threat.

Where crime and murder are at a low level and where community life is governed by respect and reverence for law, rather than by its enforcement, then severe punitive measures may be relaxed, but not abolished. . . .

Conclusion

Of course, the overwhelming statistic . . . is that 41 of the 50
states and the majority of the nations in the world have the death
penalty.

. . . All of the erudition, wisdom, experience, and knowledge of
history reveals that the death penalty is morally and legally just.
For the just man or nation this should be sufficient. Even so, justice is still justice, if no man is just—were it not so, God would
have told us.

CAPITAL PUNISHMENT:
A SOCIOLOGIST'S APPRAISAL

WALTER C. RECKLESS

Excerpted from Walter C. Reckless, "The Use of the Death Penalty—
A Factual Statement," *Crime and Delinquency*, 15, No. 1 (January 1969),
43–56. At the time of publication, Walter C. Reckless was Professor
of Sociology at Ohio State University.

CAPITAL PUNISHMENT has a rich catalogue of literature passionately critical of its use. But, except for the recording of certain
dramatic historical events, the factual information about the subject has been sparse.

Two outstanding studies, one by Clarence H. Patrick and the
other by James A. McCafferty, have attempted to supply systematized data on the world-wide legal status of capital punishment
and the legal provision for its use in the United States. In addition,
for almost a generation the U.S. Bureau of Prisons has collected
statistical information on the yearly number of executions in the
states, the District of Columbia, and the federal jurisdiction.

This paper will attempt to bring together the facts regarding the
legal status of capital punishment in the world and in the United
States as well as the available factual insights into its deterrent effect, and it will review the data and research, particularly Thorsten Sellin's which shed light on the effect of abolition or restricted
use of the death penalty on homicide and crimes of violence.

DE JURE VS. DE FACTO, INTERNATIONALLY

Patrick circulated a questionnaire through embassy sources and
received replies from 128 out of 146 countries.[1] He discovered that

[1] Clarence H. Patrick, "The Status of Capital Punishment: A World
Perspective," *Journal of Criminal Law, Criminology, and Police Science,* December 1965, pp. 397–411.

it was unrealistic to divide countries into those which have and those which do not have the death penalty, because some countries are abolitionist *de jure* and others are abolitionist *de facto*. In 1962, *de jure* abolition was found . . . in eighteen countries, the federal government of Mexico and twenty-five of its states, one state in Australia (Queensland), and five states in the United States (Alaska, Hawaii, Maine, Minnesota, and Wisconsin).

Thirty-six of eighty-nine countries with capital punishment reported that they had no executions during the five-year period 1958–62. This is certainly abolition *de facto*. The tiny country of Liechtenstein, while retaining capital punishment on the books, has not had an execution since 1798. In Belgium, the rarely pronounced death sentence is almost customarily commuted to life imprisonment; between 1867 and 1962, only one person was executed.

Actually, *de facto* status is not easy to interpret. If a country retains capital punishment on the books because its power structure believes that this law has a deterrent effect, does commutation after imposition of the death sentence constitute *de facto* abolition?

Somewhere between *de jure* abolition and *de facto* abolition fall the countries and states within a country which have legally limited application of the death penalty. In these instances, the penalty is provided for unusual crimes only, such as treason, espionage, murder of a chief of state, etc. Thirteen countries and two states in the United States belonged in this category in 1962 . . . ; some of them in past discussions have been mistakenly cited as abolitionist.

De facto abolition has a long history, evidenced in earlier times by substitute measures such as "benefit of clergy" and banishment to a penal colony. The movement to reduce the number of penal code offenses punishable by death has developed since the late eighteenth century. At that time, it is estimated, England's penal law listed over two hundred crimes calling for capital punishment. It now has four.

Decline in Number of Executions

Patrick analyzed the 1958–62 data from eighty-nine countries that have capital punishment . . . and found that, for the entire group, the annual average number of executions was 535.3, or 6 per country per annum. While six of the countries, executed more than fifty persons a year during the five-year period, thirty-six countries executed none at all. Without comparable data on the prevailing value system of each country, the operation of the police and court systems, population trends, urbanization, crime reports, etc., interpretation of these figures on execution is almost impossible, other than the fact that six executions per year for countries having the death penalty is not very many. Patrick contends that in historical perspective this average of 535.3 represents a "phenomenal decline." . . .

LEGAL STATUS OF CAPITAL PUNISHMENT IN THE U.S.

McCafferty performed the monumental task of analyzing the legal provisions for application of the death penalty in the laws of every state of the United States, the federal government, and the District of Columbia.[2] In 1952, six states out of the forty-eight were listed as abolitionist: Maine, Michigan (except for treason), Minnesota, North Dakota (except for treason and for murder in the first degree by a prisoner serving a life term for first-degree murder), Rhode Island (except for murder by a prisoner sentenced for life), and Wisconsin. Actually, to be rigorous about the matter, only three states—Maine, Minnesota, and Wisconsin—had complete abolition on their law books in 1952.

The McCafferty survey indicated that forty-four capital-punishment jurisdictions varied greatly in their coverage of various capital crimes and also in regard to whether the law defining a crime as a capital offense made the death penalty mandatory or permissive. . . . Specific findings are as follows:

1. Of the forty-four jurisdictions authorizing the death penalty for murder, only the District of Columbia and Vermont made it mandatory.

2. The nine jurisdictions which authorized the death penalty for murder but not for kidnaping were the District of Columbia, Kansas, Maryland, Massachusetts, Mississippi, North Carolina, New Hampshire, Oregon, and Pennsylvania.

[2] James A. McCafferty, *Capital Punishment in the United States: 1930 to 1952*, M.A. thesis, Ohio State University, 1954.

3. There is little likelihood of a charge of—to say nothing of a conviction for—"treason against the state." Nevertheless, twenty-six states make treason punishable by death, and, in fifteen of them, the death penalty on conviction for this crime is mandatory.

4. Most of the twenty jurisdictions which authorize the death sentence for rape are in the South.

5. In the ten states where capital punishment is authorized for lynching—Alabama, Arkansas, Georgia, Indiana, Kansas, Kentucky, Pennsylvania, South Carolina, Virginia, and West Virginia —the death penalty is not mandatory.

6. Though perjury in a capital trial is practically unknown, five of the ten states authorizing capital punishment for this offense make the death penalty mandatory.

7. The seven jurisdictions that make dynamiting a capital crime are Alabama, Georgia, Illinois, Iowa, Missouri, Mississippi, and Montana.

8. Armed robbery is punishable by death in Alabama, Kentucky, Missouri, Mississippi, Texas, and Virginia, and in the federal jurisdiction.

9. Alabama, Arkansas, Georgia, North Carolina, Vermont, and Virginia can punish arson by the death penalty; in Arkansas the death penalty is mandatory if the arsonist is a prisoner and the structure he burns is a prison.

10. Train robbery is a capital offense in Alabama, Arizona, Nebraska, Nevada, and New Mexico. (In New Mexico the death sentence is mandatory.)

11. In four states—Alabama, Kentucky, North Carolina, and Virginia—burglary is a capital crime.

McCafferty compiled the number of jurisdictions in the United States that listed the death penalty for one or more offenses. . . . One state (Georgia) applied the death penalty to fourteen offenses; another (Arkansas) applied it to eleven. One state (New Hampshire) specified only one crime (murder) subject to the death penalty; another (Massachusetts) specified two (murder and dueling). Of the forty-four jurisdictions in the United States retaining capital punishment in 1952, twenty-two listed from one to four capital offenses; the remainder listed from five to fourteen capital offenses. . . .

The Trend

Since the McCafferty survey in 1952, several states have gone into the abolitionist column. . . .

Alaska and Hawaii abolished the death penalty in 1957, before statehood; in 1964–65, they were joined by Iowa, New York, Oregon, Vermont, and West Virginia. Six states—Maine, Michigan, Minnesota, North Dakota, Rhode Island, and Wisconsin—had abolished the death penalty between 1846 and 1915. In October 1968 the count stood at thirteen states that do not have the death penalty; of fifty-two jurisdictions in the United States (including the federal government and the District of Columbia), thirty-nine retain capital punishment.

Eight states (Arizona, Colorado, Delaware, Kansas, Missouri, South Dakota, Tennessee, and Washington) restored the death penalty after having abolished it. On the other hand, three states (Iowa, Maine, and Oregon) which had restored capital punishment abolished it once again.

. . . The yearly count of the number of executions in the United States since 1930 [shows] a marked downward trend since 1936. Several increases over the previous year's figure occurred throughout the overall period of decline. Why these spurts took place is not clear; accumulation of delayed cases may perhaps account for them.

The dramatic decline in the number of executions—to almost the vanishing point [3]—does not mean a drastic reduction of the crime rate. Crimes against the person and especially crimes against property have increased more than the increase in population. The immediate reason for the decline in executions is the increasing unwillingness of juries and courts to impose death sentences. Another reason is the greater readiness of governors to commute death sentences to life imprisonment. Probably behind these factors is the growing public sentiment in the U.S. against the use of the death penalty. Thus juries, judges, and governors are responding to prevailing public opinion.

[3] No executions took place in 1968, up to Dec. 1, when this issue went to press.

Because of the long delays involved in the procedures for appeal or consideration for commutation, the prison population includes a steadily growing number of persons who have been sentenced to death. . . .

From 1930 to 1967, thirty-two women (twenty white and twelve Negro) were executed. Why so few, in proportion to the number of men? One reason is that women are much less frequently involved in crime. Another is the general attitude toward them which results in their being reported for crimes less frequently than men, arrested less frequently, held for court action less frequently, and found guilty by the courts less frequently. Women are nowhere near as saintly as the thirty-two executions in thirty-eight years seem to suggest: they have men "going for them" in many legitimate and illegitimate ways. It is doubtful that the United States will ever execute another woman.

Of 3,857 persons executed in the United States from 1930 to 1966, inclusive, 1,750 (45.4 per cent) were white; 2,065 (53.5 per cent), Negro; 42 (1.1 per cent), other. The number of Negroes executed was disproportionate to their percentage of the total population of the United States in the thirty-seven years. American criminologists have pointed out the disproportionate involvement of the Negro in most crimes, particularly in crimes against the person. The sociological criminologists see it as a result of a subculture of violence and the stresses and strains imposed on a minority group living in the slums of the large cities. In addition, victims (including Negro victims) are more willing to complain about Negro offenders than about white offenders, police are probably more ready to arrest and hold the Negro offender for court, and the courts tend to sentence Negro defendants more severely than white defendants. To get a commutation or an appeal for a death-sentenced Negro is far more difficult than for a white prisoner.

No Evidence of Deterrent Effect

HOMICIDE RATES IN CONTIGUOUS STATES

Although the proponents of capital punishment assert that it acts as a deterrent to capital crimes (particularly murder), the evidence indicates that it has no discernible effect in the United States, and presumably the same is true in other countries. Sellin compared the homicide rates per 100,000 population in abolition states with the rates in contiguous death-penalty states in the period 1920–55 and included in his tabulations the yearly number of executions in each contiguous death-penalty state. He found that homicide rates varied widely among these clusters of states and that within any regional cluster it was "impossible to distinguish the abolition state from the others" since the trends of the homicide rates "of comparable states with or without the death penalty are similar." As he interpreted the evidence, "the inevitable conclusion is that executions have no discernible effect on homicide death rates which, as we have seen, are regarded as adequate indicators of capital murder rates." [4]

Using the data from the 1967 *Uniform Crime Reports,* Table 9 [not shown] groups the thirteen abolition states with contiguous death-penalty states to compare the rates for murder, aggravated assault, and the combined major crimes of violence (including murder, forcible rape, robbery, and aggravated assault). Aggravated assault is listed separately because the main difference between it and murder is that the assault victim does not die: the intent of the assaulter may have been the same as the murderer's. One cannot point to higher sets of rates in the abolition states than in the contiguous retention states. As Sellin pointed out ten years ago, the variation between states in rates of murder and presumably all crimes of violence must be attributed to factors other than the abolition or retention of the death penalty.

However, some interesting comparisons can be singled out of the data in Table 9. Selecting nine of the thirteen abolition states (because of readiness of comparability), we can compare each with a contiguous retention state. (See Table 10.) [Not shown.] For Alaska, since contiguity cannot apply, the comparison is with a geographically large state having a small population.

Perhaps comparisons of this sort are not completely justified, but, even if they are only partly justified, the abolition states have

[4] Thorsten Sellin, *The Death Penalty* (Philadelphia, Pa.: American Law Institute, 1959), p. 34.

won the argument against deterrence: five to two with two ties, which might be considered a seven-to-two score for abolition. Perhaps the statement should be reversed: retention lost the argument in 1967 in seven out of nine abolition states.

BEFORE, DURING, AND AFTER ABOLITION

Gathering data from several European countries on homicides in the years before and after abolition of the death penalty or before and after drastic revisions in the law covering capital crimes, Sellin found that there was no clear trend one way or the other—that is, toward increase or decrease after abolition and revision of law.

The impact of abolition in the three earliest abolition states (Michigan, 1846; Rhode Island, 1852; and Wisconsin, 1853), as judged by the number of offenders imprisoned for first-degree murder, was negative. In various combinations of post-abolition years, there was definitely no increase in the yearly averages of convicted first-degree murderers. The data from Maine, which abolished the death penalty in 1876, restored it in 1883, and re-abolished it in 1887, indicate no overall increase in murder from one period to another. Ten other states have abolished capital punishment and then have restored it: Arizona, Colorado, Delaware, Iowa (which re-abolished it in 1965), Kansas, Missouri, Oregon (which re-abolished it in 1964), South Dakota, Tennessee, and Washington. Analyzing the statistics for the years before abolition, during abolition, and after restoration of the death penalty, Sellin says: "If any conclusion can be drawn, it is that there is no evidence that abolition of the death penalty generally causes an increase in criminal homicides or that its re-introduction is followed by a decline. The explanation of changes in homicide rates must be sought elsewhere."

Table 11 [not shown] shows the rate of murder and aggravated assault in four states that recently abolished the death penalty, for the two to three years before abolition and the two or three years after abolition. The murder rates show little change, before or after abolition. The trend in the rates of aggravated assault is definitely upward, but this rise seems to be completely unrelated to abolition, as it started in the years before abolition and continued thereafter. . . .

SHOOTING OF POLICE AND KILLINGS IN PRISON

One of the most persistent claims for capital punishment is that it deters criminals from shooting or killing policemen. Sellin obtained information on 128 killings of municipal police in 264 cities of the United States in the period 1919–54. The cities were located in seventeen states, of which eleven had the death penalty and six did not. The rate of police killings per 100,000 population during the period was 1.3 in the death penalty states and 1.2 in the abolition states. Claims that more police are killed in abolition than in retention states are not supported by the data.[5] . . .

Sometimes the claim is made that the death penalty deters prisoners from killing one another in prison and from killing staff members. Sellin requested data from prison administrators in the United States on the number of assaults which took place in their penal institutions in 1965. Of the forty-seven jurisdictions that supplied the required information, ten said no assaults had taken place in their prisons that year. Thirty-seven jurisdictions reported prison assaults having 603 victims, of whom sixty-one—eight officers and fifty-three inmates—died. The sixty-one killings resulted from forty-six incidents (mostly altercations), in which fifty-nine identifiable killers took part.

No fatal assaults occurred in the prisons of six abolition states: Alaska, North Dakota, Oregon, Rhode Island, West Virginia, and Wisconsin. Four other abolition states reported eight fatal assaults (out of the total of sixty-one). Seventeen death-penalty states reported no fatal assaults; nineteen death-penalty states and the federal prison system reported fifty-three prison homicides (out of the total of sixty-one). Certainly Sellin's data do not indicate that abolition of the death penalty encourages prison killings. The explanation of fatal as well as nonfatal assaults in prisons should be sought, according to Sellin, in the hazards of prison life—not in the presence or absence of capital punishment.[6] . . .

[5] Thorsten Sellin, "The Death Penalty and Police Safety," in *Capital Punishment*, Thorsten Sellin (ed.) (New York: Harper and Row, 1967), pp. 146, 154.

[6] Thorsten Sellin, "Prison Homicides," *Capital Punishment*, op. cit. pp. 154–60.

All these sources—a comparison of homicide rates in abolition states and contiguous retention states, a contrast of murder incidence in states which abolished and later restored capital punishment, the number of homicides just before and just after sentence or execution, the count on killings of policemen in cities of abolition and retention states, and the incidence of fatal assaults in prisons—contain no evidence that the absence or nonuse of the death penalty encourages murder, and no evidence that the presence or liberal use of the death penalty deters capital offenses.

IN RE GAULT

SUPREME COURT OF THE

UNITED STATES (MAY 15, 1967)

Excerpted from *In the Matter of Gault*, 387 U.S. 1 (1967).

No. 116—OCTOBER TERM, 1966.

| In the Matter of the Application of Paul L. Gault and Marjorie Gault, Father and Mother of Gerald Francis Gault, a Minor, Appellants. | On Appeal From the Supreme Court of Arizona. |

MR. JUSTICE FORTAS delivered the opinion of the Court.

This is an appeal under 28 U.S.C. §1257 (2) from a judgment of the Supreme Court on Arizona affirming the dismissal of a petition for a writ of habeas corpus. . . . The petition sought the release of Gerald Francis Gault, petitioners' 15-year-old son, who had been committed as a juvenile delinquent to the State Industrial School by the Juvenile Court of Gila County, Arizona. The Supreme Court of Arizona affirmed dismissal of the writ against various arguments which included an attack upon the constitutionality of the Arizona Juvenile Code because of its alleged denial of procedural due process rights to juveniles charged with being "delinquents." The court agreed that the constitutional guarantee of due process is applicable in such proceedings. It held that Arizona's Juvenile Code is to be read as "impliedly" implementing the "due process concept." It then proceeded to identify and describe "the particular elements which constitute due process in a juvenile hearing." It concluded that the proceedings ending in commitment of Gerald Gault did not offend those requirements. We do not agree, and we reverse. We begin with a statement of the facts.

I

On Monday, June 8, 1964, at about 10 a.m., Gerald Francis Gault and a friend, Ronald Lewis, were taken into custody by the Sheriff of Gila County. Gerald was then still subject to a six months' probation order which had been entered on February 25, 1964, as a result of his having been in the company of another boy who had stolen a wallet from a lady's purse. The police action on June 8 was taken as the result of a verbal complaint by a neighbor of the boys, Mrs. Cook, about a telephone call made to her in which the caller or callers made lewd or indecent remarks. It will suffice for purposes of this opinion to say that the remarks or questions put to her were of the irritatingly offensive, adolescent, sex variety.

At the time Gerald was picked up, his mother and father were both at work. No notice that Gerald was being taken into custody was left at the home. No other steps were taken to advise them that their son had, in effect, been arrested. Gerald was taken to the Children's Detention Home. When his mother arrived home at about 6 o'clock, Gerald was not there. Gerald's older brother was sent to look for him at the trailer home of the Lewis family. He apparently learned then that Gerald was in custody. He so informed his mother. The two of them went to the Detention Home. The deputy probation officer, Flagg, who was also superintendent of the Detention Home, told Mrs. Gault "why Jerry was there" and said that a hearing would be held in Juvenile Court at 3 o'clock the following day, June 9.

Officer Flagg filed a petition with the Court on the hearing day, June 9, 1964. It was not served on the Gaults. Indeed, none of them saw this petition until the habeas corpus hearing on August 17, 1964. The petition was entirely formal. It made no reference to any factual basis for the judicial action which it initiated. It recited only that "said minor is under the age of 18 years and in need of the protection of this Honorable Court [and that] said minor is a delinquent minor." It prayed for a hearing and an order regarding "the care and custody of said minor." Officer Flagg executed a formal affidavit in support of the petition.

On June 9, Gerald, his mother, his older brother, and Probation Officers Flagg and Henderson appeared before the Juvenile Judge in chambers. Gerald's father was not there. He was at work out of the city. Mrs. Cook, the complainant, was not there. No one was sworn at this hearing. No transcript or recording was made. No memorandum or record of the substance of the proceedings was prepared. Our information about the proceedings and the subsequent hearing on June 15, derives entirely from the testimony of the Juvenile Court Judge, Mr. and Mrs. Gault and Officer Flagg at the habeas corpus proceeding conducted two months later. From this, it appears that at the July 9 hearing Gerald was questioned by the judge about the telephone call. There was conflict as to what he said. His mother recalled that Gerald said he only dialed Mrs. Cook's number and handed the telephone to his friend, Ronald. Officer Flagg recalled that Gerald had admitted making the lewd remarks. Judge McGhee testified that Gerald "admitted making one of these [lewd] statements." At the conclusion of the hearing, the judge said he would "think about it." Gerald was taken back to the Detention Home. He was not sent to his own home with his parents. On June 11 or 12, after having been detained since June 8, Gerald was released and driven home. There is no explanation in the record as to why he was kept in the Detention Home or why he was released. At 5 P.M. on the day of Gerald's release, Mrs. Gault received a note signed by Officer Flagg. It was on plain paper, not letterhead. Its entire text was as follows:

Mrs. Gault:
Judge McGHEE has set Monday June 15, 1964 at 11:00 A.M. as the date and time for further Hearings on Gerald's delinquency
/s/ Flagg

At the appointed time on Monday, June 15, Gerald, his father and mother, Ronald Lewis and his father, and Officers Flagg and Henderson were present before Judge McGhee. Witnesses at the habeas corpus proceeding differed in their recollections of Gerald's testimony at the June 15 hearing. Mr. and Mrs. Gault recalled that Gerald again testified that he had only dialed the number and that the other boy had made the remarks. Officer Flagg agreed that at this hearing Gerald did not admit making the lewd remarks. But

Judge McGhee recalled that "there was some admission again of some of the lewd statements. He—he didn't admit any of the more serious lewd statements." Again, the complainant, Mrs. Cook, was not present. Mrs. Gault asked that Mrs. Cook be present "so she could see which boy had done the talking, the dirty talking over the phone." The Juvenile Judge said "she didn't have to be present at that hearing." The judge did not speak to Mrs. Cook or communicate with her at any time. Probation Officer Flagg had talked to her once—over the telephone on June 9.

At this June 15 hearing a "referral report" made by the probation officers was filed with the court, although not disclosed to Gerald or his parents. This listed the charge as "Lewd Phone Calls." At the conclusion of the hearing, the judge committed Gerald as a juvenile delinquent to the State Industrial School "for the period of his minority [that is, until 21], unless sooner discharge by due process of law." An order to that effect was entered. It recites that "after a full hearing and due deliberation the Court finds that said minor is a delinquent child, and that said minor is of the age of 15 years."

No appeal is permitted by Arizona law in juvenile cases. On August 3, 1964, a petition for a writ of habeas corpus was filed with the Supreme Court of Arizona and referred by it to the Superior Court for hearing.

At the habeas corpus hearing on August 17, Judge McGhee was vigorously cross-examined as to the basis for his actions. He testified that he had taken into account the fact that Gerald was on probation. He was asked "under what section of . . . the code you found the boy delinquent?"

His answer is set forth in the margin.[1] In substance, he con-

---

[1] "Q. All right. Now, Judge, would you tell me under what section of the law or tell me under what section of—of the code you found the boy delinquent?

"A. Well, there is a—I think it amounts to disturbing the peace. I can't give you the section, but I can tell you the law, that when one person uses lewd language in the presence of another person, that it can amount to—and I consider that when a person makes it over the phone, that it is considered in the presence, I might be wrong, that is one section. The other section upon which I consider the boy delinquent is Section 8-201, Subsection (d), habitually involved in immoral matters."

cluded that Gerald came within ARS § 8-201-6 (a), which specifies that a "delinquent child" includes one "who has violated a law of the state or an ordinance or regulation of a political subdivision thereof." The law which Gerald was found to have violated is ARS § 13-377. This section of the Arizona Criminal Code provides that a person who "in the presence of or hearing of any woman or child . . . uses vulgar, abusive or obscene language, is guilty of a misdemeanor. . . ." The penalty specified in the Criminal Code, which would apply to an adult, is $5 to $50, or imprisonment for not more than two months. The judge also testified that he acted under ARS § 8-201-6(d) which includes in the definition of a "delinquent child" one who, as the judge phrased it, is "habitually involved in immoral matters."

Asked about the basis for his conclusion that Gerald was "habitually involved in immoral matters," the judge testified, somewhat vaguely, that two years earlier, on July 2, 1962, a "referral" was made concerning Gerald, "where the boy had stolen a baseball glove from another boy and lied to the Police Department about it." The judge said there was "no hearing," and "no accusation" relating to this incident, "because of lack of material foundation." But it seems to have remained in his mind as a relevant factor. The judge also testified that Gerald had admitted making other nuisance phone calls in the past which, as the judge recalled the boy's testimony, were "silly calls, or funny calls, or something like that."

The Superior Court dismissed the writ, and appellants sought review in the Arizona Supreme Court. That court stated that it considered appellants' assignments of error as urging (1) that the Juvenile Code, ARS § 8-201 to § 8-239, is unconstitutional because it does not require that parents and children be apprised of the specific charges, does not require proper notice of a hearing, and does not provide for an appeal; and (2) that the proceedings and order relating to Gerald constituted a denial of due process of law because of the absence of adequate notice of the charge and the hearing; failure to notify appellants of certain constitutional rights including the rights to counsel and to confrontation, and the privilege against self-incrimination; the use of unsworn hearsay testimony; and the failure to make a record of the proceedings. Appellants further asserted that it was error for the Juvenile Court to remove Gerald from the custody of his parents without a showing and finding of their unsuitability, and alleged a miscellany of other errors under state law.

The Supreme Court handed down an elaborate and wide-ranging opinion affirming dismissal of the writ and stating the court's conclusions as to the issues raised by appellants and other aspects of the juvenile process. In their jurisdictional statement and brief in this Court, appellants do not urge upon us all of the points passed upon by the Supreme Court of Arizona. They urge that we hold the Juvenile Code of Arizona invalid on its face or as applied in this case because, contrary to the Due Process Clause of the Fourteenth Amendment, the juvenile is taken from the custody of his parents and committed to a state institution pursuant to proceedings in which the Juvenile Court has virtually unlimited discretion, and in which the following basic rights are denied:

1. Notice of the charges;
2. Right to counsel;
3. Right to confrontation and cross-examination;
4. Privilege against self-incrimination;
5. Right to a transcript to the proceedings; and
6. Right to appellate review.

We shall not consider other issues which were passed upon by the Supreme Court of Arizona. We emphasize that we indicate no opinion as to whether the decision of that court with respect to such other issues does or does not conflict with requirements of the Federal Constitution.

II

The Supreme Court of Arizona held that due process of law is requisite to the constitutional validity of proceedings in which a court reaches the conclusion that a juvenile has been at fault, has engaged in conduct prohibited by law, or has otherwise misbehaved with the consequence that he is committed to an institution in which his freedom is curtailed. This conclusion is in accord with the decisions of a number of courts under both federal and state constitutions.

This Court has not heretofore decided the precise question. In *Kent v. United States*, 383 U.S. 541 (1966), we considered the requirements for a valid waiver of the "exclusive" jurisdiction of the Juvenile Court of the District of Columbia so that a juvenile could be tried in the adult criminal court of the District. Although our decision turned upon the language of the statute, we emphasized the necessity that "the basic requirements of due process and fairness" be satisfied in such proceedings. *Haley v. Ohio*, 332 U.S. 596 (1948), involved the admissibility, in a state criminal court of general jurisdiction, of a confession by a 15-year-old boy. The Court held that the Fourteenth Amendment applied to prohibit the use of the coerced confession. MR. JUSTICE DOUGLAS said, "Neither man nor child can be allowed to stand condemned by methods which flout constitutional requirements of due process of law." . . . Accordingly, while these cases relate only to restricted aspects of the subject, they unmistakably indicate that, whatever may be their precise impact, neither the Fourteenth Amendment nor the Bill of Rights is for adults alone.

We do not in this opinion consider the impact of these constitutional provisions upon the totality of the relationship of the juvenile and the state. We do not even consider the entire process relating to juvenile "delinquents." For example, we are not here concerned with the procedures or constitutional rights applicable to the pre-judicial stages of the juvenile process, nor do we direct our attention to the post-adjudicative or dispositional process. . . . We consider only the problems presented to us by this case. These relate to the proceedings by which a determination is made as to whether a juvenile is a "delinquent" as a result of alleged misconduct on his part, with the consequence that he may be committed to a state institution. As to these proceedings, there appears to be little current dissent from the proposition that the Due Process Clause has a role to play. The problem is to ascertain the precise impact of the due process requirement upon such proceedings.

From the inception of the juvenile court system, wide differences have been tolerated—indeed insisted upon—between the procedural rights accorded to adults and those of juveniles. In practically all jurisdictions, there are rights granted to adults which are withheld from juveniles. In addition to the specific problems involved in the present case, for example, it has been held that the juvenile is not entitled to bail, to indictment by grand jury, to a public trial or to trial by jury. It is frequent practice that rules governing the arrest and interrogation of adults by the police are not observed in the case of juveniles. . . .

The early reformers were appalled by adult procedures and penalties, and by the fact that children could be given long prison sentences and mixed in jails with hardened criminals. They were profoundly convinced that society's duty to the child could not be confined by the concept of justice alone. They believed that society's role was not to ascertain whether the child was "guilty" or "innocent," but "What is he, how has he become what he is, and what had best be done in his interest and in the interest of the state to save him from a downward career." [2] The child—essentially good, as they saw it—was to be made "to feel that he is the object of [the State's] care and solicitude," [3] not that he was under arrest or on trial. The rules of criminal procedure were therefore altogether inapplicable. The apparent rigidities, technicalities, and harshness which they observed in both substantive and procedural criminal law were therefore to be discarded. The idea of crime and punishment was to be abandoned. The child was to be "treated" and "rehabilitated" and the procedures, from apprehension through institutionalization, were to be "clinical" rather than punitive.

These results were to be achieved, without coming to conceptual and constitutional grief, by insisting that the proceedings were not adversary, but that the State was proceeding as *parens patriae.* The Latin phrase proved to be a great help to those who sought to rationalize the exclusion of juveniles from the constitutional scheme; but its meaning is murky and its historic credentials are of dubious relevance. The phrase was taken from chancery practice, where, however, it was used to describe the power of the State to act in *loco parentis* for the purpose of protecting the property interests and the person of the child. But there is no trace of the doctrine in the history of criminal jurisprudence. At common law, children under seven were considered incapable of possessing

[2] Julian Mack, The Juvenile Court, 23 Harv. L. Rev. 104, 119–120 (1909).
[3] Id. at 120.

criminal intent. Beyond that age, they were subjected to arrest, trial, and in theory to punishment like adult offenders. In these old days, the State was not deemed to have authority to accord them fewer procedural rights than adults.

The right of the State, as *parens patriae,* to deny to the child procedural rights available to his elders was elaborated by the assertion that a child, unlike an adult, has a right "not to liberty but to custody." He can be made to attorn to his parents, to go to school, etc. If his parents default in effectively performing their custodial functions—that is, if the child is "delinquent"—the state may intervene. In doing so, it does not deprive the child of any rights, because he has none. It merely provides the "custody" to which the child is entitled. On this basis, proceedings involving juveniles were described as "civil" not "criminal" and therefore not subject to the requirements which restrict the state when it seeks to deprive a person of his liberty.

Accordingly, the highest motives and most enlightened impulses led to a peculiar system for juveniles, unknown to our law in any comparable context. The constitutional and theoretical basis for this peculiar system is—to say the least—debatable. And in practice, as we remarked in the *Kent* case, *supra,* the results have not been entirely satisfactory. Juvenile court history has again demonstrated that unbridled discretion, however benevolently motivated, is frequently a poor substitute for principle and procedure. . . . The absence of substantive standards has not necessarily meant that children receive careful, compassionate, individualized treatment. The absence of procedural rules based upon constitutional principle has not always produced fair, efficient, and effective procedures. Departures from established principles of due process have frequently resulted not in enlightened procedure, but in arbitrariness. . . .

Failure to observe the fundamental requirements of due process has resulted in instances, which might have been avoided, of unfairness to individuals and inadequate or inaccurate findings of fact and unfortunate prescriptions of remedy. Due process of law is the primary and indispensable foundation of individual freedom. It is the basic and essential term in the social compact which defines the rights of the individual and delimits the powers which the State may exercise. . . . But in addition, the procedural rules which have been fashioned from the generality of due process are our best instruments for the distillation and evaluation of essential facts from the conflicting welter of data that life and our adversary methods present. It is these instruments of due process which enhance the possibility that truth will emerge from the confrontation of opposing versions and conflicting data. "Procedure is to law what 'scientific method' is to science." [4]

It is claimed that juveniles obtain benefits from the special procedures applicable to them which more than offset the disadvantages of denial of the substance of normal due process. As we shall discuss, the observance of due process standards, intelligently and not ruthlessly administered, will not compel the States to abandon or displace any of the substantive benefits of the juvenile process. But it is important, we think, that the claimed benefits of the juvenile process should be candidly appraised. Neither sentiment nor folklore should cause us to shut our eyes, for example, to such startling findings as that reported in an exceptionally reliable study of repeaters or recidivism conducted by the Stanford Research Institute for the President's Commission on Crime in the District of Columbia. This Commission's Report states:

In fiscal 1966 approximately 66 percent of the 16- and 17-year-old juveniles referred to the court by the Youth Aid Division had been before the court previously. In 1965, 56 percent of those in the Receiving Home were repeaters. The SRI study revealed that 61 percent of the sample Juvenile Court referrals in 1965 had been previously referred at least once and that 42 percent had been referred at least twice before.

Certainly, these figures and the high crime rates among juveniles . . . could not lead us to conclude that the absence of constitutional protections reduces crime, or that the juvenile system, functioning free of constitutional inhibitions as it has largely done, is effective to reduce crime or rehabilitate offenders. We do not mean by this to denigrate the juvenile court process or to suggest that there are not aspects of the juvenile system relating to offenders

[4] Foster, Social Work, the Law, and Social Action, in Social Casework, July 1964, p. 286.

which are valuable. But the features of the juvenile system which its proponents have asserted are of unique benefit will not be impaired by constitutional domestication. For example, the commendable principles relating to the processing and treatment of juveniles separately from adults are in no way involved or affected by the procedural issues under discussion. Further, we are told that one of the important benefits of the special juvenile court procedures is that they avoid classifying the juvenile as a "criminal." The juvenile offender is now classed as a "delinquent." There is, of course, no reason why this should not continue. It is disconcerting, however, that this term has come to involve only slightly less stigma than the term "criminal" applied to adults. It is also emphasized that in practically all jurisdictions, statutes provide that an adjudication of the child as a delinquent shall not operate as a civil disability or disqualify him for civil service appointment. There is no reason why the application of due process requirements should interfere with such provisions.

Beyond this, it is frequently said that juveniles are protected by the process from disclosure of their deviational behavior. As the Supreme Court of Arizona phrased it in the present case, the summary procedures of juvenile courts are sometimes defended by a statement that it is the law's policy "to hide youthful errors from the full gaze of the public and bury them in the graveyard of the forgotten past." This claim of secrecy, however, is more rhetoric than reality. Disclosure of court records is discretionary with the judge in most jurisdictions. Statutory restrictions almost invariably apply only to the court records, and even as to those the evidence is that many courts routinely furnish information to the FBI and the military, and on request to government agencies and even to private employers. Of more importance are police records. In most States the police keep a complete file of juvenile "police contacts" and have complete discretion as to disclosure of juvenile records. Police departments receive requests for information from the FBI and other law-enforcement agencies, the Armed Forces, and social service agencies, and most of them generally comply. Private employers word their application forms to produce information concerning juvenile arrests and court proceedings, and in some jurisdictions information concerning juvenile police contacts is furnished private employers as well as government agencies.

In any event, there is no reason why, consistently with due process, a State cannot continue, if it deems it appropriate, to provide and to improve provision for the confidentiality of records of police contacts and court action relating to juveniles. It is interesting to note, however, that the Arizona Supreme Court used the confidentiality argument as a justification for the type of notice which is here attacked as inadequate for due process purposes. The parents were given merely general notice that their child was charged with "delinquency." No facts were specified. The Arizona court held, however, as we shall discuss, that in addition to this general "notice," the child and his parents must be advised "of the facts involved in the case" no later than the initial hearing by the judge. Obviously, this does not "bury" the word about the child's transgressions. It merely defers the time of disclosure to a point when it is of limited use to the child or his parents in preparing his defense or explanation.

Further, it is urged that the juvenile benefits from informal proceedings in the court. The early conception of the juvenile court proceeding was one in which a fatherly judge touched the heart and conscience of the erring youth by talking over his problems, by paternal advice and admonition, and in which, in extreme situations, benevolent and wise institutions of the State provided guidance and help "to save him from a downward career." Then, as now, goodwill and compassion were admirably prevalent. But recent studies have, with surprising unanimity, entered sharp dissent as to the validity of this gentle conception. They suggest that the appearance as well as the actuality of fairness, impartiality and orderliness—in short, the essentials of due process—may be a more impressive and more therapeutic attitude so far as the juvenile is concerned. . . .

Ultimately, . . . we confront the reality of that portion of the juvenile court process with which we deal in this case. A boy is charged with misconduct. The boy is committed to an institution where he may be restrained of liberty for years. It is of no constitutional consequence—and of limited practical meaning—that the institution to which he is committed is called an Industrial School. The fact of the matter is that, however euphemistic the title, a "receiving home" or an "industrial school" for juveniles is an institution of confinement in which the child is incarcerated for a greater or lesser time. . . . Instead of mother and father and sisters and brothers and friends and classmates, his world is peopled by guards, custodians, state employees, and "delinquents" confined with him for anything from waywardness to rape and homicide.

In view of this, it would be extraordinary if our Constitution did not require the procedural regularity and the exercise of care implied in the phrase "due process." Under our Constitution, the condition of being a boy does not justify a kangaroo court. The traditional ideas of juvenile court procedure, indeed, contemplated that time would be available and care would be used to establish precisely what the juvenile did and why he did it—was it a prank of adolescence or a brutal act threatening serious consequences to himself or society unless corrected? Under traditional notions, one would assume that in a case like that of Gerald Gault, where the juvenile appears to have a home, a working mother and father, and an older brother, the Juvenile Judge would have made a careful inquiry and judgment as to the possibility that the boy could be disciplined and dealt with at home, despite his previous transgressions. Indeed, so far as appears in the record before us, except for some conversation with Gerald about his school work and his "wanting to go to . . . Grand Canyon with his father," the points to which the judge directed his attention were little different from those that would be involved in determining any charge of violation of a penal statute. The essential difference between Gerald's case and a normal criminal case is that safeguards available to adults were discarded in Gerald's case. The summary procedure as well as the long commitment were possible because Gerald was 15 years of age instead of over 18.

If Gerald had been over 18, he would not have been subject to Juvenile Court proceedings. For the particular offense immediately involved, the maximum punishment would have been a fine of $5 to $50, or imprisonment in jail for not more than two months. Instead, he was committed to custody for a maximum of six years. If he had been over 18 and had committed an offense to which such a sentence might apply, he would have been entitled to substantial rights under the Constitution of the United States as well as under Arizona's laws and constitution. The United States Constitution would guarantee him rights and protections with respect to arrest, search and seizure, and pretrial interrogation. It would assure him of specific notice of the charges and adequate time to decide his course of action and to prepare his defense. He would be entitled to clear advice that he could be represented by counsel, and, at least if a felony were involved, the State would be required to provide counsel if his parents were unable to afford it. If the court acted on the basis of his confession, careful procedures would be required to assure its voluntariness. If the case went to trial, confrontation and opportunity for cross-examination would be guaranteed. So wide a gulf between the State's treatment of the adult and of the child requires a bridge sturdier than mere verbiage, and reasons more persuasive than cliché can provide. . . .

In *Kent* v. *United States, supra,* we stated that the Juvenile Court Judge's exercise of the power of the State as *parens patriae* was not unlimited. We said that "the admonition to function in a 'parental' relationship is not an invitation to procedural arbitrariness." With respect to the waiver by the juvenile court to the adult of jurisdiction over an offense committee [sic] by a youth, we said that "there is no place in our system of law for reaching a result of such tremendous consequences without ceremony—without hearing, without effective assistance of counsel, without a statement of reasons." We announced with respect to such waiver proceedings that while "We do not mean . . . to indicate that the hearing to be held must conform with all of the requirements of a criminal trial or even of the usual administrative hearing; but we do hold that the hearing must measure up to the essentials of due process and fair treatment." We reiterate this view, here in connection with a juvenile court adjudication of "delinquency," as a requirement which is part of the Due Process Clause of the Fourteenth Amendment of our Constitution.

We now turn to the specific issues which are presented to us in the present case.

III. Notice of Charges

Appellants allege that the Arizona Juvenile Code is unconstitutional or alternatively that the proceedings before the Juvenile Court were constitutionally defective because of failure to provide adequate notice of the hearings. No notice was given to Gerald's parents when he was taken into custody on Monday, June 8. On that night, when Mrs. Gault went to the Detention Home, she was orally informed that there would be a hearing the next afternoon and was told the reason why Gerald was in custody. The only written notice Gerald's parents received at any time was a note on plain paper from Officer Flagg delivered on Thursday or Friday, June 11 or 12, to the effect that the judge had set Monday, June 15, "for further hearings on Gerald's delinquency."

A "petition" was filed with the court on June 9 by Officer Flagg, reciting only that he was informed and believed that "said minor is a delinquent minor and that it is necessary that some order be made by the Honorable Court for said minor's welfare." The applicable Arizona statute provides for a petition to be filed in Juvenile Court, alleging in general terms that the child is "neglected, dependent, or delinquent." The statute explicitly states that such a general allegation is sufficient, "without alleging the facts." There is no requirement that the petition be served and it was not served upon, given, or shown to Gerald or his parents.

The Supreme Court of Arizona rejected appellants' claim that due process was denied because of inadequate notice. It stated that "Mrs. Gault knew the exact nature of the charge against Gerald from the day he was taken to the detention home." The court also pointed out that the Gaults appeared at the two hearings "without objection." The court held that because "the policy of the juvenile law is to hide youthful errors from the full gaze of the public and bury them in the graveyard of the forgotten past," advance notice of the specific charges or basis for taking the juvenile into custody and for the hearing is not necessary. It held that the appropriate rule is that "the infant and his parent or guardian will receive a petition only reciting a conclusion of delinquency. But no later than the initial hearing by the judge, they must be advised of the facts involved in the case. If the charges are denied they must be given a reasonable period of time to prepare."

We cannot agree with the court's conclusion that adequate notice was given in this case. Notice, to comply with due process requirements, must be given sufficiently in advance of scheduled court proceedings so that reasonable opportunity to prepare will be afforded, and it must "set forth the alleged misconduct with particularity." It is obvious, as we have discussed above, that no purpose of shielding the child from the public stigma of knowledge of his having been taken into custody and scheduled for hearing is served by the procedure approved by the court below. The "initial hearing" in the present case was a hearing on the merits. Notice at that time is not timely; and even if there were a conceivable purpose served by the deferral proposed by the court below, it would have to yield to the requirements that the child and his parents or guardian be notified in writing, of the specific charge or factual allegations to be considered at the hearing, and that such written notice be given at the earliest practicable time, and in any event sufficiently in advance of the hearing to permit preparation. Due process of law requires notice of the sort we have described—that is, notice which would be deemed constitutionally adequate in a civil or criminal proceeding. It does not allow a hearing to be held in which a youth's freedom and his parents' right to his custody are at stake without giving them timely notice, in advance of the hearing, of the specific issues that they must meet. Nor, in the circumstances of this case, can it reasonably be said that the requirement of notice was waived.

IV. Right to Counsel

Appellants charge that the Juvenile Court proceedings were fatally defective because the court did not advise Gerald or his parents of their right to counsel, and proceeded with the hearing, the adjudication of delinquency and the order of commitment in the absence of counsel for the child and his parents or an express waiver of the right thereto. The Supreme Court of Arizona pointed out that "there is disagreement [among the various jurisdictions] as to whether the court must advise the infant that he has a right to counsel." It noted its own decision in *State Dept. of Public Welfare v. Barlow, . . .* to the effect "that *the parents* of an infant in a juvenile proceeding cannot be denied representation by counsel of their choosing." (Emphasis added.) It referred to a provision of the Juvenile Code which it characterized as requiring "that the probation officer shall look after the interests of neglected, delinquent and dependent children," including representing their interests in court. The court argued that "The parent and the probation officer may be relied upon to protect the infant's interests." Accordingly it rejected the proposition that "due process requires that an infant have a right to counsel." It said that juvenile courts have the discretion, but not the duty, to allow such representation; it referred specifically to the situation in which the Juvenile Court discerns conflict between the child and his parents as an instance in which this discretion might be exercised. We do not agree. Probation officers, in the Arizona scheme, are also arresting officers. They initiate proceedings and file petitions which they verify, as here, alleging the delinquency of the child; and they testify, as here, against the child. And here the probation officer was also superintendent of the Detention Home. The probation officer cannot act as counsel for the child. His role in the adjudicatory hearing, by statute and in fact, is as arresting officer and witness against the child. Nor can the judge represent the child. There is no material difference in this respect between adult and juvenile proceedings of the sort here involved. In adult proceedings, this contention has been foreclosed by decisions of this Court. A proceeding where the issue is whether the child will be found to be "delinquent" and subjected to the loss of his liberty for years is comparable in seriousness to a felony prosecution. The juvenile needs the assistance of counsel to cope with problems of law, to make skilled inquiry into the facts, to insist upon regularity of the proceedings, and to ascertain whether he has a defense and to prepare and submit it. The child "requires the guiding hand of counsel at every step in the proceedings against him." [5] Just as in *Kent v. United States, supra,* at

[5] *Powell v. Alabama,* 287 U.S. 45, 69 (1932).

561–562, we indicated our agreement with the United States Court of Appeals for the District of Columbia Circuit that the assistance of counsel is essential for purposes of waiver proceedings, so we hold now that it is equally essential for the determination of delinquency, carrying with it the awesome prospect of incarceration in a state institution until the juvenile reaches the age of 21.

During the last decade, court decisions, experts, and legislatures have demonstrated increasing recognition of this view. In at least one-third of the States, statutes now provide for the right of representation by retained counsel in juvenile delinquency proceedings, notice of the right, or assignment of counsel, or a combination of these. In other States, court rules have similar provisions. . . .

We conclude that the Due Process Clause of the Fourteenth Amendment requires that in respect of proceedings to determine delinquency which may result in commitment to an institution in which the juvenile's freedom is curtailed, the child and his parent must be notified of the child's right to be represented by counsel retained by them, or if they are unable to afford counsel, that counsel will be appointed to represent the child.

At the habeas corpus proceeding, Mrs. Gault testified that she knew that she could have appeared with counsel at the juvenile hearing. This knowledge is not a waiver of the right to counsel which she and her juvenile son had, as we have defined it. They had a right expressly to be advised that they might retain counsel and to be confronted with the need for specific consideration of whether they did or did not choose to waive the right. If they were unable to afford to employ counsel, they were entitled in view of the seriousness of the charge and the potential commitment, to appointed counsel, unless they chose waiver. Mrs. Gault's knowledge that she could employ counsel is not an "intentional relinquishment or abandonment" of a fully known right.

V. Confrontation, Self-Incrimination, Cross-Examination

Appellants urge that the writ of habeas corpus should have been granted because of the denial of the rights of confrontation and cross-examination in the Juvenile Court hearings, and because the privilege against self-incrimination was not observed. The Juvenile Court Judge testified at the habeas corpus hearing that he had proceeded on the basis of Gerald's admissions at the two hearings. Appellants attack this on the ground that the admissions were obtained in disregard of the privilege against self-incrimination. If the confession is disregarded, appellants argue that the delinquency conclusion, since it was fundamentally based on a finding that Gerald had made lewd remarks during the phone call to Mrs. Cook, is fatally defective for failure to accord the rights of confrontation and cross-examination which the Due Process Clause of the Fourteenth Amendment of the Federal Constitution guarantees in state proceedings generally.

Our first question, then, is whether Gerald's admission was improperly obtained and relied on as the basis of decision, in conflict with the Federal Constitution. For this purpose, it is necessary briefly to recall the relevant facts.

Mrs. Cook, the complainant, and the recipient of the alleged telephone call, was not called as a witness. Gerald's mother asked the Juvenile Court Judge why Mrs. Cook was not present and the judge replied that "she didn't have to be present." So far as appears, Mrs. Cook was spoken to only once, by Officer Flagg, and this was by telephone. The judge did not speak with her on any occasion. Gerald had been questioned by the probation officer after having been taken into custody. The exact circumstances of this questioning do not appear but any admissions Gerald may have made at this time do not appear in the record. Gerald was also questioned by the Juvenile Court Judge at each of the two hearings. The judge testified in the habeas corpus proceeding that Gerald admitted making "some of the lewd statements . . . [but not] any of the more serious lewd statements." There was conflict and uncertainty among the witnesses at the habeas corpus proceeding—the Juvenile Court Judge, Mr. and Mrs. Gault, and the probation officer—as to what Gerald did or did not admit.

We shall assume that Gerald made admissions of the sort described by the Juvenile Court Judge, as quoted above. Neither

Gerald nor his parents was advised that he did not have to testify or make a statement, or that an incriminating statement might result in his commitment as a "delinquent."

The Arizona Supreme Court rejected appellant's contention that Gerald had a right to be advised that he need not incriminate himself. It said: "We think the necessary flexibility for individualized treatment will be enhanced by a rule which does not require the judge to advise the infant of a privilege against self-incrimination."

In reviewing this conclusion of Arizona's Supreme Court, we emphasize again that we are here concerned only with proceedings to determine whether a minor is a "delinquent" and which may result in commitment to a state institution. Specifically, the question is whether, in such a proceeding, an admission by the juvenile may be used against him in the absence of clear and unequivocal evidence that the admission was made with knowledge that he was not obliged to speak and would not be penalized for remaining silent. In light of *Miranda v. Arizona*, . . . we must also consider whether, if the privilege against self-incrimination is available, it can effectively be waived unless counsel is present or the right to counsel has been waived.

It has long been recognized that the eliciting and use of confessions or admissions require careful scrutiny. . . .

This Court has emphasized that admissions and confessions of juveniles require special caution. . . .

The privilege against self-incrimination is, of course, related to the question of the safeguards necessary to assure that admissions or confessions are reasonably trustworthy, that they are not the mere fruits of fear or coercion, but are reliable expressions of the truth. The roots of the privilege are, however, far deeper. They tap the basic stream of religious and political principle because the privilege reflects the limits of the individual's attornment to the state and—in a philosophical sense—insists upon the equality of the individual and the State. In other words, the privilege has a broader and deeper thrust than the rule which prevents the use of confessions which are the product of coercion because coercion is thought to carry with it the danger of unreliability. One of its purposes is to prevent the State, whether by force or by psychological domination, from overcoming the mind and will of the person under investigation and depriving him of the freedom to decide whether to assist the State in securing his conviction.

It would indeed be surprising if the privilege against self-incrimination were available to hardened criminals but not to children. The language of the Fifth Amendment, applicable to the States by operation of the Fourteenth Amendment, is unequivocal and without exception. And the scope of the privilege is comprehensive. As Mr. JUSTICE WHITE, concurring, stated in *Murphy v. Waterfront Commission,* . . . :

The privilege can be claimed in *any proceeding,* be it criminal or civil, administrative or judicial, investigatory or adjudicatory . . . it protects *any disclosures* which the witness may reasonably apprehend *could be used in a criminal prosecution or which could lead to other evidence that might be so used.* (Emphasis supplied.)

With respect to juveniles, both common observation and expert opinion emphasize that the "distrust of confessions made in certain situations" . . . is imperative in the case of children from an early age through adolescence. . . .

Against the application to juveniles of the right to silence, it is argued that juvenile proceedings are "civil" and not "criminal," and therefore the privilege should not apply. It is true that the statement of the privilege in the Fifth Amendment, which is applicable to the States by reason of the Fourteenth Amendment, is that no person "shall be compelled in any *criminal case* to be a witness against himself." However, it is also clear that the availability of the privelege [sic] does not turn upon the type of proceeding in which its protection is invoked, but upon the nature of the statement or admission and the exposure which it invites. The privilege may, for example, be claimed in a civil or administrative proceeding, if the statement is or may be inculpatory.

It would be entirely unrealistic to carve out of the Fifth Amendment all statements by juveniles on the ground that these cannot lead to "criminal" involvement. In the first place, juvenile proceedings to determine "delinquency," which may lead to commitment to a state institution, must be regarded as "criminal" for purposes of the privilege against self-incrimination. To hold otherwise would be to disregard substance because of the feeble enticement of the "Civil" label-of-convenience which has been attached to juvenile proceedings. Indeed, in over half of the States, there is not even assurance that the juvenile will be kept in separate institutions, apart from adult "criminals." In those States juveniles may be placed in or transferred to adult penal institutions after having been found "delinquent" by a juvenile court. For this purpose, at least, commitment is a deprivation of liberty. It is incarceration against one's will, whether it is called "criminal" or "civil." And our Constitution guarantees that no person shall be "compelled" to be a witness against himself when he is threatened with deprivation of his liberty—a command which this Court has broadly applied and generously implemented in accordance with the teaching of the history of the privilege and its great office in mankind's battle for freedom.

In addition, apart from the equivalence for this purpose of exposure to commitment as a juvenile delinquent and exposure to imprisonment as an adult offender, the fact of the matter is that there is little or no assurance in Arizona, as in most if not all of the States, that a juvenile apprehended and interrogated by the police or even by the juvenile court itself will remain outside of the reach of adult courts as a consequence of the offense for which he has been taken into custody. In Arizona, as in other States, provision is made for juvenile courts to relinquish or waive jurisdiction to the ordinary criminal courts. In the present case, when Gerald Gault was interrogated concerning violation of a section of the Arizona Criminal Code, it could not be certain that the Juvenile Court Judge would decide to "suspend" criminal prosecution in court for adults by proceeding to an adjudication in Juvenile Court.

It is also urged, as the Supreme Court of Arizona here asserted, that the juvenile and presumably his parents should not be advised of the juvenile's right to silence because confession is good for the child as the commencement of the assumed therapy of the juvenile court process, and he should be encouraged to assume an attitude of trust and confidence toward the officials of the juvenile process.

This proposition has been subjected to widespread challenge on the basis of current reappraisals of the rhetoric and realities of the handling of juvenile offenders.

In fact, evidence is accumulating that confessions by juveniles do not aid in "individualized treatment," as the court below put it, and that compelling the child to answer questions, without warning or advice as to his right to remain silent, does not serve this or any other good purpose. In light of the observations . . . it seems probable that where children are induced to confess by "paternal" urgings on the part of officials and the confession is then followed by disciplinary action, the child's reaction is likely to be hostile and adverse—the child may well feel that he has been led or tricked into confession and that despite his confession, he is being punished.

Further, authoritative opinion has cast formidable doubt upon the reliability and trustworthiness of "confessions" by children. . . . The recent decision of the New York Court of Appeals . . . *In the Matters of Gregory W. and Gerald S.*, deals with a dramatic and, it is to be hoped, extreme example. Two 12-year-old Negro boys were taken into custody for the brutal assault and rape of two aged domestics, one of whom died as the result of the attack. One of the boys was schizophrenic and had been locked in the security ward of a mental institution at the time of the attacks. By a process that may best be described as bizarre, his confession was obtained by the police. A psychiatrist testified that the boy would admit "whatever he thought was expected so that he could get out of the immediate situation." The other 12-year-old also "confessed." Both confessions were in specific detail, albeit they contained various inconsistencies. The Court of Appeals, in an opinion by Keating, J., concluded that the confessions were products of the will of the police instead of the boys. The confessions were therefore held involuntary and the order of the Appellate Division affirming the order of the Family Court adjudging the defendants to be juvenile delinquents was reversed. . . .

We conclude that the constitutional privilege against self-incrimination is applicable in the case of juveniles as it is with respect to adults. We appreciate that special problems may arise with respect to waiver of the privilege by or on behalf of children, and that there may well be some differences in technique—but not in principle—depending upon the age of the child and the presence and competence of parents. The participation of counsel will, of course, assist the police, juvenile courts and appellate tribunals in administering the privilege. If counsel is not present for some permissible reason when an admission is obtained, the greatest care must be taken to assure that the admission was voluntary, in the sense not only that it has not been coerced or suggested, but also that it is not the product of ignorance of rights or of adolescent fantasy, fright or despair.

The "confession" of Gerald Gault was first obtained by Officer Flagg, out of the presence of Gerald's parents, without counsel and without advising him of his right to silence, as far as appears. The judgment of the Juvenile Court was stated by the judge to be based on Gerald's admission in court. Neither "admission" was reduced to writing, and, to say the least, the process by which the "admissions" were obtained and received must be characterized as lacking the certainty and order which are required of proceedings of such formidable consequences. Apart from the "admission," there was nothing upon which a judgment or finding might be based. There was no sworn testimony. Mrs. Cook, the complainant, was not present. The Arizona Supreme Court held that "sworn testimony must be required of all witnesses including police officers, probation officers and others who are part of or officially related to the juvenile court structure." We hold that this is not enough. No reason is suggested or appears for a different rule in respect of sworn testimony in juvenile courts than in adult tribunals. Absent a valid confession adequate to support the determination of the Juvenile Court, confrontation and sworn testimony by witnesses available for cross-examination were essential for a finding of "delinquency" and an order committing Gerald to a state institution for a maximum of six years. . . .

As we said in *Kent v. United States,* 383, . . . with respect to waiver proceedings, "there is no place in our system of law for reaching a result of such tremendous consequences without ceremony. . . ." We now hold that, absent a valid confession, a determination of delinquency and an order of commitment to a state institution cannot be sustained in the absence of sworn testimony subjected to the opportunity for cross-examination in accordance with our law and constitutional requirements.

VI. Appellate Review and Transcript of Proceedings

Appellants urge that the Arizona statute is unconstitutional under the Due Process Clause because, as construed by its Supreme Court, "there is no right of appeal from a juvenile court order. . . ." The court held that there is no right to a transcript because there is no right to appeal and because the proceedings are confidential and any record must be destroyed after a prescribed period of time. Whether a transcript or other recording is made, it held, is a matter for the discretion of the juvenile court.

This Court has not held that a State is required by the Federal Constitution "to provide appellate courts or a right to appellate review at all." In view of the fact that we must reverse the Supreme Court of Arizona's affirmance of the dismissal of the writ of habeas corpus for other reasons, we need not rule on this question in the present case or upon the failure to provide a transcript or recording of the hearings—or, indeed, the failure of the juvenile court judge to state the grounds for his conclusion. *Cf. Kent v. United States*, . . . where we said, in the context of a decision of the juvenile court waiving jurisdiction to the adult court, which by local law, was applicable: ". . . it is incumbent upon the Juvenile Court to accompany its waiver order with a statement of the reasons or considerations therefor." As the present case illustrates, the consequences of failure to provide an appeal, to record the proceedings, or to make findings or state the grounds for the juvenile court's conclusion may be to throw a burden upon the machinery for habeas corpus, to saddle the reviewing process with the burden of attempting to reconstruct a record, and to impose upon the juvenile judge the unseemly duty of testifying under cross-examination as to the events that transpired in the hearings before him.

For the reasons stated, the judgment of the Supreme Court of Arizona is reversed and the cause remanded for further proceedings not inconsistent with this opinion.

It is so ordered.

Part V

PENO-CORRECTIONAL AND TREATMENT PROGRAMS

INTRODUCTION

CRIMINOLOGY TEXTS usually list five general policies under which societies operate to attack delinquency and crime: punishment (or retribution), incapacitation, deterrence, rehabilitation, and prevention. They are not mutually exclusive. Punishment may serve as a deterrent as well as an element of rehabilitation. Incapacitation (such as imprisonment) may be used as punishment, but it may also be employed to facilitate rehabilitation. And so on. In our own society, all five policies play some part in programs for dealing with potential and actual offenders.

Looked at another way, it may be asserted at the risk of oversimplification that in our society we seek to *prevent* unlawful behavior. Failing that in the individual case, we invoke the police power to *control* the offender by detection, apprehension, and adjudication. Up to this point there is consensus—prevention and control are fully approved by most members of our society. Ambivalence sets in when the question is raised: What shall we now do with, for, against, the adjudicated offender? Here some would answer: "*Punish* him." Others would advise: "*Treat* him, by the best means known, so he may become law-abiding and socially adjusted."

Punishment and treatment thus may be seen as two extremes on a continuum, with variations in between. At each extreme stand policemen, jurists, criminologists, penologists, social workers, psychiatrists, and laymen, who are engaged in a dialectic and actual tug of war. FBI Director J. Edgar Hoover has not noticeably retreated from the position he took years ago:

Crime being filth of mind, it must be fought in exactly the same manner that you fight filth of any other description, by boycotting those who engage in it, by segregating it, making it loathsome, outlawing it and those who practice it. A criminal should be regarded with utter revulsion; . . .[1]

[1] J. Edgar Hoover, *Persons in Hiding* (Boston: Little, Brown and Co., 1938), p. 314.

An opponent of the "treat-'em-rough" school is Dr. Karl Menninger, who would eschew punishment for the sake of punishment in favor of treatment of the offender:

What we want to accomplish is the reintegration of the . . . individual back into the main stream of social life, preferably a life at a higher level than before, just as soon as possible.[2]

Clearly, there is disagreement on what will serve society and the offender best, punishment for the sake of punishment or treatment aiming at the social readjustment of offenders. Some speak of *penal* treatment, which suggests a penalty to be exacted of the wrongdoer. Others prefer the term *correctional* treatment, suggestive of therapy in the interest of helping offenders change. The ambivalence is evident in the term *peno-correctional*, as applied to the programs established for dealing with offenders.

The fact that all shades of opinion exist in the same place, at the same time, accounts in no small measure for the confusion in the field concerning the goals of peno-correctional services and the methods to be employed in implementing them. But although the arguments over punishment-or-treatment continue, there has been a slow but discernible trend away from punishment as an end in itself to treatment as an end that offers possible benefits to the individual wrongdoer as well as society.

Incarceration has been seen as a means of punishment, as treatment, as both, and as neither, depending on who is speaking. Sykes, in "The Purposes of Imprisonment," discusses these views in Part V. In the item that follows, an anonymous prisoner reveals the actual impact upon him of his introduction to confinement. The next three items deal with the prison community, a concept developed by Donald Clemmer, whose "Imprisonment as a Source of Criminality" leads off the series. Failure to recognize the existence of a prison *community* that exerts a definite influence upon its members has retarded the possible development of institutional programs that might mitigate the evil effects of prison life.

Prisons are always and at best an abnormal environment, for many reasons. Ward and Kassebaum discuss one aspect in "The

[2] Karl Menninger, M.D., *The Crime of Punishment* (New York: Viking Press, 1968), p. 265.

Jail House Turnout: Homosexuality Among Women in Prison."
The absence of conventional sex and family life is a pervasive abnormality. In "Conjugal Visiting at the Mississippi State Penitentiary," Hopper describes one institution's attempt to mitigate this
problem.

An interesting and hopeful experiment in bridging the gap between confinement and freedom has been work-release programs,
discussed in the item by Zalba.

One of the most innovative and challenging developments in the
treatment field has been the current exploration of the use of inmates and former inmates as change agents, engaged in helping
prisoners, probationers and parolees find their way back to social
acceptance. Benjamin and associates treat with one phase of this
approach in "Inmates as 'Therapists.'"

As it becomes increasingly clear that incarceration has, on the
whole, been a failure as a means of "rehabilitation," attention is
shifting to community-centered programs. Hence "Alternatives to
Incarceration: Community-Centered Programs," a survey by the
President's Commission on Law Enforcement and Administration
of Justice.

Probation and parole are longtime, conventional community-
centered programs. In this Part, J. Edgar Hoover expresses his oft-
repeated feelings about these services in "A Police Official Looks
at Probation and Parole." Lejins discusses "Parole Prediction,"
designed to facilitate the efficient selection of inmates for parole.

Prediction techniques are actuarial procedures for estimating the
statistical chance of recidivism in individual cases. Hopefully,
proper selection and treatment of probationers and parolees will
yield a reduction in recidivism. In "Personal Characteristics Related to Parolee Recidivism," Glaser and O'Leary cite the statistical evidence to date on this subject, for parole.

Because there is a great deal of public misunderstanding of the
erstwhile murderer and his fitness ever to be at large, I have included Stanton's study of "Murderers on Parole." His findings have
been borne out by earlier investigations.

THE PURPOSES OF IMPRISONMENT

GRESHAM M. SYKES

Excerpted from Gresham M. Sykes, *The Society of Captives* (Princeton, New Jersey: Princeton University Press, 1958), pp. 9–12. At the time of publication Gresham M. Sykes was Associate Professor of Sociology at Northwestern University.

LYING SOMEWHERE between total annihilation of the offender on one hand and warning or forgiveness on the other, imprisonment is generally viewed as the appropriate consequence of most serious crimes. The issue is put more bluntly by prisoners themselves in their aphorism, "If you can't pull the time, don't pull the crime," but the thought is much the same.

Yet why is imprisonment appropriate? On what grounds is imprisonment justified? It is a cliché of modern penology that placing the offender in prison is for the purposes of punishment, deterrence, and reform. There is a beguiling neatness and simplicity about this three-pronged aim but it requires examination. . . .

The idea of punishment as the purpose of imprisonment is plain enough—the person who has committed a wrong or hurt must suffer in return. The State, through its agent the prison, is entitled if not morally obligated to hurt the individual who has broken the criminal law, since a crime is by definition a wrong committed against the State. Imprisonment should be punishment, not only by depriving the individual of his liberty, but also by imposing painful conditions under which the prisoner must live within the walls.

Now it is true that there are few persons directly concerned with handling the offender who will advance this view of the prison's purpose as baldly as we have stated it here. Penologists, prison psychiatrists, prison administrators, judges—all are far more apt to claim that we do not place the criminal in prison to secure retribution but to accomplish better things. Yet there is some reason to doubt that this denial of punishment as a legitimate aim of imprisonment accurately reflects the opinions of the general public. However harsh an insistence on retribution may appear to be, it cannot be ignored as a social force shaping the nature of the penal institution, whether in the form of community reactions to accusations of "coddling" prisoners or the construction of budgets by the state legislators.

The idea of deterrence as the aim of imprisonment is somewhat more complicated, for the argument contains three parts which need to be treated separately. First, it is claimed that for those who have been imprisoned the experience is (or should be) sufficiently distasteful to convince them that crime had best be avoided in the future. This decision to forego crime is not expected to come from a change in the attitudes and values concerning the wrongness of crime. Rather, it supposedly flows from a sharpened awareness of the penalties attached to wrongdoing. Second, it is argued that imprisonment is important as a deterrent not for the individual who has committed a crime and who has been placed in prison but for the great mass of citizens who totter on the edge. The image of the prison is supposed to check errant impulses, and again it is fear rather than morality which is expected to guide the individual in his action. Third, there is the assertion that the deterrent effect of imprisonment is largely a matter of keeping known criminals temporarily out of circulation and the major aim of imprisonment is to keep offenders within the walls where they cannot prey on the free community, at least for the moment.

Like those who argue for imprisonment as retribution, the adherents of imprisonment as deterrence tend to support those polices [sic] which would make life in prison painful, with the possible exception of those who argue for simple custody alone. They are faced with a moral dilemma when it comes to justifying punishment for the criminal in order to deter the noncriminal, for as Morris Cohen has pointed out, we feel uneasiness in hurting Peter to keep Paul honest. A more serious problem, however, is presented by the fact that the view of imprisonment as deterrence is based on a hypothetical, complicated cause-and-effect relationship. Does the prison experience actually induce the criminal to refrain from wrongdoing through fear of another period in custody? Does the image of the prison, for those who have never been within its walls, really check the potential criminal in mid-act? Affirmative answers to these questions must be secured before the use of imprisonment for the purpose of deterrence is rationally justified and this has proven to be no easy task. The usual procedure has been to make the common-sense assumption that men are rarely so good by either nature or training that they will always conform to the law without the threat of the pains of imprisonment in the background. For those who are too humanitarian to claim vengeance as the goal of confinement and too cynical, perhaps, to hope for real reform in the majority of cases, the objective of deterrence offers a comfortable compromise.

When we turn to the idea of imprisonment as reform, it is clear that there are few who will quarrel with such a desirable goal—the disputes center on how it can be accomplished, if at all. In seeking to use imprisonment for the rehabilitation of the offender, the aim is to eradicate those causes of crime which lie within the individual and imprisonment is commonly regarded as a device to hold the patient still long enough so that this can be achieved.

Unfortunately, the advocates of confinement as a method of achieving rehabilitation of the criminal have often found themselves in the position of calling for an operation where the target of the scalpel remains unknown. In recent years, with the rise of sociological and psychological interpretations of human behavior, the search for causal factors underlying criminality has grown more sophisticated but the answer remains almost as elusive as before. Yet in spite of the confusion in this area, there are many students of the problem who believe that the reformation of the offender requires a profound change in the individual's personality and that this change can be won only by surrounding the prisoner with a "permissive" or "supportive" social atmosphere. For those devoted to a psychiatric view of criminal behavior, psychotherapy in individual or group sessions is often advanced as the most hopeful procedure; for those with a more sociological bent, self-government, meaningful work, and education are frequently claimed as

minimal steps in the direction of reformation. Both factions—
divergent though they may be in their theoretical arguments—are
apt to agree that the punishing features of imprisonment should be
reduced or eliminated if efforts at rehabilitation are to be effective.

MY FIRST DAY IN PRISON

ANONYMOUS

Anonymous, "The First Day—Introduction to a Nightmare," *The Rhode Islander in Prison, A Special Issue produced by inmates at the ACI, The Providence Sunday Journal Magazine* (February 16, 1969), pp. 10–12. At the time of publication, the author was an inmate of the Adult Correctional Institution of Rhode Island.

"OKAY, EVERYBODY OUT!"

I didn't hear the sheriff until I was brought out of my fog when the three men I was handcuffed to started to slide toward the door of the sheriff's van. Although it had been several hours since I had stood before the judge and heard him say: "I sentence you to four years at the Adult Correctional Institutions," it seemed less than a moment ago.

"Let's go. You'll have plenty of time to look at stone walls even if it is from the inside. You can take my word for it, they look the same from both sides," said the sheriff.

As the line of connected men wound its way toward the plate glass doors in a bizarre game of follow-the-leader, I had a chance to look around at the outside of my new home. The large lawn smelled good with the fragrance of fresh cut grass. The cars sped along the highway, each a speedy way to get away from what was sure to be a most terrifying four years for me.

We walked through the plate glass doors into what I later came to know as the front hall. It contained an officer behind a small desk and a glass display case containing items that could be purchased by the inmate population or their visitors.

At a signal from the sheriff, another officer ensconced in a large glassed-off room flipped a switch and a large steel gate slid open. We were herded into the space formed by that door and another such door about 12 feet down the corridor.

"Line up along the wall and I'll get the handcuffs off," the sheriff ordered.

After we were free of each other and each of us was rubbing the circulation back into his hands, the electric gate opposite the one we entered opened and another officer came in. He unlocked a third door about halfway between the two gates. Then, turning to us he ordered: "As I call your name, come in here."

I watched two other men go in as they were called and then it was my turn. As I walked in I was instructed to strip. After the clothes I wore were thoroughly searched, as well as my person, I was permitted to dress in my underwear; but as I reached for my pants, I was handed a pair of green coveralls similar to the type worn by mechanics. A receipt for my personal belongings was thrust under my nose with a terse order to sign it, then get into the cage.

The "cage" referred to an end of the room that had been screened off from the rest. It was here that we all ended up after going through the commitment process. It was hard to believe that myself and the three men around me were now "inmates" when just moments ago, we were men with individuality. Now the green coveralls converted us to nearly identical images of each other.

After we were processed, we were led out of the cage and along another corridor ending with another steel gate.

"Another load for the hospital," called the committing officer.

When the turnkey approached, he got into a conversation with the committing officer, just as two friends do on any job. It seemed strange to hear them talking about a week-end boating trip they had planned when I knew that the next time that door opened for me would be four years from now.

Then came the transition that I had seen in movies and read about. As we stepped from the corridor, it was like stepping into another world, as indeed we had. While the lighting in the corridors had been bright fluorescent, the light in the cell block was dim, supplied as it was by about a dozen hanging light bulbs and whatever sunlight filtered in through the heavily barred windows.

As my eyes adjusted to the light, I could see the far wall of the cell house. Between myself and the wall there were three cell blocks, each three tiers high. It was foreboding and I was scared, more so than at any other point in my life. Somehow, I was still trying to cling to the fantasy that it was all a mistake. One that would be realized soon, and then I would be making that short trip through the corridors again, only this time on my way out. That fantasy was soon exploded when I heard the last steel door slam behind me.

Next we were led to still another steel door.

"Hospital," called the committing officer, and another officer came to let us into the hospital.

We were then instructed to line up against one wall and put the two sheets, pillow case and blanket we had been issued on the floor. "Strip to the waist," the hospital officer instructed.

Then the male nurse came out of his office and asked if anybody had been here before. When he saw one of the new arrivals, he said, "Don't even bother answering that, Charlie. We were so sure you were coming back, we didn't even put your record away."

When my turn came, I entered the office and tried to answer the questions that were put to me.

"Are you sure you have never been on junk?" the nurse asked.

"No sir."

"Then why are you in such a fog? Booze?"

"No sir."

Then the inmate clerk asked me how much time I was doing and if it was my first time in jail.

"Yes," I stammered. "I'm doing four years."

Looking at the nurse, the inmate said, "Well, that's why he's pretty well out of it."

After answering some more questions and getting a chest X-ray, we left the hospital and started walking down toward the end of the cell house. We passed row after row of empty cells.

"Where are all the other men?" asked one of the new arrivals.

"In the shop working," was the terse answer.

When we reached the cell block, the officer turned us over to the cell block officer. The cell block officer went to a small box attached to the last cell in the row. As he opened the box, I caught a glimpse of a row of handles numbered to correspond with the 33 cells in that row. Flipping several of the handles, he watched the indicated doors slide open.

We followed the officer down the row of cells as he assigned one to each of us with the instructions:

"This is your new home. Keep it clean. The bed must be made every time you are out of the cell. These have automatic locks, so when you are in the cell, keep your hands out of the doorway. Going in or coming out of the cells, make sure that you go right in or come right out. Do not loiter in the doorway. Whenever you see your door open, come out and see what is going on. Your cell will never be open if you are not supposed to come out. Do not put your arms through the bars anywhere near the door: If the door opens while your arm is out, it will snap the bone like a match stick. Throw your cigarette butts in the toilet and not out of the cell. You will follow all these rules or I will know why. Now get in your cells and make yourself at home. You'll be here awhile."

The cell consisted of three walls of quarter-inch steel plate for the sides and back. The front has six horizontal bars and 14 vertical bars. The cell is 5½ × 8 feet. The furnishings consist of a small sink and a toilet, a small table that is hinged at the wall, and the bed, which is made of a framework of angle iron with one-inch metal slatting. It too is hinged on the wall and suspended by chains. The mattress is made of some type of synthetic stuffing.

As I was looking around, I heard a slam and felt the walls vibrate. I spun around and all I could see were bars. There was no opening that you could walk through at will—nothing but bars. I think that was the point when things looked blackest. Here I was in jail. A criminal. A convict. A second-class citizen for the rest of my life. There was nothing to cling to for reassurance. I hadn't been able to see my parents for about four days. I felt then that the very things I had been brought up to believe in were not true. The teaching that one is supposed to trust is a fallacy. If you have money, then it is true. If your parents are among the socially elite, then it's true. However, if you are part of the indistinguishable working class, forget it.

Standing before the judge, I was asked, "It is understood that you have been made no promises concerning the sentencing power of this court . . . ?" Not knowing what to say, I said nothing until my lawyer leaned over and said, "Agree with him."

I agreed with the judge and never mentioned that the attorney general had promised I would get less than five years if I decided to plead *nolo* (throwing myself on the mercy of the court). I pleaded *nolo* and was sentenced to four years.

All of this went through my mind as I sat there looking at the walls; then a loud buzzer sounded. Almost at once, dozens of men started walking by the front of my cell. One man stopped and asked me if I wanted a cigarette. I had one, but when he started to pump me about my case, I told him to leave me alone, and he left.

Then I heard a knock on the wall from the cell next to me. It was Charlie.

"Watch out for the guys who come by and offer you things; they aren't trying to help you, only themselves. In a place like this where men are away from women, they try to make do with what they have available. So before you accept anything from anyone, make sure you know what he has in mind."

After this warning, I looked at everyone who passed my cell in a new light, trying to see if he might be one of the people I was warned about.

Suddenly the door snapped and started to slide open. As I walked out, I saw a line forming and was told it was the chow line. After about 20 minutes the line started to move. We wound our way along the same path that we had followed to the cells what had seemed like hours ago. We came to a door and after passing through, we emerged into the prison yard.

At first it was hard to reconcile what I saw with what I had imagined the inside of a prison to look like. There were wide, well kept lawns crisscrossed by sidewalks with several trees spotted about in a geometric layout. Around the lawns, there were several rows of green painted benches almost presenting the picture of one of the small parks found in the center of many small New England towns. This picture was shattered as soon as you lifted your gaze and spotted the huge gray wall surrounding the entire compound. It seemed almost to sneer and say, "You're here now, and you'll never get out."

If you lifted your gaze a little higher, you could see the guards walking their assigned posts atop the 20-foot wall. Each was armed with a .357 Magnum carbine and a .38 caliber revolver. Both well known for their stopping power, these guns have an unimpeded traverse of fire all around the wall.

After we had proceeded through the cafeteria-style serving line in the dining hall, we were directed to a row of tables. The chairs for these tables were hinged seats attached to the table behind us. At a signal from the guard standing in the front of the dining hall, men started filing from the tables and past a G.I. can where they threw their garbage and a table where they deposited their metal trays.

As I left the dining room I was instructed to return to the cell assigned to me. When I got back to my cell, the door was open but I was hesitant to go in until I was told to get in "or else."

"And make sure you are standing in front of your door until after the guard goes by taking a head count," the officer ordered.

I stood at the door and watched as the officer made a small check mark under my cell number on his pad. Well, this is it, I thought. Now all you are is a head to be counted and a body they must be able to account for. At this time there was nothing left. I was no longer me. I was cell number C-11, commitment number 28493, hospital record number 23507. In all truth, I was a body that the guards would be just as happy to see as a robot.

By this time it was four o'clock and I was told by Charlie that we would be in the cell until we went to breakfast at 8 the next morning. I don't know what those first few days would have been like if Charlie, an old hand at the game, hadn't been there to call over to me and let me know what was going on.

At 4:30 the buzzer again ripped the air with its strident shriek and sent me bolting from the bed to the cell door. I knocked on the wall to find out from Charlie what was going on.

"The men who are sentenced are allowed to come out from 4:30 until 9 p.m. They can watch television or go to the library or gym. After we have been here about 30 days, we will be able to go out in the evenings also. Remember what I told you about people offering you things. There will be several guys around tonight to see if anybody they know came in today."

True to his prediction, men started drifting around the front of

my cell and trying to strike up conversation. They offered me cigarettes. Thinking of the possible motives, I refused them all. After a
time, I was left alone to stare at the ceiling.

I heard another knock on the wall and saw a book being waved
in front of my cell. It was Charlie passing me something to read.
He had a friend who had brought him several books and some cigarettes. He offered to loan me a pack but assured me that that was
all it was, a loan. He told me how I could put in a store order to
get the things I needed if I had my money in the front office.

I tried to read the book he had sent but all my eyes could see
was the judge passing sentence on me. Everything was happening
in slow motion and I felt powerless as I tried to escape the judge's
stare and get away from the courtroom and the police and the
bars. Bars, something that will remain just behind my eyelids for a
long, long time. They will remain there long after I complete my
sentence.

At nine o'clock the alarm sounded again, sending the men to
their cells for the rest of the night. After five solid minutes of hearing doors slam closed one by one, there was silence. The guard
came by with his pad and seeing me in the cell, made another
small check on it. I noticed that he was a different guard from the
one who had assigned me to the cell.

The hush that had started when the last door had slammed shut
now erupted into what sounded like a full-scale riot. Radios
started blaring out the latest hit songs while men were calling from
cell to cell, talking on all subjects under the sun. This mad chatter
kept up until 10:30 when the lights went out, heralded by still another shriek from the alarm.

I came to realize that my world was going to be centered
around that alarm. It would tell me when to get up and when to
go to bed. It would call me to meals and return me to my cell. In
short, there would be little I could do without first being notified
by that bell. Each time it rang, it raised the dust in the corners, it
was so loud. It seemed to mock by saying, "I am your boss. You
will do nothing unless I tell you, and when I do tell you, you had
better jump."

The noise in the wing stopped as if a large hand was suddenly clasped over every mouth in the prison at the same moment. Now I was alone with the sounds made by 250 men preparing for sleep. Not being able to sleep myself, I listened until all I could hear was a few muted snores from the cells somewhere above me. Then I was alone with my thoughts. Thoughts of home and parents, thoughts of friends, many of whom I would or could never be friends with again. Thoughts that threatened to drive me crazy so that when sleep started to seep into me, I was actually glad to escape the harsh reality for the world of my dreams. A world where an alarm, any alarm, had no place or function.

Thus ended my first day in prison.

How old am I?

Seventeen.

IMPRISONMENT AS A SOURCE
OF CRIMINALITY

DONALD CLEMMER

Excerpted from Donald Clemmer, "Observations on Imprisonment as a Source of Criminality," *Journal of Criminal Law and Criminology*, XLI (September–October 1950), 311–19. Reprinted by special permission of the *Journal of Criminal Law, Criminology and Police Science*, Vol. XLI, No. 3 (Copyright © 1950, by Northwestern University School of Law). At the time of publication, Donald Clemmer was Director, Department of Corrections, in the District of Columbia.

THE RISE of humanitarianism during the last two centuries has had its influence on penal practices in noticeable ways. Earlier societies employed corporal punishment strictly as personal retribution and with deterrence as only a vague and secondary purpose. The development of imprisonment as a form of penalty for violation of laws is, in the historical sense, rather new. As humanitarianism has in minute and almost indescribable ways edged slowly into all human relations, so also has it influenced penal programs. The doctrine of humanitarianism has, for example, added a new concept to penal practice within fairly recent times—the concept of rehabilitation. This doctrine or trend has also recognized the youthful offender as a "juvenile," and it has been instrumental through modification of criminal codes, in reducing the single and absolute responsibility toward the offender. There have been many exceptions according to locality, and the humanitarian influence has been jagged in its slow, upward climb.

It is important to recall the historical newness of imprisonment as penal method, and it is especially important to recognize that rehabilitation as a serious purpose has only a few decades of experience behind it. These views are needed for perspective as we lay bare in a descriptive way the manner in which American prisons contribute in some degree to the criminality of those they hold.

No scientific evidence exists to show in what precise manner or to what degree the influences of the prison culture moulds [sic] the lives of those subjected to its culture. There can only be observations and rather crude deductions from those observations. Reference is indicated here, of course, to the well-understood condition that the tools of research for understanding in a scientific way how a human being comes to be exactly what he is, are limited. Human nature is too complicated a phenomena [sic] to disect [sic] and analyze, and locate with certainty the precise set of causes of any particular human reaction. There are too many and too complicated individual differences among people. Neither the psychiatrist nor the sociologist, in contrast to the chemist or mathematician, can claim full, logical understanding of causal factors. . . .

What Happens after Release?

We do have certain fundamental information as to what happens to men after they are released from prison. We know, for example, that in the United States varying numbers, between 40 and 80 percent, are returned to prisons for additional offenses. We know precisely that 83 percent of the inmates admitted to the Jail in Washington, D.C. in the fiscal year 1949 had some type of prior criminal record. Of the 19,980 admitted in the year mentioned, 46 percent had a prior felony record, and the balance a misdemeanor record only. In one of the revealing studies having reference to imprisonment it was found that four-fifths of the inmates of a reformatory in Massachusetts turned out to be failures so far as post-parole criminality was concerned, when the cases were followed up for a period of five to fifteen years following their release from the institution. . . .[1]

Statistics currently being cited in America by parole authorities indicate the country over that between 10 and 20 percent of in-

[1] Sheldon and Eleanor Glueck, Five Hundred Criminal Careers, Alfred A. Knopf, New York (1939).

mates placed on parole, violate it. These figures are accurate so far as they go, in that the calculations are made according to the length of time an individual is on parole. Thus, if a man is released from prison and has nine months to serve on parole, he is tallied as making a successful parole if he completes the nine months, even though the next month, he commits a new crime. It requires studies such as those made by the Gluecks to reveal the real facts. . . .

Prison Culture May Play a Part in These Results

It is unnecessary to belabor the point further, that the inmates flocking out from American penal and correctional institutions, go forth in tragic numbers to engage in crime again. Though no tangible facts are now presented, the later crimes of those who have been in prison are frequently more sophisticated or heinous than the offenses for which they were first committed. Just what part the prison itself plays in what appears to be this advance in criminality is not known. Certain basic conditions of the prison culture are understood, however, and it is reasonable to presume that the culture of a prison influences the people participating in it, in the same way as culture anywhere plays a part in shaping the lives of men.

It is not possible to characterize the culture of a prison community in specific detail here. Some of its characteristics are easily discernible, such as the recognition that it is a community of persons of one sex, that those held in it have been stigmatized by the broad society because of law violation, and that the persons who make it up hold, or have held, attitudes which are predatory or sexually unconventional or assaultive in nature. We know further that the prison usually concentrates these people in a restricted area, without privacy of any real kind, and that they mingle and interact in personal ways. . . .

. . . The prisoners [sic] world is a confused world . . . It is dominated and it submits. Its own community is without a well-established social structure. Recognized values produce a myriad of conflicting attitudes. There are no definite communal objectives. There is no consensus for a common goal. The inmates' conflict with officialdom and opposition toward society is only slightly greater in degree than conflict and opposition among themselves. Trickery and dishonesty overshadow sympathy and cooperation. Such cooperation as exists is largely symbiotic in nature. Social controls are only partially effective. It is a world of individuals whose daily relationships are impersonalized. It is a world of "I," "me," and "mine," rather than "ours," "theirs," and "his." Its people are thwarted, unhappy, yearning, resigned, bitter, hating, revengeful. Its people are improvident, inefficient, and socially illiterate. The prison world is a graceless world. There is filth, stink, and drabness; there is monotony and stupor. There is disinterest in work. There is desire for love and hunger for sex. There is pain in punishment. Except for the few, there is bewilderment. No one knows, the dogmas and codes notwithstanding, exactly what is important.

It is not surprising, if the foregoing evaluation is even reasonably accurate, that men or women in durance vile are influenced by the culture in which they find themselves and which, by their basic personality traits, they help to make. Prisons and prisoners are what they are because of what they have been in the past, and because of the mood and temper of society concerning them. Institutions could be so organized as to be less deliterious [sic], it is believed, but society is not ready for this step. Modern and progressive penological methods have done much in recent years to alter and counteract the harmful influences which are inherent in them. Certain paradoxes, society-wise, are apparent, however.

Even our modern prison system is proceeding on a rather uncertain course because its administration is necessarily a series of compromises. On the one hand, prisons are expected to punish; on the other, they are supposed to reform. They are expected to discipline rigorously at the same time that they teach self-reliance. They are built to be operated like vast impersonal machines, yet they are expected to fit men to live normal community lives. They operate in accordance with a fixed autocratic routine, yet they are expected to develop individual initiative. All to [sic] frequently restrictive laws force prisoners into idleness despite the fact that one of their primary objectives is to teach men how to earn an honest living. They refuse the prisoner a voice in self-government, but they expect him to become a thinking citizen in a democratic society. To

some, prisons are nothing but "country clubs" catering to the whims and
fancies of the inmates. To others the prison atmosphere seems charged
only with bitterness, rancor, and an all-pervading sense of defeat. And so
the whole paradoxical scheme continues, because our ideas and views regarding the function of correctional institutions in our society are confused, fuzzy, and nebulous.[2]

Director James V. Bennett in this statement has put the problem
well. The confusion of the free community ramifies to the prison or
correctional institutions. None-the-less, important progressive measures have been taken. Yet in the prisons of America, in spite of
classification, vocational and social education, psychiatric service,
and all the other efforts to treat inmates, prisons continue to
"breed crime," to use a moralistic phrase.

The manner and way in which the prison culture is absorbed by
some of its people can be thought of as a process of "prisonization." Prisonization is here regarded as similar to the sociological
concept of assimilation. When a person or group of ingress penetrates and fuses with another group, assimilation may be said to
have taken place. Assimilation implies that a process of acculteration [sic] occurs in one group whose members were originally quite
different from those of the group with whom they mix. It implies
that the assimilated come to share the sentiments, memories, and
traditions of the static group. It is evident, of course, that men who
come to prison are not greatly different from the ones already
there, so far as broad cultural influences are concerned. There are,
however, differences in mores, custom folkways, and group behavior patterns. As these are encountered, and when absorbed, some
aspects of acculteration [sic] or prisonization are occurring.

Every man who enters the penitentiary undergoes prisonization
to some extent. The first and most obvious integrative step concerns his status. He becomes at once an anonymous figure in a subordinate group. A number replaces a name. He wears the clothes
of the other members of the subordinate group. He is questioned
and admonished. He soon learns that the warden is all-powerful.
He soon learns the ranks, titles, and authority of various officials.
Even though a new man may hold himself aloof from other in-

[2] Annual Report, Federal Bureau of Prisons (1948), p. 3.

mates and remain a solitary figure, he finds himself within a few months referring to or thinking of keepers as "screws," the physician as the "croaker," and using the local nicknames to designate persons. He follows the examples already set in wearing his cap. He learns to eat in haste and in obtaining food he imitates the tricks of those near him.

After the new arrival recovers from the effects of the swallowing-up process, he assigns a new meaning to conditions he had previously taken for granted. The fact that food, shelter, clothing, and a work activity had been given him originally made no especial impression. It is only after some weeks or months that there comes to him a new interpretation of these necessities of life. This new conception results from mingling with other men and it places emphasis on the fact that the environment *should* administer to him. Supplemental to it is the almost universal desire on the part of the man, after a period of some months, to get a good job so, as he says, "I can do my time without any trouble and get out of here." A good job usually means a comfortable job of a more or less isolated kind in which conflicts with other men are not likely to develop. The desire for a comfortable job is not peculiar to the prison community, to be sure, but it seems to be a phase of prisonization.

In various other ways men new to prison slip into the existing patterns. They learn to gamble or learn new ways to gamble. Some, for the first time in their lives, take to abnormal sex behavior. Many of them learn to distrust and hate the officers, the parole board, and sometimes each other, and they become acquainted with the dogmas and mores existing in the community. But these changes do not occur in every man. However, every man is subject to certain influences which we may call the *universal factors of prisonization.*

Acceptance of an inferior role, accumulation of facts concerning the organization of the prison, the development of somewhat new habits of eating, dressing, working, sleeping, the adoption of local language, the recognition that nothing is owed to the environment for the supplying of needs, and the eventual desire for a good job are aspects of prisonization which are operative for all inmates. It is not these aspects, however, which concern us most but they are

important because of their universality, especially among men who
have served many years. That is, even if no other factor of the
prison culture touches the personality of an inmate of many years
residence, the influence of these universal factors are [sic] sufficient to make a man characteristic of the penal community and
probably so disrupt his personality that a happy adjustment in any
community becomes next to impossible. On the other hand, if inmates who are incarcerated for only short periods, such as a year
or so, do not become integrated into the culture except in so far as
these universal factors of prisonization are concerned, they do not
seem to be so characteristic of the penal community and are able
when released to take up a new mode of life without much difficulty.

The phases of prisonization which concern us most are the influences which breed or deepen criminality and anti-sociality and
make the inmate characteristic of the criminalistic ideology in the
prison community. As has been said, every man feels that [sic] the
influences of what we have called the universal factors, but not
every man becomes prisonized in and by other phases of the culture. Whether or not complete prisonization takes place depends
first on the man himself, that is, his susceptibility to a culture
which depends, we think, primarily on the type of relationships he
had before imprisonment, i.e., his personality. A second determinant effecting complete prisonization refers to the kind and extent
of relationships which an inmate has with persons outside the
walls. A third determinant refers to whether or not a man becomes
affiliated in prison primary or semi-primary groups and this is related to the two points already mentioned. Yet a fourth determinant depends simply on chance, a chance placement in work gang,
cellhouse, and with cellmate. A fifth determinent pertains to
whether or not a man accepts the dogmas or codes of the prison
culture. Other determinants depend on age, criminality, nationality, race, regional conditioning, and every determinant is more or
less interrelated with every other one.

Influencing Factors in Prisonization

With knowledge of these determinants we can hypothetically construct schemata of prisonization which may serve to illustrate its extremes. In the least or lowest degree of prisonization the following factors may be enumerated:

1. A short sentence, thus a brief subjection to the universal factors of prisonization.

2. A fairly stable personality made stable by an adequacy of positive and "socialized" relationships during pre-penal life.

3. The continuance of positive relationships with persons outside the walls.

4. Refusal or inability to integrate into a prison primary group or semi-primary group, while yet maintaining a symbiotic balance in relations with other men.

5. Refusal to accept blindly the dogmas and codes of the population, and a willingness, under certain situations, to aid officials, thus making for identification with the free community.

6. A chance placement with a cellmate and workmates who do not possess leadership qualities and who are also not completely integrated into the prison culture.

7. Refraining from abnormal sex behavior, and excessive gambling, and a ready willingness to engage seriously in work and recreative activities.

Other factors no doubt have an influencing force in obstructing the process of prisonization, but the seven points mentioned seem outstanding.

In the highest or greatest degree of prisonization the following factors may be enumerated:

1. A sentence of many years, thus a long subjection to the universal factors of prisonization.

2. A somewhat unstable personality made unstable by an inadequacy of the "socialized" relations before commitment, but possessing, none-the-less, a capacity for strong convictions and a particular kind of loyalty.

3. A dearth of positive relations with persons outside the walls.

4. A readiness and a capacity for integration into a prison-primary group.

5. A blind, or almost blind, acceptance of the dogmas and mores of the primary group and the general penal population.

6. A chance placement with other persons of a similar orientation.

7. A readiness to participate in gambling and abnormal sex behavior.

We can see in these two extremes the degrees with which the prisonization process operates. No suggestion is intended that a high correlation exists between either extreme of prisonization and criminality. It is quite possible that the inmate who fails to integrate in the prison culture may be and may continue to be much more criminalistic than the inmate who becomes completely prisonized. The trends are probably otherwise, however, as our study of group life suggests. To determine prisonization, every case must be appraised for itself.

Among inmates who are prisonized to the least degree, the agencies of reform existing in many American correctional institutions take hold, and it is these individuals who do not recidivate. That is, among the individuals who do not return again and again to prison, it is reasonable to presume that some force during their incarceration has acted as cause or partial cause to prevent recidivism. By case study methods it can be demonstrated that a trade learned in prison, or re-directed attitudes, or by surgical or psychiatric treatment, many inmates have been "cured," as it were, of their criminality. Others who do not recidivate, refrain from further crime simply because the one experience in prison has been so painful and unpleasant, that further desire or impetus toward crime is blocked.

Prisons do affect the people who live in them. They "breed crime," it appears, but they also retrain some few people and scare others. The culture of the prison with its unseen environment does these things through many of the same processes that operate in any social group. It is fundamentally a learning process.

In a scientific sense, the exact and precise role of the prison as cause of criminality can not be determined. Most persons admitted to prison already possess "criminality" in various degrees. After they leave, and if they engage again in crime, the "location" of criminality for such subsequent crime is difficult to determine. Presumably, the criminality which the individual brought to prison was intensified as a result of prisonization, and remained as a potential in the personality upon release. Also, when released, no forces of sufficient strength in the free community existed to thwart or divert the potential—and thus it may be said that the post-release community was conducive to crime. By observation and presumption, however, it can be stated that imprisonment, even in progressive institutions with their carefully developed training programs, frequently increases the criminality of the individuals it holds.

As humanitarianism increases and as the sciences which deal with human nature improve their techniques of treating the maladjusted, and as other better methods than prison are found to deal with violators of the law—the criminality of the offender, which is currently increased by the methods used, may well be decreased in that brave, new world somewhere ahead.

LEADERSHIP AMONG
PRISON INMATES

CLARENCE SCHRAG

Clarence Schrag, "Leadership Among Prison Inmates," *American Sociological Review*, XIX (February 1954), 37–42. At the time of publication, the author was affiliated with the University of Washington.

INEFFECTIVENESS of our penal institutions as therapeutic agencies is usually explained in terms of inadequate treatment facilities, inferior qualifications of administrators, or the criminogenic characteristics of inmates. The social climate of the prison and the interpersonal relations among the inmates have received less attention. Failure to investigate more thoroughly the dynamics of interaction among prison inmates may be a serious theoretical and methodological omission in criminological research.

Results of an investigation into inmate interaction in a western state prison are reported in this paper. Although data were obtained on several kinds of interaction . . . the discussion here is limited to leadership phenomena.

The Problem

The study is chiefly concerned with two problems: (1) How may inmate leaders and their followers be identified? (2) Assuming that leaders and followers are known, how may their interrelations be investigated so as to promote the eventual prediction and control of leadership phenomena? . . .

Research Procedures

DESIGNATION OF LEADERS AND FOLLOWERS

Data on leadership were obtained from a sociometric schedule which was administered to the residents of Trusty Quarters, a medium custody building within the prison. One hundred and forty-three respondents completed and returned their schedules. Included in the schedules is an item designed to obtain the names of inmate leaders.[1] Responses to this item were validated against the results of an official election in which members of the Inmate's Council were chosen. Results of the election, held one week after the schedules were completed, are in agreement with our sociometric data.

HYPOTHESES TO BE TESTED

Eventual prediction and control of prison leadership requires (1) identification of the general characteristics of leaders and (2) knowledge of the kinds of inmates who are most likely to be influenced by certain types of leaders. Accordingly, two sets of hypotheses were in this study submitted to statistical test. The first set is concerned with the question: Are the social and criminal backgrounds of inmate leaders significantly different from those of the other prisoners? Specifically, these hypotheses, stated in null form, assert that leaders are not significantly different from the total Trusty Quarters population with respect to age, ethnic status, occupation, marital status, educational attainment, test intelligence, type of offense, previous criminal record, or institutional adjustment. Rejection of certain of these hypotheses identifies background characteristics that are significantly associated with the status of inmate leader.

The second set of hypotheses is concerned with the question: Do variations in the social and criminal backgrounds of our respon-

[1] This item was stated as follows: "Name the inmates now in the institution who are in your opinion best fitted to represent the rest of the inmates by selection for the Council. List your first choice on the line below, then your second choice on the second line." The present analysis is restricted to first choices.

dents influence their choices for leaders? Stated in null form, these hypotheses assert that leadership preferences, as indicated by responses to our schedule, are independent of the background factors mentioned above. That is, expressions of preference are expected to be uninfluenced by variations in the backgrounds of our respondents. However, rejection of some of these hypotheses implies that the characteristics of leaders differ significantly according to the characteristics of the respondents by whom they are chosen. Thus, consensus among the prisoners does not occur with respect to their leadership preferences. . . .

PROCEDURES FOR TESTING THE HYPOTHESES

The above hypotheses, when tested by conventional chi-square analysis, may be accepted or rejected within specified degrees of probability. For example, the assertion that leaders do not differ from the rest of the Trusty Quarters prisoners was tested by classifying the two groups of inmates according to the sub-categories of a given characteristic, and then determining the significance of the difference between the two resulting frequency distributions. This procedure was repeated for each of the characteristics on which reliable information was available.

The second set of hypotheses, asserting that leadership preferences are independent of the respondents' characteristics, requires a somewhat more elaborate testing procedure. To illustrate, Table 1 . . . [deleted] presents data on leaders and followers classified according to type of offense. Leaders and the respondents by whom they were chosen are classified with respect to a given characteristic, type of offense, and the resulting data are recorded in a 3 by 3 table. Traits of leaders are plotted in rows and those of followers in columns. Obviously rows equal columns in number, and there are as many of each as there are sub-categories within the characteristic used in classifying the inmates.

Cell frequencies in Table 1 may easily be compared to a hypothetical model which is based on the assumption that leadership choices are independent of type of offense. This model is constructed by making cell frequencies proportional to the products of their row and column totals. If the hypothesis of independence is tenable, the model should duplicate the cell frequencies in Table 1. Large discrepancies between the two sets of frequencies, on the other hand, would require that the hypothesis be rejected.

Significance of the differences between the frequencies observed in Table 1 and those of the model may be determined by the usual chi-square test of independence. Chi-square for Table 1 rejects the independence hypothesis at the one per cent level of significance. Thus, leadership preferences, according to our data, are significantly related to the crimes for which the respondents were committed to prison.

What, however, is the nature of the relationship between leadership and type of offense? Further analysis of the data brings out several other important facts regarding prison leadership. For example, the most striking disparities between the independence model and Table 1 occur along the diagonal of homogeneity. That is, violent offenders [2] are almost exclusive in their preference for leaders who are also violent offenders, while sex offenders prefer sex offenders, and property offenders likewise choose leaders from their own offense category. This tendency for like to choose like is significant at the one per cent level. Furthermore, persons committed for violent or property offenses refrain from choosing sex offenders and, conversely, sex offenders avoid choosing property offenders. Despite these differences in the choice patterns of certain types of offenders, there is nevertheless a significant tendency for persons in all offense categories to select leaders who are committed for crimes of violence. Thus, statistical analysis of Table 1 shows that although a certain offense category—namely, crimes of violence—is uniformly related to leader status, important differences occur in the preference patterns of inmates who are classified by the offenses for which they were imprisoned.

Analyses similar to the above were made of the interrelations among leaders and followers classified according to each of the previously mentioned background factors.

[2] Violent offenders include, chiefly, cases of murder, assault, or robbery with a weapon.

Summary of Findings

CHARACTERISTICS OF THE LEADER GROUP

What are the determinants of leadership in a prison community? Comparison of our leaders with the total population suggests that, in general, factors related to criminal career and institutional adjustment are significantly associated with leadership, while social and economic background traits are not. Leaders, as a group, do not differ from the other inmates with respect to age, occupation, educational attainment, ethnic status, marital status, or scores on an intelligence test. However, leaders have served more years in prison, have longer sentences remaining to be served, are more frequently charged with crimes of violence, and are more likely to be repeated offenders. Significantly more leaders than other inmates are officially diagnosed as homosexual, psychoneurotic, or psychopathic. Finally, the institutional adjustments of leaders are marked by a significantly greater number of serious rule infractions, including escape, attempted escape, fighting, and assault.

Infrequently selected as leaders are first offenders, non-violent offenders, or persons with short prison sentences. Most important among the determinants of leadership are criminal maturity, comparatively permanent tenure in the institution, and habits of aggressiveness and violence. It is probable, therefore, that the group identifications of the inmates are generally organized around the activities and interests of the least improvable offenders, and that the values of the prison culture encourage rebellion and nonconformity.

PATTERNS OF PREFERENCE AMONG THE RESPONDENTS

What are the major variations in the leader preferences of our respondents? Choices of certain groups of inmates deviate significantly from the pattern outlined above. Different choice patterns of inmates classified by type of offense have already been mentioned. Other important variations occur with respect to both social and criminal background factors.

First offenders, for example, select leaders who are first offenders. Recidivists do so infrequently. Inmates serving short sentences prefer short-termers, whereas persons serving long sentences very rarely choose short-termers as leaders. Again, inmates with clear conduct records exclude those who have committed serious rule infractions. Conversely, the well-behaved inmates are excluded by the more fractious prisoners. Homosexuals, psychoneurotics, and psychopaths show greater preference for leaders from their own ranks than do the rest of the inmates.

We have already noted that leaders, as a group, do not differ significantly from the other inmates with respect to social background. However, preference patterns are significantly associated with certain social characteristics. Ethnic status is an example. Whites choose whites with rare exceptions, while Negroes tend to choose Negroes. Other ethnic groups scatter their choices throughout the prisoner population. Preferences are also associated with level of intelligence. Superior inmates choose leaders who have superior intelligence, while average and dull inmates choose leaders from their own intelligence classes. On the other hand, no significant differences were observed among respondents classified by age, occupation, education, or marital status.

Data on preference patterns, then, show that respondents, when classified by offense, sentence, previous criminal record, institutional adjustment, ethnic status, or test intelligence, tend to choose leaders who have traits similar to their own. This tendency for like to choose like is statistically significant. It provides the chief source of deviation from the general pattern of leader preference.

IMPORTANCE OF PROPINQUITY

Are leadership preferences related to the physical distances between groups of inmates? Segregation of inmates presumably regulates frequency of contact and thereby facilitates the regimentation of inmate activities. If segregation is effective, its influence should be reflected in the choices of our respondents. To test the effect of segregation, leaders and the respondents who chose them were classified according to whether they (1) reside in the same cell, (2) reside in different cells on same tier of building, (3) reside on different tiers of same building, and (4) reside in separate buildings.

The data show that degree of physical proximity is an important determinant of leader preference. The probability that a given inmate will be chosen by a certain respondent varies inversely with the physical distance between them. Thus, our findings confirm the utility of segregation as a device for regulating inmate interaction.

Conclusions

Results of this study, of course, cannot be generalized to other institutions until similar investigations are made elsewhere. Tentatively, however, we may conclude that leadership in prison is exercised by the criminally mature inmates who are serving long sentences for crimes of violence. Status of an inmate is ordinarily enhanced by acts of violence within the institution, by homosexuality, or by psychoneurotic or psychopathic behavior. Prison culture is organized around the values of its most persistent and least improvable members. . . . Socialization in prison means, for many inmates, the acquisition of the skills and attitudes of the habitual criminal.

Despite the dominance of the violent recidivists, certain groups of inmates direct their leadership choices toward persons who possess characteristics the same as their own. Short-termers, first offenders, persons convicted of non-violent crimes, and inmates who make good institutional adjustments create within the prison society a number of dissentient minorities. These minorities resist, at least to some extent, the dominant influence of the typical leader group. Thus, an effective classification program may segregate these minorities and in this way neutralize the influence of the more mature criminals.

Physical proximity is an important determinant of inmate influence and leadership. The kinds of influences an inmate encounters in prison life are largely determined by his immediate associates, especially by cell partners.

The above considerations clearly challenge the current trend toward construction of massive, multi-purpose prisons. They indicate the desirability of smaller and more specialized institutions. In a heterogeneous prisoner population, the hardened offenders may inevitably rise to positions of leadership. . . . It therefore seems likely that mass treatment, with its economy in construction and supervision, provides a misplaced emphasis in contemporary prison administration.

RESOCIALIZATION WITHIN WALLS

LLOYD W. MCCORKLE
AND RICHARD KORN

Lloyd W. McCorkle and Richard Korn, "Resocialization Within Walls," *Annals of the American Academy of Political and Social Science,* CCXCIII (May 1954), 88–98.

As THE concept "socialization" implies group membership, so the derivative concept, "resocialization," implies changes in group memberships. Many findings in the social origins of individual behavior suggest that the problem of reshaping the antisocial attitudes and values of offenders is related to the possibility of altering the patterns of group membership which they bring with them into the prison. The question therefore arises, To what extent does the prison community provide opportunities for altering the group memberships and reversing the socialization process which contributed to the criminal behavior of those incarcerated in it? A necessary starting point for this inquiry would appear to be an examination of the prison community as a functional social unit.

A prison is a physical structure in a geographical location where a number of people, living under highly specialized conditions, utilize the resources and adjust to the alternatives presented to them by a unique kind of social environment. The people creating and enmeshed in this environment include administrative, custodial, and professional employees, habitual petty thieves, one-time offenders, gangsters, professional racketeers, psychotics, prepsychotics, neurotics, and psychopaths, all living under extreme conditions of physical and psychological compression. The formal administrative structure of the prison may be comprehended in a brief glance at its table of organization. This table reveals a series of bureaucratically arranged positions with the warden at the top, and formal flow of power downward from his position. A more penetrating glance at the social structure of the prison reveals an ongoing complex of processes that can neither be described nor anticipated by a static enumeration of formal powers and functions. For interacting with this formal administrative structure—and in many ways independent of it—is another social structure, the inmate social system, which has evolved a complex of adaptational processes with which inmates attempt to cope with the major problems of institutional living.

The Inmate Social System

Observation suggests that the major problems with which the inmate social system attempts to cope center about the theme of social rejection. In many ways, the inmate social system may be viewed as providing a way of life which enables the inmate to avoid the devastating psychological effects of internalizing and converting social rejection into self-rejection. In effect, it permits the inmate to reject his rejectors rather than himself. If it is valid to assume that the major adjustive function of the inmate social system is to protect its members from the effects of internalizing social rejection, then it would seem to follow that the usages of this system are most beneficial to those who have most experienced the consequences of, and developed defenses around, social rejection. It would also follow that the system would find its strongest supporters among those who have, in the process, become most independent of the larger society's values in their definitions and evaluations of themselves. We might also expect to find that those individuals whose self-evaluations are still relatively dependent on the values of the larger, noncriminal society and whose supportive human relationships are still largely with its members would have the most difficulty in adjusting to a social system whose major values are based on the rejection of that larger society.

If these inferences are correct, we may only conclude that the inmate social system is most supportive and protective to those inmates who are most criminally acculturated—and conversely, most threatening and disruptive to those whose loyalties and personal identifications are still with the noncriminal world. Observation supports this conclusion. The nonacculturated offender is rejected not only by the society which defines him as a person, but he suffers the double jeopardy of rejection from the subsociety in which he is now forced to live. In effect, he is denied membership in both. The adaptive inmate, on the other hand, is not only protected from loss of the group membership which defined him as a person, but he is placed in an environment where that membership is assured and his personal adjustment consequently powerfully bolstered. Continued group acceptance of these individuals is based upon their adherence to inmate codes and values.

Characteristics of the System

The first and most obvious characteristic of the inmate social system is the absence of escape routes from it. The offender is not only incarcerated in a physical prison without exit; he is enmeshed in a human environment and a pattern of usages from which the only escape is psychological withdrawal. Another aspect of the inmate social system is its rigidly hierarchical character, in which vertical mobility, while possible, is highly difficult. The causes of this immobilizing rigidity are various.

The numbers of roles an individual may play are severely limited and, once assigned, are maintained—particularly at the lower status levels—with enormous group pressure. The degree to which the individual can partake in the selection of his role is similarly limited and conditional. From the moment the new inmate arrives from the court or the county jail, he is exposed to a series of very direct defining experiences. It is of interest to note that those inmates who participate in and administer these experiences are frequently those who recognize that the inmate is somewhat near their level, a perception which stimulates anxiety in them. For example, an obviously tough professional hoodlum will create no special problem to the majority of the lower-status inmates who, responding to minimal clues, will either avoid him or immediately acknowledge his higher status. The arrival of this inmate, however, will pose a threat to the wing's chief "bad man," who will be expected to challenge the newcomer to a battle of mutual definitions.

There is an additional aspect of this defining process which sheds light on another characteristic of the social structure, namely, its extreme authoritarianism. The role-defining conflicts carried on by inmates on or near the same status level point up the fact that any situation of equality is a situation of threat which must be resolved into a relationship of superordinance and subordinance. However vehemently inmates in groups demand equal treatment and condemn favoritism, inmates as individuals continuously press for special personal advantages. Where demands for increased permissiveness have been granted by authorities, the results have almost invariably been that the rigid authoritarian patterns have not been destroyed but merely transferred to a new and less stable center of gravity. The history of inmate self-government reveals that the yielding up of powers by the external ordering authority usually generates patterns of internal group coercion more punitive, more rigid, and incomparably more discriminatory than those which they supplanted. This authoritarian character of inmate relationships suggests that members of the system afford no exception to the general psychological observation that the victims of power tend to regard its possession as the highest personal value.

POSSESSION OF POWER

The dominating value of the inmate social system seems to be the possession and exercise of coercive power. There are probably no relationship functions which have escaped the influence of this factor. Even usages of mutual aid have been contaminated and made subservient to it. To illustrate: one way to proclaim possessive rights over another inmate is to help him in some way, usually by material aid. New inmates, unaware of the subversive motivations behind these services, are quickly apprised of their coercive character. Once an inmate has accepted any material symbol of service it is understood that the donor of these gifts has thereby established personal rights over the receiver. The extreme degree to which these mutual aid usages have been made dependent on power struggles is illustrated by the custom of forcing other inmates to accept cigarettes, a frequent prison invitation to submission. Aggressive inmates will go to extraordinary lengths to place gifts in the cells of inmates they have selected for personal domination. These intended victims, in order to escape the threatened bondage, must find the owner and insist that the gifts be taken back. Should the donor refuse to take them back, the receiver may be forced to fight him then and there.

One measure of the inherent cohesive strength of any social system is the degree to which behavior controls have been individually internalized, thereby obviating all but a minimal degree of inter-personal coercion. Since the basic values of the inmate social system, personal power and exploitation, are inherently inimical to cooperative group living, enormous pressures are required to prevent the inherently centrifugal forces from disintegrating the system. These pressures are supplied in part by the external control and punitive threats of the official world. In the absence of these external unifying forces, order can be maintained only by the most tyrannical inmate rule.

EVASION OF RULES

Like every other social organization, the inmate system provides not only rules and sanctions for their violation but also methods for evading those rules and escaping the sanctions. The disruptive forces inherent in the basic personal value (personal domination through the exertion of coercive power) have generated techniques for the violation of the most fundamental ordinances in support of group unity. The power of these disruptive forces is indicated by the fact that even the most sacred rule of the inmate code, the law against squealing, is daily violated and evaded with impunity. Contrary to the propaganda generated by the more solemn of the inmate clergy in defense of their code, informers and betrayers require little or no seduction by prison officials. Actually the main administrative problem presented by informers is not gaining them but avoiding them, since they come as volunteers from all levels of the inmate hierarchy.

In face of these weaknesses and internal contradictions the question arises, How does the system avoid breaking down and why have prison officials generally failed in exploiting its weaknesses? A part of the answer may lie in the fact that prison officials have generally tended to use the inmate power structure as an aid in prison administration and the maintenance of good order—not realizing that in this attempt to manipulate the structure they themselves are more used than using. Far from systematically attempting to undermine the inmate hierarchy, the institution generally gives it covert support and recognition by assigning better jobs and quarters to its high-status members providing they are "good inmates." In this and in other ways the institution buys peace with the system by avoiding battle with it.

The Work Situation

The freedom from the necessity of earning a living in prison introduces a striking difference between the requirements of material success within and without the walls. A significantly different configuration of traits and aptitudes acquires value, some of which represent direct reversals of those developed outside. In prison the direct relationship between work done and material value received has largely broken down. The relationship between individual productivity and personal status is even more markedly broken down. From a sophisticated inmate's point of view this relationship seems to become a negative one. Strategic placement and effective informal connections rather than individual productivity are the crucial methods for the attainment of material goods.

As a consumer-producer, the inmate lives and trades in two economic worlds: he is a barterer in the informal and illicit inmate market and a wage earner in the prison work system. The contrast between his behavior in these two worlds is most revealing. As a trader in the informal inmate barter system, he is resourceful, ingenious, and usually co-operative: there is a kind of "Better Business Bureau" tradition which is generally effective in encouraging the liquidation of debts. As a wage earner in the prison labor system he is, by contrast, encouraged to be nonproductive, dilatory, and contentious, articulating his work relations with the institution in terms of declarations of rights and grievances. In many modern institutions, the "workers' rights" of inmates go beyond the most extreme of those advanced by organized labor on the outside.

INMATES' ATTITUDES

The following is a summary of the sophisticated inmate's view of his economic rights—those attitudes and values concerning work most frequently articulated to institutional officials by leading spirits of the inmate social system:

The fundamental authority in defining the inmate's job obligations is *tradition.* Inmates are to be required to work only so much as the tradition concerning given jobs requires. Any departure from these traditions—especially those departures in the direction of increased work for the same pay—are violations of the inmates' work rights and justify obstructionism. (In a certain penal institution, for instance, "tradition" had established that one inmate lay out all the salt cellars on the mess tables while a different inmate was required to lay out the pepper.)

Increases in the amount of time or output may only be required under extraordinary circumstances and merit increased pay or special benefits, since these added efforts are "favors" extended by the inmates. The inmates have a right to resent and take reprisals against any of their number who "show the rest up" by doing more than the traditional amount of work. These hostile attitudes toward more energetic inmates effectively condemn them to the deteriorating work patterns enforced by the group. Any inmate who performs more than the usual expectation must prove that he has received a special reward—usually food or informal permission to evade some institutional rule.

The providing of jobs is a duty of prison officials and a right, rather than a privilege, of inmates. Once assigned to a job, there are only a limited number of legitimate reasons for which an inmate may be "fired." None of these legitimate reasons includes adherence to the accepted job tradition. Thus an inmate rarely feels that he may rightfully be dismissed for laziness, if he performs only the usual amount of work traditionally required, despite an increase in institutional needs, since the tradition protects him from any definition of himself as lazy. Inmates generally feel that the fact that they are paid less than comparable civilian workers entitles them to produce less.

The total result of the prevalence of these attitudes has been to reduce "imprisonment at hard labor" to a euphemism existing chiefly in the rhetoric of sentencing judges and in the minds of the uninformed public. The inmate social system not only has succeeded in neutralizing the laboriousness of prison labor in fact, but also has more or less succeeded in convincing prison authorities of the futility of expecting any improvement in output. . . .

SUPERVISORS' ATTITUDES

The following summarizes what the writers have found to be the prevalent attitudes of work supervisors toward convict labor:

Convicts are inherently unindustrious, unintelligent, unresourceful, and uninterested in honest work. They are, generally speaking, a worthless lot of men who have never learned, and can never learn, good work habits. In the face of these facts, the supervisory staff cannot be held in any way responsible for the low output of prison labor. Any attempts to force increases in output of prison labor are dangerous and must be resisted by realistic administrators in order to protect what little work can be secured from inmates.

But there is another reason for the low labor standards of inmates. Convicts may not justifiably be expected to do as much work as their civilian working counterparts because their pay is so much less. . . .

One is reluctantly forced to the conclusion that, in adopting a set of expectations which support inmates' attitudes, prison work supervisors have surrendered to the realities of inmate pressure rather than to the realities of the work situation. This surrender has implications that extend far beyond prison walls, since it encourages inmates to fixate work habits which severely cripple their ability to make realistic work adjustments upon release. Since the inmate's ability to make an effective noncriminal adjustment on the outside is directly dependent on his ability to hold a job, the conclusion is inevitable that the fostering of deteriorated work patterns in prison represents a considerable contribution to recidivism. . . .

There is another far-reaching evil in this surrender to the inmate social system. In manipulating supervisory authorities into support of his position, the adaptive inmate destroys a major therapeutic objective of the prison experience, namely, that of learning compliance to duly constituted authority. By learning that he can successfully deceive, connive, and evade, the inmate is re-encouraged in the hope that, by using the social skills perfected in prison, he may avoid the unfortunate "errors" that first trapped him and sent him there.

The Custodian

Probably the most important and strategically placed individuals involved in the problem of reconstruction of attitudes are the cellblock officers and shop instructors—those representatives of the external community who come in direct, face-to-face daily contact with the inmate. How these individuals relate to the inmate determines, in the long run, not only the care and treatment policy of the institution, but that of the larger society as well. Consequently, any attempt to evaluate reconstruction within walls must make a careful and exhaustive analysis of these highly significant relationships.

The responsibility of those who man the locks is as confining, in many ways, as is the imprisonment of those confined by them. The keeper of the keys is a prisoner too. By the time he retires, the custodian will have spent from eight to fifteen years totally within the prison walls. During this time he will have been personally and singly responsible for the custody and discipline of many thousands of inmates. During most of the time he has spent inside the walls he will have been continually outnumbered and continually under the threat of being outwitted by inmates whose obedience to him is protected only by his status as a symbol of power. His duties are as manifold as those of a commander . . . of troops and as hazardous as those of the commander whose forces may at any time cross the brink of rebellion. One of the hazards of his situation paradoxically is the ease with which he can be lulled into forgetfulness of its hazards.

In order to preserve his status as a symbol of authority, the custodian must surround himself with a social distance which prevents the realities of his weaknesses from becoming apparent to the inmates. The realities of his situation are most unfavorable. He is dependent in part on inmate personnel for the physical mechanics of operating his wing. He is also continuously exposed to numerous techniques of deception. However, these tangible weaknesses do not form the main hazards threatening his effective functioning. These are more intangible and, as such, difficult to detect and even more difficult to control.

The inmate social system has developed techniques to exploit the custodian's psychological as well as his physical vulnerability. These techniques are aimed at a reduction of the social distance protecting his role as guard, outflanking it with a personal relationship, and exploiting that relationship for the inmates' own purposes. Once the relationship between keeper and inmate is on a man-to-man basis, the dependency and vulnerability of the custodian become apparent. "Obeying orders" becomes transformed into "doing the guard a favor." When obedience undergoes this transformation, reciprocity becomes operative, "One favor deserves another." Should a keeper now refuse to return the favor, the inmate feels it within his right to become hostile because of the keeper's "ingratitude." Once the Pandora's box of special favoritism is open it cannot be shut again without a painful and dangerous demonstration of how fickle are the personal relations between those improbable "friends"—the keeper and his prisoner. Neither can be loyal without violating the principles and risking the rejection of the groups which define their roles and set the limits of mutual accommodation. Once these limits are passed, and it is usually the inmate who attempts to pass them, one or the other must balk. This is interpreted as a "betrayal" which terminates the relationship and transforms the friends into enemies. In the process, both become discredited by their own groups—which have now victoriously redemonstrated the insurmountability of the mutual antagonism.

It thus becomes apparent that a breakdown of the social distance between the inmate and his keeper must, sooner or later, result in the exploitation of one by the other and the ultimate degradation of one or both. It is at this point that the most hazardous consequences of this breakdown emerge. Having lost, through a personal relationship, a large measure of the control which had previously been protected by his formal, impersonal role, the keeper is far less able to cope with the powerful and eventually antagonistic emotions which that personal relationship unleashed. A violent resolution of the conflict now becomes increasingly probable, unless harmony can be reestablished by a new capitulation or coerced by a convincing show of force.

The Professional Staff Member

When the activities of the various categories of prison personnel —administrative, custodial, maintenance, and professional workers —are compared in terms of *a clear definition of function,* a curious result of the comparison emerges. Of all the personnel at work at the prison, the professional workers are charged with the most far-reaching and socially urgent responsibilities. These are, however, the very persons who are assigned roles and functions which are defined in the most ambiguous and uncertain terms. The new custodial officer, for instance, comes into a defined situation, with his expectations concerning his role reinforced by tradition. Almost anyone he meets has a more or less clear expectation of what his behavior ought to be in practically every situation, and these expectations set distinct limits to individual deviation. In well-run institutions, the very uniform he wears functions as a kind of insulation against personal failings; it is understood that security and discipline require that the official community organize its responses around the role rather than the man. Consequently, it is universally acknowledged that the institution will support the uniform, within limits, whatever the personal characteristics of the individual who wears it. A comparable situation exists in the cases of the administrative and maintenance personnel. Here, too, objectives are limited, well defined, and matched with reasonably effective powers for their realization.

But what of the psychiatrists, the psychologists, the social workers, the counselors, and classification specialists—those to whom the larger society has assigned the mission of resocialization within walls? What are the work aspirations and expectations which are to guide their operations? What are the traditions which will unify the expectations related to their work and set standards for their behavior and the behavior of the personnel interacting with them? They do not exist; they never existed.

The professional entered penal treatment through the breach in the wall forced by the zeal and indignation of the nineteenth-century religious reformers. His forebears, the humanitarian reformers, moved by a profound faith in the direct educability of human nature, sincerely believed that the problem of crime could be solved by a combination of decently treating and religiously exhorting confined criminals.

It is the tragedy of modern correction that the impulse to help has become confused with treatment and seems to require defense as treatment. One of the more ironic difficulties with this position is that, when one makes "rehabilitation" the main justification for humane handling of prisoners, one has maneuvered oneself into a position potentially dangerous to the humanitarian viewpoint. What if humane treatment fails to rehabilitate—shall it then be abandoned? The isolated survivals of flogging and other "tough" techniques which will disgrace American penology remain to remind us that this is no mere academic question.

The bleak fact is that, just as the monstrous punishments of the eighteenth century failed to curb crime, so the more humane handling of the twentieth century has equally failed to do so. Professional workers in penology have an overriding obligation to acknowledge this failure and to seek for its causes. In their inquiry they ought not to exempt their own concepts and methods from scrutiny.

We shall now attempt to examine a process by which the professional services, by defining themselves as the rescuers and helpers rather than the rehabilitators of convicts, helped to maneuver themselves into exploitation by the inmate social system and collaborated in their own neutralization.

"Treatment by Helping" Neutralized

In the first part of this paper the observation was made that the
inmate social system appears to function as an adaptation to social
rejection and punishment, enabling the offender to avoid the
pathological effects of converting the hostility of society into
hatred of himself. Rather than internalizing this hostility, as does
the typical neurotic, the adaptive inmate appears to be able to
turn it back upon society, using the misery of prison life as his reasonable pretext. If this interpretation is correct, it may help explain
the failure of any attempt to rehabilitate which is based on easing
the harshness of prison life.

In order to externalize hostility, individuals must find external
objects or conditions against which to express that hostility. The
harshness of prison life has been suggested—and is, in fact, suggested by inmates—as the external condition which satisfies this
requirement. The question now arises: given the need to externalize hostility, would the effect of improving specific conditions be to
reduce the hostility *or would it require the inmate to find new outlets for it?* Putting the question in a different form: does acceding
to the demands of the aggressive adaptive inmates result in a decrease in their protests or does it give rise to new demands around
which the hostility generates new protests? Observation and experiences with the results of acceding to inmate pressure strongly
suggest the latter.

Much as he protests bad prison conditions, the adaptive inmate
requires them, because his system of adaptation creates in him a
need to protest. By finding reasonable pretexts for aggressive protest, he is able to accomplish at least three essential psychological
objectives.

1. The cathecting of hostilities originally generated by his failures in human relations generally and his resentment at confinement in particular.

2. Reinforcement of his self-picture in the role of a martyred victim of superior force, with attendant justifications of his "heroic
counterattack."

3. Absolution of any personal sense of guilt or responsibility for his offense against society by emphasizing and concentrating on society's real or fancied offenses against him.

The implications of this widespread psychological orientation for any treatment based chiefly on permissiveness and helping will become painfully obvious for any professional staff member who enters the prison with a missionary zeal and a determination to undo, by openhanded giving, the "evils of generations of prison corruption." The inmate social system has an infinite reserve of grievances and injustices with which to capture his sympathies and divert his efforts. The new professional can walk through the corridors of the cell block reserved for the most notorious prison "bad men," and hear the noble principles of the Declaration of Principles of 1870 mouthed by the most cynical and deteriorated of inmates—men who a moment before and a moment after they speak with him will be ridiculing his naïveté to the very "brutal hacks" they complained about to his face. All too frequently the lingo and point of view of the professional becomes the property of the articulate champions of the most aggressive and corrupting inmate forces in prison. Like some strange human hothouse, the prison has a way of developing a species of flowery "bleeding hearts" which put forth especially sticky and luxurious blossoms to ensnare the new professional. It is almost as if the inmate social system recognizes the special value of these articulate inmates and puts them forth as a kind of burnt offering with which the professional can make penitential sacrifices on his personal altar of social conscience. The inmate social system throws a diversionary human screen of institutional "problem cases" around the professional staff member, eating up his time and misdirecting his efforts away from his proper target, the system itself.

Lack of Treatment Rationale

Mention has been made of the lack of any systematic theory of correctional treatment. This situation is closely related to the absence of any comprehensive and tested theory of crime causation. Since the majority of professional personnel working on the treatment of offenders have been trained in the field of psychological therapies, it would be of interest to determine to what extent their methods of correctional treatment are in harmony with the larger body of theory and practice available in social and psychological pathology and treatment.

We are not prepared, in this paper, to enter into the controversies concerning the nature of the malady—personal or social—from which the habitual, acculturated offender suffers. Assuming, for the purposes of discussion, that he is suffering from some form of personality deviation or disturbance, we may raise two questions. First, do contemporary theories of psychotherapy, however diverse, agree on any common core of requirements and procedures? Secondly, if this common core be ascertainable, what inference may be drawn from it for some general statement of a treatment rationale for offenders? Our survey of contemporary theories and methods of psychotherapy persuades us that such a common core exists, or is at least implicit in contemporary practice. The following summarizes our understanding of the principles of any form of psychological treatment. . . .

1. The person must somehow be brought to an awareness that his difficulties are related to motives and patterns of perception within himself. His attempts to account for these difficulties by blaming a hostile or unfavorable human environment must be analyzed as deriving at least in part from a natural human tendency to avoid guilt and self-rejection. He must be assisted in the gaining of an awareness and a motivation for the taking of present initiative toward change or growth within himself, and he must be shown the fruitlessness of evading this responsibility by futile attempts to change merely his environment.

2. This assistance toward understanding comes about through some relationship with the therapist (or therapeutic situation) in which the individual actually attempts to make his faulty modes of perception and behavior work. Repeated demonstrations of this failure may be necessary before he is able to abandon them. It is important that these failures be not interpreted by him as indicating that he is a worthless or helpless person.

3. Finally, the individual must be provided with opportunities

for the learning, testing, and fixating of newer, more effective modes of perceiving and relating to his human environment. As these new patterns emerge and are found rewarding in terms of increased success in relations with the self and others, they tend to become more and more established in the individual's total pattern of adjustment.

Therapeutic changes based on the processes just cited are critically dependent on the individual's taking the first step of locating the source of his difficulty somewhere within himself. But it is against this first and all-important acknowledgement that the inmate social system mobilizes all its forces and values. This mobilization takes the form of defining all situations in terms of grievances and demands justified by those grievances. On the basis of this orientation, the inmate social system divides the whole world of people with whom it relates in terms of a simple dichotomy: there are people who persecute inmates and people whom inmates may exploit. When the professional staff member defined himself as a friend and helper of the inmate he was automatically redefined by the values of the inmate social system as one to be exploited as a champion of inmates in their grievances against society in general and the custodian in particular. Any deviation from this assigned role—especially in the direction of co-operation with measures of custodial control—were then viewed, quite logically, as a betrayal by the professional of his mission to help the inmate. Treatment—defined as help—at this point becomes the enemy of control.

But it is only through strict and careful measures of control that the inmate may be brought face to face with the inadequacy of his faulty technique of adjustment, as he tries to carry out the same pattern of violation and evasion of rules within the institution that required his institutionalization in the first place. By defining himself as one who only aids and eases the inmate in his prison adjustment, the correctional therapist implicitly contributes to the frustration of the all-important objective of demonstrating to the inmate that his pattern is ineffective. Treatment, viewed in this way, now becomes an obstacle to therapy.

Conclusions

The total result of the interacting trends and processes described has been to isolate the confined offender from socially beneficial contact with individuals outside the inmate social world and to prevent the formation of relationship bonds which might redefine him as an acceptable member of the noncriminal community. This is the major dilemma of penology.

The writers see little possibility of a resolution of this dilemma within the universally prevailing context of a large institutional approach. Large institutions (walled and unwalled) are dependent on the development of a bureaucratic apparatus based on formal structuring of human relationships. This formal structuring, which is required for the efficient and secure operation of the large institution, is in turn dependent on the maintenance of a social distance which sets crippling limits on contact with members of the official community—the only available representatives of the larger society. Where these limits have been redefined—as in the case of the professional worker—the results, to date, have largely been supportive to the inmate social system and have contributed to the weakening of measures of control.

Effective measures of control are viewed as essential to any therapeutic program which would attempt to demonstrate the ineffectiveness of the coercive or conniving or evasive personal and social adjustment which the adaptive offender brings with him into prison. Only after this demonstration is made will it be possible to create the relationships and set up the learning situations required for the fixations of new patterns of behavior. In order to participate effectively in this two-phase therapeutic process—the breaking down of old and the building up of new behavior patterns—the professional and the custodian alike must work to heal the breach which traditionally divided treatment and custody and which ultimately weakened both. The custodian's definition of the therapist as an enemy of discipline and the therapist's conception of the custodian as an obstructor of treatment must be replaced by new definitions which view both as united collaborators in a unitary therapeutic program.

THE JAILHOUSE TURNOUT:
HOMOSEXUALITY AMONG WOMEN
IN PRISON

DAVID A. WARD
AND GENE G. KASSEBAUM

David A. Ward and Gene G. Kassebaum, "Lesbian Liaisons," *Trans-action*, 1, Issue 2 (January 1964), 28–32. At the time of publication, David A. Ward and Gene G. Kassebaum were research sociologists in the School of Public Health, University of California at Los Angeles.

How DO women react to the deprivations, limitations, and degradations of prison? Almost all of what is known about adaptations prisoners make, the defenses they create, the way they strike back, compensate, or resign themselves, refers to prisons for men. Much less is known about women. It is not clear whether the needs and behavior of women in prison are substantially different from those of men or whether the effects of being imprisoned are so uniform and overriding that similarities become greater than differences.

Mrs. Iverne R. Carter, superintendent of the California Institution for Women, the largest women's prison in the world, has challenged the assumption that female prisoners require the same kind of management as do males. She has said that in her experience they act differently, have different problems, and, consequently, they need different treatment.

To examine the behavior of women in prison the authors initiated a study at the California Institution for Women in 1961. Over a two year period data were gathered through the use of interviews, questionnaires, personal observation, and detailed analysis of official records. Support for the superintendent's statement was found:

> Women do not appear to have as high a level of informal community organization and solidarity as do male prisoners. They do not support "convict codes" that serve to orient the newcomers and make confinement more bearable.
>
> There is a greater amount of homosexuality among female prisoners than among male prisoners—much of it reflected in manners and dress. In most cases homosexuality is practiced by women who were not homosexual outside and who will go back to men once outside of prison. These women are the so-called "jailhouse turnouts." There is no evidence that any of these relationships are coercive in the way that young male prisoners are sometimes pressured into homosexuality. Estimates of the total amount vary—but most of the inmates themselves believed at least 50 percent were involved, and many estimates of staff and inmates ran from 60 to 75 percent.
>
> This temporary homosexuality can be understood as a response to and compensation for the pains of imprisonment itself. Without the emotional support and help they get from families and lovers in the outside world, without the organization and experience that male prisoners have, the female inmates turn to individual attachments.

Impact of a Total Institution

Prison is one of the more extreme examples of the "total institution" that Erving Goffman describes graphically in his book, *Asylums:*

The recruit comes into the establishment with a conception of himself made possible by certain stable social arrangements in his home world. Upon entrance, he is immediately stripped of the support provided by these arrangements . . . he begins a series of abasements, degradations, humiliations, and profanations of self. His self is systematically, if often unintentionally, mortified.

Soon the former identities and associations—sweetheart, daughter, mother, wife—seem to become unreal and appear to have happened long ago. New labels become relevant—prisoner, inmate, drug addict, murderer, thief—labels which are more damaging to women than they are to men.

Western culture is inclined to be more protective toward women, and generally will not justify treating them as harshly as it might the allegedly more aggressive, dangerous males. Proportionately, women are so much less often arrested, tried, convicted, and sentenced that the effect is all the greater when a woman is imprisoned.

Upon arrival at the prison the women are questioned and told what personal belongings they can keep. Jewelry and rings with precious stones are taken away. Underwear becomes a matter of official regulation—inmates may keep their own only when: (1) pastel—not red, "a symbol of homosexuality"; and (2) unpadded "to prevent narcotics from being smuggled in."

The prisoner is fingerprinted and photographed and takes a supervised bath. Then comes the most embarrassing admission experience, a pelvic examination in a room with other women—an examination not for medical reasons, but for the discovery of narcotics and other prohibited goods. Finally the new arrival is issued temporary clothing to get her to the reception cottage. Shortly after that she receives a medical examination and is issued regular clothing.

One great difference between this institution and male prisons is that the women can keep a great many personal articles and clothing, including: coats, jackets, raincoats (all "no quilting, padding or fur"), sweaters ("no turtleneck, V-neck, or tight slipover"), gowns or pajamas, bathrobes ("no quilting or padding"), shoes ("low heels, bedroom, thongs, tennis"), simple costume jewelry—earrings, necklaces, scatter pins, bracelets, non-electric clocks, dark glasses, unopened cigarettes, suitcases ("no larger than 18×26 inches"), unfinished knitting and light handsewing material, tooth brush, hair rollers, and so forth.

Thus the complete stripping of all personal possessions that takes place in male prisons does not occur here, and the pains of the admission experience are mitigated slightly.

Reactions to Imprisonment

New inmates report two major initial emotions: surprise and fear. Much of the surprise turns out to be pleasant—the physical conditions are not as bad as they had feared—a measure of the apprehension they bring to prison:

It's less difficult than I assumed; it's not like home but it's going to be easy compared to how I thought it would be. It's neater, cleaner, you got combs, towels, etc. If you just have patience. The girls as a whole are not rough or tough; they've got more heart than the people on the outside. We can talk to each other. I'll tell you what scared me—that rolled wire. I said, "Take one last look" (at the outside), but the inside looked better than the parks in the city.

Despite the favorable impression conveyed by the attractive grounds, fear and apprehension are characteristic of the newcomer: fear of mistreatment, dread of the future and of prison life, and fear generated by uncertainty, aggravated by the fact that many rules and staff explanations are unclear.

Treated Like Children

Women are especially ill-prepared to cope with uncertainty. Outside they may be able to depend on families, husbands, and lovers who might have personal regard and respect for them. In prison they immediately become dependent on the staff, whose interest is professional and casual, and whose personalities and whims soon assume overwhelming importance. The staff controls almost all the necessities and comforts of their daily lives— including many which are considered basic, inviolable and personal, outside—as well as being able to affect the length of time served. The inmates feel that the rules are what the staff interpret them to be, and that the prisoners are treated like children:

You are constantly addressed as though you were either a mental case or a child—most of the staff here formerly worked in mental institutions or taught school. They feel it necessary to constantly nag you. The routine is the same from day to day. There is little to challenge a four-year-old, much less an adult. You lose the power, if you're not careful, to make even a small decision, or harbor an original thought.

Imprisonment is also more severe for women than for men because it is much more unusual. Female inmates generally have not come up through the "sandlots of crime" or had experience in training schools or reformatories, as have prisoners in penitentiaries for men. Of a sample of 293 female inmates, only 15 percent had ever been committed to juvenile training school, and 65 percent had never been in prison before. Although jail terms for drunkenness, prostitution, and petty theft are fairly frequent, for many women prison is a completely new experience.

Most women who come to prison are unsophisticated as criminals, and their lack of prior experience in doing time has not prepared them to suffer the rigors of confinement. They are more vulnerable than men to the indignities, degradation, and loss of privacy and identity that take place in prison. These pains strike the new prisoner, fresh from arrest, trial, and conviction, with particular force.

There is a further psychological pain of prison which is particularly severe for a woman who is a mother—leaving her children. A man can serve time knowing that although the family may have great difficulty without his income, his wife can still care for the children. The imprisoned mother, however, loses her ability to fill what is, in our society, her most important function. This is psychologically meaningful even though many of the women had been sexually promiscuous and had more than one marriage. The mother is not only concerned with separation from the children but worries about how they will be cared for while her husband works. While she is in prison, unable to interfere, her children's care may be taken over by the municipality; or her husband may look for another woman to act as mother.

This concern was apparent when inmates were asked on a questionnaire, "To what aspect of prison life do you find it hardest to adjust?" Forty-three percent checked "Absence of home and family,"—four times as many as checked any other answer. The data also indicate that this frustration is not appreciably lessened as the length of time served increases.

Emotional Needs

During the early period, when the psychological pains of imprisonment are most acute, the inmate most needs emotional support. One described her feelings as follows:

Knowing I was going to be sentenced here, I made every effort to see that my first week would be one of total escape . . . The morning of my sentence I took every form of pill I could manage to get, smoked as much marijuana as my mind could possibly stand and still manage to receive my sentence as a lady. The shock of hearing the inevitable penetrated with the same force as though I had indulged nothing but my common sense. However, the aftereffects were successful . . . I managed to float through my first four days, depressed when I was awake, but slept most of the time. I felt as though I had been pushed off the edge of the world, and in many ways, it still seems this way.

Apprehensive and bewildered, new arrivals are most in need of information and reassurance about what to do and what to expect. Most of what they get comes from other inmates—in jail, enroute to the prison, and in the receiving unit. There are enough returned parole violators and second or third termers to give the new arrivals information that the staff and orientation program do not provide. Eventually they do learn the answers to most of their questions; eventually they may also find emotional support.

Effects of the Indeterminate Sentence

The most important question for each woman, however, is one that neither staff nor other inmates can answer: How long will she serve? The indeterminate sentencing laws of the state—generally considered a step forward in penology, make it not only impossible to know when one can be paroled, but, until actual appearance before the parole board, even when eligibility will be considered. Waiting to get a definite sentence becomes more trying than waiting for a release date.

If the indeterminate sentencing law results in uncertainty, the philosophy of "individual treatment" compounds it by adding inconsistency.

Individual treatment is based on the proposition that all individuals, and the circumstances surrounding their actions, differ. Therefore, treatment must take into account the peculiarities and needs of each person. The classification and disciplinary committees, and the parole board, may deal differently with women who have committed the same offense or violated the same prison rule.

Since these decisions are reached in private, few staff members and no inmates know the bases for most of them, and the suspicion arises that whim, prejudice, or favoritism decide many. In addition, the important decisions are made by upper level personnel and committees who have little sustained contact with individual prisoners. The inmates feel that the staff members who know and understand them best, the cottage and work crew supervisors, are those who are least able to do anything to help them.

Not knowing how long they must stay, not knowing what to expect from individual staff members, administrative committees or the parole board, inmates feel lost and out of sight of landmarks. Sociologists refer to this lack of standards, rules, and guidelines as *anomie*.

Male prisoners are subject to anomie, too; but they fight prison by working with others to set up a common defense against the personal degradation, self-mortification, and loss of identity. They have developed rules and maxims covering these adaptations, and these make up the so-called "inmate code." New arrivals find information available from inmate *politicians* and *right guys*, and scarce goods are available from *merchants*. Criminal behavior is rationalized and justified; methods and techniques for getting scarce goods and services are made known; and ways to deal with staff and fellow inmates are detailed. The code provides a philosophy for doing time that makes it more bearable; and the inmate social organization provides the mechanisms for assuring conformity to the code.

The standards of the men stress hostility toward staff, and fundamental cynicism toward the world. By contrast the women are *squares*. Few are cynical in the same way as men prisoners, or as sophisticated in crime, its lingo, or its rationalizations.

Evidence of how naive they are was illustrated during a search for forbidden material in the housing units. The inmates were told they would have several minutes warning before their rooms were searched to allow them to flush illegal items down the toilets. Interpreting this order as a break, they did as told instead of searching out other ways to hide or get rid of goods. The sewage from each cottage was then filtered permitting the staff to ascertain the nature, amount, and general location of contraband materials. There are undoubtedly some male prisoners who compare in gullibility, but not as many as in the women's prison.

In summary, it can be said that female prisoners suffer most of the psychological pains that men do, in addition to some distinctly their own. However, because they have distinctive needs and different histories of criminality, the kinds of adaptations they make vary somewhat from those found in prisons for men.

Homosexuality as an Adaptation

There are many personal reactions to stress, and each may come in a number of forms. Psychological withdrawal is one. Goffman describes another as "colonization"—becoming so well attuned to prison that it becomes "home." Revolt is a third. There are troublemakers at the women's prison, but most of them seem to be either emotionally disturbed or are homosexuals trying to promote or protect their interests. It is evident, however, that the principal adaptation utilized by these female prisoners is the homosexual liaison. This adaptation reflects the most severe deprivation of confinement for women—emotional deprivation. Most of the women interviewed saw this need as motivating most homosexual affairs:

Why do girls "turn out?" [sic] They need to be loved, everybody has to have someone.

There's a lot of homosexuality because women are more emotional. They find in a jail that they have to depend on themselves. They need someone to talk to, so they get friendly, which leads to sexual intimacy.

The Approach

One inmate described for a female interviewer how she (the inmate) might have approached the interviewer if the interviewer had been a newly arrived inmate:

Let's say you've four children; you're not a criminal, but passed some bad checks and you come in with everyone that matters so far away . . . Once I know you don't play, then I begin to build a friendship, knowing all the while what's going on, although you do not. Maybe we like the same music, poetry, or other things of common interest. We spend lots of time together, and then I leave you alone for a week maybe playing with someone else. You'll miss me. You'll want to know if I'm mad at you. You'll miss me—after all, we've filled up a lot of time together. By this time you like me, and you're wondering, "What's it like? What would my people think? What would I have to do? Is it really so sick?" By then I'm half being your friend again. The pressure's on. Then one day the time is right; the scene is right; I'm full of emotion (as all women are), and you say to yourself. [sic] "She really loves me. I care for her, surely it's not a wrong thing . . ."

A related question here is whether heterosexual deprivation is a major factor leading to homosexuality. Some staff members believe so, but inmate opinion does not support them. The question asking which aspect of imprisonment was the most difficult to bear included among the alternative answers: "Lack of sexual contact with men." Of the 293 women questioned a total of only 5 selected this answer, as compared to over 120 for "Absence of home and family." Not one of those questioned in interviews thought that sex hunger was of primary importance in influencing her own homosexual affairs—or of those of anyone she knew. In addition, most homosexuality first occurs at the beginning of the sentence. Presumably, it is not at the time that the frustrations arising from the absence of heterosexual contacts is most acute. It is, however, at the beginning of her sentence that the inmate is most in need of comfort, support, and reassurance.

Homosexual Roles

Homosexuality involves more than a change in the gender of the love object. For some women it represents a dramatic inversion of sexual role. These shifts are manifest in the principal homosexual roles played by women. The most obvious of them is the *butch*, *stud broad* or *drag butch*. She is the counterpart of the male and, ideally, acts in an aggressive manner and is the active sexual part-

ner. Her hair is close-cropped or worn in "pixie" or "D.A." styles;
she wears no makeup; her legs are unshaven; she usually wears
pedal pushers, or if a dress, the belt is worn low on the hips. Masculine gait, manner of smoking, and other gestures are adopted. A
variation of this is the woman who dresses femininely, but acts ag-
gressively and plays the dominant role in her homosexual relationship. Many of the *jailhouse turnouts* who are *butches* are singu-
larly unattractive, according to some of the criteria used to judge
feminine attractiveness in our society. Many are overweight or un-
derweight, have skin disorders, or appear unusually wiry or muscular. In addition, interview and personal record data suggest that
the experience of many *butches* with males has often been unhappy. These severely unattractive women, and the women possessing aggressive personality traits and inclined toward masculine
habits and demeanor, express themselves in the *butch* role when
these predisposing factors are combined with the experience of imprisonment. The role of the *butch* in the prison community thus
seems to be an effort to solve a variety of problems and conflicts of
which adjustment to imprisonment is one.

The complementary role to the butch is the *femme.* It is less difficult to describe and to understand the role of the *femme* because
she often does in the homosexual affair what she did in heterosexual relationships. She continues to play the role often expected of
women: to be relatively more submissive and passive in sexual relations, to be dependent, and to provide housekeeping services.
The role of the *femme* provides relief from the need to fend for
oneself in a strange and threatening environment. This role provides for the establishment of supportive relationships similar to
those which characterized relationships with fathers, husbands, or
lovers.

Jailhouse Turnout

The newly arrived female prisoner is placed in a situation in
which any source of relieving the pains of imprisonment holds
great attraction. The old supports from the outside world are gone;
the groupings and organization that help men do time do not exist

for women. Despite efforts of the staff to cope with the problem, there remain for many women only the comfort and help that can come from a close association with another individual. And the persons who are quickest, most available, and most aggressive in offering information and solace are homosexual. Homosexual liaisons appear initially to satisfy needs which are otherwise not met, and the form which is taken suggests that the most severe strain of imprisonment for women is emotional deprivation.

The term *jailhouse turnout* is a way of summing up this adjustment to a stressful situation. The indications are that most prison homosexuality is temporary and transitional with heterosexual relationships being resumed upon release. The problem for women's prisons is finding a socially acceptable substitute for the emotional support that women inmates derive from their lesbian liaisons.

CONJUGAL VISITING
AT THE MISSISSIPPI STATE
PENITENTIARY

COLUMBUS B. HOPPER

Excerpted from Columbus B. Hopper, "Conjugal Visiting at the Mississippi State Penitentiary," *Federal Probation*, XXIX, No. 2 (June 1965), 39–46. At the time of publication, Columbus B. Hopper was Associate Professor of Sociology at Southeast Missouri State College. Since publication of this article, a limited number of experiments in conjugal visiting have been undertaken, as for instance, in California. Elsewhere, others are in the study and planning stages.

THE MISSISSIPPI State Penitentiary consists of 21,000 acres of delta plantation land. The central plantation and the offices of administration are located at Parchman in Sunflower County in the Yazoo-Mississippi Delta. Parchman, as the institution is called, is one of the world's largest penal-farm or plantation systems. Since it is a plantation system, the buildings and other facilities differ from those at most state prisons in the United States. The buildings are of many different types: administrative, hospital, barns, storehouses, cotton gin, equipment sheds, and repair shops. Other large buildings are found in the 16 inmate camps which form the basic organizational structure of the penitentiary.

Each camp at Parchman is a separate community within the plantation, under the supervision of a sergeant responsible for all phases of the camp's operation. An individual camp consists primarily of a large rectangular building for the detention of inmates. The buildings, made of brick, are built and maintained by prison labor. The one-story camp buildings are designed so that on an average 60 inmates may be housed in one wing. In each wing there are no partitions or cells separating the prisoners; they are housed in congregate quarters with electric lights, running water, showers, and toilet facilities. Some of the camp buildings are surrounded by wire fences; most are not. . . . The number of inmates housed in a single camp is never large. While one or two confine 200 inmates, a few have less than 100, and two less than 50. The camps are segregated for the white and Negro races. Generally, a total of approximately 2,100 inmates are confined in all camps combined.

The institution is a productive plantation, not only producing all food and clothing used by inmates, but sometimes also showing a profit on its products. . . . The work may be planting, gathering, canning, slaughtering beef or hogs, or whatever chore may be most urgently needed at any particular time. Since cotton is the major crop grown, much of the work for most inmates, especially in the fall, centers around the production of this crop. Although cotton is the chief source of income for the institution, income is also derived from the sale of other crops as well as livestock. . . .

General Visitation Program

A distinguishing feature of the penitentiary in Mississippi is its visitation program. Parchman apparently has the most liberal visitation program of any state penitentiary in the United States. The institution not only emphasizes bringing visitors into the prison, but also allows the inmates to keep contact with their families by leaving the prison themselves. In a survey carried out in 1956, for example, Parchman was the only prison among 47 surveyed which permitted inmates to make home leaves for other than reasons of emergency. Under the existing leave program at Parchman, called the "Holiday Suspension Program," each year from December 1 until March 1, selected inmates who have been in the penitentiary at least 3 years with good behavior records may go home for a period of 10 days. During 1963, out of 275 inmates released on holiday suspension, only 3 did not return voluntarily.

All visiting by the inmates' families occurs on Sunday afternoons; inmates may receive visits from their families each Sunday. Although visiting hours do not begin until 1 o'clock in the afternoon, the visitors usually begin arriving at any time after mid-morning. They come mostly in private automobiles, although some come by bus and taxi. The visiting hours are from 1 o'clock until 3 o'clock except on the third Sunday in each month when they are from 1 o'clock until 5 o'clock. The third Sunday is called "Big Sunday" because of the longer visiting hours; this is the time when the largest number of visitors come. On a "Big Sunday" there may be as many as 300 or more visitors.

While waiting until the visiting hours start, the visitors wait in their cars parked on the sides of the highway in front of the administration building. As the visiting hours draw near, they drive in the main entrance and clear themselves with a guard. After a brief inspection of the car, consisting usually of the guard's looking into the car and recording the number of the license plate, the visitors drive by the administration building, past the hospital, and out on the plantation to the camp that houses the inmate they wish to visit.

On arrival at the camp the visitors must undergo another inspection by the camp sergeant or the guard on duty at the entrance of the camp grounds. This inspection is more rigid than the inspection at the main entrance, particularly if it is the first time a visitor has appeared at the camp. The visitors must identify themselves, and if requested, submit to being searched. The guard looks into the car trunk, and records the visitors' names. If the visiting hours have begun, he admits them into the camp area, and informs the inmate concerned that he has a visitor or visitors. The inmate then is allowed to come out of the camp building unguarded, receive his visitors, and visit with them anywhere within the camp area.

The grounds around each camp building are extensive enough to allow inmates and their visitors room enough to be by themselves, considerably removed from other inmates or staff members. The penitentiary provides tables and benches for inmates and their visitors. When the weather is warm, the grounds around a camp building, although less crowded, look somewhat like a city park on a Sunday afternoon. People sit on blankets eating picnic lunches; others sit on benches in the shade of trees, while others walk around. One may even see a boy and his father having a game of catch with a baseball, or children playing by themselves on swings or slides.

The penitentiary allows all members of an inmate's family to visit him, except in the case where a member of the family had one time been incarcerated in Parchman. Since released inmates are not allowed to return for visits to other inmates, a member of one's own family may not visit if the member himself has formerly been an inmate. Otherwise, however, members of an inmate's family are allowed to visit him, every week if they desire. For the married male inmate, the visiting freedom means that he may see his wife in private. He may go with her to a private room in a little building on the camp grounds and have coitus. Parchman is the only penal institution in the United States which has publicly announced such a practice. The conjugal visit is considered to be a part of the family visitation and home visitation programs. The family visit is emphasized at Parchman, and the conjugal visit is believed to be a logical part of the visiting program.

Informal Development of Conjugal Visits

The conjugal visiting privilege has developed informally in the Mississippi State Penitentiary, and it is still best described as an informal, unofficial practice. That is to say, the beginning of the practice may not be determined from the existing penitentiary records and it still does not have legal notice or control. In fact, until the last camp was built, funds were not allocated for the program. Records are still not kept as to whether an inmate uses the privilege, nor does an inmate have to make application for it or hold any particular grade as an inmate.

At the time of this study, no employee at Parchman remembered when the penitentiary did not allow conjugal visits. Most of the employees believed that the practice had been in existence since the penitentiary was first opened in its present location. One man who had been employed intermittently at the penitentiary for over 35 years and who lived near the penitentiary and had knowledge of it even before his employment, said that the privilege was allowed to his own knowledge as long ago as 1918.

While the practice has apparently been in existence for many years, it has only recently developed into a somewhat systematic program, and especially since it has begun to get publicity. In earlier days of conjugal visiting at Parchman the practice was confined largely to the Negro camps. Moreover, there was little or no institutional control over the privilege. A sergeant of a Negro camp said, for example, that when he became sergeant of his camp in 1940, conjugal visiting was being practiced but no facilities were provided. The usual practice, he added, was for an inmate to take his wife or girl friend into the sleeping quarters of the inmates and secure whatever privacy he could by hanging up blankets over beds. Upon gaining control of his camp, the sergeant allowed the inmates to construct a small building for conjugal visits. He has continued to allow the inmates in their spare time to construct such buildings or add to them. At the time of this study, his camp had three separate conjugal visiting houses, each containing several rooms.

The buildings used for conjugal visits are referred to by the inmates and staff as "red houses." No employee contacted at Parchman remembered the origin of this term. Apparently the first building provided for the visits was red in color, and inmates in talking about it spoke of it as the red building or house. Most of the existing red houses are simple frame constructions with about five or six rooms, although some have as many as 10. The rooms are small and sparsely furnished; in each is only a bed, a table, and in some a mirror. A bathroom which the wives may use is located in each building.

Since the red houses have been built in an unsystematic and unplanned manner, through accommodative relationships between the individual camp sergeants and his inmates, they are not standard in appearance. Nor do they have the quality of workmanship found in the other penitentiary buildings. They do not, on the average, present an attractive or even presentable appearance. Their condition, however, has begun to show some improvement in the past few years. . . .

The only conjugal visiting facilities at Parchman planned and specifically provided by the penitentiary are those at the first offender's camp, opened in 1963. The planning and institutional construction of the conjugal visiting facilities at this camp denote a significant point in the development of conjugal visiting at Parchman; they represent institutional acceptance of the conjugal visit as an important phase of the general visitation program. In this camp the red house was included in the camp plan from the beginning, and it is made of the same brick and other materials as the main camp building itself. The main camp building is joined on one side by a chapel, and a few yards in back of the two is the red house. The rooms in this red house are larger than the ones in the older buildings. They are also more attractively designed, furnished, and decorated.

The conjugal visiting program at Parchman should, in fact, be considered to be still in a developmental stage or process. It is likely that the practice has only begun to take on the pattern that it will take in the future. Although it has been going on for many years, only recently have the staff members begun to speak of it among themselves. Whereas for many years they felt the practice to be something that should not be mentioned, they now speak of it with frankness and even pride.

Evaluations by Camp Sergeants

In attempting to obtain the most meaningful evaluation of the program by the institutional staff, attention was directed to the camp sergeants. The position of camp sergeant is one which requires the individual to have constant association with inmates. He lives a very short distance from the camp building and is, in fact, on duty 24 hours a day. The average sergeant spends at least 12 hours a day with his inmates. He knows each inmate personally, his hometown or community, and other members of his family. It is the sergeant's duty to censor the mail of each of his inmates, that which he writes as well as that which he receives. All disturbances and problems among his inmates come to the sergeant's attention, and are usually settled by him. If an inmate has a problem he takes it to his sergeant.

Furthermore, when a member of an inmate's family comes to the penitentiary with a problem concerning an inmate, he is referred first to the camp sergeant. Consequently, the camp sergeants come to know the inmates, their problems, and their behavior much more thoroughly than do the other staff members. In the case of conjugal visiting, the camp sergeants are the only employees who know which inmates do and do not have the visits. Inquiries dealing with staff members' evaluations of the influence of the conjugal visiting program were directed, therefore, to the sergeants of the 14 camps which have conjugal visiting privileges.

Each camp sergeant was asked questions relating to the homosexuality, discipline, work, and cooperation of his inmates. Each was also asked what if any problems had developed relating to the conjugal visits, and what changes he would like to see made in the program as it was being practiced. The first question concerned the extent of homosexuality in their camps. While it is impossible for a camp sergeant to have accurate knowledge of the extent of such behavior, the sergeants were asked on the basis of incidents of it coming to their knowledge to rate homosexuality in their camps as a very big problem; definitely a problem; a small problem; or a very small problem. Of the 14 sergeants, one rated homosexuality a very big problem; six considered it definitely a problem; five said it was a small problem, while two considered it to be only a very small problem.

When asked to compare the extent of homosexuality among their inmates who had conjugal visits with that of those who did not, 11 said those receiving conjugal visits engaged in much less. The remaining three said inmates receiving conjugal visits engaged in a little less. All agreed that those receiving the visits engaged in less homosexuality.

In comparing disciplinary problems presented by inmates, six said they could tell no difference in their inmates in this regard. Four said that those having conjugal visits gave them much less trouble, and four said they gave a little less trouble.

When asked to compare the willingness to work of their inmates, five believed those receiving conjugal visits were much better in this respect. An additional five said those receiving conjugal visits were a little better workers, while four said they could tell no difference. When asked about the overall cooperation of those receiving conjugal visits as compared to other inmates, three reported no difference. All the others, however, stated that they could definitely say those receiving conjugal visits were more cooperative.

The sergeants were also asked what they believed to be the most helpful aspect of the conjugal visiting program. One sergeant said the work of the inmates was most importantly influenced in his judgment; four felt the visits were most helpful in producing cooperative attitudes in general among inmates while two others suggested the reduction of homosexual behavior. Seven of the camp sergeants, however, believed the most helpful aspect and the chief purpose of the visits was to keep marriages from breaking up.

When asked if the program caused any extra work for them, 12 of the 14 asserted it did not. They said, rather, that they had to be on the job all of the time anyway. On the other hand, one believed the practice actually saved him work in some instances. The freedom of visiting privileges in general, he added, kept the prisoners' wives and other family members from worrying so much and making inquiries about them. When an inmate and his wife can see each other in private, talk freely, and even have intercourse, he said, they do not have to come to him often for help or information. Speaking of this he said:

Most problems the inmates have are concerned with worry about their families. And most people who come to the penitentiary are concerned about how the inmate is getting along, how his health is and so on. The best thing I can do is to allow them to see each other and judge for themselves. A common thing in prison is for a married man to worry about his wife, whether or not she still loves him and is faithful to him. One visit in private with her is better than a hundred letters because he can judge for himself.

Two sergeants of Negro camps, however, indicated that the program caused them extra work in ascertaining whether a woman was the wife of an inmate. Although the sergeants of the white camps said they did not allow a woman to visit an inmate unless she had official proof of their marriage, the Negro camps still present problems in this respect. Since many Negro inmates in Mississippi have common-law marriages, which the penitentiary wishes to respect, the sergeants have to question the female visitors and try to determine whether the visitor and inmate have actually been living as a married couple. Often, one said, he checked with one or two people in the inmate's home community as additional proof of marriage. While he admitted that several of his inmates probably received visits from women to whom they were not married, even by common law, he did not believe that many of his inmates did so because most of the women who visited also brought their children with them.

The other camp sergeant who spoke of problems involved in screening out the unmarried female visitors said that at least on one occasion to his knowledge, a prostitute had slipped by his screening and spread venereal disease among several inmates. He also mentioned that several wives of inmates had become pregnant. He did not say that the wives becoming pregnant had caused any trouble at the penitentiary, but mentioned it as a problem associated with conjugal visiting.

All of the sergeants of camps having conjugal visits said that the facilities provided for the visits should be improved. Not a single sergeant rated his red house as being in satisfactory condition. Even with neglected facilities, however, all sergeants enthusiastically supported the program as being of basic importance in their camps. Each believed that the program should, in general, be continued as it was being practiced. . . .

Inmate Opinion

A question of importance concerning conjugal visiting is: "How do the single inmates feel about married inmates having the conjugal visiting privilege?" Since the program of conjugal visiting is intended only for married inmates, it is a categorical privilege which the majority of inmates do not have. It might be, for example, that the unmarried men in the institution feel that the penitentiary is unfair in its treatment of inmates. If this were the case, then one would expect that a program of conjugal visiting would, as some writers suggest, cause more tension and conflict than it would reduce. To obtain some indication of this problem, a questionnaire was submitted to a total of 1,600 inmates. Of this number, 822 were unmarried and not receiving conjugal visits; 464 were married and receiving conjugal visits, while the remaining 314 were married but were not receiving conjugal visits.

An item in the questionnaire was directed to unmarried inmates and stated as follows: "If you are unmarried, do you resent married inmates having the conjugal visiting privilege?" The possible answers were: "yes, [sic?] very much," "yes," "a little," and "no." The response indicated that the great majority of unmarried inmates did *not* feel resentment over the privilege being granted to married men. Of 822 unmarried inmates responding to the question, 737, or 89.6 percent, answered that they felt no resentment; a total of 85 inmates, however, did report resentment, 58 replying "very much" and 27 replying that they felt a little resentment.

The fact that very nearly 9 out of every 10 unmarried inmates did not indicate resentment suggests that for most inmates a pattern of relative deprivation operates within the institution in regard to conjugal visits. Apparently most unmarried inmates identify with other unmarried inmates and view a married inmate and his wife very nearly in the same way unmarried individuals do in a free community. Of several unmarried inmates talked to by the researcher, not one said he felt any resentment toward the staff or other inmates concerning the visits.

Since the embarrassment associated with and the obviousness of sex in conjugal visits have been objections to the practice, two items in the questionnaire were directed toward these aspects. The inmates who received conjugal visits were asked the following question: "If you engage in conjugal visiting, has any other inmate ever acted in any way disrespectful to your wife?" Of 462 inmates answering the question, only 18, or 3.9 percent, replied in the affirmative. When asked if the visits were embarrassing to them, 42, or 9.1 percent, replied in the affirmative. When asked if they believed the conjugal visits were embarrassing to their wives, however, 87, or 18.8 percent, answered that the visits were embarrassing to their wives.

The inmates who received conjugal visits were also asked to choose from among several items the one for which they believed conjugal visits to be most helpful. The items from which they had to choose were as follows: keeping marriages from breaking up; reducing homosexuality; making inmates more cooperative; helping rehabilitate inmates; making inmates easier to control; or making inmates work harder. As a final choice, the inmates could choose to mark that the visits were helpful for all of the above equally. . . . Of the 464 inmates responding to the question, 234 believed that conjugal visits were most helpful in keeping marriages from being broken. It is interesting to note that the inmates, as did the sergeants, ranked the preservation of marriages as the most important function of conjugal visiting.

The majority of the inmates using the conjugal visiting privilege did not believe that the facilities provided for the visits were in satisfactory condition. When asked to rate the buildings provided for the visits, only 152 out of 464, or 32.7 percent, rated them as being in satisfactory condition. Most of the inmates who were talked to about the red houses complained that the rooms were too small and that the buildings were in need of repairs.

Importance of Small Camps

The fact that so few inmates reported embarrassment and so few problems have been encountered despite neglected facilities, is perhaps best explained by the small size of the inmate camps and the informality and freedom small numbers allow. In an inmate camp at Parchman housing only 150 men, the number of visitors coming on a single day is never large. It is easier to evolve and maintain a working system of interpersonal relations, generally, when numbers are small. In conjugal visiting, small numbers are basic for sex activities are the most delicate of human activities. . . .

The penitentiary provides no contraceptive devices for the inmates nor does it require their use. If an inmate and his wife wish to use contraceptives, the wife must provide them.

The freedom and informality of conjugal visiting at Parchman are further revealed by the fact that the inmates themselves are responsible for the orderly operation of the red houses and for cooperation in the use of them. No time limit is imposed by the staff of the institution on the time an inmate and his wife may stay in a red house. The inmates are left to use their own judgment. They know how many inmates have wives visiting on a single day, and know that when there are few visitors they may stay longer in the red house. In camps having a fairly large number of men receiving conjugal visits, systems have been worked out by the inmates to avoid embarrassment in determining whether a room in the red house is being used. The usual procedure is to erect a board in front of the building that indicates which rooms are and are not empty. Each room is numbered and its number is written on a piece of wood or some other material suitable for a marker. A string or chain is then attached to the marker and it is hung on the board. Before an inmate and his wife go into the building, they select a room, remove the marker from the board, and take it with them into the room. . . .

In leaving the inmates alone without formal rules and regulations, the penitentiary has forced the inmates to cooperate with each other if they are to have the conjugal visiting privilege. Thus, the inmates cooperate in several ways. By informal agreement, married inmates whose wives are visiting are left to themselves in one area of the camp grounds. Inmates not having wives or whose wives do not visit, do not go near the areas in which the red houses are located. Inmates often cooperate by watching or attending to the children of a couple in a red house. Above all, the inmates cooperate by being respectful and courteous to each other's wives.

The conjugal visit at Parchman is not a privilege granted specifically for good behavior. The inmates in the maximum security unit do not have the privilege nor do women inmates have it. All married inmates in the other camps, however, have the privilege. While the privilege is not granted for good behavior within an individual camp, inmates whose behavior presents a persistent problem are often removed to the maximum security camp for a few days. . . .

The attitude of the staff at Parchman toward conjugal visiting privileges is that a man and his wife have the right of sexual intercourse, even though the man is in prison. Inmates are eligible to receive conjugal visits upon commitment as soon as they are assigned to a camp. No special counseling is given to an inmate using the privilege nor is any extra requirement made of him. He is like any other inmate except that he and his wife take part in the conjugal visiting program. . . .

Conclusion

. . . The conjugal visit in Mississippi seems, above all, a manifestation of the rural emphasis on the stable family. Mississippians are, and always have been, a rural people. Although the percentage of people living in urban places in Mississippi has been increasing, the rate has been slow. The census of the population in 1960 showed that only 37.7 percent of all Mississippians lived in urban places. . . . The influence of the rural environment upon marital and familial relationships is well known, and the stability of the rural family is a widely accepted fact. As a union of husband and wife, parents and children, the rural family is much more closely integrated and more permanent than the urban family, and in comparison with other social institutions, the role of the family is much more important in the country than in the city. A prison in a rural culture in which both staff and inmates have a high regard for the stability of marriage is more likely to make efforts to safeguard a marriage even though the husband is imprisoned than a prison in an urban setting. . . .

The small, semi-isolated camp structure was favorable to the development of conjugal visiting in part because it simply increased the probability of its development. Instead of being one big central prison, Parchman is several different prison camps, most of them separated by several miles. More importantly, however, the small number of inmates housed in each camp reduces security precautions a great deal. It also allows a camp sergeant to know his inmates well and to develop primary relationships with them. The fact that a sergeant knows an individual inmate and his wife is very helpful for the conjugal visit for it means less formality in the reception of wives and in security precautions. The small camps present wives with a less rigid and more informal situation than would a large prison. As a result, they are able to relax and are not constantly reminded of the prison setting of the visit. Such an atmosphere allows wives to keep their self-respect and to have the feeling that the visit has been a private one.

Since segregation of the races is a general feature of the social organization of the State of Mississippi, the functioning of the conjugal visiting program at Parchman is also dependent upon the segregation of the Negro and white races within the penitentiary. While this factor might be of no importance in a prison in a state having successful integration of the races generally, there can be little doubt of its significance in Mississippi. Segregation of the Negro and white races in Parchman precludes conflict of the races in the most carefully guarded aspect of their interaction—that of sexual behavior.

. . . With adequate facilities, careful selection, and appropriate counsel, it is possible that the conjugal visiting program in Mississippi could be developed into one of the most enlightened programs in modern corrections.

WORK-RELEASE PROGRAMS

SERAPIO R. ZALBA

Excerpted from Serapio R. Zalba, "Work-Release—a Two-Pronged Effort," *Crime and Delinquency*, 13, No. 4 (October 1967), 506–512. At the time of publication Serapio R. Zalba was a Lecturer, School of Applied Sciences, at Case Western Reserve University.

IN CONTEMPORARY America, two positive purposes guide the societal response to deviant behavior: protection of society-at-large and rehabilitation of the transgressor. How rationally these goals are pursued is another matter. Taking them as given, we may ask, in respect to the hundreds of thousands of our fellow citizens sent to jail each year, "What should we do that will afford us protection against their antisocial acts and yet will rehabilitate them so that they can be happy (for their sakes), law-abiding (for our sakes), and productive (for both our sakes)?"

The work-release program (also called *work furlough, day parole, out-mate program, private work-release, intramural private employment,* and *semi-liberté*), which combines incarceration in the local jail with work on regular jobs in the community, is an attempt to meet the above requirements.

The question of how the offender can make best use of his time is basic. More often than not, the answers to it have typified the confusion and conflict of a society that wants rehabilitation but is still struggling with its impulses for vengeance. . . .

. . . Although work-release has existed in the United States for over fifty years, a trend toward its wider adoption has developed only recently. Of the twenty-four states which were utilizing the concept in 1965, nineteen had adopted it after 1956. It was not until 1965 that Congress passed legislation authorizing work-release programming for federal prisoners. And official adoption of the work-release concept in a state does not necessarily mean actual statewide use. For instance, in California, considered by some to have one of the more active programs, only five of the fifty-eight counties have put work-furlough programs into operation.

The basic meaning of the work-release approach was expressed as follows by Wisconsin State Senator Henry Huber, the father of the idea:

Committing a man to jail with nothing to employ his time defeats the ends of humanity more often than advancing it by depriving his family of its breadwinner. Under the proposed [work-release] law he is shown the error of his ways, given his sentence, and kept employéd so his family is not reduced to want.

Traditional incarceration punishes both the offender and society. The offender loses his freedom and his job, and he may also be fined; society is required to pay the cost of his keep, treatment, and supervision, and it may also have to support his family through public assistance of some kind in addition to incurring losses to the economy in manpower, buying power, and taxes.

The psychological losses are equally damaging. Prevented from supporting his family financially, he is also deprived of the normal parental role and cannot support it affectionally. Withdrawing the opportunity and responsibility for performing the major adult-role tasks in our society is not a constructive act, yet it is the most frequent official response to crime in the U.S. today.

The social-psychological and the economic aspects of work-release are intimately related; both must be considered in evaluating it as an alternative to traditional incarceration.

Correctional Treatment

Some external control, such as institutionalization, is frequently necessary for the person whose previous behavior has been extremely unacceptable or unpredictable, especially if he has a prior history of physical violence. At the same time, along with attempts in the protected and structured environment to inculcate new patterns of social behavior and personal adjustment to social norms, he needs the opportunity for practicing adequate social performance in the "real" outside world. Ultimately the resocialization of the offender will be hampered unless adequate opportunities for appropriate social performance and autonomy of action are provided before he is finally released to the free community through discharge or parole. . . .

It is in this respect that the work-release plan makes a therapeutic contribution by releasing the offender from the county jail to go to work on a regular job in the community but to return to the institution at the end of the working day. *Some* needed institutional control is provided, and, concurrently, *some* opportunity is given to the offender to perform in socially desired roles and ways in the free community.

Work-Release Programing

The following description of typical work-furlough programs is based on those in Wisconsin and in Marin, Orange, and Santa Clara counties in California.

Most programs are for misdemeanants sentenced to county jails. The misdemeanant may be specifically committed to the program by the sentencing judge, may be placed on work-release by a county parole board, or may be automatically eligible for it (as in Wisconsin) if sentenced to "hard labor."

The offenses committed by work-release prisoners cover a wide range. The most common are nonsupport, driving with a revoked license, and drunk driving, but some programs place offenders convicted of narcotics violations, burglary, armed robbery, and even sex crimes, thus emphasizing the individual's potential for adquate performance on the work-furlough program rather than the specific crime committed.

If the furloughman already has a job, he continues his employment, leaving the jail during his working hours and returning after work. If he has no job, an attempt is made to find one for him. In some cases men are released from jail to seek employment. In Marin County, 65 per cent of the furloughmen retained the jobs they had before being sentenced; 30 per cent worked on jobs found for them by the staff; 5 per cent were self-employed.

Some furloughmen hold a number of part-time jobs or may even hold a full-time job *and* a part-time job. In a very few cases, an offender with limited employability—for example, a deteriorated chronic alcoholic—may be allowed to take work almost on a volunteer basis and accept donations for his labor, the major benefit lying in performance of a useful activity rather than in financial gain to the offender or the county.

Payment is generally in accord with current rates paid to others on similar jobs in the same company and the same community. Labor in Wisconsin and California is highly unionized, and union scales are generally adhered to. The average wage of Huber Law participants in Wisconsin is reported as $20 a day. There is always the possibility that unscrupulous persons administering work-release programs will conspire to provide labor at less than current market wages for a fee or kickback. It is usually avoided by giving the worker the right to change jobs or quit if he feels he is being exploited. Some sheriffs in Wisconsin set a $1 minimum hourly wage for work-release employment.

Transportation to and from the job can be a source of difficulty, but the offender's ingenuity and desire generally triumph over often awkward circumstances. Some furloughmen walk to work, some ride a bicycle, and some are picked up at the jail by the employer and driven back after work.

Programs differ in the amount of responsibility given offenders in handling their own earnings. In Wisconsin the furloughman's earnings are paid directly to the sheriff's department for fiscal management. In contrast, in Marin County the paycheck is turned over directly to the worker, who then cashes it and brings to the work-release officer the amount agreed upon for reimbursement to the county for his keep, payment of fines and restitution, and family support (unless he sends his support directly to the family). Personal expense money is kept by the furloughman, and the balance is held in trust pending final release from custody. The amount charged to furloughmen for keep, or administrative costs of the program, varies from program to program. In Wisconsin the charge ranges from $1.50 to $3.23 a day.

During his nonwork hours the furloughman generally remains in the jail, but the administrator of the work-release program has a great deal of latitude: he may allow him to attend night classes in the community, go for medical or psychiatric treatment, etc. If the furloughman works near his family home, he may be allowed to eat his lunches there and pick up his personal laundry. This allows for some maintenance of family contact and solidarity. . . .

Earnings and Disbursements

In Wisconsin, furloughmen earned a total of $2,800,000 during the years 1955 to 1960; the sum in 1960 was $633,000. In Marin County, the annual average for the years 1959 to 1965 was $46,000; in Orange County, the annual average for the years 1962 to 1964 was $122,000. In Santa Clara County, the total earned by persons in the program in eight years (1957 to 1965) came to over $1,-375,000, averaging $486 for each furloughman; the total earned in 1965 alone was $243,000.

The disbursement of funds varies from program to program. The major categories of disbursement are (a) reimbursement to the county for partial cost of room and board and administration of the program, (b) family support, (c) personal expenses, (d) fines and restitution, and (e) savings kept for the prisoner until his release.

. . . The major item of disbursement from earnings is family support. From a rehabilitation point of view this is desirable: responsible performance of the parental and adult roles is a major objective of the program. The proportion of earnings allocated for this purpose ranges from about one-third (in Wisconsin) to about two-thirds (in Orange County).

The second largest item is reimbursement to the county (for keep and administrative costs of the program). From a rehabilitation point of view this is also desirable. Some advanced European correctional institutions and programs—e.g., Holland's Van der Hoeven Clinic—require the inmate to work and pay for his keep *and* cost of his psychological treatment.

Personal expenses and fines and restitution play a less important part in the program. Savings held in trust for the furloughman until his release are important from a rehabilitation as well as an economic point of view. Everyone working in correction is well aware of the social and psychological problems faced by the offender released from an institution with little or no money. The releasee is much better prepared to face the stigma and readjustment problems that will confront him if he is bolstered by adequate funds and has a job awaiting him.

Failures

Work-release programs are not free of failures. Though the vast majority of furloughmen respond positively to the trust placed in them, some escape, and some violate other rules. Escape rates vary from less than 1 per cent (Orange and Marin counties) to 12 per cent (Milwaukee County, Wis.). Those furloughmen removed from the program for violation other than escape were involved in such behavior as drinking, returning to the jail late, etc. Escapes and violations of institutional rules occur, of course, even in counties without work-release programs.

A Two-Pronged Effort

Walter H. Busher, work-release administrator for Marin County, offers the following cautions to a political jurisdiction considering the development of a work-release program:

1. Do not institute a program unless the sheriff is willing to assure his fullest cooperation. . . .

5. Do not become panicked by the first adverse experience.

6. *Finally, do not let the attractive financial aspects of the program—which can be considerable—overshadow the fact that a work-release program is basically a device to strengthen society by improving the quality of citizenship of some of its members.*

Even while urging caution, Busher reports great enthusiasm for the program in his area by the offenders and their families, the probation department, jail personnel (who often seek jobs for the furloughmen *on their own time*), the courts, and the unions. The majority of the furloughmen are wage-earners (90 per cent in Marin County) rather than salaried employees; most of the furloughmen in the highly unionized geographic areas discussed in this paper are union members.

An unexpected outcome of some programs has been that, as the judges have become more and more aware of the practicability of releasing offenders under supervision, they have placed larger numbers directly on probation rather than committing them to jail. The work-release program in Marin County, for example, is becoming smaller and smaller—paradoxically, a sign of its success.

Widespread interest in the "half-way house" concept is evidence that we are aware of the difficulties of re-entry into the free society from institutional life. We now face an equally important issue: man cannot be separated from the economic life of his society without loss to both himself *and* society.

Work-release has demonstrated that it can provide (a) institutional supervision and (b) opportunity for offenders to perform the major societal economic roles. It thus offers a two-pronged effort to deal with the rehabilitation of offenders.

INMATES AS "THERAPISTS"

Excerpted from Judith G. Benjamin, Marcia K. Freedman, and Edith F. Lynton, *Pros and Cons: New Roles for Nonprofessionals in Corrections* (Washington, D.C.: U.S. Department of Health, Education, and Welfare, Welfare Administration, Office of Juvenile Delinquency and Youth Development, 1966), 35–40. The authors prepared this report for the National Committee on Employment of Youth.

A PREVALENT line of thinking holds that an individual inmate's rehabilitation can be accomplished more effectively if he is involved in the rehabilitation of other inmates, and that this can be institutionalized into an organized method of rehabilitation. Ideas advanced at a conference in Norco, California, . . . reflected this thinking and led to the proposal that the products of a social problem should be used in efforts to cope with the problem. An underlying assumption was that the offender, by virtue of his offender's status, will have avenues open to him for producing positive change in the behavior of other inmates that are closed to the staff, whether professional or nonprofessional.

Some of the thinking at the Norco conference was based on the experiences of the self-help movement: that people with common problems are influenced more readily through group process. Such movements, however, rely on the participants' desire for change. Correctional innovators are trying to arouse a similar desire through involving inmates in the work of the correctional institution. They see a potential force for good in the energy of the offender population, if that energy can be captured and redirected toward rehabilitative goals.

Not all the recent changes in inmates' roles occur as a result of advances in correctional theory and practice, however. Inmates in adult institutions frequently have served in a semiprofessional capacity and some of the roles that are now being described as "new" are little more than an extension of this practice. As services are expanded and new ones introduced, the need for manpower in correctional institutions increases. Largely for expediency's sake, but also to encourage the development of new work skills and future employability, the immate is often called on to provide the needed manpower.

The Inmate as "Therapist"

Perhaps the most significant innovations in developing new roles for inmates occur in the treatment services, because of the introduction of group methods. Group treatment requires that the inmate be a participant and even a prime mover in the rehabilitative process. In group treatment, each member of the group is expected to contribute to the process of group change and be changed in turn; each member is thought capable of a contribution because of shared values, problems, and experiences. With so much of the responsibility shifted to the offender, the natural next step is to allow the offender to direct treatment sessions. This is now beginning, particularly in the therapeutic-community type of institutional setting.

THE CALIFORNIA INSTITUTE FOR MEN

California, more than any other State, has been experimenting with new forms of intensive treatment for the institutionalized offender. One of the earliest attempts at "milieu therapy" was the Pine Hall Project, established at the California Institution for Men in Chino as part of a State-financed, four-year experiment with "intensive treatment programs." The project was to test the effectiveness of a therapeutic community with a selected group of 30 young, first-time felony offenders, housed in a separate unit.

The basic treatment elements consisted of daily mass meetings oriented toward "here-and-now" behavior, followed by small "social therapy groups." Initially, staff assumed the leadership, but eventually the inmates conducted the meetings and acted as their own "social therapists," with staff serving primarily in the role of consultants.

The positions of "social therapist" or "group coordinator" were established in response to the inmates' concern over the lack of feedback from delinquent behavior to the small group sessions. The group demonstrating the strongest attachment to the project was asked to consider how this problem might be resolved. It started by keeping a logbook to record behavior incidents it felt should have been considered at group sessions. This led the group to assume the direction of these sessions.

Besides meeting with staff for daily "tutorials," the "social therapists" also asked for further assistance to gain a better understanding of themselves, particularly in their new role as group leaders. Weekly seminars were set up for this purpose. In addition, psychiatrists and the correctional innovators who were responsible for the project were available for consultation. An extension course in social therapy, conducted by the University of California, was also available to those who wished to participate. When other inmates moved into the role of group coordinators, the veterans helped to train them.

As the project evolved, inmates played an instrumental role in selecting and orienting new inmates to the project. Feeling that they had information about prospective candidates that staff did not possess, the men organized themselves into a selection committee composed of a representative from each of the small group therapy sessions. The committee interviewed offenders who met the criteria for eligibility, usually with a staff member present, and selected those whom they felt were appropriate. It is interesting to note that the committee was less interested than staff in historical information, but more concerned about the extent of identification with the delinquent culture.

A group of men who identified strongly with the project organized themselves into a welcoming committee to counteract the "hazing" newcomers usually faced and the negative influence of the most delinquent members who usually exert the greatest pressure on new inmates. According to reports of staff, this effort met with considerable success.

The men also performed other staff functions. Inmate foremen and an inmate work-dispatcher, in cooperation with staff, planned and executed the inmates' work-crew assignments. These roles

were performed in rotation so that all could experience the role of
supervisor. The men also set up a program to screen, select, and
train members of the group who were willing and able to act as a
"night watch." One inmate undertook the assignment of serving as
the project's research clerk, investigating the behavior of both inmates and staff alike and assessing the need for change. Although
there was always an undercurrent of resistance on the part of project staff and the administration to this increase in inmate authority, staff most closely associated with the direction of the project
felt that this increasing involvement of the inmates gave them a
more realistic attitude toward authority. . . .

As an experimental program, the Pine Hall Project was given a
limited life to test its assumptions, but its influence is still being
felt in the California system and in other parts of the country. It
also has had an impact on later developments at the California Institution for Men.

Currently, for example, the Reception Guidance Center, housed
at this Institution, is experimenting with inmate-led therapy
groups. No research is being done on this program; it is simply an
innovation by an experimentally minded staff member with administrative backing. He is enthusiastic about this venture, but makes
no claims of superiority of inmates over professionals as social
therapists. He is using them because he firmly believes in the
group process as *the* method of treatment and feels it unlikely that
there will ever be a sufficient number of professionals employed to
provide service to all offenders. He prefers the inmate group leader
to the nonprofessional correctional officer, but primarily because
the inmate is undergoing therapy himself and, therefore, is more
experienced.

CHAPEL HILL, NORTH CAROLINA

Probably the greatest impact of Pine Hall has been on the program operating in Chapel Hill, North Carolina, under the Institute
of Government at the University of North Carolina. Convinced of
the value of the Pine Hall Project, the Institute's Training Center
on Delinquency and Youth Crime wanted to adapt this model to
North Carolina. With no professionals in the State corrections
agency familiar with the techniques of the therapeutic community,

the Training Center decided to set up such a program, using its staff as consultants but relying on parolees from Pine Hall to man the institution.

A separate custody-free, camp-type facility was established on the grounds of the University, housing some 20 first-time-commitment male offenders. Five parolees were brought in from California, selected by a staff member from Pine Hall.

Out of this original group of five, only one remained with the program. Of the others, one had never gone through Pine Hall and identified more with the inmate culture than with the objectives of staff. Two other parolees, who had been reared in a large city, found it difficult to adjust to the rural, relatively isolated town of Chapel Hill. Social outlets were few, and local mores, particularly regarding interracial contacts, made it even more restrictive. With only one experienced person left, the decision was made to use those inmates most responsive to treatment as "social therapists" for their fellow offenders.

By and large, the North Carolina program has followed the Pine Hall model, but with greater freedom and responsibility extended to the inmates. The professional role of consultant is more clearly marked since the Training Center's interdisciplinary staff does not live on the premises, but makes regular visits and is "on call" when needed. During the initial stages of the project, while the offender staff was in training, the professionals were at the camp daily. Gradually they passed the reins of responsibility to the parolee and the inmate staff.

The mass meetings are chaired by the parolee, who is the top staff person. The small group sessions are led by six inmate "social therapists." The boys as a group are expected to be responsible for all housekeeping, cooking, and general cleaning chores.

There is one very interesting departure from the Pine Hall model. Instead of working as crews around the institution, because of a State law permitting work-release, the boys work at regular jobs in the community. Two, in fact, have been working as "police aides," tutoring and counseling potential dropouts.[1]

[1] They have been called "police aides" because they have been working under the supervision of a local police official who originated the idea, but it has not been a police department program as such, and most referrals come from the schools.

The program at Chapel Hill has had its setbacks. The failure of the parolees is one; problems of grooming the inmate staff and achieving a common understanding of what constitutes a "therapeutic community" are others. It is not easy to distinguish between a "social therapist" and an "informer," especially if what is said in group sessions can result in expulsion from the project. There have been a number of incidents of boys' being away from camp overnight on "unauthorized leave" and, as a consequence, being committed to custody institutions. And a few, including former "social therapists," committed offenses that necessitated further legal action.

Many of these problems would be experienced in any experiment where principles, practices, and procedures are first being tested. The Training Center staff are aware, for example, that they failed to consider in advance the pressures on parolees of living in Chapel Hill.

Some observers feel, however, that the program was bound to face difficulties because of "excessive reliance" on inmates. They feel that there should have been closer, ongoing supervision by professionals. They see a built-in conflict of identification arising when inmates must perform the role of staff. Also, the work-release program, while it may mark an advance in correctional practice, added to the pressures because it put the inmates in the position of being half free and half confined.

Yet staff at the Training Center feel that, even with its checkered history, the program eventually managed to overcome the obstacles and achieve its objective—a true therapeutic community. They feel there is now a sense of common purpose among the inmates and a feeling of oneness with the project. As one indication of this, they point to the fact that the current group of social therapists, on their own initiative, decided to move from separate staff quarters into the regular living units to become a part of the community, rather than an isolated power bloc.

Now that the project has passed its trial stage, it is expected to be discontinued because of lack of funds and local support. . . .

ALTERNATIVES TO INCARCERATION: COMMUNITY-CENTERED PROGRAMS

Excerpted from the President's Commission on Law Enforcement and Administration of Justice, *Task Force Report: Corrections* (Washington, D.C.: U.S. Government Printing Office, 1967), pp. 38–43.

IN RECENT years a number of experimental community programs have been set up in various parts of the country, differing substantially in content and structure but all offering greater supervision and guidance than the traditional probation and parole programs. . . . The advent of these programs in the postwar decades and their recent growth in numbers and prominence are perhaps the most promising developments in corrections today.

These programs are by and large less costly, often far less costly, than incarceration in an institution. Evaluation has indicated that they are usually at least as effective in reducing recidivism and in some cases significantly more so. . . .

Guided Group Interaction Programs

Underlying one of the newer programs for treating the young delinquent in the community is the premise that juvenile delinquency is commonly a group experience and that therefore efforts to change delinquent behavior should focus primarily on a group like that within which the individual operates. A number of group counseling methods have been employed but the method called guided group interaction has been used most extensively in those programs which involved a research component.

The general strategy of guided group interaction calls for involving the offenders in frequent, prolonged, and intensive discussions of the behavior of individuals in the group and the motivations underlying it. Concentrating on participants' current experiences and problems, the approach attempts to develop a group "culture" that encourages those involved to assume responsibility for helping and controlling each other. The theory is that the offender-participants will be more responsive to the influence of their fellow offenders, their peers, than to the admonitions of staff, and less likely to succeed in hoodwinking and manipulating each other.

As the culture develops and the group begins to act responsibly, the group leader, a staff member, seeks to encourage a broader sharing of power between the offenders and the staff. At first, group decisions will be limited to routine matters, such as the schedule of the day, but over time they may extend to disciplinary measures against a group member or even to decisions concerning readiness for release from the program.

HIGHFIELDS

The Highfields project in New Jersey was the pioneer effort in guided group interaction. Initiated in 1950, it has been duplicated in communities and also in institutions and used with both juveniles and adults. Highfields limits its population to 20 boys aged 16 and 17, who are assigned directly to it from the juvenile court. Boys with former commitments to correctional schools are not accepted, nor are deeply disturbed or mentally retarded youths. The goal is to effect rehabilitation within 3 to 4 months, about half the average period of incarceration in the State training school.

The youths are housed in the old Lindberg mansion. They work during the day at a mental institution immediately adjacent to their residence. In the evening they participate in the group counseling sessions. On Saturdays, they clean up the residence. Saturday afternoon is free, and Sunday is reserved for receiving visitors and going to religious services. Formal rules are few.

Early efforts to evaluate the effects of the project on recidivism, as compared with those of the State reformatory, are still the subject of academic dispute. However, it is clear that Highfields was at least as effective as the reformatory, perhaps more effective, and that it accomplished its results in a much shorter period of time at greatly reduced monthly costs.

PINEHILLS AND OTHER DEVELOPMENTS

Important variations on the Highfields project developed at Essexfields, also in New Jersey, and at Pinehills in Provo, Utah. As at Highfields, program content at Essexfields and Pinehills centered around gainful employment in the community, school, and daily group meetings. The most significant difference was that, in the Essexfields and Pinehills experiments, the offenders continued to live at home.

The regimen at both Essexfields and Pinehills was rigorous. At Pinehills, for example, all boys were employed by the city. They put in a full day's work on the city streets, on the golf course, in the cemetery, wherever they were needed. They were paid 50 cents an hour. During the late afternoon, after the day's work was finished, all boys returned to the program headquarters where they met in daily group sessions. About 7 P.M. they were free to return home. They were also free on Sundays.

In the daily group sessions all group members, not just adult staff, were responsible for defining problems and finding solutions to them. By making the program operations to some extent the work of all involved, both offenders and staff, it was possible to make a better estimate of just how much responsibility for his own life a given offender could take.

The fact that these guided group interaction programs are located in the community means that the problems with which the group struggles are those that confront them daily in contacts with their families, friends, teachers, and employers. This is one great strength of a community program over an institutional program. The artificiality of institutional life is avoided, and concentration can be placed upon the issues with which every offender eventually has to deal. . . .

CONTRIBUTIONS OF GUIDED GROUP PROGRAMS

These projects, like Highfields, represent an authentic departure from traditional community programs for delinquents. The Highfields type of program is unique in that the group process itself shapes the culture and social system of the total program. The key element seems to be the amount of decision-making authority permitted the group, which has considerably more authority to decide than in traditional group therapy programs. J. Robert Weber, who made a study of promising programs for delinquents, said of the Highfields type of program:

If one asks a youth in most conventional institutions, "How do you get out?" one invariably hears some version of, "Be good. Do what you are told. Behave yourself." If one asks a youth in a group treatment program, "How do you get out?" one hears, "I have to help myself with my problems," or "When my group thinks I have been helped." This implies a basic difference in the social system of the organization, including staff roles and functions.[1]

In the large institution, Weber concluded, the youth perceives getting out in terms of the problem of meeting the institutional need for conformity. In the group treatment program the youth sees getting out in terms of his solution to his own problems, or how that is perceived by other youths in the group.

FOSTER HOMES AND GROUP HOMES

Foster-home placement has long been one of the most commonly used alternatives to institutionalization for juvenile probationers. . . .

The utilization of foster homes or group homes in lieu of institutional confinement has several obvious advantages, provided the offender does not require the controls of an institution. Such placements keep the offender in the community where he must eventually work out his future. They carry less stigma and less sense of criminal identity and they are far less expensive than incarceration. . . .

A number of States have begun to develop group homes as a variant to traditional foster-home care for youths who need a somewhat more institutional setting or cannot adjust to family life. The Youth Commission of Minnesota, for example, reported using seven group homes under arrangements with the home operator or

---

[1] J. Robert Weber, "A Report of the Juvenile Institutions Project (unpublished report to the Osborne Association and the National Council on Crime and Delinquency," Sept. 1966), pp. 225, 226.

with an intermediate agency. A nominal retaining fee was paid for each bed licensed; and, when a youth actually was placed in the home, the rate of pay was increased.

The Wisconsin Division of Corrections in 1966 was operating an even more ambitious program. Thirty-three homes for boys or girls were in use under a payment plan similar to that employed in Minnesota. With four to eight adolescents in each home, the total population handled was equivalent to that of at least one institution, but operating costs were one-third to one-fourth less.

In both States the adolescents placed in group homes were those who had been received on court commitment as candidates for institutional placement. In Wisconsin, approximately one-fourth of the group had been released from institutions for placement in a foster home. Other jurisdictions are experimenting with the group-home technique. . . .

Halfway Programs: The Prerelease Guidance Center

In corrections as in related fields, the "halfway house" is an increasingly familiar program. Initially, such programs were conceived for offenders "halfway out" of institutions, as a means of easing the stresses involved in transition from rigid control to freedom in the community. The prerelease guidance centers of the Federal Bureau of Prisons are the best-known halfway-out programs in the United States. Recently the halfway house has come to be viewed as a potential alternative to institutionalization, and thus a program for those "halfway in" between probation and institutional control.

FEDERAL PRERELEASE GUIDANCE CENTERS

The first prerelease guidance centers of the Federal Bureau of Prisons were opened in 1961 in New York, Chicago, and Los Angeles, and others were established subsequently in Detroit, Washington, and Kansas City. Each center accommodates about 20 Federal prisoners who are transferred to it several months before their expected parole date. Thus they complete their terms in the community but under careful control.

Some of the centers are located in what were large, single-family houses; some occupy a small section or scattered rooms in a YMCA hotel; and one is located in a building once operated as a small home for needy boys. All are in neighborhoods with mixed land usage, racial integration, and nearby transportation.

Offenders transferred to these centers wear civilian clothes. They generally move from prison to the centers by public transportation without escort. For a day or two they are restricted to the building, although they may receive visitors there. In the YMCA's they eat in a public cafeteria in the building and use the public recreation areas, taking out YMCA memberships. Following a day or two of orientation and counseling, they go out to look for jobs. After they are on a job, they are gradually given more extensive leaves for recreational purposes and for visits with their families. As their parole date approaches, some may even be permitted to move out of the center, although they are still required to return to the center for conferences several times a week.

These centers are staffed in large part by persons rotated from regular institution staff who are highly oriented to counseling. One full-time employee is an employment counseling specialist. Several others, such as college students in the behavioral sciences, are employed on a part-time basis and provide the only staff coverage during the late night hours and part of the weekend. In addition to individual counseling, there are several group sessions a week. Federal probation officers, who will supervise the offenders when they go on parole, participate in the center's counseling activities. By the time a resident is ready to begin his parole, almost all of his individual counseling has been assumed by his parole supervision officer.

A major function of these temporary release programs has been to augment the information available to correctional staff. This information includes both diagnostic data on the individuals temporarily released and information on the assets and deficiencies of correctional programs and personnel. In addition, they provide optimum circumstances for counseling, since the counseling can deal with immediate realities as they are encountered, rather than with the abstract and hypothetical visions of the past and the future or the purely institutional problems to which counseling in institutions is largely restricted.

Inmate misbehavior while on work release or in prerelease guidance centers is not a rare thing, particularly for youthful offenders. Although a majority adjust quite satisfactorily, some get drunk, some get involved in fights and auto accidents when out with old or new friends, and some are late in returning to the center. An appreciable number of the youth have difficulty in holding jobs, some fail to go to work or to school when they are supposed to be there, a few abscond, and a few get involved in further crime. The important point is that they would be doing these things in any case, and probably more extensively, if they had been released more completely on their own through parole or discharge. Under the latter circumstances, however, correctional staff would know of the releasee's difficulties, if at all, not nearly so promptly as is possible with temporary release measures.

When an individual returns from a temporary release to home, work, or school, his experience can be discussed with him by staff, to try to assess his probable adjustment and to note incipient problems. Many difficulties can be anticipated in this way. The inmate's anxieties can be relieved by discussion, and discussion may also help him develop realistic plans for coping with prospective problems. When persistent or serious misbehavior occurs, sanctions are available to staff, ranging from restriction of further leaves or temporary incarceration to renewed institutionalization, with a recommendation to the parole board that the date of parole be deferred. . . .

STATE PRERELEASE CENTERS

The Kentucky Department of Corrections, under a grant from the Office of Economic Opportunity, has a series of vocational training courses in its State reformatory which are identical with courses established at several centers in the State under the Department of Labor. Prerelease guidance centers ···ere established near these centers in three cities, so that reformatory inmates could continue their institution courses in the community, where as trainees they receive a small stipend, in addition to highly developed job placement services.

The Federal Bureau of Prisons assisted in establishing these centers and sends Federal inmates from these cities to the centers. Conversely, State correctional agencies share in the operation of the Federal prerelease guidance centers in Detroit and Kansas City, assigning some State inmates there, and the District of Columbia Department of Corrections plays a major role in the operation of the center in Washington. This State-Federal collaboration could well serve as a model for many types of correctional undertaking.

INTENSIVE COMMUNITY TREATMENT

Perhaps the best known of the country's efforts at controlled experimentation in the correctional field is the California Youth Authority's Community Treatment Project, now in its sixth year. Operating within a rigorous evaluative design, it offers an excellent illustration of the profitable partnership which can develop when carefully devised program innovations are combined with sound research.

The subjects of the project consist of boys and girls committed to the Youth Authority from two adjacent counties, Sacramento and San Joaquin. While under study in a reception center, each new group is subjected to a screening process which excludes some 25 percent of the boys and 5 to 10 percent of the girls because of the serious nature of their offenses, the presence of mental abnormality, or strenous community objections to their direct release. The remaining youngsters are then either assigned randomly to the community project—in which case they form part of the experimental group—or are channeled routinely into an institution and eventually paroled.

An interview by a member of the research staff provides the basis for classification of the offender subgroups. This categorization is made in terms of the maturity of the youth, as reflected in his relationships with others, in the manner in which he perceives the world, and in the way he goes about gaining satisfaction of his needs. A variety of standardized tests seeks to measure the extent of his identification with delinquent values as well as his general personality characteristics.

The program provided for the experimental group offers singly or in combination most of the techniques of treatment and control which are in use in corrections today: individual counseling, group counseling, group therapy, family therapy, involvement in various other group activities, and school tutoring services by a certificated teacher with long experience in working with delinquents. The goal is to develop a treatment plan which is tailored to the needs of each type of offender. The resulting plan is then implemented at a level of high intensity, made possible by the availability of carefully selected and experienced staff on a ratio of 1 staff member for each 12 youths.

A program center serves as the hub of activity; it houses the staff and provides a recreation area, classrooms, and a musicroom. A limited outdoor sports activities area also is available. In the late afternoon and some evenings, the center resembles a small settlement house operation as the wards come in after school for counseling, tutoring, and recreational activity.

An unusual and controversial feature of the experiment is the frequent use of short-term detention at the agency's reception center to assure compliance with program requirements and to "set limits" on the behavior of the participants. The detention may vary from a few hours to a few days.

Results have been measured in several ways. A repetition of the psychological test battery seeks to determine what movement has occurred in the socialization of the individual offender. The responses of the various categories of youth have revealed greater success with some than with others, and may eventually provide a more reliable indicator of who should be institutionalized. Finally, the "failure rate," as measured by the proportion who are later institutionalized because they have committed additional offenses, is carefully compared with similar information on members of the control group who have been institutionalized and then returned to the community under regular parole supervision.

The latest report of the project activity available to the Commission revealed that checks of parolees, at the end of 15 months of parole exposure, showed that 28 percent of the experimental group had been subject to revocation of parole, as compared to 52 percent of the control group which was afforded regular institution and parole handling.

After several years of pilot work, the California Youth Authority decided in 1964 to extend the community treatment format to the Watts area of Los Angeles and to a neighborhood in west Oakland. Both are high-delinquency areas; both are heavily Negro in population. Essentially duplications of the original experiment, the two new program units do not have a research component. Instead of random assignment of the subject, the youths committed from a given area are screened by project staff for direct release from the reception center.

In the absence of a control group, the success of the program has been measured by comparing the failure rate of the youth assigned to it with equivalent statewide rates for youths of the same middle to older adolescent age range. At the end of 15 months of parole exposure, 39 percent of project wards had been subject to parole revocation as compared to a statewide revocation rate of 48 percent for youths of the same age bracket. . . .

RECEPTION CENTER PAROLE AND
SHORT-TERM TREATMENT PROGRAMS

Diagnostic parole is a program whereby all commitments from the juvenile court are referred to a reception center where they can be screened for eligibility for parole, either immediately or after a short period of treatment. This program has reached significant proportions in an increasing number of States.

While most State systems have long had some informal arrangements for returning a few cases to the community at an early date, more organized procedures developed almost simultaneously in New York, Washington, Kentucky, and California in the early 1960's. These programs were conceived in part as a response to acute population pressures in overcrowded institutions. The seemingly successful results have led to a substantial increase in the volume of cases diverted from the training school to short, intensive treatment programs followed by parole in the community.

In New York the screening is undertaken by special aftercare staff while the youngsters are in New York City's Youth House awaiting delivery to the State school system. The youths selected to return to the community are those who are thought to be amenable to conventional casework procedures. Those selected are placed in an intensive casework program. The apparent success of the original unit in New York City has led to an expansion of the program and to the practice of returning still other youngsters to the community after the intake studies carried on in the State schools.

Washington, another State with a central reception center for juvenile offenders, is also screening those committed. A significant percentage of cases are assigned to immediate placement in foster homes or other community-based programs, including four halfway houses.

The California Youth Authority apparently is making the greatest use of the reception center release procedure. Currently some 20 percent of the boys and 35 percent of the girls processed are being released to regular parole or to foster-home placement at the termination of reception period. This is typically a month long, but in some instances release may be postponed for another 30 to 90 days. . . .

The success of reception center parole has been encouraging. . . . To date, parole from reception centers has been confined to the juvenile field. However, there is no inherent reason why this approach should not be taken with adults, and hopefully it will be so used in the near future.

A POLICE OFFICIAL LOOKS
AT PROBATION AND PAROLE

J. EDGAR HOOVER

"Statement of Director J. Edgar Hoover," *FBI Law Enforcement Bulletin,* XXVII (November 1958), 1–2.

THE PREMATURE release of dangerous criminals through frequently occurring abuses in our system of parole, probation, and other forms of clemency demands the serious attention of police and public alike. Law enforcement is a vast machinery of criminal justice established for the protection of society. The shortcomings of any part in this mechanism not only impede the police profession but also imperil the safety of the Nation's citizens. It is therefore imperative that law enforcement and the general public recognize and re-evaluate the rehabilitation procedures which allow ill-advised leniency to criminals.

The dire consequences of maladministration of the parole and probation programs, daily paraded before the public in the newspaper headlines across the land, can no longer be ignored. No less than 92 of the 109 dangerous criminals listed among the FBI's "Ten Most Wanted Fugitives" since March, 1950, had been the recipients of parole, probation, or other forms of clemency. The service martyr plaques of the Nation's police agencies are filled with the names of dedicated men slain at the hands of gunmen who were the recipients of ill-advised clemency.

The validity of the principle of parole, probation, and other forms of clemency is not a question in issue. What must be sought is not the abolition of the systems of rehabilitation but the improvement in their administration to assure that the welfare of the public, as well as the criminal, is served. To achieve this objective, a critical self-analysis of present procedures and results is essential.

The failures of "easy freedom" policies cannot be attributed to any one solitary cause. Certainly, the handicaps of the parole and probation systems resulting from insufficient manpower, paltry budgets, and excessive workloads must be removed. In addition, moreover, soft-hearted leniency, coddling of juvenile criminals, cheap solutions to overcrowded prison facilities, and other unrealistic techniques are potent factors which should be brought out in the open. An ostrich-like attitude, apologetic statements, and unwarranted resentment of concern for the abuses threatening the public upon the part of not only penologists but also a small segment of the judiciary can only aggravate an already serious problem.

The remarkable progress gained by law enforcement in recent years is due in no small degree to the intelligent evaluation of procedures and the ardent solicitation of public assistance in overcoming handicaps. In like manner, the parole and probation failures of yesterday and today can be the bases for the successes of tomorrow. In dealing with human failings, there can be no guarantee of 100% success. Each failure, however, presents a challenge and should be objectively analyzed in an effort to avoid recurrence.

The primary obligation for making the parole and probation systems serve their rightful purpose naturally lies with the established agencies and authorities in this field. In the light of current experience, the law-abiding public and the rest of law enforcement are entitled to a frank evaluation of past results, an honest appraisal of present policies, and a carefully planned program for future operation to halt the unleashing of unreformed criminals upon American communities.

In the rehabilitation phase of law enforcement, parole and probation authorities, police officials, the judiciary, and the citizenry share grave interests and responsibilities. With united and cooperative effort, success can be achieved. The only alternative is surrender to lawlessness and social disorder.

PAROLE PREDICTION

PETER P. LEJINS

Excerpted from Peter P. Lejins, "Parole Prediction—An Introductory Statement," *Crime and Delinquency*, 8, No. 3 (July 1962), 209–214. At the time of publication, Peter P. Lejins was Professor of Sociology at the University of Maryland.

THE TERM "parole prediction" is firmly established in American correctional parlance. It refers to the estimate of probability of violation or nonviolation of parole by an offender on the basis of experience tables, developed with regard to groups of offenders possessing similar characteristics. . . .

The use of the experience tables for estimating the chances of success of a parolee or a particular type of parolee is, of course, a special application of a general method that has been used by social science, especially applied social science, for quite some time. That this method would sooner or later find its way also into the studies of criminal behavior was to be expected. Although it is in wide use, the standard reference usually is to the computation of insurance rates on the basis of experience tables.

Although the computation of experience tables and their use for prediction purposes in parole has so far been by far the most popular kind of prediction in criminology, it is, of course, only a special instance of prediction of criminal or delinquent behavior in general. Other types of prediction in this area that have also received a considerable amount of attention are prediction of probation outcome, delinquent behavior, recurrence of criminal behavior in general (recidivism), etc.

Early History

In 1923 Professor Sam Bass Warner, of Harvard, describing a pioneering study that attempted to relate the background factors available in the reformatory records of a group of offenders to success or failure on parole, reported only a very limited relationship. A few months later Professor Hornell Hart suggested that improved methodology would reveal the relationship which Warner failed to find and that several background factors which *singly* do not show a significant relationship with the ultimate parole outcome should be *combined* into a prognostic score. By reason of these suggestions Hart is widely credited as the originator of the parole prediction idea.

Development of a table of expectancy rates of parole violation and nonviolation and introduction of this instrument into actual use in a state parole system was the accomplishment of Professor Ernest W. Burgess, of Chicago University, and his associates. Reported in 1928 and subsequently put to use in Illinois, it was the first large-scale study of the relationship of the offender's background factors to the parole outcome, and for many years it served as the basis for the accumulation of data and for further studies by a number of scholars.

Briefly, Professor Burgess' parole prediction procedure was as follows:

Within a parolee population for which the average violation rate was known, the violation rates for sub-populations possessing some specific background characteristic were computed; e.g., the rate for parolees characterized by "no previous work record," for parolees with a record of "casual work," for those with a record of "irregular work," and for those with a record of "regular work." Where these violation rates were lower than the violation rate for the entire parolee population, the corresponding factor was considered to be a favorable or positive one. All positive factors were placed into an experience table and each candidate for parole was given one point for each such factor in his background. Finally, a table giving the violation expectancy rate for offenders with different numbers of favorable factors was worked out for the population studied. It was assumed that future candidates for parole would have the same chance of success as those having the same number of favorable factors in the original population.

In this prototypic expectancy table the chances of success ran from 98.5 per cent, for parolees having sixteen to twenty-one favorable factors, to 24 per cent for those having only two, three, or four favorable factors. This instrument was put into practice in Illinois in 1933.

Publication of Burgess' proposals was followed soon afterward by Sheldon and Eleanor Glueck's report of what is usually regarded as another pioneer advance in the development of instruments predicting criminal behavior. The Gluecks took a somewhat different course and continued independently of the Burgess-Illinois tradition. The essentially new thought for prediction already evident in their first publications was the weighting of the favorable background factors on the basis of the extent of their relationship to success or failure. These weights can be and have been developed through various statistical techniques.

Even in these early stages of investigation the idea was expressed that the experience tables should be used not only for the computation of the chances of success of parole, but also as guides in deciding on the kind of supervision or treatment to be given the released parolee.

Later Major Ideas

An important addition to the rationale of parole prediction is Laune's observation, in *Predicting Criminality,* that almost all the background factors in the Burgess-type experience table are static; that is, not subject to change by the institutional treatment program. For example, preincarceration work history, marital status, national or ethnic origin, etc., remain the same, regardless of what is done to the offender in the way of treatment. This means that the correctional process—preparation of the offender for his return to the community—had hardly any role at all in prediction. Laune suggested that the changes produced in the inmate in the course of institutional treatment be accounted for in the expectancy table, thus introducing into the treatment process a certain element of dynamism—and also, some would say, optimism. He tried to discover the attitudes of the inmate through the "hunches" of fellow inmates, who presumably know, better than the institution's personnel, what these attitudes are. While Laune's research is important, the follow-up of his study showed that the inmate-hunch method was no more effective than the original Burgess method.

Of the score of other criminologists in the thirties who were interested in parole prediction, one might limit mention to Clark Tibbitts, George B. Vold, and Barkev S. Sanders. Their principal contribution was the discovery that parolee experiences—or predictions derived from different populations of parolees—were not always consistent; it was possible, they said, that rapid changes in administrative practices and policies and in the general conditions of life could change the role of the background factors quite rapidly.

Later this problem was picked up by Lloyd E. Ohlin, who also discovered, in a comprehensive study of Illinois parole, the need for continuously adjusting the experience tables. Ohlin maintained that research on predictive factors ought to be a part of the parole system and that it be a constant operation, to the extent that experience of parolees who have completed the first year of parole should be used in evaluating parolee backgrounds the next year. This means the development of a very sensitive instrument, quite different from what the original researchers probably had in mind.

As Karl F. Schuessler suggested in his attempt to structure the history of parole prediction by distinguishing several stages in its development, the post-World War II period was characterized by explorations of methodological refinement. Of these the most significant were conducted by Ohlin and his associates. Especially noteworthy is the Ohlin and Duncan "index of predictive efficiency." This measure consists of a percentage change in the prediction error as the result of using an experience table instead of the overall rate.

Another refinement, also brought in by Ohlin after study of the Illinois materials, was reduction of the number of favorable factors originally developed by Burgess. A more sophisticated statistical analysis of the relative weight of these factors as predictors of the behavior of the parolee demonstrated that, for practical purposes, twelve factors would be as effective as the original twenty-one. These explorations further showed the relative importance of just one or two factors among these twelve.

Use by Parole Boards

It is now time to turn to the all-important question of the applicability of the experience tables to the action of the paroling authority in an individual case.

This has been a crucial and controversial issue from the very beginning of parole prediction. The issue, characteristic of the social sciences in general, is simply this: predictions based on the experience tables are never 100 per cent correct and often fall far below. This means there is always the possibility that a certain individual, denied parole on the basis of the unfavorable past experiences of others with similar backgrounds, may be just the one who, in spite of this similarity, would not act as the majority did in the past. Refusing him parole would then constitute an injustice, of course, and at the same time an operational error.

The opposition to the use of prediction tables, on the basis of the probability sketched above, is made up of two camps. One consists of those who, hardly understanding what it is all about, clamor that the fate of an individual should not be decided on the basis of "statistics"; the other consists of those who thoroughly understand the meaning of the manipulations involved and are justifiably concerned about the proper application of experience tables to individual cases.

From the beginning many have maintained that recommendations based on experience tables should be supplemented by a thorough case study. Several researches were conducted in an attempt to shed some light on this issue. Some of these showed a remarkable similarity between predictions read from the experience tables and those derived from a diagnosis made, for example, by a psychiatrist; others failed to establish such reassuring coincidence in the results produced by the two methods. . . .

There are no signs of an end to the battle between the intransigents—on one hand, those who are obsessed in their opposition to statistical prediction "as a matter of principle," and, on the other, those who think that any parole selection procedure other than statistical prediction belongs in the same class as the talisman, the divining rod, and the wishbone. It is probably safe to state that, apart from these extremists, the vast majority of professionals in parole would agree that the opportunities offered by the experience tables could not and should not be missed.

Just as in other fields where computation of categoric risks has been found useful—as, for instance, in insurance and the assaying of aptitudes—so also in parole we cannot afford to forgo the help offered by the summation of experiences with types of offenders similar to the one whose case is under discussion. With the exception, perhaps, of the extreme ends of the continuum, a case study will always be necessary. The experience tables, however, would add considerably to the perspective on the idiosyncracies of the individual case and can serve as a guide for the exploration of the danger zones both during the formulation of the parole decision and during the subsequent treatment.

Parole prediction devices should be further explored and refined. I am convinced that they are destined to become an important part of the groundwork for parole decisions.

PERSONAL CHARACTERISTICS RELATED TO PAROLEE RECIDIVISM

DANIEL GLASER
AND VINCENT O'LEARY

Excerpted from Daniel Glaser and Vincent O'Leary, *Personal Characteristics and Parole Outcome* (Washington, D.C.: U.S. Department of Health, Education, and Welfare, 1966), pp. 5–24. At the time of publication, Daniel Glaser was in the Department of Sociology at the University of Illinois. Vincent O'Leary was Director of the National Parole Institutes.

THE FIRST information available on prisoners is that which most immediately identifies them. This comprises facts which generally can be learned quickly, such as sex, race, age, offense, prior criminal record, intelligence, and body dimensions. Some of these attributes, for example, the offense and criminal record, may actually have intricate variations. However, we shall first consider them as broad categories into which inmates may be classified soon after they reach the prison. This section is concerned with the parole prognosis value of this gross information by which prisoners may be divided into the young and the old, the thieves and the murderers, the first offenders and the repeaters, and so forth.

AGE

One of the most firmly established pieces of statistical knowledge about criminals is that the older a man is when he is released from prison, the less likely he is to return to crime. By no means should it be inferred that all old prisoners are good risks or all youngsters poor risks. Nevertheless, . . . for all parolees taken collectively, the older they are at release the less likely they are to fail on parole.

. . . The parole violation rate predominantly decreases as the age at parole increases, although there is some deviation from perfect consistency in this relationship. Such findings have been reported for many decades, and in numerous jurisdictions, both in the United States and abroad. A related finding is that, as age at release increases, it is increasingly likely that if any further criminality occurs, it will be a misdemeanor rather than a felony.

The easiest interpretation of this finding is that people become less criminal as they become more mature. Such an interpretation only has much validity if the word "mature" is used primarily in a nonbiological sense. Criminals generally are at least as well developed physically as the average person of their age. They can only be considered immature by defining normal maturation as change from delinquent youth to noncriminal adulthood.

It will suffice at this point to observe that the age group which has the highest crime rates in most industrialized societies is the vaguely defined one which is in transition between childhood and adulthood. These are the people we call "adolescents." For them to become adults, in the sense that others treat them as adults, requires not just physical maturation, but the acquisition of a self-sufficient position in the adult economic and social world. Prisoners tend to be persons who have failed in the past and may be handicapped in the future in achieving this transition, although most of them eventually do become self-sufficient in a legitimate adult life. . . .

. . . It is the consensus of both statistical analysis and personal impressions of experienced officials that youth are the least predictable of all prisoners. Although they have high rates of return to crime, this rate diminishes as they mature, and it is hard to predict when their criminal careers may end. They are in a period in which old associates and points of view may suddenly be dropped, and new ones gained. Innumerable cases can be cited where marriage, new employment, or other incidents marked a turning point which was followed by the complete metamorphosis of such offenders. Many individuals with long histories of juvenile crime, including acts of violence and drug addiction, are now leading respectable and law-abiding lives. . . .

THE CRIMINAL RECORD

The extent to which a person has devoted himself to crime is not easily measured. We only know of the offenses for which he was apprehended, or which he will admit, and he may have been involved in considerable criminality not revealed to us. Nevertheless, that which can be learned about prior criminality often is the most valuable information that a parole board has about a prisoner. . . .

There are so many standpoints from which criminal records can be analyzed, that we cannot exhaust all of the possibilities here. Instead we shall focus on three principal types of information for which this record is our primary or our initial source. These are: the *duration* of the prisoner's prior involvement in crime, his *prior experience with government agencies dealing with crime* (police, courts, prisons, etc.), *and the types of offense* he has committed.

DURATION OF PRIOR CRIMINALITY

The duration of prior criminality can be estimated imperfectly from several types of evidence. For example, offenders can be differentiated according to the age at which they were first arrested, first adjudicated, first committed to a correctional institution, or first reported in any type of difficulty for delinquent activity. Presumably, among offenders of approximately the same age, the earlier they first have any of these experiences, the longer is the span of their prior involvement in crime, and the more likely they are to continue in crime. . . .

The foregoing conclusion has occasionally been challenged by a theory that all offenders have approximately the same period of delinquency and crime to go through, so that the earlier they start this period, the younger they will be when they conclude it. This is suggested by the finding that many older chronic offenders have no juvenile delinquency or youth crime record.

Nevertheless, the predominance of evidence is against this conclusion. Despite some deviations, the overall generalization . . . is that at any age, the longer the span of prior criminality, the more likely it is that it will be extended in the future. . . .

The few rather persistent types of crime characteristically starting at a later age than the majority of offenses provide exceptions
to the foregoing generalization that early onset means more persistence in crime. These late starting offenses consist of some crimes
associated with alcoholism, especially check forgery, and some offenses that also seem to occur as an abnormal adjustment to senility. These include a petty theft and vagrancy combination, and
certain sexual indecency offenses. The old and persistent criminals
who do not have a criminal record which goes back to juvenile
days, or have a long gap between youth and old age offenses, are
not sufficiently numerous to contradict the overall generalization
that the younger a person was when his crime began, the more
likely he is to persist in it.

The number of prior felony convictions is only a rough indication of the duration of prior criminality. Of course, what we know
about a man's criminal record generally is limited to that which
was recorded by government agencies which dealt with him.
Therefore, the duration [of] past criminality often can be roughly
estimated from many types of available records on a person's experience with agents of the law.

PRIOR POLICE, COURT, AND CORRECTIONAL EXPERIENCE

Since there are many ways of classifying a criminal's record of
previous experience with government agencies, it is often difficult
to compare statistical tabulations from different jurisdictions. . . .

These tabulations indicate, on the whole, that no matter how
one counts the volume of previous experience with police, court, or
correctional agencies, the overall trend is for the parole failure rate
to increase as the magnitude of this prior experience increases.
This trend, however, is offset by the influence of age: one or more
commitments as a juvenile seems to be more unfavorable as a
prognostic sign than the same number of commitments later. In
general, the increase in violation rate with increasing number of
prior commitments becomes progressively less, or halts completely,
after a few terms of imprisonment, or even of successive felony
convictions. However, . . . this decrease in failure rate simply reflects the crime-diminishing effect of older age at release for those

with three or more prior felony convictions. Possibly the reduced
rate of return to crime with each successive commitment also reflects some rehabilitative or deterrent influence of imprisonment. It
is clear, at any rate, that we cannot conclude with certainty that
everyone in any category of prior criminal record will persist in
crime indefinitely into the future.

. . . Wisconsin data . . . show that prison commitments alone
may not be as unfavorable for parole prognosis as combinations of
prison and lesser commitments. This unfavorable prognosis is in
terms of overall violation rate only; it ignores type of violation.
Persons habitually in minor difficulty with the law, such as drunks
and vagrants, may not be as serious a problem to parole boards as
persons less likely to violate, but more likely to commit serious
new offenses if they do. This observation, of course, brings out the
oversimplification we are employing in most of this discussion by
not distinguishing different types of violation. Some correction of
this deficiency will be made in considering offense as a factor in
parole prognosis.

TYPES OF OFFENSE

Still another aspect of the vital information provided to parole
boards by the criminal record is the type of offense for which a
prisoner is currently committed, or in which he was previously involved. It is appropriate therefore to provide an overall view of the
many types of offense, and to compare their significance in predicting continuation of criminality.

The most persistent types of common crime are those in which
offenders obtain someone else's money without use of violence.
These crimes can be divided into two major categories: illegal service and predatory crimes.

Illegal service crimes consist of economically motivated offenses
in which there is no person who clearly considers himself a victim;
instead, the persons with whom the criminals deal are his customers. Examples of such crimes are the sale of illicit alcoholic beverages ("moonshine"), narcotics and stolen goods, and the provision
of illegal gambling and prostitution services. Only a minute proportion of these offenses lead to arrest and prosecution. Also, con-

viction on some of these charges, such as gambling and prostitution, seldom leads to imprisonment, so parole boards seldom confront such criminals. Because these criminal services are both more profitable and safer than most other offenses, one can reasonably speculate that they may be the most frequently committed clearly criminal acts, even though this is not confirmed by complaint or arrest statistics.

The crimes usually encountered by parole boards are predatory crimes. . . . On the whole, these offenses usually fall into three main clusters, from the standpoint of violation rates. The offenses usually associated with the highest violation rates involve taking somebody else's property by stealth or by deceit. Notable here are the crimes of theft, burglary, and forgery.

Theft, which older criminal codes usually call "larceny," consists simply of taking somebody else's property. Both in the law and in statistical tabulations, the crime of auto theft usually is treated separately. Auto thieves have the highest rates of parole violation in most jurisdictions, possibly because they generally are the youngest parolees. Their crime usually is committed for the temporary enjoyment of transportation rather than for long-term economic gains. For this reason, in approximately 90 percent of auto thefts the vehicle is recovered intact, even though the thieves usually are not caught. However, in some auto thefts the cars are stripped, and some older auto thieves are in gangs which falsify ownership papers and sell stolen cars.

Other types of theft include shoplifting, removing objects from parked cars, picking pockets, taking goods from places of employment, and many more varieties of "stealing." Most of the separate crimes are small, frequently they are not immediately discovered by the victim, and probably a major portion are never reported to the police. Only a small proportion of theft reported to the police, other than auto theft, is solved by recovery of the stolen goods, or conviction of the offenders. Furthermore, the small value of the property taken in separate offenses frequently results in a convicted person receiving only a minor penalty, so that most of the time they never go to prison or receive only a short sentence. Probably the persistence of these criminals is due in large part to the fact that they cannot readily be given certain or severe penalties.

Burglary consists of breaking and entering for the purpose of committing a felonious act, and it sometimes is designated in the law' as "breaking" or "breaking and entering." Usually it is committed in conjunction with larceny at the place entered. However, burglary almost always causes a more severe penalty than larceny alone, so the offenders usually are prosecuted only for burglary. However, some State laws make "burglary and larceny" a single compound offense. A majority of persons arrested for burglary are under 19 years of age, but an appreciable number of the burglars who are encountered in prison populations are older. These often include those for whom burglary has become a profession in which they work closely with dealers in stolen goods ("fences").

Another kind of recurrent economic offense not involving violence is the crime of forgery. Forgers differ from most criminals in the extent to which they commit their crimes alone and in being relatively older. Petty or naive forgery is notably associated with chronic alcoholism. Perhaps because cashing a fraudulent check requires a certain amount of facility at writing, and an appearance of success, forgers are also distinctive in generally having more education and less often coming from an improverished home than most prisoners. Other types of fraud, often called "confidence games" or "bunko games," are less often associated with alcoholism than simple check forgery, and are more frequently persistent criminal professions. Embezzlement is a special kind of fraud, frequently involving violation of trust by a prominent and presumably trustworthy citizen, so that he is placed in a government or business position where he handles much money. These offenders generally are good risks as far as prospects for violation are concerned, but their parole poses special public relations problems.

The selling of narcotics has already been mentioned as an illegal service crime. Other narcotic offenses include illegal possession, use, and purchase of narcotic drugs. Evidence on the relative risk of these narcotic offenders as parolees is inconsistent. There is some indication that they have very high violation rates when they are paroled to neighborhoods where narcotics usage is extensive, but that they have average or below average violation rates elsewhere.

Robbery is different from the economically motivated crimes described earlier, in that robbery involves the use or threat of violence in order to procure someone else's property. Like narcotics offenses, it is associated with diverse violation or recidivism rates in different jurisdictions, but robbers generally seem to have about the average violation rate for their age group. However, they are of concern to parole boards because of the serious injury or death which they may cause. Robbers vary tremendously in character. They include groups of adolescents in slum areas who "roll" drunks coming from taverns in the late hours of night, naive individuals who make a foolhardy effort to solve economic crises by trying to hold up a large bank (often without a working weapon), and some highly dangerous individuals who have a psychological drive to hurt their victims.

The cluster of offenses associated with the lowest violation rates on parole are crimes which least often serve as vocations. These include homicide and rape. However, the strong public demand for punishment as an expression of revenge against such offenders, plus the extreme importance of preventing recurrence of these crimes, makes parole boards exceptionally cautious in paroling those who commit these offenses.

One of the least favorable crimes, from the standpoint of parole violation probability, is the crime of escape from prison. In some States, notably California, offenders sentenced for this offense have the highest violation rate of any offense category, even higher than auto thieves. However, escapees do not constitute a large proportion of prisoners.

Thus far, this discussion has dealt only with gross violation rates, although it has been noted that the nature of the probable parole violation may be a crucial consideration in parole decisions. The type of violation likely to be committed, if any, is a concern especially in the forefront of a parole board member's thoughts when he considers the type of offense for which a prisoner was last convicted. William L. Jacks, statistician of the Pennsylvania Board of Parole, has made one of the few studies of type of violation in relation to type of offense. . . .

. . . In Pennsylvania the offenses fell into three main clusters in terms of prospects of committing a new crime on parole, and these three clusters were much like those for overall violation rates . . . However, larceny and narcotics offenses are ranked somewhat differently in these two compilations. Burglars, forgers, and narcotic drug offenders were most likely to commit the same offenses, while larceny and robbery were an intermediate cluster, followed by felonious assault and sex offenses. Homicides were lowest, only about 1 in 250 committed a homicide on parole after being imprisoned for homicide. The gravity of this offense, of course, still makes any repetition a crucial concern.

A California tabulation of adult male parolees returned to prison for new offense in 1959, 1960, and 1961 concluded: 26 percent are returned for a more serious offense than that on which they were paroled, 38 percent are returned for an offense of similar seriousness to that on which they were paroled, and 37 percent are returned for a less serious offense. Seriousness was measured by the length of the statutory maximum sentence for the offense in California, except that narcotics offenses were classified as more serious than property offenses with higher maximum sentences.

INTELLIGENCE

Intelligence tests are almost invariably administered to the inmates of correctional institutions today. They are used to determine the appropriate education, work, and treatment of each prisoner, and the test results also are reported to the parole board. Despite the convenient availability of this information, it has been found to have only a slight relationship to parole outcome. . . . In the several jurisdictions for which we have procured statistics, there was little consistent pattern of violation rate according to intelligence. Generally, the most mentally deficient inmates did not do as well on parole as most prisoners, but usually their violation rates were not extremely different from many with above average intelligence scores. . . .

RACE AND NATIONALITY

Although Negroes in the United States have a higher rate of arrest, conviction, and imprisonment for crimes than whites, most tabulations we have encountered find little marked or consistent difference in the parole violation rates of the two groups. . . . It is probable that the higher crime rates among Negroes occur largely because Negroes, more often than whites, experience conditions associated with high crime rates in all racial groups. These conditions include low income, high unemployment, low level of education, and residence in slum areas which have long had high crime rates.

These conditions conducive to high crime rates usually are also associated with high parole violation rates. The fact that Negro parole violation rates are not higher than those of whites, therefore, is somewhat puzzling. It may reflect more careful selection of Negroes for parole than of whites, or more frequent institutionalization of unadvanced offenders among Negroes than among whites. There is some evidence that the latter occurs with juvenile delinquents, but evidence as to its occurrence in prison is conflicting.

In the southwest portion of the United States, the largest ethnic minority are persons of Mexican descent. In California, where they are most numerous, they have a parole violation rate about the same as that of whites and Negroes. American Indians generally have an average or somewhat higher than average rate of parole violation.

The differences in crime or parole violation rates for various ethnic groups could readily develop as a consequence of police or parole officers not treating every person in the same fashion for a given type of behavior, regardless of the person's ethnic descent. Statistics to assess whether or not this occurs are not available on a widespread and recent basis. A common impression is that officials tend to overlook infractions committed by minority group members in their own community and to be unusually severe in dealing with infractions which members of minorities commit elsewhere. This, of course, could be conducive to the habituation of minority group members to criminal behavior, which they might engage in wherever they encounter an opportunity.

Japanese and Chinese are infrequent in correctional institution populations. In California, where they are most numerous, they have a lower violation rate than other parolees. This probably reflects the closeknit community and family support which they receive.

In a few portions of the country, notably New York, persons of Puerto Rican descent are a new and extensive component of the prison population. Experience with them as parolees has been too brief for confident conclusions as to how their violation rates compare with those of other ancestry.

In general, the evidence on race and nationality as a factor in the evaluation of parolees suggests that it is not of much predictive utility in itself. . . .

SEX

Males coming before parole boards in most States outnumber females in a ratio of about 20 to 1. This probably occurs both because females in our society commit felonies less often than males do, and because those females who are convicted of felonies are less likely to receive a sentence of imprisonment than are males. . . . Female parolees violate less often than males, but the differences are not always marked.

BODY CHARACTERISTICS

In the 19th century, there was much effort to explain crime as the expression of an inherited characteristic that could be identified by a person's physical appearance. One still frequently hears people say that somebody looks like a criminal, or that someone else looks like he could not possibly be a criminal. However, parole board members often observe a fine appearance in some individuals who have shocking criminal records.

There have been popular experiments to investigate the ability to predict criminality from physical appearance. The most useless efforts involved asking people to judge character from photographs of criminals mixed with photographs of highly respected noncriminal persons, when all persons portrayed were of about the same age and wore similar apparel. These studies demonstrated almost complete failure of this approach to character judgment.

Years ago, a study found that height and weight had no relationship to parole violation. Classification of people by their general physical condition has not uncovered clear and consistent findings of marked deviation from average violation rates. Some studies find those in poor health or having a handicap with slightly higher than average violation rates, while others found these individuals slightly more successful on parole than the average.

The most recent extensive research in this field has been that of the Gluecks, which compared the overall body dimensions of delinquents with those of nondelinquents from the same high delinquency neighborhoods. The delinquents were huskier (mesomorphic) in body build than the nondelinquents. It has not yet been demonstrated that this is not simply the result of the huskier youth in high delinquency areas being more readily accepted in delinquent street gang activity (and perhaps, also, more readily picked up by the police), than the slender (ectomorphic) or paunchy (endomorphic) youth.

Summary

Of the gross characteristics readily available for the classification of prisoners, those most closely related to parole outcome were found to be age and criminal record. On the whole, younger prisoners were shown to have the highest violation rates. However, the extent to which violation rate decreased with age was not uniform for all populations for which this information was available. Some sources of variation in this relationship were discussed.

The criminal record was found to have a wealth of information closely related to parole outcome, but capable of classification in many ways. Of course, an individual's prior criminality is only known from the crimes for which he was apprehended and his offenses recorded, and this record is often incomplete. Nevertheless, lower parole violation rates were consistently found for those with no prior criminal record. However, the violation rate for younger first offenders was much higher than that for older first or second felony offenders. The figures predominantly support a conclusion that the lower a prisoner's age at first arrest, the higher his parole violation rate is likely to be at any subsequent age, but some types of late-starting persistent offenders were noted.

Although persons with little or no prior contact with police, courts, or correctional institutions have a much better record on parole than those who have been in institutions before, the rate of violation does not always increase markedly with each increase in the number of convictions or commitments. This may partially reflect the crime diminution generally occurring with older age at release; the extent to which it can be credited to rehabilitative or deterrent effects of prior imprisonment cannot readily be determined.

Offenses were found to fall into three main clusters as far as parole violation rates are concerned. Those for which the prospect of violation is greatest are crimes involving the taking of someone's property by stealth or deception without the use of force. Notable here are theft, burglary, and forgery. Narcotic offenses and robbery generally were associated with violation rates near the average for all parolees, but they were inconsistent in this respect from one jurisdiction to the next. On the whole, the lowest parole violation rates were associated with crimes of violence, including rape, assault, and homicide.

A Pennsylvania study was cited on the extent to which persons who violate parole by committing a new offense repeat the offense for which they previously were imprisoned. Burglars, forgers, and narcotic users were found most likely to repeat their previous offenses, if they committed a new offense. Sex offenders tabulated collectively were relatively low in rate of repeating the same crime, while those convicted of homicide showed the lowest rate of repeating the same offense while on parole of any category.

Intelligence, race, nationality, sex, and body build were found not to have sufficiently marked or consistent relationships to parole outcome for large numbers of offenders to be very useful in evaluating parolees.

MURDERERS ON PAROLE

JOHN M. STANTON

Excerpted from John M. Stanton, "Murderers on Parole," *Crime and Delinquency,* 15, No. 1 (January 1969), 149–155. At the time of publication, John M. Stanton was Director of Research of the New York State Division of Parole.

THE PURPOSE of this study is to make an extensive survey of paroled murderers in New York State and to compare their delinquency rates with those of paroled nonmurderers.

Because most of those convicted of first-degree murder were originally sentenced to be executed, whereas those convicted of second-degree murder were not, the statistical data will be presented separately for each group. One may thereby learn what happened to those persons who lives were spared by governors' commutations of sentence and who were later released on parole. The Revised Penal Law in New York State, effective September 1, 1967, provides for only one degree of murder, which ordinarily draws a maximum sentence of life imprisonment; in certain exceptional cases, capital punishment may be the penalty.

Murder First Degree

From July 1930, when the New York State Division of Parole was established, to December 31, 1961, sixty-three persons convicted of first-degree murder were released from New York State correctional institutions to original parole supervision. Fifty-five were paroled as a result of commutation by governors; eight were released after September 1960 by action of the Parole Board under Chapter 292 of the Laws of 1960, which provides that a person serving a term of natural life may be paroled as though the sentence fixed a minimum of forty years and a maximum of natural life. Before enactment of Chapter 292, only the governor could parole a person convicted of first-degree murder. Of the sixty-three paroled first-degree murderers, sixty-one had been originally sentenced to be executed, but the executions had been commuted to natural life sentences by the governors.

The sixty-three murderers consisted of fifty white males, nine Negro males, one Chinese male, one Japanese male, one white female, and one Negro female. Their mean age at the time of release was fifty-one years. Thirty had not completed the eighth grade; five had completed high school and, of these, three had attended college and one was a graduate of a university in Japan. Thirty-six were single; the marital status of one was not known; of the twenty-six who had been married, six were widowed, five were separated, and six were divorced.

Fifty-six had no prior felony conviction, six had one, and one had three. Before their parole, nine served less than nine years in prison and seven served more than thirty years; the mean time of imprisonment for the entire group before release on parole was twenty-three years.

Three of the sixty-three murderers paroled between 1930 and 1961 became effective delinquents before December 31, 1962. One of these three was returned to prison with a new sentence after being convicted of burglary; two were returned to prison by the Board of Parole as technical parole violators.

Murder Second Degree

From January 1945 to December 31, 1961, 514 persons convicted of second-degree murder were released from New York State correctional institutions to original parole supervision by the Board of Parole. Of this group, 343 (66.7 per cent) were white males; 148 (28.8 per cent), Negro males; five, males other than white or Negro; eleven, white females; and seven, Negro females. Their mean age at the time of release was forty-six years. Fourteen (2.8 per cent) had graduated from high school; 295 (57.3 per cent) had not completed the eighth grade. There were 272 single persons; of the 242 who had been married, fifty-six were widowed, sixty-nine were separated, and thirty-three were divorced.

Of this group, 417 (81.1 per cent) had no prior felony conviction, seventy-seven (15 per cent) had one, and twenty had two or three. Before their parole, five spent two years and two spent thirty-one years in prison; the mean time of imprisonment for the entire group before release on parole was fifteen years.

Of these 514 murderers released on parole from 1945 to 1961, 115 (22.4 per cent) became effective delinquents before December 31, 1962. Of the 115, seventeen were convicted of felonies, thirty-three were convicted of misdemeanors or lesser offenses, and sixty-five were technical parole violators. Of the seventeen convicted of felonies, two (0.4 per cent of the 514) were convicted of first-degree murder. One of these two had been paroled after spending seventeen years in prison; the other, after thirteen years. One committed two murders less than a month after his release on parole; he was executed in Sing Sing Prison in March 1963. The other had been on parole for a little over a year when he became involved in the murder which eventually resulted in his conviction of first-degree murder; he was executed in Sing Sing in July 1955.

Two Criteria

Two rates are used here to compare paroled murderers with paroled nonmurderers. One is the overall delinquency rate, based on all the effective delinquencies occurring in one year. The other is the new convictions rate, based on the number of convictions for felonies, misdemeanors, and lesser offenses occurring from the date of release to the end of the observation period. The procedures, populations, periods of observation, etc., used to arrive at these comparative rates are explained in the next two sections.

Overall Delinquency Rates

The parolee population used for the comparative overall delinquency rate consisted of all males released from New York State correctional institutions to original parole supervision [1] during 1958 and 1959, exclusive of those released to warrants [2] and to deportations.[3] Not counting the 195 released to warrants and the sixty-one deported, the number of persons released on original parole who constituted the subjects of the overall delinquency rate comparison was 7,370.

For those released in 1958, the period of observation of delinquent parolee behavior was 1958, 1959, and 1960; for those released in 1959, the observation period was 1959, 1960, and 1961. The average length of the observation period is thirty months; it is considered an adequate period since most parolees who are declared delinquent violate within thirty months of their release. (Of the 2,420 parolees declared delinquent in 1960, 2,252—93 per cent —were declared delinquent within thirty months of their release.)

In this study delinquent parolee behavior is defined as any delinquency not cancelled during the same year it was declared. Most effective delinquencies, which may be divided into technical violations and arrests, result in return to the institution for parole violation.[4]

During 1958 and 1959, sixty-five murderers were paroled. (Eight of them had been convicted of first-degree murder; fifty-seven, second-degree murder.) In the same two-year period, 7,305 men were paroled who had been convicted of all offenses other than murder. During the three-year observation periods, nine (13.8 per cent) of the sixty-five murderers became delinquent, compared with 2,996 (41 per cent) of the 7,305 nonmurderers. In both technical violations and new arrests, . . . the delinquency rate for the nonmurderer group was three times greater than the rate for the murderer

[1] Persons released on reparole were excluded because they would have impaired the homogeneity of the parolee populations in the study.

[2] Parolees released to warrants were eliminated because they are kept in custody in other jurisdictions for varying periods of time during which they have little opportunity to violate their parole conditions.

[3] Parolees released to deportation were not included because it is unlikely that they will be declared delinquent in a foreign country.

[4] Almost 90 per cent of all parole violators returned to institutions in New York State are returned at the discretion of the Parole Board; the remainder are returned by the courts as new commitments.

group, and the chi square of the difference between the two groups was found to be statistically very significant—that is, most unlikely to occur through chance.

New Convictions Rate

In the ten-year period of 1948–57, 28,788 persons convicted of crimes other than first- or second-degree murder were released to original parole supervision and were observed by the Division of Parole for periods that varied from a few months up to five years, the mean period being approximately four and a half years. During the same ten-year period, 336 persons convicted of first- or second-degree murder were released to original parole supervision and were similarly observed for five years. . . . 7.2 per cent of the 336 murderers were convicted of felonies, misdemeanors, or lesser offenses during the five-year observation period following their release, whereas 20.3 per cent of the 28,788 nonmurderers were convicted of similar crimes during the same observation periods. In brief, the paroled nonmurderers were convicted, while under parole supervision, of almost three times as many offenses as were the murderers. The chi square of the difference between the two groups was found to be statistically very significant.

[The statistics] show that, considering both the overall delinquency and new conviction rates, parolees who had been convicted of murder are better risks than parolees who had been convicted of all other offenses.

Discussion of Findings

The sixty-three paroled first-degree murderers made exceptionally good parole risks. None of them was seriously assaultive while under parole supervision; by the end of 1962, only one had been returned to prison after conviction of a new felony.

Of course, first-degree murderers whose sentences are commuted and who are eventually paroled are a select group. During the period 1930 to 1961, when these sixty-three murderers were paroled,

327 others with the same conviction were executed in New York State. On December 31, 1962, New York State prisons contained over one hundred persons serving life sentences who had been convicted of first-degree murder and had not been paroled. Obviously, therefore, the sixty-three whose parole experiences were observed in this study were a select sample of all persons convicted of first-degree murder.

Prisoners convicted of second-degree murder also make good parole risks, but apparently not as good as those convicted of first-degree murder. One of the reasons for this difference is probably that they are not as select a group. Everyone convicted of second-degree murder is eventually eligible for parole, whereas anyone convicted of first-degree murder and sentenced to be executed could not be paroled unless his sentence was commuted by the governor. Other possible reasons for the disparity between rates of the two groups are the greater age and less extensive previous criminal record of the first-degree murderers, which may partially explain their better parole experiences.

Although the 514 second-degree murderers had relatively good parole records, two of them committed crimes while on parole which resulted in their being convicted of first-degree murder and later executed. One was involved in an armed holdup and, although he did not actually perpetrate the killing, was convicted of first-degree murder. The other killed two drinking companions during an altercation shortly after his release on parole.

Why Murderers Are Better Risks

A previous study of mine found that delinquency rates of parolees are at their highest in the age groups under forty-one; as the ages increase, the delinquency rates regularly decrease. The median age of all persons paroled in 1958 and 1959 was twenty-six; the median age of the paroled murderers observed in this study was forty-five. Because of this age factor alone one would expect that the paroled murderers would make better parole risks than the nonmurderers. The study also found that the lowest delinquency rate was maintained by those who had spent the longest time in prison before their parole. The median period of institutional treatment of all parolees released in 1958 and 1959 was twenty-eight months, whereas the median period of imprisonment of the paroled murderers was fifteen years. Although length of institutional treatment is probably closely related to the age factor, on the basis of their greater length of confinement murderers would be expected to do better on parole than all other offenders.

In my opinion murderers are better parole risks than nonmurderers because a majority of them are first-felony offenders and many are occasional or situational offenders whose crime may be most aptly described as a "crime of passion." In this study fifty-six (89 per cent) of the sixty-three persons convicted of first-degree murder and 417 (81 per cent) of the 514 convicted of second-degree murder had no previous felony conviction. Numerous studies have demonstrated that prior criminal record is positively correlated with delinquencies on parole; multiple offenders are more likely to violate parole than first offenders. Also, another recent study of mine has shown that parolees classified as occasional or situational offenders have the lowest delinquency rates of all other categories. However, this study is concerned with paroled murderers, and not all of them are first, occasional, or situational offenders. Some murderers are professional criminals or potentially so, or are psychologically abnormal. These types are recognized as being serious threats to community safety and are not usually released by the New York State Parole Board. The two murderers mentioned in this study who were paroled and again committed murders appeared, at the time of their release, to have developed positive attitudes toward society and to have been relatively safe parole risks. That they proved to be otherwise is one of the risks society must take if it follows a policy of rehabilitation based on the individualized treatment and evaluation of each offender.

Other Homicides

This study is concerned with the parole experiences of murderers and not with persons convicted of manslaughter. Yet in New York State the majority of offenders committed to state institutions for homicides are convicted of manslaughter. For example, in 1966, of the 4,919 persons placed in New York State correctional institutions, seventy had been convicted of murder and 334 of manslaughter. To describe the legal distinctions between murder and manslaughter is unnecessary, but generally speaking, persons convicted of murder are guilty of a more serious crime against society than those convicted of manslaughter. However, a study of the descriptions of homicides would not enable one, in many instances, to determine exactly how manslaughter differs from murder. The efficiency of the police and the prosecutor, the legal sophistication of the offender and the skill of his lawyer, the willingness of the offender to plead guilty to manslaughter rather than stand trial for murder—all have considerable effect on the final legal conviction regardless of the substance of the crime itself.

Thus, regarding the enormity of the offense, many persons convicted of manslaughter are guilty of crimes just as serious as those committed by convicted murderers. Since they represent a greater proportion of offenders than those convicted of murder, some attention should be given to them whenever the parole experiences of murderers are discussed. Although this study does not include manslaughter cases, through observation I have found that, like those convicted of murder, they are primarily first-time felons, many of whom fit into the accidental-situational offender classification and make better parole risks than nonhomicide offenders.

Conclusions

Using both the overall delinquency rate and the new convictions rate as the criteria, this study has demonstrated that paroled murderers in New York State commit significantly fewer delinquencies on parole than other offenders.

That the excellent parole records of murderers are not confined to parolees in New York State is supported by two surveys reported in 1968. One was conducted by the National Council on Crime and Delinquency and the other by the Massachusetts Department of Correction. In the NCCD survey, which was based on a one-year follow-up of men and women paroled from twenty-two agencies in twenty-one states during 1965, the best parole performance (90.89 per cent) was found among those convicted of offenses classified as willful homicide. In the Massachusetts survey, which reported on the experiences of 238 persons committed for murder from 1943 to 1966, the murderers were found to have much less serious criminal records than other offenders, and the recidivism rate of the murderers (10.3 per cent) was significantly lower than the overall recidivism rate of other offenders (59.5 per cent).

Part VI

PREVENTION

INTRODUCTION

MARK KOENIGIL, the author of a book on the role of the motion picture,[1] approvingly quotes an official of the French Ministry of Justice who asserted that his Survey Department found that 20 percent of the minors who entered prison had attended the movies daily—at times more than once. And at least 80 percent attended shows once a week. This, Koenigil declared, proved that watching movies made children delinquent and this fathered criminality. A basic thesis of his book was that crime "correlates directly with the increase in the number of theatres and the progress and development of the cinematographic industry."[2] To prevent crime, he suggested, we should (a) keep children and suggestible adults away from "bad" movies or (b) produce nothing but "good" movies.

This nostrum is admittedly far-fetched, but even much more scientific and sophisticated investigations and experiments have left us little better off as to ways to prevent delinquency and crime.

But we continue trying, and Part VI is devoted to a cursory survey of some of the suggestions advanced and efforts exerted. Governor Ronald Reagan gives an audience of correctional workers some general and specific guidelines that he believes are worth considering. Following this, a man who has had extensive contacts with the agents and agencies of "law and order" states his views on the same subject. John M. Martin follows with a critique of three prevalent approaches to delinquency prevention. And as a finale, Martin and colleagues offer "A Structural Approach to Delinquency Prevention and Treatment."

[1] Mark Koenigil, *Movies in Society* (New York: Speller, 1962), p. 25.
[2] *Ibid.*, pp. 22–23.

A PUBLIC OFFICIAL DISCUSSES DELINQUENCY AND CRIME PREVENTION

RONALD REAGAN, GOVERNOR OF CALIFORNIA

Excerpted from a press release, issued for Governor Ronald Reagan, consisting of an advance copy of his remarks on June 12, 1967, before the National Institute on Crime and Delinquency, convened at Anaheim, California.

. . . WITHOUT QUESTION, the problem of crime and delinquency has grown steadily since the end of World War II until it is now perhaps the major domestic problem that faces our nation. . . .

Since 1960, crime in the United States has increased by 35 percent for every 100,000 population. These are the FBI's national figures.

Most of this increase is accounted for among those who have been born or reached maturity since World War II—the 10 to 39 year old age bracket. In California, 80 percent of all crimes are committed by men and boys between 14 and 29.

The biggest increases in crime have been crimes against property—burglary, auto theft and the like.

At the same time that crime has been rising, police ability to meet the challenge posed by the criminal has diminished. It has diminished to the point where it is difficult to say any more that crime does not pay.

Only about 25 percent of our reported crimes are solved. I will leave it to you to decide whether some court decisions rendered in recent years are at least partly to blame for this shocking fact. . . .

. . . The annual correctional bill nationally runs something over a billion dollars.

And, of course, this is only a small fraction of the total cost of crime prevention and control. If you add in the cost of property losses, personal injuries and deaths, the total reaches staggering proportions.

Obviously, something must be done to halt this trend. The alternatives eventually are anarchy or a police state. Neither is particularly inviting.

In fact, the trend must be more than halted; it must be reversed. It is obvious from recent studies that a large proportion of our citizens fear for their own safety in their homes and on the streets.

Few women are brave enough or foolhardy enough to venture out alone at night any more. Many neighborhoods are not even safe in the day time.

There has been a significant increase in the purchase and training of watchdogs. More and more citizens are buying firearms not for hunting or target practice, but for protection of themselves and their families.

In many areas citizens have banded together, rightly or wrongly, to patrol streets and in other ways attempt to protect the residents of their neighborhoods and communities.

Women are urged to carry whistles as a means of calling for help. Self-protection classes such as Judo and Karate flourish. Law-abiding citizens are genuinely concerned. And so are those of us who are ultimately charged with providing protection, maintaining law and order, solving and preventing crime and finding causes of crime and juvenile delinquency.

We are concerned not only because we face the problem, but also, and more importantly, because so far, we have failed either to solve it or to find the cause.

Not all our penologists, not all our social workers, not all our new theories have managed even to slow the trend.

We are here, hopefully, to see if there are ways to look at new ideas, to re-examine some time-tested methods that might have been more effective than some of our theoreticians would have us believe.

Crime, its prevention and control, and the correction of the offender are all highly complex problems. Crime and the criminal are found in all walks of society, all economic strata, and in both city and rural areas.

I certainly am not here to offer any cure-alls or panaceas.

However, I would like to take a few minutes to give you some of my thoughts. . . .

I do not hold with the theory that society is to blame when a man commits a robbery or a murder and therefore we must be understanding and as sympathetic for the criminal as we are for the victim.

Nor do I hold with the spirit of permissiveness abroad in the land that has undoubtedly added to the juvenile delinquency problem.

This is an era, not only of permissiveness, but also of affluence. As a result, many young people often have time on their hands. Many who might otherwise find jobs have no need to work. May I point out respectfully that we should question perhaps that part of the President's crime report that lays such emphasis on curing crime by eliminating poverty. This is a worthy goal in itself but it is interesting to note that during the great depression, we had an all-time low in crime.

I cannot help but believe that goods and privileges carelessly given or lightly earned are lightly regarded.

A boy who works for the money to buy a car and keep it in gasoline is much more likely to appreciate it and care for it than the youth whose car has been given to him and whose gas is purchased on his father's credit card.

Likewise, the boy or girl who can go out at night only if he or she behaves is more apt to behave than those who have not set rules to follow, and no responsibilities to accept.

This brings me down to two points. First, are we doing enough for our children by doing too much for them? Aren't they really better off if they are taught to accept responsibility and to learn that in the long run we all must earn what we get and that we usually get what we earn?

The second point is, haven't we made it almost impossible for many of our young people to earn legitimately the things they need and want?

In some cases we have taught them by example that they don't have to learn, [sic?] that instead they have a right to expect to be given. I challenge that this is wrong. I challenge that nobody does any young person any favor by this approach.

But also, haven't our laws, aimed with the best intentions at preventing exploitation of children and providing old age security and of insuring meaningful wages—haven't these, by being too narrowly drawn and too rigidly implemented, put many kids to loitering on the street corners because they couldn't get jobs after school or during the summer?

I suggest that if exceptions were made in some of our laws regarding social security and minimum wages, and if some of our unions would cooperate by recognizing that a boy seeking a part-time job should fall in a little different category than the full-time skilled or semi-skilled adult, that we would take a lot of our young people off the streets and out of trouble.

You know, there are a lot of old maxims that are still true today and it is not corny to note that it is idle hands that do the devil's work and, as a result, there is often the devil to pay and it is you and I who usually do the paying.

In urging that we allow our young people the right to work and to earn and to gain the sense of pride that you only get through your own accomplishments, I am not overlooking the value of recreation.

I think, without question, that we need better and more recreational facilities. We need to make it possible for a boy or girl to play hard as well as to work hard, and to develop and take pride in his athletic skills or hobbies.

I suggest to you that this is another area where government, with its limited tax fund, can turn to business and industry to sponsor teams, to make available recreational facilities and to work with youth on an informal basis.

A slum boy living next door to a factory wouldn't be throwing rocks through the factory windows if the factory owner and foreman were friends who now and then extended a friendly hand.

Here is an area in the independent sector that offers tremendous possibilities.

Now I do not mean by all this that there is no such thing as a bad boy or that there is no place in our society for punishment. Far from it.

I do believe in the carrot and the stick philosophy—you know, where you offer the carrot as a reward for being good and come up behind with the stick for being bad.

There is talk these days that punishment is not a deterrent, however, and I believe that that talk is partly responsible for our increase in crime.

Certainly, as punishment becomes more difficult to mete out, those who would be deterred by its threat feel freer to resort to crime and acts of violence.

Some court decisions have narrowed the difference between liberty and license and in some areas have overbalanced the scales of justice so that the rights of society are outweighed by decisions granting new rights to individuals accused of crimes.

California . . . is the leading state in terms of major crimes. On a percentage basis, we have nearly twice our share—nine percent of the population and about 17 percent of the crime.

I am convinced that enactment of legislation we have introduced will help deter crime, will slow the flood of pornographic material now available on our newsstands, will speed and strengthen the administration of justice and will assure California citizens the best, most efficient law enforcement agencies in the nation.

This legislation includes:

> —First: an effective law to restore to the cities and counties the ability to enact local laws designed to meet local problems. This is commonly referred to as the "implied pre-emption issue."

> Such a law will allow local law enforcement agencies to more thoroughly police their jurisdictions, especially in the areas of vice, sex offenses and offenses against public decency.

> —Second: laws increasing penalties for those criminals who, during the commission of a robbery, burglary or rape, inflict great bodily harm upon their victims with dangerous weapons.

I believe society must be protected from those who would inflict personal violence on its members. These bills, by the way, have already been passed and signed into law. We think they will be of major help in our war on crime.

—Third: comprehensive legislation dealing with pornography and obscenity, with special emphasis on prohibiting dissemination to minors of "harmful" material. A careful effort is being made to avoid any suspicion of censorship. . . .

—Fourth: we recognize that from time to time persons are arrested unjustly or as victims of circumstances. Yet, despite their innocence, they must live the remainder of their lives with a public police record. Our bill, by closing certain records, will provide relief for such persons, while, at the same time, preserving those records for use by law enforcement and authorized persons.

But we are convinced that even more effort on the part of all of us is needed if we are to control crime. . . .

Scientific and technological advances are being utilized by and adapted for use by the criminal element.

Modern methods of transportation and communications, and modern tools and weapons are used daily by those who prey on society.

If we are to reverse this trend, it is essential that society also use to the fullest our scientific and technological advances in the prevention, detection and control of crime. And in the correction and rehabilitation of criminals.

In addition, there is need for basic research involving the joint effort of various scientific and professional disciplines into the nature of crime, and crime apprehension and treatment. . . .

Of course, major efforts are constantly being made to stem crime by law enforcement agencies, both state and local, by departments of state government, by educational institutions and by private organizations.

Outstanding organizations such as yours, the State Bar of California, the California Council on Crime and Delinquency, are all concerned.

We are convinced, however, from talking with state leaders in the fields of law enforcement and crime prevention that these efforts must be coordinated, that new efforts must be stimulated if we are to have an effective crime prevention program. Those engaged in this broad field must be able to share results of the research and benefit from the progressive practices of others. . . .

The war on crime is a never-ending one. And it is necessary that we pursue it constantly and with vigor if our citizens are to be safe on our streets and in their homes, and if man is to be able to live free from fear of his fellow man in an ever contracting world and an increasingly more complex society. . . .

AN OFFENDER DISCUSSES
PREVENTION

ANONYMOUS

Part of a tape recording of a 27-year-old man who has a record of over 100 arrests as a juvenile delinquent, youthful offender, and adult criminal. He has served several terms in a reformatory and once in a state prison. Identifying features have been altered.

WHEN THESE experts start spouting off about gangs and crime and delinquency, I wish I was mayor of this town. I'd show them what to do.

If I was mayor, I'd do something about parents, first of all. A whole lot of this hanging out starts right with the parents. Parents can be too strict or too soft. A lot of them let their kids sass them too much. The kid thinks, "Well, I can run this place! I can leave, come back or do whatever I want to do." Then there's parents that get too strict. Some of them get after their kids for smoking. Well, they should know he's going to smoke, no matter what. They should let them do it right in front of them. Then he won't have to sneak out somewhere and smoke. If a kid's going to smoke, he's going to smoke. You might just as well let him do it in the house.

If I was mayor, I'd tell parents about things like that. Like not pushing children to go to school. I don't think they should push them. But I think they should talk to them in a way where the kids understand. Tell what would happen to them if they didn't go to school, what they'd end up like. I don't think they should say, "Either you go to school or you stay in for a week." That only makes a kid resent their parent.

I'd tell parents what a big mistake they make when they argue and all. It's the wrong way to handle children. It makes kids want to run the streets instead of staying home. I've seen families broken up because of too much arguing between the mother and father. Or else maybe the mother or father is drinking too much. Or just not caring how the house looks. A kid loses all faith in everything when they see stuff like that going on. And then, if he sees it when he's young, he thinks that's going to be right for him when he's older. Lots of parents do their kids harm by fighting all the time.

Some of my buddies, do they get upset when their parents quarrel? Oh, and how! I mean! I've seen kids that when their parents get in a quarrel, they're just as jittery as hell. They can't sit still. They want to be on the go all the time. I've been in kids' houses when their parents were arguing like that. When they'd start arguing, the kids would just start jumping around and everything, smoking one cigarette after another. Then they'd say, "Well, let's get out somewhere and have a cup of coffee or something. Christ! I don't want to stay around in this place! Maybe by the time I come back, maybe they've settled down a little."

Take Oogie's folks. The old man is always sitting around with a can of beer in his hand. He's always three sheets to the wind, and when he's like that, he wants to beat the old lady up. Any time I've been there, the old guy's been there, in his undershirt, stinking from beer, roaring at the old lady, beating up on her, why is the supper late, why didn't she wash his shirts, some other such goddamn thing. And she's crying, and he's throwing her around. And Oogie laughs at it all. He ain't afraid of the old man. But like as not, after one of them scenes, he'll go out and scream along the highway in his hot rod and have an accident or get twenty traffic tickets. Or he'll get feeling ornery and sock some guy he don't even know, for no reason at all. Dumb stuff like that. Well, you know it's because he's upset.

Why do parents act like that? Don't they know what it does to their kids? If I was mayor, I'd make those parents go to some goddamn school or something, whatever it is, until they damn well learn how to behave and get along and handle their kids right. I'm sick and tired of all this bullshit about kids being hoodlums and all like that. Well, if they get mean and ornery, nine times out of ten, it's the parents. I lay it to the parents.

If I was mayor, I'd give kids more recreation. Open up pool rooms, ping pong rooms, stuff like that. But right in the neighborhoods where them things are needed. Build a nice, big place for fellows, where they'd always be welcome. It would be public. Everybody would be eligible, not just the nice little boys. If a parent objected to his kid being there with roughnecks, I'd tell that parent to drag him out then, goddamn it! I'd say, "Tie him to your apron strings. We don't give a shit. Keep him!"

I'd build a great big center in every neighborhood, that's what I'd do. Dance floor, club rooms, gym, pool. I'd tell gangs to come on in, dress like you want, cuss if you want. There will be rules— no broken windows, no drinking. But follow them rules, behave yourself, and you're always welcome. Guys would come in if you put it to them like that. They know that anywhere they go there's going to be laws and rules that they're going to have to abide by. But the reason they don't go to the Ys and centers and places like that now is that the rules are stupid. The guys that run them places don't want to understand kids. They don't want to take them the way they are.

If I was mayor, I'd have guys working there that could understand kids, talk to them, reason with them. Go out on the streets and show the guys they can come in and not be made to act like a bunch of sissies. Explain how much better off they'd be. Explain half that stuff to them and I think they'd realize it.

Another thing. I'd build an older guys' college, so a kid that didn't finish college and wanted to, he'd have a chance to finish it, nights. I know there are places like that. But them are stiffer than they should be. Lots of guys, they feel as though they'd like to go to college, but they feel it's too stiff. I'd have this easier college. I'd have it so, if they wanted to learn, all they'd have to do is walk in and learn. They wouldn't have to finish high school. They could just walk in and take a course.

Another thing I'd do. I'd close down half of these shady soda places. The kind that cops know all about, where all kinds of things are going on there. Transactions for dope. Drinking in the back room. Like that one around the corner from where I live. They used to sell on the average of 24 pints of whiskey a day, they claimed. Sell it in the back room for $10 a pint. To kids. Well, how does a school kid get $10 to pay for whiskey? He's got to steal for it. And that place didn't give a damn what went on in the back room once a guy paid for that pint. Shit! The guys brought in girls, 14, 15. Gave them some whiskey. Laid them right on the couch, on the floor. That was part of the idea. If you bought a pint, you were supposed to be left alone back there. I'd close them goddamn places up if they didn't clean house.

I wouldn't do much about the police force. I think it's just about where it should be. They're not too rough. Not too mean. Oh, I might have to fire some cop now and then because he was getting too mean. That's something that can make a kid go wrong—bad cops, mean ones. Some towns have got a lot of cops like that.

I'd do things about our courts, I'll tell you that. I'd put in a judge that understands kids and can figure out what a guy is headed for. Look at his record, and here it is, drunk, drunk, drunk. All right. That guy don't belong in jail. He needs a hospital. Then here comes a guy, robbery, robbery, robbery. Shit! Put him in the can. That's good enough for him.

That's another thing. I'd like to build a hospital for narcotics users and habitual drunkards. Instead of the judge saying 90 days in the county jail, I'd say 90 days in the mental hospital out there.

I'd have me a judge, if he had a kid before him, and seen 20 times he's been arrested for petty theft, never more than a couple bucks, he wouldn't just send him to prison. I'd have that judge see if this kid was nuts. If he's a—what you call that?—kleptomaniac? I'd have him examined, see if he is. If he is, hell! Jail ain't no place for him. But if he's doing it just for orneriness, I'd put him in the clink for a while.

I think I'd throw out that Juvenile Court altogether. It's no goddamn good. You come up there, you can't have your case argued, you ain't got no jury. You haven't got one single right. The judge, he's got a fistful of goddamn papers. He's reading them, mumbling something to you. Then he says, "Shit! You ain't no good! I'm sending you away!" I'd cut that stuff out. A juvenile is entitled to as much of a fair trial as a grownup, ain't he?

Another thing I'd do if I was mayor, I'd build a race track for hot rods, what they call drag strips, where guys can clock their cars, race, tinker with their cars in garages. Different car clubs race against each other. All on this special track, where it's safe, and you can't hurt no other drivers, because only hot rods are on that track. I'd have one of them, if I was mayor. It lets a club make its reputation without being hauled in all the time for speeding.

You know that outfit they've got here, the Coordinating Council, or something like that? How come they haven't accomplished a goddamn thing? I'll tell you why. They're not working at it as hard as they should. And that's because everybody on that Council is one of them so-called experts. Them guys ain't experts. They consider them experts because they've got a college education, they've done this, they've done that, they've got degrees. That still doesn't tell them how kids act and what they do. What they should do to prevent it. The real expert is the guy that's done it himself. Not them chicken-shits that sit there with the white collar and white shirt and everything.

You know what I'd say to do? Put a half dozen kids that's been in trouble on that Council. They'd get it right flat, them other experts. Then they'd have a better idea what to do. You can't go by a guy that's got a college degree and says, "I *think*." You've got to have a guy in there that says, "I *know*. I did it."

That guy's judgment wouldn't always be as good as a cop's or a social worker or a chief of police or things like that. But he would have some ideas that would help. The other fellows would be checking on him and he'd be checking on them. Each one putting into the kitty what he knows best.

You sit around, discuss the whole thing, then everybody vote on what they think should be done. I wouldn't be the best, but I think I could make a fair member of a Council like that. I could help them quite a little.

Another thing. If I was mayor, it would be pretty much to ask, I guess, but say they needed something for war that could be manufactured by kids, they could be trained for it. I'd open up some kind of plant and give a lot of kids a chance. Where they can make themselves spending money. Where they ain't going to feel they have to go out and steal. Where they can make some money and buy themselves a car. A lot of kids haven't got no car, so they wander around at night. A lot of tempting things, boy, when you wander around at night and you see things laying around.

You know, I might make a good mayor at that! I don't know, though. Probably the people wouldn't like it, because I'd go all out for the kids' benefit. Some of them would think I was giving kids too much breaks. But I'd rather give a kid a break and straighten him up than give him a half-assed break and have him end up half good and half bad.

THREE APPROACHES TO DELINQUENCY PREVENTION: A CRITIQUE

JOHN M. MARTIN

Excerpted from John M. Martin, "Three Approaches to Delinquency Prevention: A Critique," *Crime and Delinquency,* 7 (January 1961), pp. 16–24.

ASIDE FROM punishment and strict repression, delinquency prevention is usually defined in these three different ways:

1. Delinquency prevention is the sum total of all activities that contribute to the adjustment of children and to healthy personalities in children.

2. Delinquency prevention is the attempt to deal with particular environmental conditions that are believed to contribute to delinquency.

3. Delinquency prevention consists of specific preventive services provided to individual children or groups of children.

General Description

The logic underlying preventive activities of the first type is disarmingly simple: anything that contributes to the adjustment of children and to their healthy personality development prevents delinquency. Basically this approach links delinquency prevention with general improvements in the institutional fabric of our society, particularly as these affect child welfare. In large part this approach rests on a continuation and extension of measures, now commonplace on the American scene, which are designed to reduce the economic inequities of our social system. Such activities include procedures for raising the income levels of poverty stricken families, better low-rent housing, improving job tenure and work arrangements, and other means for reducing the rigors of poverty and economic insecurity. The approach also embraces attempts to reduce prejudice and discrimination against minority group people, increase the educational achievements of oncoming generations, improve marital relations by premarital counseling and family social work, and increase the impact of religious doctrines on both adults and children.

Preventive activities of the second type, by and large, aim to overcome factors in the immediate environment of children that seem to contribute to their delinquency. Such activities include attempts at community organization, such as the Chicago Area Projects . . . work by "coordinating councils" for harmonizing the efforts of welfare and child care agencies in delinquency prevention; the work of recreational and character-building agencies of all types; and attempts to reduce the commercial activities of adults which are clearly illegal and detrimental to the welfare of children who may get caught up in such traffic as, for example, the sale of liquor to minors, dope peddling, and receiving stolen goods.

Preventive activities of the third type include probation and parole services to children and youths, the programs of residential institutions and special schools for delinquents, child guidance clinics insofar as they are concerned with the diagnosis and treatment of delinquents, direct work with antisocial street gangs, and a variety of other services whose principal purpose is the adjustment of individual children or groups of children.

Relative Merits

It would be enormously difficult, if not impossible, to measure the effectiveness of these three types of preventive activities in terms of their ability actually to reduce delinquency, and no attempt will be made to do so here. However, general comment will be made about the relative merits of the three approaches.

In the main it is correct to conclude that improvement in the collective welfare, particularly in the welfare of depressed minority people, will reduce delinquency. In areas such as metropolitan New York the reduction of juvenile delinquency is most intimately linked with the successful assimilation of low-status groups, in particular the ever increasing number of migrant and uprooted Negroes and Puerto Ricans. Whatever contributes to the welfare and assimilation of these people reduces the delinquency rate among their children and, correspondingly, in the communities in which they live; conversely, whatever impedes their progress inflates the delinquency rate in those areas.

But the relationship between delinquency and improvement in the general welfare is more complicated than it appears at first glance. For example, although it is tempting to claim that improved housing and the reduction of poverty will reduce both crime and delinquency, evidence that delinquency is highest during periods of extreme prosperity and *not* during depressions, as well as awareness of the variety and number of offenses committed by middle- and upper-class persons, should warn us against the facile assumption that the elimination of poverty is the Rosetta stone of crime prevention.

The relationship between delinquency, at least in terms of official statistics, and poverty and poor housing has, of course, long been noted by students of social problems. However, it is erroneous to conclude that the abolishment of these living conditions will also abolish delinquency among low-status children. As Bernard Lander pointed out in his study of differential juvenile delinquency rates by census tracts in Baltimore, delinquency appears to be fundamentally related to social instability or *anomie* and not basically to poverty and poor housing.

It is within this context that we can best understand the disillusionment of those who expected too much by way of delinquency prevention from public housing. Their disappointment is well reflected in the pungent remark reportedly made by one student of New York's slums: "Once upon a time we thought that if we could only get our problem families out of those dreadful slums, then papa would stop taking dope, mama would stop chasing around, and Junior would stop carrying a knife. Well, we've got them in a nice apartment with modern kitchens and a recreation center. And they're the same bunch of bastards they always were." [1]

Emphasis upon *anomie* or social disorganization as a basic contributing factor to the high delinquency rates characteristic of some urban areas, with a concomitant de-emphasis of the obvious poverty of these areas as the underlying factor in their high delinquency rates, would, then, appear to be of cardinal importance for understanding and preventing delinquency in such places.

Anomie and Delinquency

Useful as Lander's statistical analysis of census tracts in Baltimore may be for destroying the myth that poverty and inadequate housing are the root causes of delinquency, the relationship between *anomie* and delinquency may also be more complicated than it seems. Lander emphasized the "internal" disorganization characteristic of high delinquency areas. Yet relatively *stable* neighborhoods may also be characterized by comparatively high rates of delinquency. A good example of just such a neighborhood is the tightly knit Italian slum of "Eastern City" examined by William Foote Whyte in his classic, *Street Corner Society.*

The existence of stable but delinquent neighborhoods suggests that there are at least two kinds of areas that produce delinquency:

One is the rapidly changing and thoroughly chaotic local area of the kind isolated by Lander, perhaps best illustrated by New York City's racially mixed and tension-ridden Spanish Harlem . . .

The other is the rather well-organized neighborhood such as the Italian ethnic community studied by Whyte, "disorganized" primarily in the sense that the way of life there is judged "out of step" when contrasted with the essentially middle-class culture of the greater society.

It is in the second kind of area particularly that well-developed relationships are likely to exist between criminally precocious adolescents, corrupt politicians, and the seemingly inevitable racke-

[1] D. Seligman, "The Enduring Slums" in The Editors of Fortune, *The Exploding Metropolis*, Garden City, N.Y., Doubleday, 1958, pp. 111–132.

teers. These relationships go far in explaining the easy transition many delinquents make from juvenile misbehavior to the more sophisticated forms of adult criminality. It is in this type of area, too, that personality and family structures are less likely to split and disintegrate under the stresses and strains characteristic of more chaotic and tension-ridden neighborhoods.

But distinctions of this sort, important as they may be for understanding differences in the social structure of delinquency areas, must not obscure a more basic fact: quite aside from the stability or instability of social relations in delinquency-prone areas, the traditions, standards, and moral sentiments of such areas are notoriously delinquent and criminal in "complexion" and "tone." This peculiar cultural climate has long been recognized by students of urban life, particularly by the ecologists and social psychologists of the "Chicago School" of American sociology.

Recently this recognition has linked up with a more general discussion of social-class subcultures and particularly with more detailed analyses of lower-class culture as a breeding ground for delinquency. A good example of this is found in an article by Walter B. Miller which called attention to the delinquency proneness of lower-class culture in a discussion of the "focal concerns" of the urban lower-class way of life. Miller's emphasis is not upon the so-called "subculture of the delinquent gang" as discussed by Albert K. Cohen, but upon the content of the whole mode of existence of urban lower-class people. Miller believes that in the lower class, in contrast with the middle class, people are likely to have commitments to focal concerns such as physical "toughness," "smartness" interpreted as the ability to "con" or dupe others, and "excitement" in terms of seeking thrills, taking risks, and courting danger. When these commitments are combined with the intense need for "in-group" membership and status or "rep" so characteristic of lower-class adolescents, Miller feels that conditions are especially ripe for the development of juvenile misconduct, particularly gang delinquency.

Thus the concept of social disorganization can be used to describe both stable and unstable delinquency areas. If we accept such disorganization as basic to an understanding of law violation in both kinds of areas, then we must question the value of other delinquency prevention methods besides those aimed at the reduction of poverty. In particular we should examine the limitations inherent in current attempts to prevent delinquency by the use of "individual-centered" techniques, such as social casework and related psychological-psychiatric services.

"Individual-Centered" Techniques

Practitioners of such techniques work toward individual adjustment, not social change. Seldom do they try to reduce the delinquency-producing features of the delinquent's environment, especially his extrafamilial environment; instead they emphasize adjustment to prevailing environmental conditions. For most delinquents, who are generally without emotional disturbance and who reflect the patterned deviancy so often found in their lower-class neighborhoods, this means that they are expected to make a nondelinquent adjustment to a highly delinquent life situation. Our recidivism rates testify that at best this adjustment is precarious. Furthermore—and this is perhaps the more basic point—because such efforts fail to come to grips with the underlying social and cultural conditions giving rise to delinquency, they do little to prevent the outcropping of delinquency in the first instance. Most try to take hold only after maladjustment, even delinquency itself, has become manifest in the lives of the youngsters they seek to help.

This, however, should not be taken as a rejection of probation and parole, of training schools and reformatories, of child guidance clinics, and of other kinds of institutions and agencies given over to the care and "correction" of delinquents. Far from abandoning this line of approach, we must work hard at improving existing facilities of this sort and act imaginatively regarding the "invention" of new ones. Furthermore, we must, as we have seldom paused to do in the past, rigorously test and verify the effectiveness of various approaches aimed at the rehabilitation of individual delinquents. In this regard the basic question still to be answered is: To what extent and under what conditions do our correctional agencies really correct?

But despite all of this, we must not be so carried away by our desire to rehabilitate delinquents that we fail to see individual treatment in a proper perspective, lose sight of its limitations, and ignore the fundamental proposition that *the prevention of delinquency should include both individual treatment and general or social prevention.* Unfortunately this is just what has happened. To a truly remarkable degree public and private delinquency prevention agencies have spent comparatively little money or energy on community-centered programs of social prevention. For decades most of these agencies have put their effort into establishing various kinds of facilities for rehabilitating delinquents on a case-by-case basis, with the "model" and most prestigeful approach in recent years being that of the psychiatrically-oriented child guidance clinic.

In sum, if we grant the primary role social disorganization plays in the development of delinquency, then the prevention of delinquency is not fundamentally a problem of bettering the general welfare of children or rehabilitating individuals, although the wisdom of continuing our attempts at both seems obvious. Nor for that matter is delinquency prevention essentially a problem of coordinating the activity of welfare agencies, although, like the application of "individual-centered" techniques, this too has an important role to play in prevention. . . .

Basically, the problem of delinquency prevention is a problem of social organization or reorganization, and other approaches have merit only to the degree that they contribute to such reorganization.

Social Reorganization

How can social reorganization best be accomplished? Although we may be both unable and unwilling to reduce substantially the drift toward *anomie* that Robert K. Merton and others have suggested is a pervasive characteristic of American society, we may be able to make partial inroads upon such disorganization, particularly insofar as it is related to the problem of juvenile delinquency, if we focus directly on the local areas in which delinquency is most pronounced. The logic underlying this proposal is that a local area "does not need to control the entire culture of a nation (which would be impossible) in order to control its delinquency rate. The things that need to be done are local and relate to personal inter-action rather than to the larger institutions." [2] The essence of this approach to social reorganization, then, is to stimulate social change in delinquency-prone neighborhoods.

Unfortunately we have no rich arsenal of tried and proven tech-niques for accomplishing such change. Much needs to be learned and many innovations need to be developed toward this end. De-spite these difficulties, however, we do know much about stimulat-ing change in delinquency areas. The framework within which the reorganization of such neighborhoods can be accomplished has been well described by Frederic M. Thrasher in his outline of a proposal for coordinating neighborhood activity for delinquency prevention.

This proposal envisons that any attempt to prevent delinquency in local areas must fix responsibility for social change at the neigh-borhood level where such changes can be implemented by local community leaders assisted by experts. Implicit in this approach is the assumption that in even the most delinquency-prone neighbor-hoods not all the residents are criminals or delinquents, and that in such areas there is actually a duality of conduct norms—one favor-ing law-abiding behavior, the other favoring delinquency.

Although Thrasher's plan utilizes, as subsidiary techniques, the best services offered by the usual community agencies—especially those of school, court, training institutions, and child guidance clinic—his proposal "represents a radical departure from the meth-ods of social work and community organization as formerly conceived." [3]

This comment made almost three decades ago is nearly as appli-cable now as it was then. When one surveys current social work ef-forts at community organization, it becomes abundantly clear that,

[2] E. H. Sutherland, "Prevention of Juvenile Delinquency" in A. Cohen et al. (eds.), *The Sutherland Papers*, Bloomington, Indiana University Press, 1956, pp. 131–140.

[3] F. M. Thrasher, *The Gang*, second revised edition; Chicago, University of Chicago Press, 1936, p. 538.

far from being focused in local areas, this activity is largely county- or city-wide in scope. Furthermore, all too often "community organization" in social work means that professional social workers meet with one another and with upper- and middle-class laymen for the purposes of mapping fund-raising campaigns, educating the public, coordinating agency activity, and similar objectives. Even when particular neighborhoods are the targets for such organization, seldom is the basic responsibility for such work placed in the hands of leaders who are truly representative of the people living in such areas.

Fundamentally the difference between the kind of plan outlined by Thrasher and traditional social work proposals for community organization is that in the former the real work is done by local residents who, banded together in a committee or council, act to (1) get the facts about delinquents and delinquency in their neighborhood; (2) organize existing preventive forces serving their neighborhood; (3) stimulate the development of new programs and services as required; and (4) in cooperation with professional agencies, look to the adjustment of their own delinquents, organize the leisure-time activities of their own children and young people, and improve the neighborhood environment, particularly by encouraging the enforcement of laws outlawing the activities of "slum landlords," petty racketeers, and other adults that are clearly detrimental to the welfare of their neighborhood and their children. . . .

The inclusion of children and youths in neighborhood organizations for delinquency prevention is most vital. Too often they are simply left out of the planning and management phases of such activity. As a result, the isolation of their adolescence is compounded and a real opportunity for establishing closer ties between the generations is overlooked.

Chicago Area Project

Perhaps the best known of the relatively few delinquency prevention programs predicated on local community organization that are actually in operation are the Chicago Area Projects developed by Clifford R. Shaw and his associates. Basically these projects aim

at producing internal cohesiveness and conventional behavior in
delinquency areas through the development of *indigenous leadership*. Outside professional leadership is mimimal. Chiefly it is used
to interest and develop local talent. Program activities are not ends
in themselves but are used to achieve local unity. Some direct
work is done with children and adolescents on a one-to-one counseling basis, and psychiatric and other types of referrals are made
when needed. But the central aim is to draw local youngsters into
various project activities so that they will identify with conventional rather than with delinquent groups and cultural patterns.

Outside leaders have a definite but limited role. This approach
to area reorganization places principal emphasis on the role of natural community leaders who are carriers of conventional conduct
norms. Not only do such leaders serve as nondelinquent models for
emulation by youngsters attracted to programs offered by projects
of this type, but because these indigenous leaders have prestige in
the local area, they easily attract adults, as well as children and
youths, to project programs in the first instance. It is around natural community leaders, then, that legitimate social structures can
be germinated and multiplied in delinquency-prone areas. And it
is in relationship with such leaders and within such structures that
youngsters can develop the close and intimate attachments with
conventional models, achieve the satisfactions, and acquire the
sense of personal worth and purpose necessary to counter the drift
toward delinquency characteristic of their life situations.

Some Basic Questions

Two basic questions arise relative to preventive programs like
the Chicago Area Projects: First, *can they be established, and once
established will they last?* Second, *do they actually prevent delinquency?*

In regard to both parts of the first question, the answers seem to
be definitely affirmative. Thus, in their recent evaluation of the
Chicago Area Projects, Witmer and Tufts found that:

1. Residents of low-income areas can organize and have organized themselves into effective working units for promoting and
conducting welfare programs.

2. These community organizations have been stable and enduring. They raise funds, administer them well, and adapt the programs to local needs.

3. Local talent, otherwise untapped, has been discovered and
utilized. Local leadership has been mobilized in the interest of
children's welfare.[4]

A definite answer to the second question is much more difficult
to obtain. However, two types of evidence tentatively suggest that
it too may be affirmative. First, statistics from 1930 to 1942 indicate
that delinquency rates declined in three out of four of the communities in which projects were then being carried on; second, in
some of the projects, work with men and boys on parole from institutions has been very successful, with one project noting that out
of forty-one parolees worked with between 1935 and 1944, only one
was recommitted to an institution.[5] However, evidence such as
this, without comparable controls, must obviously remain
inconclusive. . . .

Another question that arises with respect to delinquency prevention programs geared to local leadership is: *How can they best be
originated?* In this regard Walter C. Reckless has warned against
waiting for the "spontaneous generation of experimental action";
outside help must get such programs started by stimulating local
leaders to action. Likewise it seems necessary that outside assistance should also include sufficient money, at least in the beginning, to help defray costs. Again and again programs of this type
have foundered because the few hundred dollars raised by raffles,
cake sales, thrift shops, and local donations were simply not
enough to meet day-to-day expenses.

Who should provide such assistance? To this there are a number
of answers. The potential role of private foundations, boards of education, fraternal organizations, and private industry and labor
unions in supporting or initiating such activity is enormous. Of special significance is the potential but presently underdeveloped role
urban churches can play in this field. The force of organized reli-

[4] H. L. Witmer and E. Tufts, *The Effectiveness of Delinquency Prevention
Programs*, Children's Bureau, United States Department of Health, Education
and Welfare, Publication 350, Washington, D.C., Government Printing Office,
1954, p. 15.
[5] *Ibid.*, p. 16.

gion in the prevention of delinquency will be more fully realized if, and only if, more churches make realistic financial appropriations for such purpose and if, on the personal level, more churchmen base their approach to delinquency on love, direct service, intimate communication, and example, instead of on benign indifference, social distance, and exhortation.

Assistance should also be available from other sources. For example, communities in states with Youth Authority plans might well call upon such authorities for help insofar as these state agencies actually make provision for realistic assistance to local communities; and in New York the new State Youth Division, one purpose of which is to stimulate communities to take action with regard to delinquency, should be a prime source of both money and advice, as should the Youth Board in New York City. Although the Federal Youth Corrections Act makes no provision for rendering assistance to local communities, the capacity of the federal government in this and other facets of community programs for delinquency prevention is tremendous.* Finally, professional social workers themselves, as citizens, as agency representatives and educators, and as spokesmen for their highly influential professional associations, might become less remiss about endorsing, inaugurating, and experimenting with community-centered crime prevention programs.

In any event, if neighborhood programs run by residents are to develop to their full potential, it seems almost axiomatic that outside assistance must be provided.

In Summary

Students of delinquency are becoming increasingly aware of the necessity of reaching out beyond the child and his family in their efforts at prevention. It is submitted that the most efficacious approach for modifying the operating milieu of the bulk of our delinquents is through the widespread establishment of community-

---

* Since this was written, the federal government has provided millions of dollars to local communities for delinquency prevention programs, partly out of "War on Poverty" funds. Ed.

centered programs of prevention. Supported by continued improvement in the collective welfare—particularly in terms of the successful assimilation of low-status groups—and incorporating the best of "corrections" and individual treatment, the community-centered approach offers the most hope for reducing law-violation by our children and adolescents.

A STRUCTURAL APPROACH TO DELINQUENCY PREVENTION AND TREATMENT

JOHN M. MARTIN, JOSEPH P. FITZPATRICK, AND ROBERT E. GOULD, M.D.

Excerpted from John M. Martin, Joseph P. Fitzpatrick, and Robert E. Gould, M.D., *The Analysis of Delinquent Behavior, A Structural Approach* (New York: Random House, 1968, 1970), pp. 3, 175–188. At the time of publication John M. Martin was Professor of Sociology, Fordham University; Joseph E. Fitzpatrick was Professor of Sociology in the same institution; and Robert E. Gould, M.D. was Assistant Professor of Clinical Psychiatry, New York University Medical Center.

A REVOLUTION is stirring in national thinking about crime and delinquency. Instead of the old emphasis on changing the individual offender, the new movement stresses changing the manner in which various social institutions, including courts and correctional agencies, relate to him. The causes of delinquency and youth crime in particular are sought in conditions of social and political inequality, especially in lack of economic and educational opportunity, rather than solely in individual pathology and personal failure. The dysfunctional consequences of bureaucratic decisions and practices for the disadvantaged are being given much closer scrutiny. Leaders of the new movement are likely to take their guiding principles from social science and law, as well as psychology. They see that the need to reform social institutions through community action and to win fair decisions for the poor is just as important as therapy, casework, and counseling for individual offenders. . . .

. . . The structural approach to delinquency . . . does not simply suggest minor changes in the existing practices of juvenile
courts, juvenile correctional institutions, private youth-serving organizations of various sorts, and other agencies presently man-
dated to prevent and control delinquency. New formats for social
investigations, reduction in the size of case loads, the advantages
of group therapy, the use of halfway houses, or similar technical
problems are not issues of major consequence. The structural approach is concerned with fundamental questions of policy: Will existing agencies dealing with delinquency continue to function to
maintain, and to reinforce, the *status quo*—that is, will these agencies continue to remain committed to conservatism? Or will these
agencies, or many of them at least, come over to the side of domestic reform in the struggle for equality and justice for the nation's
poor? If the latter goal is chosen, what strategies should be followed? What specific changes in agency organization and functioning should be addressed? What modifications in work role
should professionals and others employed by such agencies begin
to develop and apply?

The difficult and frequently exasperating task of changing the
traditional tight case orientation and social control function of
most existing delinquency agencies is only one facet of the job facing an agency that has made the decision to participate in alleviat-
ing social conditions adversely affecting disadvantaged youth.
Gaining endorsement of an appropriate political constituency, including the poor themselves, to support an agency committed to
social reform is a second facet of the task. The third is to get on
with the work. . . .

The first operating principle is the vigorous rejection of the
premise that the major social norms governing the national society
express the sentiments of the total collectivity. Conflicting norms
within the larger society, . . . are readily identified. Clashing values on a broad scale are clearly visible. Given these conditions, it
seems essential to recognize that, in many areas of society, subgroups within the system may accept prevailing norms only because powerful dominant groups have imposed these norms upon
them by force or else because the subgroups have passively sub-

mitted to such norms. Frequently, a deviant subgroup, such as nonconforming teen-agers, will subtly avoid confrontations, wherever feasible, and continue to adhere to its own standards. Sometimes the deviancy is massive and overt, as with recent wholesale looting during episodes of intense racial strife. With apparent strong support from many of their fellow ghetto-dwellers, the looters of the riots of 1964–1968, who were often young males from various socioeconomic segments of their home communities, seemed through their pilferage to be rejecting established patterns of white-black accommodation. During the widespread riots of April 1968, the police, National Guard, and regular troops on riot control duty enacted a new master plan, which sought to contain civil disorders with a minimum of personal violence—a plan that temporarily set aside traditional law enforcement practices which have long defined property rights as superior to the human rights of property violators. No doubt this devaluation of property by both looters and riot control personnel startled and bewildered many middle-class citizens who continue to hold tightly to their belief that private property is almost sacred.

Failure to recognize the existence, even the vitality, of normative conflicts among different segments of society makes it difficult for a program in the delinquency field to avoid the hazards of an ethnocentric exercise of power. Despite the best intentions, given programs may grind down upon their clientele. Charity is no substitute for justice; compassion and understanding do not automatically bestow dignity; there is no substitute for a fair share of the Gross National Product. The present, almost completely unilateral process of decision-making by agency personnel operating in juvenile courts and related public and private agencies increases considerably the chance of unfairness. Among the many contributing circumstances to such unfairness, none is more significant than the fact that clients lack effective and reliable representation of their interests. Their situations, problems, and point of view often do not receive adequate consideration. In such cases, when judges, psychiatrists, social workers, and others with broad and frequently ill-defined authority sit in judgment on adolescents and their families suspected of social deviation and when the adjudged are poor

Negroes, Puerto Ricans, or members of other politically disadvantaged groups, the risk of *mis*judgment and even prejudicial condemnation is acute. . . . Similar risks are present, of course, even when socially deviant groups drawn from the white middle class, such as present-day hippies and college draft resisters, are judged by officials. When those doing the judging are committed, consciously or not, to preserving the interests and sentiments of the dominant strata and seemingly are unaware that these norms and values are not shared by other groups within the society, then actual injustice may be done. Moreover, since the effects of official treatment may often be hazardous for the individual and of doubtful rehabilitative benefit, the influence of the system of criminal justice cannot be presumed to be benevolent. . . .

When agencies of criminal justice attempt to understand and otherwise relate to offenders drawn from the seriously disadvantaged strata of society, they face many complex problems. A technical examination of what might be called the discontinuities in the theory and practice of correctional casework reveals one aspect of these difficulties. The dependence of the correctional field, both adult and juvenile, upon social casework methods for a systematic probing of individual cases makes any flaw in these methods extremely significant. Such a flaw affects the entire process of social investigation and recommendation, sentencing or disposition, and rehabilitation, confinement, and release. The usual casework methods appear to be almost completely concerned with the adjustment of the individual to prevailing social standards, rigorously defined in middle-class terms. Yet they operate under the guise of an idealized model of case analysis, which is essentially a scaled-down application of psychodynamic psychiatry. Psychodynamic psychiatry stresses *intrapersonal* psychic adjustment as a basis for change in individual functioning. To a surprising degree, casework methods in correction end up doing something quite different: they measure and stress overt conformity to middle-class standards, values, and life styles. . . .

It may be that the nation in its conventional wisdom intends to use and enforce middle-class norms, values, and life styles when it requires that authorities make judgments about who is to get what kind of treatment or sentence, as the case may be, in the criminal justice system. It may consider these to be the norms, values, and life styles which represent the consensus of the citizens and which must be enforced as the basis of the national life. Clearly, when these standards are enforced, the socially, culturally, and politically disadvantaged will suffer, since they will be coerced into conformity. No orderly society can avoid this human phenomenon. The Mormons were compelled to give up the practice of polygamy because they did not have the political strength to support their set of values; critics of the Vietnam war today are being compelled to accept the military draft as a fact of life, since the established government and its constituency support this position. If this is the principle which guides the official handling of delinquents, it should be openly stated and enforced, not disguised as an aspect of good mental hygiene. It really has nothing to do with mental hygiene, good or bad. It is a problem of a conflict of values and the issue is the extent to which the community at large is willing to admit the legitimacy of norms and values peculiar to one subgroup or subculture in its midst. When these conflicts of value are made explicit, political processes exist by which they can be accommodated or resolved, sometimes, as noted, by legal coercion. Real damage, however, is done not only to delinquent youth, but also to society at large, when one segment of the population, one ethnic group or social class, identifies its *own* definition of values as the national consensus and proceeds to enforce it. This can easily become a practice of politically enforced ethnocentrism or the protection of class interests. There is abundant evidence that, in the correction of delinquents, this is often the case.

A sound public policy designed to remove unfair practices from the system of criminal justice cannot tolerate this or other forms of dominant-group ethnocentrism, where they have become institutionalized in correctional practice. This means that the very models of social investigation and treatment most agencies use in judging delinquents and in doing something to or for them are incompatible with a sound system of legal justice. Through the use of drastic new models and within a wide range of normative limits specifying what contemporary American society will not tolerate in adolescent behavior, new dimensions of pluralistic tolerance might be built into day-to-day decision-making in the delinquency field. But more than cultural pluralism is needed. The structural nature of the delinquency problem, especially among the disadvantaged, also needs to be considered, not only in terms of relevant psychic and familial variables, but also in terms of their relationship to a wide range of personal, social, and cultural variables at the level of the reference group and neighborhood and in terms of the greater community itself. It would be best to examine each youth in these terms, in order to understand him properly in the context of his own community. . . .

However, studying cases in isolation is not sufficient. An environmentally oriented agency policy requires recognition of the fact that most official delinquents tend to come from urban slums and that the cases originating in any given slum, or section thereof, need to be studied *collectively*. This would permit diagnostically relevant patterns to emerge and would reveal links between individual cases. It would also show the relationship between individual case data and prevailing environmental conditions. And most significant, the malfunctioning of the local environment itself could then become an object of investigation, as well as the malignant relationship of this environment to the wider community. If this line of analysis were initiated, new programs aimed at creating environmental change, as a central objective of delinquency agency function, might then logically follow. Conservative and narrow self-interests may insist that institutional reforms must not occur or, as it is more often put, that all changes be slow, gradual, and nondisruptive. Translated pragmatically, this means no real change at all. This view may prevail for a year or for a decade or two, but not forever. The ebb and flow of reform in America testifies that nothing, and nobody, is capable of stopping indefinitely the acquisition of power by shut-out sectors of the population. And with power achieved, suitable institutional rearrangements usually follow.

Modern American ghettos, where official delinquency is concentrated, need almost everything in the way of environmental change and social reform. Almost anything that can be accomplished in this regard is an improvement over what is now there. But from the vantage point of the structural analysis of delinquent behavior, several new forms of programming appear to be essential in order to reduce sharply delinquency in urban slums. Each would certainly constitute a vital aspect of any community development-type program put into effect by a delinquency agency.

The first is obvious: a massive national outpouring for urban slum people of welfare, educational, housing, and work programs. . . . The Negro violence which struck well over a hundred cities during April 1968 should remove the last vestige of doubt that only sustained national action can end the enduring crisis of the ghetto.

On the level of the local ghetto, highly specific programs clearly need to be established for a variety of purposes, including the delivery and fair distribution to all disadvantaged minorities of the national wealth which seems destined to be reallocated to slum communities. From region to region, from city to city, from neighborhood to neighborhood, the needs are so widespread that no one group among the poor, no one neighborhood among a large city's many slums, should be given preferential treatment. . . .

Second, these programs, if administratively situated outside the system of criminal justice in the so-called private sector of welfare, could be used to divert local youth out of the official system when they got "in trouble." Thus modern ghetto-dwellers could follow the lead presented by the Jews, Irish Catholics, and other earlier immigrant groups who developed their own large-scale private welfare systems which served to divert their children and youth from the courts, public training schools, and reformatories of earlier days. Such local programs might not only help local youth in some worthy welfare sense, but they might also, quite literally, be used, wherever feasible, to keep local youths out of official trouble by taking them out of the hands of overworked police youth bureaus and precincts, off the overcrowded dockets of juvenile courts, and otherwise out of the official processes of justice. . . .

This leads to the third, and perhaps the most significant, purpose which could be served by local, privately controlled welfare services to ghetto youth. Such service delivery systems could themselves become increasingly important bases of institutionalized power for presently disadvantaged groups, which could use these service structures and the taxes which would support them to help create their own welfare enterprises. Following an argument advanced by Frances Piven and Richard Cloward, private agencies of this order would be as much political as social welfare institutions, inasmuch as they would serve as organizational vehicles for the expression of the group's viewpoints on social welfare policy and also as the means for other forms of political association and influence. Once developed, the strength of these new welfare organizations, working in combination with similar local and community-wide enterprises in education, health, religion, and other fields, could be used by the disadvantaged to improve their own general bargaining position vis-á-vis other, more established, interest groups. It is the enhancement of this bargaining position and the consequent enrichment and empathic modification of institutions and practices that offers the key to social change in the ghetto. . . .

This general course of action has been followed in the past, and remains the case today, in New York, for example, with the Catholics, Jews, and also, of course, with the white Protestants. The political advantages to be gained by today's disadvantaged groups through the development of their own, privately controlled, tax-supported welfare delivery systems cannot be matched by launching new programs and continuing old programs for the disadvantaged through long-established agencies, either public or private, particularly where the recipients of service exercise little or no voice in policy. Put bluntly, the issue is one of control and influence: Who is going to run what for whom? And consequently, who is going to profit politically, psychologically, economically, and in many other ways from the enterprise?

Indigenous minority leaders say that what they want is *money* and *dignity*. Some say they want *power*. The right kinds of welfare, education, housing, and work are four good vehicles for obtaining all three. The right kind of locally controlled welfare agency seems to be one very good device which a neighborhood might use to compete successfully for these types of broadly scaled programs, many of which will have to be paid for by state and federal mon-ies. Such highly diverse and specialized programs, once obtained, need not necessarily be run by the local welfare agencies which were instrumental in securing them. Welfare is only one institutional set in any community and certainly not the largest. Other locally controlled institutions in education and in housing, for example, might operate their own nonwelfare neighborhood programs. This division of labor would keep each separate institutional set focused upon its own area of expertise, much as is the case in the broader community. Such an arrangement of minority-group power, with the proper political coordination at both the neighborhood and wider community levels, might actually provide greater stability and strength for a ghetto than one giant, omnipotent, neighborhood agency. In any case, once a locally run ghetto agency is brought into being in the private sector of welfare, the people who own it can decide which particular political strategy they may wish to follow at any given time.

Until locally owned welfare agencies can be run on an independent basis in slum communities, it will probably be necessary for coalitions of more powerful groups and institutions to work closely with disadvantaged people in various neighborhoods to design, establish, operate, and fund such enterprises. Funding offers an apt illustration of the difficulties which disadvantaged groups are likely to experience in creating such organizations on their own. Except for antipoverty money, which is very unstable and not a large part of any city or state operating budget, most of the stable funding patterns in education, welfare, and medical care—to cite three crucial areas—are not now within the grasp of the disadvantaged. As is the case in manufacturing, banking, defense, higher education, and other great American industries, the disadvantaged are also seriously disadvantaged when they try to own and operate any major sector of private welfare. If properly qualified, they may be either the recipients or the social workers of private welfare, but they are not yet able to own the structures dispensing the services. Given this state of affairs, coalitions which join together the disadvantaged and the advantaged are probably not only desirable but necessary for establishing the type of local welfare agency described above. Some might believe that such coalitions are in fact highly desirable in their own right on a permanent basis, since they may serve to reduce the polarization of racial conflict now openly characteristic of many American cities. That may or may not be true. It does seem, however, that such coalitions are pragmatically essential for enabling the disadvantaged to get at the resources of money, professional expertise, and institutionalized power necessary for bringing effective local programs on a massive scale into urban ghettos. Participation at all levels—from policy-making to typing—in such coalitions by representatives of the disadvantaged could, in turn, serve to direct the content of the new programs and to prevent them from becoming just another phase of the domestic colonialism now so characteristic of ghetto life. Starting as full partners, these participants could progressively take over larger measures of control and responsibility. The design would call for effective transfer of program ownership, from the advantaged to the disadvantaged, with all possible speed.

INDEX OF AUTHORS